LABOUR LAW AND FREEDOM

Lord Wedderburn

LABOUR LAW AND FREEDOM

Further Essays in Labour Law

Lawrence & Wishart
LONDON

Lawrence & Wishart Limited
144a Old South Lambeth Road
London SW8 1XX

First published 1995
Copyright © Lord Wedderburn, 1995

ISBN 0-85315-744-8

Photoset in North Wales by
Derek Doyle & Associates, Mold, Clwyd.
Printed and bound in Great Britain by
Redwood Press, Trowbridge.

CONTENTS

PREFACE

This volume of essays in labour law contains a sequence of articles – some written specially for this volume, some published recently, some written in earlier years – all of which speak to themes which are germane to labour law in Britain and its context in Europe and transnationally. Many of the essays deal with issues relevant to the emergence of a labour law in Britain which might claim to be called an alternative labour law – alternative, that is, to the policy of the last fifteen years. In that sense, even in re-examining aspects of the past, they aim to illuminate issues for the future. The volume is published in association with the Institute of Employment Rights, as was the volume *Employment Rights in Britain and Europe* 1991; both draw on *The Worker and the Law*, of which a new edition is in preparation.

Just as the current legislative regime in Britain abhors, as did the law of the nineteenth century, combination by workers, so an alternative labour law sees collective organisation as a necessary condition both of workers' freedom and of a free society more generally. A reform not founded on that principle cannot be an alternative labour law, no matter how attractive the packaging. It is from that starting point that these essays set out: they do not, of course, purport to be a legislative programme; but they are founded on that principle. Reviving the importance of collective relationships may no doubt be unpopular among those who, even now ignoring the bequests of Kahn-Freund and Sinzheimer, see labour law as some technical body of rules without ideological significance or as a mere adjunct to the organisation of the market, with trade unions relegated to the role of friendly societies or messengers. Of course, since the subject was first widely recognised in Britain in the 1960s, labour law has become increasingly ideological, in an overt manner, a natural sequence in a society in which government has renounced consensus and which has itself become increasingly fragmented by new divisions of class and injustice. Movement towards the 'political', however, has not been a phenomenon of the 1980s alone. The judges, for example, bear their share of responsibility in the scrapping of the social pact – or 'equilibrium' as Kahn-Freund thought – reflected in the case law, when they seized the opportunity in the litigation of the 1960s to renew the attack on that rare liberal precedent of 1898, *Allen* v *Flood*. As an appendix to chapter 1 suggests, *Rookes* v *Barnard* still has its relevance. Other chapters inquire into aspects of the common law which could obstruct the development of alternative labour law, with occasional comparisons with other European systems. The greatest difficulties for an alternative policy are not created by Thatcherite legislation alone, but by the comfortable alliance which it made with the common law. The chapters which look at European law more directly try to make a similar assessment without, it is hoped, either 'Eurofabulism' or 'Eurodium'. Meanwhile, the realities of multinational capital, the most dangerous obstacle to the survival of the values of alternative labour law, appear in many chapters, including an early essay first published in 1972. An alternative labour law cannot be enacted in a void; it carries conviction only if based on hard legal analysis allied to an alternative social vision. For those who aim to give it effect in government in the real world we must reserve our patience and our sympathy, so long as they do not give up the fight.

The essays deal specifically with labour law's evolution and relationship to the common law, liabilities of trade unions in industrial action in a comparative context, regulation of trade unions' internal autonomy, problems of transnational collective bargaining and multinational labour relations, convergence and divergence of European systems and evolving issues of workers' protection. Two new papers, the first and last chapters, raise questions about the starting points and the goals of British labour law, past and future, not least the role of what is understood by 'collective *laissez-faire*' and what assistance can be expected from European sources. These are central issues for those architects who will shape labour law's future relationship to the competitive market, global networks of capital, individual freedom and workers' rights – and brooding over all of these, the disease of unemployment. In such a collection of essays there are inevitably matters which are discussed in more than one; for the most part each has been left in its own context but, where it seemed necessary, I have added a few cross references and notes updating sources or references.

My thanks again go to colleagues and friends in many countries – trade unionists, managers, legal practitioners and labour law scholars. I have tried to learn from them, whether I agreed with them or not. On the matter in these essays I have particular reason to thank Bob Simpson, Paul Davies, Mark Freeland, Silvana Sciarra, Félice Morgenstern, Peter Brannen, Bruno Veneziani, Antoine Lyon-Caen,

Jean-Claud Javillier, Gérard Lyon-Caen, Bill McCarthy, Simon Deakin, Colin Turpin, Simon Auerbach, David Lea, Jim Mortimer, David Cockburn, Brian Thompson, John Hendy, Peter Pain, Roy Lewis, Jon Clark, the participants in the comparative labour law 'Pontignano' seminars and my fellow members of the pioneering Comparative Labour Law Group of 1965 to 1978 – including Folke Schmidt who is so much missed. I am grateful for the agreement of the journals in which some of the essays first appeared to their inclusion here, namely the Law Quarterly Review, the British Journal of Industrial Relations, the Industrial Law Journal, the Bulletin of Comparative Labour Relations, Federation News, and the Dublin University Law Journal; also to the TUC for a speech originally published by it. I am especially happy to include my Sinzheimer lecture for 1993 with the agreement of the Sinzheimer Institute of the University of Amsterdam.

My thanks and more than thanks go to my wife:

.... sonitu suopte
tintinant aures, gemina teguntur
lumina nocte ....

For errors and infelicities I am, of course, alone responsible.

Bill Wedderburn
London October 1994

ABBREVIATIONS

A C	Appeal Cases
ACAS	Advisory Conciliation and Arbitration Service
AEEU	Amalgamated Engineering and Electrical Union
All E.R.	All England Law Reports
Ass. Plén	Cour de Cassation in full session (France, High Court of Appeal)
AUEW	Amalgamated Union of Engineering Workers (now AEEU)
Aus. J. L. L.	Australian Journal of Labour Law
BJIR	British Journal of Industrial Relations
Bull. Comp. Lab.R.	Bulletin of Comparative Labour Relations
CA	Court of Appeal
CAC	Central Arbitration Committee
Cort. Cass	Corte di Cassazione (Italian High Court of Appeal)
CBI	Confederation of British Industry
CEC	Confédération des Cadres
CEEP	Centre Européen des Entreprises à Participation Publique (Public Employers European Centre)
CESI	Confédération Européenne des Syndicats Indépendents
CFE-CGC	Confédération Française de l'Encadrement
CFDT	Confédération Française Démocratique du Travail
CFTC	Confédération Française des Travailleurs Chrétiens
CGIL	Confederazione Generale Italiana di Lavoro
CGT	Confédération Générale du Travail
CGT-FO	Confédération Générale du Travail-Force Ouvrière
Ch.	Chancery Division (High Court)
CISL	Confederazione Italiana Sindacati Lavoratori
CLJ	Cambridge Law Journal
CMLR	Common Market Law Reports (and Review)

CO	Certification Officer
COHSE	Confederation of Health Service Employees (now UNISON)
Comp. Lab. L. Jo.	Comparative Labor Law Journal (US)
Cons. const.	Conseil Constitutionel (France, Constitutional Council)
COPAUIA	Commissioner for Protection Against Unlawful Industrial Action
Cort. cost.	Constitutional Court (Italy).
CPSA	Civil and Public Services Association
CRE	Commission for Racial Equality
Crim.	Cour de Cassation Criminal Chamber (France)
CROTUM	Commissioner for the Rights of Trade Union Members
CT	Code du Travail (France, Labour Law Code)
D.	Dalloz
Dr. Soc.	Droit Social
Dr. Ouvr.	Droit Ouvrier
EAT	Employment Appeal Tribunal
EC	European Communities (previously EEC)
ECHR	European Convention of Human Rights, and Court, Strasbourg (Council of Europe)
ECJ	European Court of Justice, Luxembourg (EC and EU)
ECR	European Court Reports
EEC	European Economic Community
EIRR	European Industrial Review and Report
EOC	Equal Opportunities Commission
EOR	Equal Opportunities Review
EPA	Employment Protection Act 1975
EPCA	Employment Protection (Consolidation) Act 1978
ETUC	European Trade Union Confederation
EU	European Union
EUROCOMMERCE	EC Retail, Wholesale and Trade Representation
FWR	Fair Wages Resolution
GCHQ	Government Communications Headquarters

Giorn. di. dir. del. lav. e di rel. ind.	Giornale di diritto del lavoro e di relazioni industriali
GMB	GMB (British union, formerly General, Municipal and Boilermakers Union)
GPMU	Graphical, Paper and Media Union
HL	House of Lords (Law Lords as 'Judicial Committee', the final appeal court)
HS Info. Bull.	Health and Safety Information Bulletin (with IRRR)
ICF	International Federation of Chemical and General Workers
ICR	Industrial Cases Reports
ILJ	Industrial Law Journal
ILO	International Labour Organisation
IMF	International Metal Workers Federation
Ind. Rel. L.J.	Industrial Relations Law Journal (US)
Ind. Rels. Jo.	Industrial Relations Journal
Int. J.C.L.L. I.R.	International Journal of Comparative Labour Law and Industrial Relations
Intl. Lab L.R.	International Labour Law Reports
IPMS	Institution of Professionals, Managers and Specialists
IRLR	Industrial Relations Law Reports
IRRR	Industrial Relations Review and Report
IT	Industrial Tribunal
ITW	International Transport Workers Federation
IUF	International Union of Food and Allied Workers
J.	Judge of the High Court ('Mr. Justice ...')
JRWLA	Joint Regulation of Working Life Act (Sweden)
Lav. Dir.	Lavoro e diritto
LC	Lord Chancellor
LIB	Legal Information Bulletin (with IRRR)
LJ	Lord Justice (Court of Appeal judge)
LOLS	Ley Organica de Libertad Sindical (Spanish Law)
LQR	Law Quarterly Review

LRD	Labour Research Department
MLR	Modern Law Review
MMC	Monopolies and Mergers Commission
MR	Master of the Rolls (senior judge of CA)
MSF	Manufacturing Science and Finance Union
NALGO	National and Local Government Officers Association (now UNISON)
NAS/UWT	National Association of Schoolmasters/Union of Women Teachers
NCU	National Communications Union
NGA	National Graphical Association (now GPMU)
NIRC	National Industrial Relations Court (Britain 1971-74)
NUJ	National Union of Journalists
NUM	National Union of Mineworkers
NUPE	National Union of Public Employees (now UNISON)
NUR	National Union of Railwaymen (now RMT)
NUT	National Union of Teachers
Ox. Jo. L. S.	Oxford Journal of Legal Studies
P.	President
Parl. Deb.	Parliamentary Debates (Hansard)
PC (JC)	Privy Council Judicial Committee (mainly Law Lords)
PPLR	Public Procurement Law Review
QB	Queen's Bench Division (High Court)
Riv. dir. lav.	Rivista di diritto del lavoro
RMT	Rail, Maritime and Transport Workers Union
SC11	Social Chapter of Eleven Member States (Protocol and Agreement on Social Policy to Maastricht Treaty)
SNB	Special Negotiating Body (under proposed SC11 Directive on information and consultation rights of employees in undertakings of Community-scale)

SOGAT	Society of Graphical and Allied Trades (now GPMU)
Soc.	Cour de Cassation Social Chamber (France)
Sté.	Société
TGWU	Transport and General Workers Union
TUC	Trades Union Congress
TULRA	Trade Union and Labour Relations Act 1974
TULRCA	Trade Union and Labour Relations (Consolidation) Act 1992
TUPE	Transfer of Undertakings (Protection of Employment) Regulations 1981, SI. 1794
TURER	Trade Union Reform and Employment Rights Act 1993
UCATT	Union of Construction, Allied Trades and Technicians
UCW	Union of Communication Workers
UK	United Kingdom
UIL	Unione Italiana del Lavoro
UNICE	Union des Confédérations de l'Industrie et des Employeurs d'Europe (EC Employers' Association private sector)
UNISON	(British public sector union, amalgamation of NALGO, NUPE, COHSE)
USDAW	Union of Shop Distributive and Allied Workers
VC	Vice Chancellor (High Court and Court of Appeal)
WLR	Weekly Law Reports
ZIAS	Zeitschrift für ausländisches und internationales Arbeitsund Sozialrecht

1

CHANGE, STRUGGLE AND IDEOLOGY IN BRITISH LABOUR LAW

Why has it been so difficult to draw up a labour law programme with a coherent philosophy as an alternative to the regressive British laws of the last fifteen years? There has been time enough in face of the legislative flood of 1979 to 1993 – and possibly more to come.[1] Time to see through the 'step-by-step' presentation and locate the compass of ideology which has guided these steps at many crucial moments since 1982, when 'monetarist ideology delegitimized trade unionism, public expenditure, the provision of social services and the commitment to full employment'.[2] Have we perhaps made too flip a judgement on the labour law that went before this sorry period? A new journey must begin with a clear perception of its starting point.

IDEOLOGY AND MARKET LABOUR LAW

It is manifest that there has been in recent British labour law a common general direction, different from provisions imposed by European Community sources or the trends in most other Member States, and that this has been influenced broadly by an ideology. Indeed, whilst it is 'not claimed ... that his doctrines concerning political economy were the sole determinants of government policy in the 1980s', the philosophy of Hayek, with its appeal to the market as the only real 'spontaneous order', has clearly been central to the new Conservatism in social policy: 'It does not explain everything, but it illuminates much'.[3] Objections that this attributes 'a more detailed programme to Hayek' than he himself articulated, may mistake the function of ideology,[4] both in the past and for the elaboration of a new alternative policy. The job of the ideologue is not to draft Bills but to guide, often by an invisible hand, or a nudge in a general direction, at just those moments of choice when the politician is pressed by events and the civil servant dusts off position papers. Hayek's avowed aim was 'not to provide a detailed programme of policy but rather to state the criteria by which particular measures must be judged if they are to fit into a regime of freedom'; so it may be surprising that he came as near as he did to concrete proposals – on secondary action, picketing, the closed shop, protection of non-unionists, an end to union 'privileges' and to contracts 'in restraint of trade' – especially when he saw British unions as merely the sharpest examples of what he detected to be global 'union coercion' and 'monopoly'.[5] That is why recent British governments have so often collided with the consensus approach evident in the rather different 'social-market' governments in the European Union (though the Berlusconi administration in Italy may prove to be a new ally). The Thatcher *genre* of free market policies guaranteeing the 'spontaneous order' – like the dogma of economists who reject the 'welfare compromise',[6] and insist that only 'competitive capitalism' can promote freedom because it 'separates economic power from political power'[7] (a mystification that shields economic power from the accountability of democratic political control) – is now widely identified as a major inspiration of the new labour law agenda after 1982, built on the 'market rate' not the 'rate for the job'. The simple message which became the basis of legal policy, dressed up in the semantics of 'trade union reform', preached that: 'the legalised powers of the trade unions ... are the prime source of unemployment', and responsible 'for the decline of the British economy in general'.[8] The plans for a new, regressive labour law policy developed under that influence.[9] In this vision, 'employee involvement' at work is a matter for the employer's choice, never a matter for workers' rights;[10] and if need be, new laws must increase the employer's authority unilaterally to change employment relationships.[11] Market labour law is master and servant law writ large.

But there are still uncertainties about what went on before and during the Thatcher era and some of these bedim the vision of the future. Some unhelpful debates have only recently been clarified, such as the need for an alternative policy to make use both of 'positive rights' and of 'immunities' both substantively and semantically – only political confusion kept that artificial issue alive for long.[12] Other debates about an alternative labour law have proceeded on rather questionable premises about the earlier era, not least by lumping 'abstentionism' in with 'collective *laissez-faire*' and the ideology of autonomous trade unionism. There has even been a felt compulsion to jettison every facet of the 'old religion' – or to give it its most neutral title, 'voluntarism' – as though thereby some dialectical process would automatically cleanse the tribal imagination and install a cult of Cromwellian Regulation in labour law, though as always we perceive only the derivatives of these sources.[13] By itself this might be merely a harmless urge to settle accounts with the paternal past, but it is more damaging if it insists too (as if often does) that the earlier ideologies were quite irrational. Any 'dialectic of progress' needs to eschew hubris and learn from past societies at all levels.[14] And proponents of a new labour law cannot afford indiscriminate discardment of lessons from the past in face of today's challenges: the globalisation of economic markets; multinational enterprises able to reduce national governments 'to the status of parish councils';[15] the needs of transnational negotiation and the difficulty of collective action for workers, when for capital internationalisation adds an armoury of new, mobile weapons;[16] the return of aggressive macho management comfortable with the notion of 'authority' as understood by the common law;[17] and the growth of employment relations which make the individual worker's labour power an ever more flexible commodity, whether deskilled or reskilled, a plastic convenience for the employer – but glad to have the job. Similarly, we need to look realistically at our new source of law – and policy – the dimension of European law.[18] And at the centre broods the spectre haunting Europe, pervasive joblessness reducing millions – and not only the unemployed – to poverty and fear. Is it not somewhat ironic that in reply to workers' claims for shorter hours the offer is made of 'zero hours' employment contracts? No Act of Parliament can produce simple answers to all these problems. But the new British legislation for an alternative policy can be expected to keep in focus its own values, just as the regressive British laws of 1982 to 1993 never lost sight of theirs.[19] At the core of these values for the future is freedom of association – gauged by ILO standards: rights to organise, to strike and to enjoy representation for collective bargaining.[20] It must have an international cognisance, hitherto largely lacking, supportive of workers' transnational action and machinery,[21] now maturing (not trade policy which, without constituting disguised protectionism by industrialised nations, could exert pressures, as the President of the ILO puts it, towards 'social progress in spite of the countervailing influence exerted by the globalisation of the economy'.[22] Such labour clauses for the defence of fundamental labour standards are supported now even by the United States,[23] but not by the current British Government.

TAKING CARE WITH EUROPEAN LAW

We may begin with a limited, practical question. The need to take greater care with the terms of debate has frequently been in evidence in discussing regulation originating from the European Community.[24] There has even grown up among some a tendency to assume that legislation from the Community, or judgements of the Luxembourg Court of Justice ('ECJ'), on employment matters must always be positive steps, just as there are some for whom Community law cannot be anything but an invasion. Neither the Eurofabulism of the former nor the Eurodium of the latter are good guides. The former is now more common among lawyers, immersed in the details of Community law and procedures, such as 'qualified majority voting' in the Council or the competence of the Parliament, when what matters most is the substance of the policies.[25] Even so, attacks of Eurofabulism are understandable among those in Britain who have never experienced anything other than these recent years of crude, anti-union and deregulatory labour legislation. For them a different social policy that says it accepts rights for workers, shines like an oasis in the desert. But to ensure that this is not a mirage we must assess the meaning of each European measure, driving through the jargon which invariably accompanies them. It must be said that one of the unfortunate things about recent scholarly debate on 'European' law is the new style of religious fervour that infects some participants (not least practitioners), as if a posture that is *communautaire* was a substitute for analysis.

The need to analyse carefully was illustrated recently by the apparently anodyne Directive 91/533 of 14 October 1991. That imposed, in the interests of 'transparency', a Community requirement that employers must be obliged to inform employees of the 'conditions applicable to the contract or employment relationship'. Since the first of the modern statutes inserting a 'floor of rights' in 1963. British law has required the employer to give a statement of written particulars to the employee; this represents the 'best evidence' of the contractual terms (at first enforced by criminal sanctions but now only by feeble orders of an industrial tribunal). Many Continental systems have required written form for a few specialist, employment contracts but otherwise regarded the giving of written terms to the employee in the private sector as a matter mainly for collective bargaining, a feature attracting little attention in English commentary.[26] For once the Directive is constructed almost to a British pattern, and the

Commission has warned all Member States except Denmark, the UK and Spain that they have not properly implemented the Directive.[27] One feature of the Directive was indeed welcome: its extension of the right to a statement to all employees working eight hours or more for at least a month, and the duty of the employer to give it within two months. But beyond that it may be doubted whether this Directive will be a catalyst for useful reforms in industrial practice and employment law.[28] Rather the opposite. It introduced, for example, the unhappy possibility of a written statement in 'instalments', if the employer chooses, albeit that the core terms must be in one document. This results in a fragmented 'transparency' for the worker.

The method of implementation has also left the law in a worse condition on the critical issue of changes in the terms in the employment contract. Since 1963 management has been able to avoid 'a flood of paper' in Britain by including in the written particulars a statement that the terms of a collective agreement applied 'as varied from time to time'. So, for most terms of the employment, if the collective agreement was kept up to date and a copy of it was available at the place of work or otherwise reasonably accessible, that was enough, a sensible procedure of reference.[29] This procedure is certainly in the interests of workers. After a negotiated change of the employment terms the employer could arrange for the accessible agreement to be updated for a whole work group so long as their employment particulars made it clear that this was the system, without writing to each of what may be thousands of workers. But the manner in which the Directive has been implemented appears to have closed off much of this sensible machinery of 'reference'. Now a statement may refer to a document, so long as it is reasonably accessible or available at work, only on matters concerning sick pay or pension schemes, and to collective agreements only on notice periods for termination of employment. So too, the matters on which changes can be made within the procedure of reference and availability relate now only to sick pay, pension schemes, notice periods, and disciplinary rules and procedures.[30] This change will produce uncertainty and is not in the interests of workers. Written particulars figure prominently when worker and employers are in dispute, and the chance is increased of employees finding then that the employer is not contractually bound to collective terms they had assumed were incorporated by reference. Beyond that it seems that the employer must inform each individual employee not later than one month after any change – individually. Not only does this require a flood of paper sufficient to make any manager blanch, part of which arguably the Directive may not demand.[31] It appears also to represent a positive policy of the government to individuate the employment relationship wherever this can be done, a preference which even sceptical observers may recognise as touching upon their individualist ideology.[32] Despite its relevance to everyday practice in the office or factory, this measure seems to have escaped rigorous analysis at times because of a belief that, coming from Brussels in what appears to be a policy of well intentioned worker-protection, it must be a 'good thing'. But this 1066 evaluation of European labour law measures is no better than Eurodium. What is needed with such instruments is a close look at the fine print and a practical answer workable between managers and workers' representatives.

COLLECTIVE *LAISSEZ-FAIRE*

If such recent innovations need to be reviewed, it is hardly surprising that we should feel obliged to take a look again at what are said to be the foundations of British labour law. Many precepts laid down for the future rest on analyses of the past, and many current concepts received their definition then in different social frameworks. Take, for example, the well-known doctrine of Kahn-Freund, stemming from 1954: the 'abstention' or 'non-intervention' of the law, fashioned when he could believe in the 'equilibrium' of British society. In 1959 he offered more felicitously the concept of 'collective *laissez faire*'. This he described as:

> allowing free play to the collective forces of society and to limit the intervention of the law to those marginal areas in which the disparity of these forces, that is, in our case the forces of organised labour and of organised management, is so great as to prevent the successful operation of what is so very characteristically called 'negotiating machinery' ... if you like, collective *laissez-faire*.[33]

These concepts arose from his review, and instinctive grasp, of the primacy of 'voluntary' collective bargaining in British industrial relations, especially compared with other systems.[34] This degree of self-regulation arose primarily from social, not legal, causes, not least from the 'cardinal fact' that in Britain the 'industrial revolution preceded the extension of the Parliamentary franchise to the working class',[35] where, crucially, the 'trade unions were an industrial power before they became an effective political pressure group'.[36] That is still a fundamental influence, as is the fact that it took for granted, despite the fragile legal base, strong trade unions able to act autonomously and effectively. This has become the preferred explanation of labour lawyers, labour historians and industrial sociologists alike of the special shape of British labour law, emerging from the struggle for trade union freedom with immunities where visitors expect to find positive rights.[37] But of course that special history, though it makes a mould, does not determine the form of all later developments: 'founding conditions are different from maintenance conditions'.[38] The formative period, in Britain 1870-1918, may control the script sufficiently to make difficult a total change of style or big bang proposals for change, unless social relations have been torn up by the roots (even the 'new' German labour law system has some of its roots in Weimar). But significant changes in style and story line do occur when social forces require; that surely is why proposals for 'positive rights' have come on to the agenda in Britain in the 1980s, which while they would not in themselves be a 'panacea',[39] could mark the introduction of new legal supports for trade unionism with rights to organise, to representation in collective bargaining and to strike.

Like it or not, Kahn-Freund's analysis, honed to its high point in 1959,[40] still runs the language of the debate. It was 'an original and elegant portrait of the classical British system in peace-time during the first half of the century'.[41] He led the field but he was not wholly alone; other social scientists had made a parallel analysis.[42] It may sometimes be useful to divide industrial relations into periods, of which 'collective *laissez faire*' is one, but its traces tend to appear throughout the last century and a half. It is useful, too, to be reminded that the Conservative administrations of the 1980s laid claim to a place in the oldest tradition in British labour law. With their adherence to 'freedom of contract' they claim to be voluntarists, pursuing more deregulation and eroding what they find is a stifling consensus and union 'privileges' in immunities. 'We want to get back,' cried Earl Gowrie for the Thatcher government in 1980, at the outset of the programme to curb workers' liberties, 'to a voluntary system'.[43] This is the voluntarism of master and servant, utterly divorced from 'collective *laissez-faire*' in its hostility to combination on the part of workers. There never has been an agreed version or canon of 'voluntarism'. Analysis is led astray by failing to notice that it has always been a relative concept.

This alone would justify an attempt to sort out the cross currents and ambiguities. Indeed, for all the meagre 'social contract' legislation of the 1970s, the system was in central respects less legally regulated in 1980 than in 1950. In 1950 the wartime Order 1305 of 1940 still made strikes in connection with a trade dispute into criminal offences (even after a report to the Minister, and thereafter still if the dispute was sent to arbitration, which was binding).[44] That Order was linked with other complex wartime legislation protecting jobs and working practices.[45] True, this all looked temporary; but it all lasted long into the peace; and it was crucial for demobilised workers who sought employment. Nor could anyone know at the time whether it would last into the 1960s or beyond as wartime regulation of labour law did elsewhere.[46] We may say that, like most great rationalisations, the thesis in the 1950s of 'collective *laissez-faire*' has to be allowed a latitude even as a description. But it manifestly differed from 'abstention', which 'obscures questions of power and substance', whereas collective *laissez-faire* has no meaning if need and the right of workers to bring pressure to bear collectively are rejected.[47] Indeed, with hindsight it is apparent that the social parties, unions and employers, and even governments, always wanted from the outset to secure a place for regulation in this system of non-intervention on their *own terms* – as it were, to enjoy a text of 'abstention' with hefty footnotes intervening in their favour. Thereby they wanted departures from what some have called 'pure abstentionism',[48] though the adjective reminds one of Baron Rolfe's dislike of 'vituperative epithets'.[49] In noting the terms on which real participants were willing to engage in collective *laissez-faire*, we do not refer merely to the exceptional institutions which, even in Britain, long established a partially regulated floor to wages and other conditions – the Fair Wages Resolution or Wages Councils, and the other exceptional, largely auxiliary, legal interventions, rationalised almost from their inception as 'props' to the voluntary system. The 'first objective' of a Wages Council was to start up collective bargaining in the industry concerned and then 'commit suicide'.[50]

THE SIGNIFICANCE OF THE 1950s

What we find on closer re-examination of the 1950s is that the categorisation of the period as one of 'classical' abstentionism or voluntarism, with industrial relations 'conducted largely through a system of autonomous self-government',[51] may in large measure be justifiable only by emphasising parts of the picture. Ministers adopted the description of a 'voluntary' system in the 1950s – but then, so they did in 1980 and they still do today. This residual term is open to infinite interpretation. In the 1950s in truth the description emphasised three separate factors. First, the apparent (we may now say, atypical) disinclination of the courts to intervene. Second, the small number of relevant statutory features marginally altering such items as 'truck' legislation, though not touching the deep regulatory structures of safety legislation. And third the end of penal sanctions on strikes with the revocation of Order 1305. Judicial attitudes were believed not to be hawkish in the *Taff Vale* manner, marked especially by the Court of Appeal's unwillingness greatly to expand tort liability for industrial action, though it sowed the seeds of liabilities never previously imposed.[52] This assessment overlooked the extent to which judges still felt the lingering bequest of war-time rhetoric on social cohesion. The Law Lords had already limbered up ready to strike anew, counsel significantly advising the TUC not to demand legislation against their intervention for fear 'of inviting other reforms in the law affecting trade unions'.[53] As for Order 1305, Kahn-Freund in the formative period of his analysis saw it as dangerous; for in that kind of setting the parties to collective bargaining tended to become 'instruments for the realisation of the social and economic policy of the government.'[54] The revocation of Order 1305 did not, however, come about for that democratic reason. It came after Attorney General Shawcross's foolhardy prosecutions of gas workers and then, in 1951, of dockers for strikes that might be crimes under the Order. The prosecution failed to convince the jury that there was a trade dispute – without which (paradoxically) there could be no crime, so the prosecution had to be dropped.[55] So, 1951 was the year when wartime ended for labour law. The deal between the TUC and the Labour government to keep Order 1305 alive could not survive. Strikes in trade disputes ceased to be crimes; the wartime power to prosecute was 'tolerated so long as it was not used'.[56] The common account is that the system could thereafter set sail into 'abstention'. But the manner in which this was done may fairly stand as an example of the way terms of the post-war 'voluntarist' system were determined, not by an uncontroversial line of social deregulation or dejuridification, but intermittently and 'in the course of a struggle'.[57]

How far did the system evolve into collective *laissez-faire* with a shifting balance or uneven equilibrium between the parties? In one sense manifestly it did, for trade unions became even more vigorous and effective in collective bargaining, from national level to plant –

especially through workers at plant level – in the economic conditions of the 1950s, without further legal assistance. But at the outset, the legal consequences of Order 1305 and its abolition left the parties manoeuvring in a juridical half-light, not as joint and avowed partisans of unconditional 'abstention'. On its side, authority was willing to use various legal weapons, redolent of master and servant, that were still to hand against (especially) unofficial strikers for whose actions evil Communists were blamed by all sides, especially Labour governments playing 'the "Red Scare" card'.[58] Striking seamen, for example, found themselves struck off the register of seamen, and were in consequence served with their conscription papers within days.[59] Employers had also evaded the arbitrated terms binding under the Order, especially by means of sacking workers and then hiring them at the old rates.[60] True, after 1958 the nationalised coal employers ended a long tradition in the industry of suing striking miners for breach of contract, but elsewhere the mood of employers toughened. The unions had made gains. Freed from the embarrassment of penal sanctions on strikes, a new Order (No. 1376) in 1951 set up a system of compulsory arbitration on 'issues' and 'disputes' in employment to replace the provisions of Order 1305. It is interesting that writing on labour law in 1954, Kahn-Freund gave a close account of all these provisions, judging them to be of 'outstanding importance for the shaping of industrial relations in the course of the last thirteen years ... compulsory arbitration has not in this country killed voluntary bargaining'; he hoped these provisions, or something like them 'may one day become a *permanent* feature of the law'.[61] This did not inhibit him from advancing the thesis that 'reliance on legal sanction' might be a sign of 'weakness' on the part of the unions. Of course, there is a great difference between overall compulsory arbitration and compulsory extension of minimum terms of collective agreements; but the picture painted by him simply was not one of unrelieved 'abstention'; the 'gloss' on voluntarism which we saw added by legislation was on the contrary intervenient. Its 'auxiliary' character stemmed not from its inherent nature but from its consequences – it was helpful to collective bargaining. That might distinguish it from systems like the French, where the *Code du travail* may have obstructed the growth of bargaining. But there were, and are, many systems where extensive legal regulation was the very basis of collective bargaining – in Sweden, for example, which came to be the object of such intense interest for both the Donovan Commission and Bullock Committee alike.

By this point one has left 'abstention' in any real sense far behind and moved into the more modulated philosophy of 'collective *laissez-faire*'. Many years later, some would try unsuccessfully to rationalise prices and incomes legislation in this way, as an intervention necessary to *preserve* collective bargaining (perhaps from itself). But although the pretended capacity to suppress voluntary bargaining was objectionable to most adherents of 'voluntarism', such interventions did not reshape the labour law of the period 1960 to 1979.[62] After the demise, however, of Order 1376 in 1958 (its Industrial Disputes Tribunal continued transitionally into 1959) compulsory arbitration provisions, though more narrowly couched, were enacted under a statute of 1959. After that, there were some parallel procedures under the Industrial Relations Act 1971; and more vigorous provisions for extending collectively bargained minimum conditions appeared in the 'social contract' legislation of 1975 until the axe of 1980 came down impatiently on all these market-obstructive devices.[63] So for four decades, in war and peace, British labour law knew of compulsory arbitration of one kind or another, as a central area of legal intervention – if you like, mainly 'auxiliary' but nevertheless crucial – in collective bargaining law. This fact has been widely undervalued by us all. There is no objection whatever in principle in our traditional labour law to compulsory arbitration and legal enforcement so long as it is balanced against the values of autonomous trade unionism, which are at the core of collective *laissez-faire*.

PERIODS OF STRUGGLE

Moreover, this succession of legal provisions was not the happy stream of voluntary adjustment sometimes depicted. There was no straight line of juridification or dejuridification.[64] The feature missing from such accounts is the re-entry of hard fought industrial struggle which was central to the legal developments. Authorities date the return of major strike activity as early as 1953, confirming the social pressure from workers.[65] Employers then complained soon after 1951 about being bound by arbitration when it was no longer a crime to strike and about wages forced from them that were 'inflationary'. The Conservative government accepted that it was wrong in peace time for 'one party to be coerced by law'.[66] By the mid-1950s the 'middle class acquiescence' tolerating stronger unions had fragmented. Cabinet papers declared the 'old sanction for discipline in industry' had disappeared with the advent of full employment.[67] But trench warfare was threatened in 1957 with the massive dispute in engineering, justifiably known as 'the employers' challenge', the strike resulting 'from an attempt by British employers to alter the system of industrial relations' in their own favour, their self-interested renewed protests about inflation accompanying their pursuit of authority and 'power'.[68] They felt let down by government (whose incomes policy they claimed to have maintained) – the latter excusing their withdrawal of support as a consequence of Suez. The employers recorded:

> Twice in four years the Federation have been prepared to 'fight it out' with the unions ... Like the Czechs in 1938 their complaint was that they were not allowed to resist in 1954 and 1957 after they had received every encouragement to have a firm purpose and to make it known to the unions.[69]

The 1957 dispute was the first occasion since the war that the engineering employers had revived their traditional intransigence, exemplified in the lock-outs of 1897 and 1922.[70] It was the end of an era. Social struggle had returned in depth, if not in every union headquarters then for shop stewards on most shop floors. Into the 1960s the number of official stoppages in engineering and elsewhere rose sharply.[71] Certainly, even this early, it was not 'strictly true' that the law was wholly 'abstentionist'.[72]

At just this period of the late 1950s, often accepted as one of legal 'non-intervention' at its highest, a group of influential Conservative lawyers (including some destined for high judicial office) chose to put together some 'thoughts on the constitutional and legal position of Trade Unions'. This challenged openly, as others had more discretely, the doctrine put forward in the Conservative Party earlier that there should be no new trade union legislation without agreement with the unions.[73] It registered the phenomenon to be found in any newspaper of the period, the return of anti-unionism in the establishment. The new document, emanating from the Temple, *A Giant's Strength* (1958),[74] adopted the tone of an elegantly aggressive legal attack on the unions' position. It was destined to have great influence – not least in teaching every Conservative candidate that it was Disraeli's government, not Gladstone's, which enacted the Act of 1875, when the TUC Congress then 'expressed the warmest eulogies of the Government'. The analysis in 1958 by these top Conservative lawyers saw unions as powerful bodies occupying 'a privileged position under the law' – an inevitable conclusion for common lawyers on 'immunities' that rescue unions from illegality under the 'ordinary (common) law of the land'. Their conclusions have a modern ring: no immunity should apply to unofficial strikes; unions should be made to register with vetted rules as the price for slender legal protection; secondary action was indefensible in days of full employment; and all strikes should be illegal unless preceded by a *tribunal of inquiry*. This, the first post-war blast of a comprehensive legal policy by Conservative lawyers, was an interesting mixture of 'corporatist' (the union register and the tribunal) and more radical free-market thinking (removing immunities). It was in the tradition of those who had opposed the repeal of the anti-union Act of 1927 by Labour in 1946, and against the policies of the conciliators, especially Monckton ('the oil can' fixer). There was one chapter in *A Giant's Strength*, however, which is less remembered and which could, if adopted, have revolutionised the map of labour relations law. Significantly, an echo may now perhaps be found in European Community law, discussed below.[75] One wonders whether it will be reflected in the next Conservative Bill. It is the proposal to extend 'restrictive practices law' against the unions. To this we return in Chapter 10.

VOLUNTARISM: ON WHOSE TERMS

By 1958 the struggle in many sectors had sharpened. Workers found that 'many employers' organisations were talking about getting rid of [Order 1376] and fighting it out with the unions – and those words were actually said'.[76] The employers had for years been pushing for the end of all compulsory arbitration under Order 1376, and the government had agreed that its form (then still a Defence Regulation) had to be reconsidered. Quickly.

> the employers in general came to the conclusion they could not continue to support the compulsory system ... [and] the Government, on consideration, decided to abandon the Order [1376] without replacement.[77]

The fact that government intended to end unilateral arbitration and 'return to the position of forty years before' engendered a 'feeling that it was now a "free-for-all" ' in many unions leaders.[78] What was left of the wartime consensus seemed to be disintegrating. But significantly the TUC did not raise a shout of 'abstention'. It opposed revocation because the Order (assisting the work of conciliation officers) had encouraged employers to bargain and unions were keen to use such procedures.[79] Already the move from Order 1305 to Order 1376 had made it more difficult for unions to use the procedure to exert pressure to gain recognition.[80] The Parliamentary contradictions were notable. The Opposition protested against the ending of legal regulation and called the 'scrapping of this Order, without anything of a permanent legislative nature taking its place ... a retrograde step in industrial relations'.[81] A Labour Member complained that 'after seventeen years of arbitration and negotiations' union members would look for settlement by arbitration, 'but they will find that it is non-existent ... We shall be faced with a trial of strength'.[82] Indeed, despite the rupture in 1958 of the tacit pact between government and unions to maintain legal regulation for the fixing of minimum conditions, before the Donovan Commission the unions continued their demand for the return of an improved Order 1376.[83]

But government took its stand on 'voluntarism'. So did the Opposition – but on its own terms. Each had its preferred style of intervention. 'The whole basis of our industrial system is voluntary negotation and agreement between the sides', said Macleod, narrowing the area of debate. 'Where we differ is ... whether there should be the prop of compulsion behind it in certain events.'[84] The victory for the Tory hawks in revoking the Order reflected significant social changes of attitude. Their victory was not complete, however, in the very next year the government squeezed into its legislative programme for 1959 a narrow provision (materially different from the Order) for arbitration under certain conditions by the Industrial Court of claims for terms not less favourable than 'recognised terms and conditions' of collective agreements. A 'Wages Councils (Amendment) Bill' was conveniently proceeding through Parliament; the new clause was added to it and the name changed to Terms and Conditions of Employment Act 1959; eventually this new clause was all that remained of the Act. Some suggested the unions should have called not for compulsory arbitration but for broader minimum income arrangements;[85] but this would, of course, have involved an even greater, or at least more open, modification of 'voluntarism'. But we must note that the unions, though not taking up that position, had gone wider in another respect. They repeatedly proposed the reintroduction – understandably – of an Order similar to order 1376 under which 'independent' arbitration could be required of a wider range of 'disputes', *in addition* to arbitration supportive of minima derived from collective bargaining. From 1960 this policy can be found regularly in the TUC General Council's Reports, until the issue was overtaken by other aspects of the Labour Government.[86] Of course, the arguments advanced for the legislation by the TUC struck a chord in 'voluntarism' in a loose sense: the machinery would promote 'peace' and employers would settle 'voluntarily because employers were aware that otherwise they would be sent to arbitration'.[87] In some respects the arguments were aimed at securing recognition of unions; but 'voluntarism' was restricted to a different sense: a demand that arbitration must be 'independent of direct Government influence' in face of the new Prices and Incomes Board, and that arbitrators should be available at local level to 'give a decisive verdict within seven days or so'.[88] The unions' – sensible – policy was a good illustration of voluntarism on terms. It was based on collective *laissez-faire*, not on 'abstention of the law'.

More important, commentary has at times obscured the significance of these events. Even Kahn-Freund was to write as if the really important feature was the replacement of the Orders by an Act,[89] and commentators have spoken (not unnaturally in terms of pure legal analysis) of the 'replacement' of the arbitration provisions of the Order by the Act, or of the former being partly 'carried over' into the latter.[90] It is understandable that concentration on the forms should present this development as a smooth takeover that can be analysed in some process of juridification. In fact, however, the crucial gap between the revocation of Order 1376, inspired by the employers, and the government's capitulation by enacting the 1959 Act, is evidence of a renewed social struggle. We can detect a gradual acceleration of opinion and action against the unions – a 'conflation of the image of the trade union Goliath with the new theme of small groups of "militants",[91] leading directly to Prime Minister Wilson's 'tightly knit group of politically motivated men' in his analysis of the 1966 seamen's strike. This trend was soon to affect the courts and then the legislature, as it entered the era when minimal protection of individual workers on redundancy pay, sick pay and safety in offices, illustrated 'government intervention to make private industry do what it has ... so signally failed to do for itself'.[92] Of course, legislation on safety is and was an accepted exception to any doctrines about non-intervention of the law, one dictated by history rather than by logic.

CIVIL SERVICE CONTINUITIES

Civil service contributions to policy were of some importance here (as they are today) aiming at maintaining social peace and buying off working-class protest,[93] especially in the measures on redundancy payments and industrial tribunals.[94] If the object had been primarily protection of the workers concerned, further research on alternative, less 'legal', methods might have been appropriate.[95] The arguments for the redundancy payments legislation of 1965 were put by judges as the 'implementation of the policy more acceptable to trade unions' in reducing the 'widespread practice of overmanning',[96] and by official research as intended to take the edge off 'union and workplace opposition ... in the redundancy situation ... to achieve some reduction in its intensity'.[97] From 1956 to 1965 the challenge to the unions' effectiveness grew gradually stronger alongside a growing challenge from the shop floor against policies first of a 'return to orthodox market policies, and secondly, limited elements of corporatism'.[98] There followed the high tide of 'incomes policy',[99] then the social contract legislation (which must, of course, be judged in the context of general policies, including incomes policy)[100] and in the 1980s the Thatcher administrations which aimed to sweep trade union influence out of the market arena. In all these periods there was no total abstention from legal influence on labour relations – even if one puts safety at work aside. What there was was a continuing spirit of priority for autonomous bargaining, collective *laissez-faire* that allowed nevertheless for attachment to particular legislation (not all of it strictly auxiliary) by one or other, sometimes both, of the bargaining sides. And from the employers' insistence upon revocation of unilateral arbitration and *A Giant's Strength* to the first judgment in *Rookes* v. *Barnard*, when the ambiguous face of judicial 'non-intervention' was shattered, was no more than three years.[101]

Middle class opinion was swimming in the same stream as employers' opposition to compulsory arbitration. The period 1951 to 1959 was not a time of a shared ideology based on strict 'voluntarism'. It did confirm the healthy ability of the labour movement to match its claim to priority for collective bargaining with a pragmatic approach to legislative protection and assistance. From the very outset, once the penal wartime controls were lifted the cards of 'abstention' were marked by each side, even in the time of 'Butskillism', with their own terms for intervention. Errors in union calculations followed (as in the unco-ordinated response on legislation for unfair dismissals) but as far as they were concerned, there never was any period or doctrine of absolute or strict 'abstentionism'.[102] How could this be, many asked at the time, with huge tomes of legal regulation on safety at work standing in the shelves? It was of course easy to claim 'priority' for 'autonomous machinery over statutory machinery'; but the idea that compulsory arbitration would disappear from the British system was said in 1954 to be a 'semi-utopian belief'[103] – though some twenty five years later Mrs Thatcher achieved it at a stroke. Like employers and unions in the 1950s, Kahn-Freund marked his own cards by calling for the adoption of a permanent system of compulsory arbitration on terms of 'freely negotiated collective agreements', which his command of the subject knew could not possibly be confined ultimately within the boundaries of Order 1376. A review of this period, however, makes one focus on the stance of the trade union movement. Had it before this time taken its stand on more positive forms of basic labour rights in the ILO Conventions (with all the difficulties for Member States that have arisen here in the European Community)[104] would it perhaps have been in a marginally better shape to defend its members' freedoms and advance their interests?

THE TRUE DOCTRINE

Once freed from the historical myth of strict 'abstentionism' on the part of all whose centre of gravity has been autonomous trade unionism, the era of the 1950s has other lessons for us, not least on strike ballots. They are not a new idea. In 1955 the Cabinet considered the proposal to require secret ballots of union members before strikes. The civil service had a paper in the drawer to give to any Minister interested in the idea of obligatory ballots – just as it has had since 1915 other standard, if burgeoning papers on emergencies and the use of troops to break strikes.[105] Such civil service policies aim at social order, not excluding reform in the interests of what they perceive to be social cohesion. They have been of importance elsewhere, for example on the introduction of industrial tribunals proposed to be a 'nucleus of a system of labour courts'.[106] From an early date – perhaps as early as Askwith or the Whitley Reports – the ruling ideology of the Ministry of Labour was a preference for voluntary machinery in bargaining and disputes. In 1933 an ILO expert described the British system as resting on the 'mutual recognition and widespread regulation of working conditions by collective agreements' which was 'the result of a century of struggle and evolution'.[107] The ideology survived the times of 'incomes policy' in the Department of Employment, as it became,[108] though, as Freedland has shown, civil service promotion of the voluntary system[109] has been largely replaced by promotion of competitive enterprise in the process of 'de-institutionalising' the Department under the Thatcher governments, a process that 'started long before the *Götterdämmerung* of the eighties.'[110] In the old tradition, it was avowed in 1955 that 'persuasion and the technique of skilled conciliation' were the 'true doctrine of the Ministry of Labour'.[111] The plans brought out of the drawer in 1955 about containing strikes were manifestly similar to the paper which was put before the Labour Government in 1946, and one which turns up later.[112] Of course, many unions have long had rules requiring ballots before 'major strikes' but these were enforceable only by members.[113] The orthodox reasoning was presented to the House of Commons[114] by Monckton under the two main headings found at the earlier date, arguments coming down against both the banning of unofficial industrial action and the imposition of 'a secret ballot of members' before official strikes. The former, seriously considered by the Attlee government in 1950, was rejected because it risked making all strikes official, especially when it was uncertain which penalties and what methods of enforcement could possibly be used. (This adumbrated the experience of 'martyrdom' for the dockers' shop stewards imprisoned in 1972, which in turn led to moves away from enforcement against persons and towards attachment of the property of unions in the Act of 1982, changes in the court rules in 1981 to enforce contempt of court fines and in 1983 the idea for even stronger action such as 'taking over by an outside authority of the running of the business of a trade union', a plan largely overtaken by the judicial extensions of the availability of receiverships).[115]

On the option of strike ballots, Monckton had in 1955 offered the, again traditional, three reasons for caution, none of them mentioning basic labour freedoms, though he did take pride in having given a recent lecture at the ILO 'about industrial relations and human relations'. They were: such ballots would not affect unofficial strikes; they would not apply to action less than a strike, such as a work to rule or go slow; and they might make it 'more difficult for negotiators to settle on compromise terms'. Macmillan reconsidered the issue in 1957, and 'successive governments over the next 30 years were to consider the same proposal ... as a means of clamping down on strike action', but none legislated.[116] In a *Green Paper* of 1983 the Thatcher government advanced the same three reasons in virtually the same words, to prove why a proposal for strike ballots 'did not attract wide support' and why 'no country ... has legislated to require universal "automatic" strike ballots ... before *any* strike'; also limitation to official strikes would encourage unofficial action, and ballots on action short of a strike were 'impracticable'.[117] It was therefore wholly unprecedented for the government to revive the idea in 1983 in its search for another 'step' in anti-union legislation to clear the market of what they saw as workers' collective obstruction. This time, there was a very different outcome. Six months after its *Green Paper* the government said that, of the 150 responses, there was 'general agreement' that there should after all be a ballot always 'before union members are called out on strike'.[118] Some employers, like those in engineering, had not seen ballots as a priority, though they would use the weapon once the rule was enacted.[119] Four months later the Secretary of State justified imposition of strike ballots on *all* official industrial action, including action short of a strike, not by citing any new social problems or errors in the traditional reasoning, but by saying that unions, enjoying an immunity 'unique in English law', should 'consult their members before calling on them to risk their own livelihood by going on strike, often causing public disruption'. In truth, the debates of 1983–1984 disclosed no substantial reason other than the government's demand that unions go through this procedure to 'safeguard' the members and the public. The primary plaintiffs would of course be the employers. So in what became the Act of 1984 all official strike action was covered; it was not 'practicable to require the same of leaders of unofficial action' – disciplining unofficial strikers (not just their leaders) had to wait for the selective dismissal provisions of the 1990 Act. The government did not believe this would encourage unofficial action or impede settlements.[120]

Asked why he disagreed with the traditional reasoning of the *Green Paper*, the Secretary of State spoke merely of taking a different view 'in the light of those consultations'. Analyses of the subsequent proceedings reveal no answers to the traditional Monckton-civil service points.[121] Nor were these points ever answered, certainly not in 1988, 1990 or 1993, when Acts made strike-ballots a centre-piece of policy and turned the legal screw tighter to the point of mandatory postal ballots within four weeks before the call to action, eventually obliging the union to hand over the names of members about to strike to the employer.[122] Instead the government put broad emphasis on 'handing back the unions to their members' and on not creating special courts or agencies to enforce the new laws. In its obvious implicit criticism of the 1971 Act (with a corporatist special court, the NIRC, and the Registrar), this emphasis reveals a key point.

IDEOLOGIES OF ENFORCEMENT

There were no events to which the ministers could point in 1983 to knock out the Monckton-civil service arguments that had been convincing for many decades. So why turn, after all these years, to a positive 'No-ballot: no-immunity' rule for all union action, even for a one-hour go slow? At one level, 'ballots' were a device the government had used before. The imposition of ballots in 1980-82 to validate a dismissal in a closed shop, with extravagant demands for 80 or 85 per cent majorities, was never meant to *legitimise* such union security arrangements, only to hamstring them. This became clear in 1988 when all legal and industrial pressures to support them were made unlawful, and the provisions for ballots was quietly dropped.[123] though this 'liberation from trade union power' often left managers 'running in all directions or sometimes more energetically on the spot'.[124] In similar vein, the emphasis in 1984 on enforcement machinery provides an important clue. The government was by now deeply committed to controlling unions in steady steps whilst avoiding corporatist machinery, and in 1983 it scented success. Unions were to be handed 'back to their members' so that they, not some special agency or court, would be a central enforcement mechanism to enforce 'their' rights. After 1988 they could be aided by the CROTUM; but that officer is *never* a party to the proceedings (that would step over the corporatist threshold). After 1990 they are helped by the tighter rules on vicarious liability. The reality, of course, is that it is employers who benefit and they normally who seek the injunctions (available from judges by virtue of judge-made rules for merely an 'arguable case') whenever the complex strike-ballot procedure is arguably infringed. Indeed, curiously the hurdles over which a defendant union has to jump are higher where the complainant turns out to be an employer than where he or she is a union member,[125] a ridiculous provision in principle since the union cannot know at the time of the ballot who the plaintiff is going to be.

The plan was to leave the unions to the common law, the 'ordinary law of the land', cleansed of immunities. At the heart of this legal ideology is reliance on the hostility to trade unions in that law which has never altered its view that they are unlawful by reason of 'restraint of trade'. So deep-seated is this judge-made doctrine that judges now say it should not be altered by 'intervention by the judges'![126] Deprived of 'privileges' (and in the British case with no collective rights) unions were to be subject to this regime as they were in the 1900, but with additional, special liabilities and procedures, as in the members' ballots on terms made as difficult as possible (by postal ballots and with the State money for costs of which Prior had been proud, now withdrawn). This process was not to be effected, as in the emergency procedures of 1971, by direct government 'coercion'. It is sometimes objected that none of the ideologues, Hayek, Friedman or Nozick etc, proposed these precise measures. Nor did they; but legal ideology works more by osmosis than by mirrors. Those in power sniff out the way forward for the imposition of their interests where their chroniclers may have given only general guidance. Strike ballots give us an example. Hayek's concept of withdrawing 'coercive' powers from unions – what a distinguished follower called restoring the 'principle underlying the British Combination Acts 1799 and 1800'[127] – aimed also at the union members' individual relationships with their employer. No obedience to the union must rank above his or her employment obligations (this was translated directly into law in the 1988 Act as the right of strike-breakers not to be 'unjustifiably disciplined' by the union).[128] Labour law in the United States had been aware of the argument that a 'strike-ballot clause' involved an inroad upon collective bargaining and weakened the union in bargaining, especially because 'it enables the employer, in effect, to deal with its employees rther than with their statutory representative'. This was the basis on which the Supreme Court refused, to Hayek's displeasure, to make such a clause a mandatory subject of bargaining.[129] It happens that Hayek was fond of referring critically to such 'errors' detected by his disciples in American labour law and from the references he gives it is clear that he would approve of this use of ballots.[130] (Of course, whether the British legislation has effectively decollectivised the workforce is another question.)[131] There was a decisive difference between the 1980s governments and that of the preceding Conservative administrations, which showed in their labour law legislation. To deny the importance of the ideological component in this difference does less than justice to the seriousness of the policy. There is a theme and it is likely to continue.[132] until the chance for an alternative is afforded.

ABSTENTIONISM OUT?

In the light of that history, it may be thought regrettable that Kahn-Freund ever applied the title of 'abstention' of the law (or more rarely, 'non-intervention') to the system. True, much of the legislative intervention could be and was explained as supports or 'props' for collective bargaining. But the very term 'abstention' allowed the whole analysis to be robustly pigeonholed as a 'serious misunderstanding of the role of law in constituting society', when what was needed were 'effective legal mechanisms enforcing democracy, the Rule of Law and fairness' in the workplace.[133] Such a claim had a potent ring, though, on its own premises it would need judges devoted to a quest for Justice of positively Platonic proportions. It may also miss out the role of autonomous, collective unions to 'provide a qualitatively different kind of employment protction'[134] – including the legal role institutionalised in other legal systems by forms of *l'action syndicale* (unions' right of audience to protect members' interests). Indeed, we must not fall into what might be called 'vulgar abstentionism' by ignoring the mixed system of forty years ago.

The term 'abstention' itself was often a provocative misdescription; legislation simply did not 'abstain' and judges did so only interstitially. Westminster never debated (not even in the House of Lords) the absurd motion: 'That the law do now abstain from industrial relations'. What the crucial legislation *has* done is different in kind: it took to 'excluding' the decisions, in whole or in part, of the common law *judges* after their interventionist, 'creative' judgments which would have made trade unionism unlawful. It repelled judicial liabilities in tort which could be ruinous for trade unions – in 1875, 1906, 1965 and again in 1974 and 1976; the first move in 1871 saved them from unlawfulness under the common law's doctrine of 'restraint of trade', from which they still are only precariously protected.[135] The writer suggested in 1965 that, faced with hostile judgments, 'the counter-attack by trade unions and their supporters used political power to *exclude* them by legislation'.[136] Whatever else, this signified a political and interventionist response to repressive common law innovation. Equally, repressive laws need a similar response. The phrase 'collective *laissez-faire*' stuck and felt right, not only by reason of its incisively descriptive insight but because it spoke to that history and to the values or, as Flanders put it, the 'complex pattern of beliefs', which constituted 'voluntarism', above all the preference for collective bargaining.[137] The primacy of voluntary arrangements was central; but rejection of some ideal type or Platonic 'Idea' of Regulation or Legislation as such was not part of it. The problem of finding 'imagination and constructive formulations'[138] in labour legislation has always been part, albeit usually auxiliary, of a 'positive' approach to collective labour relations. But – and this is crucial – what was enshrined also in collective *laissez-faire* is the necessary reference to basic labour standards, freedoms internationally established in the ILO Conventions and other international instruments – freedom of association (which subsumes a right to organise and a right to strike) and autonomous collective bargaining encouraged by the State.[139] It is this which distinguishes its form of 'voluntarism' from the Thatcher brand. In its response to the ILO, the British government has even denied the long accepted interpretation of freedom of association as including a right to strike by asserting: 'at no point in its text does Convention 87 refer to a "right to strike" or a "right to lock out",' adding the remarkable statement: 'UK law guarantees all employees an absolute freedom to choose to take strike action.'[140]

On the other hand, a different understanding of 'abstentionism' as a much more diffuse concept has often been employed to refer to *all* legislation on employment rights: in this sense "abstentionism related as much to individual employment law as to the institutions of collective bargaining and industrial conflict.'[141] It might refer to whether workers could be more effectively protected by negotiation or by legislation, though they never could be in Britain by total 'abstention' because of the nature of the common law.[142] By hypothesis, however, individualist concepts of 'abstention' so understood did not share the link with collective organisation. Whereas some (at times even Kahn-Freund himself) saw the growth of statutory rights for individual workers in the 1960s and 1970s as changing the 'old tradition of legislative non-intervention',[143] others from the outset regarded it as – or said it must become – a 'floor of rights' affecting the process of collective bargaining but not, if well constructed, damaging it.[144] Reliance on legislation alone loses the umbilical connection with values of autonomy, the link with the labour movement, at any rate in Britain. Our employment law does not reflect what is found in some systems, where the law accepts

> from the outset, the inequality of the parties to the individual employment contract ... [it] became a 'law for unequals', distinguishable from private contract law which posed as the law of free and equal citizens.[145]

A juridical chasm divides the techniques and concepts of such systems of labour law from the common law apparatus with its strong aura of master and servant law, on to which collective *laissez-faire* was grafted.[146] In democratic countries through the Tunnel collective legal values invariably rest upon guarantees, frequently in a constitution. In Britain, collective *laissez-faire* was not a constitution but it was, to borrow from a later Chapter, at times 'a language, at others a code, for the defence of the autonomous trade union.'[147] Lacking a legal presumption in favour of the weaker party to the hiring transaction in which labour power is sold, this 'code' attempted to reduce the inequality by demanding a guided primacy for collective relations, not total because it accepted the formal presence of 'freedom of contract', a feature which leaves it vulnerable to individual contract's derogations.[148] This was a credo, however, under which the attainments of British trade unions were such as they could still feel proud.

PARODIES OF COLLECTIVE *LAISSEZ-FAIRE*

Although there was wide-spread acceptance of the collective *laissez-faire* doctrine by the 1960s – it is now often forgotten how heartening it was to read an analysis giving a shape to a system which conventional lawyers were still wont to describe as 'the law of contract and tort', if not 'master and servant' – subsequently misunderstandings have crept in. For example, it was suggested in 1990: 'The issue today is not 'law or no law', but fair law or unfair law'.[149] Politically that makes a nice point, but juridically it illustrates an inadequate analysis widely found in the media. It encourages avoidance of inquiry into the *nature* of different laws by such assertions as: 'acceptance of the role of law in industrial relations has been one of the most significant developments of the 1980s'.[150] One could have said the same of the 1880s if one had concentrated upon factory legislation. The issue never was, never could be, 'law or no law'. No industrial society can exist with a legal void at the workplace. Calls for 'autonomy' are calls not for empty space but for freedom of association and protection from dominant social regulation that builds in the masters' prerogatives.[151] Although it has always suited its detractors to paint it as a lawless jungle, collective *laissez-faire* involved not 'no law', but a particular type or quality of law, one which put a premium on protecting autonomous collective bargaining and which necessarily, therefore, demanded areas of liberty for trade unions.[152] Indeed, even at the peak of so-called 'abstention' volumes of regulations about safety at work and hours, for instance on conditions for women and young workers, sat on the statute book. They gave the lie to the thesis that there was 'no law' in labour relations, while legal 'immunities' protecting (barely) basic collective liberties in social conflict after 1906 illustrated the singular character of British labour law elsewhere in leaving the pattern and outcome of bargaining very largely to the parties. That was the key point. Kahn-Freund himself mentioned some thirty five major Acts in his classic analysis of 1959; and even in the 1940s and 1950s, the British labour market was subject to not unimportant legal regulation, to which further regulation on individual employment rights were added in the 1960s.

The central claim was historically undeniable: 'The proud edifice of collective labour regulation was built up without the assistance of the law ... No Wagner Act, nor Weimar constitution, no Front Populaire legislation.'[153] From the outset, it was as a comparatist that he was at his brilliant best. Two decades later the point was reaffirmed: 'auxiliary legislation' was an 'absolutely dominant feature of British labour law' which did not affect the 'normal processes of collective bargaining at all'.[154] Perhaps more account should have been taken of the manner in which Ministers had promoted Whitley Councils; or of the various Bills which had been presented in the 1930s, unsuccessfully, to give collective agreements greater legal effect, when in the prevailing economic circumstances intervention on bargaining might have gone further but for the war.[155] Recent commentaries make an interesting but rather different analysis, describing forms of 'collective laissez faire', some of which are said to be a 'pure abstentionist position' of those holding 'totally abstentionist views'. This 'pure' or 'total' form, abstention with the epithet, is never precisely defined, and at times is said to exist 'in the realm of ideas rather than in the real world'.[156] It may perhaps intend to encompass the more extreme formulations of Kahn-Freund himself in the first flush of his grand design, or later before he thought a 'fundamental change' might be evident in new legislation.[157] In a sense, 'pure abstentionism' never got purer than his optimistic – and surely erroneous – statement: 'What the State has not given the State cannot take away',[158] if only because that did spring from a realm of ideas, especially Laski's,[159] rather than from history. 'Abstentionism' (with or without an epithet) insisted upon withdrawal by, or at most an unreal 'neutrality' from, the State. Collective laissez-faire could afford a more sophisticated inquiry into the nature of its interventions, knowing that the 'tendency of regulation cannot be determined a priori'.[160]

The concept of 'pure' abstentionism has, however, been more doubtfully extended to exclude legislation on any social problems touching the workplace, a meaning invariably adopted by the opponents of collective laissez-faire. Proponents are depicted as swimming in 'deep water', for example 'having to defend [their] support for legislation to curb racial discrimination' to the inquiries of the Donovan Commission, as the writer did, against the blanket view that 'the law had little part to play in regulating industrial relations'.[161] The waters were hardly so deep. First, the explanation of 'abstention' that was proffered was the common historical version: it 'did little more than exclude common law liabilities' and leave collective bargaining to the parties.[162] Second, at that time proposing laws to outlaw discrimination on grounds of race aroused enraged objections from such people as Lord Tangley, a Commission member, who objected to the 'preferential treatment' involved in laws outlawing racial discrimination. It is easy today to see the errors in the belief that proposals for laws to curb racism or sexual inequality impaired any rational philosophy of collective *laissez-faire*.[163] The truth is such people used 'abstentionism' as an Aunt Sally, torturing 'voluntarism' to make it mean 'no law'. The 'pure abstentionism' mockingly advanced by the Tangley school of jurisprudence would if taken seriously allow no room at the workplace for laws on rape. Since part of the objective, it was clear at the time, was to make 'abstentionism', 'voluntarism' and 'collective *laissez faire*' all look ridiculous, the pronouncements would scarcely be worth serious attention except as examples of distortion and of the need for more effective legislation than we yet have on racism. As for Kahn-Freund, he bracketed regimes of 'active racial discrimination', wherever it was practised, with dictatorships.[164]

From the very outset of the debates on collective *laissez-faire*, the need for an 'imaginative and constructive formulation of positive labour law'[165] has been on the agenda. Far from aiming at theoretical 'purity', some of the exponents of this view had proposed in the 1960s that, without 'discarding' the old tradition or its immunities, 'serious consideration should now be given to the introduction of certain, carefully drawn "positive" rights for trade unions' which would be 'more fitting in modern society'.[166] Unhappily, there followed the Industrial Relations Act 1971, putting a legislative framework to a very different use, far from the purposes of collective *laissez-faire*. Since trade union autonomy was directly threatened, proposals for 'positive laws' cautiously took a back seat.[167] Few opponents of the corporatist 1971 Act can claim that they foresaw the brutal assaults on trade union liberties that followed in the 1980s; but aspects of the former can, with hindsight, now be seen to have alerted the ideological senses to the nature of the later, market driven legislation.[168] The option of positive rights for collective liberties did not find its place on to the menu of either the Donovan Report or the politicians – except perhaps in a subfusc way in that chameleon document, *In Place of Strife*.[169] There was a highly literate discussion in the Green Paper of 1981[170] just before Conservative policy broke finally with the past in the Employment Act of 1982 to put unions into the frame as defendants and lock them in to tort liability by adjusting special doctrines of 'vicarious' responsibility[171] progressively greater in severity than the common law.[172] Apart from some remarks on an agenda of employers,[173] the issue was left to academic commentary in the early 1980s to pick up the earlier threads.[174]

DIVERSE APPROACHES TO COLLECTIVE *LAISSEZ-FAIRE*

With these developments in mind, one may usefully refer to three types or uses of collective *laissez-faire*.[175] They may be loosely called the descriptive, the prescriptive and the ideological. It is the ideological prescription – not at all the same as 'abstentionism' – on which we can draw for analyses and struggle in the future. Let us at once remark in parenthesis however that British labour law scholarship, strong in its healthy pragmatism, tends to look in a rather Nelsonian manner at the messages of 'ideology'.[176] It has often been said that pragmatism rather than theory moulded the system. But, unlike the times of Tawney and Laski, today even the term 'political economy' has become suspect, reflecting perhaps an old, specifically English, trauma, not limited to 'left' or 'right', and in need more of Freud than of Marx. It is as if the very inquiry into ideologies – without which few Continental scholars would be respectable[177] – had become in England an offence against scholarly values, as if a timid disinclination to analyse an ideology inherent in the opponent's labour law policies sprang from fear that its devotees might in reply open up an alien or 'extremist' ideology in one's own position. In fact, pragmatism (at its best in the Warwick school) has been afforded a false hegemony that has limited the political and at times trade union arguments for social change,[178] and now affects even the public face of scholarship. This was, and is, a sad limitation that rendered England the more unready for the ideological assault of Thatcherism, not least in labour law. There were few diffused ideological weapons able to engage with the false semantics of 'trade union reform'. With this English empirical characteristic goes an uncertainty about processes of a class society, whereby 'widespread legitimation and acceptance exists of institutions, mechanisms, principles and beliefs so necessary and convenient for the owners and controllers of resources'. This derives largely from 'their very power [which] affords them the facilities for creating and maintaining social attitudes and values favourable to that acceptance.'[179]

Sinzheimer had no doubts on the point: 'No scholarship is possible without conviction, without a view of the totality'.[180] Remembering that its roots are in life not consciousness, ideology is essential even to the pragmatist. Labour law affords many practical examples. The Conservative manifesto of 1983 promised consultation about removing trade disputes 'immunities' in specified 'essential services'; but no such legislation has appeared.[181]

There are of course many practical difficulties – the defining of 'essential services' and the invention of 'an acceptable means of determining the pay and conditions' of the workers if negotiation failed;[182] but the venture is unattractive to Thatcherite philosophy also because the solutions will inevitably become embroiled in tripartite or other unacceptable 'corporatist' machinery. Instead, the new proposals became a right for 'individuals' to bring an action even though not entitled to the supply of the lost or impaired services or goods; this section, which began under a heading of 'public services', is presented now as an alternative attaching to any disruption of any supply of goods or services by means of an unlawful act (even if the 'unlawful' character, such as failing to notify an employer of the names of union members about to strike, is actionable on normal principles only by other persons).[183] New machinery invented by the Thatcher legislation is unashamedly ideological but not corporatist, as with the CROTUM or COPAUIA whose job it is to assist union members or other individuals to sue trade unions,[184] and amendments to existing bodies express the same sentiment, though often masked by the vocabulary of step-by-step reform.[185]

The first two uses of collective *laissez-faire* are well established. The descriptive form is found in Kahn-Freund's compelling accounts of British industrial relations and their relationship with the law, given in 1954 and 1959. The second, in the same sources, is the prescriptive form of a recommended 'abstention' which he described (rarely and somewhat rashly) as the distinguishing mark of a 'mature' or 'healthy' system of industrial relations, a feature which by 1978 he accepted he had 'overestimated' in the case of Britain.[186] Less remarked however is the third, the ideological form and function of collective *laissez-faire*, through which in our practice and our very language there is offered an understanding *and* justification of collective organisation in general, and in particular the need and right of workers to form, join and act in combination through autonomous trade unions, free from control by employers or by the State.[187] This flavour appears most strongly in

Kahn-Freund's writings when he objects to anti-union intervenionist judgments. He had persuaded himself that the judges' tendency so to act was defunct but was eventually persuaded (against his initial disbelief) that cases like *Rookes* v. *Barnard*[188] put 'in jeopardy' the right to strike, that 'essential element in collective bargaining'[189] though he little knew with what a winter that swallow was to be followed in the 1980s. It is in these frontier areas, where collective *laissez-faire* is compelled to fight off assaults, that its meaning as a 'code' or 'language' for the defence of autonomous trade unionism becomes clear.[190] Perhaps the critics of the *Rookes* decision were more aware than its defenders of the ways in which technical legal argument combined with policy appreciations; to the latter the idea that there was any 'policy' in the judgments was little less than treasonable.[191]

ADDING ON POSITIVE RIGHTS?

One obvious answer to such problems is the enactment of a set of 'positive rights' in the area of labour relations providing, in particular, rights for free trade unions at the level of international minima (which the United Kingdom has ratified in the ILO Conventions on freedom of association and collective bargaining, Nos. 87 and 98, and has been found to contravene in every Report of the ILO Committee of Experts since 1988). On the surface it seems an easy step, if the political will can be mustered. Positive rights could remove the precarious nature of legality for workers in combination, so long as they were interpreted according to their purpose and the sanctions made employers comply at the workplace. Trade unions are still in a weak sense 'unlawful' at common law by reason of the doctrine of 'restraint of trade'; the Act of 1871 provided – and now the Act of 1992 provides[192] – an immunity for trade unions (so that if a union in any way fails to meet the Act's definition, its rules are still unenforceable at common law).[193] But the solution of 'positive rights' is more complex, quite apart from the fact that it would undoubtedly be met by false, but media-friendly allegations that unions were being put 'above the law' – a powerful reason today why most politicians fight shy of the idea. At first it was suggested that such rights would be safe 'regardless of common law developments';[194] but the 'creativeness' of the judiciary reminds us that provision has to be made for the entire area of substantive law and, perhaps more important, in view of the dominance of the interlocutory injunction in collective labour relations,[195] of procedure too. New positive rights will need to seal off labour law from the common law's double helix of liability that constantly reproduces itself in novel forms of wrongdoing, outside whatever was Parliament's last immunity. We can see the process from criminal conspiracy by gas workers organising a strike against victimisation in 1872[196] to the Court of Appeal's 'dock strike injunction' of 1989,[197] forever outflanking narrowly couched protective statutes. There has grown up, therefore, a broad consensus among those who wish to see British labour law provide rights elementary to a modern system of jurisprudence, that positive rights and protection against unfair procedures must be enacted[198] – not instead of 'immunities', but in addition. The primary examples are rights to associate and organise in trade unions, to take strike and other industrial action within a reaasonable definition of legality and to have the opportunity to represent members, including collective bargaining. Even before the legislation of the Thatcher era, these rights were not secure in British labour law. Rules which are on their face the same law, when applied to patents, to income tax or to labour rights can produce justice in the one case and injustice in the other, as is the case with interlocutory injunctions.[199] Observers remained unconvinced that all was not as it should be in High Court procedures when an *ex parte* injunction in 1986 was granted to an employer without notice to the union, despite a statutory provision which required it, from the judge's home over the telephone, on a Sunday afternoon.[200] Few cases illustrate so graphically the property-based ideology of common law procedures. The same principles of discretion formally apply for granting interlocutory injunctions as in other areas; but the results in labour law are class biased for that very reason.

From here it is no great stride to conclude, as a widening consensus seems to agree, that in order to operate a new system of positive rights we probably need to establish specialist 'labour courts', with their own magistracy (why not in part career judges?) dealing with collective industrial relations as well as the statutory rights of employees within the jurisdiction of the industrial tribunals.[201] But there are many types of 'labour courts', different in their composition, competence and philosophy. Some of today's judges have supported labour courts tripartite in composition, such as a broadened Employment Appeal Tribunal[202] or, even more to their taste, courts which would intervene in the merits of collective disputes and tell the public 'who is right'.[203] That is not what is proposed. What is sought is a style and composition of tribunals with a general jurisdiction able to recognise the conflicting interests before them and seek resolution of disputes while upholding a level of labour standards reconciled with international sources, much more like the Central Arbitration Committee than the High Court.[204] Elsewhere a parallel ambition has been expressed: *'un Droit collectif nouveau, fondé sur la conciliation, la discussion plus que sur la 'juridiction.'*[205] This is the philosophy, not of the common law, but essentially of collective *laissez-faire*. The common law still harbours more than a trace of 'master and servant'[206] and its approach to collective labour relations still speaks of the defence of property. What has to be devised is a tribunal which counts among its highest values that 'free play to the collective forces of society'[207] in which labour possesses rights as well as capital, and rests more upon conciliation than orders to punish contempt of court.

COLLECTIVE LABOUR STANDARDS

Here we see the crucial difference between 'abstentionism', on the one hand and, on the other, collective *laissez-faire*. The latter overtly accepts and avows the reality of conflict, of classes and groups in society, but can encapsulate, too, even the philosophy of a 'labour court' not chained to the common law, freed from review by the orders of the High Court. For however liberal its judges try to be, the common law cannot escape from its class ideology. Indeed, creation of a separate labour jurisdiction would be unacceptable to 'abstentionism' (and one would imagine, anathema to 'pure abstentionism'). But it is a step which is manifestly on the agenda for collective *laissez-faire* seeking to sustain labour standards, including an effective 'freedom to strike' – and for that, whatever else had changed, Kahn-Freund to the end declared a 'vital need'.[208] When in the 1960s the judges let Kahn-Freund down in his belief that they would not rampage again in the manner of *Taff Vale*, it was suggested that labour courts – the Swedish Labour Court is an example – might offer a defence of collective *laissez-faire* itself. This makes it all the more unfortunate that some programmes proposing an 'Industrial Court' have rather misunderstood the object of the operation. Such labour courts would be chaired by a High Court judge and would, except in very few respects, operate under the common law rules.[209] They would be High Courts dressed in proletarian wrappings. That would be a mistake. The magistracy required is not the common law judiciary but one expressing a relationship between labour law and society in which the former, especially in reflexive form, can feed back those values to the social base. In this context, a continuing careful distinction between 'abstention' and collective *laissez-faire* reminds us, too, of Kahn-Freund's hope that there would emerge 'a new generation of lawyers' not insulated from the facts of industrial life.[210] (In a system of 'pure abstention' they would not find much to do.) So too, a plan for new 'labour courts' will be still-born unless it is part of an overall programme for a new labour law and that cannot be seen outside the context of the law of the European Union. The sustenance of international labour standards must also go with the grain of implementing such values, when the ILO itself, the primary source, seems ready to develop new mechanisms for their enforcement. For that body the 'crucial question', in the words of the Director-General, is

> whether, given the voluntary acceptance of obligations arising from its standards, the ILO can maintain the spirit of 'emulation' towards social progress in spite of the countervailing influence exerted by the globalization of the economy and the growth of international competition.[211]

Lacking positive collective rights in law, workers in Britain nevertheless implemented at the high point of collective *laissez-faire* in the early 1950s standards in *practice* of a freedom of association proximate to ILO standards.[212] These could be matched against the apparent liberties which other workers supposedly enjoyed in lands with grand but often unenforced legal Labour Codes.[213] The pedigree of collective *laissez-faire* stretched back into the history of that tradition, to the Lancashire delegates in the Ten Hours Bill campaign who advocated in 1844 'forming a union between masters and men to abridge the hours of factory labour without the aid of parliament'.[214] Although they figured in a highly empirical form in the proposals of the Donovan Commission, Kahn-Freund himself was well aware of the values for which the philosophy of collective *laissez-faire* stood and of the dangers for those who discard those values in the name of some unitary social principle or lighthearted employment of 'abstention' with no guarantees of any alternative point of reference for the defence of workers' freedom of association.[215] There is force in the claim that the picture of a British social equilibrium being maintained by the State was historically suspect, at best a short term vision or even 'simply a myth',[216] an ideological mystification to which Kahn-Freund fell prey, to be frank, as other exiles have done. More important now than a staged re-run of the question whether pluralists must believe in a mystic, social 'equilibrium',[217] is the quest for a freedom that reaches back to the rhetoric of older traditions, to Winstanley[218] and to early claims to have 'generated a love of freedom [and] have knit together the victims of capital, when masters have forgotten honour and justice and the world compassion and sympathy'.[219] This quest was once succoured by the claim that 'no adequate ground has been shown for the continuance of special laws relating exclusively to the employment of labour',[220] and the Donovan Report's assertion that no better way was known than collective bargaining to meet the different interests in industrial relations. Workers themselves need few lessons on the limitations of collective *laissez-faire* in a society of class injustice, though they may despair of changing them; but in each generation throughout these periods the philosophy was, and is, a weapon not for utopian claims but an argument within prevailing social relations justifying collective action. For over a century it sustained Harrison's case against 'special laws relating exclusively to employment' – precisely the point denied by every Secretary of State for Employment between 1982 and 1993 to justify special discrimination against unions merely because they were 'special'[221] – and arguing that unions are 'essentially clubs and not trading companies' and should not therefore have imposed upon them 'the degree of regulation possible in the case of the latter'.[222] In such societies the defence of workers' interests nourishes a philosophy that asserts the need for collective '*laissez-faire*'. The doctrine has fed international standards and has encouraged workers to seek new horizons in their relationships at work. Indeed, in a sense Kahn-Freund struggled against his own progeny when he opposed 'worker participation' in decision making.[223]

COLLECTIVE *LAISSEZ-FAIRE* AND CULTURAL ASSUMPTIONS

It is possible to feel this philosophy in embryo operating at times even as a small internalised brake upon capital and the State, albeit in a calculation of self-interest, when faced by effective, or even defeated trade unions. For example, take the curious historical period in which after Lord St. Leonard's Act of 1867 the authorities failed to usher in an era of compulsory arbitration – and why did they not, when just such measures of regulation were about to appear in Australia and New Zealand?[224] Instead, even at that early time, we find a 'settled preference for employers and workpeople ... to set up machinery of their own devising'.[225] Moreover, in the hour of the unions' great defeat, the philosophy appears as a thread in the arguments persuading Baldwin not to extend the Bill of 1927 to abolish all 'immunities', as the employers wanted, because that could be represented to public opinion as 'persecution of the unions'?[226] It will be said, correctly, that the employers were often using the idea for their own class interests; yet the tinge of concession and self-control was not matched in the hubris that infected our rulers during and after the miners' strike of 1984-85. The 1927 Act was a nasty piece of revenge on the trade union movement, but we need not ignore the fact that government spokesmen felt it necessary to insist they would not ban 'legitimate and industrial strikes', even 'sympathy' strikes,[227] and the Lord Chancellor repeatedly argued that the government meant 'no attack on trade unions or trade unionism'.[228] While Ministers criticised the protection from tort liability enjoyed by unions under the 1906 Act, section 4, they significantly did not move to delete or amend it, an 'abstentionist' trace not shared by their successors fifty three years later.[229] Even in those periods before 1939 the place of what we see as ideological collective *laissez-faire* in the history of the labour movement is curiously, if silently, acknowledged, especially on various Parliamentary occasions, introducing into the individualistic society of England a 'collective element'.[230] The lead given by the Whitley Committee's Reports was followed by the decision of employers to negotiate even if that stemmed from confidence in their own ability to maintain control without outside assistance.[231] Their ideology makes no sense without 'conflict and accommodation' by independent unions.

That ideological aspect of collective *laissez-faire* becomes even more important in a country which lacks a written constitution (other, at any rate, than the European Treaties, which, we shall see, are here of little value).[232] The point is even stronger if it lacks a Charter of Rights, above all when international instruments ratified by the State, such as the Council of Europe Social Charter 1961, or European Convention of Human Rights 1950, are not automatically part of domestic law. Here what becomes a usage acquires a meta-constitutional flavour; beyond the positive law, protections of civil liberties in Britain have often depended upon conventions and the very language of accepted customs. One must consider, therefore, the effect new structures of labour law may have upon social discourse and values, just as consideration of the employment relationship involves considering 'the culture, the values and the norms of the wider society and the institutional arrangements which ensure that appropriate obligations are internalised and developed and reinforced by each generation.'[233]

If there was any doubt that legislators should consider this dimension of their activity, the rout of the 1971 Act and ideological victories won by the new labour law of 1980-1994 should end it. 'Reform of the trade unions' has been a flag which fluttered over the descent of labour law into depths far below international minima, convincing the general populace, and even many members of the unions concerned, that these authoritarian measures were no more than a Prior's progress step-by-step to 'safeguard the liberty of the individual from the abuse of industrial power' and 'to improve the operation of the labour market'.[234] The economists and sociologists now debate whether, or how far, these laws had the effects their authors claim,[235] and how future legislation can help build the necessary collective organisations in the labour market, with adequate regulation and positive economic effects.[236] Psychologically and ideologically, however, the effect of the 1980s legislation, fanned by the media, has been to cast out 'collective bargaining' from the common cultural vocabulary, as anyone knows who said the words to a class of students in 1974 and in 1994. There are young people who believe that in the winter of 1979 not a single corpse was buried in England. The belief (which has or had little to do with 'facts') has been made widespread again that 'picketing implies *in principle* an interference with [non-unionists'] right to dispose of their labour as they think fit and is, therefore without justification; and ... is a violation of the [employer's] right of free resort to the labour market for the supply of such labour as he requires'.[237]

Collective *laissez-faire* implies certain relationships between 'the collective forces'. In terms of labour law, it assumes the need for independent trade unions in bargaining with a sufficiently broad band of employers or employers' associations in an autonomous relationship that is not based on some *Carta del lavoro* or *Chartre du travail*.[238] It is no accident that the first topic – 'the vital problem' – to which Kahn-Freund turned after collective *laissez-faire* was union recognition. This was followed by 'freedom of organisation'. In 1959, he believed, in common with his belief that British society had reached a new equilibrium, that recognition for collective bargaining had in general 'moved from the contested into the accepted sphere',[239] optimistic even at the time, not only for white collar workers. In 1978, 'the British paradox' was sensed to be that even 'the small degree of intervention' of the social contract legislation may have been 'too strong a burden for the traditionally "voluntary" system of collective labour law to bear.'[240] So it proved. Even before its repeal by the Act of 1980 the mechanism enacted to enforce recognition was widely agreed not to work well. But today, the willingness of employers to bargain is even more patchy. Total derecognition or refusals to bargain or partial and creeping derecognition by way of the agenda for bargaining, are all an established, and probably a growing feature of modern British industrial relations.[241] The conclusion to be drawn from the failure of the 1975 machinery is not that the law should 'abstain' – that would be to jettison the spirit of collective *laissez-faire* with the bath water of discarded semiotics – but that it should be adequately adjusted to policy. The question is *how* the law can intervene productively, directly or indirectly.

ENTER GLOBAL CAPITAL

Moreover, the new global market in which multinational capital is unleashed makes this a peculiarly ill-chosen moment to leave workers' organisations alone to their fate. It was suggested some twenty years ago that in a world entrenching the right for capital to enjoy 'free movement', as in the European Community, the 'logical correlative ... would be a legal right of trans-national, *collective* industrial action for "labour" ', not merely the right, as the Community provided, to free movement for individual workers.[242] Without the collective dimension to workers' rights even the prized 'social dialogue' between employers' organisations and trade unions in the Community is weakened, and if employers are free to abandon recognition of workers' unions at their whim, they may leave the unions to indulge in a monologue of doubtful value. In any event, we yet have to see whether 'European' collective bargaining will truly be effective, or whether it will develop into further powers for the Commission to propose enactment by law of measures, in part or whole, 'prenegotiated' by capital and labour at geographical levels higher than heretofore. We already have an example of the ways in which employers might torpedo such an enterprise in the withdrawal of the European employers' organisation (UNICE), instigated by the CBI, from the negotiations for rights of consultation for workers in 'Euro-scale' undertakings.[243] Plans for 'European labour law' cannot assume that employers, multi- or uni-national, will necessarily do what planners want. The question has not been entirely out of the minds of British legislators, for the 1982 legislation revised the definition of 'trade dispute' so as to narrow the occasions when it could relate to 'matters outside the United Kingdom', just as the 1976 Act had expanded them.[244] This may have looked at the time as – to adapt the Webbs – mere petty higgling between the political parties. But behind the amendment and counter-amendment deep streams of policy flowed, crucial to collective values. Kahn-Freund agreed that 'the power of multinational enterprise is in no way balanced by a corresponding power of labour'; nor do national government's writs run internationally; so 'the entire basis of our thinking on collective labour relations and collective labour law is destroyed by this development'.[245] 'Recognition' is a parallel problem, a matter to which we return, both in its domestic and its European context.[246] 'Recognition' is, of course, an unfortunate term. We do not demand that employers merely say to the union: 'nice to see you'. We mean they should bargain with it, at any rate on certain matters or, given its representativeness, in certain circumstances.[247] These are even more difficult to define transnationally.

The reason for re-examining Kahn-Freund's thinking in particular on these matters is not a belief that his judgment was always correct, as it were some theological point of reference, but because the debate about labour law policy has been dominated, and the debate about alternative policies today is highly influenced, by frames of reference which he was most prominent in establishing in the 1950s. Even government Ministers in the 1980s felt the need to claim for their policies roots in 'voluntarism', thought not of course the old collective *laissez-faire* supported by 'privileges'.[248] He did not apply the same analysis to all analogous situations: compare his analysis of multinational labour law with that of the European Community, despite his early command of it,[249] his touch was sometimes more secure in legislation than in case law,[250] as in his erstwhile belief, shared by many in industry, that adequate 'strike notices' could validate strike action by workers, when only a notice to terminate the employment contract, not normally available to the union, could do so,[251] or in the view that 'advice' could escape the tort of inducing breach of an employment contract – both of those are writ large in the Donovan Report as part of its reasoning to reject a positive right to strike.[252] Even on legislation, he had a tendency to take class out of it, describing the factory legislation of the 19th century as 'deliberate experimentation' or 'trial and error', rather than a product of social forces in struggle.[253] He was of course not alone in these beliefs or in his repeated – now questionable – assertion that our society does not 'contrary to Marxist assumption' require the 'industrial reserve army' of unemployed.[254] But then, which of us, if used according to our lapses, 'shall 'scape whipping'?

VALUES IN NEW LABOUR LAWS

A reappraisal of collective *laissez-faire*, distilled out of 'abstentionism', discloses values that place autonomous trade unions at the centre of a democratic society, the precise opposite of current policies and at odds with fashionable liberalism which occupies itself by explaining why we cannot replace the Thatcher legislation. Its influence caused parts of our labour law to have an odd look, not least in the 'immunities'. Some are not, on inquiry, as odd as they look. Take the principle that an employer can escape the tribunal's jurisdiction on unfair dismissal only by dismissing all the relevant employees participating in industrial action, without discrimination.[255] Gradually that policy has been whittled away, for example by giving employers power in 1990 to dismiss unofficial strikers selectively to preserve the employer as master in his house.[256] Some commentators today dismiss the principle with well intended impatience as insufficiently protective of workers. But at the crossroads where unfair dismissal rights and the liberty to strike meet, it was essential in 1974 to refuse to the judges the competence to decide which strikes were 'reasonable' and which not. That would have handed over to judges' discretion – ultimately the appellate courts – the definition of 'reasonable' strikes. Many are the judges who would bask in such jurisdiction; Lord Donaldson (ex-President of the NIRC) believes a court should have the power to tell the public 'who is right' in a dispute, making industrial action justiciable and judges into arbiters of social conflict beyond the dreams of *A Giant's Strength*.[257] Even under the present formula judges still try to assume that function, for example by maintaining the court's right against workers unfairly dismissed by an employer (because only some of the strikers were dismissed or others were improperly re-engaged) to reduce their compensation for unfair dismissal by reason of their contributory 'conduct', *viz* their industrial action. Otherwise, declared Wood J., 'dismissal for industrial action would become automatically unfair'.[258] The shocked tone says much about the present law and its judiciary. The proposition will not shock an alternative labour law any more than it shocks a French lawyer accustomed to find that the wrongful dismissal of a worker on strike is null and void.[259] For the 'right' to strike to become a right we must put in place *both* positive rights *and* immunities – though some recent commentary, which cannot be analysed here,[260] seems oddly to balk at this point – and see that they are well drafted and administered by courts not hostile to it.[261]

In a search for an alternative labour law it is the spirit of 'collective *laissez-faire*', not of 'abstentionism' nor of mere regulation, that can underpin freedom of association (within which the ILO includes a right to strike), the restoration of autonomy to union rules[262] and an end to interlocutory procedures for unfair labour injunctions (if we need signposts, Irish law has made a start).[263] With the improvement and extension of collective bargaining and conciliation we must aim (though it is unfashionable to say so) at new ventures in worker participation. Official research demonstrates what damage the policy of excluding organised workers has done, not least in the failure to offer adequate opportunities to workers' representatives on training, with 'Training Committees' at workplace level.[264] Alternative labour law must reassert, too, that improved employment protection can unlock the talents of working people; such intervention 'by securing equity in treatment, ensures efficiency in performance'.[265] There is, of course, also one dominant priority in shaping our labour law: a contribution to the restoration of full employment. This goal must be pursued despite what even friendly critics call the 'deflationary bias of the convergence provisions in the [Maastricht] Treaty'.[266] It is no cause for concern that progress will on some occasions invoke methods of autonomous collective bargaining, on others the methods of enactment, usually the two together as has so often been the case. This enterprise will not be a route 'back' to 'collective *laissez-faire*' so much as a way forward with it, unimpeded by sectarian formalities whether homespun or 'European'. It will not make 'voluntarism' a substitute for social policy 'any more than law is a substitute for strong trade unions'.[267] It must not be the victim of ambitious politicians who misuse the rhetoric of 'positive laws' to deprive workers of effective collective rights at the workplace. It will look to the values of 'collective *laissez-faire*' in real life, not to the apparition of 'abstention' or spooks of 'Legal Intervention'. Dispelling the mirage of 'abstentionism' for a better realisation of collective *laissez-faire*, it may find that critics of the former hold equally to the perspectives of freedom inherent in the latter.[268] More, we can thereby modify bureaucratic interventionism and well-intentioned juridification that is forgetful of the values of autonomy. For, without those values, legislation can leave dangerously open the prospect of authoritarian demands for 'compulsory labour service' or coercion to work in Essential Services (couched often as bans on industrial action[269] or, smug defenders of the market economy should bear in mind, to the free market equivalent of workfare schemes which make survival dependent on accepting jobs designated by the State, in new forms of 'contract' imposed upon the jobless, as in the proposed 'job seekers agreements'.[270] We should recall that in the era of Beveridge it was accepted that those who declined 'suitable work' should suffer deductions from benefit, but only such that they were not 'flung into grievous want'.[271]

COLLECTIVE *LAISSEZ-FAIRE* AS A POINT OF DEPARTURE

Since 1951, then, our labour relations have seen a marcescent 'abstentionism' flicker and fade. More recently, the common law has been invigorated by a legislative replacement of policies 'excluding' it, aiming instead to install by regulation 'free market' conditions cleansed of collective resistance. Just like the common law, the new policy disempowers individual workers in the name of individualism. The core values inherent in 'collective *laissez-faire*', therefore, now have a new relevance; proclamations of their death by apologists of comfortable reform by regulation unwittingly help to make a new labour law bereft of direction and workers' unions exposed. Those values presuppose, as few other ideologies do, the practice of freedom in autonomous trade unionism as 'a central feature in an equitable society'.[272] Trade unions, which demonstrate the value of collective action of individuals, cannot adopt the mantle of those who claim they can cure social injustice by the impact of legislation alone. Alternative labour law can inspire the forces of social reform if it is infused with an extension of collective freedom at work, not thereby opposed to 'individual rights' but blending 'individual' and 'collective' law together more readily than in the past and making adequate provision for workers' security in their trade union. It must, too, have a social purpose, pursuing the 'institutional changes' without which 'these human rights are entirely ineffective'.[273] It will thrive only as part of a concordance of social policies set to rescue working people from new depths of powerlessness and inequality – setting out from a standard that cannot even match Gladstone's claim in 1863 that, in an era of 'intoxicating augmentation of wealth and power ... the rich have been growing richer, the poor have been growing less poor'.[274] It will acknowledge – in the tradition of collective *laissez-faire* – that individual rights at work cannot be enforced adequately except in the presence of free trade unions particularly in a fragmented labour market increasingly peopled precariously by part-time, temporary or casual workers. It must look over the walls and beyond the rhetoric of Europe to movements abroad and international labour standards, observing their values and resolving their current ambiguities for developing countries. The drive for 'social clauses' protecting the oppressed in international trade is in its tradition of accommodating a legal floor, whether it be for safety at work or other employment conditions. At the same time imagination at home must devise a civilised floor of regulatory measures for the protection of the poorest and for the rights and opportunities for workers, above all the opportunity to work. The chance for this change will come soon. It will demand resolute courage in the struggle – and clarity in the ideology. No-one can stand aside from it, least of all those who purport to lead. It must not be squandered.

NOTES

1. For a 'second guess' on the next step, see Paul Smith and Gary Morton, 'Union Exclusion in Britain – the Next Steps' (1994) 24 Ind. Rels. Jo. 3,10-11. See too Chapter 10. Labour deregulation is continued wherever possible: see Deregulation and Contracting Out Act 1994, s.36 (repealing the provision making dismissals unfair which break the employer's agreement on criteria for selection).
2. T. Keenoy, 'Constructing Control' in J. Hartley and G. Stephenson (eds.), *Employment Relations* (1992) 98.
3. See Wedderburn, 'Freedom of Association and Philosophies of Labour Law: The Thatcher Ideology' Chapter 8, *Employment Rights in Britain and Europe* (1991) cited at 204, 228, also (1989) 18 ILJ 1. See the discussion by S. Auerbach *Legislating for Conflict* (1990), who at first acknowledges this limitation, 227, but then at times seems to overlook it in discussing the political and economic factors at work.
4. S. Auerbach *op.cit.* 235-6. The subsequent Employment Act 1990 and the Trade Union Reform and Employment Rights Act 1993 ('TURER') do much to clarify the ideological element in policy, not least in controlling union rules about membership and demanding that a trade union must describe to the employer the members being balloted or called to strike, in a ballot that must be postal, 'so that he can readily ascertain them' (ss. 17, 18, 20): see the delicate analysis of the 1990 Act by B. Simpson (1991) 54 MLR 418, and of strike ballots and policy in the recent Acts: (1993) 22 ILJ 287, especially 294-7. As he points out, the proposals in the draft Code of Practice 1988 which were withdrawn – such as the proposal to demand a ballot about a ballot – were as revealing as the legislation.
5. See *The Constitution of Liberty* (1960) 'Introduction' 5, and for his general programme 'Labor Unions and Employment' 276-9. He matched the union position in Britain, the United States and 'most European countries by the 1920s' (268), but made an exception for unions which acted only as friendly societies or as machinery to transmit the employer's offers of 'alternative benefits which the employer could provide at the same cost' (276).
6. Such as Milton Friedman and his school: H. Gospel and G. Palmer, *British Industrial Relations* (2nd ed. 1993) 164-9, 252-4.
7. M. Friedman, *Capitalism and Freedom* (1962) 9ff; for an economist's critique see E. Mishan, *Economic Efficiency and Social Welfare* (1981) Chap. 20 on 'The Folklore of the Market'.
8. F. Hayek, *1980s: Unemployment and the Unions* (1980) 52, and *Law, Legislation and Liberty* (1979) Vol. III; see for an analysis Wedderburn *op.cit.*, note 3, 204.

9. See Chapter 8 of R. Taylor, *The Trade Union Question in British Politics* (1993).
10. See *Competitiveness: Helping Business to Win* (Cm. 2563 1994) para. 5.17-18; *People and Companies: Employee Involvement in Britain* (1989, Dept. of Employment).
11. See for the best example, s. 13 TURER Act 1993, allowing the employer to discriminate in favour of non-unionists when he is 'furthering changes' in his relationship with employees.
12. See the discussion in Wedderburn, *Employment Rights in Britain and Europe* (1991) 367-74, (also (1991) 54 MLR 1, 17-25) and notes 166ff below. For earlier phrases, see Chapter 4 'The New Politics of Labour Law: Immunities or Positive Rights'. A 'positive rights' programme is not necessarily more, or less, 'radical' than any other; it depends on the legal content.
13. In the sense of psychological derivatives, see Melanie Klein, 'The Relations Between Obsessional Neurosis and Early Stages of the Super-ego', Chapter 8, *The Psycho-analysis of Children* (1980).
14. J. Habermas, in T. McCarthy, *The Critical Theory of Jürgen Habermas* (78) 259, 423; and see K. Klare, 'Labor Law as Ideology' (1981) Ind. Rel.L.J. 450.
15. Tony Benn, Parl. Deb. H. C. 27 November 1968, col. 491.
16. See on national laws and transnational industrial relations, Chapter 7 below.
17. See Chapter 2 below.
18. As the main legal source under the Maastricht Treaty is still the 'European Community', that term will be employed below. On the direction of the Community and labour law, see Chapter 10.
19. The Employment Act 1980, although carrying many of the features of later Conservative policy, arguably contained a mix of objectives that sets it (somewhat) apart. In any event, it was made clear in 1980 that more legislation would follow. The new era begins unconditionally in 1982.
20. See ILO, *Freedom of Association and Collective Bargaining: General Survey by the Committee of Experts* (1983) Chapters III to XII. These were the three areas of freedom with which even N. Tebbit, Secretary of State for Employment, said he had no quarrel: Parl. Deb. H.C. 8 February 1982, col. 744, on the TUC's claim to rights 'to combine', 'to be recognised ... for collective bargaining', and 'not to work except on terms ... agreed with an employer', adding: 'There is nothing in the Bill [of 1982] that prevents trade unions from organising, gaining recognition, bargaining collectively or from organising industrial action ... in pursuit of pay and conditions or in defence of their jobs'. The 1982 Employment Act was the first to dig deep into British labour law in contravention of ILO standards.
21. Perhaps the most 'progressive' step taken by the European Commission is the money granted for transnational meetings of employees' representatives: Social dialogue and employment budget 'B3 4004': see EIRR 238 (1993) 15-19.
22. M. Hansenne, *Defending Values, Promoting Change* (ILO, Report of the Director General 1994 Part 1) 57. For unsuccessful pressures by the

United States to attach rather primitive social clauses to GATT (with little support by the European Union States, except France), and for opposition from developing and many industrialised countries to a 'new protectionism', see *Financial Times*, March 16, 25 and 28, and April, 7, 1994.

23. R. Reich, United States Secretary of Labour, proposed restricting this use of trade to defend a core 'short list': a ban on child or slave labour and freedom of association and collective bargaining, see *Financial Times*, 10 June 1994.

24. See especially Chapters 6, 8, and, for some conclusions, 10 below.

25. See E. Szyszczak on the 'fairy tales' in the 'social dimension' of the single market, in D. O'Keefe and P. Twomey, *Legal Issues of the Maastricht Treaty* (1994) 313, 324-7; and on concentration by some commentators on such procedures as the need for unanimity, instead of the more important issues of substance, see P. Davies in W. McCarthy, *Legal Interventions in Industrial Relations* (1992) 345-6.

26. Wedderburn, B. Veneziani, S. Ghimpu, 'Hiring Procedures' in *Diritto del lavoro in Europa* (1987, in English) 51 6. See too, ss. 1-6, and s. 11 EPCA (1978) as amended by TURER Act 1993, Sched. 4, in order to implement the Directive.

27. Commission, *Eleventh Annual Report on Monitoring the Application of Community Law* COM(94) 500 final, 29 March 1994, p. 56; a complaint against the UK was withdrawn after the TURER Act 1993, Sched. 4.

28. See J. Clark and M. Hall, 'The Cinderella Directive?' (1992) 21 ILJ 106, 118.

29. The original ss. 1 and 4 of the EPCA 1978; see Wedderburn, *The Worker and the Law* (3rd. 1986) 136-8. 330-1.

30. See the new ss. 1 and 4, EPCA 1978, inserted by Sched. 4 TURER Act 1993.

31. Articles 3 and 5 of the Directive together may allow for something more like the previous British practice. It is, as is usual, open to a Member State to enact provisions or 'permit' agreements that are more favourable to workers than the Directive: art. 7.

32. Employers could 'make reference to collective agreements, as they may still do for particulars of pensions, sickness entitlement or certain details relating to disciplinary and grievance matters', but *not* otherwise: Bnss. Denton for the Government, Parl. Deb. H.L. 6 May 1993 col. 849. The reason for the constriction was never explained. A government amendment on collective agreements, passed at 1 a.m. on Third Reading without debate, appears to have made the problem worse, not better, though the Opposition (*nostra culpa*) did not oppose it, conceding maybe if not an own goal, at least a corner, HL 24 May 1993 cols. 150-1.

33. O. Kahn-Freund, 'Labour Law' in M. Ginsberg, *Law and Opinion in England in the 20th Century* (1959) 224, and see 227-9. It is noteworthy that he followed immediately with a discussion of the 'related though different topic of freedom of organisation'. On the undesirability of an 'abstract debate' about 'abstentionism', see Wedderburn, *The Worker and the Law* (3rd. ed. 1986) 846. See too Chapter 10 below.

34. For a useful account see W. McCarthy (ed), *Legal Interventions in*

Industrial Relations (1992) Chapter 1; see too, Wedderburn, R. Lewis and J. Clark, *Labour Law and Industrial Relations: Building on Kahn-Freund* (1983).

35. O. Kahn-Freund, *Labour and the Law* (1st ed. 1972) 43; (3rd ed. 1983, P. Davies and M. Freedland eds.) 53.

36. O. Kahn-Freund, 'Collective Labour Relations' (1959) 3 Riv. di Dir. Int. e Comp. del Lav., no. III, 353, 356 (General Report to the 2nd. International Congress on Social Legislation, 1958).

37. E. Hobsbawm, *Worlds of Labour* (1984) 153; C. Maire, 'Preconditions for Corporatism', Chapter 2 in J. Goldthorpe (ed.) *Order and Conflict in Contemporary Capitalism* (1984) 449-56; Wedderburn, 'The Social Charter in Britain' (1991) 54 MLR 1-10, and 'Industrial Relations and the Courts' (1980) 9 ILJ 1, now Chapters 3 and 11 in *Employment Rights in Britain and Europe* (1991). See too O. Kahn-Freund in Renner, *The Institutions of Private Law and their Function* (1949); the legal difference between Britain and say, France, Germany and Austria 'reflects the histories of the various working class movements'; later, for reasons that were not clear, Kahn-Freund seemed to be less comfortable with this.

38. C. Maire, *op.cit.* note 37, 50.

39. S. Fredman, 'The New Rights: Labour Law and Ideology in the Thatcher Years' (1992) 12 Ox. Jo. L.S. 24, 41, and see 40-44 for a helpful discussion of the 'way ahead'.

40. O. Kahn-Freund, 'Labour Law' in M. Ginsberg (ed.), *Law and Opinion in England in the 20th Century* (1959) 215, overtaking his chapter in A. Flanders and Clegg, *The System of Industrial Relations in Great Britain* (1954).

41. Wedderburn, 'Laws about Strikes' Chap. 4 in W. McCarthy (ed.) *Legal Interventions in Industrial Relations* (1992) 185, on exaggerated reports of the death of collective *laissez-faire*.

42. Notably, H. Phelps Brown, *The Growth of British Industrial Relations* (1959) Chaps III, VI, VII; and see R. Lewis, 'Reforming Industrial Relations, Politics and Power' (1991) 7 Ox. Rev. Econ. Pol. 55.

43. On the Employment Bill, Parl. Deb. Vol. 409, HL, 21.5.1980, col. 902.

44. See the useful accounts of such legislation in the first and the second World War by D. Pritt, *Law, Class and Society: I Employers, Workers and Trade Unions* (1970) Chapters 6 and 8; and on the 1950s, his *The Labour Government* (1963).

45. See Conditions of Employment and National Arbitration Order 1940, no. 1305; and Reinstatement in Civil Employment Act 1944; Restoration of Pre-War Trade Practices Act 1942, which were effective for many years and not finally repealed until 1981 and 1986. On the parallel 1919 Act, see A. Fox, *History and Heritage* (1985) 291-3. The dock labour scheme, originating in 1940, gave dockers a status by statute, though the remnants of employment contract were paradoxically later to serve to retain some legality for industrial action: *Associated British Ports* v. *TGWU* [1989] WLR 939 HL. For an evaluation of Order 1305 at the time, O. Kahn-Freund (1943) 6 MLR 112, expressing the hope that aspects of arbitration enforcing 'freely negotiated collective agreements' would survive into peacetime, 142.

46. The Netherlands, for example, where after an emergency Decree of 1945, complete control over wages and conditions was exercised through a Board of Conciliators and the bi-partite 'Foundation of Labour' until 1970, and Ministerial powers to freeze wages lasted until 1982. See, H. Bakels, 'The Netherlands', in R. Blanpain and K. Engels (eds.), *Encyclopaedia of Labour Law* (1987) 71-3, and see below Chapter 10, on incomes policy, 364ff.

47. J. McIlroy, *Trade Unions in Britain Today* (1988) 75: 'The absence of one kind of law may help trade unions. The absence of another kind of law may handicap them'.

48. See especially, P. Davies and M. Freedland, *Labour Legislation and Public Policy* (1993).

49. He could see 'no difference between negligence and gross negligence'; they were the 'same thing with the addition of a vituperative epithet': *Wilson* v. *Brett* (1841) 11 M and W 113, 115.

50. Wedderburn, *The Worker and the Law* (1965) 134.

51. P. Davies and M. Freedland, *op.cit.* note 48, 132 and 29; for their rather different evaluation on similar premises, see Chapter 2, and on 'pure' abstentionism, below note 156ff.

52. *DC Thomson & Co Ltd* v *Deakin* [1952] Ch. 646 CA (indirect inducement of breach of contract, which for some reason no-one could explain, had not been included in the trade dispute immunities in the 1906 Act and had, equally mysteriously, not been relied upon by plaintiffs in the interim: Donovan Royal Commission *Report* (1968 Cmnd. 3623) para. 887 *et seq*. There were good precedents on which the Court of Appeal could have rejected the indirect tort altogether. The answer to the first mystery may be that Sir Charles Dilke knew he could not secure passage for his vital amendment if he set it that wide (see Wedderburn, *The Worker and the Law* (1986 3rd ed.) 586-7. Liability was quickly extended in *Stratford* v *Lindley* [1965] AC 269 HL, *Torquay Hotel Co* v *Cousins* [1969] 2 Ch. 106 CA and *Rookes* v *Barnard* [1964] AC 1129 HL, the last adding the 'spine-chilling' semantics of 'intimidation' to the tort vocabulary: Wedderburn (1964) 27 MLR 257, 279. The *Thomson* decision did, however, reserve a core of legality for industrial action despite later judicial assaults: see *Middlebrook Mushrooms* v *TGWU* [1993] IRLR 232 CA: see too the Appendix below to this Chapter.

53. *Bonsor* v *Musicians Union* [1956] AC 104 HL; TUC General Council *Report* 1956, para. 437, see too Wedderburn (1957) 20 MLR 118-123.

54. See 'Collective Agreements under War Legislation' (1943) 6 MLR 112, 142, referring both to the ban on strikes and the compulsory arbitration provisions of the Order; see R. Lewis in Wedderburn, R. Lewis, J. Clark (eds.), *Labour Law and Industrial Relations* (1983) 120-2.

55. For the most notorious wartime prosecution, that of Betteshanger miners, see Appendix 6 *Donovan Report, op.cit.* (Cmnd 3623, 1968) 340. Lord Shawcross, as he became, also made the odd submission in 1951 that 'strikes not in connection with trade disputes ... [if] calculated to cause a breach of contract, or ... to interfere with or affect the policy of the State, or affect the interests of the State, might constitute a grave criminal offence': see D. Pritt, *Law, Class and Society* (1970), note 44, 93-7. This

attempt by Shawcross to revive liabilities of the early 19th century seems to have been taken seriously by no-one.

56. The remark by O. Kahn-Freund, 'Labour Law' in M. Ginsberg (ed.) *Law and Opinion in England in the 20th Century* (1959) 215, 256.

57. See A. Wilson, 'Contract and Prerogative' (1984) 13 ILJ 1, 24.

58. J. Davis Smith, *The Attlee and Churchill Administrations and Industrial Unrest: 1945-1955* (1990) 98-104.

59. See the exchanges between Sir Walter Monckton and various Opposition members in *Hansard*: Parl. Deb. HC 23 June 1955 col. 1523-5.

60. H. Turner, *Arbitration: A Study of Industrial Experience* (1952, Fabian Pamphlet).

61. In A. Flanders and H. Clegg, *The System of Industrial Relations in Great Britain* (1954) 96, and 84 respectively (emphasis supplied) and on 'weakness', 44; see too below on the 1959 Act, note 89; also W. McCarthy, *Compulsory Arbitration in Britain* (1968, in Research Paper 8 for the Donovan Royal Commission); K. Wedderburn and P. Davies, *Employment Grievances and Disputes Procedures in Britain* (1969) 210-13.

62. See on this subject, Chapter 10: where we need to assess this 'new departure in that it limits the freedom of collective bargaining', O. Kahn-Freund, *Labour Law: New Developments and Old Developments* (1968).

63. Employment Protection Act 1975, Schedule 11, repealed by s. 19 Employment Act 1980. See the account by P. Wood. 'The CAC's Approach to Schedule 11 and the Fair Wages Resolution 1946' (1978) 7 ILJ 64 (the 'volume of claims' was determined 'by the existence of an incomes policy', 82). On the 1971 Act, R. Simpson and J. Wood, *Industrial Relations and the 1971 Act* (1973) 93-5.

64. See on juridification in British labour law, J. Clark and Wedderburn, in G. Teubner (ed.) *Juridification of Social Spheres* (1987), 163-191.

65. See J. Durcan, W. McCarthy, G. Redman, *Strikes in Post-War Britain* (1983) 398-400.

66. W. McCarthy, *op.cit.* note 61 above, 32-3; The evidence for 'inflationary' awards by the Industrial Disputes Tribunal was little more than an allegation by the *Economist*: J. Durcan *et.al.*, *op.cit.*, note 65 above, 367.

67. J. Davis Smith, *The Attlee and Churchill Administrations and Industrial Unrest: 1945-1955* (1990) 120, on 1955 when there had been major official strikes on the railways, in newspapers and docks, and unofficial strikes in the mines and by seamen. See for a parallel analysis, Wedderburn (1972) 10 BJIR 1, now Chapter 3 below.

68. H. Clegg and R. Adams, *The Employers' Challenge: A Study of the National Shipbuilding and Engineering Dispute of 1957* (1957), see especially 144-5. A consideration of the industrial events of 1955-7 leads one to question the description of these years as 'the easy decade': P. Davies and M. Freedland, *Labour Legislation and Public Policy* (1993) Chapter 3. 'Public policy' was not unaffected by the industrial struggles; the 1957 strikes resulted in 6.15mn. days idle. See Ministry of Labour *Evidence* to Donovan Royal Commission (1965) 37.

69. Engineering Employers' Association, *Looking at Industrial Relations* (1957) 40.

70. A. Marsh, *Industrial Relations in Engineering* (1965) 43; Donovan Royal Commission *Report* (Cmnd 3623 1968), Harold MacMillan feared it would be 'a fierce struggle', see K. Jeffrey and P. Hennessy, *States of Emergency* (1983) 227.
71. H. Clegg, *The System of Industrial Relations of Great Britain* (1972) 338-9.
72. P. Kahn, N. Lewis, R. Livock, P. Wiles, *Picketing and the Law* (1983) 31, and see 34-5.
73. *A New Approach* (1951, introduction by Sir David Maxwell-Fyfe), after the adoption of mixed policies in the *Industrial Charter* (1947).
74. Inns of Court Conservative and Unionist Society, *A Giant's Strength*, 1958; citations are from pages 11, 22-27, 54-6, and from Chapter IV 'Restrictive Practices'. A diminished version on restrictive practices appeared in the outline Conservative programme, *Fair Deal at Work*, 1968, 50-1.
75. See Chapter 10, 370-9 below, especially discussing *Merci Convenzionali Porto di Genova SpA v Siderurgica Gabrielli SpA* (C-179/90) [1991] ECR I-5889 ECJ; *Höfner v Macroton* (C-41/90) April 23 1991; Slot (1991) 29 CMLR 964.
76. *Evidence* of TGWU to the Donovan Royal Commission, 15 March 1966, Day 30, 1199 (H. Nicholas. Gen. Sec.).
77. *Industrial Relations Handbook* (1961, Ministry of Labour) 146; it was revoked by Order 1796 of 1958; see too, W. McCarthy, *Compulsory Arbitration in Britain* (1968), note 61 above.
78. D. Macdonald, *The State and the Trade Unions* (1960) 161, 163; Wedderburn, *The Worker and the Law* (3rd ed. 1986) 344. The TUC protested; there appear not to have been the then customary consultations in the National Joint Advisory Council.
79. See TUC, *Evidence* to Donovan Royal Commission, Day 61, paras. 324-7.
80. G. Bain, *The Growth of White-Collar Unionism* (1970) 175; so too in the machinery imposed by statute in 1959 when there was no collective arbitration, only an award for the individual employee. See below note 89ff.
81. A. Robens MP, Opposition spokesperson, Parl. Deb. HC 19 Nov. 1958, col 1168, moving to annul the revocation Order.
82. F. Tomney MP, *ibid*, col. 1184; he accused the Minister of being 'concerned not with matters of negotiation or procedure, but with economics', col. 1183.
83. See for example, TGWU, *Evidence* to Donoval Royal Commission *op.cit.* note 76 above, 1184.
84. I. Macleod, Minister of Labour, Parl. Deb. HC 19 Nov. 1958, col. 1172, claiming that further consultation with the unions would have been 'of no value', col. 1172.
85. See G. Latta, 'The Legal Extension of Collective Bargaining' (1974) 3 ILJ 215.
86. Especially by *In Place of Strife* (Cmnd. 3888, 1969).
87. TUC, *Annual Report* 1965, 147.
88. See the debate on a motion passed unanimously in TUC *Annual Report* 1966, 408-10; on local arbitrations by 'dispute teams, such as those associated by Jack Scamp', see H. Nicholas (TGWU) 410.
89. See his Note in (1959) 22 MLR 408-411: perhaps to emphasise the importance of this partial 'extension' of collective agreements, he omitted

the social background, adding oddly: 'The trade unions were perhaps not very interested in this matter'. He did briefly touch on the real position in 'Labour Law' in M. Ginsberg (ed.), *Law and Opinion in England in the 20th Century* (1959) at 235. He added that this was 'the most important enactment concerning the enforcement of collective agreements ever to have been passed by Parliament' (22 MLR 408), a sentiment not entirely consistent with the idea that he found it of secondary importance or even that the times were 'not very exciting'. See P. Davies and M. Freedland, *Labour Legislation and Public Policy* (1993) 29.

90. See P. Davies and M. Freedland, *op.cit.* note 89, 119; B. Bercusson, *Fair Wages Resolutions* (1978) 277; and a certain ambiguity in K. Wedderburn and P. Davies, *Employment Grievances and Disputes Procedures in Britain* (1969) 204. Even the Donovan Royal Commission *Report* (Cmnd 3623 1968) reads as if the employers' opposition to Order 1376 arose *after* the Act of 1959 had just 'preserved' part of the 'former arrangements' (para, 239-40).

91. Wedderburn (1972) 10 BJIR 270, 278, below Chapter 3.

92. *The Times*, April 22, 1963, describing the efforts of the Minister (Mr Hare) against the caution of both employers and unions.

93. See the analyses, much under-rated at the time, by R. Fryer in (1973) 4 ILJ 1, and R. Martin and R. Fryer, *Redundancy and Paternalistic Capitalism* (1978).

94. Civil service policies led ministers to overtake the voluntarist stance of the tripartite National Joint Advisory Council on 'arbitrary dismissals' in Labour's Industrial Relations Bill of 1969 (statutory arrangements 'would cut across and undermine voluntary procedures', see NJAC *Dismissal Procedures* (1967) 44).

95. See now J. Clark and R. Lewis, *Employment Rights, Industrial Tribunals and Arbitration: The Case for Alternative Dispute Resolution* (Inst. of Employment Rights 1994). See too Wedderburn, R. Lewis and J. Clark, *Labour Law and Industrial Relations* (1983) 173-84.

96. *McRea* v *Cullen & Davidson Ltd*, [1988] IRLR 30, 32 (NI CA).

97. S. Parker, C. Thomas, N. Ellis, W. McCarthy, *Effects of the Redundancy Payments Act* (1971) 10.

98. C. Crouch, *Class Conflict and the Industrial Relations Crisis* (1977) 211; see too G. Dorfman, *Wages and Politics in Britain 1945-1967* (1973) on the TUC rejection of incomes restraint in the early 1950s. Harold MacMillan attacked the unions in 1956 when the priority of full employment was questioned in the White Paper, *The Economic Implications of Full Employment* (Cmnd. 9725 1956): see further Crouch *op.cit.* Chapters 11 and 12.

99. Insofar as this involved further, though inherently temporary, legislation many see it as part of the process of juridification or expression of a change in the nature of labour law; see below Chapter 10 for further discussion of such views.

100. J. Clark and Wedderburn, in Wedderburn, R. Lewis and J. Clark, *Labour Law and Industrial Relations* (1983) 190-6.

101. The new judicial onslaught began with Sachs J. [1961] 2 All E.R. 825 and *The Times* April 26, May 5 and 6 1961; disapproved [1963] 1 QB 623 CA;

restored *Rookes* v *Barnard* [1964] AC 1129 HL. See the Appendix at the end of this Chapter.

102. Compare the rare appearance of what some call the 'pure form' of market capitalism: C. Crouch, *Class Conflict and the Industrial Relations Crisis* (1977) 196.

103. O. Kahn-Freund in A. Flanders and H. Clegg, *The Systems of Industrial Relations in Great Britain* (1954) 88 and 92; see too on the Act of 1959 his note (1959) 22 MLR 408, also, on the differences between Order 1376 and the Act, 409-10.

104. In particular the insistence by the Commission, partly supported by the Court of Justice Opinion on the ILO Convention 170 of 1990, that where there is 'joint competence', the Member States cannot act in the ILO or ratify Conventions without jointly concerting their relations through it. See Wedderburn, 'Labour Standards, Global Markets and Labour Laws in Europe' in D. Campbell and W. Sengenberger, *International Labour Standards in the Global Economy* (1994 IILS).

105. See the dominant study by K. Jeffrey and P. Hennessy, *States of Emergency* (1983): contemporary contingency planning on the inside of the government involves employers, but not trade unions: see on the analogy with problems under Order 1305, 268-9.

106. Ministry of Labour, *Written Evidence* to Donovan Royal Commission (1965) 92.

107. J. Richardson, *Industrial Relations in Great Britain* (1933, ILO Report, Series A No.36) 91; see too Chapter V on voluntary, consultative 'Works Councils'.

108. Discussed below in Chapter 10.

109. Including opposition to parts of the Industrial Relations Act 1971. See M. Moran, *The Politics of Industrial Relations* (1977) 95-6; compare D. Barnes and E. Reid, *Government and Trade Unions* (1977) 134-5. (Barnes was a hawkish senior civil servant in this period.)

110. M. Freedland, 'The Role of the Department of Employment' in W. McCarthy (ed.) *Legal Interventions in Industrial Relations* (1992) 291; the loss may involve an entire transformation of the role of the State, 292-4, citing K. Middlemas, *Power, Competition and the Strong State* vol. 3, *The End of the Postwar Era: Britain since 1974* (1991) Chapter 12.

111. H. (later Lord) Watkinson Parl. Deb. HC 23 June 1955 cols. 1628-29.

112. J. Davis Smith, *The Attlee and Churchill Administrations and Industrial Unrest; 1945-1955* (1990) 9, 20.

113. H. Clegg, *The System of Industrial Relations in Great Britain* (1972) 75, 352 (the function of such rules was frequently to control payment of strike pay).

114. Adjournment debate on industrial relations after the railway strike. See Sir Walter Monckton (Minister of Labour) Parl. Deb. HC 23 June 1955 cols 1509 *et seq.*, especially 1525-7; see too, J. Davis Smith, *op.cit.* note 112, 120-1.

115. See for details Wedderburn, *The Worker and the Law* (1986 3rd ed.) 56-8, 77, and on the law created in the miners' strike on receivership over union assets 739-46. See also the Green Paper, *Democracy in Trade Unions* (Cmnd. 8778 1983) pp. 14-15; and on its plans to take control of

unions, Wedderburn, *Employment Rights in Britain and Europe* (1991) 81-2.

116. J. Davis Smith, *op.cit.* (1990), note 112, 123.

117. *Democracy in Trade Unions, op.cit.* note 115, para. 60. The Green Paper went on to consider ballots 'triggered' by the Government or by employers or by a 'proportion of union members' (which was raised again in the draft of the Code on industrial action in 1988, but so far has not been taken up).

118. J. Gummer MP, Written Answer, Parl. Deb. HC. 19 July 1983, col. 91.

119. J. Elgar and B. Simpson, 'The Impact of the Law on Disputes in the 1980s', D. Metcalf and S. Miller, *New Perspectives on Industrial Disputes* (1993) 100-1.

120. T. King MP, Secretary of State for Employment, Parl. Deb. HC 8 November 1983, cols. 158-62, where he gives no explanation other than that the idea had arisen in 'consultations'. On some of the inconsistencies in the government's position; see S. Auerbach, *Legislating for Conflict* (1990) 136-50. But the link between ballot and breach of contract was broken by the Employment Act 1990, Sched. 2, para. 2, by which ballots were required for any inducement to take part in industrial action now TULRCA s. 226) though inducing breach of contract would still be the normal tort arising therefrom (other than where the plaintiff is a union member, s. 62, or is relying on s. 235A TULRCA 1992 as amended in 1993).

121. See on this point the complementary but otherwise very different analyses by K. Coates and T. Topham in *Trade Unions and Politics* (1986) 84-100, and S. Auerbach, *Legislating for Conflict* (1990) 133-56. These useful analyses of the debates need to take the argument back to 1947, if they are not to find, as Auerbach claims, that the 1984 Act is just a 'dismal swamp' based on economic and political assumptions 'precarious in anything beyond the short term'. Coates and Topham also add a wider ideological vision.

122. See the helpful note by B. Simpson (1993) 22 ILJ 287; and now on the union's duty to provide the employer with the striking members' names, *Blackpool and Fylde College* v *NATFHE* [1994] IRLR 227 CA.

123. Employment Act 1988, ss. 10 and 11 [now s.222 TULRCA 1992].

124. S. Dunn and M. Wright, 'Managing Without the Closed Shop' in D. Metcalf and S. Miller, *New Perspectives on Industrial Disputes* (1993) 48.

125. The union can succeed against the member without proving it notified the relevant employer of the result of the ballot: s. 62(2)(a) TULRCA as amended in 1993; see s. 226(2)(a)(ii), on inter alia s. 231A; such notification is required if the ballot is to be effective against employers – an odd structure which the Government confirmed it had fully intended.

126. *Boddington* v *Lawton* [1994] ICR 478: 'It cannot be right for the courts … to attempt to re-assess the requirements of public interest in this field … I cannot think of a subject where interventions by the judges would be more ill-advised', *per* Nicholls VC, 491.

127. W. Hutt, *The Theory of Collective Bargaining 1930-1975* (1975) 123. See F. Hayek, *Law Legislation and Liberty* (1979) Vol. II, 150-152, and Vol III, making clear that there must be a right to reserve special measures

against large organisations of workers. Among the new liabilities in Britain, see now s. 235A TULRCA 1992, added in 1993: a right for 'individuals' to sue for an order to stop industrial action if it is unlawful as respects *any* person.

128. Now s. 64 TULRCA 1992. 'To do the bidding of others is for the employed [person] the condition of achieving his purpose', F. Hayek, *The Constitution of Liberty* (1960) 120. It is not clear how Hayek would have reacted to the great increase of 'self-employed' workers.

129. *NLRB* v *Wooster Division of Borg-Warner Corpn*, 356 US 342, 350 (1958) S.Ct.; for later developments, see L. Merrifield, T. St. Antoine, C. Craver, *Labor Relations Law* (1989) 556-64. The ballot-clause under review was what the employers wanted in the agreement.

130. Especially by his references to approved disciples, see *The Constitution of Liberty* (1960) 268 (objecting to the notion that the aim of unions 'must be supported for the good of the public'), 279, and see 505, note 7 where he cites fifteen works on labour law and labour economics to support his criticisms, in particular S. Petro, *The Labor Law of a Free Society* (1958). It should not be thought that Hayek did not read the works he cited.

131. See G. Morton and P. Smith, 'Union Exclusion and the Decollectivisation of Industrial Relations' (1993) 31 BJIR 97.

132. See P. Smith and G. Morton, 'Union Exclusion — The Next Steps' (1994) 25 Ind. Rels Jo. 3, 6, 10-12, guessing at new legislation, especially in the public sector, from the government's 'ideology' and its 'policy statements and action'; Wedderburn, 'The New Policies in Industrial Relations' in P. Fosh and C. Littler (eds.) *Industrial Relations and the Law in the 1980s* (1985), 'The rules of the game slowly, but logically, are changed', 48; and see generally 44-54. On Hayek, see (1989) 18 ILJ 1, and contrast S. Auerbach, *Legislating for Conflict* (1990) 239, who, writing before the Acts of 1990 and 1993, saw no 'common theme' for the legislation in the 'lofty realms of ideology', merely 'problems' and a 'complex patchwork of influences'; on that view most of the subsequent 1990 and 1993 legislation is virtually inexplicable. Compare H. Carty on the 1990 Act, (1991) 20 ILJ 1, 20; 'the Act lacks justification'.

133. H. Collins, 'Against Abstentionism in Labour Law' in J. Eekelaar and J. Bell (eds.) *Oxford Essays in Jurisprudence* (3rd. Series 1987) 79, 87-8, 99-101.

134. L. Dickens, M. Jones, B. Weekes, M. Hart, *Dismissed* (1985) 251. The exact effects of union representation in industrial tribunals may need reconsideration after N. Tremlett and N. Banerji, *The 1992 Survey of Industrial Tribunal Applications* (Employment Department, Research Series 22, 1994). On *l'action syndicale*, see G. Lyon-Caen and J. Pelissier, *Droit du Travail* (1992 16th ed) 566-72.

135. S. 11, Trade Union and Labour Relations (Consolidation) Act (TULRCA) 1992. In 1994 the Prison Officers Association discovered that, as its members had the powers of a police constable, they were not 'workers' within the Act's definition and therefore the Association did not fall within the definition of a 'trade union'. At once the common law doctrine of restraint of trade caught the Association, since s. 11 of the Act could not apply, rendering its rules unenforceable: Nicholls VC

Boddington v *Lawton* [1994] ICR 478. For the earlier judgments, see (1991) 54 MLR 1, 17-23, and below Chapter 2, note 99 et seq.

136. K.W. Wedderburn, *The Worker and the Law* (1965) 20; (1972 2nd ed.) 25.

137. A. Flanders on 'The Traditions of Voluntarism' in *Management and Unions* (1970) 289, referring to his *Evidence* to the Donovan Royal Commission, Day 62, 6 December 1966. See too, W. McCarthy in *Legal Interventions in Industrial Relations* (1992) 6.

138. The phrase is from P. Davies and M. Freedland, *Labour Legislation and Public Policy* (1993), 666 speaking about the future and 'positive labour law': see too Chapter 10 below.

139. ILO Conventions 87 (1948) and 98 (1949); also for these rights in whole or part, Council or Europe Convention on Human Rights 1950, art. 11, and Social Charter 1961, arts. 5, 6; Universal Declaration of Human Rights 1948, art. 23; International Covenant on Civil and Political Rights 1966, art. 22; International Covenant on Economic, Social and Cultural Rights 1966, art. 8; N. Valticos, *International Labour Law* (1985) paras. 204-213.

140. United Kingdom, *Reply to Committee of Experts' General Observations 1992, Report to ILO for 1 July 1991 to 30 June 1992*, Annex Ci, paras 9, 10. On the right to strike as one of the essential means of protecting workers' interests in the ILO philosophy, see R. Ben-Israel, *International Labour Standards: The Case of Freedom to Strike* (1987).

141. P. Davies and M. Freedland, *Labour Law: Text and Materials* (2nd ed. 1984) 259: 'with hindsight'.

142. Compare the tripartite National Advisory Joint Council Report, *Dismissals Procedures* (Ministry of Labour, 1967) which advocatd extended collective bargaining, not legislation, to deal with 'arbitrary dismissals', at least until a further review.

143. See his *Labour Law: Old Traditions and New Developments* (1968) 52; but elsewhere he appeared to accept such legislation, enforced through the industrial tribunals, as within collective *laissez-faire* in the nature of a floor to, and supportive of, collective bargaining; see *Labour and the Law* (1983) 50 and 170-5.

144. K.W. Wedderburn, *The Worker and the Law* (1972 2nd ed.) 482.

145. F. Carinci, R. de Luca Tamajo, P. Tosi, T. Treu, *Il rapporto di lavoro subordinato* (2nd ed. 1990) 2; see the almost parallel passage in G. Lyon-Caen and J. Pélissier, *Droit du Travail* (1992 16th ed.) 32, and on *l'automonie collective*, see p. 37.

146. See below Chapter 3.

147. See below Chapter 9, 294.

148. See below on 'inderogability' in other systems; Chapter 6.

149. Tony Blair MP, then Labour Party spokesperson on Employment, speech 5 April 1990.

150. *Industrial Relations in the 1990s* (*Green Paper* Cm.1602 1991) 1.19.

151. Wedderburn, 'Labour Law – From Here to Autonomy', Chapter 5 *Employment Rights in Britain and Europe* (1991).

152. Compare J. Clark on 'Juridification' (1985) 14 ILJ 69, 87-8.

153. O. Kahn-Freund, 'Collective Agreements under War Legislation' (1943)

6 MLR 112, 143.
154. O. Kahn-Freund, *Labour Law: Old Traditions and New Developments* (1968) 7.
155. See I. Sharp, *Industrial Conciliation and Arbitration in Britain* (1950) 332-5; see too the exceptional Cotton Manufacturing Industry (Temporary Provisions) Act 1934: *ibid.* 135ff.
156. P. Davies and M. Freedland, *Labour Legislation and Public Policy* (1993), 642, 643; see above note 49 on the 'vituperative epithet'.
157. O. Kahn-Fruend, *Labour Relations: Heritage and Adjustment* (1979) 72. He saw signs a decade earlier that the tradition had not been 'maintained' in face of legislation. See *Labour Law: Old Traditions and New Developments* (1968) 52.
158. O. Kahn-Freund, 'Labour Law' in M. Ginsberg (ed.) *Law and Opinion in England in the 20th Century* (1959) 215, 244. The State does not give life.
159. See H. Laski, *Grammar of Politics* (1925) 90-94. Kahn-Freund often recorded his debt to conversations with Laski and others at LSE, but scarcely ever referred to his writings.
160. K. Klare, 'Labor law as Ideology' (1981) Ind. Rel. L.J. 450, 481; and see Wedderburn, *The Worker and the Law* (1986 3rd ed.) 860-1, which is a development from earlier editions, see note 136 above and p.64 below.
161. P. Davies and M. Freedland, *Labour Legislation and Public Policy* (1993), 226, referring to the episde of Lord Tangley's questions, in K. Wedderburn, *Evidence* to Donovan Royal Commission Day 31, 22 March 1966, though it does little to illustrate the concept of 'pure abstentionism'. Lord Tangley's vehement questions included: 'Why do you make an exception in fact in favour of racial or ethnic discrimination?' (Q 4888) This illustrated his attitude to racial discrimination and his undeveloped understanding of collective *laissez-fair*. Probably 'the most reactionary member' of the Commission (W. McCarthy, (1993) 15 Emp. Relns. 3, 4) he favoured legislation to weaken trade unions and outflank the immunities (see his 'Supplementary Note' to the 'Donovan' *Report* of the Royal Commission (Cmnd 3623 1968) pp. 284-7). He was visibly annoyed by proposals to restore the union liberties lost in *Rookes* v *Barnard* [1964] AC 1129 HL, equating union pressures to chasing people from the workplace 'with a whip'; and he vigorously objected to laws that gave 'black, yellow, brown, any colour ... treatment preferential over another' (Q 4889). The writer's answer suggested: 'this community faces a problem of racial discrimination which, if we do not face up to it, is going to have the most dreadful consequences in ten years time', see too p.294 below.
162. K. Wedderburn, *Evidence* to Donovan Commission Day 31, *op.cit. Memorandum* para. 7.
163. The issue on racial discrimination of course was how far well devised legal sanctions would assist in destroying racism, a point parallel to, but distinct from, the questions raised by collective *laissez-faire*. More, this was a time when only the futile Act of 1968 confronted what many had begun to identify as a social evil, potent with harm for workplace and society.

164. *Labour and the Law* (1972) 234. In discussion with the writer he appreciated the distortions by Lord Tangley.
165. The phrase is from P. Davies and M. Freedland, *Labour Legislation and Public Policy* (1993), 66, who rightly repeat the overall ambition.
166. Wedderburn, *The Worker and the Law* (1965) 342; the central question remained: 'Who is to control what at the place of work?'. For bold proposals of new rights by trade unionists including a Right to Organise Act, see C. Jenkins and J. Mortimer, *The Kind of Laws the Unions Ought to Want* (1968) 51.
167. See K.W. Wedderburn, *The Worker and the Law* (1972 2nd ed.) 401, 481-3; see too, in 1964 pp.75-80 above; also p.158 below. On the use of semantic choices, see Chapter 10 below, pp.353-9.
168. See below, Chapter 3 on the themes of 'order' and 'individualism' in the 1971 Act; and on the different ideology and political orientation of the 1980s legislation, even more hostile to the values of autonomous trade unionism, see Chapter 5 below, and Chapter 8 in Wedderburn, *Employment Rights in Britain and Europe* (1991).
169. Cmnd 3888, 1969: on recognition rights, for example, see paras. 53-62.
170. 'An Alternative System of Positive Rights', Chapter 4, *Trade Union Immunities* (Cmnd 8128 1981).
171. See Chapter 4 below on the remarkable differences of approach in Britain and in France to this issue, of great importance if 'European-level' collective bargaining is envisaged. See Chapters 5 and 10 below.
172. The government certainly believed that the noose of vicarious liability had been gradually tightened around the unions: see *Unofficial Action and The Law* (Cm. 821, 1989) Chap. 2. The view that the 1982 Act was 'softer' than the common law may overlook the effect of s. 15(3)(c)(d) thereof [now s. 20(2)(b)(c) TULRCA 1992], which made a union liable strictly for any act of the two senior officers and of all employed officials, while the common law test in *Heatons Transport Ltd* v *TGWU* [1973] AC 15 HL depended on notions of express or implied authority which gave the union a chance: see *General Aviation Services* v *TGWU* [1976] IRLR 224 HL (not cited by P. Davies and M. Freedland, *op.cit.* above note 165, 480-1; compare their *Labour Law: Text and Materials* (1984) 831). An unauthorised official can make the union liable under the new law, not under the common law test. Of course, the Employment Act 1990, s.6 (now TULRCA 1992, s. 20(3)(b)) turned the screw even tighter and was even harsher in regard to repudiation by unions of acts done by unauthorised persons (now s. 21 *TULRA* 1992). Vicarious liability is crucial in motions for an injunction. See too, Chapter 4 below for comparisons with France.
173. See for example the CBI discussion document, *Trade Unions in a Changing World: the Challenge for Management* (1980) 22-3.
174. For further discussion, see Wedderburn in *Employment Rights in Britain and Europe* (1991) 367-74, also (1991) 54 MLR 1, 17-25.
175. See too for this analysis, the Sinzheimer Lecture for 1993, below Chapter 9. The core of that view appeared in papers by the writer of 1972, now Chapter 3 below, and in 1983, 'The New Politics of Labour Law', now Chapter 4 in *Employment Rights in Britain and Europe* (1991).

176. The term is used here in a sense somewhat closer to Popper than to Marx, not, or not necessarily, implying 'false' consciousness: see K. Popper, *The Open Society and Its Enemies* (5th ed. 1966) 141-3; T. Bottomore and M. Rubel, *Karl Marx: Selected Writings in Sociology and Social Philosophy* (1961) 5-25.

177. Fortunately Italian scholars have largely remedied the converse lack of pragmatic research; for an example see T. Treu (ed.) *L'uso politico dello Statuto dei lavoratori* (1975) and *Lo Statuto dei lavatori: prassi sindacale e motivazioni dei giudici* (1976).

178. In the robust 'Wembley programme' of 1982, the General Council were 'aware that at present trade union members do not fully grasp the dangers that the Employment Bill poses to them and their unions. This highlights the need for a mass campaign of publicity, meetings and education to inform union members and the wider public of the reasons for TUC policy', *Industrial Relations Legislation: Report by the TUC General Council*, 5 April 1982, para. 65. See too, Chapter 10, below.

179. Alan Fox in his incomparable analysis, *Beyond Contract: Work, Power, and Trust Relations* (1974), 277: 'there remains, from the power-holders' point of view, a never ending need for what might be called "fine tuning" ', 278.

180. See H. Sinzheimer, *Philip Lotmar and the Discipline of Labour Law in Germany* (1922), 9 Arbeitsrecht 587, in R. Lewis and J. Clark *Labour, Law and Politics in the Weimar Republic* (1981) 102; see too Chapter 9 below.

181. *Conservative Manifesto 1983*, 12; for criticism of the failure, see C. Hanson and G. Mather, *Striking Out Strikes* (1988) 83-6; generally G. Morris, *Strikes in Essential Services* (1986), 188-204.

182. ACAS *Annual Report 1983* 12. On the linking of 'essential public services' to constitutional rights, and a *Commissione di Garanzia*, see the Italian Law 146 of 1990, discussed in Wedderburn, *Employment Rights in Britain and Europe* (1991) 321-5 (also the problems that have beset Spanish law in trying to give the workers a role in defining essential services).

183. In the TURER Act 1993, s. 22 (now s. 235A TULRCA 1992). This was first proposed in the Green Paper as a right to sue in respect of 'public services within the scope of the Citizen's Charter' (*Industrial Relations in the 1990s*, 1989 Cm.1602 para. 4.6-4.10: refuse collection, health and education services, 'publicly-owned transport services', social security benefits and gas, electricity, water, telecommunications; 'the right would also apply if the service was contracted-out to a privately owned company': 4.11). This last would have heightened the need and the difficulty of defining the 'public services' involved.

184. The Commissioner for the Rights of Trade Union Members (ss. 109-114, 266 TULRCA 1992) and the Commissioner for Protection Against Unlawful Industrial Action (inserted in 1993 as ss. 235B, 235C TULRCA 1992). For tripartite machinery in other jurisdictions, see Wedderburn, *Employment Rights in Britain and Europe* (1991) 316-25.

185. See for example, the repeal of the 'collective' jurisdiction of the CAC in s. 3 Equal Pay Act 1970 (Sex Discrimination Act 1986, s. 6 and Sched. 9; see

P. Davies, 'The CAC and Equal Pay' *Current Legal Problems* 1980, 165) or the truncation of ACAS' remit on collective bargaining (TURER 1993 s. 43).

186. Notably in his 'Legal Framework' in A. Flanders and H. Clegg, *System of Industrial Relations in Great Britain* (1954) 42, 43-4, where industrial relations are pronounced 'healthy' because they are less regulated by law; see the Note in his *Selected Papers* (1978 ed. M. Partington) 76, on his 'Intergroup Conflicts and their Settlements' (1954) 5 BJS 193. See too, Wedderburn, 'Otto Kahn-Feund and British Labour Law', Chapter 3 in Wedderburn, J. Clark and R. Lewis, *Labour Law and Industrial Relations* (1983).

187. See the references in Chapter 9, 'Labour Law and the Individual' below, notes 52-71, for further discussion, especially on the weakness caused in Kahn-Freund's position by his belief that English society had reached an 'equilibrium' which rendered the State 'neutral'; see also chapter 10 below.

188. [1964] AC 1129 HL.

189. '*Rookes* v *Barnard* and After' (1964) 14 *Federation News* 30, 40: 'we are now facing the revival of the "labour injunction",' p. 41. See below, appendix to this Chapter.

190. See Chapter 9 below.

191. Compare O. Kahn-Freund (1964) 14 *Federation News* 30; K. Wedderburn (1964) 27 MLR 257, with L. Hoffman (1965)81 LQR 116; C. Hamson [1961] 190; J. Weir [1964] CLJ 225.

192. TULRCA 1992, s. 11.

193. See the fate of the Prison Officers Association; it was not a trade union because in law its members were not 'workers' (*Home Office v Evans* November 18 1993, Evans J.) so the doctrine of restraint of trade applied to it: (*Boddington v Lawton* [1994] ICR 478 [see now ss. 126-128 Criminal Justice and Public Order Act 1994].

194. P. Elias and K. Ewing, 'Economic Torts and Labour Law' [1982] CLJ 321, 358; Ewing later made it clear that the rights must not be 'easily outflanked': 'Rights and Immunities in British Labour Law' (1988) 10 Comp. Lab. Law Jo.1, 35. But, given the agility of common law judges, how? For detailed treatment of this problem, see Wedderburn, *Employment Rights in Britain and Europe* (1991) Chapter 11, 374-90 (also (1991) 54 MLR, 1, 25-47).

195. Wedderburn, 'The Injunction and the Sovereignty of Parliament', Chapter 7 in Employment Rightsin Britain and Europe (1991); C. O'Regan, 'Contempt of Court and the Enforcement of LabourIn-junctions' (1991) 54 MLR 385.

196. *Regina* v *Bunn* (1872) 12 Cox 316 (combination to break contracts by organising a strike held to be a criminal conspiracy, both by reason of those breaches and independently by reason of the 'unjustifiable annoyance and interference with the masters in the conduct of their business' (Brett J.).

197. The Court of Appeal extended tort liability to stop the strike, *Associated British Ports* v *TGWU* [1989] 1 W LR 939 (reversed by the HL on other grounds, *ibid*.). For the repeated instances in between, see *Employment*

Rights in Britain and Europe (1991) 370-1. The forms extend beyond the law of tort, reaching to restitution for 'economic duress' and various forms of 'unlawful means'.

198. See Wedderburn, *Employment Rights in Britain and Europe* (1991) especially Chapter 6 'Freedom of Association or Right to Organise', and Chapter 11, 'Social Charter, Labour Law and Labour Courts?'; K. Ewing, 'Rights and Immunities in British Labour Law' (1988) 10 Comp. L.L.J. 1.

199. See *American Cyanamid Co v Ethicon* [1975] AC 396 HL; Wedderburn, 'The Injunction and the Sovereignty of Parliament', Chapter 7 in *Employment Rights in Britain and Europe* (1991).

200. *Barretts & Baird (Wholesale) Ltd v IPCS* [1987] IRLR 3 (Henry J.). An '*ex parte*' injunction is one which the union has not had an opportunity to defend as defendant.

201. See Wedderburn, *Employment Rights in Britain and Europe* (1991) 374-390, and (1991) 54 MLR 25-4; W. McCarthy, 'The case for labour courts' (1991) 21 Ind. Rels. Jo. 98; B. Hepple, 'Labour Courts: Some Comparative Perspectives' (1988) 41 *Current Legal Problems* 169.

202. For example, Popplewell J., 'Random Thoughts from the President's Chair' (1987) 16 ILJ 209, and Wood J., 'The Employment Appeal Tribunal as it enters the 1990s' (1990) 19 ILJ 133.

203. Lord Donaldson (the ex-President of the NIRC 1971-4), 'Lessons from the Industrial Court' (1975) 91 LQR 181, especially 190-2, and 'The Rôle of Labour Courts' (1975) 4 ILJ 69.

204. For a more detailed analogy with the CAC, see Wedderburn, *Employment Rights in Britain and Europe* (1991) Chapter 10, 'Social Charter, Labour Law and Labour Courts?' 374-90, and (1991) 54 MLR 1, 25-47.

205. 'A new collective law based upon conciliation and discussion rather than the courts': G. Lyon-Caen, 'Du Rôle des Principes Généraux du Droit Civil en Droit du Travail (Première Approché)' (1974) Rev. Trim. de Dr. Civ. 229, 231, discussed in Wedderburn (1987) 16 ILJ

206. See below Chapter 2.

207. O. Kahn-Freund, 'Labour Law' in M. Ginsberg (ed.) *Law and Opinion in England in the 20th Century* (1959) 214, 224. Here he employs a phrase from a much earlier phase in his thinking: see 'Collective Agreements Under War Legislation' (1943) 6 MLR 112, 142: 'collective bargaining' leaves employment conditions 'to the free interplay of social forces, collective forces, it is true, not individual forces'.

208. O. Kahn-Freund, *Labour Relations: Heritage and Adjustment* (1979) 77.

209. See for example, *Labour's Better Way for the 1990s* (1991 Labour Party Policy Review) 38-40, where the court would have a conciliation rôle, sequestration of union assets would be limited short of 'paralysing' its lawful activities, and *ex-parte* injunctions would not be allowed. *Each* party would have an option in interlocutory cases to a 'hearing on the full merits' which would 'have to follow immediately'. Since the employer chooses the time to strike in the courts on short notice, this last change would normally benefit him, rather than the union. In any event, an injunction would on present practice run during the hearings if the

employer has even an 'arguable' case, a level of proof untouched by this proposal. None of the proposals featured in the Party's 1992 election manifesto.

210. 'Industrial Relations and the Law – Retrospect and Prospect' (1969) 7 BJIR 301, 316.

211. See the Director-General's *Report* to the 81st Session 1994, *Defending Values, Promoting Change* (Part I, 1994, ILO) 57, also 52-4; and on 'social clauses' 57-63: above notes 22, 23, and below Chapters 7 and 10.

212. For the contrasts between 'freedom of association' and the 'right to organise' see Wedderburn (1987) 18 Ind. Rel. Jo. 244, and *Employment Rights in Britain and Europe* (1991) Chapter 6.

213. For ILO cases involving many such States, see R. Ben-Israel's invaluable *International Labour Standards: The Case of Freedom to Strike* (1987) Part III.

214. P. Grant, *The History of Factory Legislation* (1866)cited in G.D.H. Cole and A. Filson, *British Working Class Documents: 1789-1875* (1965) 328. One of the earliest judicial destructions of a statutory protection for workers was the decision of Parke J. permitting 'relays' to evade the Ten Hours Act, *Ryder v Mills* (1850) 3 Ex. 853; see W. Cornish, *Law and Society in England 1750-1950* (1989) 307.

215. See for example the argument in *Labour and the Law* (1972) 165-195, (1983 3rd ed.) 220-236.

216. R. Lewis, 'Kahn-Freund and Labour Law: An Outline Critique' (1979) 8 ILJ 202, 218; but to be fair, Kahn-Freund himself did recognise that equilibrium was not a 'pre-established fact' of any economic system, *Labour Law: Old Traditions and New Developments* (1968), 11.

217. See A. Fox, *Beyond Contract: Work, Power and Trust Relationships* (1974) especially 263-5; and on pluralism H. Clegg (1975) 13 BJIR 209; R. Hyman (1978) 16 BJIR 16, 17-22; F. Prondzynski in P. Fosh and C. Littler (eds.) *Industrial Relations and the Law in the 1980s* (1985) 179-85.

218. G. Winstanley, *Love of Freedom* (1649), see C. Hill, *A Nation of Change and Novelty* (1993 rvsd. ed.) Chapter 7 'Gerrard Winstanley and Freedom'.

219. G. Holyoake, address to the trade unions of Sheffield, 28 November 1841, in W. Milne-Bailey, *Trade Union Documents* (1929) 47.

220. The *Minority Report* to the *Report of the Royal Commission on Trade Unions* (1869 c.4123) xxix, by F. Harrison, T. Hughes and the Earl of Lichfield.

221. '[S]pecial measures may be needed to regulate union affairs in recognition of the unique purposes of unions, which are quite unlike those of, for example, companies, sporting clubs or even political parties', Lord Strathclyde Parl. Deb. HL 23 July 1990 col. 1274, on the special extension of vicarious liability for unions.

222. *Minority Report, op.cit.*. For Harrison's separate memorandum, see W. Milne-Bailey *Trade Union Documents* (1929) 454.

223. See O. Kahn-Freund, 'Industrial Democracy' (1977) 6 ILJ 65, and the response by P. Davies and Wedderburn, 'The Land of Industrial Democracy' (1977) 6 ILJ 197.

224. It was in part the 'failure of "voluntary" systems of arbitration' in those

countries which promoted the movement towards compulsory arbitration. See W. Creighton, W. Ford, R. Mitchell, *Labour Law: Text and Materials* (2nd ed. 1993) 11. The prevalence of violent disputes about recognition was one reason registration was acceptable and rights were then bestowed on the unions so that they were 'safely incorporated within the system': S. Macintyre and R. Mitchell, *Foundations of Arbitration: The Origins and Effects of State Compulsory Arbitration* (1989) 15.

225. Lord Amulree, *Industrial Arbitration in Great Britain* (1929) 81.

226. G. McDonald, 'The Role of British Industry' in M. Morris, *The General Strike* (1976): Special Study I, 306-12.

227. See Sir D. Hogg, Att.-Gen., Vol. 205 Parl. Deb. HC 2. 5. 1927, col. 1318; 'genuine industrial strikes' or a 'sympathetic strike if it is called for industrial purposes'; also Viscount Cave LC Vol. 68 Parl. Deb. HL 30.6. 1927 cols. 5-6; Marquess of Salisbury, *ibid*, 5.7.1927, col. 165-6, defending the 'delay' in presenting the Bill, as the Government 'were so anxious that there should be no violation of the true rights of labour'. In the light of the banning of sympathetic strikes in 1980 (the valueless 'exceptions' were repealed in 1990: see now s. 224 TULRCA 1992) it is noteworthy that the Attorney-General defined a 'sympathetic strike' as one by persons 'not directly interested in the subject-matter', Vol. 205 *ibid*. cols. 1314-5, though the Solicitor-General, Sir Thos. Inskip, thought the concept 'inexact'; the 'fantastic epithets' intruded because 'sympathy is a gracious thing ... human in its appeal'. 205 *ibid*. 5.5.1927, col. 1884.

228. Viscount Cave LC *ibid*. 30.6.1927, col. 12. The Earl of Halsbury adopted a very different tone, and was especially outraged at 'massed picketing', Vol. 68 *ibid*. 4.7.1927, cols. 59-65.

229. For example, Lord Peel (First Commssr. for Works) who supported the recommendations of the Dunedin Royal Commission which did not recommend complete protection from tort liability for unions, as enacted by s.4, Trades Disputes Act 1906: Parl. Deb. Vol. 68 HL 4.7 1927, cols. 79-80. The repeal in 1982 of union funds' protection in tort was the turning point away from any ambivalence in the ideological thrust of the Thatcher legislation: see Wedderburn, *Employment Rights in Britain and Europe* (1991) Chapter 8.

230. The phrase is used to describe such processes by Renner, *The Institutions of Private Law and their Social Functions* (1949, ed. O. Kahn-Freund) 122; and see the editor's note 154, where he adds the point that 'in this country collective regulation was much less closely linked with State intervention than on the Continent' (171).

231. R. Hyman, *Industrial Relations: a Marxist Introduction* (1975) 135.

232. See Chapter 10 below.

233. R. Brown, 'The Employment Relationship in Sociological Theory' in D. Gallie (ed.) *Employment in Britain* (1989) 61. For further discussion of the language and 'rhetoric' of labour law, see Chapter 10.

234. N. Tebbit, Secretary of State for Employment, Second Reading of the Employment Bill, Parl. Deb. HC, 8.2.1982, col 741.

235. W. Brown and S. Wadhawani, 'The Impact of Recent Industrial Relations Laws on the Economy' 1990, Nat. Instit. Econ. Review, 131; also (1990) 40 *Federation News* 18.

236. W. Brown, in W. McCarthy, *Legal Interventions in Industrial Relations* (1992) 310-11.
237. Royal Commission on Trade Unions, *Eleventh Report* (1869, c. 4123) p. xxi para. 70.
238. Italian Fascist and Vichy codes. See the revealing account by T. Ramm in B. Hepple (ed) *The Making of Labour Law in Europe* (1986) 255, 287-96.
239. O. Kahn-Freund, *op.cit.* note 33 above, 227-9, supporting his thesis with the well known dictum of Goddard LJ *Evans v NUPBWPW* [1938] 4 All E. R. 51, 54, about the 'great benefit' of collective bargaining.
240. Wedderburn, 'The New Structure of Labour Law in Britain' (1978) 13 Israel L. R. 435, 456.
241. See N. Millward, *The New Industrial Relations?* (1994).
242. Wedderburn, 'Multinational Enterprise and National Labour Law' (1972)1 ILJ 12, 19 (emphasis supplied), now Chapter 7 below.
243. This matter is discussed further below, Chapter 10.
244. S. 18 Employment Act 1982, now s. 244(3) Trade Union and Labour Relations (Consolidation) Act 1992; and see s. 1(d) Trade Union and Labour Relations (Amendment) Act 1976.
245. 'A Lawyer's Reflections on Multinational Corporations' (1972) Ind. Rels. Jo.(Aus.) 358-9.
246. See on the question of representatives for bargaining and the effects of bargaining, below Chapters 6 and 10. For a valuable review of legal and trade union problems on recognition, see B. Simpson, *Trade Union Recognition and the Law* (1991, Institute of Employment Rights).
247. See below, Chapter 10. In the United States, the law requires election of the bargaining union in an enterprise and makes certain topics 'mandatory' for bargaining.
248. Earl Gowrie *op.cit.* note 43 above. In an early exposé and defence of the 1980s policies, R. Tur claimed that unions without immunities would merely be 'voluntary associations ... within the limits of the ordinary law of the land'. See Wedderburn and W. Murphy (ed.), *Labour Law and the Community* (1982) 163.
249. See his monumental Chapter VI, 'Labor Law and Social Security' in E. Stein and T. Nicholson, *American Enterprise in the Common Market* (1960) 297-458.
250. See on 'no-strike' clauses *Rookes v Barnard* [1964] AC 1129 HL, where the point was not 'conceded', as he held, but could not be denied because of an express incorporation in the employment contracts; *contra* Kahn-Freund in *Labour Relations and the Law* (1965) 27, 'quite exceptional'; also *Labour and the Law* (1972) 149, compare (3rd ed. 1983) 176.
251. 'Any form of industrial action by a worker is a breach of contract', Lord Templeman, *Miles v Wakefield MDC* [1987] ICR 368, 389; on the lack of authority in the union to act as agent: *Boxfoldia Ltd v NGA* [1988] ICR 752. On the widespread, reasonable but legally erroneous view that due notice legitimates strikes, see Wedderburn, *The Worker and the Law* (1986 3rd ed.) 191.
252. See the *Report* of the Donovan Royal Commission (1968 Cmnd. 3623) paras. 802-4, 878-894, 928-52. Also, Wedderburn, in W. McCarthy (ed.) *Legal Interventions in Industrial Relations* (1992) 187-92, on the 'missed

opportunity' in the Donovan Report. Despite the comparisons with France and Italy where doctrines of 'suspension' are fundamental, he said little about the crucial aspect of breach of employment contracts in British strikes: compare O. Kahn-Freund and B. Hepple, *Laws against Strikes* (1972). As early as 1897 the Webbs had drawn attention to the breach of contract involved in a strike, and the frequent civil actions brought by employers against workers in the mining industry. See *Industrial Democracy* (1914 ed.) 659, n.1.

253. For his recantation from his explanation, see (1979) 8 ILJ 193, 201.

254. For example, *Labour Law Old Traditions and New Developments* (1968), 11.

255. Now TULRCA 1992, s. 238; originally para.8 Sched.1 TULRA 1974 (until 1975 the test was whether the 'reason' for dimissal was the industrial action).

256. Now s. 237 TULRCA 1992, see too s. 223 banning strikes against such dismissals, originally introduced in the 1990 Act: see B. Simpson (1991) 54 MLR 418. There was no growth in unofficial action outside the norm of the previous decades to justify this even as a 'problem-solving' measure: see the poor case made in *Unofficial Action and the Law* (1989 Cm. 821) and the distorted comparative accounts at p. 2. Compare the more careful use of comparative law in Appendix to *Trade Union Immunities* (1981 Cmnd. 8128) 93.

257. 'Lessons from the Industrial Court' (1975) 91 LQR 63, 68. Kahn-Freund always insisted upon the fundamental premise that industrial disputes were not justiciable. See *Labour and the Law* (3rd ed. 1986, eds. P. Davies and M. Freedland) 138.

258. Wood J., *TNT Express (UK) Ltd* v *Downes* [1993] IRLR 432, 436. That is exactly what most Continental systems of labour law would expect. See Wedderburn, 'Laws About Strikes' Chapter 4 in W. McCarthy, *Legal Intervention in Industrial Relations* (1992). Note that Wood J. says dismissal 'for' (i.e. by reason of) industrial action. That was the old test before the formula became in 1975, dismissal *when* taking part, etc. As such it is much more culpable in the employer.

259. See Wedderburn in Chapter 10, 'The Right to Strike – is there a European Standard?', *Employment Rights in Britain and Europe* (1991), and further in '*Limitation législative et judiciaire en matière d'action syndicale et droit de grève*' 1990 Rev. Int. de Droit Comparé, 1, 67ff. Of course, a very narrow definition of 'strike' permitting such suspension could also obstruct the purposes of any such policy.

260. Except perhaps in a footnote: see the interpretations of C. Summers in (1992) 21 ILJ 157, with whom it is easy to agree that there is at root more than a mere 'semantic difference' between immunities and rights; but the two may be alternative or supplementary ways to an objective. Nor is it helpful to Britain's recognition problem to recommend other jurisdictions where there is a dominant 'practice of recognition': *ibid*, 165-7; other comments may reflect a misunderstanding in thinking that the writer's *Employment Rights in Britain and Europe* (1991) was at fault in not including the United States as one of the European comparisons. United States' labour relations law, fascinating in itself, is of limited

comparative utility in Britain, partly because of the very low trade union density in the United States, especially in private sector employment. For an interesting assessment; see P. Fosh *et al*, 'Union Autonomy: A Terminal Case in the UK?' (1993) 15 *Employee Relations*. 3, 15-17. The position in Canada is of course rather different, with much higher union membership.

261. The Government's announcement that it will advertise for certain (for the present, lowly) judges re-emphasies the case for labour courts cut off from the common law ideology. See Wedderburn, *Employment Rights in Britain and Europe op.cit.* 374-90. If some benches can be filled by advertisement, is it impossible to imagine others elected?

262. On control of internal union rules, see Chapter 5 below, and the helpful discussion by S. Fredman, 'The New Right: Labour Law and Ideology in the Thatcher Years' (1992) 12 Ox.J.L.S. 24, 41-42. *Quaere* whether the doctrine of 'pure autonomy' is realised in any system. On problems of strikes and industrial action, Wedderburn, 'The Right to Strike – Is There a European Standard?', Chapter 10, *Employment Rights in Britain and Europe* (1991).

263. See the Irish Industrial Relations Act 1990, s. 19; T. Kerr (1991) 20 ILJ 240.

264. See J. and R. Winterton, *Collective Bargaining and Consultation over Continuing Vocational Training* (Employment Department, Research Brief February 1994).

265. S. Deakin and F. Wilkinson, *The Economics of Employment Rights* (1991 Institute of Employment Rights) 43; also J. Michie and F. Wilkinson, *Unemployment and Workers' Rights* (1993 Institute of Employment Rights).

266. J. Grieve-Smith, 'Policies to Reduce European Unemployment', in J. Michie and J. Grieve-Smith (eds.) *Unemployment in Europe* (1994) 274; and see Chapter 10 below.

267. F. von Prondzynski, in P. Fosh and C. Littler (eds.) *Industrial Relations and the Law in the 1980s* (1985) 189.

268. See for example, the interesting analysis by H. Collins, 'Against Abstentionism in Labour Law' *op.cit.* note 133 above, 101, which does not however make clear the relationship of industrial justice to workers' autonomous organisations.

269. Kahn-Freund was acutely aware of compulsory labour schemes, both from events in Nazi Germany and even in the British 'Essential Work Orders' and direction of labour during wartime periods 1916-1918 and 1940-1947: 'Labour Law' in M. Ginsberg, *Law and Opinion in England in the 20th Century* (1959) 224-6, notes 14-22. On replacement of 'free hiring' with 'compulsory labour service', see L. Trotsky, *The Defence of Terrorism* (1921) 127-32, in L. Kolakowski, *Main Currents of Marxism* (1978) Vol. 2, 511-12.

270. See the position already on unemployment benefit: Social Security Contributions and Benefits Act 1992, ss. 27, 57(1)(3); for example, the concept of suitable work has been tightened, and pressure to take very low paid jobs has increased. See NACB *Benefit of the Doubt* (1994) Chap. 7. The government intends to introduce even stricter measures in

1995-96, whereby unemployment benefit is restricted to 6 months as a 'jobseeker's allowance' and the unemployed person must make an 'agreement' with financial penalties for lack of substantial efforts to find work. See, *Competitiveness: Helping Business to Win* (Cm. 2563 1994) para. 5.23, and *Jobseeker's Allowance* (Cm. 2687 1994) Chaps. 3 and 4: this will 'emphasise the responsibilities of unemployed people to take effective steps to find a job' (para. 6.2).

271. See the pungent analysis in the Beveridge era by Barbara Wootton, *Freedom under Planning* (1946) generally in Chap. VI, 'Choice of Employment', and Chap. VII 'Freedom of Collective Bargaining' (if it comes to the choice, she held, 'compulsory arbitration is much to be preferred to industrial direction', 108). On her later proposals for a more egalitarian system and policy, see *The Social Foundations of Wage Policy* (1954).

272. S. Fredman, 'The New Rights: Labour Law and Ideology in the Thatcher Years', *op.cit.* above note 39, p. 39.

273. E. Hobsbawm, 'Labour and Human Rights' Chapter 17, in *Worlds of Labour* (1984) 312.

274. From Gladstone's Budget speech as reported in *The Morning Star* and *The Times* 17 April 1863; this and the subsequent year's speech became notorious through being savaged by Marx in *Capital* (1946 ed) 667-9, a passage which was the subject of complaints about Marx's alleged 'misquotations' of Gladstone which were in turn later shown to be misconceived (see *ibid*. Appendix II, F. Engels, 825-839).

APPENDIX TO CHAPTER 1

FROM ROOKES V BARNARD
TO A ROYAL COMMISSION?*

In the April issue of this journal Professor Kahn-Freund discussed the decision in *Rookes* v *Barnard*, the most critical judicial decision for trade unionists since the *Taff Vale* decision in 1901, one that is, as he said, 'a frontal attack on the right to strike'.[1] Many of us concluded shortly after that decision last January that 'only new legislation can effectively restore the right to strike which the trade union movement thought it had secured in 1906'.[2] Since then two things have happened. First, the TUC General Council has proposed a specific amendment of the Trade Disputes Act, 1906, to restore the right to strike. But the Minister of Labour, Mr Godber, would agree only to an inquiry without prior legislation. Secondly, the House of Lords has decided another case, *Stratford Ltd* v *Lindley*,[3] the 'Watermen's Case', which on inspection turns out to be of as great importance to trade union law, and as great danger to union activities, as *Rookes* v *Barnard* itself. This article aims to re-examine the position in the light of the Watermen's Case; to ask what are now the better short-term measures to restore the situation; and then to touch upon a few questions that will need further inquiry or action. Only by such a careful re-examination of the current position can we decide how strong is the case for a general inquiry into trade union law.

The case for such an inquiry has not been made out in detail. It is true that the recent judgments by the Law Lords have increased the area of uncertainty in the law. Lord Donovan sat in the Court of Appeal in *Rookes* v *Barnard*, and had his judgment therefore reversed by the Lords; but he had become a Law Lord by the time of the Watermen's Case, in which counsel had invited the judges to clear up the law so that the electors could decide about it at the election. Lord Donovan replied:

> The prospect ... of finding out from an election address just how the law stands with regard to trade disputes is a prospect which I find attractive, but not very likely.[4]

Nevertheless, it is desirable that trade unionists should have the opportunity to examine what has happened to the law. In a democracy, the choice between

* First published in 1964 in *Federation News* Vol. 14.

even complicated alternatives cannot be left just to experts. And if it is shown that there are ways of restoring effective liberty of action in industrial affairs without a general 'inquiry', a case for having such an inquiry will at least have to be properly argued.

HOW THE ROOKES CASE UPSET THE BALANCE

British labour law is the creation of the history of the trade union movement and its relationship with the courts. In the last century that relationship was even less happy than it is at present. Again and again, the judges extended liabilities of their own creation (the 'common law' liabilities) in a manner hostile to trade unions, which were at that time in many ways still unlawful. Union pressure, as the movement grew, extracted from a Parliament increasingly dependent on the votes of ordinary people after 1868, statutes to protect the unions against the judge-made liabilities. This happened with conspiracy, for example. In 1872, gas workers were convicted of the crime of conspiracy for organising a strike to defend a victimised colleague. In 1875, Parliament enacted that in *trade disputes* a court could not convict for the crime of conspiracy unless the combination did or aimed to do an act that was *itself criminal* (such as assault). The judges responded by making trade union defendants liable for the *tort* (civil wrong) of conspiracy, until in *Quinn v Leathem*, 1901,[5] the Law Lords made it seem impossible to organise industrial action without running into that liability. So, in 1906 the Trade Disputes Act declared that an act done in *contemplation or furtherance of a trade dispute* shall not be actionable as a civil conspiracy by reason of the agreement or combination:

> unless the act, if done without any such agreement or combination, would be actionable (Section 1).

There were other judicial liabilities fended off in the same way. After 1853, for instance, the judges made it civilly a tort to 'induce' (or cause) a person to break his contract with someone else. Union officers ran the risk of this every day, for in calling men out on strike, or getting them to take other action like blacking work, they were often inducing them to break their employment contracts, and so risking liability at the suit of employers. Also, some judges, especially in *Quinn v Leathem*, appeared to be ready to go back on a fundamental decision of some years before[6] and declare 'interference with business or employment' a tort in itself. By 1906, therefore, Parliament had to give protection against those torts. It did so in Section 3 of the Act which reads:

> An act done by a person in contemplation or furtherance of a trade dispute shall not be actionable on the ground *only*—
> (*Limb 1*) that it induces some other person to break a contract of employment,

(*Limb* 2) that it is an interference with the trade, business or employment of some other person, or with the right of some other person to dispose of his capital or labour as he wills.

As every trade unionist knows, Section 4 of the Act also gave complete protection to union funds against tort actions for damages (though, judges are now saying, possibly not against injunctions, a new danger of some gravity). But they know too that the effective right to strike depended not on Section 4, but on Sections 1 and 3, because those were the sections that protected union officers and members in their daily activity. They did so not by declaring positive rights to strike, and so on, but by giving apparent 'immunities' against the liabilities that judges had created. The rules of the industrial game were constituted by these 'immunities' from judge-made doctrines which would have made the game impossible. In the *Rookes* case and the Watermen's case, the judges have added new rules which materially alter the moves which the trade union side can make in industrial negotiation. Let us recapitulate briefly the way in which this was done in *Rookes* v *Barnard*.

(a) *The Common Law*
Rookes, it will be recalled, sued as a non-unionist who had been given lawful notice after the union members threatened immediate strike action if he was not removed, in order to maintain their 100 per cent membership. Barnard and Fistal (two draughtsmen employed by BOAC, and both local voluntary union officials) and Silverthorne (a full-time official of the Draughtsmen's Association, then AESD) were the defendants, and they were made liable for a conspiracy. (The extent of their liability awaits a new trial on the amount of damages; but that matter is not directly relevant here.) But, as we saw, Section 1 protects against conspiracy in a *trade dispute*, as this was, unless the act is 'actionable' in an individual. The House of Lords said the threat to strike was actionable as 'intimidation' because it involved a threat to strike in breach of employment contracts. Never before had such a tort appeared in English trade union law. The only known cases of intimidation had been threats of violence. The Court of Appeal refused to treat a threat to break a contract as the same as a threat of violence. But the House of Lords preferred to do so, as the Irish courts had done in 1938 and 1940, treating, as Mr George Woodcock said at the TUC Conference, a threat to break a contract as the same thing as a threat to smash a man's face into pulp. 'I find therefore,' said Lord Devlin, 'nothing to differentiate a threat of a breach of contract from a threat of physical violence or any other illegal threat'; and Lord Hodson remarked: 'The injury and suffering caused by strike action is very often widespread as well as devastating, and a threat to strike would be expected to be certainly no less serious than a threat of violence'.[7] Clearly, this is a very different attitude from that expressed in 1942 by a great judge, Lord Wright, who recognised that: 'The right of workmen to strike is an essential element in the principle of collective bargaining'.[8]

(b) *Intimidation as a Threat to Break a Contract*

But, it may be said, this new liability for 'intimidation' can only arise where there is a breach of contract, because it rests on a new equation of breach of contract with an act totally 'illegal'. This is true. But it is very difficult to organise a strike – or other industrial action – without some breach of contract. Since this is important in the Watermen's case too, three comments are appropriate here:

(i) In *Rookes* v *Barnard* there was a collective agreement stipulating that there should be *no strikes*. Counsel *admitted* (rightly or wrongly) that this clause became part of each employee's employment contract. Therefore a strike would have been a breach of contract; therefore the threat of it was intimidation, said the House of Lords. The admission means that the point can be fought again another day. But it does not limit the intimidation doctrine to that kind of case.

(ii) If there were no such collective agreement (or no 'procedure' agreement which might operate in the same way) would a strike be in breach of contract? The answer seems to be – very probably; certainly if it is a limited strike (e.g. a one-day strike) or a strike without notice. The only way of validating a strike appears to be to give proper notice to terminate employment, i.e. to quit the job. This is important under the Contracts of Employment Act, 1963, because the new rights to notice can be lost by a strike in breach of contract. And even notice of the strike may not be notice to quit the job – very naturally, because men going on strike do not think they are asking for their cards! Lord Devlin, in *Rookes* v *Barnard*, said that the notice given there was only notice 'to break the contract by withholding labour', not to terminate employment. The Engineering Employers' Federation's Supplementary Guide to the Contracts of Employment Act, 1963, suggests that if an employee 'takes part in a strike *after* the Procedure has been duly utilised ... he will *not* be acting in breach of his contract'; but even this seems very doubtful, unless the Engineering employers all regard themselves as bound to this as an implied term in employment contracts in the industry. (Even then, do the trade unions accept that *no* strike is lawful unless the procedure is fully exhausted?) Lord Devlin's remarks suggest that *all* strikes are breaches of employment contracts unless [workers] quit the job.

(iii) The new illegality of threats to strike certainly operates outside cases where there is a no-strikes collective agreement. It did so, for instance, in the Irish case of 1940, where the strike was just one called without notice to quit, on which the Minister (Mr Godber) relied so much in August. And breach of contract may arise not from a strike, but from other ordinary industrial action, e.g. a go-slow or (as in the Watermen's case) an embargo on certain work. Although it has always been true, and remains true, that an employer can sue his workers for breach of contract individually for such actions, this possible liability has never been a serious impediment to union action. The damages that can be recovered are small; and few employers are foolish enough to issue writs against their work-people. The union official was protected, as we saw, by Section 3 (Limb 1) of the Act of 1906. But now, workers and officials alike are open to the new threat of 'intimidation' liability, a much more serious liability.

(c) *The Act*

The House of Lords refused to accept any section of the Trades Disputes Act, 1906, as a protection for the defendants in *Rookes* v *Barnard*. First, they held that Section 1 was no defence, even though it seemed that the damage arose only from the combination, and no act could be 'actionable' without the combination. They held that the section was ousted by intimidation because that was 'in its nature' actionable in an individual. Lord Reid even re-phrased the section so that the words 'the act done' ought to be understood, in his view, to mean 'the nearest equivalent act' done without combination:[9] 'The section cannot reasonably be held to mean that no action can be brought unless the precise act complained of could have been done by an individual without previous agreement or combination'! Yet that *is* what the section says. Their Lordships' interpretation left Section 1 almost valueless as a protection.

Similarly, the House of Lords regarded Section 3, Limb 2, as being a protection that defends trade unionists when they do acts that are lawful *anyway*. Why such a section should be interpreted so as to give it no effect instead of protecting what might be unlawful 'interference with employment' (such as Rookes had suffered) was beyond the comprehension of Lord Donovan in the Court of Appeal. He had asked: 'If the second limb refers only to lawful acts, that is, something that anyone could do anyway, why bother to enact it?'[10] Nevertheless, that *is* the meaning assigned to it by the Law Lords – a meaning that leaves this part of the section quite valueless as a protection for trade union activity.

Lastly, there was the position of Silverthorne. He was not an employee. He had not threatened to break any employment contract. Had he not merely threatened to induce men to break their contracts – an act which Section 3, Limb 1, says he can do in trade disputes? The House of Lords refused to take that view. This full-time official was, in their view, someone who had combined with employees who were intimidating by threatening to break *their* employment contracts. Therefore, he was liable with them for the conspiracy!

It is this last point which has come to the fore after the Watermen's case. That decision did not, as we shall see, turn on intimidation at all; but some of the judges commented on the problem of officials in Silverthorne's position. Both in the Court of Appeal and in the House of Lords, the judges appeared to accept in *Stratford* v *Lindley*, that a union official who individually threatened to call a strike in a trade dispute – or, as Lord Donovan put it, 'mentioned to an employer the possible alternative of a strike' – would be protected as against *the employer* by Section 3, Limb 1, because he was only threatening to do what it permits. But Lord Pearce added that Section 3 would not protect him if some *other* person were the plaintiff. Such a third person might be anyone aimed at and injured by the threat to strike – from a non-unionist like Rookes to customers or suppliers of the employer concerned. The position of the full-time official is therefore still one of great danger. And this danger is increased by the fact that any judge at any time may decide to take the 'Silverthorne view' of him; that is to say, to treat him as a conspirator with his workers, in which case he cannot possibly be protected by Section 3 at all! And it is to be remembered that *local* union officials who are *also* employees receive no protection from the section against the new intimidation.

What the Law Lords have done, therefore, is create a new common law liability which can be used, almost at will, to turn the flank of all the protections in the Trade Disputes Act, 1906. This they did by treating breach of contract as wholly 'illegal' for the first time in England. Having done that, they could treat a threat of it as 'intimidation', like a threat of violence. Since no-one dreamed that this was the law in 1906, there is nothing in the Act of 1906 which protects against that liability in exact terms. All the other protections were thereby evaded; and, where necessary, they were limited by very narrow interpretations.

THE WATERMEN'S CASE AND RESTORING THE BALANCE

(a) *The Watermen's Facts*

The defendants here were Lindley and Watson, respectively Secretary and President of the Watermen, Lightermen, Tugmen and Bargemen's Union, who organised some 3,000 of the 3,350 lightermen employed in the Port of London on work of the kind that arose in this case. They and the TGWU had made a joint approach to a firm, Bowker and King Ltd, on a number of occasions between 1956 and 1962, to get negotiating rights. The firm, and its chairman, Mr Stratford, refused. In 1963 Bowker and King Ltd did negotiate an agreement with the TGWU but not with the Watermen. Out of the 48 workers at Bowker and King Ltd about three belonged to the Watermen's Union. The Union refused to accept exclusion from negotiation and, without further communication with the firm, placed an embargo on all barges hired out or repaired by another of Mr Stratford's companies, Stratford Ltd. In effect they froze this business by the embargo, which was operated by their members employed by customers who took the barges on hire or sent them for repair.

Although liability in the Watermen's case did not turn in the end on intimidation, it is interesting to note how easily a breach of employment contracts can be found in these – quite normal – industrial situations, once the lawyers move in. All the Law Lords were satisfied that the workers employed by the customers would be in breach of their contracts in operating this embargo. Lord Reid put it down to the terms of the Dock Workers' Order, 1947 because he thought that 'a man working under the scheme is not free to make his own contract with his employer' and therefore had to obey any usual orders given (an opinion which must be causing some concern among dockworkers' unions). The other judges said simply that *any* workers who refused to do ordinary work when ordered to do so were in breach of contract, even though the employer knew that the union had put an embargo on it, and even though he accepted the men's refusal to do the work without dismissing them. The importance of the new equation of breach of contract with something wholly 'illegal' is immediately obvious. Workers may encounter it any day of the week.

(b) Short-Term Reform to Reverse the Rookes Case

Before the decision in the Watermen's case, there were two main proposals for reversing the decision in *Rooks* v *Barnard*. Let us examine them, and see the effect on them of the Watermen's case. They were:

(i) Proposals to amend Section 3 of the 1906 Act, so that in *trade disputes* the new intimidation would be restricted either to violence (as Professor Kahn-Freund proposed) or, at least, to things other than breach of contract. The TUC General Council's proposal followed the latter form, aiming to add to Section 3 words to protect in trade disputes an act which only '*constitutes or contributes to intimidation by a threat to commit (or to procure) a breach of any contract*'.

(ii) Proposals, made by the present writer,[11] to abolish the new form of intimidation altogether, not just in trade disputes. In other words, to pass a measure of law reform which concentrated on reforming the common law, putting it back into the form which the Court of Appeal gave it. After such a reform, a breach of contract would still leave the party who broke it open to action by the other party to the breach – as has been the law for centuries – but *not* open to new liabilities for 'intimidation' and the like.

There were three main reasons why it seemed important to the present writer that the second method of reform should be chosen, and two of them are supported by the judgments of the Watermen's case.

(a) Legal 'Privileges' for Unions?

Trade unions are often accused of having legal 'privileges'. Except for the unimportant area of union immunity to tort actions outside trade disputes, this accusation is quite unfounded. But the legal *form* of our labour law gives rise to the impression. As we saw, the liberty of action which is absolutely necessary for trade union activity and modern collective negotiation has been provided by 'immunities' or 'privileges' in trade disputes for union officials and workers, to protect them from judge-made liabilities which would have made modern collective bargaining impossible. What appear as rights in other systems of law (e.g. a 'right to strike') appear in our system as liberties protected by these 'immunities'. But now the judges have introduced *new* liabilities. It does not follow that the right response of the trade union movement should be to call for what will appear to be new 'immunities'. To avoid the old misunderstandings about 'privilege', it might be better to abolish the new judicial doctrines, rather than accept them and give an immunity in trade disputes. No case has ever been made out for the new 'intimidation' in commercial law generally. Indeed, its introduction is causing concern.

Business men might be as happy as trade unionists to abolish it outright.

(b) Liabilities Other Than Intimidation May Follow the Rookes Case
Proposals of the first kind would do nothing to reverse the doctrine that breach of contract is wholly 'illegal' for all areas of law. A coercive threat of breach is intimidation, says the House of Lords; but intimidation is not the only tort which relies on the concept of 'illegal means'. For example, a combination to injure by use of illegal means is one form of the tort of conspiracy. It is possible that any combination to use any breach of contract would fall within that tort. Furthermore, in the Watermen's case, many of the Law Lords suggested ways in which more and more liabilities might be fashioned out of this new illegality. For example, Lord Reid made it clear that he would make the Watermen's officials liable because they 'threatened to use unlawful means to interfere with the appellants' business'.[12] The unlawful means was inducing their members to operate the embargo in breach of their employment contracts. It is true that the Law Lords held (as we shall see) that there was no trade dispute here, so the 1906 Act could not help. But even if there had been a trade dispute, it would not seem that this new form of tort would be protected by anything in the Act, because (as we have seen) the Lords said that Section 3 (Limb 1) would only protect union officials if sued by the *employer* – and the employer here was not Stratford Ltd but the customers hiring the barges. So, either by way of conspiracy to break a contract, or by way of 'interference with business by using illegal means', the judges have a vast new armoury of weapons with which to attack trade union activity all the while breach of contract retains its new 'illegal' status. The second proposal would cut the ground from beneath all these possible liabilities. The first would do nothing to protect anyone from them, workers or officials.

(c) The Meaning of Trade Dispute
The House of Lords astounded the trade union world by holding that there was *no* trade dispute being pursued in the Watermen's case. The 1906 Act defined such a dispute as:

> any dispute between employers and workmen, or between workmen and workmen, which is connected with the employment or non-employment or the terms of the employment or with the conditions of labour of any person. (Section 5(3))

It is important to emphasize here '*any person*'. The terms of employment need not be those of the workers in the dispute. Indeed, the Act goes on to make clear that the 'workmen' involved need not even be employed by the employer with whom the dispute has arisen. Since cases in the 1920s the courts have been willing to accept a trade union as conducting a dispute as agent for its members; and in 1960 an attempt by a union to obtain negotiating rights was accepted as adequate to constitute a trade dispute within the definition.[13] In the Court of Appeal, the Master of the Rolls, Lord Denning, had treated it as clear that this was a trade dispute, of which Lindley and Watson had acted in furtherance or, at least, in contemplation. This the House of Lords refused to accept. They said that this was merely an inter-union dispute, 'merely the advancement of their union's prestige in rivalry with another union' (Lord Pearce). Their Lordships were sure that the workers at Bowker and King Ltd were 'adequately protected' by the collective agreement that was made with the TGWU (a question that one might have thought was to be decided by trade unions rather than by judges); and laid great stress on the fact that the three Watermen members had not appeared to complain of those terms. 'There was here no practical need for any intervention by the respondents (the Watermen)': Lord Pearce. 'I cannot find sufficient grounds for holding that it (the dispute) was connected with the terms of employment or with the conditions of labour of any person': Lord Reid.[14] There might have been something to be said for such a conclusion if the Act had demanded that the dispute be *about such* terms or conditions. The idea that it was not *connected with* them seems far-fetched in the extreme.

But, for the moment, the importance of this finding rests in the way in which it renders even less reliable any protections afforded by Sections 1 and 3 of the Trade Disputes Act, 1906. Sections 1 and 3 only operate within the area of trade disputes. If the judges now begin to narrow down the boundaries of that area by interpretations like this, amendments of Section 3 which aim to reverse *Rookes* v *Barnard*, or any other case, will be left stranded and ineffective. Whatever else this remarkable decision about the meaning of 'trade disputes' implies (and we return to it later), the sword of Damocles that 'intimidation' has suspended over the heads of workers and union officials, would be more effectively cut down, by a short-term measure of the second kind, rather than the first, since the second does not, but the first does, operate only within the trade dispute area.

LIABILITY IN THE WATERMEN'S CASE

Unhappily, however, the story does not stop there. An interlocutory injunction was granted against the officials in *Stratford* v *Lindley*, not for 'intimidation' but for a tort which is not protected by the Act of 1906 *even if there is a trade dispute*, and one which would not be protected by any of the proposals mentioned above. They were made liable for the tort of *inducing a breach of the commercial contracts*, here the contracts of hire. This is not the same as the 'interference with business' discussed above, because Lord Reid was there discussing interference with *new* contracts, business about to be done. This liability is for procuring breach of contracts already made.

(a) *The Liability from 1853 to 1964*
The tort originates in modern form with *Lumley* v *Gye*, 1853,[15] and consists in *knowingly and intentionally inducing a breach of contract made between two*

other persons to the damage of one of them. We have seen that the 1906 Act, Section 3, Limb 1, gave a protection to union officials against one form of the tort – namely inducing breach of *employment* contracts, when the employer will be the plaintiff. But, it is a common-place of industrial conflict that Union action is often aimed at holding up the employers' business in ways that are likely to lead to his commercial contracts being interrupted or made difficult to perform. Why has that activity not fallen more often into the clutches of this judicial doctrine, unprotected as it is by the Act?

The answer seems to be that it has not been very important in the last fifty years partly because few writs have been issued based upon it, and partly because the judges, when they have had to deal with it, confined it until recently to a very narrow area of liability. For example, in *DC Thomson Ltd v Deakin* in 1952,[16] the Court of Appeal faced a case not unlike the Watermen's case. Thomson Ltd, the firm of Edinburgh printers, ran a non-union shop and refused to allow workers to join any union. In the course of a long battle, the trade union movement operated a boycott of the firm, declaring supplies to them black. Certain lorry drivers employed by one of the supplier to Thomsons, who had contracts already for supplying goods to them, would therefore have been unhappy to drive the next load of supplies. The suppliers therefore did not send the supplies, and broke the contracts. Thomson's sued the officials of various unions for inducing the breaches, asking for an interim injunction to stop the boycott.

The court refused the remedy. The judges, in effect, narrowed the liability at every point of the definition. For instance, they said that it had not been proved that the officials *knew* enough about the supply contracts to be liable for knowingly inducing the breaches. Also, they had not by persuasion induced one of the contracting parties to break contracts (i.e. they had not tried to persuade the suppliers); they had merely approached their servants (the lorry drivers). This might be an *indirect* inducement of the breach between suppliers and Thomson's. But to be liable for *indirect* inducement, a defendant must be shown to have used an 'unlawful' means somewhere along the line; and that had not been shown here, because it was not proved that the lorry drivers had in turn broken their employment contracts. Also, the commercial breach induced must be shown to be a 'necessary' consequence' of the inducement. Perhaps the suppliers could have got the supplies to Thomsons otherwise than by lorry. For all these reasons, the defendants escaped and the liability for inducing breach of commercial contracts seemed no great impediment to industrial trade union action.

(b) *The Watermen's Case; Extensions of Liability*
At every point the judges in the Watermen's case took a different approach to liability. The officials there had been held by the Court of Appeal not to have sufficient knowledge of the contracts of hire, and so not to be liable, like the officials in *Thomson v Deakin*. But the Law Lords disagreed. Lord Reid said: 'it must have been obvious' there were contracts and it was 'reasonable to infer' that they knew there would be breaches. They had 'sufficient knowledge'

(Viscount Radcliffe).

Since the Law Lords held that the customers' workers *did* break their employment contracts, the officials could therefore be made liable here for an *indirect* inducement of the breach of the hiring contracts. But the Law Lords went further. Three of them held that because the union had informed the Employers' Association of the embargo, the inducement should be regarded as a *direct* procurement of the breaches. 'The fact that an inducement to break a contract is couched as an irresistible embargo rather than in terms of seduction does not make it any the less an inducement', said Lord Pearce.[17] So the reach of *direct* inducement is lengthened, and the liability widened. Furthermore, Lord Pearce also explained that there was no need for such a plaintiff to show that the breach was a *necessary* consequence; it was enough that the defendants 'intended to procure the breach and successfully procured it as a reasonable consequence of their acts and their communications to the hirers through their association and in answer to subsequent inquiries on the telephone'.

Once liability has reached this width, a new hazard is introduced into union action. Certainly, it appears to be more dangerous now to inform an Employers' Association of impending industrial action, because such communication may, as here, be treated as evidence of a direct procurement of breach of commercial contracts. But such breaches are the everyday consequence of union action, and very often the intended consequence. What else can a union do to put pressure on an employer but make it more difficult for him to carry on his business, very often at the expense of existing contracts? Some of the Law Lords said that this, by itself, *without* any actual *breach* of contract, *might* be unlawful in their eyes; Lord Reid merely said that he 'need not consider whether or how far the principle of *Lumley* v *Gye* covers deliberate and direct interference with the execution of a contract without that causing any breach'. (There may, in other words, be more to come yet!) But where there is a breach, union officials are under a new threat, not this time because of a newly-constructed liability, but because of a new judicial approach to an old liability that has been there since 1853. Any action on their part which is aimed to hold up the employer's business may, in legal terms, bring the most serious risks.

(c) *Restoring the Balance of the Watermen's Liability*

The House of Lords' decision came too late for much discussion at the 1964 TUC conference. But there is every sign that, as an understanding of its implications has spread in the trade union movement, concern has grown that it represents a threat as big as the *Rookes* v *Barnard* judgment. As we have mentioned, none of the proposals so far made would completely protect against the wide doctrine of inducing breach of commercial contracts. Once proof of 'knowledge' is made easier, and 'direct' inducement widened, the tort assumes huge and unknown possibilities.

This is particularly serious because it is a tort used predominantly in interlocutory proceedings in industrial cases. That is to say, as in the

Watermen's Case and *Thomson* v *Deakin*, the plaintiff is coming to court asking for an injunction to stop the defendants carrying on their activity until the trial of the action. All the evidence in these actions is given on paper (by 'affidavits') not by witnesses in person; and very often the interlocutory proceedings are the only ones that ever take place, because the trial is never proceeded with at all. The effect of such an injunction is to bring the law and the judges right into the thick of an industrial battle *while it is still going on*, not, as in *Rookes* v *Barnard*, to ask for damages as compensation when it is all over. The 'labour injunction' has been the curse of labour relations in the USA; and it would be disastrous to introduce it into Britain. Yet, in practical terms, that is just what a widening of the liability for inducing breach of commercial contracts means. If for no other reason, this offers the strongest argument for reversing the judgment in the Watermen's Case as quickly as that of *Rookes* v *Barnard*. The trade union movement made it quite clear that it was not prepared to enter any general inquiry into the law if the *Rookes* judgment stood. It would not be unreasonable for it to make the same point about the Watermen's Case.

But how can this be done? Once again there are two main ways of doing the job:

(i) An amendment of Section 3 could again be tried. This time it might take the form of omitting the words 'of employment' in Limb 1. The effect of this would be to make *all* forms of inducing breach of contract protected in trade disputes. Two problems would arise, however. First, the amendment would only be effective if combined with the second proposal made above for reversing *Rookes* v *Barnard*. (Otherwise the judges could use the terminology of 'interfering with business by use of breach of contract' to produce the same liability.) Secondly, such a protection would only operate in *trade disputes*, with all the problems which that now implies.

(ii) Another method, which would be particularly appropriate for an interim measure, would be to amend, or even abolish, the *common law* liability for inducing breaches of contracts. If there is to be an inquiry into labour law generally it would certainly do no harm to have it held in an atmosphere free from the irritant of interlocutory labour injunctions. If it be thought a strong step to abolish such a liability entirely, it could be replied that such a liability has only been created by the judges since 1853, and if they have now developed it in a new form that inhibits modern collective bargaining, it had better go. The trade union's right to take industrial action, an 'essential element' in that process, must take precedence; and the tort is, after all, mainly used in labour law cases.

Legislation along either line would do something to redress the imbalance created by the Watermen's judgment. It would need to be supplemented by the legislation suggested to restore the rights threatened by *Rookes* v *Barnard*. There are other steps which could be taken as well. The 'labour injunction' could profitably be specifically forbidden, a reform which would be particularly welcome in the light of the recent judicial remarks that suggest trade unions themselves may, after all, be open to actions for injunctions.[18] There is a case, too, for amending Section 1 so as to give it life; and to restore some meaning to Section 3, Limb 2, instead of leaving it (as Lord Evershed said it would be after the interpretation in *Rookes* v *Barnard*) 'nugatory'. Room could be found for these additional measures in an enactment passed speedily by a new Parliament. But unless the new Parliament passes a Bill to deal effectively *both* with the 'intimidation' doctrines of *Rookes* v *Barnard* (by abolishing the equation of breach of contract and other illegalities) *and* with the Watermen's Case (by removing the threat of liability for inducing breach of commercial contracts), there will never be any fruitful discussion of labour laws as a whole. Instead there will be more and more writs and injunctions, leading to industrial chaos.

A GENERAL INQUIRY?

Many people have come to *assume* that there ought to be a general inquiry into trade union law. Some of them are people who think it is 'time to clip the unions' wings'; but others feel that, since there has been no general review for over fifty years, there ought to be one now. Of course, in one sense, the latter attitude begs a big question. It has been a tradition of modern British labour relations to keep the law out of industrial affairs, or at least out of industrial conflict, as far as possible. One of the worst features of the judgments in *Rookes* v *Barnard* and *Stratford* v *Lindley* is the indication contained in them that the judges, departing from this long and admirable tradition, are now determined to develop the common law in a way that will bring the courts back into the middle of industrial disputes. Is this desirable? At the end of the furious battles of the period 1870 to 1906, there was no doubt that most people shared Mr Winston Churchill's view in 1911: 'It is not good for trade unions that they should be brought in contact with the courts, and it is not good for the courts'. Many commentators would say that this was still true.

But if there could be a balance restored and, as it were, 1964 could be forgotten and obliterated from the annals of British labour law, there might be a chance for profitable discussion and action on many other aspects of labour law. We cannot touch upon all of them here. Four have been chosen for comment, each of which throws light on the desirability of an inquiry, or the form of inquiry that might be adopted.

(i) *A Comprehensive View is Needed*
Firstly, the area for investigation is far larger than many commentators suggest. What people tend to do is pick a special area of law and discuss that against the background of their own policies. Take Mr Rookes' position, for example. Many commentators, including some in the labour movement, have said that his case involved both a question of the right to strike and one of 'human rights'. But what does this mean? Is a worker to have a 'right' to work at a place where he will get the fruits of collective bargaining but stop the union by law from forcing him to join? To take, as Mr Grunfeld has put it, a 'free

ride' on the backs of his fellow workers?[19] In the USA and especially in some States, the law enforces a 'right to work' at a place without joining a union. But is a 'right to work' to be translated as a right not to join a union? Or has it more to do with the degree of unemployment in a country, and the provisions against arbitrary dismissal, or for compensation or protection in redundancy? All of these things come in, and they tend to be cloaked by discussion of 'human rights' which very rarely include a right not to be unemployed! The whole field of employment law and practice must, in other words, be seen as one.

Even so, however, there are many things which can be done at once. The law can provide new protection against arbitrary dismissal, for example. There is bound to be some amendment of the Contracts of Employment Act, 1963, before long; for never was a measure so ill-planned as that one. Should not an employer need to give some reason for dismissal, even with notice? Has not the worker some proprietary right to retain his employment unless a socially adequate reason appears for depriving him of it (as is the case in Germany)? Even the last Government showed that urgent measures can be put through quickly in this area when they enacted the Trade Union Amalgamation Act, 1964, which swept aside much of the old law inhibiting easy amalgamation of unions. There is little more need to wait before enacting measures on redundancy, on job-security, and perhaps (an urgent question in view of the appalling injury figures) on workers' safety representatives at the workplace. All of these questions fall inside, not outside, any general discussion of employment and trade union law. But action need not await an inquiry.

(ii) *Trade Disputes and the Courts*
Similarly, there are many questions that need attention in the field of trade dispute law, quite outside the questions raised by the two recent cases. Should not contracts of employment be automatically suspended in a trade dispute? (*Not* just on notice of a strike, for that would put the workers' side at an immediate disadvantage.) How far should the liabilities in tort be retained at all? Should not the labour injunction be scrapped? Would new limits to strike action be justified in some 'public interest' or would they merely be a way of curtailing union bargaining strength? At the centre of many of these questions would be the notion of a 'trade dispute'. There are certain technical amendments to the definition in Section 5 of the Act (set out above) which plainly ought to be made, and which again would need no inquiry. For instance, the Act talks of workers 'employed in trade or industry'. It is not therefore clear which white-collar workers are included (nurses and local government officials, for example, may be excluded). More fundamentally, should the concept of 'trade dispute' be expanded in view of the judges' approach in the Watermen's case? Perhaps – but how could this be done? The form of words in the 1906 Act is wide. What would a wider formula include?

Because of this difficulty, some observers have suggested that it is not the definition of trade dispute that is wrong, but the policy of the courts in the last few years. The judges have adopted in those years a notably more hostile attitude to trade unions and strikes and (as we have seen above) have stretched the common law at almost every point to their disadvantage. Is it now time to institute new tribunals, bodies which understand and have sympathy with the trade union movement and with collective bargaining, to take jurisdiction in these matters? There are already some trade union questions in which the courts are forbidden to interfere. For example, under the 1913 Act, members' grievances about alleged discrimination under the political levy rules are dealt with by the Registrar, to the complete exclusion of the courts. Similarly, the ordinary judges have been displaced in favour of the Registrar if complaints are made by members about the electoral arrangements set up by the new Amalgamation Act, 1964. Is it now time to have Labour Courts, on which workers' representatives might sit, as in other countries? The cost might be less; the cases might be heard more expeditiously; the policies might be aimed at making collective bargaining work and strengthening union structures. Would not the new law or arbitrary dismissals be a good starting point for such an experiment? In the atmosphere produced by their latest judgments, the House of Lords cannot be surprised if those interested in Labour Law are asking, with all respect to their Lordships, whether they have not come to the end of the road and whether the next stage in the history of British Labour Law does not demand Labour Courts. If it does, then of course there will have to be a general inquiry before their institution, and it will be of critical importance to bring the trade union movement into their administration from the very beginning.

(iii) *A Positive Code of Labour Law?*
Should we now jettison our tradition of 'abstention' by the law? Should we have a code of *positive* rights in Labour Law? Certain voices in trade union circles have already called for such a code. The Draughtsmen's Journal in April, 1964, said for example: 'Trade union rights ought to be protected by law … four fundamental rights – the right to organise, to bargain collectively, to conduct union activities at the place of employment, and to strike – ought to be protected affirmatively by law … Now that the law will almost inevitably have to be changed, surely the trade union movement and its sympathisers have something more constructive to say than: "Back to 1906".'[20] There is great power in such an argument. The institution of legal duties on employers, for example, to bargain with a union, would be a momentous step and one for which a good case can be made. Such a code of positive union rights would certainly have to be administered by tribunals that understood its purposes.

But there would be other matters proposed for inclusion in the code. Would collective agreements become legal contracts binding on the union? (The main effect would be, of course, to see more legal actions springing from strikes that infringed procedure.) Would a code of 'unfair labour practices' be demanded as a price of these new positive rights? If so, how far would 100 per cent, membership practices come under attack, instead of being strengthened as recent research suggests they should be?[21] How far would the new Labour

APPENDIX TO CHAPTER 1

Courts then administer new limitations on the legal right to strike more stringent than the House of Lords today? Would there be demanded a new control over the rule book as part of the code?

(iv) *Internal Union Affairs*

The last question brings us finally to the place of law in internal union affairs. Once again the tradition has been to keep the law out, though since the *Bonsor* case in 1956[22] the possibility that a member wrongly expelled can demand damages from his registered union has increased the chance of legal intervention. Once again, there are a number of technical questions that need consideration (e.g. the protection of part-time officials in regard to disciplinary functions; the legal status of the registered – and even more the unregistered – trade union; the outmoded inability of a member to sue for benefit to which he is entitled under the rules). But most of these could be cleared up by legislation after discussion between the TUC and a serious Minister of Labour. They are not Royal Commission material. The fundamental question which unions have to face is whether they are prepared to give up any part of their status as voluntary autonomous bodies. For there can be no doubt that the main point, if there were a general inquiry into their internal affairs, would be the demand for new statutory control over the rule-book.

The state of many union rule-books is such as to give strong weight to such arguments. There is need for a spring-cleaning of rules. But that is not the same thing as accepting the need for new State control of rule-books. The ETU scandal does *not* show that British unions are all undemocratic and fraudulently administered. If, of course, undemocratic rules are adopted, the case for new control will grow; but at present it really is not strong, especially when there is no way of controlling union electoral *processes* by law without also controlling union constitutions by law. (There is no point in the law demanding fair procedure in elections and then allowing a body not to hold elections.) What is strong is the case for a speedier and less expensive method by which members can complain of improprieties in the administration of the union which have injured them. Here again, the precedent of the Registrar's jurisdiction (excluding the judges) suggests that some similar procedure could be pressed into service. The Registrar has retained the confidence of the trade union world. But once again, one is bound to ask whether this could be effected not after a long-drawn-out inquiry, but on the basis of discussions between the Minister and the TUC and unions.

CONCLUSION

The case for a general inquiry is not, then, obvious, as some commentators suggest. There are many matters on which some quick action would be worth a dozen Royal Commissions (as in the case of job-security). On the other hand, if some of the fundamental bases of our labour law system are to be changed, if for example, we are to have a code of 'positive' labour law, or a system of Labour

Courts to take jurisdiction from the present courts, there must plainly be an inquiry; but it must then be one that looks at the law and practice of employment as a whole.

Whether or not there is any inquiry, the two new judgments of the House of Lords must be reversed at once, in order that collective bargaining can be effectively carried on without constant recourse to writs and labour injunctions. *Rookes v Barnard* would be best reversed by an Act abolishing its *common law* innovations. The Watermen's case could be dealt with in the same way by amending the common law at least as a temporary measure until a more satisfactory definition of 'trade dispute' were instituted. It is both sad and astounding that in 1964 we face the need to clear away judicial pronouncements of this character. If there ever is a general inquiry into trade union law, it might be set the task of answering the question: *why*, suddenly in the 1960s, have the judges seen fit to develop the law in this way?

NOTES

1. *Federation News*, Volume 4, April, 1964, p. N30, 'Rookes v Barnard and After'. *Rookes v Barnard* [1964] 1 All E.R. 367 (HL).
2. K.W. Wedderburn, 'Intimidation and the Right to Strike', (1964) 27, MLR, 257 at p. 281.
3. *J.T. Stratford and Sons Ltd.* v *Lindley* [1964] 3 All E.R. 102 (House of Lords).
4. [1964] 3 All E.R. at p. 117.
5. [1901] AC 495 (HL).
6. *Allen* v *Flood* [1898] AC 1 (HL)
7. *Rookes* v *Barnard* [1964] 1 All E.R. p. 400 and p. 395.
8. *Crofter Hand Woven Harris Tweed* v *Veitch* [1942] AC 435, at p. 463 (HL).
9. [1964] 1 All E.R. at p. 376.
10. [1962] 2 All E.R. at p. 601 (CA).
11. New Society, 3 September 1964, p. 8. 'The TUC and Trade Union Law'. K.W. Wedderburn.
12. [1964] 3 All E.R. at p. 107.
13. *Beetham* v *Trinidad Cement Ltd.* [1960] AC 132.
14. [1964] 3 All E.R. at p. 113 and p. 106, respectively.
15. *Lumley* v *Gye* (1853) 2 E & B 216.
16. [1952] Ch. 646 (CA).
17. Lord Reid at p. 106; Lord Pearce at p. 112.
18. *Boulting* v *Assoc. of Cinematograph Television and Allied Technicians* [1963] 2 QB 606 (in the Court of Appeal. Lord Denning thought the protection extended to injunctions; but Upjohn and Diplock LJJ thought it did not).
19. *Trade Unions and the Individual in English Law*, C. Grunfeld (1963) p. 50.
20. See *The Draughtsman*, April 1964, pp. 3 and 4, ASSET has also made similar suggestions.
21. See W. McCarthy *The Closed Shop in Britain* (1964) and *ibid The Future of the Unions* (Fabian Tract 334, 1962).
22. [1956] AC 104.

2

COMPANIES AND EMPLOYEES: COMMON LAW OR SOCIAL DIMENSION?*

The Earl of Birkenhead concluded with customary finality and arrogance that Sir William Blackstone was 'a graceful though not profoundly learned, expositor of the Common Law, and a judge, conscientious indeed, but not of great distinction.'[1] Not that Birkenhead's evaluations are beyond question; the only judge to whom he gave the palm of 'master of the common law' was the Earl of Halsbury. But it is the tradition of just that common law judge which is central to this paper, by the nature of the common law system a personal expositor of the law as it stands – highly personal compared with his anonymous continental colleague[2] – while his function as to the future is to move with the times 'belatedly'.[3] Blackstone advertised his courageous venture to teach 'the Laws of England' in a university as aiming 'to compare them with the Laws of Nature and of other Nations; without entering into undue Niceties, or the minute Distinctions of particular Cases.'[4] It is that comparison with the 'Laws of other Nations' which proves helpful in the law concerning companies and employees, so long, of course, as we avoid 'the abuse' of ignoring their social and political contexts[5] or of assuming that their grass is always greener.

These are complementary areas of the law concerning, on the one hand, the production and distribution of economic resources and, on the other, people who in blue collar or white sell their labour power in a world of internationalised capital and global markets, with an increasing transnationalisation of the 'employer' whether in legal form or economic reality. The transnational movement of employees is less

* First published in 1993 in *Law Quarterly Review* Vol. 109, as a revised version of the Blackstone Lecture delivered in Oxford, October 1992.

pronounced than the fathers of the European Community envisaged in requiring free movement of labour in the Treaty, though the internal labour markets of transnational enterprises have contributed to an acceleration of shorter term 'postings' across frontiers.[6] Nor is it easy to harmonise the law in these fields. Labour law is deeply rooted in its local labour relations and labour movement; and although capital for its part flows relatively freely across frontiers now at the touch of a key board, the Community programme for harmonisation of company laws has encountered many barriers.[7]

When the two – labour law and company law – are brought into unaccustomed proximity, accepted principles – especially principles with common law roots – tend to be challenged. Let me take an example *de lege Communitatis lente ferenda*. In most jurisdictions the shareholders control the company's constitution and its control of the place of the registered office. In plans for the *Societas Europaea* (the optional European Company) the European Commission has proposed three different models of employee participation, from which one is to be chosen by agreement between management and workers on formation. But each Member State would have the right to limit the options available to companies registered on its national register. It follows that, if the shareholders changed the seat of the registered office to a new State which did not permit the model chosen by that agreement, they could unilaterally torpedo the participation agreement, and so have an effective veto over the model of employees' participation. In later drafts, therefore, once the company is in being with a participation agreement, there can be no transfer of the registered office to a State with a different set of options without the agreement of the employees' representatives.[8]

In both these fields our fundamental concepts derive from common law principles consolidated not long after Blackstone's death: the year 1825 saw the repeal of the Bubble Act 1720, heralding the birth of modern company law (eventually the incorporation by mere registration with limited liability in 1855, comparatively a very late date for this privilege)[9] and in labour law, the repeal of the Combination Acts by the Act of 1824 and its less liberal successor in 1825, secured in part by the energy of Francis Place in the determinist belief that if only 'every vexatious enactment' were repealed workmen would cease to 'hate their employers' and laws of supply and demand would ensure the disappearance for ever of trade union 'combinations' (rather the opposite of beliefs dominant today among free market ideologists).[10] Shortly after, in 1833, the Master and Servant laws were re-enacted without relaxation of their rigour. The bequest to our modern law from that era is of particular importance, not only to domestic law but also to plans for a gradual harmonisation of commercial laws in the Community, let alone revisiting the concept of the 'employee' or the interests recognised by the law *within* the 'employer', the interest evaluations of 'internal company law'. Many systems of law personify the 'employer'; in the private sector 'he' is normally a company, an aggregation of capital treated as a focus of rights, steered by controllers who enjoy the immunity of 'limited liability', the prize which Lord Diplock identified as 'the reason' why the law of England 'and that of all other trading countries' permits the creation of corporations with a personality separate from its members.[11] It is arguable that employment law should jettison the concept of 'employer' and seek, not veils of personality, but centres of decision-making in the company or (more realistically) group of companies, of which the corollary would be more personal liabilities for top management.[12] But English law seems not to be going in that direction. The Court of Appeal has recently apparently re-emphasised its deep commitment to the mystique of corporate personality, refusing

> to lift the corporate veil against a defendant company which is the member of a corporate group merely because the corporate structure has been used so as to ensure that the legal liability (if any) in respect of particular future activities of the group ... will fall on another member of the group rather than the defendant company[13].

There is no legal issue more urgent for the legislature than that of company groups. The courts today reject any wide use of the devices that could control the use of corporate persons, even by way of implied agency between parent and subsidiary, in contrast with the flexibility of earlier times when parties were found to have created a trust or agency in Lord Du Parcq's phrase 'as Monsieur Jourdain talked prose, without knowing it.'[14] The British courts' inability to reopen the *Salomon* decision is in part caused by their refusal to reconsider the economic and social policies presented by huge concentrations of capital;[15] we may contrast the way such issues are addressed, albeit modestly, elsewhere such as the treatment of linked enterprises by the *Cour de Cassation* constituting a *unité économique et social*.[16] This is not to suggest that nothing has changed in the common law since Bramwell B. rejected the claim of a boy whose fingers had been mangled by an unfenced machine left in the street, saying:

It may seem a harsh way of putting it, but suppose this machine had been of a very delicate construction and had been injured by the child's fingers, would not the child, in spite of his tender years, have been liable to an action as a tortfeasor?[17]

Since then the law on negligence has undergone several conceptual revolutions created largely by judge made common law. But, as we shall see, it has to be asked: why has there not been any similar revolution in employment law or company law? And especially in that part of company law concerning the employees? Where is the Atkin and the *Donoghue v. Stevenson* in this part of our 'Laws of England'?

Despite the mass of legislation in these areas, the common law judge is still a privileged 'expositor' of the law and it is because he is such (invariably still *he*) that we are entitled to ask why he chooses one direction for policy rather than another. The explanation that focuses on social 'background' of the men involved is a frail guide. Lord Devlin, an expositor more than usually gifted with judicial introspection, insisted:

> judges will still be of the same type whether they come from major public schools or from minor public schools, grammar schools or comprehensives.... They will all be the type of men – there will be exceptions of course, but the type – who do not seriously question the status quo, men whose ambition it is to serve the law and not to be its master.[18]

A personal expositor of his version of the law, the common law judge vouches for his judgment with his name, and this very specific tradition is one reason why many common law judges, despite their robust natures, tend to have thin skins: why else should they increasingly criminalise their common law doctrine of contempt of court (extending imprisonable offences without any reference to Parliament) when their anonymous Continental counterparts run civil courts without any such doctrine at all?[19] The problem is not – or not at root – one of personal prejudice; a more fruitful lesson lies in the contrast between our bench, drawn from practitioners in litigation-oriented guilds, and the career-judiciary within the 'modern continental systems ... developed in the universities by legal scholars for the use of officials.'[20] Of course, judges alone cannot be asked to reform everything. Let us take an example in the debates about Community law, in the frail 'social dimension' of the Community.[21]

In the absence of general Community legislation on employment, many now set great store on the 'social dialogue' between 'management and labour' or 'social partners'. The 'Social Chapter' Protocol and Agreement in the Maastricht Treaties, agreed by 11 Member States, was itself based on the agreement between the European trade union and employer organisations on October 31, 1991; the Agreement would upgrade this 'dialogue' – more than consultation, but not necessarily as much as collective bargaining – as part of the procedures for social legislation, stating 'should management and labour so desire, the dialogue between them at Community level may lead to contractual relations, including agreements.'[22]

This somewhat tautologous phrase intends that agreements concluded at Community level would be implemented *either* by law (in a 'decision' of the Council of Ministers) *or* through 'procedures and practices specific to management and labour' in each Member State, that is by appropriate, local collective agreements.[23] For some this heralds a breakthrough to European collective bargaining[24]; others doubt if we shall see more than 'co-ordinated' bargaining at national level, rather than European-level bargaining.[25]

Whoever is right, framework collective agreements of some kind concluded at European or transnational level are not wholly out of the question in the next decade, though multinational employers currently resist them. The problem arises: how to ensure that norms negotiated at supra-national level are translated into enforceable terms and conditions of employment at national, perhaps sectoral, level. For most Member States the problem is not great, not (as is usually thought) because their collective agreements are 'legally binding' (at least in theory) between employers and unions whilst usually in Britain ours are not.[26] That is not the main problem. The difficulty arises from the fact that the common law's doctrine of 'freedom of contract' leaves no room for a principle which almost all Continental systems contain in a weak or strong form. That principle, which we may call 'inderogability', requires that the employee must not be deprived of his or her rights under an applicable collective agreement, *even if* he or she has agreed to alternative, less favourable conditions.[27] A strong version is to be found in the *Code du Travail:* 'When an employer is bound by the terms of a collective agreement, those terms apply to the contracts of employment made with him, in the absence of provisions more favourable [to the employee].'[28]

No individual contract can be made to derogate from those terms.

That is the starting point for the collective agreement in various systems – in France, Germany, Italy, Belgium, Spain – as a source not just of agreement but quasi-law. In some – France, Spain, the Netherlands and Germany, for example – collective agreements can also be 'extended' to new employers not themselves parties to them by decision of a Minister after the necessary consultations.[29]. Each system has acquired its own crop of exceptions and qualifications (until 1980 even Britain had institutions faintly resembling extension, and even today some CAC awards cannot be displaced *in peius* by individual contract).[30] Such an approach is at variance with common law 'freedom of contract' (though this has not prevented its adoption in some common law jurisdictions, for example in New Zealand and, to a degree, in the United States). In Britain with few exceptions it is for the individual contract to incorporate the terms of the collective agreement, expressly or impliedly. That allows managements, when opportunity offers, more easily to push for 'personal contracts', displacing negotiated terms, as public policy now encourages them to do.[31] Judges still apply this rule strictly. There must be a 'recognisable contractual intent as between the *individual* employee and his employer' to incorporate these terms.[32] If European-scale collective bargaining ever took off, something in that approach would have to give. The unbridled force that the common law gives to freedom of contract is not suitable for the transmission to local law of minimum conditions built upon European-level collective agreements.

In many of those jurisdictions it appears to be sometimes easier for courts to change the direction of the legal policy. But we should not assume this degree of greater uncertainty necessarily creates greater difficulty than our current methods. In Italy, for example, judicial meanings have proliferated on the constitutional right to strike, for instance in decisions of the *Corte di cassazione* and even of the Constitutional Court. A change in direction, or an experimental change, is a regular part of such systems. In 1980 the former court expunged previous *a priori* definitions of a 'strike' in order henceforth to use 'the word and the concept in the meaning which they bear in ordinary language adopted in their surrounding social setting.'[33] In France in 1986 the *Cour de Cassation*, and in 'full assembly' at that, appeared to introduce a new doctrine giving courts competence in interlocutory cases to declare strike notices illegal by reason only of their being 'unreasonable'. Labour lawyers confidently predicted the atrophy of this interventionist doctrine and the novelty – although stemming from the highest civil court – was not accepted by 'lower' courts of appeal which continued to apply the opposite principle. In 1992 the aberration was renounced by the *Cour de Cassation* itself.[34] As it happened, in the same period British courts faced a not dissimilar curiosity in the understanding given to the common law by the House of Lords in *Lonrho Ltd v Shell Petroleum Co Ltd* (No. 2). Lord Diplock laid it down that in the law of civil conspiracy, even if unlawful means are used, liability ensues only when the conspirators have a predominant intention to injure (thereby equating it to the 'Crofter' type of conspiracy to injure, and giving burglars an escape route from this tort on proof that they had a predominant intent to serve their own selfish interests). The Court of Appeal felt compelled to follow this reasoning at some expense to the litigants (though courts in New Zealand, Ireland and Canada did not). In Britain no one could know whether the Law Lords could be persuaded to reconsider. Fortunately they did in 1991 when they found that Lord Diplock had not after all said what he appeared to say in 1982.[35]

To cure incipient misunderstandings, let it be made clear that it is not averred that the common law is in all ways inferior to systems of law from which it is different. Each system has its strengths and oddities, especially in labour law and company law. Italian law has inherited a distinction between a lawful strike which damages the 'production' of the enterprise and a strike illegal because it damages its 'inherent productive capacity' (*dano alla produttività*) – a distinction leading Italian writers find difficult to understand. In French law there is a constitutional *right* to strike but the courts refuse to include within it a stoppage which achieves the objectives of the strikers: so that a stoppage on Saturday in furtherance of a demand for an end to Saturday working is illicit, whereas a stoppage on Friday to the same end is legitimate.[36] But prominent features of the common law hinder its coming to terms with social change. For our purposes we may term this the 'social dimension' in the law. If it is true that 'the common law is more like a muddle than a system,'[37] it is a muddle in which some economic and social interests repeatedly have an easier time than others and in which it is more difficult to shift social gears than in comparable systems. By 'social dimension' of our law we do not mean in this context *l'espace sociale européenne* which was supposed to open the third phase of social policy in the Community[38] after the Council of Ministers unanimously agreed: 'the same importance must be attached to the social aspects as to the economic aspects' of the internal market.[39] It is far from clear how much remains of the 'social dimension' of the internal market. The Commission sought to promote parts of it (though with notable omissions) in its *Action Programme* on the declaration of 11 States in the 'Social Charter' in which the place of the employee at the interface with the company-employer was in many respects central.[40]

In contiguous fields, those of equality of the sexes, and safety at work, programmes of Community law preceded by many years the 'social dimension' of 1992; both these have long ago established independent norms of Community pre-eminence.[41] So too, regulation of safety at work does not pose great conceptual problems for English law, one reason why unanimity on that has been easier to attain in the Council of Ministers. Safety at work is the one area in which common lawyers, reared on the nineteenth century Factory Acts and even factory inspectors, assume that regulation is the way to do things (though they tend to think about compensation rather than accident prevention). At the turn of the century it was still uncertain whether our employment law would absorb general regulatory legislation – if you like, regulation in the French manner, across the board, for example on hours of work for adult men (rather than the British regulation which for decades sought to protect young or women workers, now almost all repealed in 1989 and on women now unacceptable to Community law).[42] By 1921, when Britain refused to ratify the first Convention of the ILO for a 48 hour week, collective bargaining was already preferred to regulation for the terms of the ordinary employment contract.[43] The impact of Community legislation on labour law is still uncertain.[44] Indeed, commentators have argued that such Community legislation on labour law as we have is not merely for the protection of workers but is part of the arrangements for an integrated economic free market. It has been persuasively argued, for example, that the 1975 Directive requiring consultation about proposed redundancies with workers' representatives (for example, when closing a coal mine) is enacted not merely for protection of the workers but for – perhaps primarily for – the safeguarding of undistorted competition, putting employers on a level playing field, a law 'promoted on the basis that it contributes to the integration of markets.'[45] The Court of Justice in the 'Genoa Docks' judgment of 1991 has taken a step on this road by recognising the proximity of competition law to labour law in the Community, applying the Treaty articles on free movement of workers and on competition to declare unlawful the practices of an obsolescent dock work scheme. This has been described as subjecting labour law to rules of competition[46] – an echo of the *Danbury Hatters* decision in the

United States that heaped anti-trust legislation on to the unions in 1908.[47]

THE INTERESTS IN THE COMPANY

Company law offers some surprising parallels, not least at Community level, for example in the promotion of employee participation in public companies by the Commission after 1975. Naturally enough, this initiative was differently received in different countries. It can as easily be seen as part of the tradition of Catholic social reformism as of any socialist tendency,[48] well within the main stream of post-war Continental plans for *la réforme de l'entreprise*.[49] But in company law one critical question is: how far are the controllers obliged to consider the 'interests of the company' in any sense separate from what they as shareholders see as their interests? The question is of special importance in two contexts: when shareholders exercise their votes in general meeting; and when directors reach decisions within their powers of management of the company's affairs. As to the first, British company law emphasises the property which an individual shareholder has in his right to vote. He can vote according to his perception of his own interests; he can even sell that vote and an injunction will lie to enforce performance of the contract.[50] But the directors must not sell their votes in the boardroom, for their fiduciary duty to the company – the envy, one must interpolate, of some Continental systems –[51] is to act *bona fide* 'in what they consider, not what a court may consider, is in the interests of the company.'[52] When the director comes to consult (as he must) the 'interests of the company', those are normally understood in our system to be the 'interests of the shareholders', generally the interests of 'the corporators as a general body' or 'the shareholders present and future'.[53] Neo-liberal ideologues have mirrored the common law by demanding that the directors must indeed act as 'trustees for the shareholders and for their benefit' alone.[54] Apart from a small extension to include the interests of creditors if there is a risk of insolvency, English courts have applied this same formula since the nineteenth century.[55] But ordinary business parlance has long replaced that legal meaning of the 'company's interests'. Business men and City institutions tend to define a public company's interests much more widely, inserting as legitimate interests to which a company's controllers should pay regard not just those of shareholders, but of other constituencies.[56] Public company chairmen declare: 'this company has duties to its members, employees, consumers of its products and to the nation', or even 'shareholders, creditors, employees, investors, management, suppliers, customers, the community and the state'.[57] Of course, such duties may not be more stringent; a director whose legal duty is to make an honest business judgment balancing all these interests will rarely be open to challenge unless he is a crook who has been careless with the minutes. The field is full of fudge. In 1973 a CBI committee offered a useful fudge: a public company must pursue profit, but it must also act 'like a good citizen in business'.[58] What is remarkable is that these developments have had no 'significant impact upon the common law formulation of directors' duties'.[59]

Most company law systems elsewhere have explored a wider legal duty, for instance in the United States, France, Italy and Germany. The best known debate on the issue arose in the United States when the 'bad corporate structure' was seen by analysts there (but not, it seems, in Britain) as one cause of the Great Crash of 1929.[60] The contemporary analysis founded on the divorce of 'ownership and control' (although not wholly justified by later inquiry – if one dare say it of Berle and Means)[61] sparked the impassioned *Berle v Dodd* debate in the *Harvard Law Review* on the theme: 'For Whom Are Corporate Managers Trustees?'[62] – a question doubly central in a time of multinational corporations. The debate did not lead to an overall restructuring in United States jurisdictions, but a glance at American case law on, say, the duties of directors shows the effect it had on the legal culture. The significant distinction, however, between the American and the European debates has been this: the former has from the outset been concerned with a wide variety of interest constituencies whereas the European debate has tended to concentrate on shareholders and employees as the primary interests within the enterprise.[63] Thus we may say loosely that since the War most of western Europe has, but the United States has not, enjoyed a vigorous debate about 'industrial democracy.' In Britain our debate (which goes back to the Webbs)[64] went underground in the 1940s, but reappeared to climax, some believe to breathe its last, in the 'Bullock Report' on industrial democracy in 1977 which encountered bitter opposition.[65] Representation of employee interests was the nub of the European Commission's prescriptions in 1975 on the evolution and reform of 'certain social institutions, companies included'; they must all respond to the 'democratic imperative'; employees had interests as substantial as those of shareholders, 'sometimes more so'. All this led to such proposals as the draft Fifth Directive for employee representation in the company's institutions.[66] In Britain that proposal was categorised by the Institute of Directors as a 'Trojan Bullock'.[67]

Other company laws of Western Europe either look to interests wider than merely those of the shareholders or at least couch the overall 'interests of the company' in terms of a plurality whose interests the controllers must take into account, something more than their individual proprietary interests as shareholders. For example, in France and Italy the company's interests (*l'intérêt social* or *l'interesse sociale*) have a varying, but usually a more objective interpretation. The proprietary right of the Italian shareholder is limited; article 2373 bans his voting when there is a conflict of interest – although the supreme court has recently accepted that 'he may cast his vote to achieve even a personal interest so long as this does not sacrifice the company's interests to his own.'[68] This precept is sometimes put more strictly to protect the *interesse sociale* where the company suffers damage: 'The sacrifice of the company's interests is not justified even where all the shareholders are unanimous in wanting to inflict damage on the company with a view to personal gain.'[69]

Furthermore, since the liberalisation of company law in 1869 the Italian company has also had a body of official auditors (*il collegio sindacale*), officials who protect all relevant interests in their control of the company's affairs. In France, writers differ about how far the similar doctrine excluding conflict of interest goes, but a shareholder's right to vote is limited by the 'interests of the company' as a separate entity and voting agreements are acceptable only exceptionally as a safeguard for *l'intérêt collectif*.[70] As part of 'the protection of the different interest groups' in the company, those of the employees are met first by the place of the *comité d'entreprise* (at establishment, enterprise and group level) two members of which attend directors' meetings[71] and, secondly, by the encouragement of profit-sharing and share option schemes; after 1967 employees participated as of right in profits and growth (*aux fruits de l'expansion*) and after 1986 a distribution to employees became obligatory under a calculation of great complexity. This method of accommodating workers' interests began a century ago, the 'Briand law' of 1917 permitting distribution of (voteless) 'labour shares'. Today, some 10,000 participation agreements cover 4.5 million workers, 'Pepper' schemes on which the European Commission keeps a close and approving watch.[72]

In Germany, the courts have developed a more powerful notion of *Unternehmensinteresse* ('enterprise interest') which serves as a point of reference for a plurality of interests 'somehow integrated by the organisation of the firm'.[73] In 1861 the German Commercial Code moved to suspend shareholders' voting rights in cases of self-interest; by 1918 German writers asserted that the interests of the 'enterprise as such' must include those of various persons, including the employees; today they put forward a wide range of interests to be included. The official reason why Company Law does not expressly impose social responsibility as such on directors of companies is said to be that 'the principle was already expressed in the constitutional clause imposing social responsibility upon private property.'[74] But the German employee is also a recognised actor on the company scene by way of codetermination (in similar vein, but to a more modest degree the same could be said in the Netherlands, Denmark and Sweden through representation on company boards). First come the powers of Works Councils: permitted in 1891, made general in 1916 and given extensive functions in the Weimar law of 1920 (to represent workers and help to attain the 'works objective').[75] In the present scheme (ironically first enacted under the influence of British advisers) workers' interests are represented through two channels: first the Works Council, now with some powers of co-decision, and secondly, by representation on the Supervisory Boards of larger companies. This is the system of Codetermination.[76] In coal and steel companies employee representatives have long been one half of the Board; in other companies with 500 employees or more they are one-third; and after 1976 in companies with at least 2,000 employees nearly one-half – 'nearly' because one seat is reserved for higher management and in case of deadlock the shareholders control the chair with a casting vote. Alongside the Works Councils, institutional representation on Supervisory Boards puts German company law at the ultra-red end of the comparative spectrum on industrial democracy.

British company law is, by contrast, in the ultra-violet band. In 1962 a shareholder complained in a derivative action that on the sale of two newspapers, the company's main asset, the directors aimed to give the free balance of the purchase price, some £1m, to ex-employees who had lost their jobs (there being no statutory redundancy payments at the time). The judge ruled that the directors' decision was not taken 'in the interests of the company'.[77] They were giving the company's money 'to its former employees to benefit those employees rather than the company ... prompted by motives, which, however laudable and however enlightened from the point of view of industrial relations, were such as the law does not recognise as a sufficient justification.'

At root, this is still the approach of English law. True, in 1980 the legislature gave to a company a statutory power to make such payments even if they are 'not in the best interests of the company' (a rare case of directors being permitted to act *otherwise* than in the 'best interests' of the company – but one confirming the central place of the shareholders' interests even today). In the same Act the law on directors' duties was amended, requiring them to 'have regard in the performance of their functions' to the interests of the employees in general, as well as the interests of its members.[78] Commentators rightly saw this provision as little more than 'window dressing',[79] doubly so when the section provides that the redefined fiduciary duty is owed to the company and enforceable only in the 'same way as other duties owed to the company', that is by the use of shareholder's 'derivative action'. It is as though the legislature expected shop stewards to come to work with a share certificate in one hand and the exceptions to the rule in *Foss v Harbottle* in the other.[80] It must be added, however, that this is peculiarly an area where procedural problems beset many legal systems. Even the French trade union which has long had the capacity to bring or defend actions for the defence of workers' 'collective interests', has been rebuffed by the courts when trying to enforce infractions of company law.[81]

British company law is characterised by a leading French comparatist as based 'on the law of partnership' with 'a certain flavour of *laissez faire*'.[82] It is based on the raw ownership of shareholders who were, before the repeal of the Bubble Act 1825, partners at common law but in equity's eye beneficiaries behind a trust in the unincorporated deed of settlement 'company', that skilful adaptation which Maitland believed (incorrectly, we can now see) might even have done the job of the limited liability company.[83] From that era comes the particularly strong legal ideology identifying shareholders as individualist owners. In 1837, the common law courts, now released from the prohibition on transferable shares,[84] shaped the 'share' itself into a more readily transferable chose in action, just as company law stood on the threshold of incorporation by registration. Until that date, the shareholder was regarded inconveniently as a joint owner in equity of the property of which the legal title was in the corporation, or in the deed of settlement company the trustees,[85] but, moving out of that backwater, the judges held that the shareholder in a company, even one which owned equitable interests, was the owner of a separate chose in action with rights under the company's constitution.[86] What has been aptly called this 'reification' of the share as 'fictitious money capital' facilitated investment[87] and confirmed the legal view of the shareholder as a proprietor with his own proprietary stake. On the other hand, the same period saw equity treat directors who misused their powers as liable, if not as constructive trustees, then by way of breach of their fiduciary duty by analogy with the duties of trustees.[88] But although they owed fiduciary obligations to the company, it was equally stressed that they were 'persons selected to manage the affairs of the company for the benefit of their shareholders'.[89]

British company law came to see the 'company's interests' normally as the aggregation of these proprietary rights of the shareholders. The structure of the capital market may in comparative terms have been more favourable to such a view in England than elsewhere. In Germany, for instance, shares or share certificates have since the nineteenth century been deposited with banks, giving the bank an open proxy at general meetings, a practice which continues today. This pattern increased the pressures on company law to treat the 'company's interests' as an amalgam of financial interests with a more general 'social' content; indeed, it is said that 'there was only one factor which the boards of companies had to take into consideration, namely, the influence of the banks'.[90] In the 1950s it was said that 'banks collect *Aufsichrat* places the way other people collect stamps',[91] though their representatives sometimes encounter difficult conflicts of interests.[92] The concept of a 'general collective interest' (other than the aggregated interests of individual proprietary shareholders) had been fortified in Germany by the place of the banks; the same may well have been the case in Italy and France, in part through stronger 'Statist' interventions in the markets[93] and a long tradition of credit management through the banks (especially in the latter through the *Crédit National*).[94] In Britain, not long after the introduction of limited liability at the late date of 1855 and when the Stock Exchange had already assumed a modern form, a process of division between finance and industrial capital fed a habit of shorter term investment,[95] part of a process which illustrated the importance to the London market of overseas bills and investment.[96] There was nothing in the structure of British capital markets to exert on directors of companies or on shareholders any pressure to consider the company as part of a set of social relationships wider than their own circle, nor indeed to formulate such notions; no Briand 'labour shares' took root, no *collegio sindacale*. Indeed, the ethos of the rugged entrepreneur was so dominant that in 1856 the Joint Stock Companies Act repealed the obligation to appoint auditors (which was restored for banks in 1879 but for companies generally only in 1900). In Britain 'the wealthy private banks of the City of

London had shown little interest in provincial business and small country banks had proliferated.'[97] These were more accessible to the needs of British industrial enterprise and there the values of individual ownership were paramount.

THE COMMON LAW AND LABOUR

Curiously 1825 was a crucial time for labour law as well, the year of the repeal of the Combination Acts, the first bare liberty to form trade unions, though the liberty to act effectively was still denied by vague crimes of 'intimidation' and 'molestation'. The tradition of the common law was already in place to interpret narrowly any statutes that afforded a protection or 'immunity' to trade unions or persons acting on their behalf. On that little has changed. If such legislation is wide enough to be effective it is regarded, in Lord Diplock's memorable words, as 'intrinsically repugnant to anyone who has spent his life in the practice of the law or the administration of justice'.[98] Its consequences 'tend to stick in judicial gorges'.[99] It is wrong to see this tradition as based on some personal 'bias'; its grip is more lasting. For example, the Act of 1871 gave protection to trade union purposes from the doctrine of *restraint of trade*. In their interpretations at the turn of the century the courts even adjusted and redefined the doctrine so as to acquire anew their jurisdiction over union internal affairs.[100] Restraint of trade rested and rests on 'public policy' and that is 'a variable notion, depending on changing manners, morals and econmic conditions'.[101] In face of that description, one is entitled to ask why the courts did not go on in modern times to adapt public policy and abolish the application of restraint of trade to trade unions altogether. That is what one would do if one accepted trade unions as economic associations acceptable within the values of freedom of association in a democratic society. The judges have exclusive control of what is in restraint of trade. Yet to this day they have never lifted the sword of the common law suspended over trade unions. For the common law will not legitimise trade unions. A special immunity is still needed to make them lawful. On the contrary, in 1954 they extended the scope of the doctrine and held that the 'rules' of a union were not protected by the statutory immunity of the time even though a union's 'purposes' were protected.[102] Yet another statutory amendment was needed to prevent unions from being illegal by this judicial sleight of hand.

What happened in trade union law is well known: new common law liabilities (or 'extended' liabilities to use Lord Denning MR's word)[103] were regularly created – save during war time periods – for such defendants as unions, many of them parallel to the doctrines of Sir William Erle who expounded principles of liability in 1867 which would invariably render illegal effective trade union activity.[104] Many such judgments ran counter to manifest Parliamentary policy – a new type of criminal conspiracy for annoying masters of ordinary nerve in 1872; in 1901 a new liability for civil conspiracy and a new status as defendants for the unions; in 1910 a bastard form of *ultra vires* to stop union political action; new torts of intimidation in 1964; of interference with contract in 1965; special 'extensions' of liability proposed in 1969; new tort liability for inducing an unenforceable breach of statute in 1989.[105] Perhaps the most serious extension of all occurred in 1975 whereby interlocutory injunctions may be granted to kill off industrial action on the flimsiest of cases proffered by the employer under the *Ethicon* decision[106] – a classic illustration of labour law being changed by common law developments which may (or may not) be defensible in the area in which the case itself originates (here patents) but manifestly unfair when applied to industrial disputes and, indeed, many other social disputes. One does not need to search for the common law judicial policy. Writing in 1962, Lord Devlin candidly hoped for the chance to restrict or overturn *Allen v Flood*. It came two years later in *Rookes v Barnard*.[107]

The process is alive and well, indeed more actively so than in the 1930s. Take the wrong of 'economic duress' introduced into labour relations by the Law Lords in 1982.[106] Once there was no wrong of *'economic* duress' but after 1976 the courts extended restitutionary claims in commercial cases to cover economic pressure which 'vitiated consent'. [109] Canadian courts sensibly refused the new doctrine entry into labour relations because it would then render most threats of industrial action wrongful.[110] In one sense coercion of the will by lawful pressure is the essence of collective bargaining, and it is still uncertain how far an act unlawful in itself is a constituent of the new wrong. Dismissed employees cannot rely on it since, Lord Donaldson MR has remarked, they have a 'real alternative', namely to draw social security.[111] It is not clear how far the trade dispute 'immunities'[112] protect such 'duress' even if done in furtherance of a trade dispute; but in extra-judicial writings Lord Goff has strongly favoured liability, saying it does not follow that

> because it is enacted that a union should not be liable in tort for the *loss* which its action causes another, it should be allowed to retain an

enrichment, in this case money, which it gains from an act that is prima facie unlawful, particularly if that act is characterised as illegitimate, though not tortious.[113]

It may not follow as the night the day, but it does illustrate the predator principles of the common law in face of the principle of freedom of association. Five years later it was perhaps less than fortunate that his was the leading speech in the *Dimskal* decision holding that industrial action undertaken lawfully in Sweden could subsequently be treated as unlawful duress by an English court.[114] This pays no respect to the principle of a right to strike in ILO conventions (and the European Social Charter 1961) given that the Committee on Freedom of Association has repeatedly recognised that right as central to freedom of association, 'one of the essential means available to workers and their organisations for the promotion and protection of their social and economic interests'.

It is in its approach to the liberty (let alone a right) to withdraw labour in social conflict that the common law is in comparative terms most repressive. Continental colleagues find it astonishing that we profess the values of 'freedom of association' in international instruments to which we have put our name yet leave our law in the archaic condition that causes every strike to be a breach of employees' contracts of employment no matter how legitimate the dispute. Beyond that, the only protection for the organisers of industrial action are fragile immunities, victims of judicial hostility and now squeezed dry by the legislation of 1980-1990. All this the ILO experts have pronounced a contravention of the minimum standards of Convention 87.[115] The civil rights needed to meet these standards of the ILO and 1961 Social Charter[116] must be based upon a *right* of some kind which allows the British jurist to say, when complaint is made of damage flowing from the exercise of it, as his Italian colleague says: *qui iure suo utitur neminem laedit*.[117] We even permit lawful dismissal of a whole group of strikers for the very act of withdrawing their labour and the employer's right to dismiss 'unofficial strikers' selectively without challenge was expanded in the 1990 Act.[118] Lord Denning once made an attempt to review this area of law so as to introduce suspension of the employment contracts in disputes,[119] but he gave up on the task. It may well be that only legislation can dig our law out of this hole. For there is no help from Brussels on the horizon.[120]

The French doctrine of suspension of the contract in industrial disputes is well known – *la grève ne rompt pas le contrat de travail sauf faute lourde imputable au salarié.* What is less well known is that it was introduced first by the courts and by *la doctrine*[121] before the positive law of the 1946 Constitution declared the right to strike, after which a Law of 1950 confirmed the doctrine and the Law of 1985 reconfirmed that the dismissal of a worker exercising his right to strike is void, which the *Cour de Cassation* in turn has now accepted as ground for compulsory reinstatement.[122] But industrial action short of a strike (a go slow, work to rule or organised working without enthusiasm) are all a breach of contract in the eye of the law of contract, as much in France as in Britain. They are not a 'strike' within French principles because there is not the necessary combined 'abstention' from work. The recognition of a positive right to strike does not open floodgates to any and all types of action. It all depends upon the definition of 'strike'.

The question often arises whether the employee is to receive any part of the salary in partial industrial action. In 1992, a manageress wished to return to work after a strike in a pay dispute but refused to sign an unconditional guarantee that having 'reflected about the industrial action' she would now 'work normally in accordance with the terms of my contract' (though she later handed in a letter drafted by the union stating she would work as normal). She was held to have evinced an *intention* to engage in a continuing 'withdrawal of goodwill' even after her attempt to return. That meant she could not prove she was willing to 'serve her employer faithfully within the requirements of the contract'.[123] She was therefore not entitled to recover any of her wages even though the employers preferred not to terminate the employment.[124] The decision enlarges upon the case five years earlier where a Registrar – adopting a form of industrial action as novel as the recent 'thinking strike' when workers abstained from their customary helpful suggestions to management – refused to perform marriages on Saturdays, a small proportion of his duties. This cost him, the Law Lords decreed, the whole of his salary. There was a respectable line of cases supporting a proportional deduction, whether by set off or counterclaim, but the Law Lords preferred the *Bullen and Leake* argument that the employee cannot recover anything if he or she is not ready, able and willing to fulfil the contract.[125] Lord Templeman remarked that the precedents supporting the more merciful solution were 'ancient and irrelevant',[126] adding (in a passage anxiously studied by labour historians): 'Industrial action is largely a twentieth century development introduced with success by the Bermondsey matchworkers at about the turn of the century'.[127] There is little hope that the Law Lords will reconsider the *Miles* principle, as the *Cour de*

Cassation might, even if – perhaps because – the reasoning in it is cloned from authorities stretching back to 1829.[128] The point is particularly important when employers are more willing to pursue legal remedies and are reportedly reducing conditions, increasing the cost of a partial stoppage.[129] The decisions ousting the principle of proportional reduction, strengthen the legal whip hand of the employer in a recession. True, a single act of disobedience may no longer be enough to justify summary dismissal of the employee, as it was in 1845 when Baron Alderson upheld the dismissal of a maid for a defiant visit to her sick and dying mother[130]; but a repudiation, especially associated with defiance, can still justify withdrawal of wages or even instant dismissal.[131]

Pollock CB said of the decision from which there ultimately sprang the doctrine of common employment[132] (which freed the master from liability because an injured servant was assumed to have given consent to the risks of his employment, and particularly the risk of injury by a fellow servant): 'There never was a more useful decision or one of greater practical or social importance in the whole history of the law.'[133] This decision and its subsequent judicial development 'severely curtailed' the opportunities for workers to secure damages just at the point where injury rates were increasing in the new factory units of production and workers were often employed by companies,[134] all of which increased the range of the 'common employment' doctrine. This was a class doctrine; as Goodhart put it, 'infamous'.[135] But so urgent was the need for it that the House of Lords forced it into Scots law; it was 'inexpedient' to have a different rule north of the Tweed.[136] Nor did the judges ever renounce it (statute had to end its life in 1948).[137] As in the case of restraint of trade, one is entitled to ask: why not? True, some judgments cut down its ambit, for example by developing non-delegable duties, the duty to provide a safe system of working and competent staff,[138] and confining the boundaries of the doctrine itself. But the law reports 100 years on reveal the doctrine firmly imbedded in the Court of Appeal, and in 1948, the year of its abolition by statute, unshaken in the House of Lords, Viscount Simon resolutely insisting that 'apart from statute, the common law rule, within proper limits, still applies.'[139] Lord Devlin had no doubt that the judges could have killed off common employment. Instead, he said, they left it 'as a nerveless tooth which could still bite even when in decay'.[140] But in every generation it is a mark of the common law judge that he takes in only with great difficulty the social need for radical change in the law he administers. Baron Bramwell cried passionately to convicted pickets: 'Pray attend to this, it is said in all kindness … there is no class legislation. There is no law which gives to one set of men an advantage for their own particular benefit. Now, you know that as well as I.'[141] And in applying the newly invented tort of conspiracy to strikers, Lord Lindley was no less concerned in 1901: 'The law is the same for all purposes … it applies to masters as well as to men.'[142] Recent times have offered parallels, not least in the treatment of pickets.[143]

Here judges have rarely discarded doctrines deep in the common law tradition hostile to workers' interests. Few are likely to accept the analogy that private sector managerial power should be 'likened to government power' and so avoid 'the dead weight of tradition in the common law.'[144] We must not overlook such small changes as occur. There has been something of a new approach in the recent willingness of High Court judges to grant injunctions to employees in a few types of wrongful dismissal despite the personal nature of the employment contract.[145] That development has no doubt been assisted – but also limited – by the proximity of judicial review in employment which is said to fall within 'public law' – though few can explain what is public and what is private.[146] Recent decisions also illustrate the use of the injunction where the employer 'cannot be relied upon to act fairly and rationally' in relation to the employee.[147] That is encouraging. But we are a long way from the day when the ordinary servant can obtain reinstatement for a wrongful dismissal. Paradoxically the chance of reinstatement for an unfair dismissal under statute is equally bleak because the judges' interpret employment protection statutes in the image of the common law.

It is as if the traditional common lawyer walks, as a Greek parable has it, backwards into the future – like the Lord Chamberlain walking backwards before the Queen at the opening of Parliament, steered by his eye fixed on a guiding figure in a portrait behind her. Past injustices are reflected in the old precedents within the judges' sight, carefully recorded, sometimes retouched. New legislation swims into view sideways, reflected in the colours of old principles, and current complaints perceived with a kind of strabismal uncertainty. The banners of past trade union heroes may have become mellow, even noble with age; but the strident demands of their current counterparts today are the more frightening because they can be heard but not yet seen. In such cases we hear Lord Salmon's words: ' … if this is the law, surely the time has come for it to be altered.'[148] Current industrial conflict creates that slightly panic-ridden 'nostalgia for the law as it stood … before the Trade Disputes Act 1906'[149] – the untrammelled common law. In this new generations come to play their part, genuinely imbued with the 'desire to be part of the profession', and not to offend the Benchers.[150] For this common law culture passes on a traditional, inner core of values from which even liberal judicial expositors wrestle free only rarely, and then at risk of their liberalism being dubbed radicalism. Central to the social philosophy is an extreme, often aggressive, protection of property, allied to assertive individualism and in the employment field presumptions about disciplinary powers.

But, it may be objected, all this was long ago. Lords Abinger and Alderson, even Lindley, like Rosencranz and Guildenstern are dead. True, the first said of common employment: 'to allow this sort of action to prevail would be an encouragement to the servant to omit that diligence and caution which he is in duty bound to exercise on behalf of his master.'[151]

That was in 1837. Has the ethos radically changed? When a lorry driver was held liable to indemnify his master after he had negligently injured a fellow employee and was denied the protection of his employer's insurance policy by the (majority) Law Lords because of his 'status' as a 'servant', it was said 'to grant the servant immunity from such an action would tend to create a feeling of irresponsibility in a class of person from whom, perhaps more than any other, constant vigilance is owed to the community.' That was Viscount Simonds, proceeding resolutely backwards towards a parallel with common employment, in 1956.[152] 'The common law demands that the servant should exercise his proper care and skill', he added, refusing to imply a term in the worker's favour partly because he could not formulate one as 'a necessary condition of the relation of master and man'.

This decision was a 'major extension' of earlier decisions about the worker's implied warranty of his skill[153], but Lord Tucker saw no 'general change in circumstances affecting master and servant to justify a court in introducing some quite novel term into their contract ... absolving the servant.'[154] The subsequent abstention of insurance companies from enforcement of their rights did not alter the fact that this decision was seen as a judgment to a large extent based on 'policy'.[155] But whose policy? It is not ill mannered to ask how far judicial policy had come in the 120 years since Lord Abinger.

The emergence of more liberal social attitudes ultimately affects the common law; but it twists and turns, often unpredictably, often edging crabwise back to the past. Take the interpretation of statutes on factory conditions. In 1850 the Exchequer judges wrecked the Ten Hours Act

1847 by legitimising relays of child and women workers. They were impelled by their clear understanding of 'freedom', for as Parke B. had said: 'as it is a law to restrain the exercise of capital and property, it must be construed stringently'. Otherwise the employers would be deprived of 'full control of their property'.[156] Yet after a period of resistance to civil actions for damages based on breach of statutory duty,[157] after decades of mangled operatives, in 1898 the Court of Appeal struck out on a new path by upholding the right of an injured workman to sue for breach of a strict factory duty,[158] and that despite the existence in that case of an alternative remedy in the statute which might have offered them an argument of escape from that conclusion.[159] And it was in such cases, too that the courts began to reject the simple defence of 'consent' on the part of the worker, decisions in which we may detect a delayed reaction against the horrors of industrial accidents.[160] Yet it was in just this more liberal period that judges made the worst of the Workmens' Compensation Acts, for example abolishing the right to compensation for workers guilty of a 'foolhardy act'. The same attitudes led to the deduction from workers' damages of State benefits (but not private insurance begotten of 'thrift'), an approach now supported by the Social Security Act 1989.[161]

In the modern law the new legislation on employment protection has obviously made a difference, though its modest proportions scarcely support extravagant claims that it is a 'burden on business.' Yet it is in this very area, in the frail laws on unfair dismissal for example, that common law attitudes re-emerge. The story has been told often enough of the terms of the legislation being redesigned by judges in a common law image. Where Davies and Freedland, Hepple, and Collins agree, I shall not dissent, at least today. The evidence is overwhelming. The meaning of 'employee'[162] with which our predecessors wrestled under the Poor Laws and in workmens' compensation cases, has long been in crisis.[163] The common law exported that crisis into employment protection, together with an approach to the definition of 'dismissal' and the supposed rule that the appellate courts deal only with questions of law.[164] Of course, the problem – the resistance of the old law to concepts of effective worker protection – is not unique to England. The French courts were embattled for 25 years about whether the *droit commun* in the Code Civil was excluded by laws specially protecting workers' representatives from dismissal. The *Cour de Cassation* at first held that an employer could evade the procedures required for such dismissals (not least, permission from the labour inspector) by resorting to judicial rescission of the contract (*résiliation*).[165] Eventually on re-examining the issue the court supported the opposite view, even banning further applications for the old common law remedy; the status of the representative was protected by public policy, something in which all workers in the enterprise had an interest.[166]

In England it is not the problem, but the judicial reaction which is peculiar. The dominance of common law attitudes reappears even at this stage of remedy. The statute on its face provides reinstatement (or re-engagement) as the primary remedy, contrary to common law philosophy; but in practice the effective remedy in the overwhelming majority of unfair dismissal cases is compensation.[167] To this we must add a further common law element, the promotion of managerial authority. Although the courts have maintained a residual control over the need to observe fair procedures,[168] in a string of decisions they have also established the principle that the employer (whose conduct the Act says must be reasonable according to 'equity and the substantial merits of the case')[169] satisfies the requirement that he has acted 'reasonably' if he proves that his conduct comes within 'a range of reasonable responses' of management.[170] What is more, his conduct does not cease to be reasonable merely because it contravenes the employee's contractual rights.[171] For the purpose of what is fair, even 'contract' gives way to the employer's inherent right to make law in his own enterprise, his inherent powers of direction and of discipline. Again we see something behind the formal contract, something not in the statute. The judges have insisted that an industrial tribunal must not replace the employer's judgment on these issues with its own idea of fairness so long as his conduct falls within the '*band of reasonable responses*' which a reasonable employer might make even if another equally reasonable employer might not.[172] No wonder commentary concludes: 'British unfair dismissal law has developed in a way which legitimates managerial authority to regulate the labour market.'[173] Others have found that what was once thought to be a movement 'towards a greater protectiveness of employees' interests or pursuing social policy objectives', has crumbled in the judicial grasp.[174] Of course, reinstatement in employment of an unlawfully dismissed worker is a difficult process; it evokes human responses with which the law is not always apt to deal. One finds this in other jurisdictions; in German and Italian law, for example, though both appear to produce stronger remedies than ours, Italian law especially because of the ban on 'anti-union conduct' by the employer.[175] But if an order for reinstatement or re-employment is made, what if the employer disobeys it?[176] Will lack of work in a recession cure the employer's duty to re-employ? The British statute tells the tribunal to take account of a number of issues before awarding reinstatement or re-engagement, including its 'practicability'; and in case of a refusal or failure by the employer to obey an order the industrial tribunal may award a substantial additional compensation – unless the employer satisfies the tribunal that it was 'not practicable to comply' with it.[177] This gives the tribunals and the appellate courts a considerable discretion.

The English decisions have long swung the benefit of 'impracticability' in the employer's favour, as when he has no work for the employee unlawfully dismissed without his penalising other workers.[178] This crucial part of the Act was tested in the case of 12 dockers' shop stewards dismissed by reason of their trade union activities (and therefore unfairly) following the dock strike and the repeal of the Dock Labour Scheme in 1989.[179] The tribunal ordered their re-engagement, but the port employers (PLA) claimed that the order should not have been made, let alone enforced, because it was not 'practicable' to re-employ these workers. The PLA could not and would not take them back into the workforce. It had derecognised the union, instituted extensive redundancies and introduced 'personalised contracts'. An employer could not be expected to disrupt his business by complying with such orders. It was an 'error of law' for the tribunal to 'substitute its own view for that of management providing that the particular management in the particular circumstances is reasoning, deciding and acting within a reasonable bracket.'

> An employer is entitled to say what in his commercial judgment is in the best interests of his business when viewed against its existence, survival and success in a competitive market. That success is to be seen not only against the interests of its owners, whether or not shareholders, but against the interests of the maintenance of employment and the well-being and contentment of it workforce.[180]

The tribunal was entitled to question this commercial decision; but it would be 'an enormous and unnecessary burden' to investigate the internal affairs of every business: 'Provided the decision or judgment of the employer is within the reasonable brackets ... it should be respected.' He should not be asked to 'disrupt his workforce' by searching for 'vacancies' for those dismissed, making for uncertainty among existing employees 'and their families'. This Bramwellian exposition (whether or not it is upheld on further appeal) illustrates the courts' common law drift towards a special blend of discipline and contract, in that order, stressing the preservation of the employer's disciplinary prerogatives, his right to be master in his house, to expel those he believes to be disruptive. We are fortunate that not all employers live by law alone. In neighbouring systems of law judges find difficulty with re-employment; but once a dismissal is seen to be void, they are more readily persuaded that an unlawful dismissal has not caused an interruption in the employment contract. This element has been present in the recent trend in France to interpret laws concerning employees reinstated after dismissal by reason of lawful strikes or union activity.[181] The remedy has long been available for dismissed workers' representatives. This is part of a general characteristic in many such jurisdictions attaching to labour law. It is perceived as a law overtly protective of the weaker party. Its origins are found, not in freedom of contract, but '*à l'origine du droit du travail ... la protection du faible contre le fort.*'[182] For example, when the employer came before them with a fixed term employment contract, the German Labour Courts drew the conclusion from principles of equality that they would interpret it to be a 'standard' indefinite contract in favour of the worker, unless the employer could prove a 'justification' – objectively, not within some theoretical brackets of reasonable management conduct showing why the fixed term was necessary.[183]

EXAGGERATED CONTINUITY

In contrast, the modern law of employment in England carries with it a very different inheritance. It enjoys the curse of exaggerated continuity. If we take, for instance, the well known division of three periods of collective labour law offered by Calamadrei – first where collective action is repressed by penal laws; second when it enjoys liberties; and third when it acquires rights of action[184] – the parallels among European systems as they emerge from the first to the second period are remarkably close, including Britain. Everywhere for example courts try to inflict one last sting of criminal sanction. So, in the 1870s French pickets who cried: '*Nous t'aurons*' to blacklegs were convicted of crimes; so too, German pickets who cried out to strikebreakers: '*Pfui*'; also, Belgian pickets who hurled insults and British pickets who cried 'Bah' to scabs or cast them 'gestures' and 'black looks'.[185] But in the subsequent periods, different in date but comparable in social and industrial phases, the British development diverges sharply. It becomes necessary to look for special features of differentiations. In collective labour law, the special history of the British labour movement with its crucial anticipation by the industrial wing, is one well-known reason why our system did not acquire collective rights in the third phase.[186] But our social and legal history infused employment law with a further factor – a wide range of disciplinary prerogatives for the employer. Whoever was right in the argument concerning the contract of employment in Blackstone's day,[187] in the century following his death this feature was implanted so deeply into the criminal law that it was destined to be bequeathed to the modern civil system. The master's authority is part of the common law's double helix.

Of course all modern systems provide the employer with powers of discipline and direction at work. When criminal sanctions fell away Continental employers were left with massive powers of discipline and control (in the second half of the nineteenth century in France, the Netherlands, Italy, Germany and Belgium). But when one considers *le pouvoir de direction* or *le pouvoir disciplinaire* in French law, although at first they are put on a contractual base,[188] they have now been affected by 'institutional' analysis, making them part and parcel of the plurality of interests balanced in the enterprise. It has been argued, for example, that they vest in the *chef d'entreprise*, as the hierarchical head of the occupational community, with their limits fixed by their functional character.[189] The Law of August 4, 1982, part of the *Auroux* reforms, introduced compulsory procedures to ensure greater fairness in disciplinary measures,[190] and such measures are linked by some to that analysis,[191] and beyond that to the concept of *l'intérêt collectif* within the enterprise, a plurality of interests which we have found behind the juridical entity of the French company.[192] In Germany, a similar debate was encouraged by the appearance of works councils, first in Weimar under the Law of 1920, later in the 1950s with rights to consultation and on some matters to co-decision, alongside the notions of 'enterprise interests' in company law.[193] In Italy, after the escape from the 'corporativist' thinking of the fascist period and the effects of its *Carta del lavoro*, the arrival in 1970 of Article 7 of the Workers' Statute put the employer's powers of direction (defined shortly in the Civil Code Arts. 2104-2106) on a new base.[194] Writers advanced theories, as in France, both of a 'contractual' basis and of 'the law of the enterprise ... understood as a collective interest distinct from that of the employer'[195] The 1970 reform was seen as an extension of interests recognised within the enterprise; it required obligatory procedures in the use of disciplinary powers in a manner similar to the French reform.[196] Of course, workers can be treated unfairly by disciplinary measures in any system of labour law. But the introduction of 'institutional' or 'enterprise-based' starting points for the employer's powers of direction and discipline, despite the extensive uncertainties over the precise limitations, seems to have cut the historical cord; modern debate has relatively little to do with the penal laws of the last century.

In Britain, however, the employer's powers of discipline and direction are not based upon such balancing of enterprise interests. Here the legal culture is part of a society that has uninterrupted bonds with the past; it suffered no historical rupture equivalent to France and Italy, let alone Germany, no *Chartre du Travail*, no invasion of its territory, no totalitarian assault on its labour relations system.[197] It proudly retained its modern base – the contract of employment and (until recently) collective bargaining – even in war-time; if strikes were made illegal then in trade disputes, this was arranged by consensus and even extended in a government deal with the TUC until 1951. This had been the only European system not to have used the *livret* (worker's work book) or its equivalent, common on the continent well into the nineteenth century. But the price of this continuity has been a survival of concepts of authority of which many were bred in the criminal jurisdiction of the Master and Servant Acts and became endogenous to the employment tradition. There, not in the civil courts, do we find before 1875 the major enforcement mechanism to sanction workers' indiscipline, withdrawal from work or faulty execution of work. But 1875 made no clean break. Not only were a few crimes passed on (even today we have, recently consolidated from the Act of 1875 though unused, criminal sanctions for a breach of employment contract which endangers human life or seriously damages property).[198] More important, the 1875 legislation itself, far from destroying the links with criminal courts, continued a special jurisdiction on discipline and deemed the magistrates to be civil courts for day-to-day disputes between employer and workman or apprentice.[199] Not only was breach of the contract of service as such a crime as recently as 1874; discipline under the wage-work bargain was passed on and still has its roots not in the private law of contract but in penal laws that linked the servant's duties to the master's authority, the prevention of civil disorder and an abiding distrust of the working class.

That criminal law was extensively used. In the 20 years after 1855, workers convicted in England for disobedience or leaving their work rose in number from 9,900 a year on average in 1857-67, to 10,400 in 1872.[200] As all readers of the Webbs know, the worker could be imprisoned for a breach but the master was answerable only in damages; the employer could give evidence in his case, the worker could not; workers were imprisoned again and again if they refused to do the work because (at least in Queen's Bench) imprisonment was no discharge.[201] The lineage of the legislation extends to the Ordinance of Labourers 1349, Elizabeth's Statute of Artificers 1563 through the Master and Servant Acts of the eighteenth and nineteenth centuries.[202] In 1833, the ruling authorities decided to take no chances by passing new and severe Master and Servant legislation under which, on the complaint of an employer, a magistrate was given new powers to 'issue his Warrant for the apprehending every such Servant' for disobedience at work, 'neglect to fulfill the same or ... any other misconduct or misdemeanour in the execution thereof or otherwise respecting the same.'[203] As Lord Ellenborough had said in 1817 in *Spain v Arnott*: 'The question really comes to this whether the master or the servant is to have the superior authority.'[204]

Central to this use of the criminal law was authority. This did not change after 1875. And when decisions of the 1950s speak of the implied terms of the contract between master and servant, as in *Lister's* case, or assert, as in the dockers judgment of 1992, the primacy of the employer's 'commercial judgment' over remedies for employees unfairly dismissed, excusing him from any step that would 'disrupt his workforce' (that is, employees he has chosen to keep in '*his* workforce') who can doubt the link with the earlier tradition which shaped the contract of service in the shadow of criminal imprisonment? Fox has pointed out that, while the transmission to civil contract jettisoned many commitments of the status relationship, the 'pure milk of the contract gospel' was diluted so that the entrepreneur could continue to 'enjoy practical and moral support in his unfettered command' over labour resources. This was done by marrying contractualism to the traditional master-servant notions.[205] Similarly, Deakin has shown the continuing influence in decisions on the Wages Act 1986 of the old magisterial prerogatives to make deductions from wages and the magistrates' powers to cancel a right to wages of absconding servants; the modern cases rest on 'the shaky foundations of the common law'.[206] So too, recent decisions on 'no work no pay', dispensing with concepts of set-off or apportionment, reach back to similar sources.[207] In Britain we have had no effective debate about the 'enterprise as such' and the powers of direction or discipline which might functionally be required in different types of enterprise. Instead we have had continuity of the master's prerogatives.

In the law of combination and conspiracy, after the exclusion by the 1875 Act of criminal conspiracy from trade disputes, the Law Lords in 1901 'invented a new civil offence (civil conspiracy) and then created a new kind of defendant against whom it could be alleged (the trade union).'[208] But it is less remarked how the common law of the individual employment contract was reviewed and strengthened long *before* the repeal of the Master and Servant Acts in 1875, when the penal master and servant principles laying down the master's prerogatives flowed over – how could they not? – into what became the civil contract. Even a century later, on the eve of employment protection legislation, the old authorities survived explicitly: in one textbook of 1962 the law on the employee's 'misconduct' and 'disobedience' cites 23 cases decided after 1875, but 35 authorities decided before 1875, while another authoritative work of 1976 set out as common law cases on 'dismissal for disobedience' – 10 decided before, and 10 after 1875.[209] In later books the influence of earlier cases tends to be implicit, their influence found often in interpretations of employment protection legislation based upon parallel principles.

The common law laid down in this period further weapons by which the master could rely on contractual duties to obey, well before the penal sanction was removed. Both Parliament and judges contributed to the process, in which the law of tort was prominent. In 1859 the Molestation of Workmen Act purported to make lawful peaceable persuasion short of 'intimidation' in furtherance of claims for better wages or hours; but it took seven years to steer it through Parliament in the face of strong opposition. It passed largely because a proviso was added excluding attempts to induce 'any workman to break or depart from any contract'. This addition was made on the model of the master and servant laws and 'in the wake of *Lumley v Gye*' six years before.[210] The *Lumley* decision created what we know today as the tort of knowingly and intentionally inducing a breach of contract without lawful justification, providing the employer a new right against the organisers of defecting servants. The potentialities of this new civil liability were appreciated only after a curiously long delay – as late as 1906 Lord Loreburn L.C. did not trust in such a wide liability; it was not until Dilke introduced his amendment for immunity against the tort in trade disputes that its possibilities began to be understood, and even then only in respect of employment contracts, not commercial contracts.[211] What had set out in 1351 as a wrong against the master's proprietary interest was, as Holdsworth says, 'adapted to the purely contractual basis' of a new tort which was an 'enormous extension' of civil liability.[212] It was a creative decision; on a strict reading of the precedents there was force in the dissenting judgment of Coleridge J. This tort became the central weapon for common law containment of trade union organisation in industrial action (one which Lord Denning MR wished to 'extend' still further in 1969) and which would be wider still under the Bill of 1993.[213]

As if to prepare instinctively for the day when imprisonment would no longer be available for the servant's misconduct and as if sensing that criminal sanctions would soon be blunt instruments against workers of an advanced industrial society, the common law began in the 1850s to lay up in store sources of discipline and order clothed in the rhetoric of equality and contract both against workers and against those who might foment their disaffection. The special English factor facilitated this: whereas the tort of conspiracy was invented in 1901 *after* the death of its criminal progenitor, discipline under the contract of employment required less inventiveness because for more than 40 years it had grown coterminous with the criminal law on master and servant by which its features were significantly moulded. What is more, as it was still a crime there could be no question of mitigating the doctrine that departure from the workplace was wrongful, not just a suspension. But no parallel 'enormous extension' of liability was ever created then or later to favour the servant or employee. The tort of inducing breach of contract was central, a liability some legal systems reject (in Sweden for example) and others have softened by way of doctrines of 'justification'.[214] But in England Lord Halsbury snapped shut the latter defence in 1905 when he 'absolutely refused to discuss' justification of inducing breach of contract on economic grounds and no judge since has dared to prise it open.[215] Only in one case during 140 years of modern employment law has a judge dared to inspect the agenda for the introduction of a principle of suspension of contract in industrial conflict 'as an implication read into the contract by the modern law.'[216] Judicial policy might have provided a partial amelioration – just as easily as the policy applied in *Lister*'s case – but once again, where the interests of workers taking action are concerned, the judiciary has put its common law creativity on a leash. British strike law seems destined to remain the child of master and servant law.[217]

Lastly, it is useful to note that there are parallels in public law. The old legislation regulating the labour market was moribund by the end of the eighteenth century, and wage fixing had virtually died out by the time of its formal burial in 1813.[218] But there was another institution, which had long expressed the policies of those who regarded 'idleness among the lower orders as wicked'.[219] Elements in the Poor Laws supported this stern attitude to work; in 1834 it was still true that 'the able-bodied pauper was compelled by law to work'.[220] Indeed, 'the stamp [of the Poor Law] is readily apparent throughout our social welfare system'.[221] Its external effects upon employment ran well alongside the pressures within the law moulding the emergent contract of employment. The external pressure to work – and moral disapproval of the idle poor – descend into the modern legal doctrines excluding from social benefit or assistance those whose unemployment is 'voluntary',[222] and are reflected in the disqualifications from today's social security benefits of workers guilty of 'industrial misconduct', not to speak of the additional requirements now that the unemployed applicant must be 'actively seeking work'.[223] This tradition of public discipline for the unemployed poor has complemented the tradition of authority to control those who are employed.

CONCLUSIONS

We may attempt three brief conclusions. First, it has long been clear that the ideology of the common law in employment is hostile to workers' combinations and collective action, leading judges to interpret restrictively all legislation which has provided their leaders (though not them) with slender, and in the last decade ever-shrinking, immunities from certain wrongs. Just as important, built into today's common law is an approach to managerial authority, discipline at work and the employer's prerogatives which regularly make an appearance in a law which cannot be satisfactorily explained on any base of contract. That tradition still expresses a version of the civil obligations required of the servant, as sanctioned in the old criminal law of master and servant in the arms of which they were reared before 1875. The archetypal models of master and servant have since 1825 run deep into the culture of judicial assumptions, including the interpretation of employment protection legislation. On occasion, as when the enterprise is restructured, the employer reaps the benefit of these even when he is in breach of his contract.

Secondly, the interests of the employee find little solace in our company law as it has been developed since the repeal of the Bubble Act in 1825. The status of the shareholder and the nature of the share were anchored by the common law firmly into an individualist idelogy of proprietorship which ran with the grain of society and especially with the capital market of the day. The shareholder's property in his share and the 'interests of the company' as the shareholders' interests alone, became pillars of the modern law with no plurality of other interests acknowledged (such as those of the employees) as they have, in whole or in part, been accepted by neighbouring company laws as a natural and necessary part of their enterprise law, either through the law on companies or on contiguous institutions such as works councils or 'Pepper' schemes. In England, the company law developments did nothing to assuage, and something to sharpen, hierarchic structures of authority. Modern company legislation in Britain has barely addressed these social dimensions of the law, and the next companies Bill is likely to concentrate on deregulating private companies, not making a contribution to consensus.

Thirdly, policies which might do a little to amend the common law philosophies, such as Community proposals for employee participation in the proposed European Company or the draft Fifth directive on the harmonisation of company law, necessarily find themselves embroiled in Britain in a battle with these common law principles and their dominant ideology, the common law tradition of authority at work. In that tradition company law and master and servant law form complementary halves. Certainly those who practise worker participation elsewhere in the Community find it strange that the issue of 'workers' participation' is so explosive in Britain. The 'social dimension' of community policies is currently a sickly infant; but many Member States have long ago introduced such participation into their company industrial relations. It might have been thought wise in Britain, in a society which fragments at every turn of the calendar, to seek a new settlement for employees' rights in the company. It need not be as bold as what M. Auroux called in 1982 rights to make 'the worker who is a citizen out there in the city, a citizen too here at the workplace'. Modest changes reaching out for a wider consensus can, no doubt, be fully accomplished only by legislation whether at domestic or (if 'subsidiarity' allows) at Community level, aided perhaps by new levels of collective bargaining. But from time to time there have been judges in England and in Scotland who have dared to understand the unseen grip of the past, who have sought to break open old traditions at least at the edges. It is not impossible that new judges might apply their creativity today in a search for adventurous social dimensions which the old common law manifestly cannot offer unaided. We may have little confidence that this will happen. But we need not yet wholly despair.

NOTES

1. Lord Birkenhead, *Fourteen English Judges* (1926), p. 223.
2. See D. Harris and D. Tallon, *Contract Law Today: Anglo-French Comparisons* (1989), pp. 10-11, 391. For criticism of the traditional French one-sentence, anonymous judgment: A Touffait and A. Tunc, 1974 Rev.Tr.Dr. Civ. 1010, quoted in O. Kahn-Freund, C. Lévy and B. Rudden, *A Source Book on French Law* (3rd ed. by B. Rudden 1991), pp. 281-288.
3. So J.A.G. Griffith, *The Politics of The Judiciary* (4th ed. 1991), p. 328.
4. On June 23, 1753. See W. Holdsworth, *History of English Law*, Vol. XII (1938), p. 746.
5. O. Kahn-Freund, 'On the Uses and Abuses of Comparative Law' (1966) 82 L Q R 40 at p. 61.
6. See Treaty of Rome, Arts. 48-51; and the proposed Council Directive concerning the *Posting of Workers in the Framework of Provision of Services* COM (91) 230 final, June 20, 1991, based on Arts. 57 and 66; see generally, D. Marsden, 'European Integration and Integration of the Labour Markets' (1992) 6 *Labour* pp. 3-35.
7. In 1992, 16 company law directives have been implemented, seven more have been agreed or adopted at Community level and eight more are proposals or draft proposals, including those requiring forms of employee participation, *e.g.* the proposed *Fifth Directive* ([1983] OJ C240/2, amended [1991] O J C321/9), and the proposed Directive and Regulation for the *European Company* ('*Societas Europaea*') ([1991] O J C176/1).
8. See proposals for the *European Company (Societas Europaea)* [1991] O J C176/1, which try to provide for this problem. Two separate instruments are needed to satisfy the requirements under Community law for a 'base' in the Treaty of Rome, especially one which would allow for adoption my majority voting. Hence the 'company law' aspects in the Regulation are proposed under Art. 100a of the Treaty, and those on employee participation in the draft Directive under Art. 54. On British government reactions on the latest text: see *Revised Proposal for a European Company Statute: a Consultative Document* (D T I 1992). On transfer of the registered office, see the new Arts. 5, 5a and 81 of the proposed Regulation and in the proposed Directive Art. 3(3): but note the competence of the general meeting on the 'law' applicable to the registered office and Art. 3(7) of the Directive.
9. On English company law 1720-1825, see L.C.B. Gower, *Modern Company Law* (5th ed., 1992) Chaps. 2 and 3: and for other systems, A. Levy, *Private Corporations and Their Control* (1950), Vols I and II.
10. See E.P. Thompson, *The Making of the English Working Class* (1963), pp. 56 *et seq.*
11. *Dimbleby & Sons Ltd.* v. *NUJ* [1984] 1 WLR 427 at p. 435. Compare the classic analysis by H.L.A. Hart, 'Definition in Theory and Jurisprudence' (1970) 54 LOR 37.

12. See G. Lyon-Caen, '*Du Rôle des Principes Généraux du Droit Civil en Droit du Travail (Première Approche)*' (1974) Rev. Trim. de Droit Civil 229 at p. 240, discussed by Wedderburn in 'Labour Law: From Here to Autonomy?' (1987) 16 I L J 1 at pp. 20-22 (Chapter 5 of *Employment Rights in Britain and Europe* (1991)); and see B. Bercusson, 'Workers, Corporate Enterprise and the Law' in R. Lewis (ed.), *Labour Law in Britain* (1976), pp. 134-160.

13. Slade L J in *Adams v. Cape Industries Plc* [1990] Ch. 433 at p. 54, (1990) 5 B C C 786 at p. 826 C.A.; see H. Collins, 'Responsibility of Groups in Complex Economic Integration (1990) 53 M L R 731. Contrast the view of Cumming-Bruce L.J. in *Re A Company* [1985] 1 B C C 99, 421 at p. 99, 425.

14. Du Parcq L J in *Re Schebsman* [1944] Ch. 83 at p. 104.

15. *Salomon v. Salomon Co. Ltd.* [1897] A C 22 (H L).

16. Primarily in calculating the obligatory number of workers' representatives: G. Lyon-Caen and J. Pelissier, *Droit du Travail* (16th ed. 1992), pp. 758-60. On other systems and the corporate veil, see. E. Cohn and S. Simitis, 'Lifting the Veil in the Company Laws on the European Continent' (1963) 12 I C L Q. 19; K. Hopt (ed.), *Groups of Companies in European Laws* (1982); D. Sugarman and G. Teubner (eds.), *Regulating Corporate Groups in Europe* (1990).

17. *Mangan v. Atterton* (1866) L R 1 Ex. 239 at p. 240.

18. Lord Devlin, 'Judges and Lawmakers' (1976) 39 M L R 1 at p. 8.

19. See Wedderburn, 'The Injunction and the Sovereignty of Parliament' (1988) 23 *The Law Teacher* 4 Chap. 7 in *Employment Rights in Britain and Europe, op. cit.*; also G. Lightman, 'A Trade Union in Chains' [1987] *Current Legal Problems* 25; K. O'Regan, 'Contempt of Court and Enforcement of Labour 'Injunctions' (1991) 54 M L R 385.

20. O. Kahn-Freund, 'Introduction' to *The Institutions of Private Law and their Social Functions* (1949), p. 13, citing Max Weber, *Wirtschaft und Gesellschaft* (1920), p. 508.

21. See for a detailed examination, Wedderburn, 'Inderogability, Collective Agreements and Community Law' (1992) 21 I L J 245. [See chap. 6 below.]

22. The Maastricht Agreement on Social Policy, Art. 4(1).

23. *Ibid.* Art. 4(2).

24. *F. Guarriello, Ordinamento comunitario e autonomia collettiva: il dialogo sociale* (1992) p. 177; B. Bercusson, 'Maastricht: a Fundamental Change in European Labour Law' (1992) 23 Ind Rels. Jo. 177 at p. 188; and on fundamental rights, B. Hepple. 'The Crisis in E.C. Labour Law' (1987) 16 I L J 3; P. Teague, 'Constitution or Regime? The Social Dimension to the 1992 Project' (1989) 27 B.J.I.R. 310 at p. 323.

25. M. Weiss in G. Spyropoulos and G. Fragnière, *Work and Social Policies in the New Europe* (1991), pp. 62-72; and see A. Adinolfi 'The Implementation of Social Policy Directives through Collective Agreements' (1988) 25 C M L R 291. On transnational relations, see M. Gold and M. Hall, *Report on European Level Information and Consultation in Multinational Companies: an Evaluation of Practice* (1992), and the European Trade Union Institute, *The European Dimensions of Collective Bargaining after Maastricht* (1992).

26. See now Trade Union and Labour Relations Act 1992, s.179 (consolidating s. 18(1)-(3) of the 1974 Act).
27. For this principle in various systems of labour law and on incorporation in English law, see Wedderburn *op. cit.* n. 21.
28. Art. L. 135-2 *Code du Travail.* In Italy, too, the principle of *inderogabilitá in pejus.* The terms of the individual contract are 'substituted by those of the agreement, unless they contain conditions more favourable to the worker': Civil Code Art. 2077. For some difficulties see G. Giugni *Diritto sindacale* (9th ed. 1991) pp. 147-160; G. Ghezzi and U. Romagnoli, *Il diritto sindacale* (3rd. ed. 1992) pp. 161-70, and Wedderburn (1992) 21 I L J 245 at pp. 258-63. The Italian development has been complex by reason of a more general legal prohibition against 'compromises' in which workers lose their rights: see V. Leccese, *'Transazioni collettive e disposizione dei diritti del lavoratore'* (1991) 50 Giorn. D L R I 283-330.
29. See Wedderburn and S. Sciarra, 'Collective Bargaining as Agreement and as Law' in A. Pizzorusso, *Law in the Making* (1986), pp. 185-237 (also 1989 35 Riv. D.C. 45-102).
30. See Sched. 11 to Employment Protection Act 1975 (unilateral arbitration; repealed by s.19 of the Employment Act 1980) and s.21 *ibid* (inderogable awards sanctioning union claims to information). On the law in the United States and New Zealand: (1992) 21 I L J 245 at pp. 250-251.
31. For example, pressure on journalists in Britain to accept 'personalised contracts of employment': A C A S *Annual Report 1991*, pp. 17-22, 35-36; and see the White Paper *People, Jobs and Opportunity* (Cm. 1810, 1992) on the official government preference for individual over collective bargaining. For limits to the employer's powers to introduce 'personal contracts', see *Assoc. Newspapers v Wilson* and *Assoc. British Ports v. Palmer* [1994] ICR 97 [on appeal to H L]; but see the new powers immediately introduced by s. 13 TURER Act 1993, amending s. 148 TULRCA 1992.
32. Hobhouse J. in *Alexander v. Standard Telephones and Cables Ltd (No. 2)* [1991] I R L R 286 at pp. 292, 294 ('not apt for incorporation') on 'incorporation' generally, see Wedderburn, *The Worker and the Law* (3rd ed. 1986), pp. 326-43.
33. Cass. January 30, 1980, no. 711, Riv. giur, lav. 1980, II, p. 11; G. Ghezzi and U. Romagnoli, *Diritto sindacale* (3rd. ed. 1992), pp. 203-206, 228-230. On the Italian courts: G. Certoma, *The Italian Legal System* (1985), pp. 187-91.
34. The new doctrine that *juges des rèfèrés* could disallow a strike notice because it was 'unreasonable', espoused by the Cour de Cassation (Ass. plénière July 14 1986, *SNOMAC c Air France*, Dr. Soc. 1986, 745 G. Lyon-Caen) was not applied in the 'lower' courts which continued to hold that the judge has no competence to decide the reasonableness of workers' claims (Cour d'Appel Paris, January 27, 1988, *Air Inter c. SNOMAC*, Dr. Soc. 1988, 243 J-E. Ray). In 1992 the Cour de Cassation upheld the traditional principle, excluding judicial competence to determine the reasonableness of the claim (June 2, 1992, *SA Ipem Hom c Mercier, Zaluski c SA Ipem Hom*; Dr. Ouvr. 385, J-E. Ray 1992 Dr. Soc. 700: 'A ten year parenthesis has just been closed'). Strike notices may be unlawful, for example as an 'abuse' of the constitutional right to strike, of particular

relevance in the public sector: Cass. Soc. May 30, 1989; Wedderburn, *Employment Rights in Britain and Europe* (1991), pp. 175, 315.

35. See *Lonrho Ltd* v *Shell Petroleum Co Ltd (No. 2)* [1982] AC 173 HL; *Metall und Rohstoff AG* v *Donaldson Lufkin & Jenrette Inc.* [1990] 1 QB 391 CA; *Lonrho Plc* v *Fayed* [1992] 1 AC 448 HL. On other jurisdictions, see: *Taylor* v *Smyth* [1991] 1 IR 142 (Ir. Sup. Ct.); *S.S.C. & B. Lintas* v *Murphy* [1986] 2 NZLR 436; *Westfair Foods Ltd* v *Lippens Inc* (1990) 64 DLR (4th) 335 (Man. CA).

36. See respectively: G. Giugni, *Diritto sindicale* (9th ed. 1991), pp. 240-241; G. Lyon-Caen and J. Pelissier, *op.cit.* n. 16 at pp. 810-811; H. Sinay and J.-C. Javillier, *La Grève* (2nd ed. 1984), p. 178; so too J.-M. Verdier, *Droit du Travail* (9th ed. 1990), pp. 355-356. Two recent decisions prove the doctrine does not apply when the stoppage overlaps only fortuitously the work period in issue: Soc. June 21, 1989 *SNCF c Coudurier* and *IBM c Cortes*, D. 1990 Somm. 167: Soc. June 27, 1989, *SA Fonderie Pasquet c Sotto*.

37. B. Simpson, 'The Common Law and Legal Theory' in W. Twining (ed.), *Legal Theory and the Common Law* (1986), p. 24.

38. See on the 'social dimension' of justice, M. Cappelletti, in E. Fazzalari (ed.), *Italian Yearbook of Civil Procedure*, Vol. I (1991) pp. 115, 120. For the three periods of Community social policy: R. Neilsen and E. Szyszczak, *The Social Dimension of the European Community* (1991), pp. 15-37.

39. Conclusions of the Madrid Summit 1988, repeated by Eleven States in the *Community Charter of the Fundamental Social Rights of Workers* (the Community '*Social Charter*') 1989, Preamble 2nd. ind.

40. Wedderburn, *Social Charter, European Company and Employment Rights* (1990). The United Kingdom did not of course adhere to the *Social Charter*.

41. On equal treatment as an independent Community value, see the valuable survey by C. Docksey, 'The Principle of Equality between Women and Men as a Fundamental Right under Community Law' (1991) 20 ILJ 258-280.

42. See, for example, the rejection of legislation and collective agreements providing special protection of women workers on night work in France: the *Alfred Stoeckel* judgment (Case C-345/89, [1991] OJ C220/7). In England, all such legislation (even for young workers) was repealed in the Sex Discrimination Act 1986 and Employment Act 1989. The ILO urged the adoption of Convention no. 171 of 1990, providing for improved conditions for all night workers. [See W. Wuiame (1994) 23 ILJ 95.]

43. A. Alcock, *History of the ILO* (1972), pp. 14-15, 50-55. What is now seen as exceptional legislation regulating men's hours is to be found in the Railway Servants (Hours of Labour) Act 1893 and Coal Mines Regulation Act 1908, as amended by the Coal Mines Act 1919 (maximum hours underground).

44. E. Vogel-Polsky 'What Future is there for a Social Europe following the Strasbourg Summit?' (1990) 19 ILJ 65 at p. 75; and on the 'social dialogue' between management and labour at Community levle, E. Vogel-Polsky (ed.) *Quel Avenir pour L'Europe Sociale: 1992 Et Apres?* (1992), pp. 104-108.

45. See especially P.L. Davies, 'The Emergence of European Labour Law' in W. McCarthy, *Legal Intervention in Industrial Relations* (1992), p. 347; also Wedderburn, 'European Community Law and Workers' Rights: Fact or

Fake in 1992?' (1991) 13 U. Dublin LJ. 1; G.F. Mancini, 'Labour Law and Community Law' (1985) 20 *Irish Jurist* 1 at pp. 2, 12; and C. La-Macchia, *'La Carta comunitaria dei diritti sociali'* (1990) 48 Giorn. DLRI 769-807. On the purpose of a Directive in interpreting English law, see *Litster* v *Forth Dry Dock and Engineering Co.* [1990] 1 AC 546 HL; and now *R* v *Secretary of State for Trade and British Coal Corpn., ex p. Vardy and NUM*, [1993] IRLR 104.

46. G. Lyon-Caen, *'L'infiltration du Droit du Travail par le Droit de la Concurrence'* (1992) Dr. Ouvr. 313-321, with the judgment of *Merci Convenzionali Porto di Genova* v *Siderurgica Gabriella SPA* (Case C-179/90, December 10, 1991).

47. *Loewe* v *Lawlor* 208 US 274 (1908) and 235 US 52 (1915); L. Merrifield, T. St. Antoine and C. Craver, *Labor Relations Law* (1989), pp. 601-604. So, too, Australian Trade Practices Act 1974, s. 45D. [See pp. 370-410 below.]

48. See for instance M. Bloch-Lainé, *Pour une Réforme de l'Enterprise* (1963) proposing to put companies into the joint hands of the shareholders, employees and public authorities. Compare J. Maxwell, 'Should Christians Press for Revision of Company Law' (1962) 40 U. Det. L.J. 1-165. On proposals for constituency representation in the United States, see Wedderburn in G. Teubner (ed.), *Corporate Governance and Directors' Liabilities* (1985), pp. 12-32. See too A. Schonfield, *Modern Capitalism* (1965), pp. 381-382; and A. Anastasi (ed.), *Modelli di democrazia industriale e sindacale* (1988) Vols. I and II.

49. See P. Sudreau, *Rapport: la réforme de l'entreprise* (1975); *The Biedenkopf Report: Co-Determination in the Company'* (1970, translated D. O'Neill, Belfast); the 'Bullock' *Report on Industrial Democracy* (Cmnd, 6076, 1977).

50. *Puddephatt* v *Leith* [1916] 1 Ch. 200; *North West Transporation Co* v *Beatty* (1887) 12 App. Cas. 589 PC. The rule was strongly asserted in a judgment making a 'rare exception': *Standard Chartered Bank* v *Walker* [1992] 1 WLR 561 (Vinelott J.).

51. A. Tunc, 'A French Lawyer Looks at British Company Law' (1982) 45 MLR 1.

52. Lord Greene MR in *Re Smith and Fawcett Ltd.* [1942] Ch. 304 at p. 306.

53. Dillon LJ in *Lee Panavision Ltd* v *Lee Lighting Ltd* [1991] BCC 620, 634, citing the well known passage of Evershed MR in *Greenhalgh* v *Arderne Cinemas Ltd.* [1951] Ch. 286 at p. 291. On present and future shareholders, see *Report on the Savoy Hotel Co.* (1954, Milner Holland, QC) discussed in L.C.B. Gower, (1956) 68 Harv. L. Rev. 1176. Many regard the interests of the company as an 'elusive concept', *e.g.* J. Farrar in B. Pettet (ed.), *Company Law in Change* (1987), p. 55. Compare C. Bradley, 'Corporate Control: Markets and Rules' (1990) 53 MLR 170.

54. F. Hayek, *Law, Legislation and Liberty* (1979), Vol. III, p. 82; M. Friedman, *An Economist's Protest* (1972), p. 177. For the influence of Hayek on labour law policy, see Wedderburn 'Freedom of Association and Philosophies of Labour Law' (1989) 18 ILJ 1 (Chap. 8, *Employment Rights in Britain and Europe, op.cit.*, n. 12).

55. See V. Finch, 'Directors' Duties: Insolvency and Unsecured Creditor' in A. Clarke, *Current Issues in Insolvency Law* (1991) pp. 87-119; D.

Prentice in E. McKendrick (ed.), *Commercial Aspects of Trusts and Fiduciary Obligations* (1992), Chap 4.

56. See H. Wincott, *Evidence to the Jenkins Committee on Company Law* (September 23, 1960), p. 49 (shareholders, customers and employees; co-equal interests); City Panel, *Rules on Take-Overs and Mergers* (1990) General Principle 9 ('shareholders' interests taken as a whole together with those of employees and creditors').

57. See L.C.B. Gower, *Modern Company Law* (5th ed. 1992), p. 554; P.L. Davies, 'Directors' Fiduciary Duties and Individual Shareholders' in E. McKendrick (ed.), *Commercial Aspects of Trusts and Fiduciary Obligations* (1992), Chap. 5, p. 85. For a management approach to social responsibility, see D. Clutterbuck and D. Snow, *Working in the Community: A Guide to Corporate Social Responsibility* (1990).

58. CBI Committee, *The Social Responsibilities of the British Public Company* (1973), p. 23.

59. P.L. Davies, *op.cit*, n. 57, at p. 85; the 'Cadbury Committee' in *Financial Aspects of Corporate Governance* (1992) finds a role only for directors (executive and non-executive), shareholders and auditors.

60. J.K. Galbraith, *The Great Crash 1929* (1954), pp. 179-188.

61. A. Berle and G. Means, *The Modern Corporation and Private Property* (1932, rev. ed. 1967); and see the qualifications in E. Herman, *Corporate Control, Corporate Power* (1981). Among the rather dated managerialists, see R. Gordon, *Business Leadership in the Large Corporation* (1961), p. 550.

62. A. Berle in (1931) 44 Harv. L.R. 1049, and E.M. Dodd, (1932) 45 Harv. L.R. 1145. For the later debate: Wedderburn, 'Trust, Corporation and the Worker' (1985) 23 Osgoode Hall L.J. 204 at pp. 223-4. On the position of the banks in the U.S.A., E. Herman, *Corporate Control Corporate Power* (1981), Chap. 7. *The Law Institute draft 'Principles of Corporate Governance'* included an obligation to 'take into account ethical considerations as are reasonably regarded as appropriate to the responsible conduct of business': Art. 2.01; and see D. Branson, 'Countertrends in Corporate Law' (1983) 68 Minn. L.R. 53; W. Cary and M. Eisenberg, *Corporations* (1980) and *Supp.* (1986), pp. 208-226; *Klinicki v Lundgren* 695 P. 2d 906 (S.C. Oregon 1985).

63. O. Kahn-Freund often pointed out the identity of view in opposition to worker participation of 'Marxist doctrine and American trade unions': *La Participation: Quelques Experiences Étrangères* (1976), p. 27. He might have added English company law.

64. See S. and B. Webb, *Industrial Democracy* (1901); on the 'origins of industrial democracy in Britain', see S. Sciarra, *Democrazia politica e democrazia industriale* (1978), pp. 7-44.

65. *Report of the Committee of Inquiry on Industrial Democracy* (1977, Cmnd. 6706); and the retreat in *Industrial Democracy* (1978, Cmnd. 7231).

66. *Employee Participation and Company Structure* (1975, E.C. Bulletin Supp. 8/75), p. 9; on current proposals, see n. 8, above.

67. Institute of Directors, *The EEC Vth. Directive – a Trojan Bullock?* (1980).

68. *Cort. cass.* May 4, 1991, no. 4927, *Casa di cura La Vernella c. San Carlo,*

noted D. Preite 1991 18 Giur. Comm. 887 at p. 889. For differing interpretations of *interesse sociale* and its 'fluctuating' meaning, see P. Xuereb, in R. Drury and P. Xuereb (eds.), *European Company Laws: A Comparative Approach* (1991), pp. 145-154, 185-191; also (1987) 8 *Company Lawyer* 16, at pp. 23 *et seq.* For the ban on voting where interests conflict see. *Codice Civile* Arts, 2373, 2377, 2469.

69. *Cort. cass.* October 25, 1958, no. 3471, Giur. It. 1959 I, 1, 869; and see G. Cottino, *Diritto Commerciale* (1976) Vol. I, pp. 631-635, 681-692.

70. On *l'intérêt social*, see J. Paillusseau in R. Drury and P. Xuereb, *op.cit.*, n. 68, pp. 31-38 (on 'interest groups'); P. Xuereb, *ibid.*, pp. 190-200 (*abus de droit*) and (1988) 51 MLR 156. See also, the Law of July 24, 1966, Art. 82; G. Strauss, *Les Droits de la Minorité dans la Société Anonyme* (1970).

71. Labour lawyers tend not to consider these as organs integral to the enterprise (G. Lyon-Caen and J. Pelissier, *Droit du Travail* (16th ed. 1990), p. 841); *contra*, company lawyers who do (A. Tunc, *op.cit.*, n. 51; (1982) 45 MLR 1 at p. 16; N. Catala, *L'Enterprise* (1980), pp. 477-485, 590-596, 847-853).

72. See the Ordonnance of October 21, 1986, obligatory for companies with more than 50 employees: J-C. Javillier *Manuel, Droit du Travail* (4th ed., 1992), pp. 368-374; and see 'Promotion of Employee Participation in Profits and Enterprise Results'. *The Pepper Report* (1991, ed. M. Uvalic) in *Social Europe Supp.* 3/91 (European Commission and European University Institute), pp. 66-87 (France) and 'Conclusions', Chap. 16.

73. See F. Kübler, 'Dual Loyalty of Labour Representatives' in K. Hopt and G. Teubner (eds.), *Corporate Governance and Directors' Liabilities* (1985), pp. 432-437, 439-441. The precise place of the employee interests within 'enterprise' interests is debated: pp. 439-440. On directors' conflicting loyalties, see the valuable review by K. Hopt, 'Self-Dealing and the Use of Corporate Opportunity and Information' in K. Hopt and G. Teubnerk (eds.) *ibid.*, pp. 285-325.

74. On the German developments: A. Levy, *op.cit.*, n. 9, Vol. I, pp. 177-185, citing W. Rathenau, *Von Aktienwesen* (1917), and Vol. II, pp. 667-698, 847-848; for the law now, F. Kübler in K. Hopt and G. Teubner (eds.), *Corporate Governance and Directors' Liabilities* (1985), pp. 439-440.

75. See R. Lewis and J. Clark (eds.), *O. Kahn-Freund, Labour Law and Politics in the Weimar Republic* (1981), pp. 21-35, and the useful summary, pp. 214-221. Representation on the Supervisory Board was also seen as a counter to Nazi moves in the Company Law of 1937 to increase the powers of the Management Board according to the *Führerprinzip*.

76. On the modern system, see M. Weiss, *Labour Law and Industrial Relations in the Federal German Republic* (1987), pp. 149-183, and 'Recent Trends in the Development of Labor Law in the Federal Republic of Germany' (1989) 23 Law and Society Rev. 759 at pp. 768-70; on the background, H. Spiro, *The Politics of German Codetermination* (1958); on participation in groups of companies, see P.L. Davies in K. Hopt (ed.), *Groups of Companies in European Laws* (1982), pp. 222-226.

77. *Parke v Daily News* [1962] Ch. 927. The case must now be seen as one concerning breach of directors' duties, not *ultra vires*.

78. See ss. 309 and 719 of the Companies Act 1985.

79. J. Birds, 'Making Directors Do Their Duties' (1980) 1 *Company Lawyer* 67 at p. 73; and D. Prentice, 'A Company and its Employees: the Companies Act 1980' (1981) 10 ILJ at p. 7, stressing the important limitation that money used under s. 719 must be money available for a dividend or otherwise at the shareholders' expense, now s. 719(3)(4); Wedderburn in K. Hopt and G. Teubner (eds.), *Corporate Governance and Directors' Liabilities* (1985), pp. 28-32.

80. See Gower, *Modern Company Law* (5th ed. 1992) pp. 643-662 on this difficult area of company law; also, in the context of take-overs, C. Bradley, 'Corporate Control: Markets and Rules' (1990) 53 MLR 170 at pp. 179-182.

81. Code du Travail, Art. L. 411-11. The *Cour de Cassation* has rejected union actions to enforce criminal sanctions against directors: Crim. March 14, 1979, D. 1979. *L'action syndicale en justice* is available to enforce criminal sanctions where the functions of the Labour Inspector have been obstructed: Crim. October 11, 1983; see J.C. Javillier, *Manuel du Droit du Travail* (4th ed., 1992), p. 386; G. Lyon-Caen and J. Pelissier, *Droit du Travail* (16th ed. 1992) pp. 570-571.

82. A. Tunc, 'A French Lawyer Looks At British Company Law' (1982) 45 MLR 1 at p. 8.

83. F. Maitland, 'The trust in effect enabled men to form point stock companies with limited liability': *Selected Essays* (eds. A. Hazeltine, G. Lapsley, P. Winfield) (1936), p. 135; compare C. Cooke, *Corporation, Trust and Company* (1950), pp. 130, 186; the possibilities of ensuring limited liability were restricted: Gower *op.cit.*, n. 80, pp. 34-38; *Re Sea, Fire and Life Insurance Co* (1854) 3 De G.M. & G. 459. On the deed of settlement company, see A. Dubois, *The English Business Company after the Bubble Act, 1720-1800* (1938).

84. By the repeal in 1825 of the Bubble Act 1720: *Josephs v Pebrer* (1825) 3 B. & C. 639; on the common law aversion to transferable shares, R. Formoy, *The Historical Foundations of Company Law* (1923) p. 32. But 'scrip companies' appear to have flourished before 1825, shares being transferable by delivery: Lindley on *Companies* (1902), p. 183.

85. *Child v Hudson's Bay Co.* (1723) P. Wms. 703; *Ashby v Blackwell* (1765) Amb. 503.

86. *Bligh v Brent* (1837) 2 Y. & C. Ex. 268; and see *Ashworth v Munn* (1880) 15 Ch.D. 363.

87. See P. Ireland, I. Grigg-Spall and D. Kelly, 'The Conceptual Foundations of Modern Company Law', in P. Fitzpatrick and A. Hunt (eds.), *Critical Legal Studies* (1987) at pp. 149, 152-160.

88. See L. Sealy, 'The Director as Trustee' [1967] CLJ 83, making clear the difference in the deed of settlement company of the position of trustees and of directors.

89. Romilly M.R. in *York & North Midland Railway v Hudson* (1853) 16 Beav. 485 at p. 491.

90. A. Levy, *op.cit.* n. 9, Vol. I, pp. 180-184.

91. D. Schneider, *Die Welt der Arbeit*, July 24, 1959, quoted by A. Schonfield, *Modern Capitalism* (1965), pp. 251-252. The banks became the 'prefects' of the system: *ibid*, p. 246.

92. K. Hopt, 'Functions of the Supervisory Board in the Bank-Industry Relationship' in N. Horn and J. Kocka (eds.), *Law and the Formation of the Big Enterprises in the 19th and Early 20th Centuries* (1979), and in K. Hopt and G. Teubner (eds.), *Corporate Governance and Directors' Liabilities* (1985), p. 306, on conflicts of interests for the representatives of the banks.
93. See F. Stockman, R. Ziegler and J. Scott, *Networks of Corporate Power* (1985), Chaps. 2, 10, 11 and 15; and on Germany, Chap. 5.
94. See A. Schonfield, *Modern Capitalism* (1965), on France, pp. 166-75, on Italy, pp. 177-194.
95. See for example, P. Cottrell, *British Overseas Investment in the Nineteenth Century* (1975); G. Ingham, *Capitalism Divided? The City and Industry in British Social Development* (1984).
96. See for example, A. Caincross, *Home and Foreign Investment 1870-1913* (1953).
97. W. Cornish and G. de N. Clark, *Law and Society in England 1750-1950* (1989), p. 253. On the banks and their roles in London and the provinces, see P. Mathias, *The First Industrial Nation* (1969), Chaps. 5 and 13.
98. *Duport Steels Ltd v Sirs* [1980] ICR 161 at p. 177.
99. Lord Diplock in *Express Newspapers Ltd.* v *McShane* [1980] ICR 42 at p. 57; Wedderburn (1980) 9 ILJ 65.
100. For example in *Gozney v Bristol, etc, Society* [1909] 1 KB 901; see the analysis by O. Kahn-Freund, 'The Illegality of a Trade Union' (1943) 7 MLR 192-205.
101. G. Treitel, *Law of Contract* (8th ed., 1991) p. 424.
102. Sachs LJ in *Edwards v SOGAT* [1954] Ch. 354 at pp. 381-382; see also Lord Denning MR at p. 37; Trade Unions and Labour Relations Act 1974, s. 2(5) (now TULRCA 1992 s. 11) [and *Boddington v Lawton* [1994] ICR 478.]
103. *Torquay Hotel Co Ltd.* v *Cousins* [1969] 2 Ch. 106 at p. 138, CA.
104. *Memorandum, Report of Royal Commission on Trade Unions* 1867-1869 (C 4123), lxxi.
105. See *R v Bunn* (1872) 12 Cox 316; *Quinn v Leathem* [1901] AC 495 HL; *Taff Vale Railway Co.* v *Amalgamated Society of Railway Servants* [1901] AC 426 HL; *Amalgamated Society of Railway Servants v Osborne* [1910] AC 87 HL; *Rookes v Banard* [1964] AC 1129 HL; *Stratford v Lindley* [1965] AC 269 HL; *Torquay Hotel Co Ltd v Cousins* [1969] 2 Ch. 106 CA; *Associated British Ports v TGWU* [1989] 1 WLR 939 CA (revs'd on other grounds HL, *ibid.*).
106. *American Cyanamid Co v Ethicon Ltd* [1975] AC 396 HL. See on this process Wedderburn, 'The Injunction and the Sovereignty of Parliament: Control of Judicial Discretion?', Chap. 7 in *Employment Rights in Britain and Europe* (1991), pp. 154-197.
107. *Samples of Lawmaking* (1962), pp. 11-14; *Allen v Flood* [1898] AC 1 HL; his was a notably hawkish speech in *Rookes v Barnard* [1964] AC 1129 HL.
108. *Universe Tankships Inc. of Monrovia v Laughton* [1983] 1 AC 366 HL. See Wedderburn (1982) 45 MLR 556; I. Sterling (1982) 11 ILJ 156.
109. See for a summary of the development in the commercial cases; G.

Treitel, *Law of Contract* (8th ed., 1991), pp. 363-366. Nowhere in the case law, however, is there a satisfactory explanation of just how the 'will' of a multinational corporation is coerced. In *Universe Tankships Inc. of Monrovia* v *Laughton* [1983] 1 AC 366 HL: 'duress' was conceded in view of the 'catastrophic' financial loss threatened. It is perhaps surprising how often this concession is made; see below n. 114.

110. *Manalaysay* v *The Oriental Victory* [1978] 1 FC 440 at p. 446 (Can.); Wedderburn, *Employment Rights in Britain and Europe* (1991), p. 329, n. 254.

111. Lord Donaldson MR in *Hennessy* v *Craigmyle Ltd* [1986] ICR 461 at pp. 468-469; 'in real life it must be very rare to encounter economic duress of an order which renders actions involuntary' at p. 470.

112. Now ss. 219-235 of the Trade Union and Labour Relations (Consolidation) Act 1992.

113. Lord Goff and G. Jones, *Law of Restitution* (3rd ed., 1986), p. 224; but see p. 236 for a more ambiguous view.

114. *Dimskal Shipping* v *International Transport Workers Federation* [1992] ICR 37 HL. He doubted whether it was helpful to ask whether the 'plaintiff's will had been coerced': at p. 46. As in *Universe Tankships Inc of Monrovia* v *Laughton*, above, n. 109, counsel had made concessions, including the illegality of 'blacking' without statutory protection.

115. See K. Ewing, *Britain and the ILO* (1989) (on the Committee of Experts Report); Wedderburn, *Employment Rights in Britain and Europe* (1991), pp. 277-279 and 353 (on the decision of the Freedom of Association Committee in Case no. 1540, 1991, *National Union of Seamen and UK*). On the right to strike as part of freedom of association: R. Ben-Israel, *International Labour Standards: The Case of Freedom to Strike* (1987), Part II.

116. Council of Europe, *Social Contract* 1961, Art. 6(4). The European '*Social Contract*' 1989 Art. 13 proclaims a right to stike, but with greater limitations: see Wedderburn in W. McCarthy (ed.), *Legal Interventions in Industrial Relations* (1992), pp. 159-165.

117. E.g. G. Giugni, *Diritto sindacale* (9th ed., 1991) p. 218: no one is liable for damage caused merely by the exercise of a right. On the right and the liberty to strike, see P. O'Higgins, 'The Right to Strike – Some International Reflections' in J. Carby-Hall (ed.), *Studies in Labour Law* (1976), pp. 110-117.

118. On unfair dismissal, see now Trade Union and Labour Relations (Consolidation) Act 1992, ss. 237-239.

119. *Morgan* v *Fry* [1968] 2 QB 710 CA; for the problems see the 'Donovan' *Report of the Royal Commission on Trade Unions and Employers Associations* (1968, Cmnd. 3623) para. 943. See too, *Ticehurst* v *British Telecommunications Plc.* [1992] IRLR 219, below, n. 124.

120. The 'Maastricht Social Chapter' (in the Protocol, Agreement and Declarations) to which the United Kingdom is not a party, does not extend its legislative machinery to rights to associate or rights to strike or lock-out: see Art. 2(6). The Presidency *Conclusions* of the European Council at Edinburgh, December 11-12, 1992, merely note the Commission's continuing 'priority' for 'implementing all the provisions'

of the Social Charter (DOC/92/8 Annex 2, *Subsidiarity*).
121. See H. Sinay and J.C. Javillier, *La Grève* (2nd ed., 1984) pp. 292-99; P. Durand, Dr. Soc. (1950), p. 118.
122. The Law of May 25, 1864, introduced a liberty to organise a strike but the stoppage normally remained a breach of contract; the right to strike was made constitutional by the Preamble to the constitution of 1946 (continued in 1958); the Laws of February 11, 1950, and July 25, 1985, confirmed a suspension of the contract (in the absence of *faute lourde*) and rendered dismissals infringing the right to strike 'void', now requiring reinstatement: Soc. October 10, 1990, *Sté Thermo Formage c. La Rocca*, Dr. Ouvr (1990), p. 495: Soc. *Cie. Lyonnaise des Goudrons c. André* Dr. Ouvr. (1990), p. 457; J.-E. Ray, '*La réintegration du salarié gréviste illégalement licencié*' Dr. Soc. 1991, 64; see G. Lyon-Caen and J. Pelissier, *Droit du Travail* (16th ed., 1992) pp. 802-805.
123. The phrase of Buckley LJ, *Secretary of State of Employment v ASLEF (No. 2)* [1972] ICR 19 at p. 62.
124. Ralph Gibson LJ in *Ticehurst v British Telecommunications Plc* [1992] IRLR 219 at pp. 224-225. She might have fared better had she intended to engage in the 'blunt and straightforward weapon' of a strike rather than action less than a strike: p. 227.
125. *Henthorn v Central Electricity Generating Board* [1980] IRLR 381 CA; *Bullen & Leake on Pleading* (3rd ed. 1868 now 13th ed. 1990) (eds. J. Jacob and I. Goldrein).
126. *Miles v Wakefield M.D.C.* [1987] AC 539 [1987] ICR 368 HL; J. McMullen, (1988) 51 MLR 234 at p. 239; and B. Napier [1987] CLJ, 44; *Wiluszynski v Tower Hamlets LB* [1989] IRLR 269 CA (council employees allowed back into the workplace but entitled to no wages by reason of minor breaches of contract).
127. [1987] ICR at p. 392: 'most of the 50-odd authorities cited in the course of this appeal were ancient and irrelevant'. Many were opposed to his reasoning. The celebrated match-girls' strike, supported by Annie Besant, took place in 1888 (S. & B. Webb, *History of Trade Unionism* (1920 ed.), p. 402) and methods of struggle more limited than the all-out strike, which seems to be referred to, were known in the early nineteenth century (*e.g.* S. & B. Webb on the 'strike in detail': *Industrial Democracy* (1914 ed.), pp. 171-172). Incomplete execution of work in industrial action was regularly the subject of prosecution (*e.g.* for 'neglect to fulfil the same ... [and] any other Misconduct or Misdemeanour in the execution thereof': Master and Servant Act 1823, see D. Simon, 'Master and Servant', J. Saville (ed.), *Democracy in the Labour Movement* (1954), pp. 161-173.
128. *R v St. John Devizes* (1829) 9 B. & C. 92 (an early form of *Kapovaz* or 'beck and call contract' still lawful in Britain but controlled in Germany, M. Weiss, *op.cit.* n. 76, p. 49); see M. Freedland, *The Contract of Employment* (1976), pp. 227-244; and on pleadings, M. Lobhan, *The Common Law and English Jurisprudence 1760-1850* (1991), pp. 171-174, 270-274.
129. See the discussion in E. Szyszczak, *Partial Unemployment* (1990), pp. 47-56, reporting on survey material. Contrast the unlawful conduct of an

employer who does not even go through the motions of notice and rehiring: *Rigby* v *Ferodo* [1988] ICR 29 HL.
130. *Turner* v *Mason* (1845) 14 M & W 112 at pp. 115-117: she did not even 'show the mother was likely to die that night', *per* Alderson B. See now on repudiation, *Laws* v *London Chronicle* [1959] 1 WLR 698 CA; *Pepper* v *Webb* [1969] 1 WLR 514 CA; *Wilson* v *Racher* [1974] ICR 428 CA; Baron Alderson cultivated common employment in *Hutchinson* v *York and Newcastle Rlwy* (1850) 5 Exch. 343 at p. 351.
131. See *Gorse* v *Durham C.C.* [1971] 1 WLR 112 at p. 117; on 'self-dismissal' S. Anderman, *Unfair Dismissal* (2nd ed. 1985), pp. 49-62; *Sovereign House Security* v *Savage* [1989] IRLR 115 CA.
132. *Priestley* v *Fowler* (1837) 3 M & W 1; see the telling account in P. Bartrip and A. Burman, *The Wounded Soldiers of Industry* (1983), pp. 103-106; also W. Cornish and G. de N. Clarke, *Law and Society in England 1750-1950* (1989), pp. 495-499; and Pollock on *Torts* (14th ed. 1939, ed. P. Landon), pp. 79-86.
133. *Vose* v *London and Yorkshire Ry. Co.* (1858) Exch. 249 at p. 252; the judges were pleased to find a similar doctrine in the common law of the United States: Shaw C.J. in *Farwell* v *Boston and Worcester RR. Corpn.* 4 Met. 49, 38 Am. Dec. 339 (Sup. Jud. Ct. Mass. 1842).
134. See Bartrip and Burman, *op.cit.* n. 132, pp. 106-110.
135. A.L. Goodhart, *Essays in Jurisprudence and the Common Law* (1937), p. 2.
136. *Bartonshill Coal Co.* v *Reid* (1858) 3 Macq. 265 HL; see Cornish and G. de N. Clarke, *op.cit.*, n. 132; pp. 498-499; Bartrip and Burman, *op.cit.*, n. 132, pp. 112-120 on the Scots resistance.
137. Law Reform (Personal Injuries) Act 1948, s. 1, in respect of personal injuries. The Employers Liability Act 1880 left the doctrine in being, though its effects were mitigated by various statues, *e.g.* the Workmen's Compensation Act 1897, though this did not cover agricultural workers and seamen: see P. Bartrip and S. Burman, *op.cit.*, n. 132, Chaps. 7 and 8; R. Howells, '*Priestley* v *Fowler* and the Factory Acts' (1963) 26 MLR 367.
138. As in *Wilsons & Clyde Coal Co* v *English* [1938] AC 57 HL.
139. See *Graham (Miller)* v *Glasgow Corpn.* [1947] AC 368 at p. 372 HL Sc.; *Lancaster* v *LIPB* [1948] 2 All E.R. 796 HL; *Bloor* v *Liverpool Derricking Co.* [1936] 3 All E.R. 399 CA (workman killed when working with director acting as foreman; held to be in common employment; 'an unfortunate rule of law, but nevertheless ... still part of the law': *per* Greer LJ at p. 402). On the similar early cases involving managers, see Bartrip and Burman, *op.cit.*, n. 132, pp. 118-124. On the tortuous lines of case law, see Batt on *Master and Servant* (4th ed. 1950), pp. 461-472. Mid-nineteenth century judges exhibited an extreme *laissez faire* policy: P. Atiyah, *The Rise and Fall of Freedom of Contract* (1979) pp. 124-125; but when later judges applied the doctrine of common employment with modifications instead of abolishing it, they felt they were acting – as within common law ideology, they were – as reasonable men.
140. Lord Devlin, *The Judge* (1979), p. 20.
141. Bramwell B. in *R* v *Druitt* (1867) 10 Cox 592, see D.N. Pritt, *Law Class and Society* (1970), p. 36.
142. *Quinn* v *Leathem* [1901] AC 495 HL.

143. *R* v *Mansfield JJ.*, *ex p. Sharkey* [1984] IRLR 496 at p. 502; see S. McCabe and P. Wallington, *The Police, Public Order and Civil Liberties: Legacies of the Miners' Strike* (1988), pp. 95-99, 144-146; on the predictably wide effect of the new law R. Simpson (1981) 44 MLR 189 at p. 196. Where the law is interpreted more liberally, it is for pickets who are acting in non-industrial disputes: *DPP* v *Fidler*, [1992] IWLR 91 (anti-abortion pickets), modifying a leading precedent, *Lyons* v *Wilkins* [1896] 1 Ch. 811, CA; [1899] 1 Ch. 255, CA, and reinterpreting s. 7 of the Conspiracy and Protection of Property Act 1875, now s. 241 of the Trade Union and Labour Relations (Consolidation) Act 1992. See the similar developments on contempt of court; S. Auerbach, 'Legal Restraint of Picketing' (1987) 16 ILJ 227 at pp. 239-244.

144. See H. Collins, 'Market Power, Bureaucratic Power and the Contract of Employment' (1986) 15 ILJ 1 at p. 14; compare his *Justice in Dismissal* (1992), especially Chap. 8.

145. See *Powell* v *Brent LB* [1988] ICR 176 CA; *Jones* v *Lee* [1980] ICR 310 CA: *Dietman* v *Brent LBC* [1987] IRLR 259 and [1988] IRLR 299 CA; *Lansing Linde* v *Kerr* [1991] IRLR 80 CA; *Hill* v *CA Parsons* [1972] Ch. 305 CA was a distortion of the law in favour of a non-unionist.

146. See *R* v *East Berks Health Authority, ex p. Walsh* [1984] IRLR 278 CA; *McLaren* v *Home Office* [1990] IRLR 338; *R* v *Derbyshire CC, ex p. Noble* [1990] IRLR 332; H. Carty, 'Aggrieved Public Sector Workers and Judicial Review' (1991) 54 MLR 129-136. See too now *R* v *Secretary of State for Trade and British Coal Corpn., ex p. Vardy* [1993] IRLR 104.

147. See *Jones* v *Gwent CC* [1992] IRLR 521 CA. On the need for continued trust and confidence: *Ali* v *Southwark LB* [1988] ICR 567; compare *Micklefield* v *SAC Technology Ltd.* [1990] 1 WLR 1002; A Phang (1991) 20 ILJ 214-219.

148. *Express Newspapers Ltd* v *McShane* [1980] ICR 42 at p. 61. The first of many Bills to change the law had already been introduced in 1979: Wedderburn (1980) 9 ILJ 65 at p. 93, n. 58.

149. H. Laski, *Trade Unions in the New Society* (1950), p. 126.

150. See D. Sugarman, 'Legal Theory, the Common Law Mind and the Making of the Textbook Tradition' in W. Twining (ed.), *Legal Theory and the Common Law* (1986) 26 at p. 36, and generally his discussion of the common law, at pp. 61 *et seq.*

151. *Priestley* v *Fowler* (1837) 3 M & W 1 at p. 6; see too Bramwell B. in *Degg* v *Midland Railway Co.* (1857) 1 H & N 773. The law in France reached a contrary conclusion, but not in Germany: see B. Hepple (ed.) *The Making of Labour Law in Europe* (1986), pp. 126-127.

152. *Lister* v *Romford Ice Co Ltd* [1957] AC 555 at p. 579. Of the 22 cases cited in the Law Lords' speeches, eight were reported before 1860.

153. *Ibid.* at p. 573, so described by M. Freedland, *The Contract of Employment* (1976), p. 201; compare *Harmer* v *Cornelius* (1858) 5 CB (ns) 236, which itself extended the right to dismiss for misconduct: *ibid.*, p. 200.

154. [1957] AC 55 at p. 594. The *Lister* decision made it doubly difficult to devise implied terms of greater equity for the employee: see *Scally* v *Southern Health and Social Services Board* [1991] IRLR 522 HL.

155. G. Treitel, *Law of Contract, op.cit.*, n. 109 at p. 192. See J. Stone, *Legal Systems and Lawyers' Reasonings* (1964), p. 307, citing R. Parsons, 'Individual Responsibility versus Personal Responsibility' (1956) 29 AIJ 714.
156. *Ryder* v *Mills* (1850) 3 Exch. 853; and for Parke B. see J. Ward, *The Factory Movement* (1962), p. 371.
157. *Atkinson* v *Newcastle Waterworks* (1877) 2 Ex.D. 125 appeared to throw doubt on earlier tests of strict duty (*e.g. Couch* v *Steel* (1854) 3 E. & B. 402). But in the early cases construction of the statute was crucial to determine whether the plaintiff came within the scope of it: *Coe* v *Platt* (1851) 6 Exch. 752. (1852) 7 Exch. 460, 923.
158. *Groves* v *Lord Wimborne* [1898] 2 QB 402.
159. On the 'construction test' today: *Lonrho* v *Shell Petroleum* (No. 2) [1982] AC 173 HL; on its effects: Winfield and Jolowicz on *Tort* (13th ed. by W. Rogers, 1989), pp. 198-201; 'You might as well toss a coin' *per* Lord Denning MR, *Ex p. Island Records* [1978] Ch. 122 at pp. 134-135 CA.
160. *Baddeley* v *Earl Granville* (1887) 19 QBD 402 at p. 405; *Smith* v *Baker* [1894] AC 325 HL.
161. See *Stephen* v *Cooper* [1929] AC 570 HL; Cornish and Clark, *op.cit.*, n. 132 at pp. 509-538, and see P. Bartrip and S. Burman, *op.cit.* n. 132 at pp. 190-206. For abolition of the doctrine and deduction of one half of benefit, see Law Reform (Personal Injuries) Act 1948, s. 2. Common lawyers have tended to regard the deductions of social security benefits (but not other benefits) as defensible: see Salmond and Heuston on *Torts* (20th ed., eds. R. Heuston and R. Buckley, 1992), pp. 549-550. They are likely to approve the full deduction prescribed under the Social Security Act 1989, s. 22 and Sched. 4 (most State benefits are covered and the scheme bites on damages over £2,500).
162. See B. Hepple, 'Restructuring Employment Rights' (1986) 15 ILJ 69 at pp. 71-75.
163. See Clark and Wedderburn, 'A Crisis in Fundamental Concepts' in Wedderburn, R. Lewis and J. Clark (eds.). *Labour Law and Industrial Relations* (1983), pp. 144-155; Wedderburn, *The Worker and the Law* (1986), pp. 110-147.
164. B. Hepple, 'The Rise and Fall of Unfair Dismissal' in W. McCarthy (ed.), *Legal Interventions in Industrial Relations* (1992) 79 at p. 92. See too S. Anderman, *Unfair Dismissal* (2nd ed., 1985), Chap. 3; P. Davies and M. Freedland, *Labour Law: Text and Materials* (2nd ed., 1984), pp. 445-458; on compensation see especially H. Collins (1991) 20 ILJ 201-208.
165. See Wedderburn (1987) 16 ILJ 1 at pp. 11-13 on the decisions in the *Perrier* judgments, Soc. June 21, 1974, Dr. Soc. 1974 454, 593; and *Code Civil* Art. 1184. The use of *résiliation* for employment contracts had a long pedigree; Williston and Thompson, *Contracts* (1935), Vol. 3, pp. 2545-2546, citing Cour de Paris, February 1, 1873.
166. G. Lyon-Caen and J. Pellisier, *Droit du Travail, op.cit.*, n. 16 at pp. 616-617.
167. In 1990-1991, of 2,530 successful claimants against unfair dismissal, 63 secured orders for re-employment; the median compensation awarded was £1,773: *Employment Gazette* 1991, p. 681; see too L. Dickens, M.

Jones, B. Weekes, M. Hart, *Dismissed* (1985), Chap. 5; H. Carty, 'Dismissed Employees: The Search for a More Effective Ranage of Remedies' (1989) 52 MLR 449-468.
168. See especially *Polkey* v *AE Dayton Services Ltd* [1988] AC 344 HL. An employer who failed to consult the employee about his redundancy and had him frog-marched off the premises, saying the employees did not want to be consulted, was guilty of an unfair dismissal, but only after the EAT allowed an appeal from the tribunal: *Ferguson* v *Prestwick Circuits* [1992] IRLR 266 EAT (Scot.).
169. Employment Protection (Consolidation) Act 1978, s. 57(3).
170. See the tests emerging in *Iceland Frozen Foods Ltd* v *Jones* [1983] ICR 17; *British Leyland UK Ltd* v *Swift* [1981] IRLR 439. For the best analysis of the formative period: H. Collins, 'Capitalist Discipline and Corporate Law' (1982) 11 ILJ 78 at p. 170; and later (1986) 15 ILJ 1; on *Matthewson* v *RB Wilson Dental Laboratory* [1988] IRLR 512, in (1990) 19 ILJ 39; and on 'job security' (1991) 20 ILJ 127-139.
171. See *Hollister* v *National Farmers' Union* [1979] ICR 542 CA; *St John of God Ltd* v *Brookes* [1992] IRLR 546.
172. *Saunders* v *Scottish National Camps Assoc.* [1980] IRLR 277 Ct. of S.
173. Hepple, 'The Rise and Fall of Unfair Dismissal', *op.cit.*, n. 164 at p. 85, who also suggests that collective bargaining had been marginalised in the processes of dismissal. On the right to transfer the business, see now *Newnes* v *British Airways* [1992] IRLR 575 CA.
174. M. Freedland, 'Individual Contracts of Employment and the Common Law Courts' (1992) 21 ILJ 135 at p. 136. The Swedish employer is obliged to go much further in finding alternative work and training the employee for it: F. Schmidt and A. Victorin in S. Strömholm (ed.), *An Introduction to Swedish Law* (2nd ed. 1988), p. 339, on the Swedish Employment Protection Act 1982.
175. F. Raday, 'Individual and Collective Dismissal' (1989) 10 Comp. Lab. LJ 121-165; A. Dose-Digenopoulos and A. Höland, 'Dismissal of Employees in the Federal Republic of Germany' (1985) 48 MLR 539; Wedderburn, 'The Italian Workers Statute' (1990) 19 ILJ 154-180; B. Hepple, *op.cit.*, n. 164 in McCarthy (ed.), *Legal Intervention in Industrial Relations* (1992), at pp. 79, 83-86.
176. There is a distinction between 'reinstatement' which treats the worker as if he had not been dismissed and 're-engagement' which means he will have employment 'comparable' to that from which he was dismissed: Employment Protection (Consolidation) Act 1978, s. 69. The word 're-employment' is used here to include both.
177. See Employment Protection (Consolidation) Act1978, ss. 73, 74 and 75A; 'Remedies for Unfair Dismissal' (1992) 445 IRLIB 2-9.
178. *Cold Drawn Tubes Ltd* v *Middleton* [1992] ICR 316.
179. *Port of London Authority* v *Payne* [1992] IRLR 447. The tribunal hearing lasted 197 days. The EAT felt the employer must not be 'ambushed' at a later stage by 'practicability': that could 'only lead to exacerbation of industrial relations' at p. 464. One has to remind oneself that this was a case where the employers had dismissed workers on grounds automatically unfair. See too, *Rao* v *Civil Aviation Authority* [1992] ICR

503. [On appeal the CA reached substantially the same result favouring the employer's commercial interests by different reasoning: [1994] ICR 555 CA.]

180. Wood, J., *ibid.* [1992] IRLR 466.

181. The Cour de Cassation so concluded recently on the laws of october 28, 1982, and July 25, 1985 (Cour du Travail Arts. L 4521-1 and L 122-45): Soc. October 10, 1990, *Sté Thermo Formage Mediterranéen c. La Rocca*, Dr. Ouvr, 1990 495; Soc. September 26, 1990, *Cie. Lyonnaise des Goudrons et des Bitumes c. André*; also Soc. April 10, 1991, see J.-E. Ray, '*Les pouvoirs de l'employeur à l'occasion de la grève: 1988-1991*' Dr. Soc. 1991, 768 at p. 772. In ordinary dismissal cases reinstatement is not obligatory, but where fundamental rights are infringed the worker can secure reinstatement: *l'affaire Clavaud*, April 28, 1988, J-M. Verdier D. Chron. 1988 (public criticisms of employer, right of free speech). See too, H. Sinay, '*La Réintegration dans l'Entreprise*' in *Les Transformations du Droit du Travail: Études offertes à Gérard Lyon-Caen* (1989), pp. 415-450. On workers' representatives, see above, notes 165, 166.

182. J. Rivero and J. Savatier, *Droit du Travail* (10th ed., 1987), p. 26; so too in Italy, M. Rusciano *Universalità* v *specialitá degli statuti giuridici del lavoro dipendente* (1992) Lav. e Dir. 418 at p. 432. On the protective functions of employment rights in the Italian Constitution 1948: G. Ghera, *Diritto del lavoro* (1989), pp. 17-19.

183. M. Weiss, *Labour Law and Industrial Relations in the Federal Republic of Germany* (1987), pp. 46-48. The Protection of Employment Act 1985 has relaxed some of the limitations surrounding 'atypical' employment of this kind.

184. P. Calamandrei, 'Il significato costituzionale del diritto di sciopero' (1952) Riv. giur. lav, I, 221.

185. See the cases described by A. Jacobs in B. Hepple (ed.), *The Making of Labour Law in Europe* (1986) pp. 212-213; T. Ramm in B. Aaron and K. Wedderburn, *Industrial Conflict: A Comparative Legal Survey* (1972), p. 264, on the German Supreme Court reasoning similar to that in *Lyons* v *Wilkins* [1896] 1 Ch. 811 CA; [1899] 1 Ch. 255 CA.

186. See Wedderburn, *Employment Rights in Britain and Europe* (1991), Chap. 3 (also (1991) 54 MLR 1 at pp. 2-10).

187. O. Kahn-Freund, 'Blackstone's Neglected Child: The Contract of Employment' (1977) 93 LQR 508-528; and J. Cairns, 'Blackstone, Kahn-Freund and the Contract of Employment', (1989) 105 LQR 300-314.

188. Doyen Ripert, *Aspects juridiques du capitalisme moderne* (1946), p. 206, cited by G. Lyon-Caen and J. Pelissier, *Droit du Travail op.cit.*, n. 16 at p. 339. On *pouvoirs de direction* see pp. 339-351, and *sanctions disciplinaires*, pp. 356-366.

189. P. Durand, *Traité de droit du travail* (1947) at pp. 422 *et seq.*: the courts moved to an institutional base in 1945: Soc. June 16, 1945. See too, on disciplinary powers, N. Catala, *L'Entreprise* (1980), pp. 361-373.

190. Now *Code du Travail*, Arts. L.122-42 (obligatory procedures), L 122-42 (ban on pecuniary sanctions imposed by employer).

191. See, J-M. Béraud, 'La discipline dans l'entreprise' in *Transformations du*

droit du travail: Études Offertes à Gérard Lyon-Caen (1989), pp. 381-393.
192. M. Despax, *L'entreprise et le droit* (1957) at pp. 383 *et seq;* above p. 91.
193. See R. Lewis and J. Clark (eds.), *O. Kahn-Freund; Labour Law and Politics in the Weimar Republic* (1981), pp. 82-88; M. Weiss, *op.cit.*, n. 183, at pp. 87-89, 149-169.
194. See G. Ghezzi and U. Romagnoli, *Il rapporto di lavoro* (2nd ed., 1987), pp. 196-200; Art. 7 of the 1970 Workers' Statute introduced compulsory procedures for the exercise of discipline in place of earlier powers now thought to be 'incompatible with the principle of equality between the parties to a contract'; p. 199.
195. F. Carinci, R. De Luca Tamajo, P. Tosi, T. Treu, *Il rapporto del lavoro* (2nd ed., 1990), pp. 200-201, and on disciplinary powers, 213-221. For an extended treatment, see A. Petrulli, *Il potere direttivo dell'imprenditore* (1992), esp. pp. 71-92 and Chap. III *Limiti del potere direttivo.*
196. See R. Bortone in G. Giugni, *Lo Statuto dei lavoratori: Commentario* (1979), pp. 58-87.
197. On the importance of social continuity and on labour law in the totalitarian periods in Germany, Italy and France, see the valuable discussion by T. Ramm in B. Hepple (ed.), *The Making of Labour Law in Europe* (1986), pp. 289-298; for an example of the *livret*, see *ibid.* Appendix IV.
198. Conspiracy and Protection of Property Act 1875, s. 5 (now Trade Union and Labour Relations (Consolidation) Act 1992, s. 240) has been scarcely, if ever used (crime of breach of employment contract, alone or in combination, with the probable consequence of endangering human life, causing bodily injury or exposing property to serious injury).
199. Employers and Workmen Act 1875, ss. 3, 4-7 (in part repealed by the Industrial Relations Act 1971, Sched. 9; the rest of the Act repealed by the Statute Law Revision Act 1973). In the special civil jurisdiction it was not necessary to plead a cause of action or even specify the legal nature of a claim, in 'disputes' between employer and 'workman': *Ketes* v *Lewis Merthyr Consolidated Collieries* [1911] AC 641; *Clemson* v *Hubbard* (1876) 1 Ex. D. 179. Nor did normal periods of limitation run in a magistrates court when deemed to be a civil court: *Charles* v *Mortgagees of Plymouth Works* (1890) 60 LJMC 20.
200. See the authoritative study by D. Simon, Chap. 6 in J. Saville (ed.), *Democracy and the Labour Movement* (1954), pp. 161, 186. On other statutes used in the prosecutions of the period, such as the Unlawful Oaths Act 1797, Unlawful Societies Act and Seditious Meetings Act 1817, see J. Orth, *Combinations and Conspiracies* (1991), pp. 110-117.
201. See S. and B. Webb, *History of Trade Unionism,* (1920), pp. 250-251, nn. 1,2; *Unwin* v *Clark* (1866) LR 1 QB 417; and *Hawley* v *Baker* (1857) reported in Trygve Tholfsen, *Working Class Radicalism in Mid-Victorian England* (1976), p. 182. The Exchequer judges appeared to hold a rather less draconian view.
202. See R. Hedges and A. Winterbottom, *The Legal History of Trade Unionism* (1930), Chap. I; W. Cornish and G. De N. Clark, *op.cit.*, n. 132, Chap. 4, Part 1; B. Veneziani in B. Hepple (ed.), *The Making of Labour Law in Europe* (1986) pp. 43-45, 60-64. It has been suggested that where

master and servant laws were used in a rather less general manner, as in Australia, unions were led more easily to accept compulsory arbitration: E. Phelps Brown, *The Origins of Trade Union Power* (1983), pp. 271-273.

203. D. Simon, *op.cit.*, n. 200 at pp. 161-166; T. Tholfsen, *op.cit.*, n.201 at pp. 184 *et seq.*

204. *Spain* v *Arnott* (1817) 2 Stark. 256 at p. 258; compare *R* v *St John Devizes* (1829) 9 B. & C. 896, Bayley, J. quoting Parke J. as saying: '... a contract to obey the orders of the master, which is a term implied in every contract of hiring'. The order must be within the scope of the employment: *Price* v *Mouat* (1862) 11 CB (NS) 508; this became the duty to obey reasonable lawful orders, 'lodging managerial prerogative firmly in the centre of the structure of the contract of employment': P. Davies and M. Freedland, *Labour Law: Text and Materials* (2nd ed., 1984), p. 311.

205. A. Fox, *Beyond Contract: Work, Power and Trust Relations* (1974), pp. 184-190, especially at p. 187. The 'prerogative contract' gave masters in the era of factory employment a new 'sovereign powert': P. Selznick, *Law, Society and Industrial Justice* (1969), p. 136.

206. S. Deakin, 'Logical Deductions? Wage Protections Before and After *Delaney* v *Staples*' ([1992] 2 WLR 451 HL)' (1992) 55 MLR 848 at pp. 850-852, 857.

207. *Ibid.* at p. 852 on *Miles* v *Wakefield MDC* [1987] AC 539 HL, see above, pp. 98-99.

208. E. Jenks, *Short History of English Law* (1928), p. 337.

209. See G. Fridman, *The Modern Law of Employment* (1962), pp. 447-451, and M. Freedland, *The Contract of Employment* (1976), pp. 197-200, who commented: 'There is apart from this extremely little guidance as to the managerial prerogative which is (in theory) enforceable by summary dismissal.'

210. Amending s. 4 of the Combination Act 1825; J. Orth, *Combination and Conspiracy* (1991), pp. 119-128. On *Lumley* v *Gye* (1853) 2 E. & B. 216 and the modern law, see Clerk and Lindsell on *Torts* (16th ed. 1989), Chap. 15.

211. See Lord Loreburn, Parl. Deb. HL, Vol 167 col. 295; Sir Charles Dilke's amendment to the Trade Disputes Bill, 1906, Parl. Deb. HC Vol. 162 col. 1678; on the concentration upon employment contracts, see *Report of Royal Commission* ('Donovan Report' Cmnd. 3623, 1968) para. 887. On the 1906 Bills: Wedderburn (1980) 9 ILJ 75-81; R. Kidner (1982) 2 *Legal Studies* 46-52.

212. W. Holdsworth, *History of English Law* (3rd ed., 1945) Vol. IV, p. 384. Coleridge J. dissented in *Lumley* v *Gye* (1853) 2 E. & B. at pp. 759-769, wishing to confine the action to relationships under the Statute of Labourers, 1351; the view of the majority rested upon several different principles, *viz*, intentional enticing of a person not to serve in breach of a contract, p. 753; maliciously procuring a breach of a contract, p. 759; actionable conspiracy, pp. 754-755; and a violation of a right (intentionally or maliciously) by an actionable wrong, pp. 755-756.

213. Lord Denning MR in *Torquay Hotel Co Ltd* v *Cousins* [1969] 2 Ch. 106 at pp. 136-139; see also Hoffmann J. in *Law Debenture Corpn* v *Ural Caspian Ltd.* [1993] 1 WLR 138 at pp. 149-152. On the latest legislative proposals. Trade Union Reform and Employment Rights Bill 1993 [now

the TURER Act 1992].

214. Sweden: Folke Schmidt, *Law and Industrial Relations in Sweden* (1977), pp. 185-186; on justification in the Commonwealth, *Petes Towing Services Ltd* v *Northern Industrial Union* [1970] NZLR 32; *Thermo King Corpn* v *Provincial Bank of Canada* (1982) 30 DLR (3rd) 256 at p. 271.

215. *South Wales Miners' Fedn.* v *Glamorgam Coal Co* [1905] AC 239 at p. 247; P. Cane, *Tort Law and Economic Interests* (1991), Chap. 3.

216. Lord Denning MR in *Morgan* v *Fry* [1968] 2 QB 710 at pp. 727-728; it may be that Davies LJ was reaching for a limited form of the same principle, see p. 731. On the problems which would still need to be overcome: Wedderburn, *The Worker and the Law*, op.cit. n. 32 at pp. 191-193.

217. Wedderburn, 'Laws about Strikes' in W. McCarthy (ed.), *Legal Intervention in Industrial Relations* (1992), pp. 148-171, and *Employment Laws in Britain and Europe*, op.cit., n. 12 at pp. 276-334.

218. On wage fixing see W. Cornish and G. De N. Clark, op.cit., n. 132 at pp. 290-295, and on the Poor laws, pp. 425-435. See also, W. Holdsworth, op.cit., n. 212, Vol. IV at pp. 144-147, 381-387.

219. G. Elton, *England Under the Tudors* (2nd ed., 1974), p. 188; and see pp. 259-60 on the Elizabethan poor laws.

220. D. Simon in *Democracy and the Labour Movement*, op.cit., n. 200 at pp. 195-196; T. Tholfsen, *Working Class Radicalism in Mid-Victorian England*, op.cit.. n. 201 at pp. 189-196.

221. J. Fulbrook, *Administrative Justice and the Unemployed* (1978), p. 83, and the valuable Chaps. 5, 6 and 7; see too the description in P. Ashcroft, *The English Poor Law System* (1888, from the German), pp. 283-284.

222. The concept was particularly attractive to the judiciary: see *Att.-Gen.* v *Guardians of the Poor of the Merthyr Tydfil Union* [1900] 1 Ch. 516.

223. See now s. 28(1)(a) and s. 57(1) of the Social Security Contributions and Benefits Act 1992, the latter, redolent of the Poor Laws, having been introduced by s. 10 of the Social Security Act 1989. [On future legislation for 1995, see *The Job-Seekers' Allowance* (Cm. 2687, 1994). The 'job-seekers' agreement" 'will enable their activities to be monitored effectively' (para. 4.16), and they may be 'directed' to take steps to 'present themselves acceptably to employers' (para. 4.18)].

3

THE LEGAL FRAMEWORK OF INDUSTRIAL RELATIONS AND THE ACT OF 1971*

A revolutionary change is being attempted in British labour law by means of the Industrial Relations Act 1971. Among the more patently indefensible comments made about this statute is the frequently heard judgment that it introduces a 'legal framework' for the *first time* into industrial relations. Of an equally fallacious character is the analysis that the Act flows naturally from the recent introduction in the 1960s of 'more law' into labour relations, as though 'law' were a fluid commodity which, once it had breached the dykes around a social problem, would by force of nature flow in, until the area were saturated. This notion appeared both in *Fair Deal at Work* and in *In Place of Strife*, but not – be it noted – in the *Report* of the 'Donovan' Royal Commission. The mistake in both fallacies is, of course, to ignore the different types of law which can form part of a labour law 'framework' in a social system. Law is not monotypic. In order, therefore, to measure accurately the nature of current changes in labour law it is necessary to inquire carefully into the character of the legal framework which it attempts to replace. This inquiry is made the more important when the Government in its Consultative Document of 5 October 1970 described the Act as 'the main instrument in achieving its objectives' of reforming industrial relations.

In truth there developed after 1871 a clearly enunciated legal framework for British industrial relations, a structure so intimately related to the surrounding social institutions engaged in bargaining and conflict that 'framework' suggests too remote a character for laws that grew as threads inherent in the social web. Whatever else, there was

*First published in 1972 in *British Journal of Industrial Relations* Vol. 10; the Second Shirley Lerner Memorial Lecture given in Manchester, January 1972.

plenty of 'labour law'. We may distinguish two parts of it, of which the second part falls into two convenient sub-categories.

THE FLOOR OF EMPLOYMENT RIGHTS

First, comes the law concerned with the employment relationship without reference to collective organization by workpeople. The individual contract of employment is here the fundamental legal institution – as it is in most Western European systems of law, as it will still be in Britain after 1971 (especially in view of the reliance placed upon it for certain critical new definitions such as 'irregular industrial action short of a strike')[1] – but as it is *not* in the United States, which has seen 'the virtual disappearance of individual contracts of employment'.[2] Gradually, to the old fashioned law of contract came the accretion of a series of statutory obligations, from the duty to pay manual workers in cash, in the Truck Acts from 1831 onwards, to the duty to give employees written particulars of their employment or varying minimum periods of notice in the Contracts of Employment Act 1963.

Alongside these statutes grew others, which in foreign legal systems, such as the French, would be analysed as adding obligations to the individual employment relationship or even the employment contract, but which in our system were introduced as imposing extraneous statutory obligations. For example, we have the Factories Acts from 1833 onwards, and today all the myriad regulations which govern health, welfare and (in aspiration at least) safety at various places of work (which, it is to be hoped, will be assisted by the forthcoming Report of the Robens Committee to become a coherent and unified body of law). The Redundancy Payments Act, 1965, and the new right about to be given by the 1971 Act to employees to challenge 'unfair' dismissals are merely recent additions to this vast body of labour law establishing *a floor of statutory rights and duties* to employment, whether there is any collective bargaining or not.

These objectives *might*, of course, have been reached by collective agreements (just as, in the absence of a National Health Service, American workers sought cover against sickness by bargaining for medical insurance); but the pattern of dealing with welfare at work and social security by legislation was well established in Britain before 1918, the beginning of the modern era of labour relations. While legislation was – and is – acceptable to regulate employment conditions of workers in need of special protection (in dangerous trades, or where women workers are involved – even to obtain equal pay and treatment in the Act of 1970) the laws and pay of adult male workers became (after the watershed of the Railway Servants (Hours of Labour) Act 1893 – marcescent as soon as it was enacted) a matter for collective bargaining.

Nor was this a choice made for theoretical reasons by the trade unions. The Objects of the TUC still include: 'A legal maximum working week of 40 hours. A legal minimum wage for each industry or occupation' (Rule 2). Expediency not theory drew the boundaries of what we have come to regard as the ground natural to employment legislation. After the failure of the National Joint Advisory Council Report on *Dismissal Procedures* (1967) to make the case for 'voluntary methods', an extension of the statutory *floor of rights* to include challenging unjust dismissal was inevitable (though the narrow ambit and inadequate remedies of the 1971 Act[3] were not among the necessary consequences). Curiously enough, where the conventional boundary was exceeded, a statute might even be ignored, as has been the case of the Shop Clubs Act, 1902. Under this, 'thrift funds', including certain pension schemes, in thousands of firms ought to be certified after approval by a three-quarters majority of the workpeople affected; but the statute is largely ignored [it was repealed in 1986].

COLLECTIVE 'NON-INTERVENTION'

Secondly comes the law concerned with *collective* labour relations, the area in which until 1971 the traditional theme was 'non-intervention'. Once again, however, there was no absence of a legal framework; the law was that which had grown organically within the interstices of the voluntary collective bargaining system. If we may put aside the aberrations of war-time law (from 1917 to 1919 and 1940 to 1951, the year which is, for labour law, the 'end' of the Second World War with the final disappearance of the illegality of strikes under Order 1305) and the unused provisions of the Trade Union Act 1927 repealed in 1946, the skeleton of the traditional law falls clearly into two segments.

(*a*) The negative protections of the statutes relating to trade unions and trade disputes in 1871, 1875 and 1906.[4] Just as the factory legislation in the first category was the bequest of those factory reform movements from Chartists to Tory philanthropists, so these Acts were the result of historical factors peculiar to Britain of which the effects are still felt.

The *problem* was not peculiarly British – namely the doubtful legality of the civil status of unions and the criminal or civil illegality of industrial action: such problems arose at comparable periods of development in the United States, France, Germany, Sweden and elsewhere. But the emergence between 1850 and 1900 of, first, the New Model Unions and, then, the great general unions, and the extension of the franchise in 1867 and 1884 long before the birth of a political wing to the labour movement – all this meant that the bourgeois political parties found themselves responding to political demands from an increasingly strengthened and enfranchised but organizationally industrial working class movement. Despite the involvement of leading individuals (Applegarth and others in 'The Junta' of 1867-71 participated actively for a short period in the 'International Association of Working Men') the movement itself never espoused the ideological programme common among European movements where political organization matched or ante-dated the industrial.

Aided by cautious lawyers and pragmatic Positivists the British movement demanded, and to some extent obtained, not positive rights to organize and strike but a removal of legal doctrines which would otherwise continually impede such activity – that of restraint of trade (1871) and, in 'trade disputes', criminal or civil conspiracy (1875 and 1906), and the tort of inducing breach of employment contracts (1906). Such laws introduced a 'liberty' of, rather than a 'right' to, industrial organization and industrial action. They are still with us even today in sections 132 and 135 of the Industrial Relations Act 1971.

But such statutory protections which are in fact the minimum basis of *social* rights to organize and act collectively have the *legal* form of 'privileges' – an 'exemption' from doctrines of 'restraint of trade' and conspiracy. This false way of regarding such liberties as 'privileges' is a mystification introduced by lawyers; and one central attitude of the new 1971 Act can be traced back directly to the Conservative Lawyers' doctrinal booklet of 1958, *A Giant's Strength*, which said: 'we would like to see these substantial privileges ... given only to registered unions' (p.23).

(*b*) The same industrial movement had by the beginning of the twentieth century tasted recognition for bargaining of the modern flavour and had allied itself to other opponents of the many nineteenth century attempts to legislate for compulsory conciliation of disputes.

The most that occurred *before* 1914 was what Lord Amulree described as the creation of 'public opinion' (by which he meant middle-class opinion) 'favourable to arbitration and conciliation' – expressed in the 1896 statute. After 1918, out of war-time machinery and the Whitley Committee Reports and following the short one-year period of Compulsory Arbitration,[5] there evolved the Industrial Arbitration Court and other institutions of *voluntary* arbitration and conciliation such as Joint Industrial Councils, in which many trade unions at first joined in the 1920s in order to prevent serious reductions of wages after the First World War.[6] Even if both parties consented, the Minister could not refer a dispute to the old Industrial Court for arbitration until the parties' own 'arrangements for settlement by conciliation or arbitration' were exhausted.[7] British law slotted naturally into the emerging dominance in industrial practice of 'procedures' – procedures which paid scant attention to the lawyers'

> distinction between conflicts of interests and conflicts of right, which is fundamental in European labour law ... the main thing is to find an acceptable and if possible a durable compromise by means of direct negotiation ...[8]

Indeed, one may seriously doubt whether labour law systems which purport to be based on any such distinction really operate according to their tenor[9] and it is interesting to note that the 1971 British Act does not try unrealistically to compel the introduction of such distinctions into our industrial practice.

This tradition came to be rationalized by commentators, trade unionists and managers alike, as the 'non-intervention' framework in *collective* labour relations – or 'abstention of the law' as Professor Kahn-Freund has described it – where the law provided machinery for voluntary settlements and 'held the ring' by way of negative statutory protections that gave the collective parties 'liberties' of action but few positive 'rights'.

As such it could be made to sound very old-fashioned: how absurd that the law should not impose a general duty on employers to recognize their workers' trade union! But such critics often fail to observe that even the 1971 British Act has not enacted any such enforceable duty to bargain in the North American style.[10] Recognition won by strength rather than law is a principle to be neither despised nor lightly displaced.

Nor did the traditional English law try to set up compulsory routes though which disputes had to be channelled, as opposed to such foreign systems as the French where the minutely discriminated legal obligations for processing collective disputes through 'la conciliation', 'la médiation' and 'l'arbitrage' had been overtaken in practice by

English-style 'procedures souples' between the parties long before the events of 1968 showed their irrelevance.[11]

So too, until 1971 the English law was envied by many whose legal systems tried to provide compulsory procedures or prohibitions for industrial conflict that gave rise to an 'emergency'. After a long debate in the 1930s the Swedes gave up the search for a statutory definition of strikes seriously endangering the public interest (though the matter came to be dealt with voluntarily in the collective agreements of 1966 when municipal and State employees first obtained a legal right to strike). Similarly, in the United States debate about the Taft Hartley Act, Title II, providing for 80-day 'cooling off' injunctions against strikes in emergency situations, two points command general agreement: (i) The definition of 'emergency' is as much a political decision as anything else; and (ii) If such a law is to be useful, the Executive should have a choice not of one remedy (the injunction) but an 'arsenal of weapons' to be used to get the parties to a dispute back within talking distance.[12]

Comparative scholars have noted with hollow laughter that Part VIII of the British Industrial Relations Act 1971 defines 'emergency' so widely as to include almost any major piece of industrial action but then provides the Minister not with an arsenal of weapons but with the rusty old flintlock of a 60-day 'cooling-off' injunction. As a former Director of the Federal Mediation and Conciliation Service has said of the US 80-day period, the last half of it is usually a 'heating up' period.[13]

The importation of foreign labour law without due regard to the lessons learned in its mother country is a remarkable event. Partly it may be said to be just an example of adherence to the Party policies in *Fair Deal at Work* announced long before the Donovan Report declared 'we do not think that the introduction of [such laws] ... would be beneficial' (para. 425). But it is more than that. It is a response to the demand of a constituency, namely middle-class opinion, that 'something must be done about it' – 'it' being here strikes that endanger the 'national interest' or 'the community' (as defined by middle class opinion).

The Government which introduced Part VIII was sophisticated enough to know that its provisions were unlikely to be of use to promote the golden, if verbose, principles of section 1 of the 1971 Act. But Part VIII would at least make it look as if 'something' had been done. And if it be questioned whether 'middle-class opinion' was truly the constituency of which regard was being taken, may it not be a partial answer that the Act, this comprehensive new code to set right industrial ills, included no 'emergency powers' to deal with mass lay-offs, plant-closures or dismissals by which unemployment of a scale amounting to a national emergency has already been created?

The Basis of Judicial Non-Intervention

The 1971 Act, in fact, carries here within it the hint of a lesson which needs to be stated in relation to the traditional law of collective 'non-intervention' which it replaces. That traditional framework of British labour law really rested upon a middle-class acquiescence in the current balance of industrial power. That framework was already under severe attack before 1971 because middle-class opinion – and especially its upper segment of nine per cent which owns well over half the personal wealth in Great Britain[14] – no longer acquiesced in the 1950s in the new muscles which trade unions had, but rarely efficiently flexed, in days of full employment.

The early days of the judicial policy of non-intervention in the 1920s coincided with an era of self-aware reflection by the judiciary itself. In the year when the High Court first accepted the legitimacy of the trade union objective of a 'closed shop',[15] a conservative-minded Lord Justice could declare:

> Labour says: 'Where are your impartial Judges? They all move in the same circle as the employers and are all educated and nursed in the same ideas as the employers. How can a labour man or a trade unionist get impartial justice?' It is very difficult sometimes to be sure that you have put yourself into a thoroughly impartial position between two disputants, one of your own class and one not of your class.[16]

This era of judicial reflection upon the hostile policies of courts to trade unions in the earlier years of the century coincided with the defeat of the unions in 1926. That served only to strengthen the determination of most of the judges not to 'develop' the common law – that is, create new law – so as to destroy the so-called 'privileges' of the Trade Disputes Act 1906 for those acting in furtherance of trade disputes.

The resolutions of the 'Industrial Conference' between the TUC General Council and the 'Mond' Group of Employers on 4 July 1928[17] ushered in a decade in which trade unions both were weak and had – not unnaturally – turned their back on the old militancy in favour of joint consultation. The so-called 'Mond-Turner' discussions were far more significant than the vindictive little Trade Union Act 1927, which was never used until its repeal in 1946. The TUC General Council Report on those discussions, in the hour of defeat, rejected the policies of trying 'to bring the industrial machine to a standstill' or of 'standing aside and telling employers to get on with their own job while the unions would pursue the policy of fighting sectionally for improvements', in favour of the only practicable third course for the Movement, as the TUC saw it:

> ... to say boldly that not only is it concerned with the prosperity of industry but that it is going to have a voice as to the way industry is carried on.... The ultimate policy of the movement can find more use for an efficient industry than for a derelict one ...[18]

Although the unions grew in strength during the 1930s, there was little in their effective policies which caused middle-class opinion to fear that the decisive balance of power at the workplace was being changed.

> The degree of acceptance now accorded to British trade unionism as a whole ... and the cautious policies adopted on both sides of the bargaining table, are clearly indicated in the statistics of industrial disputes in the period.[19]

Between 1934 and 1939, working days idle in disputes only once exceeded an annual two million, whereas between 1919 and 1926 they had never fallen below seven million. The comparison illustrates both the good ground for that middle class belief as well as the slow, careful and collaborative policies of the TUC leadership which was probably its only choice other than stark defeat in another General Strike.

It was on that social balance of power that judicial 'non-intervention' was finally established. Then, in the 1940s, all the pressures of a desperate war caused both sides to be unwilling – or not often willing – to upset that balance. It is not fortuitous that the high point of judicial non-intervention occurred in 1941 when the House of Lords finally extended to unions and labour relations the same rules as those applied to capital and trade competition under the doctrines of civil conspiracy (something it refused to do in 1901). Where the 'predominant object' of union officials was to 'benefit their trade union members by preventing undercutting and unregistered competition.... The result they aimed at achieving was to create a better basis for collective bargaining', said Lord Simon, and that could not be unlawful as a conspiracy. Lord Wright agreed and went so far as to say that English law:

> has for better or worse adopted the test of self-interest or selfishness as being capable of justifying the deliberate doing of lawful acts which inflict harm.... The right of workmen to strike is an essential element in the principle of collective bargaining.... It is true that employers and workmen are often at variance because the special interest of each side conflicts in the material respect, as for instance in questions of wages, conditions of hours of work, exclusion of non-union labour; but, apart from these differences in interest, both employers and workmen have a common interest in the prosperity of their industry, though the interest of one side may be in profits and the other in wages. Hence a wider and truer view is that there is a community of interest.[20]

This 'community of interest' clearly does exist; but it was upon that concept as made concrete in a particular social structure, one acceptable to prevalent and articulate 'public opinion', that judicial non-intervention was based.

But the 1950s saw the emergence of a new power, one that full employment gave to the trade unions. Then middle-class opinion changed. The social bottom was knocked out of the judges' attitudes of 'non-intervention'. It is no accident that the newspapers of the 1950s presented so regularly a harsher image of trade unions – the cart horse was turned into Goliath who held sway over members by intimidation and (later) 'noose trials' that were found on due inquiry to be as objectionable and unseemly as a public school 'de-bagging' ceremony. (Alternatively, sometimes 'militants' were found to be forcing decent union leaders into indecent wage demands – for consistency is the logic only of the small mind.)

With a characteristic flash of insight, Harold Laski sensed in his lectures of 1949 not only the impending change of opinion but foresaw also – by glancing across the Atlantic – precisely the consequential legal development which is at the centre of the Industrial Relations Act 1971 and to which I refer at length below. He said:

The Taft Hartley Act was passed to protect the freedom of the American workingman; and the leader of the Conservative party in Great Britain has promised that if the Labour government is defeated at the next general election he will free the British workingman. If you inquire from what fetters he is to be released, the answer is that it is from the obligations he assumes as a trade-union member.[21]

The conflation of the image of the trade union Goliath with the new theme of small groups of 'militants', made vivid in press and on television, gave rise by the 1960s to the now widespread doctrine that the 'new shop floor power' is essentially different from the earlier 'responsible' trade unionism. The latter resulted – it is said – from 'heroic sacrifices ... for a better share of the wealth'; the former stems from 'the disruptive power of determined groups organised at particularly sensitive points' in advanced modern societies 'assisted by the writings and urgings of theorists of the extreme left wing spectrum', with the 'possible infiltration ... of men for whom industrial negotiation may have a second purpose of political opportunism of an indeterminate nature', with the newly powerful workers sustained in their disruptions by their own savings from affluence, levies on other affluent workers or welfare payments to families.[22]

It is not important that such a picture would not be recognized by most British working men. It is important that such a view gained wide currency. In less sophisticated form the image degenerates into a much simpler conspiracy-theory of industrial problems. (As George Woodcock said of the tightly-knit 'Red Plot' analysis of the 1966 seamen's strike: 'Until I see some evidence, I flatly refuse to believe in this nonsense.') But all these images – the over-powerful trade union Goliath, the strategically placed militant with objectives of 'an indeterminate nature', the conspiracy of subversive elements that links the two – these are the common-places of middle-class commentary from the early 1950s onwards. No doubt some union policies contributed to the change; but few disagreed with George Woodcock in 1959 when he wrote: 'there is a hardening in the attitude of the non-union half of the population against the trade unions'.[23] The new attitudes had their effect, first upon the judge-made law and then upon the legislature, in ways which are quite unrelated to the fundamental *institutional* problems of British industrial life as analysed, for example, in the Donovan Report.

From the early 1920s, until 1952 (when the Court of Appeal went to great lengths so to manipulate the legal technicalities as to avoid intervention in labour disputes of a kind that would make the courts more of an arbiter of the strength of the parties)[24] the judges may be said, as we have seen, fairly to have applied the common law in a spirit of 'non-intervention'. The tradition did not die easily, for the effect of a change in social attitude is slow to seep through into case law. So, even in 1969 the High Court accepted that collective agreements were presumptively not enforceable contracts in the *Ford* case,[25] a judgment replete with 'non-interventionist' attitudes.

But the judicial tradition had already begun to weaken. Writing in 1968, a commentator who displays little sympathy for the trade union movement commented

> To a society which understands prices but is not interested in privileges, the internecine disputes of Demarcationists and Closed Shoppers have caused Trade Unionism to forfeit much sympathy.

Small wonder that he could also write:

> If the literature of the House of Lords be scanned over the last dozen years an impression may be received that Trade Unions are no longer the darlings of the law.[26]

Trade unionists who did not see their social rights as legal 'privileges' would scarcely remember any era in which their relationship with the law had been quite so romantic. But they did feel the chill wind of change with which new social attitudes, born of their own new-found strength, inspired the new judge-made law of the 1960s.

The first major explosion marking a sharp departure from the old policies in favour of the creation of new liabilities hostile to unions came in a case of which the facts arose in 1956, the High Court Judge gave judgment in 1961, and the final appeal was decided in 1964. In that year the House of Lords created in *Rookes v Barnard* the new tort of 'intimidation by threats to break employment contracts' admirably adapted for use by a non-unionist David against the organizational Goliath. This was a decision so serious that the Trade Disputes Act 1965 was demanded and obtained from the Labour Government to preserve a liberty for threatened industrial action by granting a traditional 'negative' protection against it in trade disputes.[27]

Even more important, in the 1960s, tort liabilities associated with knowingly inducing breach of existing commercial contracts, against which the Trades Disputes Acts provided no protection, were enlarged in ways that would have been unthinkable to the Court of Appeal in 1952: the concepts of 'inducement' and of 'breach' were widened; the type of knowledge and intention demanded of the defendant were reduced; interference with performance short of causing breach, even mere 'hindrance', was held by some judges to be wrongful in itself; and interference with contracts where none had yet been made was prohibited by injunction on the ground that the defendant union officials looked as though they might interfere if one were made.[28]

In the 1960s the 'labour injunction' came back into its own in England and Scotland. Theoretically a temporary remedy to preserve the *status quo* until trial, the interlocutory injunction is often the effective remedy sought by the employer to help break a strike. The practice of judges in the Chancery Division grew more frequent in this decade of granting such injunctions not merely on a basis of the wider liabilities but even *ex parte* (i.e. in proceedings where the defendant had had no time to appear) and in *mandatory* form, for example ordering defendants to withdraw instructions to strike, which instructions the (absent) defendants might well deny ever having given.[29] The extension of procedural remedies useful for employers matched the extension of equivalent substantive liabilities. Of course, it is hardly likely that judges who did this felt that they were favouring employer-plaintiffs. But if in retrospect we can agree with Professor Kahn-Freund that the judicial attitude from 1870 to 1918 'reflected that of the middle class',[30] why should we expect a different macroscopic pattern in the judicial developments of 1960 to 1971?

The same is true in regard to legal actions brought by aggrieved members unjustly treated by their own unions. In place of the careful extension of the law suggested by the Donovan Report,[31] judges who were dominated by a David and Goliath model of intra-union affairs stretched and occasionally destroyed traditional doctrines in order to grant a remedy to individual members (whose interests are much more readily intelligible to the common lawyer than are the collective interests of the majority whose need is for organizational strength). Some Court of Appeal judges, in 1970, went even to the extent of asserting an entirely novel control by the courts over the content of union rule-books in respect of admission, disciplines and expulsion – and that in a case where traditional doctrines were quite adequate to secure a remedy for a meritorious plaintiff (who had indeed been unjustly treated by the union).[32] All of these were judge-made legal developments *before* the 1971 Act, and all illustrated that in labour law as elsewhere, try as they may (and some try more than others), judges have 'no more been "above" the conflicts of capitalist society than any other part of the state system.'[33]

THE INDUSTRIAL RELATIONS ACT 1971

By placing a new court, the National Industrial Relations Court (NIRC), as the keystone of its structure, the Industrial Relations Act, 1971, in a sense insisted that courts and judges be involved in those conflicts. Once again, this insistence may be seen as a reflection of the legislature responding to the middle-class demand for more 'Law and Order' in industrial life. Such attitudes never understood the careful distinction in the Donovan Report *between* more 'order' and more 'law' when it stressed the need to effect:

> a change in the nature of British collective bargaining, and a more orderly method for workers and their representatives to exercise their influence in the factory; and for this to be accomplished, if possible, without destroying the British tradition of keeping industrial relations out of the courts (para. 190).

But the 1971 Act is not uniform in its philosophy. Many important decisions have been assigned not to the NIRC but to the Registrar (from whom there is often an appeal to the court) or to the CIR (from whose decisions no appeal ever lies). For example, the determination of the *boundaries* for a proposed bargaining unit – the critical decision – which in the first version of the Bill rested with the NIRC is now exclusively in the hands of the CIR.[34] The unifying theme of the Industrial Relations Act, 1971, is the weakening of the power of trade unions at shop-floor level, especially of unregistered 'organizations of workers'. Indeed, the latter are not only to be subject to a mine-field of legal liabilities in the sphere of industrial action, they are so little trusted that any member is expressly allowed to sue them for wrongs done in breach of the Act or breach of a rule which injured not him but some other member (the so-called 'common informer' action against unregistered unions), the only snag being that the draftsman forgot to provide for any effective remedy in such a case[35] – just one of dozens of minor nonsenses which are the bequest of totally inadequate Parliamentary discussion of the Bill.

Behind the dominant theme of the 1971 Act there are really two different, similar but not wholly compatible, philosophies; as it were, two different phantom draftsmen who work together but who represent different aspects of middle-class opinion. The first may be thought of as a civil servant or 'organization-man' concerned mainly to bring 'order' and a tidy structure into collective British industrial relations. The second is quite different, a Conservative lawyer imbued above all else with doctrines of *individual* rights, often without regard to the shop-floor problems of collective bargaining.

Let us concentrate here upon the aspects of the statute which bear the imprint of the latter. His hand is to be found throughout the statute. Let the organization-man establish a system for selectively imposing 'bargaining units' or 'agency shop agreements', the individualist inserts rights, respectively, for 'any person claiming to be an employee' in such a unit or for 'any worker to whom the agreement applies' to demand a ballot, or even a ballot in a *section* of a unit, thereby weakening the stability of the whole structure.

And it is no accident that it is in each case easier for the complainant to upset a *voluntarily* established 'bargaining unit' or 'agency shop' than to upset one backed by statutory order; in each case he needs at any time merely the support of one-fifth of the relevant work-force, whereas in a unit or shop resulting from a statutory application the hurdles in his way are higher.[36] So much for the notion that the Act favours voluntary collective arrangements. The first draftsman distrusts them because they may not be tidy; the second fears that they may override the minority's individual rights.

Union Membership and the Law
But one major victory of the individualist draftsman permeates the statute and, as it comes into force, is illustrating its remarkable doctrinaire character. I refer, of course, to section 5 whereby a worker acquires the right as against his employer, on the one hand, to join the (registered) trade union of his choice and participate in its activities and, on the other, to refuse to join any registered union or unregistered organization of workers. These rights are naturally backed up by the expected 'unfair industrial practices' for infringement and improper pressures inducing their infringement. Except where there is an agency shop agreement or the (almost impossible) approved post-entry shop, made with a registered trade union, it is illegal for any employer to 'prevent or deter' a worker from joining or (more important) refusing to join, or to 'penalize' or to 'discriminate' against him in any way in hiring, firing or during work.[37] Each of these words carries its own aura of uncertainty. The section merely gives express permission to

'encourage' membership of a *registered* union which the employer chooses to recognize for negotiation, but even then there must be no 'suggestion of reward for compliance or penalty for non-compliance'. The status of various methods of encouragement to join an unregistered union (which is the first practical problem for most managements after 28 February 1972) is left to the lawyers to argue.

The two rights – to join and to refuse to join – are not even formally equivalent, since there is no right to join the *unregistered* union of one's choice. But even if they were, the formal equivalence would be sociologically false, when, as the Donovan Report said, in comparing it to the closed shop principle, the right to refuse to join a union

> is designed to frustrate the development of collective bargaining which it is public policy to promote, whereas no such objection applies to the latter (para. 599).

The liberty of the majority of unionist individuals to organize in strength, even up to 100 per cent membership, is bound to run directly counter to a legal right of an individual worker to refuse to join. The 'agency shop' is not a compromise solution; it is a victory for the individual over the majority since it takes for granted as paramount the right to *dis*sociate. Yet why did the Government enact this vast extension of *individual* rights that inevitably inhibit the *collective* strength of workpeople, when it was protesting (perhaps too much) that it supported the 'principle of collective bargaining freely conducted on behalf of workers and employers and with due regard to the general interests of the community' (s. 1(1)(a))?

Control of Job-Entry
The legal right to be a non-unionist in section 5 is at the heart of the Act. At times it is discussed as if it were concerned largely with 'closed shop' situations. We may recall that the Donovan Report concluded, that there were no grounds for limiting the closed shop by legislation (para. 602) though there was room for improved protection for individuals in respect of trade union disciplinary powers. This last matter the Government dealt with in section 65 of the Act whereby all 'arbitrary or unreasonable' discriminatory refusals of membership by registered or unregistered unions of workers 'appropriately qualified for employment' as a worker of the 'description' specified in the rules of the organization, and all 'unfair or unreasonable disciplinary action' (whatever these portmanteau phrases mean) against any members can

be challenged as an unfair industrial practice. Dr McCarthy has distinguished three main functions of practices giving rise to a closed shop or 100 per cent unionism, namely,

a)   the function of recruitment and retention of members;
b)   the function of discipline, including the threat of exclusion;
c)   the function, in the case of the pre-entry closed shop of controlling (or in other cases of sharing some degree of control of) entry to the job (or retention of the job).[38]

In regard to this third and distinct function he concluded: 'The scope of union interest in entry control is ... largely determined by the extent to which it is felt to be necessary to maintain effective job regulation.'[39]

Section 65 itself introduces a savagely rigorous control of internal union affairs. Certainly it goes far beyond the Donovan recommendations. It was at least in connection with that section, *not* section 5, that the Solicitor General advanced the most frequently heard, and perhaps most substantial, argument against a union's untrammelled power to refuse membership and so affect control of job-entry, a power which, as we have seen, the judges had independently begun to control by judicial legislation.[40]

'The premise of this debate is that there are situations', he said 'in which unions can control a man's right of access to a job by controlling his right of access to membership of a union.... We cannot acknowledge a union's right, any more than did Donovan, totally to control access to membership of people qualified by skill, craft and training for work in such a way to allow the union unreasonably and arbitrarily to exclude those people from jobs. That is both the starting and finishing point of the matter.'[41]

So access to jobs was to be dealt with by striking down 'arbitrary' union practices especially as regards admission. Then, to make assurance doubly sure, section 7 of the Act provided that all provisions of pre-entry closed shop agreements are 'void'. True such agreements are not by themselves illegal and open as such to legal action; but industrial action by way of any strike or any 'irregular' industrial pressure short of a strike, to induce an employer to enter into or comply with such a provision is made illegal.[42] The powers of British unions, registered or not, to control or even to maintain their share in controlling job-entry are thus severely limited by sections 65 and 7, which resolutely swing the pendulum of the legal right to hire back towards managerial prerogative.

What then is the purpose of section 5? It is an open secret that this is a question that has been puzzling British management for many months. Many managers have been seeking advice on 'Under-the-Counter' methods to persuade and encourage their workers and new recruits to maintain membership or join unregistered unions – or, as the *Code of Practice* puts it, 'Welcome' such membership[43] – without falling foul of the prohibitions on deterrence or discrimination in section 5(2), or of the offer of discriminatory 'benefits' contrary to section 5(4). They have been right to seek such advice, because someone has to get on with the real job of negotiating with the great majority of unions which so far have chosen to remain free from State-licence.

Indeed, whereas lay middle-class opinion still analyses the 'closed shop' proper and many other 100 per cent union practices against the David and Goliath model of the 1950s, a large segment of modern managers by 1972 arrived at a very different appreciation of such practices where their union was willing to collaborate on workaday but critical issues. That is why the check-off has recently spread so quickly. In 1972, forms of 100 per cent membership are no longer objectionable to such managers. But the 1971 Act exemplifies the thinking of the 1950s, such as the conservative lawyers' pamphlet of 1958, *A Giant's Strength*, to which the closed shop and all its works were anathema.

Sometimes the new managerial approach goes to the opposite extreme of conceiving of the union as an institution for complete integration of workers – for organizing, rather than representing, workers – what might be dubbed the 'Pilkington syndrome'. This thinking typifies many clauses of the Act no doubt drafted by the phantom Organization-man. One example is section 36(2), the remarkable 'policing' obligation whereby unions are to keep members in line with a binding collective agreement by 'all such steps as are reasonably practicable' (the perfect phrase for the promotion of uncertainty and of interpretative litigation).

But once the Act has dealt with the abuses connected with *job-entry* as have been rightly or wrongly identified (i.e. in sections 65 and 7), where lies the need to enact further inhibitions on union strength? What *is* the point of section 5?

The Purpose of Section 5

The answer is that Section 5 emerges as a section clearly concerned not, as is sometimes alleged, with job-control, or with union discipline, but with union recruitment and union strength. That is why the right to *refuse* to join is granted both in respect of the 'goodies' (unions licensed by registration, with approved rule books, specially protected against the more severe illegalities for ordinary industrial action)[44] and the 'baddies' (organizations which have the temerity to refuse to submit their rules to the detailed control of Schedule 4 of the Act and to demand elementary industrial rights without State-licence – for elementary rights, such as the right to picket, are here involved),[45] while the right to join applies only to the trusty registered trade union.

If the section is concerned with recruitment and union strength, it is at once apparent why the right to *refuse* to join is far more important than the right to join – and why the inclusion of the unregistered organization in respect of the right to refuse is logical in terms of the section. The right to join is concerned largely with the minority problem of employers who try to prevent union membership; and in so far as it is not concerned with that problem, it can be shown to impede rather than strengthen union organization within the terms of the Act itself.[46]

But the right to *refuse* to join a union is concerned primarily with the relations between worker and union or, often today, between worker and employer-plus-union, as in the recent events at C.A. Parsons. There the judiciary joyfully devised yet more legal innovation to buttress the work of the individualist draftsman, one of the judges going out of his way to stress, in justification of granting the hitherto impermissible remedy of an injunction against the wrongful dismissal of a worker effected at the wish of the employer and the union (before section 5 had come into operation):

> that in matters of practice and discretion it is essential to take account of any important change in that climate of general opinion which is so hard to define but yet so plainly manifests itself from generation to generation.... Over the last two decades there has been a marked trend toward shielding the employee, where practicable, from undue hardships he may suffer at the hands of those who may have power over his livelihood – employers and trade unions.[47]

His Lordship specifies with precision the decades over which middle-class opinion has built up (in ways so hard to define yet so plainly manifest) the unreal model of unions that have a Goliath power at the place of work equivalent in some way to the enormous prerogatives possessed by management. Where management acted under such union pressure the rules of a century prohibiting injunctions were, by judicial fiat, changed by a majority of the Court of Appeal judges.

Yet, ironically, ten days earlier the Court of Appeal had been asked to review the century-old principle that a master can justify the summary dismissal of an employee by reasons that become known to him only long after the dismissal takes place. Although the Irish Courts had recently reconsidered the justice of this severe legal enforcement of managerial disciplinary power, no inter-generational vibrations of social change caused the English Court by subtle osmosis to detect any need to depart from the traditional principle.[48] But this was a straight case of employer dismissing employee for incompetence. No union pressure was involved.

The right under section 5 to *refuse* to join is, therefore, concerned not with job control, not with union discipline, not with the few employers who try to impose any 'yellow dog' employment contracts, but with the power of a union to organize in strength at the workplace to whatever percentage of membership is needed to provide a countervailing power to management whereby meaningful bargaining and an extension of the scope of collective arrangements can be effected. The extreme individualism of section 5 has, paradoxically, its effects at collective level. That is why it is at the heart of the many ways in which the statute limits the countervailing power of organized workpeople. The section reaches out even to the extent of displacing protection for members of unregistered organizations against unfair dismissal in case of a strike,[49] and, rather oddly, even of demanding proof of a 'substantial derogation' from his rights under section 5 before a worker can have pre-entry provisions of a closed-shop agreement declared 'void'.[50] The suggestion that the section was concerned – as the Secretary of State persuaded himself – with the peripheral issue whether a union would feel 'stronger with a 95 per cent membership of a shop with voluntary members than with a 100 per cent membership when the last 5 per cent of the 100 per cent have joined against their will'[51], can now be seen to be misconceived.

The Implications of Extreme Individualism

These victories in the Act of a philosophy of extreme individualism which inhibits collective organization are surely not accidents. Although they do not always fit neatly into the provisions relating to legal regulation of bargaining *structures*, the individualist draftsman found that they caused his colleagues few difficulties in the other two main areas of the legislation: the control of union rules and practices (notably in section 65), and the control of industrial action (notably sections 96 and 98). The inter-connections of section 5 and sections 96 and 98 are particularly important in the light of a factor which has become so fashionably trendy that one hesitates to mention it. I refer, of course, to the internationalization of capital which expresses itself in the multinational enterprise.

The advantages enjoyed by the multinational enterprise in bargaining with trade unions are now appreciated.[52] I have argued elsewhere that the flexible power of the multinational employer makes it less than ever appropriate for national systems of labour law to curtail 'solidarity' or 'sympathy' strikes and similar industrial action by unions with interests that spread with the movement of capital across frontiers; and indeed that: 'the international function of the trade union movement as a countervailing power to management in the multinational enterprise demands recognition by *national* systems of labour law of a right to take collective action in support of industrial action in other countries against companies which are, in an economic sense, part of the same unit of internationalized capital'.[53] Far from moving in that direction, sections 96 and 98 of the new British Act – the latter with its strange definition of 'extraneous parties', against whom industrial action is outlawed, which is so remarkably favourable to 'associated' companies of a type often found in a multinational economic complex – lead in exactly the opposite direction.

But it is not only that part of the 1971 Act which will be of interest to the giant corporations with their multinational Protean forms. Are we not likely to see more, rather than less, of such companies as the Texas Instrument company, which displaces collective bargaining by the more elegant forms of advanced paternalism? It is no accident that so many American corporations which set up business in Britain, as TUC Reports have consistently reported, resist gratuitous recognition of trade unions for bargaining. After 28 February 1972, they are not likely to overlook the protection of non-unionist workers provided by section 5, law of a kind which management can enjoy back home in the United States only in those nineteen States where local law provides (by their mis-named state 'Right-to-Work' laws) an even stronger legal charter for resistance to unionization.[54] But in Britain, as the TUC stated in December 1971: 'The establishment of 100 per cent *membership* in the areas in which they organize is a general objective of trade unions.'[55]

Is it not self-evident, in a world of internationalized capital in which the development of strong and effective trade unionism with an international dimension may be the most urgent priority in order to create a countervailing power capable of developing industrial democracy, and where, on the other side, working people's demands to extend their share of power at the place of work are becoming daily more insistent, that British labour law, whatever *else* is right or wrong in the 1971 Act, has taken a wrong turning up the blind alley of a misguided theology of individualism? The world wide multinational augments the tension in industrial relations which exists when local management (often far from its centre of power) faces local negotiators who express a new shop-floor power increasingly backed by official union policies, demanding, not subversion or disruption, but wider rights to democratic participation at the place of work in the making of decisions.

Individuals must be protected in all this by the law against unfair treatment by employers or unions. But the duty of a labour law system is *first* to the individuals in the collective majority; and only *second* – not to be forgotten, but *second* – to individuals who wish to opt out of collective labour relations. The new unfair dismissal law shows how labour law can fulfil both these duties; and one expects that new law to survive in some form. There is wide agreement that whatever the political complexion of future Governments, the Act will be amended, altered, or perhaps repealed. In any reconsideration of the Act, one point of departure must and surely will be the reconsideration of section 5 and all that goes with it. That section has so far ignored the first duty of the law as to introduce a new tension, one devised by labour law itself, one reaching far beyond problems of the closed shop and internal protection of union members, into the very vitals of the British system of industrial relations.

NOTES

1. s. 33(4) Industrial Relations Act 1971.
2. B. Aaron (ed.), *Labour Courts and Grievance Settlement in Western Europe* (1971) p. xix.
3. Sections 22-30 Industrial Relations Act 1971, especially the narrow definition of 'dismissal' (s.23), the limited compensation (s. 118) and absence of a remedy of re-engagement (or even of effective re-instatement, ss. 106(4), 116(4)) [see now ss. 54-79 EPCA 1978].
4. Trade Union Act 1871, especially ss. 2, 3, 4; Conspiracy and Protection of Property Act 1875, especially ss. 3, 17; Trade Disputes Act 1906.
5. Wages (Temporary Regulation) Act 1918, extended from 6 to 12 months, establishing the 'Interim Court of Arbitration'.
6. Lord Amulree, *Industrial Arbitration* (1929) p. 120 and Chapters XVI and

XVII. On the later experience see K. W. Wedderburn and P. L. Davies, *Employment Grievances and Disputes Procedures in Britain* (1969) Chap. 9. The Court is now the 'Industrial Arbitration Board', Industrial Relations Act 1971, s. 124.

7. Industrial Courts Act 1919, s. 2(04).

8. Allan Flanders, *Industrial Relations: What is Wrong with the System?* (1965) p. 28.

9. See K. W. Wedderburn, 'Conflicts of Rights and Conflicts of Interests in Labour Disputes' in B. Aaron (ed.), *Dispute Settlement Procedures in Five Western European Countries* (1967).

10. The selective procedure whereby a union may become a 'sole bargaining agent' in a bargaining unit under ss. 44-50 Industrial Relations Act (see R. Lewis and G. Latta, 'Bargaining Units and Bargaining Agents', (1971) 10 BJIR 1, pp. 84-106) may impose a duty to bargain under s. 55(1) (b). But that duty is not itself enforceable by order, the remedy being an unsatisfactory procedure for arbitration of the substantive claim: ss. 105(5), 125, and 127 – unsatisfactory because an employer can contract out of the arbitration award with individual employees: s. 127(3)(a)!

11. G. Camerlynck and G. Lyon-Caen, *Droit du Travail* (1972), p. 608. See too X. Blanc-Jouvan in B. Aaron (ed.), *Labour Courts and Grievance Settlement in Western Europe* (1971) Chap. 1, Sections 4 and 5.

12. These matters are discussed in detail in Chapter 6 of *Industrial Action – A Comparative Legal Survey* B. Aaron and K. W. Wedderburn (eds.), (1972). For some recent assessments of the US law on 'Emergency Stoppages in the Private Sector' see *Labor Law Journal*, 1971, pp. 453-83 (Papers to Industrial Relations Research Association).

13. W. Simkin, *Mediation and the Dynamics of Collective Bargaining* (1971), p. 205.

14. A. B. Atkinson, *The Distribution of Wealth and the Individual Life Cycle* (1971). See too J. Skinner, *Collective Bargaining and Inequality*, Fabian Research Series 298 (1971).

15. *Reynolds v Shipping Federation* [1924] 1 Ch. 28. See too the judges' attitudes in *White v Riley* [1921] 1 Ch. 1 (CA).

16. Scrutton, LJ [1923] CLJ, p. 8, discussing problems of judicial 'impartiality'.

17. The more important sections of the 'Scheme for Prevention of Disputes' and the 'Resolution' adopted are set out in W. Milne-Bailey, *Trade Union Documents* (1929) p. 257 and p. 430.

18. TUC *Annual Report*, 1928, p. 203.

19. H. Pelling, *A History of British Trade Unionism* (1963) p. 211.

20. In *Crofter Hand Woven Harris Tweed Co. Ltd v Veitch* [1942] A C 435, at p. 447, p. 472, p. 463, p. 479; see K. W. Wedderburn, *The Worker and the Law*, p. 28-9.

21. H. J. Laski, *Trade Unions in the New Society* (1950) p. 101. The development centres around s. 5 of the 1971 Act, see below.

22. See C. Grunfeld, 'Australian Compulsory Arbitration: Appearance and Reality' (1971) 9 BJIR 3, p. 330, n 1.

23. *Forward*, 23 October 1959.

24. *Thomson & Co. v Deakin* [1952] Ch. 646; see K. W. Wedderburn, *The*

Worker and the Law, pp. 353-6.

25. *Ford Motor Co. Ltd. v AUEFW* [1969] 2 Q B 303; see R. Lewis, 'The Legal Enforceability of Collective Agreements' (1970) 8 BJIR 3, p. 313; B. Hepple, [1970] CLJ, p. 122.

26. G. Abrahams, *Trade Unions and the Law* (1968) p. 156 and p. 95.

27. [1964] A C 1129, H L, reversing a unanimous Court of Appeal; see Wedderburn, *op. cit.*, pp. 361-73; and on this era generally, *op. cit.*, Chapter 8.

28. *Torquay Hotel Co. Ltd v Cousins* [1969] 2 Ch. 106, (C A); *Stratford v Lindley* [1965] A C 269, (HL); *Emerald Construction Co v Lowthian* [1966] I WLR 691 (CA); *Square Grip Co. Ltd. v Macdonald* (1968) SLT 65.

29. Despite the criticisms by the Court of Appeal in *Boston Deep Sea Fisheries Ltd v TGWU, The Times*, 13 March 1970 (summarized in Wedderburn, *The Worker and the Law*, p. 381-4) interlocutory injunctions were granted in a series of unreported cases *ex parte* in 1971 (for example *Astons Transport Ltd v Cowdrill*, 15 October 1971, Foster J.). But Brightman J. (one of the judges of the new National Industrial Relations Court) refused to grant this extraordinary remedy in *Hull and Humber Cargo Handling Co Ltd. v TGWU, The Times*, 16 December 1971, possibly influenced in his Chancery jurisdiction by the rule of the NIRC that interim orders should not be granted in *that* Court without hearing the defendant: Industrial Relations Act 1971, Schedule 3 para. 22(3).

30. O. Kahn-Freund, in M. Ginsberg (ed.) *Law and Opinion in England in the 20th Century*, p. 241.

31. See a restaurant of such cautious proposals for new limits on trade union rules: O. Kahn-Freund, 'Trade Unions, the Law and Society', (1970) 33 MLR, p. 241.

32. *Edwards v SOGAT* [1970] 3 WLR 713 (CA) where Megaw L.J. shows how the new doctrines were not necessary for a decision in favour of the expelled member. See Wedderburn, *op. cit.*, p. 454-61, for the respects in which the assertion of the judges' right to control union rules ran counter to earlier authority; and *Breen v AEU* [1971] 1 All E.R. 1148 (CA).

33. R. Miliband, *The State in Capitalist Society* (1969) p. 145.

34. Compare Clauses 42 and 43(3) Industrial Relations Bill (1 December 1970) with sections 45, 46 and 48, especially 48(3), Industrial Relations Act 1971.

35. Section 107(3) establishes the possibility in the case of *unregistered* organizations of 'common informer' actions; but s. 109(3)(a) allows the tribunal to grant remedies only in favour of 'the person who presented the complaint', when by definition that person is complaining of a wrong done to someone else!

36. See s. 51 and s. 14 respectively. An agency shop based on the statutory procedure cannot be challenged within two years; s. 14(3). The bargaining agency established by order needs the support of *two-fifths* of the relevant employees after two years: s. 51(3). After this paper was presented, such issues were further discussed by O. Kahn-Freund in *Labour and the Law* (Hamlyn Lectures for 1972).

37. s. 5(2)(3) and s. 33(3)(a) Industrial Relations Act 1971, with s. 105(1) and s. 119 providing the procedural corollaries.

38. W. E. J. McCarthy, *The Closed Shop in Britain* (1964), pp. 97-106; see too on post-entry shops, p. 152.
39. *Ibid.*, p. 259.
40. Especially in *Edwards v SOGAT*, above, note 32.
41. Sir Geoffrey Howe, QC, Solicitor General, *Parliamentary Debates*, Vol. 811, Col. 688, 10 February 1971.
42. s. 33(3)(b). The mark of 'irregular' industrial action is, of course, breach of employment contracts by two or more workers: s. 33(4). Space prevents discussion of another critical matter, the requirement of such an unfair industrial practice to be 'in contemplation or furtherance of an *industrial dispute*'. But it must be remarked that the definition of 'industrial dispute' in s. 167(1) differs materially from that of 'trade dispute' in s. 5(3), Trade Disputes Act 1906, not least by excluding disputes judged to arise between workers and workers, a category which could be made to include many inter-union disputes (in connection with which litigation would then go not to the NIRC but to the ordinary High Court applying all the liabilities of the law of tort without any negative statutory protections).
43. It is of interest that both the final draft of the *Code of Practice*, para, 4(iii), and the TUC *Handbook on the Industrial Relations Act*, p. 6, para. 10, published on almost the same day, take the view that an employer can state that he 'welcomes' membership of an unregistered union without risking breach of s. 5(2).
44. Such as knowingly inducing breach of contract in s. 96(1). The ability of an unregistered union to avoid breach of members' contracts by giving due strike notice under s. 147(2)(5) will be seriously hampered by the ineffectiveness of such notice wherever a procedure further restricts an employee's right to strike in his individual employment contract: s. 147(3). Such restrictions are likely to become more frequent by reason of the incorporation of 'grievance procedures' into employment contracts by the notes demanded by s. 20(2)(b)(c) of the Act, which will be evidence of the terms of such an individual contract. The fact that a procedure is 'not legally binding' in a collective agreement as between union and employer will not necessarily prevent its becoming a binding term of an *individual* employment contract. 'Grievance procedures' will often impose some restriction on the right to strike, especially if their later stages are linked with collective disputes procedures as is advocated by the *Code of Practice*, para. 123. The web thus woven by s. 20(2)(b)(c) and s. 147(3) may be seen as another victory for the 'individualist' draftsman – this time to control the right to strike of unregistered unions.
45. It is a common misconception that the right of peaceful picketing is protected in industrial disputes by s. 134. While this is true in the ordinary courts as regards liability in crime or tort, it does not answer the problem posed for members of an unregistered union who, in picketing, might frequently be seen to be engaged in a threat to induce another person to break a contract, which is *per se* illegal, after 28 February 1972, within the purview of the jurisdiction of the NIRC: s. 96. Further, of course, picketing might on some occasions attract liability under s. 98 (solidarity action against 'extraneous parties') or s. 97 (action in support of other acts which are themselves unfair industrial practices, e.g. a strike illegal under s. 96).

46. It also concerns the right to join as against pressures from other unions. Once again, the extreme character of s. 5 is illustrated since that right to be a member of a *registered* union is retained even where a different registered union has established an 'agency shop', so long as the worker concerned pays appropriate contributions either to the union or to charity: ss. 5(1)(a), 6, 8, 9, 10. Thus, a group of members of a splinter union cannot be forced to give up their membership even in an agency shop and can supply the springboard from which a 'one-fifth' application for a ballot can be built up under s. 14 (see above). This is another example of the way in which the individualist theme in the Act can encourage continuing inter-union competition.

47. Sachs L J in *Hill v C. A. Parsons Ltd.* [1971] 3 All.E.R. 1345 p. 1355 (CA), where the normal doctrine of English law that no court will grant an injunction to restrain a wrongful dismissal was displaced. An injunction was granted where union pressure had led the employers to give less notice than that to which the plaintiff was legally entitled. Both Lord Denning MR and Sachs LJ relied on the fact that section 5 was *about* to be brought into force and therefore an injunction should be granted to preserve the plaintiff's position until he could enforce his rights under the section. Apart from its usurpation of the Parliamentary power to decide the date from which laws operate, this argument runs into another difficulty. By analogy, it would be arguable that *any* dismissal after 5 August 1971, when the Act was enacted, should have been prevented by injunction if the employee so requested, in order to preserve the situation until he could utilize his rights to challenge the 'fairness' of the dismissal when ss.22-30 were brought into effect, even though he *had* been given proper notice. The orthodox law is stated in the dissenting judgment of Stamp LJ.

48. *Cyril Leonard & Co v Simo Securities Trust Ltd* [1971] 3 All.E.R. 1313.

49. s. 26(3).

50. s. 7(3). It is not clear why this heavier burden is cast upon him under s. 7(3) than under s.5(2). On the other hand, s. 7(3) is one of those few cases in which the NIRC has no discretion at all as to remedy but 'shall make an order declaring the provisions void', a declaration which at once puts at risk a union's industrial pressures on the employer: s. 33(3)(b)(c).

51. Mr R. Carr, Secretary of State for Employment, Parliamentary Debates, Vol.810, Col.672, 27 January 1971. But he added that the Government had to 'maintain the Clause as it stands first of all on grounds of individual liberty': *ibid.*, col. 673; to which he added the somewhat remarkable ground of 'industrial democracy' because workers must be free to move to the union of their choice: Col. 674-5. Even if the Bridlington arrangements did, contrary to the evidence, unduly inhibit workers' choice, such mobility for 'democracy' is provided for in s. 65(3), which guarantees the right to resign from any union.

52. See e.g. J. Gennard and M. D. Steuer, 'Industrial Relations of Foreign Owned Subsidiaries in the United Kingdom' (1971) 9 BJIR, p. 143. See too, J. B. Mitchell, 'Labour Standards and International Coordination of Collective Bargaining', in *Essays on Labor and International Trade*, Monograph 15, Institute of Industrial Relations (1970) Chap. 4; and J. Gennard, *Multinational Corporations and British Labour*, British North

American Committee (1972).

53. In 'Multi-National Enterprise and National Labour Law' (1972) 1 ILJ, pp. 12, 19 [now chapter 7 below].

54. The 'union security' arrangements allowed by the Taft Hartley Act, compare favourably in certain respects with the Agency Shop agreement recognized by s. 11 of the British Act of 1971. For the latter, trade unions must be registered. In the former, new employees can be required to join the elected union after a 'grace period' at the place of employment but, in effect, non-payment of dues to the union is the only ground on which the employer can discharge: s. 8(a)(3). See Summers and Wellington, *Labor Law*, 1968, pp. 906-66. Section 14(b), however, allows States to enact 'right to work' laws outlawing, or limiting further, the legality of union security agreements. It would not be surprising to find that British managers' attitudes were not dissimilar to those found among their American counterparts, approval in principle of the rhetoric of the 'right to work' law protecting non-unionists, but a penchant for the advantages in practice of 100 per cent union arrangements: See F. Meyers, 'Effects of Right-to-Work Laws: the Texas Act', *Industrial and Labor Relations Review*, 1955, p. 77, and his *Right to Work in Practice*, 1959. The US Railway Labor Act, 1926, as amended 1951, s. 2(11), permits post-entry closed shop agreements whereby workers must join a union within 60 days, a law which State 'right-to-work' laws cannot override.

55. *Good Industrial Relations: A Guide For Negotiators*, TUC 1971, p. 21 (emphasis supplied).

APPENDIX TO CHAPTER 3

ON THE INDUSTRIAL RELATIONS BILL*

In the Trade Union Act 1871, just 100 years ago, trade unions first achieved a lawful status in Britain. Thirty-five years later a charter of elementary rights for industrial action was won in the Trade Disputes Act 1906. Without those Acts and others like the Act of 1965 made necessary by *Rookes* v *Barnard*, modern trade unionism would have been practically illegal. All three of those statutes would be repealed by this Industrial Relations Bill. Similar protections would be partially restored in the ordinary High Court; but their protections would be quite replaced by new laws in the court to which jurisdiction would be assigned for most industrial disputes, the National Industrial Relations Court – the NIRC for short – the centre-piece of the whole scheme which goes to the very roots of the rights established in 1906.

Of course, not everyone liked the Act of 1906. The leading Professor of Constitutional Law of the day, Professor A.V. Dicey, protested against it vigorously as giving 'privileges' to trade unions. Just think what it would mean, he demanded to a Liberal Party women's meeting in 1906, if trade unions regulated 'the terms on which women laboured – domestic servants for instance'. A fate worse than death, he seemed to think.

Crisis for unions – and the law
At such moments of crisis, Professors of Law should no doubt speak their minds, and this is a great crisis for the labour movement and for British law. The new Industrial Relations Bill would make it much more difficult for workers, especially weaker and lower paid groups like women workers, to organise into strong trade unions. Unlike Professor Dicey in 1906, I believe that to be a monstrous perversion of the law.

But it is a very complicated Bill. Indeed, only now can we see just how complicated it is, because some critical features were revealed only when the Bill itself was published last month. For example, the classical definition of a 'trade dispute' – a central feature of trade union law since 1906 – is to be replaced in the Bill by an entirely new, more restrictive definition of 'industrial dispute'. Yet, not one single word of that proposed change appeared in the Consultative Document of October 1970. You must read the small print.

The small print in the Bill
I want to appeal to every person in the country to get to know about the small

---

* Text of a speech on the Industrial Relations Bill, Royal Albert Hall, London 1971, published by the TUC in 1971.

print in this Bill. Professor Dicey said about the 1906 Bill that not one Englishman in a hundred knew its true legal effect. Well, that Bill had five clauses. This one already has 150 clauses and eight Schedules; and I doubt whether one person in 100,000 has any idea at all of its true legal effects. That is partly because the false image with which this Bill has been sold has been the biggest piece of public mystification of the century.

The Solicitor General has claimed that the Bill merely introduces a 'framework of law' of which 'the major part' is 'directly in line with Donovan recommendations'. Nothing could be less accurate. We already have a 'framework of law', law which may well need reform, but which sets out not to regulate but to support a voluntary system of industrial relations. But this Bill sets out to *replace* totally our existing legal framework with a new system, largely based upon ill-chosen snippets of American laws unsuitable to British conditions; and as the Consultative Document frankly puts it, the Government aims to use legal regulations and legal sanction as the *'main instrument'* of policy for changing industrial relations. Now that was *exactly* what the Donovan Royal Commission unanimously told Government not to do. And that report was supported by very weighty research. The Government's Bill has been prepared on the basis of *Fair Deal at Work*, a scrawny little pamphlet written before Donovan even reported, unsupported by any worthwhile research at all.

National Industrial Relations Court
The *causes*, as opposed to the symptoms, of industrial disputes are not going to be improved by arguments in court-rooms, but by patient new initiatives in voluntary negotiation and local arbitration – the sort of thing the CIR and TUC have begun to promote but will be prevented from promoting by this Bill. I suggested to the Donovan Commission that: 'One Scamp is worth a dozen injunctions' of the High Court. By 1972, if this Bill and the NIRC come in, one Scamp will be worth ten dozen orders from the NIRC.

How would the NIRC enforce its orders? Against a trade union, by seizure of its assets (true, with a limit of £100,000 if it is registered – but £100,000 each time). And against anyone organising or financing a prohibited industrial action the orders will be enforced by penalties or even by imprisonment, unless he is a trade union official who proves he acted exactly within the scope of his authority (another field day for lawyers). The Government is quite correct in saying that any ultimate imprisonment would not be for a crime. It would be for civil contempt of an order of the NIRC. But even if you explain that nice legal distinction for his imprisonment to a gaoled shop steward, his reply, I suspect, would be anything but civil. Whether it is technically civil or criminal, the NIRC can be the first step to gaol for those who step out of line.

The Bill would make the NIRC the arbiter of deep issues of policy which are properly the subject of negotiation; and that is something likely to damage the very fabric of our legal institutions. Worse still the Bill would weaken at every turn the strength of organised groups of working people. When you read the

small print, these are the two salient characeristcs of the Bill – *not* the introduction
of some framework of fair rules of cricket into an hitherto uncontrolled ball-
game – but an attempt at tight legal regulation of a hitherto voluntary system of
industrial relations, and tight restraints on workpeople's rights.

The right to organise
Tonight, since I have no time for details, let me summarise just three areas of
law where the Bill would have these effects – on the right to organise in
strength; on the right to strike; and on collective agreements.

First, the Bill is a charter for blacklegs and non-unionists. It would enact a
right for a worker *not* to be a trade unionist as well as a right to be a trade
unionist. The Donovan Report explained very clearly the false character of this
apparent equation. The right to *be* a trade unionist promotes collective
bargaining; a *legal* right *not* to be a unionist is, as the Report put it, 'designed
to frustrate the development of collective bargaining'. Under the Bill it will be
normally unlawful to take industrial action to protect trade union strength
against non-unionist free riders. Thousands of workers will lose the right to
insist on working alongside only union colleagues – a right they have had for
fifty years. And for the first time ever the British statute book will include a
law designed 'to frustrate the development' of collective bargaining.

Donovan also rejected prohibition of the closed shop; but the Bill prohibits
pre-entry closed shops. It will allow only an 'agency shop' system. Even that is
not 100 per cent membership; and it is permitted only if voted for by 51 per
cent of *all* the relevant workers (abstentions count as votes against); it is open
to challenge in a new ballot by a small 20 per cent minority at any time (clause
14) – a standing threat to stable bargaining arrangements, a standing invitation
to breakaways; and if the union ever fails to attract 51 per cent of the electorate
in a ballot it is unlawful to raise the matter again for two whole years. The same
loading of scales against strong trade union organisation and the same threat to
established stable procedures appear in the clause that would allow the NIRC
– on the CIR's advice – to make legal orders defining bargaining units and to
certify what union or unions can bargain. An employer can even make an
application under Clause 42 for the sole recognition of a workers' organisation
which is not even *independent* – for a 'house union'; and from the moment of
that application it is unlawful for a genuine union to take industrial action
about recognition.

Registrar in control
The new legal rights for free riders are really the first of two pincers thrust into
trade union strength by the Bill. The second pincer is the control through
NIRC over the rules and conduct of all workers' organisations and the
enormous new powers of the Registrar and NIRC over unions that register.
Admission to unions will no longer be a matter for union rules but for legal
decision by the Registrar and the NIRC as to whether someone is 'reasonably
well qualified' and should 'reasonably' be admitted. The same goes for whether

someone has been 'unfairly' or 'unreasonably' disciplined. For registration as a State-approved trade union, an organisation will need not only to have rules which meet the rigid new regulations in the Bill but will have to meet 'any other requirements' the Registrar likes to impose (Clause 64). Union rules will be so controlled that voluntary inter-union arrangements, like those of the TUC, will exist almost at the discretion of the Registrar and of NIRC. And not content with that, the Government is now apparently considering a second register for 'professional' unions like the BMA with special exemptions.

The right to strike
Secondly, the right to strike: the Bill makes it unlawful to strike for anything that is an unfair industrial practice (for example, to stop an influx of non-unionists); it is also unlawful then to take what the Bill coyly calls any other 'irregular' industrial action (which includes almost all other industrial action since that action usually involves some breach of employment contracts). Notice: for workpeople the limits apply to calling, financing or threatening strikes or *any other* 'irregular' industrial action. For employers, they apply only to lockouts, and not to the thousands of other ways (short of dismissal) in which an employer can put pressure on his workers.

Next, under Clause 85, inducing any breach of contract – an inevitable consequence of most strikes – is an unfair industrial practice except (and the Government always stresses this) for a registered union and its authorised officials. But the next two clauses of the Bill effectively negative that protection even for the registered unions. Clause 86 makes it unlawful to *aid and abet* an unfair practice. The Secretary of State was asked in Parliament whether this clause did not mean a union was almost certain to lose its protection under Clause 85 if it made a strike by members official. All he could say was the question 'is a very difficult one ... which needs the reply of a lawyer'. The Secretary of State may have passed his written examination on the Bill with the help of his civil servants but he certainly could not pass his oral. But we should not criticise too harshly. The Secretary of State was only in the position thousands of managers and union officials will be in if this Bill becomes law – face to face with laws he could not interpret with any certainty at all, without legal advice – and probably not even with it.

Then comes Clause 87. That would outlaw strikes interfering with the business of any employer who is an '*extraneous party*' to a dispute. Some people think that sounds fair – until you read the small print. 'Extraneous party' does not mean just 'innocent third party'. It is defined so that it can include a company under the same financial control as the employer in the dispute, even if it is situated next door. Clause 87 would make unlawful sympathetic and other secondary strike and solidarity action which has been lawful in Britain for decades. Two leading American professors at Yale Law School put it well when they said about the similar Taft-Hartley law in the USA, that curtailing secondary action makes unions 'enter the economic struggle with one hand tied'.

When you look at all these legal restrictions in the Bill, it is highly likely that the severe limits it proposes on the rights to organise and to strike infringe the international obligations of the British Government under ILO Convention 87, Articles 2, 3 and 7; and under the European Social Charter, 1961, Article 6.

Collective agreements
Thirdly, collective agreements. Without waiting to hear what Donovan had to say, *Fair Deal at Work*, 1968 declared that Conservative policy was to subject collective agreements to the law applying to ordinary contracts 'no more and no less'. But the Bill attaches a conclusive presumption of legal enforceability to written collective agreements and to any written decisions of any negotiating body – from works committees to joint councils up and down the land – unless *both* parties agree otherwise in writing. That is not only legalism run mad – legalism which will destroy the flexibility which is one great virtue of our present system; it is not the ordinary law of contract.

Then the Bill allows an employer or the Secretary of State to apply to the NIRC for an order to *impose* procedures at a place of work and that order is to be binding 'as if a contract' had been made by the union and employer. Well – that is not the ordinary law of contract.

Then again, wherever a collective agreement is a binding contract, it is to be unlawful for the union not to take 'all such steps as are reasonably practicable' to stop not only members or officials but any other person 'purporting to act' for the union from breaking the agreement. This is not just legalism run mad (the interpretation of these words alone will keep NIRC going for a few years); it is also an attempt to make trade unions *police* industrial procedures, which, Donovan warned, is likely to increase industrial difficulties; and it is certainly not the ordinary law of contract.

Those are just three of many headings under which the Bill would restrict trade union rights and run labour relations into a swamp of legal squabbling. The Bill is at best an irrelevance, at worst a legal nightmare – as much for line managers as for workpeople – and it will not deal with any of the *causes* of industrial disputes. This attempt to cut all the knots of what are often frustrating problems by a sharp swing of a legal axe is more likely to commit butchery than surgery on the fabric of British industrial relations, and the axe will fall on the strength of the trade unions.

Industrial democracy
In conclusion, let me add this. Some people say that to oppose the Bill, to adhere to the ways of voluntaryism, to the long haul of negotiation – that this is a 'negative' attitude. I believe history will show this view to be wrong. I see opposition to this Bill not as something negative, but as based upon a positive affirmation, that only a strong, free trade union movement can secure for working people, blue collar or white, deliverance from the status of second-class citizenship at work.

The way to industrial democracy requires strong unions in which members and officials participate together in ever-widening areas of decision-making at the workplace. This demand that democracy be extended not only in political but in industrial life, is being heard across Europe; for it is an extension without which those who wield powers in modern society are likely to impose an increasing dehumanisation on workers who live by selling their labour. But the positive vision of an expanding industrial democracy is not the vision of this Bill. I believe as its small print is revealed and as its false image becomes clear, thousands of people will recoil from this Bill, and will understand and applaud an opposition to it which expresses the very different spirit of a positive demand by ordinary men and women for a more just, a more democratic society in what still can be made a greener and more pleasant land.

4

TRADE UNION LIABILITY IN STRIKES IN BRITAIN AND FRANCE*

It is now a shared premise of comparative study that the first step towards understanding a system of labour law is to grasp its social history, above all the history of its labour movement. There is, for instance, manifestly 'a correspondence between the juridical structure of laws on strikes and models of trade union organization: in a regime of union pluralism ... the strike cannot be the subject of a union legal monopoly'. There the right to strike (although exercised collectively) vests in the individual worker; for pluralist systems his ownership of the right necessarily becomes, in Giugni's phrase, 'a dogma founded on reason'.[1] In contrast is the 'organic' right to strike which only the union may exercise, springing fully armed from the soil of a different social, and a unitary trade union, culture – Germany and Sweden as against Italy, Spain and France.

On the other hand, those five systems all treat the legitimate strike as a suspension, not a breach, of the employment contract. The French worker's employment contract is suspended save where he or she is 'guilty of serious default'; that has been the law since 1950 (not before) buttressing the constitutional right to strike.[2] This central feature of the modern system was supplemented in 1985 by legislation asserting that a dismissal by reason of a lawful strike is an unlawful discrimination and 'null and void'.[3] In 1990, the *Cour de Cassation* at long last affirmed that reinstatement is here a proper remedy;[4] before that, the battle in the courts about its availability had been severe.[5]

When we consider the precepts of British common law on master and servant, with industrial action invariably a breach of contract (notice or no notice), legislation of 1990 that beefs up the employers'

* First published in 1991 in *Industrial Law Journal* 20.

powers to dismiss strikers (ILO Conventions notwithstanding)[6] and a common law judiciary relentlessly pursuing interpretations normally noxious to collective action,[7] we may note that it took almost half a century of determined legal policy to transform the French law on suspension and that this could never have been done without battles being won inside the Social Chamber of the *Cour de Cassation* (the highest civil appellate court). In the decisions, we catch glimpses of the flesh and blood of the judiciary. If the labour movement writes a vocabulary for its system of labour law and then 'other factors change the story, even the grammar', among these factors are juridical developments.[8] No doubt the legal principles too have their own social explanations, but labour law feels their impact only after they are formulated, and primarily through legal not social mechanisms. Take the meteoric impact of 'economic duress' in Britain. Expanded in commercial law decisions after 1975 and sprung on labour relations by willing judges and forensic concessions, its pedigree has little to do with the shape of the labour movement.[9]

Another such doctrine is vicarious liability. When does the law make a union liable in civil terms for the acts of its members or its officials in (say) industrial action? That is a day-to-day practical matter for everyone concerned in collective bargaining. The contrast between France and Britain seems here to provide a revealing indication of the way strike laws are mediated by the courts' interpretations of relevant common law doctrines.

First, though, a reformist British lawyer must not assume that the grass on the Continent is everywhere greener. He will find, for example, that forms of industrial action *less* than a strike are excluded from the French legal meaning of a constitutionally protected 'strike' and are as illegal there as here, if not more so.[10] We see a faint parallel of French concepts now that British law regards 'strikes' and 'action short of a strike' as legally distinct (though without meaningful definitions).[11] In France action short of a strike is not a *grève licite*. Work-to-rule, go-slow, working without enthusiasm – all such action is categorized as a 'misperformance' of employment duties rather than the complete abstention from work (however short) needed for a 'strike'. This cast of mind progresses to its own natural conclusions: for instance, *autosatisfaction* is illegal – securing a bargaining demand by the stoppage itself (such as stopping work on Saturday when the demand is for an end to Saturday working, though striking on Friday would have been lawful). There is a good case for British law to adopt a 'positive right to strike'; but advocates would do well not to suggest that in France (still less 'in Europe') a legitimate strike includes all forms of industrial action.

The forms of actions short of strike and an 'abusive' exercise of the right to strike generally constitute 'serious default' (*faute lourde*) leaving the worker at the mercy of the employer, even if he or she has been led into it by others.[12] Doctrines of *abus de droit* may also lead the court to consider whether the strikers intentionally caused excessive harm to the enterprise[13] (not a doctrine to put in the hands of our High Court even if renamed 'Industrial Court'). So too, although there is no general requirement in France for strike ballots or notice (except in public services),[14] a stoppage is not a legitimate strike if it is not in pursuance of '*revendications professionelles*' (occupational demands), though since 1989 the courts – in the jurisprudence of a system which knows of precedent but uses it in a more relaxed style – have made it clear that workers need not wait for the employer's response before stopping work.[15]

With that minimum context let us inquire into vicarious liability. In England the principle that a person must be liable (with the agent) for actionable loss caused by an agent whom he engaged to act on his behalf can be found in 'medieval common law and the law merchant', and its relatively early acceptance meant that the law soon concentrated on the boundaries of liability (save for such class curiosities as 'common employment'): that is, on the authority of the agent or course of the servant's employment.[16] It may well be that its early adoption is, like the timing of the industrial revolution, a crucial feature of the British development. In any event, when the occasion arose for them to consider the tortious liability of registered unions in the short period between *Taff Vale*, 1901 (when the new liability was invented) and the Trade Disputes Act 1906 (when it was removed) the judges turned naturally to agency, looking (at times cautiously) to see whether union officials had acted within their authority so as to bind the union as principal or whether the union had ratified the acts, understandably applying the ordinary common law rules.[17]

When the Industrial Relations Act 1971 reimposed quasi-delictual responsibility, a semantic battle on whether authority came 'from the top down' or 'from the bottom up' masked the essential question whether vicarious liability would be used to expand a union's liabilities by extending the *implied* authority of the 'agents' who were by now industrially at the hub of affairs, the shop stewards.[18] When in 1982 the legislature put the collar of common law tort once more round the necks of the unions, it was not satisfied with the common law vicarious liability merely for agents acting with authority; it added a strict liability for the acts of the President and General Secretary and NEC – plus a liability for other officials unless they were repudiated.[19] In 1990 still further extensions of vicarious liability have been enacted, arguably the most important part of the Act [now ss. 20 and 21 TULRCA 1992], plus a demand for repudiation of the acts of officials who are not authorized agents in the rules (even where the officials have done no act save be in the company of strangers who have acted), with repudiations available only at the end of a legal assault course.[20]

Of course, in England behind vicarious liability in tort lurk costs, damages and interlocutory injunctions, and behind them in turn the threat of punishment for contempt of court even unto sequestration or receivership of the union's property, sanctions of nuclear proportions compared with the monetary payments in French courts for non-performance of an order (*l'astreinte*: payments to the other party; the State knows its place in civil matters).[21] But in part French law tackles union liability head on, by immunity. Unions are not to be ruined by litigation that removes their property, especially poor unions as theirs are rather proud to be. In accordance with ILO principles it is, therefore, provided that the union's core property is not available for distraint (defined by three attractive measures: the property which is indispensably necessary for meetings, a library and occupational training).[22] 'In many countries the law tempers the civil liability ... by provisions for immunity from distraint of property indispensable to the proper functioning of a trade union.'[23] This international standard seems unlikely to be restored in Britain. Yet we might have had a more literate debate about it all by reference to ILO principles than to Dicey doctrines about putting unions 'above the law'.

True, French unions can incur tort liability.[24] It normally arises under article 1382, *Code Civil*, that law of tort packed into twenty-four words and based on three elements: fault, damage and a link of causality between the two – as Tunc wrote, 'How simple it is!'.[25] The union is not liable for its members' acts but, as a legal person, it is liable '*dans les conditions du droit commun*' for its own acts, those of its 'organs', so long as they do not act outwith their 'functions' (as defined by law and the rules). The organs are the President, Secretary, executive council and 'general assembly'.[26] Liability may arise either from a strike illicit in itself or from illegal acts done in the course of a licit strike. All this rests on the 'general law', though union liability in strikes is 'especially delicate'.[27] English law has an undisciplined knowledge of liability in tort for the acts of 'organs' rather than agents, the so called *alter ego* doctrine.[28] In one sense the 1982 Act imported a special range of union liability for the industrial torts by way of its own zealous 'organic' doctrine, to supplement an enlarged doctrine of vicarious liability: i.e. the union is liable strictly for the acts of its President, Secretary or NEC – but without the sensible French qualification that they must in some way act within their *'fonctions'*.[29] This could make the union liable even if action were authorized by a demented General Secretary or possibly even a rump of NEC members well below the quorum in the rules.

In France one does find pressures to enlarge liability. The traditional proposition that the law on strikes 'centres not on the liability of the union but on whether the individual stands to lose his job' (through *faute lorde*)[30] has not survived a complex jurisprudence of furious judicial activity and creativity that began in 1972.[31] In the *Corfu* case of that year damages of over 500,000 francs to non-strikers were upheld against union delegates who led an unlawful occupation.[32] By 1980, *l'affaire Regie Renault* saw an employer initially claim damages for loss caused by go-slows to the tune of 100 million francs – and against a union for its *'rôle moteur'* in inciting the workers.[33] Here was a new dimension to fault. Moreover, any of the strikers could be chosen as defendants to pay for the whole loss under the classical rule that in delict guilty defendants are liable *in solidum*.[34] Writers reacted in ways not unlike those in Britain who spied the threat to workers' freedoms in *Rookes* v *Barnard*; and they warned their countrymen, in comparative terms, not to follow 'the example of England with its strikes more and more tangled up in the courts' – and that was before 1980.[35]

Such was the concern that into one of the Bills enacting the *Auroux* reforms of 1982 there was inserted a provision for an immunity in terms familiar to us: in industrial disputes no action was to be permitted against workers, their representatives or a union for compensation unless the damage was caused by criminal acts or 'acts that are manifestly not capable of being part of the exercise of the right to strike or right to take trade union action'. But the clause was never enacted; it was declared unconstitutional by the *Conseil Constitutionel* as contravening principles of equality, a much debated assessment.[36] At once two judgments of the *Cour de Cassation* swung the pendulum back, holding in *l'affaire Dubigeon-Normandie* that a union or union delegate can be liable for personal fault but not for merely organizing a licit strike even if illegal acts result; and in *l'affaire Trailor*[37] that even if a union or union delegate acts in combination with those who commit the tortious acts, they are liable for acts done in a lawful strike only if they personally instigated them (in the case of a union, by an organ) and not for acts inherent in the 'normal exercise of the constitutional right to strike' (and it was held later that this requires something more than a passive presence of union officers).[38] The *Cour de Cassation*, in other words, adopted almost the very formula constitutionally denied to the legislature just fifteen days before.

Given that situation, would the courts extend principles of vicarious liability? Quite the opposite. Take *la Société Escobois*.[39] It obtained judgment against a union delegate who organized an occupation during a strike and then against the regional union by reason merely (said the Court of Appeal) 'of his being the agent of the union'. On further appeal the award against the union was reversed. To be liable 'the union must be the direct author through its organs of acts considered wrongful. It is liable only personally not [vicariously] for the strikers' acts.' The judgment is not overtly in terms of vicarious liability, but of 'fault' (article 1382 *Code Civil*), and there was no personal fault on its part.

What then is the position of the 'union delegate'? Is he not an agent of the union? The relevance of the question grows in the light of article 1384 of the *Code Civil* on responsibility of the acts of another. Here we find cases of true vicarious liability set out – liability of the parent for a child, instructor for apprentice and (in para. 5) a master for a servant and principal for an agent, at least 'within the functions for which he is employed'. Although an insurance scheme has taken over liability for car accidents (law 677 of 5 July 1985), the English lawyer can find plenty here that looks familiar – drivers on frolics of their own or employees who cause damage when 'abusing' their functions.[40] Does article 1384 then open new avenues to union liability for the delegate?

Apparently not, or not yet. The delegate is not only not a 'subordinate' agent,[41] he is not a union agent at all. The dominant view is that article 1384 para. 5, does not, save in the most unusual case, make the union liable as principal. One – but only one – of the reasons for this is the nature of the right to strike itself. In *Dubigeon-Normandie* the court said: 'The unions are not the principals of the strikers who exercise their own individual rights to strike'. The delegate, as a striking worker, exercises his right (and if he abuses it, incurs his own personal liability). 'Article 1384, paragraph 5, therefore appears to be wholly excluded.'[42] 'As to art. 1384: even if the workers cause damage to the enterprise illegally, they are not agents with the union as their principal.'[43] And that goes for all types of representatives, appointed union delegates and elected workers' representatives: 'they are neither organs nor officials nor agents of the union'.[44]

This is an interesting adherence to general legal principle. For the delegate is, after all, appointed by the 'representative' union to 'represent it as against the employer'.[45] His functions include defence of the interests of union members and, indeed, of all employees, together with the general *fonctionnement social* of the enterprise, initiating bargaining demands, negotiating with the employer, arranging elections for other representatives (personnel delegates, works council members and members of the committee on safety, health and working conditions).[46]

Inevitably the union delegate has a high profile during strikes. Yet despite all this, he is still not in law the union's agent. Nor is he the workers' principal, nor their agent. 'His functions give him no power of representation of striking workers and even less the quality of principal responsible for illegal acts which they commit.'[47] There have been a few indications of a stricter tendency, but they remain exceptional. In administrative law the *Conseil d'État* has expressed the view that a delegate must play a 'role of moderation' within the enterprise.[48] There seems to be pressure from below: witness the need for the *Cour de Cassation* to reverse many judgments by Courts of Appeal which have widened liability, though it has itself imposed liability firmly where the delegate has promoted a strike in deliberate breach of procedures agreed in a collective agreement (these – on notice, safety and the like – are valid so long as they do not effectively prohibit strikes).[49]

The issues in tort were tested again in 1990 in three Cour de Cassation judgments on claims under article 1382 by the *Société Générale Sucrière* relating to a wave of strikes (nine years earlier) at their plants.[50] The defendants were CGT unions: a local union at a plant at Montareau, the Marseilles area union and the engineers' union at Nassandres. In each case workers had effected an unlawful occupation and resisted orders of eviction. Various Courts of Appeal had held the unions liable: the Montareau local union had issued a tract supporting the workers after their expulsion; the Marseille union had organized the strike during which workers locked themselves in (with a placard 'Occupied by the CGT' actions for which the union had never disavowed its 'paternity', claimed the Aix appeal judges); and at

Nassandres the union launched the strike in which illegalities occurred with the 'participation of local officials'. The *Cour de Cassation* concluded that none of these judgments could stand. There was not enough to make the unions liable; they were not 'instigators' of the illegalities. The tract at Montareau, for example, was issued after the occupation ended, and no organ of the unions had participated in any of the illegal acts. Moreover: 'the strikers (even if they were union delegates as against the employer, or other representatives of workers in the enterprise) had not ceased to exercise individually their right to strike and did not make the unions of which they were members liable by the illegal acts in which they personally had indulged'.

What comes out of this? A contrast with England to be sure. But also an example, clear because its reasoning is foreign to us, of technical legal rules combining with the social stuff of labour law to govern industrial conflict. The individualization of the right to strike stems mainly from social history, natural to and necessary for pluralist unionism. Consider: 'the right to strike does not rest in the union; it cannot abuse a right it does not possess'.[51] That sets one dimension (though the law of 1963 proves it is not immutable). From altogether elsewhere come principles about agency, fault, 'organs', the *Code Civil* articles 1382 and 1384. These are given to strike law by the *droit commun*. No doubt they have had their own social origins. But by the time they bump into the social phenomena of industrial conflict – and into union structures where the confederal pyramids keep headquarters legally, though not necessarily industrially, rather more distant than in Britain from the shopfloor acts of individual delegates or workers[52] – those origins are of no more relevance than the Code Napoleon itself. Of course, there is ample room here in the confluence of social and juridical streams for judicial policy to steer the direction of union liabilities in strikes. The *Cour de Cassation* proved in 1986 that it is quite capable of moving the legal furniture creatively to the discomfort of the unions (though its new ideas seem subsequently to have been abandoned).[53] But currently its judgments on vicarious liability still protect an advantage (compared with British law) afforded to unions in large measure by the *droit commun*. Will that enlightenment last? And if so, in face of these diverse national laws on strikes and collective bargaining, will the playing field of competition in the Community's internal market remain level?[54]

I am most grateful for the kind assistance of Antoine Lyon-Caen and Hélène Cohen on French law. I remain responsible for errors.

NOTES

1. L. Mariucci, *'Il conflitto collettivo nell'ordinamento giuridico italiano'* (1989) 41 Giorn. di dir. lav. e di rel. ind. 1, 17, 18, quoting the phrase used by G. Giugni in a discussion, *Forme giuridiche del conflitto*, 9 Sept. 1988. On the 'two ideologies' on the right to strike, see O. Kahn-Freund 'Strikes and the Law – some Recent Developments in Western Europe', *Jus et Societas: Essays in Tribute to Wolfgang Friedman* (ed. G. Wilner, 1979) 201-19; Wedderburn, *'Limitation Législative et Judiciaire en Matière d'Action Syndicale et de Droit de Grève'* 1990 No. 1 Rev. Intl. de Droit Comp. 37 (report to 1989 European Congress in Paris).

2. Now *Code du Travail* ('C.T.') art. L.521-1: *'la grève ne rompt pas le contrat de travail, sauf faute lourde imputable au salarié'*. The right to strike received constitutional protection in 1946: G. Lyon-Caen and J. Pelissier *Droit du Travail* (1990 15th ed.) p. 1016ff. The *locus classicus* in English on suspension is X. Blanc-Jouvan, Chap. 4 in B. Aaron and K. Wedderburn, *Industrial Conflict: A Comparative Legal Survey* (1972).

3. CT Art L 521-1 al. 3 (*'nul de plein droit'*; the law of 25 July 1985); in face of the 'normal exercise of the right to strike' the employer may neither dismiss nor apply any other sanction: CT art. L 521-1 al. 2 (law of 17 July 1978) and L 122-45 (as amended by law of 3 January 1985, declaring any such act *'nul de plein droit'*).

4. The breakthrough came in the Cour de Cassation in *Cie. Lyonnaise des Goudrons et des Bitumes c André* Soc. 26 September 1990, Dr. Soc. 1990, 63 (report P. Waquet, 59) and *Sté Thermo Formage Méd (TFM) c La Rocca* Soc. 10 October 1990, Dr. Ouvr. 1990 496 (the employment contract 'could not be lawfully terminated'; therefore reinstatement was available).

5. See J-E. Ray, *'La Réintegration du Gréviste Illégalement Licencié'*, Dr. Soc. 1989, 349 and Dr. Soc. 1991, 64; H. Sinay, *'La Réintégration dans l'Entreprise* in *Les Transformations du Droit du Travail: Études Offertes à Gérard Lyon-Caen* (Dalloz 1989) 415-30. Before 1985 such dismissals were not 'null and void': *l'affaire Talbot*, Soc. 31 March 1982; some courts continued to refuse reinstatement: J-C. Javillier, *Manuel: Droit du Travail* (1990 3rd ed.) pp. 416-7, e.g. Paris Court of Appeal: no reinstatement because 'no legal relation results from the employment contract other than a personal one', 5 May 1988. In *l'affaire Clavaud* Soc. 28 April 1988, reinstatement was obtained by a worker dismissed for criticizing the employer in a newspaper; that infringed his fundamental rights: J-M. Verdier D. Chron. 1988, 63. Workers' elected representatives are protected by special procedures and reinstatement: see G. Lyon-Caen and J. Pelissier, *op.cit.* n. 2, pp. 790-814; though these escaped from restrictions in the Civil Code only in 1974: *les arrêts Perrier*, Soc. 21 June 1974 (Wedderburn (1987) 16 ILJ 1, 7-13). The *délégués syndicaux*, appointed by each 'representative' union with a 'section' in the enterprise, receive similar protection against discrimination and dismissal: J-M. Verdier *Syndicats et Droit Syndical* Vol. 2, *Le Droit Syndical dans l'Entreprise* (1984 2nd ed., and Supp.) pp. 321-428.

6. The ILO Governing Body adopted on 27 February 1991 the 277th Report of the Committee on Freedom of Association with findings on Case 1540,

National Union of Seamen against the UK. The Committee rejected the British Government's bizarre argument that Convention 87 on freedom of association 'does not apply to dismissals *during* a strike' (para. 90). It agreed with the Committee of Experts' report, 1989, that section 62 of the EPCA 1978 must be amended to give protection to workers dismissed for participation in a strike (K. Ewing, *Britain and the ILO*, 1989) and that section 62A (section 9, Employment Act 1990) should also be amended to bring our law into conformity with principles of freedom of association (para. 96) [see now ss. 237, 238 TULRCA 1992].

7. See: *Boxfoldia v NGA* [1988] ICR 752, CA; Employment Act 1990, section 9; *Miles v Wakefield MDC* [1987] AC 539 HL; *Wiluszinski v Tower Hamlets LBC* [1989] ICR 493, CA; *Associated British Ports v TGWU* [1989] 1 WLR 939, CA (revs. on other grounds, ibid. HL); B. Simpson (1989) 18 ILJ 234.

8. For some examples, Wedderburn, 'The Social Charter in Britain: Labour Law and Labour Courts?' (1991) 54 MLR 1, 7-13.

9. *Universe Tankships Inc. of Monrovia v Laughton* [1983] 1 AC 366, HL; and the extraordinary decision in *Dimskal Shipping SA v ITWF* (No. 2) [1990] ICR 694 CA (Neill LJ dissenting) [affirmed [1992] AC 152 HL].

10. See H. Sinay and J-C. Javillier *La Grève* (1984 2nd ed.) pp. 156-290 (difficulties in distinguishing short stop-and-go strikes from go-slows: p. 194); Soc. 16 May 1989 (dismissals upheld where workers provoked an '*engorgement*' of production by go-slow, a 'defective execution of their employment contracts' not a strike). For further discussion of concepts of 'strikes', see Wedderburn, 'The Right to Strike – Is There a European Standard?' Chap. 11 in *Employment Rights in Britain and Europe: Selected Papers in Labour Law* (Lawrence and Wishart, 1991).

11. Separate questions are required in a ballot: section 11(4) Trade Union Act 1984 (as amended by Employment Acts 1988, Sched. 3, and 1990, section 5 and Sched. 2); *Post Office v UCW* [1990] IRLR 143 CA; S. Auerbach (1990) 19 ILJ 120. The definition of 'strike' in section 11(11) of the Trade Union Act 1984 and section 1(7) Employment Act 1988 remarkably includes a 'stoppage' for any purpose whatever, while the description of 'industrial action' in the latter is circular [see TULRCA 1992, ss. 62 and 246].

12. G. Lyon-Caen and J. Pelissier, *op.cit.* n. 2, p. 1041, 1048; for recent judicial restrictions: J. Pelissier, '*La Grève: liberté trés surveillée*' Dr. Ouvr. 1988, 59: *Villon c Bordellay* Soc. 25 June 1987 (participation of dismissed worker; *faute lourde* even though stoppage began as a licit strike and she knew little of subsequent illegalities). On *autosatisfaction des revendications*: see G. Lyon-Caen and J. Pelissier, *op.cit.*, pp. 1039-40.

13. *Syndicat CGT c Sté Le Tabac Reconstitué Inds.* Soc. 30 May 1989 (strikes necessarily lead to disorganization of production, as distinct from gratuitous injury to the enterprise as such); *Sté Protection Surveillance c Mary* Soc. 1 March 1989, Dr. Ouvr. 1989 415 (repeated short strikes licit; not an abnormal disruption; safety measures maintained; no attack on the right to work of other workers). It must be remembered that strikes may also be unlawful if they infringe the right to work of others (*le délit d'entrave*): H. Sinay and J-C. Javillier, *op.cit.* n.2. pp. 743-5.

14. In addition to duties about continuity of service of employees who are

subject to administrative law, in a wider range of public services the law of 31 July 1963 bans all 'rolling' strikes and requires five days' notice of all strikes from a 'representative' trade union (the law of 19 October 1982 requires the parties to 'negotiate' in that period). By putting legality into the hands of a union the 1963 law introduced an alien 'organic' feature into the individualist French system: J-C. Javillier, *op.cit.* n. 5, pp. 403-4. The notice must state the date and hour of the strike 'as well as the duration envisaged, limited or not' (CT. art. L. 521-3, al. 4). It is noteworthy that the new Italian law 'on the exercise of the right to strike in essential public services and safeguarding personal constitutional rights' (Law of 12 June 1990, no. 146) requires ten days' notice 'with an indication of the duration of the stoppage' (art. 2(1)(5)).

15. Soc. 11 July 1989 (*faute lourde* by workers commencing a strike before demands made; but not by a worker who joined the next day, after the demands had been made); see J. Déprez Dr. Soc. 1989, 717; and *Sté Baze*, Soc. 7 February 1990.

16. See W. Cornish and G. de N. Clark, *Law and Society in England 1750-1950* (1989) pp. 489-93; although ameliorated in other developments, the doctrine of 'common employment' was not abolished until the Law Reform (Personal Injuries) Act 1948: pp. 496-9.

17. *Airey v Weighill* (1905) 49 Sol. Jo. 279 CA (whether the acts of a branch were ordered, authorized or ratified by the union; but the defendants were the trustees). Branch officers were not as such treated as agents to bind the union: *Smithies v National Assoc. Operative Plasterers* [1909] 1 KB 310 CA; *Denaby and Cadeby Main Collieries v Yorkshire Miners' Assoc.* [1906] AC 384 HL. On vicarious liability alone the case law of 1900-1909 was more principled than the law as it is in 1991.

18. *Heatons Transport (St. Helens) Ltd v TGWU* [1973] AC 15, HL; *General Aviation Services v TGWU* [1976] IRLR 224, HL; see P. Davies (1973) 36 MLR 78; on the dangers of the use of such concepts as 'authority from the bottom' see *Howitt Transport v TGWU* [1972] IRLR 93, Donaldson P.

19. Employment Act 1982 section 15; see Wedderburn, *The Worker and the Law* (3rd ed. 1986) pp. 524-40 [now ss. 20, 21 TULRCA 1992].

20. Employment Act 1990, section 6; see H. Carty (1991) 20 ILJ 1, 7-9.

21. See G. Lightman, 'A Trade Union in Chains' (1987) *Current Legal Problems* 25; Wedderburn, 'Injunctions and the Sovereignty of Parliament' (1989) 23 *Law Teacher* 4, 22-31. Some limitation on damages is provided by section 16 Employment Act 1982. The effectiveness of *astreinte* is clear: D. Tallon in D. Harris and D. Tallon (eds.) *Contract Law Today: Anglo-French Comparisons* (1989) p. 270.

22. *L'insaisissabilité du patrimoine*, CT art. L 411-12 al. 2; J-M. Verdier *Syndicats et Droit Syndical*, Vol. 1, *Liberté, Structure, Action*. (1987) pp. 295-7, 374 (but mortgages and charges may be enforced; also a garnishee order made: Trib. G.I. Nanterre 13 February 1989).

23. J-M. Servais, *Inviolability of Trade Union Premises and Communications* (1980 ILO) p. 10; and the ILO study after the Resolution of 1970, *The Public Authorities and the Right to Protection of Trade Union Funds and Property* (ILO 1976), on 'immunity' p. 97. On Dicey and *Taff Vale*, Wedderburn, *op.cit.*, n. 19, pp. 526-8.

24. See on what follows: J-M. Verdier Vol. 1, *op.cit.*, n. 22, pp. 286-94; H. Sinay and J-C. Javillier, *op.cit.*, n. 10, pp. 364-86; G. Lyon-Caen and J. Pelissier, *op.cit.*, n. 2, pp. 1063-70; J-C. Javillier, *op.cit.*, n. 5, pp. 419-23. On unions as *personnes morales*: CT art. L 411-10 and -11. British unions are not corporate bodies but they can sue and be sued in contract and in tort: sections 2(c) TULRA 1974 (on *ultra vires*, see Wedderburn (1985) 14 ILJ 127).

25. A. Tunc, *La Responsibilité Civile* (1981) p. 11. Art. 1383 declares that negligence can ground liability. On art. 1384, see below n. 40. Generally on *la responsabilité délictuelle*, see M. Le Galcher-Baron, *Les Obligations* (5th ed. 1986, P. Level) pp. 189-292.

26. See Verdier, *op.cit.*, n. 22, pp. 289-91. The precise personal liability of the organ is less certain. As to the *délégués syndicaux*, see below n. 41.

27. G. Lyon-Caen and J. Pelissier, *op.cit.* n. 2, pp. 705-6. In France a legal person is 'liable for acts of its organs ... without that raising any issue about their status as agents within article 1384 alinéa 5 [of the *Code Civil*]': Cass. Civ. 17 July 1967 (see below n. 40 on art. 1384).

28. He is not an *'alter ego*; he is the company's 'servant, agent, delegate or representative ... [or its] embodiment': *per* Lord Reid, *Tesco Supermarkets Ltd* v *Nattrass* [1972] AC 153, 170-1. The Companies Act 1985 section 35A (as amended 1989) attempts to make organs out of agents in transactions with third parties by giving the board of directors power to authorize others to bind the company free from limitations on authority. On powers of organs in French limited liability companies (board of directors, president and, if appointed, general-directors) see law 119 of 24 July 1966, arts. 98, 113, 117.

29. Employment Act 1982, section 15, amended by section 6 of the Employment Act 1990; the precept 'notwithstading anything in the rules' applies to the NEC and two top officers: section 15(3B). A quorum for NEC meetings might be set out in the rules, or some other document here included in the 'rules': section 15(7) [now s. 20(7) TULRCA 1992].

30. O. Kahn-Freund, *Jus et Societas*, n. 1, p. 216 (except in the public sector, *supra* n. 14). Taking part in an illegitimate strike amounts *ipso facto* to *faute lorde* (*Mazet c. Sté Euro. de Propulsion* Soc. 19 November 1987); but either all or none of the workers participating in it must be found guilty; no discrimination is allowed (Soc. 1 December 1988; Soc. 6 June 1989).

31. On the comparative creativity of judges in France and in Britain, see Wedderburn, '*Le Législateur et le Juge*' in *Les Transformations du Droit du Travail: Études Offertes à Gérard Lyon-Caen* (Dalloz 1989) pp. 123-58; on the style of the French judiciary, see the helpful article by A. Jeammaud, '*Les Contentieux des Conflits du Travail*' Dr. Soc. 1988, 689.

32. Soc. 8 February 1972, J. Savatier Dr. Soc. 1972, 544. An occupation is normally unlawful but in practice common; interlocutory injunctions are not always granted (J. Savaiter Dr. Soc. 1988, 655), and negotiation by the employer may be made a condition (A. Jeammaud and M. Le Friant, '*La grève, le juge et la négociation*' Dr. Soc. 1990, 167-177). On the interlocutory orders in the two jurisdictions, Wedderburn, '*Le Législateur et le Juge, op.cit.*, n. 31 above, pp. 147-155. French judges have often been restrained in their interlocutory orders 'in the interests of social peace':

J-M. Verdier, *Droit du Travail* (9th ed. 1990) p. 357. On forms of *'fautes des grévistes'*, see J. Pelissier Dr. Soc. 1988, 650.

33. Angers Court of Appeal 22 October 1980 (the case was settled after a reduction of the claim to 6 mn. francs), G. Lyon-Caen D. 1981, 153; J. Savatier Dr. Soc. 1980, 545 (union could be liable for a go-slow if it 'incited workers to violate their contractual duties', 547).

34. It has often been held that each striker may be liable for the whole amount under such responsibility: see Soc. 8 December 1983 (liability to non-strikers); *Di Fruschia c Arnaud*, Soc. 6 June 1989, Dr. Ouvr. 1990, 31 (seven strikers sued for whole damage flowing from illegal occupation). But the Court de Cassation has lately restricted the scope of liability *in solidum* in such cases: see *Sté Sapro c Charbelet et Union locale CFDT* Soc. 23 June 1988 (symbolic one franc awarded against a defendant *délégué syndical* whose acts had not 'caused' the whole damage), *Browet c Capelle Caron* Soc. 9 March 1989 (court must decide which unlawful acts engaged the personal participation of each defendant) and *Robin c Sté Les Papeteries de Mauduit* Soc. 30 January 1991 (judgment making seven pickets collectively liable reversed as the court below had failed to inquire 'in regard to each defendant worker', precisely which of the unlawful acts it was in which he was said to be a participant; nor had it instructed its 'expert' to inquire into the damage flowing from each such act (on use of experts, see Wedderburn (1991) 54 MLR 1, 37-40). These decisions have been said to halt an earlier 'abusive extension' of liability *in solidum*, insisting on strict proof of the wrongful acts of each defendant linked causatively to the damage – 'judgment *in solidum* is only for co-authors': Dr. Ouvr. 1991, 108 note F.S. Compare the robust ease with which the Law Lords made the defendants, especially the union official, all liable as 'conspirators' (or was it as joint tortfeasors?) in *Rookes v Barnard* [1964] AC 1129, HL.

35. See the classic articles by G. Lyon-Caen, *'La recherche des responsabilités dans les conflits du travail'* D. Chron 1979, 255, 257, and H. Sinay, *'La Neutralisation du Droit de Grève'* Dr. Soc. 1980, 250. Despite the variable policies of the judges, most French critics seem to prefer to rely on the courts than on the legislature: G. Lyon-Caen, *'Réglementer le droit de Grève?'* Dr. Soc. 1988, 709; contrast G. Viney, *'Responsabilité civile et relations collectives du travail'* Dr. Soc. 1988, 416. On *Rookes v Barnard* [1964] AC 1129, HL, see O. Kahn-Freund (1964) 14 *Federation News* 30; Wedderburn (1964) 27 MLR 525; and above p. 64.

36. See generally, H. Sinay and J-C. Javillier, *op.cit.*, n. 10 above pp. 92-9, 371-78. For the *Conseil Constitutionel* decision, 22 October 1982, Gaz. Pal. 1 sem. 60, see L. Hamon Dr. Soc. 1983, 155; F. Luchaire D. 1983, 189, for a rather different evaluation, M. Forde (1984) 13 ILJ 40. Legislation is within the purview of the *Conseil Constitutionel*, the courts are not.

37. These two decisive judgments of Soc. 9 November 1982 were crucial, see J. Savatier Dr. Soc. 1983, 175, who puts the emphasis in *Dubigeon-Normandie* on lack of causal link while others insist there was no 'fault': H. Sinay and J-C. Javillier, *op.cit.*, n. 10, pp. 295-6. See now, *Sté Sabro* Soc. 23 June 1988 and *Sté Les Papeteries de Mauduit* Soc. 30 January 1991 above, n. 34; below n. 50).

38. Most of the jurisprudence has maintained these principles: Soc. 8 November 1984 (union liable, main officers involved personally); Soc. 26 July 1984 (wrongful acts of strikers alone, union not liable); Soc. 16 January 1985 (union liable as 'instigator, promoter and organiser' of illicit *auto-satisfaction*); *Sté Sapro*, Soc. 23 June 1988 (union delegate, passive presence insufficient, no fault). F. Saramito Dr. Ouvr. 1988, 446; and now *Sté des Kaolins du Finistère*, Soc. 19 December 1990; Bull. V no. 698, p. 421. Some commentators seek a wider liability: B. Teyssié, *'La raison, la grève et le juge'* Dr. Soc. 1988 562, 571.

39. *Sté Escourcois des Bois ('Escobois')* Soc. 21 January 1987, J-E. Ray, *'La responsabilité civile du syndicat et de ses délégués à l'occasion d'un conflit du travail'* Dr. Soc. 1987, 426 ('hundreds of cases' since 1978, marking the 'rediscovery of article 1382' in labour law, 429-30). Each federation and union is viewed separately in the various federations of French union structure: J-M. Verdier, *op.cit.* n. 22, Vol. 1, pp. 270-369. It is notable that the delegate retains his *'mandat'* even during a strike: G. Lyon-Caen and J. Pelissier, *op.cit.*, n. 2, p. 839. On occupations as unlawful invasions of property and (even more) as interferences with the right to work, see *l'arrêt Ferodo* Soc. 17 May 1977, A. Jeammaud D. 1977, 645.

40. A clash between the Criminal and Civil Chambers of the Cour de Cassation was settled in favour of the latter's narrow view: the principal is not liable where the agent 'acting without authorisation, for purposes foreign to his competence, goes outside the functions for which he was employed': Ass. plén. 27 October 1983 and 15 November 1985, J. Aubert D. 1986, 81; liability for contractual fault may be wider, see M. Le Galcher-Baron, *Les Obligations cit.* n. 25, pp. 205-32.

41. See J-E. Ray, *op.cit.*, n. 39, Dr. Soc. 1987, p. 428. Generally on *responsabilité du fait d'autrui*, M. Le Galcher-Baron, *op.cit.*, n. 25, p. 216-40.

42. H. Sinay and J-C. Javillier, *op.cit.*, n. 10, p. 377.

43. G. Lyon-Caen, *op.cit.*, n. 35, D. 1979 Chron. 255.

44. G. Lyon-Caen and J. Pelissier, *op.cit.* (1990) n. 2, p. 1067. So too, G. Viney, *'Responsabilité civile et relations collectives de travail'* Dr. Soc. 1988, 416-425; J-M. Verdier, *Liberté, structure, action* (Vol. 1) *cit.* n. 22, pp. 291-5; *Le Droit syndical dans l'entreprise cit.* n. 5 (Vol. 2) pp. 292-3; and his *Droit du Travail* (1990 9th ed.) pp. 369-70. On the personal liability of union delegates: G. Durry Dr. Soc. 1984, 49.

45. CT art. L 412-11 (in undertakings with at least 50 employees; but after 1982 each representative union can appoint *délégués syndicals centrals* in an enterprise of more than 2000 employees; they also have a union 'section' in the enterprise to look after the 'material and moral interests of members': art. L 412-6). Unions become 'representative' not by election, but by satisfying complex series of relative tests, ranging from general support to their affiliation to national confederations: see for a helpful short account, J-C. Javillier, *Manuel, op.cit.*, n. 5, pp. 286-302.

46. See J-M. Verdier, *op.cit.* n. 5, Vol. 2, 1984, pp. 157-428.

47. Dr. Ouvr. 1988, 446, 447, on *Sté Sapro* Soc. 28 June 1988.

48. 27 June 1979, M.A. Latournerie Dr. Soc. 1979, 42 (administrative courts control the labour inspectors without whose authority dismissal of a

delegate is null and void; CT art, L 412-18). 'One can only regret the position of the Conseil d'État', J-M. Verdier (1990), *op.cit.*, n. 32, p. 370.

49. *Tanneries de Sireuil* Soc. 8 December 1983 (collective agreement on perishable goods ignored); G. Lyon-Caen and J. Pelissier, *op.cit.*, n. 2, pp. 1064-5. 'A renunciation of the right to strike, collective or individual, is of no validity', J-M. Verdier, *Droit du Travail* (9th ed. 1990) 353.

50. Three judgments involving the same company: *Union Locale CGT Monterau c Sté Générale Sucrière, Syndicat des Ouvriers Raffineurs (Marseille CGT-UGICT) c ibid.; Syndicat CGT de la Générale Sucrière (Nassandres) c ibid.*, Soc. 17 July 1990, (Bull. Civ. Vth., nos. 371 and 375), reversing judgments of Courts of Appeal of Paris, Aix-en-Provence, and Rouen; see Dr. Ouvr. 1990, 375 (P. Waquet, conseiller). For a union held liable because acts of obstruction were carried out on its officers' *instructions*, see *Synd. CGT des Papeteries de Mauduit c Sté Les Papeteries de Mauduit*, Soc. 30 January 1991, Dr. Ouvr. 1991, 108 (though individual strikers there escaped liability: above, n. 34).

51. G. Lyon-Caen, *op.cit.*, D 1979 Chron. 255.

52. See J-M. Verdier, *op.cit.*, n. 22, Vol. 1, on union structure, especially pp. 306-69 on local, departmental and other confederations, and the different structures of the CGT and CFDT. 'The union which participates in the conflict is, in general, a local union. In law it represents neither its federation nor its confederation': J. Goineau, *'La responsabilité civile des grévistes et des syndicats'* Dr. Soc. 1988, 702, 706-8 (this may be an ambivalent advantage because that structure can fragment solidarity). See too, M. Forde, 'Trade Union Pluralism and Labour Law in France' (1984) 33 ICLQ 134. A *section syndicale* has no legal personality: *Sté. des Kaolins du Finistère*, Soc. 19 December 1990, Bull. V no. 698, p. 421 (local union not liable; it had not organized strike nor participated in illegal acts; the plaintiffs sought unsuccessfully a creative ruling that the *section syndicale* had become a separate 'enterprise union').

53. See *SNOMAC c Air France* Ass. plén. 4 July 1986, C. Lyon-Caen Dr. Soc. 1986, 745 (interlocutory order by a *juge des référés* pronouncing strike notice illegal as *unreasonable* surprisingly upheld); but see now *contra* Paris Court of Appeal 27 January 1988; J-E. Ray Dr. Soc. 1988, 242; J-C. Javillier D. 1988 351 (a judge has no jurisdiction to judge the merits of the strikers' demands). The judgment of this 'lower' court seems to have had the last word on the point: G. Lyon-Caen and J. Pelissier, *op.cit.*, n. 2, p. 1041, n. 1 and 1063-4; and Wedderburn, *'Le Législateur et le Juge'*, *op.cit.* n. 31, pp. 149-52 [it has now been adopted: soc. 2 June 1992, Dr. Soc. 1992, 700].

54. Much may depend on the renegotiation of the Treaty, though current indications are that no floor of collective labour rights will be inserted. Given their astonishing diversity, without any common legal framework (whether on general principles, such as freedom of association or more technical rules such as vicarious liability) the various labour law systems of Member States might well provide unacceptable advantages to parties in their own labour markets: see G.F. Mancini, 'Labour Law and Community Law' (1985) 20 (N.S.) Irish Jurist 1; Wedderburn, 'European Community Law and Workers' Rights – Fact or Fake in 1992?' (1990 Moran Lecture, Trinity College Dublin, (1991) 13 Univ. Dub.

LJ 1) chapter 8 below, and 'The Right to Strike: Is There a European Standard?' (1991, *op.cit.* n. 10 above) [and now chapter 10 below, pp. 385-41. The French jurisprudence has not undergone radical change, see G. Lyon-Caen, J. Pelissier and A. Supiot, *Droit du Travail* (17th ed. 1994) 843-869].

5

TRADE UNION DEMOCRACY AND STATE REGULATION*

Every Western society with a capitalist mixed economy lays claim to democratic values both in its political system and in its trade union structures; yet these two component forces give rise to markedly divergent results. The line which is perceived as protecting that democratic autonomy which is the essence of free trade unionism is drawn very differently in the different countries. The primary purpose of this paper is to evaluate what has happened to it in Britain, in a comparative context. Comparative study has not revealed satisfactory explanation of this phenomenon of divergence. It is sometimes suggested that neo-corporatist State policies bring with them a special danger of integration of trade unions and, therefore, an imposition upon them of concepts of democracy devised by the State for its own purposes. Recent experience in Britain suggests that legal regulation of internal union affairs based on a vision of 'democracy' as seen by the political system may, on the contrary, be the product of decreasing neo-corporatist tendencies in the character of the State.

A SPECTRUM OF UNION 'DEMOCRACY'

Trade union democracy, in a free society, manifestly has a different purpose from that of government. A traditional British view emphasises this:

> Trade union organisation is not based on theoretical concepts prior to it, that is on some concept of democracy, but on the end it serves ... the end of trade union activity is to protect and improve the general living standards of its members and not to provide workers with an exercise in self-government.[1]

*Paper delivered at a conference in Bologna 28 April 1988, and published in 1988 in *Bulletin of Comparative Labor Relations* Vol. 17.

Other writers accept that the functional needs of the union and of its members do not necessarily fit *a priori* political concepts, for example where the State imposes on unions forms of balloting (as in the British laws of 1984 and 1988) and 'methods appropriate to the national system are transposed to the industrial relations system ... [when] the analogy is of only limited relevance.'[2]

At the other end of the spectrum stands the belief that union democracy must assume forms essentially parallel to those of political democracy. Factions are inevitable in unions; but it is another matter to demand 'the institutionalisation of opposition' within the union, as Lipset put it, with a party system with a permanent opposition.[3] To avoid the iron law of oligarchy and defeat bureaucracy the political mechanisms are imposed upon the union. Without going that far, the Landrum Griffin Act 1959 sets standards for union decision-making, through democratic procedures and financial controls.[4]

This second view, criticised in the United States for being too mechanical, too insensitive to environmental problems,[5] is regarded as far from ideal by most European commentators.

Kahn-Freund remarked that the State or municipal government does not have to reckon with a secession or a breakaway, it punishes treason and can afford parties so long as there is no civil war. But a union is a 'fighting body' from which the opposition can secede.[6] Others have set the limits of 'faction' that are consistent with representative elections themselves and the achievement of a union's purposes.[7] Clegg concluded that 'too much success [for an opposition] may undermine democracy'.[8]

In British unions for a century there has been only one major scandal, a ballot-rigging case of 1959, very different from the 'boss-ridden' bribery and violence in the 1920s, and corruption in the 1950's, in the United States.[9] It was, therefore, something of a surprise when the British government declared in 1983 its doubt about the representative character of the union leaders.[10] The new policy adopted thereafter threw in issue the extent to which the tests employed still represented a consensus, as they had in the past by addressing and imposing postal ballots for elections to central union committees.

UNION AUTONOMY AND STATUS

The long-standing refusal to pick up Professor Chafee's 'hot potato'[11] was not confined to Britain. Most Western European democracies have shared a hands-off policy, requiring only that the union must act within its purposes and its rules and observe in its treatment of members – '*les droits de la defense*', or the 'rules of natural justice'.[12] The principle of autonomy and *democrazia sindacale* have caused the courts in Italy as in France, Germany and Sweden, to practise 'abstentionism';[13] and whilst it is true that in Germany and Britain the courts have been rather more active in controlling expulsions (and in the former admissions), in general the internal autonomy of the union is respected by the law. Even today the English judges can still hold that it is 'not in the interests either of the members of such voluntary societies or of the administration of justice' for a court to intervene in a disciplinary matter before it has been heard by the 'domestic tribunal of the society according to the rules'.[14] This model of autonomous trade unionism was exported from Europe into the basic concepts of the International Labour Organisation, notably in Convention 87 of 1948 and Convention 98 of 1949, to give workers the right to establish unions and federations of their own choosing without previous authorisation; the right to draw up their rules, to elect representatives and to carry on union activities, free from dissolution by administrative authority, became the bedrock. Interference by 'public authorities' is acceptable only where it aims solely at ensuring respect for 'democratic rules'.[15]

One legal feature which illustrates the variety of application is the extent to which unions consider themselves able to accept or resist formal incorporation as a 'legal person', or corporate body, a status which by ILO standards must not be the subject of conditions which restrict the liberties of free association.[16] French unions are sufficiently secure in their independence to enjoy the status of *la personalité civile* created by the law of 12 March 1920, one of the 'necessities' of *la liberté syndicale*. So too in Sweden.[17] But here no heavy price is paid to the State. Contrast systems where recognition as a 'person' is part of a package of benefits and controls, as in the compulsory arbitration structures of Australia, or even in the United States.[18] Here, corporate status or legal personality flows from the precept that the 'democratic myth and aspiration of the union movement ... constitutes a general holding forth ... a promise made to the public as well as to the member'.[19] In Australia '[unions] were seen as existing primarily to serve public purposes as defined by governments or by courts ... entitled only to a "quasi" autonomy in relation to the state and its instruments'.[20]

Sensing a danger to their autonomy, therefore, unions in some countries have tended not to strive for, or not to accept, corporate status, as in Germany where it was associated with persecution. In Italy the status of *'associazione non riconosciuta'* is not unrelated to anxieties about the consequences that might flow from a scheme of registration under Article 39.2 of the Constitution. Nowhere is this relationship between union resistance to control and legal corporate status clearer than in Britain. There has never been a system of compulsory registration (not even by formal deposit of constitutional documents, as in France); but in 1871 Parliament offered minor benefits to unions that entered on a register. When the judges decided thirty years later that this was enough to make the union a quasi-corporate person, amenable to the rigours of common law liability against its property,[22] Parliament responded with protection against civil liability in tort – a shield later repealed in 1982.[23] The Law Lords also held that the doctrine of *ultra vires* applied to the 'quasi-corporate' unions to prohibit their 'political' activity – a prohibition partially removed by a statute which permits political activity so long as each member can 'contract-out' of political contributions without disadvantage.[24] The unions continued to insist that they were still unincorporated bodies, in the Webbs' phrase 'spontaneously arising associative entities'.[25] Companies and other corporations were command-structures; they were not. Employers had earlier proposed that a union be made by law a *persona ficta* to facilitate control.[26] The attempt in the Industrial Relations Act 1971, however, did not impose full corporate status on all unions, a surprising feature of that neo-corporatist statute, as we shall see. It offered full incorporation only to unions which registered on the new Register, which also brought them liberties to organise and to strike not enjoyed by recalcitrant unions (which were to exist in a juridical Siberia until the repeal of the Act in 1974).[27] Most unions affiliated to the TUC refused to register.

In 1974, inaugurating the modern system, Parliament enacted that unions are not and 'shall not be treated as if they are' bodies corporate; but they were given legal capacity to sue or be sued in court, and to make contracts. This compromise, breaking the formal categories and allowing the unincorporated union some incidents of corporate status without corporate capacity, appears not dissimilar to the compromise reached for *associazioni non riconosciute* and *Gewerkschaften*, – an 'intermediate type' of body or a 'centre of interests [with] limited personality'.[28]

These are not academic or technical questions. They relate to the ease with which legal doctrines can be used in the courts, to attack the autonomy of unions via their property, in actions for damages and injunctions, or fines or sequestration of property for disobedience to court orders, as is evidenced by the liabilities opened up for unions in

Britain after the Act of 1982. Such issues are likely to be more important where the political system confronts a 'unitary' structure of unions which derive their strength from membership and property based upon contributions, whether centralised with industrial unions as in Germany or Sweden, or fragmented, under a confederal umbrella, by 'multi-unionism' in Britain, Australia and the United States. Such remedies may be acceptable where the drain on union property is small, and the central role of the unions accepted in a social *consensus*. We may note the systems in Scandinavia, where care is taken to maintain the level of damages as modest to avoid 'reactions of defiance thereby creating antagonisms between classes and groups within society'.[29] No such self-discipline clothed English courts in their seizure of the assets of unions under the labour laws of the 1980s.[30]

Where unions in an ideologically pluralist system are financially weak or of uncertain monetary strength, as in Italy, discussion of such issues is sparse.[31] Even in such jurisdictions, however, an increase in civil liability gives it new relevance. In France, for example, the judicial tendencies since 1972 to impose liability in compensation (in some cases of millions of francs) led to an unsuccessful attempt to legislate a new, British-style 'immunity' limiting liability to acts that were either crimes or 'manifestly incapable of being connected to the exercise of the right to strike or trade union rights'. Faced with decisions that limit the right to strike, the French rule protecting the *patrimoine* of the union from legal attachment may assume greater importance than in the past.[32]

POLITICAL EXTENSIONS FOR 'EXTERNAL' DEMOCRACY

It was until recently possible to argue that a new common feature was emerging. This lay in the promotional or auxiliary legislation to extend the range of democracy in industrial relations, and the participation in it of workers through their unions in forms of industrial democracy. Such parallels there undoubtedly were, despite the divergencies of form.[33] In the same period, the EC Commission confronted the new 'stress' in industrial relations and the need to seek both economic growth and 'improvement of the quality of life and working conditions' by asserting that decision making processes in enterprises must 'have a broader democratic base'.[34] By the early 1980s one finds the law promoting forms of industrial democracy in auxiliary and promotional legislation, creating rights to disclosure of information or extending a right to bargain with the employer. In some countries

(Germany, the Netherlands, Austria) the route lay through the structure of the enterprise; in others (Sweden, Italy) the goal was pursued primarily through the avenues of collective bargaining, with assistance from the law. In yet others, the most important advances were co-operation agreements between the 'social partners' as in Denmark.[35]

But the meaning of the auxiliary law varied widely. In Britain, the 1975 obligation on employers to disclose information to 'recognised' unions has done little to expand the external range of democracy for unions' influence because it was confined to matters on which the employer already bargained.[36] By contrast, a bargaining union after 1976 in Sweden is entitled to disclosure on the employer's activities. Summers has contrasted starkly the extensive information and consultation rights accorded to the German Works Council, in its role of 'trustful co-operation' with the meagre rights to disclosure for unions in the United States even on the matters directly relating to the duty to bargain.[37] Legislation realising EEC Directives about obligatory consultation by employers has sometimes been ineffective in application, sometimes even non-existent, but the pressure in the Community for the realisation of the 'Vredeling' draft directive has shown that support for expanding trade union rights to information and consultation is not dead, even though the new demands for 'flexibility' now hamper the process and certain member governments maintain their attempts to stifle it.[38]

Analysis by reference to the reality rather than to the models of external democracy is also needed on participation within the enterprise and the duty on employers to 'recognise' or bargain with the union. It has been said of the German 'second tier' Supervisory Board: 'The decisions which affect the workforce most particularly are not within its jurisdiction'; and the real point of codetermination is 'the decisive power of works councils'.[39] The alternative route of a legal duty to bargain needs similar evaluation. The fragile duty to bargain enacted in Britain in 1975 failed after five years largely by reason of hostile decisions of the courts and, even more, the inability of employers' and union representatives on the Council running the scheme to agree upon the criteria for recognition.[40] The right to negotiate across the board on the employer's business activity won by Swedish unions in the Act of 1976, extending to a duty on the employer to initiate 'primary negotiations' with an established union on changes in the business, comprises (when added to the unions' right to small representation on company boards for informational purposes; and strong legislation on the working environment and employment protection) a bold attempt to widen democratic control.[41] Here the objective is an extension of the employer's duty to initiate bargaining as part of social reform, an aim shared in France when the *Auroux* reforms of 1982 instituted legal obligations to review industry level agreements and to bargain annually at enterprise level (though with the right, natural to a system of union pluralism, for a non-signatory, representative union to object to an agreement introducing new terms within eight days and, with the support of half the constituency of workers in the most recent elections to the *comité d'entreprise*, to secure its revocation).[42] The Auroux Report was unequivocal in stating: *la politique contractuelle doit devenir la pratique privilégiée du progres social.*

That is hardly the case for the union in the United States, with its right to bargain and the duty to represent all workers in the unit fairly.[43] Not that the idea of representing members and non-members alike is unknown to Europe; the *'rappresentanze sindacali aziendali'* assure Italian unions a presence at the workplace but in bodies which on the initiative of workers are elected by all, union members and non-members, even though they must operate within the 'ambit' of 'representative' unions.[44] Whereas the American system is seen as having introduced pluralist 'joint sovereignty' into industrial relations, for employees to 'participate', Feller asserts, where management would otherwise rule unilaterally,[45] the limitations on the duty to bargain facilitate the criticisms even of those who identify its nature as an inducement to workers 'to participate in their own domination at the workplace'.[46] The fact is the duty to bargain in the United States does not point towards an expanding external union democracy because it does not aim to trespass upon the prerogative of the employer to make most of the strategic decisions in the enterprise. This is particularly striking when contrasted with the profound debate surrounding the legitimacy of corporate power which has continued in that country above all, ever since Dodd posed the searching question in 1932: *For Whom Are Corporate Managers Trustees?*[47] The 'mandatory' subjects of bargaining are not meant to make the union 'an equal partner in the running of the business'.[48]

There are, however, more subtle ways of advancing external democracy than the somewhat cumbersome weapon of a general duty to bargain. Various Italian laws of the 1970s, together with laws of 1983-84, refer matters on which general direction is undertaken by the law to agreements at plant or other level for implementation, creating, if not a strict duty, at least an 'onus' to bargain.[49] Such laws permit 'a derogation from existing employment terms' where plant bargaining fixes new terms, as in the case of solidarity contracts.[50] Although there is some analogy with a Works Council in German law, this important Italian development is more flexible, allowing in a variety of areas supple obligations which 'may not all flower in the garden of labour law strictly under the name of "duty to bargain", but on the shop floor they may smell as sweet'.[51]

BARGAINING AGENTS AND STABILITY

A collective bargaining system requires reasonable stability with parties who are identifiable. On the trade union side this raises the issues both of certainty and of representativeness. The latter reaches back into the internal structure of the union, and its claim to 'represent' members. Here, the impact of State law discloses the variations imposed particularly by industrial structures bequeathed by history. Systems blessed with strong and relatively unified industrial unionism can afford to propound constitutional rights to associate and to legislate little about which unions may bargain with particular employers. The Federal Republic of Germany is the clearest example; and in Sweden the small cloud of 'autonomous unions' has not yet thrown shadows over that type of solution. In the United States and Britain, on the other hand, union structures based equally on membership differ radically in their competitive multi-unionism. Such competition may even lead a union to make agreements as exclusive agent before a workforce is even hired, perhaps after a 'beauty contest' of unions paraded before management as in Britain today; this raises delicate problems of democracy unlikely to escape political attention.[52] The solution in the United States is sought through the elected exclusive bargaining unit plus the AFL-CIO 'no-raiding' agreement; but commentators suggest this structure (founded on less than 20 per cent unionised density) may need further change to meet workers' needs, when 'rapid internationalisation of the world economic system through multinational business is undermining the effectiveness of wholly nationalistic trade unions'.[53]

In Britain the law has made little of a contribution to identification of the bargaining agent, apart from the exceptional period 1971-74. The 'Disputes Procedures' of the TUC operate contractually to regulate competing claims of affiliated unions, a consensual code using tests based on a mixture of historical accident and membership in the relevant employment unit. Otherwise, the union security device of the 'closed shop' (amongst its many other functions relating to job control, controlling the 'alternative workforce' etc.),[54] has provided one mechanism for 'effective and stable organisation', a useful link, so long as there are (as in practice there have always been) safeguards for workers who object to membership out of conscience, between 'effective collective bargaining and strong trade unions'.[55] The 1982 legislation imposed a rigorous test of representativeness here – a ballot in which workers approved the closed shop by either 85 per cent of those voting or 80 per cent of the electorate. But, the Employment Act 1988 will abolish the demand for that ballot and merely renders illegal any step by the employer (dismissal) or the union (industrial action) to enforce such an agreement.

The British legislation usually regarded as the most 'neocorporatist', the Industrial Relations Act 1971, took a different approach. It made the pre-entry closed shop 'void'; but it permitted registered unions and employers to enter (after a ballot producing a simple majority where two thirds of the workers voted) into 'agency shop' arrangements, where dissentient workers paid a sum to charity.[56] More important, the Act established a system generally for the new Industrial Court and Commission to appoint a union as 'sole or joint bargaining agent' after a ballot of the employees producing a simple majority in favour. On the application of two-fifths of the workforce, the status of bargaining agent could be removed. Duties to bargain and to disclose information were imposed on the employer. Since few unions registered, little experience was gained of this scheme, derived in great measure from American concepts, before the repeal of the Act in 1974. But, as we shall see below, it was linked to specific but perhaps surprisingly gentle provisions to regulate *internal* trade union democracy.

It would be quite wrong to imagine that these same pressures have not expressed themselves in other systems. In contrast to the 'majority' approaches, systems with ideologically pluralist unions, where the right to adhere to the union of one's choice or to none is an inevitable consequence of the legal and social structure, a different device has been needed. In France, Spain and Italy, the bearer increasingly of various rights, sometimes to bargain, sometimes in other fields, has become the 'representative' or 'most representative' union.[57] This status is not tested in France or Italy by reference to any 'majority' of workers involved, but to such considerations as affiliation to national union confederations or more flexible tests at enterprise level; nor are the tests identical in each system, or even within a given system for all purposes. As it is put in Italy: 'There does not exist one legal concept of the representative union (SMR) but a variety of concepts relevant variously to the concrete reasons for which the legislature resorted to selective criteria among unions'. Yet this concept, *'conception proportionelle et non majoritaire'*, which has for many years been 'one of the cornerstones on which the legislative order of Italian labour relations is founded',[58] is as strange to Anglo-Saxon eyes as union security clauses or the 'union membership agreement' are to the French or Italian.

It would, therefore, be as foolish to evaluate the Italian SMR by reference to American notions of democracy pertinent to 'exclusive bargaining agents' as to apply the concepts of ideologically pluralist systems to the closed shop and union security in Britain, the United States or Sweden – or indeed to apply the logic of any of those systems to the need for an Irish union to be 'authorised' by the State before it can bargain, or an Australian union to be approved by the Registrar before it can enter the ring of compulsory arbitration.[59] This search for the acknowledged representative, the respectable bearer of collective interests, creates problems within each system itself which test the consensual basis even of the political system. The wild swings in legislative purpose on union security in Britain between 1971 and 1988, first constraining, then enlarging, now almost abolishing, its lawful operation, represent policies so divergent as to question the social consensus on the issue. So too, there is a nagging perplexity in a system founded constitutionally upon the equality of freely constituted unions when it becomes necessary – understandably – to describe unions as: *'egaux en droit mais inegalement aptes a servir de porte-parole aux travailleurs'*?[60] This choice of method to protect workers' interests did not develop by reason of the French system having no experience of majority voting. The elections for *comités d'entreprises, délégués du personnel*, union delegates, delegates on health, safety and working conditions, not to speak of the *conseils de prud'hommes*, constitute one of the richest systems of workplace elective democracy. The adjustment of union 'equality' and promotion of the representative union on a non-elective basis have been required by the need to fashion a mechanism of democracy that serves both workers' interests and the stability of the system, not abstract precepts of democracy.

EXTERNAL AND INTERNAL DEMOCRACY

There are, however, common factors which emerge from the attempts in many countries to adapt labour law, both in the era of promotional or auxiliary legislation and in the current trend towards deregulation and 'flexibility', when the State begins to require stronger guarantees about union representativeness. But it may be noted that 'deregulation' does not always take the same form. For example, traditional legislation originating from the earliest era of legal protection customarily included safeguards for children, women and young workers, in regard to dangerous or heavy work, hours of employment, later maternity leave. Although lines of development were similar, 'general political developments' (not least the varying extension of the political franchise in different countries) and the diverse nature of the labour movements, differentiated the resulting legislation. Much of the early model was British; but, as Ramm notes, the 'decisive difference' later in other countries was the extension of protective legislation to all workers.[61] The prohibition against heavy work and night work being undertaken by women, found in many systems by the end of the nineteenth century, achieved the status of an international norm, for example in the many ILO Conventions and in the European Social Charter. From their inception, however, such laws were challenged, on the one side by those who wished to retain the exploitation of female labour or feared regulation as 'a pretext' for securing improvements for men,[62] on the other as a contravention of 'equality of treatment' and barrier to women's promotion (as in Denmark). The pressure to repeal such laws has now given rise to two different policies.

In Britain the statutory limitations were removed without qualification, where necessary with a denunciation of the relevant ILO or European Social Charter provision, as with restriction on night work, hours and rest intervals at work, meal intervals, and Saturday work. In 1987, further legislation was proposed to repeal more such provisions in statutes and regulations.[63] Many of these workers, especially women, are vulnerable; often not union members, with conditions less favourable than the standard employment terms. They have access neither to external democracy at work nor to internal union democracy, but are left to the unilateral forces of the market. It is to the political system that critics then increasingly look for their protection.[64] A different model was well known long before the current crisis. In 1967, in pursuit of equality, Sweden denounced the ILO Convention prohibiting employment of women in underground mines, but made it clear that protection of standards for all workers would be maintained and that it recognised that the Convention remained necessary wherever women worked 'under unsatisfactory conditions and in work for which they were not physically equipped'.[65] This approach to deregulation with maintenance but flexibility of standards, may be found in those systems with a regulatory base, such as Germany or France where the deregulation needed to widen the use of part-time or fixed contract work still leaves in place a structure of control, protective of the worker, which has never existed at all in such 'freedom of contract' jurisdictions as Britain.[66]

The giant strides along this road of particular relevance to this theme have been taken in Italy. The 'crisis' labour law of the 1970s, born of fear of growing unemployment, internationalised markets and contracting economic growth, led to new legislative intervention.[67] In return, laws from 1977 onwards envisaged an active labour market policy. The breakthrough in the 1983 Agreement (as it happens, concluded within a few days of the 'Social Compact' on similar issues in Australia) and the Protocol of 1984 led the unions into new involvement in 'tripartite responsibilities'. The relaxation of employment guarantees (as on the scala mobile) or of regulation (as on hiring procedures) was matched by continuing efforts to maintain consensus. But throughout this development one finds space reserved for bipartite or tripartite variations or adjustments of new norms. Thus, collective agreements can vary the repeal of prohibition on women's night or heavy work. Revision of the provisions on part-time work leaves collective agreements in charge but in a framework of protection. Training contracts for young workers are regulated by tripartite commissions under collective agreements. Seniority rights of workers on transfer of the enterprise are made vulnerable, but there must be a collective agreement with an SMR. 'Solidarity contracts', bringing financial help where employers make an agreement to hire new workers on reduction of working hours, or subventions where hours are renegotiated to prevent redundancies, in effect involve tripartite bargains.[68]

In contrast to unilateral deregulation in Britain, these policies have the appearance of deregulation by *consensus*. The comparison indicates that the relationship between trade union democracy and the political system in which it operates must be analysed by reference, not merely to the labour legislation which directly affected unions, but to the overall social policies. Furthermore, these legislative trends suggest new solutions but also new tensions which cannot be contained within the once fashionable theories of 'neo-corporatism'.[69] The Italian

Agreement of 1983 and Protocol of 1984 must be analysed 'from the perspective of the progress of relations between trade unionism and the political systems.[70] The tripartism evident at macro-economic level is matched by tripartite mechanisms at micro-level; and in the midst of deregulation, concerted action is encouraged between unions and employers. Although such a system is qualified by areas of unilateral control by employers, especially in areas of 'a-typical' employment, the contrast with the relatively inflexible structures of the British 'Social Contract' of 1974, and even the earlier period of 'concerted action' in Germany, are at once clear.[71]

'The Social Pact', however, writes Giugni 'is not the final solution to the institutional problem; it is a method of working by approximation ... in order to consolidate a Social Pact policy, one cannot avoid getting involved in problems of institutional reform. A clear and unquestionable definition of the representative conditions of the social forces would make it much easier for them to create the necessary consensus'.[72] It is not surprising that on such a basis the national debate seeks new rules of the game.[73]

INTERNAL UNION DEMOCRACY – THE BRITISH CASE

In any such programme, all institutions will be on the agenda (though perhaps it is time to put in a more prominent place on it the 'conditions on which private capital in a mixed economy can be allowed the privilege of incorporation with limited liability').[74] That is why it is no accident that union 'representativity' or 'democracy' is a central issue in the industrial relations debate in most European countries, both for those who wish to preserve their role and for those who wish to exclude them as 'monopolists' to be banned from the market except in a 'friendly society' role.[75] The fear of regulation has often been heard in the long period of the 'relatively weak form of corporatism – tripartism which existed after 1961' in Britain.[76] Since the Labour Government's proposals in *In Place of Strife* in 1969 it has perplexed the unions. Others have feared greater 'legalism' and 'professionalism' as the harbingers of authoritarian control,[77] or the exclusion of unions from 'the charmed circle of those incorporated', in a 'restructuring of constitutional patterns'.[78]

One of the main objections to the Industrial Relations Act 1971 was that it involved registration of unions under State conditions which eroded union freedom, a phenomenon which even after its repeal was alleged to have bequeathed 'a limited but distinct shift towards unions becoming creatures of the State rather than social entities'.[79] As we shall see, far more severe control was to come, but not in a 'corporatist' form. If one contrasts, however, the more recent developments in Britain with those of 1969-74, one finds that the 'corporatist' tendencies of the earlier period resulted in less legal intervention in union autonomy than occurred in the later period.

The industrial relations policy of government in the 1980s has been the very opposite of 'corporatist'.[80] Unions have been excluded from effective consultation in national affairs; government has maintained the appearance of abstention from disputes in the private sector (but inevitably not in the public sector); tripartite structures have been gradually abandoned, except in the Manpower Services Commission where unions have contributed to policies on unemployment, social security and training (but even there the Act of 1988 will ensure that this body, renamed the 'Training Commission', will in future have a majority of employers as members). Gradually since 1989 the liberty to take industrial action has been drastically curtailed, measures supportive of minimum standards rescinded as inconsistent with a free market, and workers' individual employment protection rights reduced. But it was not until 1984 that the new legislation made direct and major inroads into internal union democracy.

A perspective

We need a brief perspective because it is necessary to assess that 'democracy' cautiously. Comparative analysis reminds us that it is a highly relative concept. Summers has demonstrated this in his searching comparison of Sweden and the United States.[81] Both countries have statutes imposing a legal duty to bargain; both are committed to democratic unions, freedom of association, and collective bargaining. But the laws were enacted for different reasons. Employers regard unions very differently. American 'exclusive representation' is unthinkable in Sweden. More important in the present context, the American unions are surrounded by the requirements of the Landrum–Griffin Act 1959, setting 'minimum standards of democratic decision-making, due process and financial accountability'. Democratic procedures are laid down because, possessing 'powers akin to those of government [unions] should observe the standards expected of democratic government'. The equivalence between political and union democracy is made direct. But in Sweden, on all of this there is 'almost a total void of legal rules'. As in France and Italy, and in great measure Germany, these matters are regarded, as the ILO Conventions suggest they might be, as the proper realm of the freely chosen rules of the union, subject only to the general law. Summers rejects as the reason for this remarkable divergence the contingent fact that the United States intervention was directly caused by corrupt and criminal practices in American unions which have no counterpart in Sweden. Subsequent events might suggest this factor could be of rather greater importance, after the 'Labor Racketeering Amendments' of 1984.[82] But even so, the more interesting contrast lies deep within union structures themselves.

American concern was with 'democratic process' so: 'according to American standards, Swedish unions are not democratic'. Union officials are elected for life, violating the 'American principle that elected officials should be required periodically to stand for election'. Swedish unions are 'a model of one-party bureaucracy'; the officers have a monopoly of channels of information, select candidates, and can act contrary to a members' referendum. They act and decide *for* members, not as their mouthpiece. There are 'no competing political parties'; the union is a 'one-party State'. While this can be true also in an American union, the law insists on 'a measure of democratic process'. The solution to the puzzle, Summers suggests, is the acceptance of union decisions in Sweden by the members and by 'the larger society'. Beyond that lie 'inarticulate assumptions and attitudes'. Whether or not Swedish trade unionists would accept this picture without amendment, the comparison is relevant in two ways to Britain.

There, one could find unions which had some similarity to the model of the Swedish union as there described, but others whose affinity was more to the American model. The Amalgamated Engineering Union has long had semi-party factional strife (it has strict rules about election addresses, with postal ballots). Other unions appoint, not elect, their major executive officers. In some unions branches meet rarely, in others they never stop meeting. Some executives have a discretion which permits them to act otherwise than in accordance with a referendum of members. Both the political and industrial structures owe something to Burke: 'Your representative owes you not his industry only, but his judgment.'

Volumes describe such kaleidoscopic practices in British unions.[83] Critics have often repeated what Clegg called the 'pessimistic' view that there should be compulsorily inserted further 'competition' for top posts. He commented: 'This test of democracy is not very suitable for British trade unions'. If a wider test is employed, including the ability of opposition groups to push union administrations into actions they would not otherwise favour, one would find 'a growth in democracy in British unions since the war'. In addition, the strong workplace organisation of British unions, with shop stewards, has increasingly 'promoted democracy' – very direct democracy – by exercising influence on the leadership.[84]

It cannot be doubted that a union in which the leadership is free from challenge, irreplaceable by the members and free from their influence on policy, does not merit the epithet 'democratic'. On the other hand, the extent to which this blood of living democracy can be injected into the body of a union by constitutional provisions imported from the domestic political system is open to doubt. The comparison of union affairs with the national political system as such may be of 'limited relevance'. The principles of the ILO on the right to select representatives and constitutions 'in full freedom' and without interference by the public authorities, taken as obvious in France, Italy, Sweden and Germany, allow for narrow exceptions to protect the democratic interests of individual members and democratic rules; otherwise intervention 'creates a serious risk of improper interference in the internal affairs of organisations'.[85] What is more, governments that insist on unions practising 'a particular conception of democratic procedures' may find that this 'desire to promote democracy becomes linked to the desire to produce a specific outcome'.[86]

The background

The legal background of British unions has long been consistent with their status as voluntary, contractual associations.[87] Their governmental systems have developed from the early informality of 'collecting the voices' and regular referenda, into modern systems of representative government of elected officials (though in many different forms) plus the more 'direct' democracy of the shop steward system. The political system has greatly influenced the former, and distrusted the latter, for which it knows no counterpart. Both are essential to the democratic and to the 'representative' functions of British unions. The struggle for lawful status in Britain culminated in 1871 in a form crucial to the unions' future. Parliament gave them an 'immunity' in relation to the common law prohibition upon 'restraint of trade' – not, it must be noted *a right* to associate. But Parliament did not desire too close a contact between unions and the law. Unions had the same view; they wanted little contact with courts that were hostile to them. The Act of 1871 (s.4) therefore, satisfied all sides by prohibiting the 'direct enforcement' of most union rules by a court.[88]

After 1871, therefore, a British union resembled an *'associazione non riconosciuta'*. The basis was contractual, but much of the contract was unenforceable in court. However, as we have seen this did not deter the judges from ascribing to unions a 'quasi-corporate' personality sufficient to incur tort liability and to prohibit as *ultra vires* their political activities. The voluntary registration for which unions could opt under the 1871 Act required that there must be rules about the union's objects; members' rights to benefits; forfeitures and fines; appointment and removal of trustees, a treasurer, other officers and a management committee; audit of accounts; and provision for inspection of books of account and the membership list. But the precise content of the rules was for the union to choose. The 1871 Act was repealed in the Act of 1971, itself to be repealed in 1974.

In 1974 this traditional structure was reintroduced and modernised; 'registration' was replaced by a 'list' of unions without any of the guidelines on the rules. The 1871 Act, section 4, was not re-enacted. This meant that the union rules were now a fully enforceable contract. Ironically, this gave the courts unexpectedly greater powers, e.g. to appoint a receiver of union property in cases of 'contempt of court'. The enforceability of the rule book contract gave a dissident member new opportunities to 'restrain the union from a policy of supporting industrial action', as was demonstrated in the miners' strike.[89] The illegality of that strike (which led to seizure of the national union's assets) was pronounced in interlocutory judgments holding that the miners' unions had arguably not observed their own rules in respect of ballots of members.

The neo-corporatist period
The intervening period, 1971-1974, was that of the Industrial Relations Act. This was an attempt to reform the whole of industrial relations law by introducing a comprehensive regulatory structure, with a special Industrial Court (NIRC) and Commission (CIR). The 'immunities' were largely rescinded. Workers were given rights to join a *registered* union and not to join any union. Only registered unions, which in the event were few, had effective rights to take industrial action. If unions and employers made collective agreements that were legally enforceable (scarcely any did, though it was encouraged) unions were liable for infringements by any members unless they took all 'reasonably practicable steps' to stop them.[90] The Act was operative for less than three years and was generally adjudged to have 'failed'.[91] It was an attempt to integrate the unions into a coordinated system,

part of the Conservative Government's 'strongly corporatist policy'.[92]
It is therefore somewhat surprising that its provisions on *internal* union rules were markedly less stringent than on their external activities. All unions were obliged to observe a list of 'guiding principles', relating to reasonable admissions and exclusions, reasonable practice for members' participation in elections, meetings and ballots, reasonable disciplinary action, and the like. By themselves these demands went little further than the *Donovan Report*; and they were not dissimilar to the scheme of 1871. The law set the standards, but the union chose the form of its own rules. Whether it elected its national committee directly or indirectly, for example, was still for it to choose. For registered unions the Act went a little further. The Registrar was required to see that there were rules on financial accountability, elections and disciplinary proceedings, and powers and duties of officials, including specification of the circumstances in which strikes could be called and by whom. Although these provisions were more specific, and the Registrar had power to investigate a registered union's rules – both points to which TUC unions understandably objected – the 1971 law still left a wide area in which concrete rules could meet the requirements of each union. In the few major unions which registered, few changes of rule were ever made.

British laws of the 1980s
The advent of the Conservative administration of 1979 brought into government very different policies. Corporatist structures were eschewed in favour of market liberalism, deregulation and privatisation. In labour law, this led to the Acts of 1980, 1982, 1984 and, now, the Act of 1988.[93] In the first two statutes one found very little intervention on internal union democracy (the controls in the 1980 Act on exclusion from a union where a closed shop existed related more to the debate on that institution). But the Government 'Green Paper' in 1983, *Democracy in Trade Unions*, took the view that 'in many unions the role and influence of the rank and file seems to be minimal', and that ballots and other procedures must be imposed. Critics complained that the conclusion was not supported by 'empirical evidence' and aimed at ensuring unions 'pursue more moderate policies'.[94] The result was the Trade Union Act 1984 which intervened more rigorously in three respects.

i.   It obliged every union to elect its national executive committee by mandatory procedures, imposed rules as to candidatures and electorate and permitted only a *direct* vote of all members, not any indirect election. The procedure was to be by postal ballot, though the union could opt for a workplace ballot under certain safeguards. For any breach of these provisions a court can make an order on application of a member.

ii.   The union retained its 'immunity' of lawfulness in respect of authorised strikes or industrial action only if a majority of members approve it in a union ballot which put to them the mandatory question ('Are you prepared to strike in breach of your contract of employment?')

iii.   Existing political funds, most of them established decades earlier under the 1913 Act, had to be re-authorised by a ballot of members within one year and then re-validated by a ballot every ten years. The meaning of 'political' was widened, thereby restricting the availability of unions' general funds for political activity.

The Employment Act enacted in the summer of 1988, goes further than the 1984 measure and represents the highest level of legal intervention in internal union affairs in modern British history. In brief, its main provisions are:

1.   obligatory direct election is extended to include all the senior officers and all persons who attend the national committee even without a right to vote (unless they do so merely to render professional or 'technical' advice). All ballots except strike ballots must be *postal* ballots, and the union must appoint a 'scrutineer' to supervise election and political fund ballots from among persons qualified in accordance with Government criteria;

ii.   a strike or industrial action is lawful if authorised by the union in different places of work only if a separate ballot approves it in *each* place of work, except that workers in the same bargaining unit may be balloted with an aggregate majority. Unions are prohibited from adding comments or qualifications to the new mandatory question the Act prescribes must be put on their ballot paper;

iii.   the union may not lawfully expel or discipline a member, even if in accordance with its rules, for refusing to obey the union's call for strike action, even if a majority of members have approved the action in a ballot satisfying the new legislation. So too, if he refuses to break any duty owed to his employer, or if a member accuses the union of unlawful action, unless the union proves it to be false. In all such cases the law invalidates the application of union disciplinary rules. The rules remain lawful; but the member may recover compensation for his 'unjustifiable discipline';

iv. various rules of law which apply to all associations are disapplied from unions. For example, the right to indemnify officials who have innocently committed unlawful acts in the course of their duties, available to other associations, is removed from unions;

v. a new State official is created: the Commissioner for the Rights of Trade Union Members. Her function is to assist members of unions with financial support to pursue actions in the courts against their union. She has no power to assist such workers in legal actions against their employer or other persons;

vi. action by the employer, through discipline or dismissal, or by the union, through industrial action, to conclude or to sustain a closed shop is made unlawful;

vii. the Minister has power to issue 'codes of practice' which the courts must take into account in interpreting the law. He is widely expected to make codes in relating to nominations and candidatures in union elections and on strike ballots.

THE PARADOXES OF THE BRITISH CASE

Observers have noted that there was little 'empirical evidence' of the need for the stringent measures of 1988. None of the recent allegations of serious malpractice in union elections, for example, was proved. But this may be the wrong approach. The demand for 'evidence' was part of a long tradition of industrial relations research and of pragmatic practice in Britain. The Donovan Commission commissioned a major research programme; the parties to the debate on the Industrial Relations Bill avowedly stood on their interpretations of the social evidence. The fulcrum of consensus, even in 1971-74, comprised the agreed need to find the secret of 'good industrial relations' and its relationship to the law. That shared perspective is now less prominent and may have disappeared. The new policy of 'market individualism' puts the accent not upon a 'balance' in labour relations but upon 'the individual'. The legislation goes further than the American Landrum-Griffin Act in according to the individual union member absolute priority.

That was the way the 1988 clause on 'unjustifiable discipline' was presented.[95] A union member, Ministers argued, owes duties to his family, his employer and his union; when called upon to strike he must have a 'paramount' right to make his own choice. This means, it was concluded, that the union cannot lawfully 'coerce' him under the union contract, by discipline or expulsion. No curb must be placed, though, on the employer's power to discipline under the contract of employment. The individual employment relationship is regarded as sacrosanct, whilst the paramount right of the individual to escape from obligations undertaken in a collective association of workers is advanced as a fundamental value. The Act gives rise to curious paradoxes. First, instead of the withdrawal by the State, which the rhetoric of policy claims for general economic and social policies in favour of competitive market forces and individual enterprise, in this field the State intervenes increasingly to protect the individual, society and the market from 'coercion' by collective labour organisation. Many British observers express surprise at the mounting intervention, not only in trade union law but in other fields, such as education, public order and local government. But such interventions are arguably part of the policy's inherent logic. The 'free market' implies a strong – not a weak – State, intervening to protect it. Secondly, the effects upon policies for internal – and external – union 'democracy' are profound. It admits of no argument about trade union law by analogy with other voluntary associations, on the one side, or commercial companies, on the other. The ancient 'dilemma between protecting standards of behaviour and protecting autonomy and self-regulation'[96] is solved. No argument can dent the shield which *a priori* must protect 'the individual' and curtail the union. Such policies may not find the law fully satisfactory even after the Act of 1988; voices are already heard demanding yet another Bill in 1990.

The chasm between this approach to trade unionism and a range of alternative, pluralist or radical views has become wide. For the alternative policies are not confined within the trade union movement itself (indeed it has occasionally shown signs of shrinking into a corner, and begins to insist that it, too, is concerned mainly with 'individual' employment rights). Any alternative programme to that of exclusion is likely to call upon trade unions to undertake new tasks, the twin roles of cooperating in technological and labour market change and of adequately representing their members, possibly even the wider class of working people. A British equivalent of the joint regulation agreements made by Swedish unions in 1982, for example, would require a framework of law which encouraged both officials and members that the task is worthwhile.[97] It is likely that such a framework would say more about union rules than has been the British tradition, but that it would leave adequate space for democratic choice in application.

Ironically, those who, in defence of trade union autonomy, saw as their adversary ten years ago the regulation of 'neocorporatism' may have turned their eyes in the wrong direction. Today it is in the social systems of 'Social Pacts' that care is being taken to accommodate the rights of autonomous unions. It may be true that: 'Neo-corporatism is as innate to Democracy as the ideology of Corporatism is its negation.[98] But in Britain in 1988, the continuing advance of an ideology very different from both of these illustrates the power of the political system to inaugurate an essentially individualist, and therefore negative, form of trade union 'democracy'.

NOTES

1. V. Allen, *Power in Trade Unions* (1954) p. 122, and see V. Allen, *The Militancy of British Miners* (1981) Chap. 19: 'at different times unions have been attacked for being too centralised or too decentralised, for having strong leadership or weak leadership, for having too much consultation with the members or too little ... (always) in the name of democracy ... The unions could never win the argument', p. 260.
2. R. Undy and R. Martin, *Ballots and Trade Union Democracy* (1984), p. 168. See also R. Martin, *Union Democracy: An Explanatory Framework* (1968), 2, 'Sociology' 205-20.
3. See M. Lipset, *The Law and Trade Union Democracy* (1960), 47 Va. LR 1; M. Lipset, M. Trow and J. Coleman, *Union Democracy* (1956), p. 13. See also H. Wellington, *Labor and the Legal Process* (1968), pp. 159-63.
4. See Clyde Summers, *American Legislation for Union Democracy* (1962), 25 Modern LR 273; also his *The Usefulness of Law in Preserving Union Democracy* (1959), 48 American Econ. Rev. 44, and *The Public Interest in Union Democracy* (1958), 53 N.W. Univ. LR 613; B. Aaron, *The Labor-Management Reporting and Disclosure Act* (1960), 46 Va. LR 195. On demands for further measures, *see* L. Jacobs and G. Spring, *Fair Coverage in Internal Union Periodicals* (1981) 4 Ind. Rel. LJ 204.
5. M. Perlman, *Democracy in the International Association of Machinists* (1962), p. 100.
6. O. Kahn-Freund, *Labour and the Law* (1972), pp. 214-6, 273-4; (3rd edn. 1983, eds. P. Davies and M. Freedland).
7. J. Hughes, *Trade Union Structure and Government* (1968), paras. 101-10. See the careful review of 'factions' in R. Undy, V. Ellis, W. McCarthy and A. Halmos, *Change in Trade Unions* (1981), summarised pp. 120-6.
8. H. Clegg, *The Changing System of Industrial Relations in Great Britain* (1971), p. 210. See also O. Kahn-Freund, *Trade Union Democracy and the Law* (1961), 22 Ohio State LJ 1, 7-8; the *Donovan Royal Commission Report* (Cmnd. 3623, 1968) adopted that approach, but proposed a review body on arbitrary discipline or exclusion of members and on alleged election malpractice: 'it is unlikely that abuse of power ... is widespread' (para. 1069).
9. D. Bok and J. Dunlop, *Labor and the American Community* (1970), pp. 64-69.

10. *Democracy in Trade Unions* (Cmnd. 8778) p. 3.
11. Z. Chafee, *The Internal Affairs of Associations not for Profit* (1930), 43 Harv. LR 993.
12. J.M. Verdier, *Syndicats et droits syndical* (1987, 2nd ed.), pp. 352-68; Wedderburn, *The Worker and the Law* (1986, 3rd ed.), pp. 792-813.
13. F. Carinci, R. de Luca Tamajo, P. Tosi, T. Treu, *Il diritto sindacale* (1987, 2nd ed.), p. 105; Folke Schmidt, *Law and Industrial Relations in Sweden* (1977), pp. 49-55 ('use of arbitration on expulsion' etc.).
14. T. Ramm, *International Encyclopaedia for Labour Law and Industrial Relations* (1979, ed. R. Blanpain), 'Federal Republic of Germany', pp. 154-5; W. Däubler, *Das Arbeitsrecht I* (1980), pp. 85-100; and in *England Longley v NUJ* [1987] IRLR 109, 114 (CA) per R. Gibson LJ.
15. Covention No. 87 on 'Freedom of Association and the Right to Organise' 1948, Arts. 2, 3; Wedderburn, *Freedom of Association or Right to Organise?* (1987) 18. Ind. Rel. J. 244, See also on public servants, Convention No. 151 (1978) Art. 4.
16. Convention No. 87, 1948, Art. 7.
17. See Verdier, *op.cit.* note 12 p. 270; Code du Travail L 411-10; and Folke Schmidt, *op.cit.* pp. 47-8.
18. Conciliation and Arbitration Act, s. 136 (Australia; Federal unions); Taft Hartley Act 1947, s. 2(1), defining person.
19. H. Wellington *op.cit.* note 3, p. 196.
20. D. Rawson, *British and Australian Labour Law: Background to the 1982 Bills* (1982), *Industrial Relations Papers* (ANU), pp. 2-3.
21. G. Giugni, *Diritto Sindacale* (1984, 7th edn.), pp. 72-81; and see the stronger fears of G. Ghezzi and U. Romagnoli, *Il Diritto Sindacale* (2nd edn., 1987), pp. 68-70.
22. Trade Union Act 1871, s. 6; *Taff Vale Railway Co v ASRS* [1901] AC 426 (HL).
23. S. 4. Trade Disputes Act 1906, (and later s. 14(1). Trade Union and Labour Relations Act 1974) repealed by s. 15 Employment Act 1982. In ss. 16 and 17, damages in any one tort action by one plaintiff are limited to (£250,000 for larger unions) and certain funds (for provident benefits or political expenditure) are excluded from enforcement of damages, but not fines or sequestration for contempt. See Wedderburn *op.cit.* note 12, pp. 530-40, 681-4; J. Bowers and M. Duggan *The Modern Law of Strikes* (1987), pp. 174-7 [now ss. 20-23 TULRCA 1992].
24. *ASRS v Osborne* [1910] AG 87 (HL); Trade Union Act 1913, as amended by Trade Union Act 1984, ss. 12-19; *see* Wedderburn, *op.cit.*, note 12, pp. 748-71 [see now ss. 71-86 TULRCA 1992].
25. S & B Webb, *History of Trade Unionism* (1920), p. 615.
26. H. Clegg, *A History of British Trade Unions* Vol. 1 (1964), p. 313; P. Mantoux and M. Alfassa, *La Crise du Trade Unionisme* (1903), p. 31.
27. See R. Simpson and J. Wood, *Industrial Relations and the 1971 Act* (1973), Chaps, 9, 10, 11; TULRA 1974, s. 2 [now TULRCA 1992].
28. See Giugni, *op.cit* note 21, p. 80. The union can also appear to defend workers rights under art. 28, *Lo Statuto dei lavoratori*, L 300, 1970; and on use of the union name in internal disputes, *see* Carinci, de Luca Tamajo, Tosi, Treu, *op.cit.* note 13, p. 107.

29. T. Sigeman, *Damages and Bot: Remedies for Breach of Collective Agreements in Nordic Law* (1987), 8 Comp. Lab. LJ 155, 156 (describing the Danish origins of *bot*).

30. See on the miners' union sequestration and receivership in 1984-5 the authoritative review by G. Lightman QC, *A Trade Union in Chains* (1987), Current Legal Problems 25.

31. See F. Carinci, R de Luca Tamajo, P. Tosi, T. Treu, *op.cit.*, n. 13, p. 100.

32. See G. Camerlynck, G. Lyon-Caen, J. Pélissier, *Droit du Travail* (1986, 13th edn.), pp. 969-75; H. Sinay and J.C. Javillier, *La Grève* (1984, 2nd edn.) Chap. 3; J. Deprez, 'L'existence des revendications professionelles prealables', Dr. Soc. 1986, 610; J. Ray, 'La responsabilité civile du syndicat et de ses delegués', Dr. Soc. 1987, 426. Later decisions stemmed the tide of interlocutory judgments against strikes by the *juges des référés* [see above p.171 n.53]. On the *patrimoine*, Verdier *op.cit.*, 12, pp. 295-7.

33. For an approach, see Wedderburn and S. Sciarra, 'Collective Bargaining as Agreement and as Law: Neo-contractualist and Neo-corporative Tendencies of Our Age', in A. Pizzorusso (ed.), *Law in the Making: A Comparative Survey* (1988), pp. 186-237. See also B. Veneziani, *Stato e autonomia collettiva: diritto sindacale comparato* (1986), esp. pp. 85-204.

34. See *Employee Participation and Company Structure* (1975), 8 Bull, EC Supp 8/75, p. 11.

35. For example, the Danish Cooperation Agreement, (1971, now 1986) providing for full information to the joint 'cooperation committees', including the important *group* committees for company groups – compare the French *comité de groupe* required after 1982, C.T. Art. L 439-1 to 439-5. – and the Danish Basic Agreement, now revised in 1987 (EIRR No. 159, p. 13). 'Legislation in effect ratifies the results of the agreements', C. Bratt, *Labour Relations in 18 countries* (1986, SAF), p. 35.

36. Employment Protection Act 1975, s. 17 (see H. Gospel and P. Willman (1981) 10 ILJ 10); Swedish Joint Regulation Act 1976, ss. 19-22. For a comparative review; C. Docksey, *Employee Information and Consultation Rights in EC Member States* (1985), 7 Comp. Lab. LJ 32, and the tabulation pp. 49-69. But see also the important developments in Italy, notably in the public sector, experimenting with extensive rights of information and consultation that fall *between* the areas of conflictual bargaining and of codetermination or 'participation' in decision making by the union. See the fascinating account in M. Ricci and B. Veneziani, *Tra Conflitto e Participazione* (1988).

37. C. Summers, *An American Perspective of the German Model of Worker Participation* (1987), 8 Comp. Lab. LJ 333, 345-55; cf. K. Hofsteller and R. Klubeck, *Accommodating Labour and Community Interests in Mass Dismissals: A Transnational Approach* (1987), 9 ILJ 451.

38. See C. Docksey, *Information and Consultation of Employees: the UK and the Vredeling Directive* (1986), 49 Modern LR 281; A. Jeammaud and A. Lyon-Caen, *L'Information et la consultation des travailleurs dans les entreprises transnationales* (1987); B. Hepple, *The Crisis in EEC Labour Law* (1987), 16 ILJ 77.

39. O. Kahn-Freund, 'Industrial Democracy' (1977), 6 ILJ 65, 79, 81-2; P. Davies and Wedderburn, 'The Land of Industrial Democracy', *ibid.* 197.

For doubts about the effectiveness of workers' influence *via* supervisory boards, P. Davies, 'Employee Representation on Company Boards and Participation in Corporate Planning (1975) 38 MLR 254. See now generally, G. Teubner, 'Industrial Democracy through Law?' in T. Daintith and G. Teubner (eds.) *Contract and Organisation* (1986); and on British debates on industrial democracy, S. Sciarra, *Democrazia Politica e Democrazia Industriale* (1978) pp. 2-44.

40. P. Elias, B. Napier and P. Wallington, *Labour Law Cases and Materials* (1980), pp. 30-59 'Grunwick – a case study'; *cf.* Wedderburn, *op.cit.* note 12 (1986), pp. 282-289.

41. Folke Schmidt, *op.cit.*, note 13. Chaps. 6, 7, 9; on tripartite mechanisms in the labour market, see Ann Numhauser-Henning, *Hiring Procedures in Sweden* (1986), Part A.

42. G. Camerlynck, G. Lyon-Caen, J. Pelissier, *op.cit.*, no. 32, pp. 840, 890-9; *cf.* A. Lyon-Caen and L. Mariucci, 'The State, Legislative Intervention and Collective Bargaining' (1985), 1 Int. Jo. Comp. Lab. Law and IR 87, 93-7.

43. See W. Gould, *A Primer on American Labor Law* (1982) Chaps. 5, 6 and 9.

44. G. Giugni, *Diritto Sindacale, op.cit.*, n. 21, pp. 88-92. *Cf.* M. Rusciano, 'Sul problema della rappresentanza sindacale' (1987) 34 Giorn. DLRI 229.

45. D. Feller, 'A General Theory of the Collective Bargaining Agreement' (1973) 61 Cal. LR 663, 724.

46. K. Klare, 'Labor Law as Ideology' (1981) Ind. Rel. LJ 450, 461; see also the analysis by C. Stone, 'Industrial Pluralism' (1981) 90 Yale LJ 1509.

47. E. Dodd (1932) 45 Harv. LJ 1365, in reply to A. Berle, 'Corporate Powers in Trust' (1931) 44 *ibid.* 1049. See on this debate, Wedderburn, 'Trust, Corporation and Worker' (1985) 23 Osgoode Hall LR 203, 223-252; and Chap. 1 in K. Hopt and G. Teubner (eds.) *Corporate Governance and Directors' Liabilities* (1985); E. Herman, *Corporate Control, Corporate Power* (1981) pp. 280-301.

48. *First National Maintenance Corp v NLRB* 452 US 666 (1981); *cf. Textile Workers Union v Darlington Mfg.* 380 US 263 (1965); T. Kohler (1983) Ind. Rel. Jo. 402, 420-5; J. McGuire (1987) Lab. LJ 747; C. Craver (1985) Lab. LJ 604, 609-612; see also on bankruptcy and bargaining, C. Craver, 'The Use of Bankruptcy Proceedings to Modify Bargaining Agreement Obligations in the United States' (1987) 50 MLR 855.

49. See S. Sciarra, *Contratto collettivo e contrattazione in azienda* (1985) pp. 84-139, and 'Plant Bargaining; The Impact of Juridification on Current Deregulative Trends in Italy' (1987) 8 Comp. Lab. LJ 122, 130.

50. G. Giugni, 'Juridification of Italian Labour Relations' (1987) 8 Comp. Lab. LJ 309, 329; *Cf.* G. Ferraro, 'Fonti Autonome e Fonti Eteronome' (1986) 32 Giorn. DLRI 667, 695.

51. Wedderburn and Sciarra, in A. Pizzorusso, *op.cit*, note 33 p. 220.

52. See Wedderburn, *The Worker and the Law, op.cit.*, n. 12, pp. 824-31; L. Mariucci, 'Il progetto Saturn nel quadro delle relazioni industriali negli USA' (1986) Rev. ital. dir. del lavoro 315.

53. C. Craver, 'The Vitality of the American Labor Movement in the 21st Century' (1983) Univ. Illin. LR 633, 695; and see *op.cit.* (1987) 50 MLR, pp. 856-60.

54. See W. McCarthy, *The Closed Shop* (1964); and now S. Dunn, 'The Law

and the Decline of the Closed Shop', Chap. 2 in P. Fosh and C. Littler (ed.), *Industrial Relations and the Law in the 1980s* (1985). On the TUC 'Bridlington' Disputes Procedures, Wedderburn, *The Worker and the Law, cit.* p. 824 *et seq.*

55. *'Donovan' Royal Commission Report* (1968, Cmnd. 3623) p. 161; R. Benedictus (1977) 8 ILJ 160; S. Dunn and R. Gennard, *The Closed Shop in British Industry* (1984) Chap. 7; Wedderburn, Chap. 6 in Folke Schmidt (ed.) *Discrimination in Employment* (1978).

56. Industrial Relations Act 1971, ss. 7, 11-18. Enforcing any union security arrangement by an unregistered union was virtually impossible; R. Simpson and J. Wood, *Industrial Relations and the 1971 Act* (1973).

57. See Camerlynck, Lyon-Caen, Pélissier, *op.cit.* n. 32, pp. 636-47; Carinci, de Luca Tamajo, Tosi and Treu, *op.cit.*, n. 13, Chap. V; compare Spain where the test is majoritarian: A. Baylos Grau, 'Mayor Representatividad Sindical e Participacion Institucional' (1985) 2 *Relaciones Laborales* 32-49.

58. G. Giugni, *Diritto Sindacale, op.cit.*, 21 Chap. 5, p. 93. *Cf.* Camerlynck, Lyon-Caen, Pélissier, *op.cit.*, n. 32, pp. 636-7.

59. A. Kerr and G. Whyte, *Irish Trade Union Law* (1985) pp. 50 65; W. Creighton, W. Ford, R. Mitchell, *Labour Law, Materials and Commentary* (1983) Chaps. 15, 27, 28.

60. Camerlynck, Lyon-Caen and Pélissier, *op.cit.*, note 32, p. 634.

61. Thilo Ramm, Chap. 2, 'Laissez Faire and State Protection of Workers', in B. Hepple (ed.), *The Making of Labour Law in Europe* (1986) p. 88 (and on Denmark's women workers, p. 95). See too, P. O'Higgins, Chap. 20 in R. Lewis, *Labour Law in Britain* (1986).

62. B. Hutchins and A. Harrison, *History of Factory Legislation* (1903), p. 186.

63. Sex Discrimination Act 1986, ss. 7, 8; Wedderburn, *The Worker and the Law cit.* pp. 403-12; Consultative Document on *Restrictions on Employment of Young People and Removal of Sex Discrimination* (DE 1987) [and the Employment Act 1989].

64. See for example, S. Deakin, 'Labour Law and the Developing Employment Relationship in the UK' (1986) 10 Camb. Jo. Economics 225.

65. N. Valticos, *International Labour Law* (1979) 175.

66. On the German Promotion of Employmet Act 1985 and French deregulation laws of 1986, see W. Däubler and M. Le Friant, 'Un recent exemple de flexibilisation legislative' Dr. Soc. 1985, p. 115.

67. See T. Treu, 'Recent Development of Italian Labour Law' (1985) 10 *Labour and Society* 27, 31-40. For the remarkable differences in West and East European countries' hiring mechanisms and laws: Wedderburn, B. Veneziani, S. Ghimpu, *Lavoro del diritto in Europa* (1987) Chap. 1.

68. See for details, M. Garfalo (ed.), *Crisi, Occupazione, Legge* (1985); G. Ghezzi and U. Romagnoli, *Il rapporto del lavoro* (2nd edn. 1987); and S. Sciarra, (1986) 15 Bull. Comp. Lab. Rels. 53-89.

69. See M. Regini, *I dilemmi del Sindacato* (1981) on 'neo-corporatism'; also his Chap. 6 in J. Goldthorpe (ed.), *Order and Conflict in Contemporary Capitalism* (1984).

70. A. Lyon-Caen and L. Mariucci, *op.cit.*, 42 (1985) 1 Int. Jo. Comp. Lab. Law and IR, pp. 101-3.

71. See J. Clark, H. Hartmann, C. Lau, D. Winchester, *Trade Unions, National Politics and Economic Management* (1980) for a comparison.
72. G. Giugni, 'Social Concertation and Political System in Italy' (1987) 1 Labour 3, 11.
73. See L. Mariucci, 'Le regole sindacale: reflessioni e proposte' (1987) 1 Lav. Dir. 429-461; M. Grandi, 'Nuove regole dell'organizzazione sindacale' (1987) 1 Lav. Dir. 609, 620; R. Pessi, *ibid.*, 620-634. If untutored observers might wonder whether the debate was beginning to put too much emphasis upon new 'rules of the game', as compared with economic and social forces, the contrast with Britain is remarkable where lack of consensus, and perhaps of courage, has prevented any similar debate about problems which are not dissimilar.
74. Wedderburn, 'The Social Responsibility of Companies' (1985) 15 Melbourne ULR, 1, 6.
75. For example, F. Hayek, *Law, Legislation and Liberty* (1979) Vols. I-III; see Wedderburn, [1989] 18 ILJ 1.
76. D. Coates, 'Corporatism and the State in Theory and Practice' in M. Hanson (ed.), *Corporatism and Welfare* (1984), p. 131.
77. See for example, C. Crouch, *Class Conflict and the Industrial Relations Crisis* (1977).
78. N. Lewis and P. Wiles, 'The Post Corporatist State' (1984) Jo. Law and Soc. 65, 86; *cf.* G. Lembruch and P. Schmitter (eds.), *Patterns of Corporatist Policy-Making* (1982).
79. C. Crouch, *Class Conflict and the Industrial Relations Crisis* (1977), p. 192. There were no proposals in *In Place of Strife* (1969 Cmnd. 3888) to regulate the substance of internal union rules, though compulsory registration was proposed.
80. For a review, see Wedderburn, *The Worker and the Law, op.cit.*, n. 12, Chap. 1.
81. Clyde Summers, 'Comparisons in Labour Law: Sweden and the United States' (1985) 7 Ind. Rel. LJ 1.
82. See the Comprehensive Crime Control Act 1984, ss. 801-5; D. Panter (1985) Lab. Law Jo. 744.
83. See for example, among many, H. Clegg, *The Changing System of Industrial Relations in Britain* (1979), Chap. 5; I. Boraston, H. Clegg, M. Rimmer, *Workplace and Union (A Study of 14 Unions)* (1975); R. Undy, V. Ellis, W. McCarthy, A. Halmos, *Change in Trade Unions* (1981); E. Batstone, I. Borston, S. Frenkel, *Shop Stewards in Action* (1977).
84. See H. Clegg, *The Changing System, op.cit.*, p. 208-9, 220.
85. *General Survey by Committee of Experts on Freedom of Association and Collective Bargaining* (1983, 69th Session, ILO) p. 57.
86. R. Martin in P. Fosh and C. Littler (eds.) *Industrial Relations and the Law in the 1980s* (1985) pp. 79-80.
87. For detailed legal references to this section, see Wedderburn, *The Worker and the Law, op.cit.*, n. 12, pp. 521-40 and Chap. 9; and see the colourful accounts of early structures in S & B. Webb, *Industrial Democracy* (1902), and *History of Trade Unionism* (1920).
88. On judicial interventions, *see* O. Kahn-Freund, 'The Illegality of a Trade Union' (1943) 7 MLR 192, 201-2.

89. R. Benedictus and B. Bercusson, *Labour Law Cases and Materials* (1987) p. 675; Wedderburn, *op.cit.*, n. 12 pp. 728-48; K. Ewing, 'The Strike, Courts and Rule Books' (1985) 14 ILJ 160.
90. Industrial Relations Act 1971 s. 36(2), for procedure agreements, see ss. 37-43. Now the Employment Act 1988, s. 1 [now s. 62 TULRCA 1992], obliges the court, where a ballot has not been held, to require the union to ensure that members do not take part in 'official' industrial action and do not adopt 'any conduct' associated with such action.
91. See B. Weekes, M. Mellish, L. Dickens and J. Lloyd, *Industrial Relations and the Limits of Law* (1975).
92. C. Crouch, *Class Conflict and the Industrial Relations Crisis, op.cit.*, n. 77.
93. For detailed references to this section, see Wedderburn, *The Worker and the Law, op.cit*; K. Miller, Chap. 11 in R. Lewis (ed.) *Labour Law in Britain* (1986); J. Bowers and M. Duggan, *The Modern Law of Strikes* (1987), Chap. 7 'Ballots' [now ss. 219-235 TULRCA 1992]. On the 1913 and 1984 Acts; see also M. Biagi, *Sindacato, Democrazia e Diritto* (1986).
94. P. Davies and M. Freedland, *Labour Law: Text and Materials* (2nd edn. 1984) p. 683.
95. See for example the Secretary of State, Mr N. Fowler, *Parl. Deb. HC*, 1 December 1987, col. 203. Under British law, an employer does not act unlawfully if he dismisses workers because they are on strike, though he may be liable to pay compensation for unjust dismissal if he dismisses some but not others.
96. O.Kahn-Freund, 'Trade Union Democracy and the Law' (1961) 22 Ohio State LJ, 1, p. 8.
97. On Sweden, see A. Victorin, 'Restructuring Labour in the Enterprise' (1986) Bull. Comp. Lab. Rel. 85.
98. G. Giugni, 'Social Concertation and Political System in Italy' (1987) 1 Labour p. 4.
[For the equivalent provisions to the main provisions of the 1984 and 1988 Acts discussed above, see now: ss. 15, 16, 24-31, 46-47, 71-81, 219-234, TULRCA 1992].

APPENDIX TO CHAPTER 5

THE REGULATION OF INTERNAL UNION AFFAIRS IN BRITAIN: 1989-1993

Of all the jurisdictions in Europe, the British saw the fastest increase in legal regulation of internal affairs of trade unions after 1988, maintaining the acceleration evident in the four main Acts of the earlier period, 1980-1988. The Employment Act 1988, described above (p. 198) was the subject of a complaint by the TUC to the ILO as contravening Convention 87, of 1948, on freedom of association, especially article 3 which established the right of workers' organisations to draw up their constitutions and rules, elect representatives in full freedom, organise their administration and activities and formulate their programmes. The Committee of Experts found no incompatibility between the Convention and the provisions of the 1988 Act on election of officers, removal of trustees, members' access to accounting records, members' access to the courts, ballots on industrial action and the new Commissioner (CROTUM). The caution and the limitations of ILO standards here should be noted. But they also held that there were contraventions of the Convention in provisions banning 'unjustifiable discipline' (s. 3, now s. 64 TULRCA 1992) under which members can claim compensation from a trade union if it applies its rules to discipline them for refusing to join an official strike or to do any act in breach of their employment contract with their employer. There was a breach of the Convention both in these provisions because they deprived unions 'of the capacity lawfully to give effect to their democratically determined rules',[1] and in the ban on indemnification of officials for penalties incurred on union business (s. 8, now s. 15 TURLCA 1992). The British government refused to accept these conclusions arguing on 'unjustifiable discipline' that 'unions remain free to adopt any rules they wish' (although, as the Committee pointed out in 1992, they 'face serious financial penalties if and when they reinforce them') and that members should be protected from 'penalties for refusing to act unlawfully against their convictions by breaking contracts of employment'.[2] Indeed, the government replied to the ILO experts by actually extending the reach of 'unjustifiable discipline' (TURER Act 1993, s. 16: now s. 65(2) TULRCA 1992).

Yet again the central feature of British law is relied upon as the central plank of argument, that is: the character of the strike as a breach of the employment contract. In most European systems it effects a suspension of that contract within the area of legitimate industrial action. Both on 'unjustifiable discipline' and on the right to strike, the Committee has maintained its view that British law contravenes the Convention. In the 1990 Act, the government went further in giving to an employer the right to dismiss selectively but lawfully any employee participating in an 'unofficial' strike or action short of a strike (s. 9, now s. 237 TULRCA 1992: the rule hitherto, still applying to 'official' union action, being that the employer must dismiss all or none of those taking part if the jurisdiction of the tribunal is to be excluded: *ibid* 2. 238).

In the Employment Act 1990, an applicant for employment who is rejected on grounds of union membership or non-membership may claim compensation in an industrial tribunal (ss. 1-3, Employment Act 1990, now ss. 137-139 TULRCA 1992). With the amendments in ss. 10 and 11 of the 1988 Act, this made the closed shop unenforceable by either legal action or lawful industrial action (see now ss. 152, 222 TULRCA 1992). Vicarious liability in civil law for officials was broadened in 1990 to include acts of officials done without any authority, express or implied, from the union and extending strictly the requirements for a lawful 'repudiation' of unauthorised acts (s. 6, now ss. 20, 21 TULRCA 1992: notice of repudiation must be given to members and to all relevant employers in the precise terms of the Act). A special Commissioner (CROTUM, now ss. 266-71 TULRCA 1992) was established whose only function is to support financially and with advice legal actions in the courts by members against their unions. In the Trade Union Reform and Employment Rights Act 1993 ('TURER') another Commissioner was established to give similar support to individuals pursuing new rights of action against unions (COPAUIA s. 22, now s. 235B TULRCA 1992). Lawful industrial action was restricted by a new range of measures, including the removal of exceptions to the rule that 'secondary' action is not protected by the remaining 'immunities' in a trade dispute (s. 4 1990 Act, now s. 224 TULRCA 1992) and in 1993 the requirement that the union must notify to the employer the members who will be voting in the ballot and, then seven days before the strike, who will be taking strike or other industrial action (TURER Act 1993, ss. 18, 21; now ss. 226A, 234A TULRCA 1992).[3]

Ballots on official union strikes *and* industrial action short of strike are now required to be conducted by post (s. 17 TURER 1993, inserting s. 230 TULRCA 1992). So too, like ballots for elections of officials (TULRCA 1992 s. 51) ballots for mergers of unions must be postal (now ss. 100 to 100E TULRCA 1992, introduced in 1993) but in this case the union may not include any recommendation or material stating an opinion in the notice to members about the merger (s. 5 of the 1993 Act, now s. 99(3), TURLCA 1992). Voting in the obligatory ballot on a 'political fund' must also be by post (s. 71 TULRCA 1992). Government financial assistance for union ballots, however, for which much had been claimed in the 1980s, is now being withdrawn over the period ending 1996 (s. 7 TURER Act 1993). Further requirements on union accounts and annual reports were introduced by TURER 1993 and officials committing certain offences connected with them are disqualified from holding office on a set scale up to ten years (ss. 8-12, now ss. 32A, 32, 37A-E, 45A-C, TULRCA 1992). For the internal affairs of unions the most important feature of this Act is its novel control over the rules on admission and exclusion of trade unions' membership (s. 14, now ss. 174-177 TULRCA 1992). Enforceable criteria on membership are limited to employment in a trade, industry or profession, or employment in a certain region or 'conduct'. Conduct, however, does not include membership of, or exclusion from, another union. This last provision conflicted with the TUC's 'Bridlington' *Disputes Principles and Procedures*, which required unions to act against 'poaching' of members and to have rules under which they could terminate the membership of workers who had joined without clearance from another union of which they had been a member. The remedy under the new ss. 174-177 TULRCA 1992, however, is an action for compensation from an industrial tribunal by the person wrongly excluded. It appears that the person wrongly excluded cannot obtain an injunction or other order from the High Court to prevent his exclusion because the remedy for infringement of s. 174 is the compensation sanction under 'that section, sections 175 and 176 and this section, and not otherwise': s. 177(3). The TUC has issued a new code of procedure for inter-union relations, including a 'moral obligation' on a union which improperly poaches members to pay compensation to the aggrieved union.[4]

The introduction of new administrative hurdles, hardly justified by any difficulties arising in practice, now affects the areas of 'check off' (agreement between employer, employee and union whereby the employer will deduct a subscription and pay it to the union, usually for a small fee), and the political fund. The Act of 1993 gave an employee a right (already existing at common law) not to have a subscription deducted except with his or her consent, but required that the consent be validated by an authorisation signed within three years previous to the deduction (and in the first instance confirmed within one year from the passing of the Act (s. 15 and Sched. 9 TURER Act 1993). Changes in the amount to be deducted must be notified to the employee by, somewhat surprisingly, the employer. The requirements for scrutineers qualified under rules issued by the Secretary of State, the register of members, the storage and counting of votes etc. are made broadly similar for political fund ballots (TURER Act 1993, Sched. 1) and other ballots.

One of the most invasive provisions in the 1993 Act was that inserted at a late stage in the Parliament debates[5] giving the employer the right to take action which is discriminatory against employees who are union members if his purpose is to 'further a change in his relationship with all or any class of his employees' (s. 13, now s. 148(3)-(5) TULRCA 1992). The actions of employers which have contributed most to this question have been those which have attempted to lure employees away from collective bargaining to 'individual contracts of employment'.[6]

NOTES

1. See *Report of the Committee of Experts on the Application of Conventions* ILO 1989, Report III (Part 4A) 235-237; and *Report* ILO 1993, 235-6. The Committee maintained its stance on indemnification of officials: *ibid*, 237.

2. *United Kingdom Response to the ILO Committe of Experts Observation 1992 on Article 3*, para. 4 (b) and (c); *Report of the Committee of Experts etc.* ILO 1992, 243-4. See the masterly account by W.B. Creighton, 'The ILO and Protection of Freedom of Association in the UK' in K. Ewing, C. Gearty, B. Hepple, *Human Rights and Labour* (1994) 1-28 and, K. Ewing, *Britain and the ILO* (1989 Institute of Employment Rights, 2nd. ed. 1994).

3. If it is necessary to ascertain them, the union must identify the members by name: *Blackpool and the Fylde College v NATFHE* [1994] IRLR 227 CA.

4. For a detailed review of s. 14 TURER Act 1993, see B. Simpson, 'Individualism versus Collectivism' (1993) 22 ILJ 181; see too his 'Employment Act 1990 in Context' (1991) 54 MLR 418-438.

5. Six days after the Court of Appeal gave judgment in *Wilson v Associated Newspapers* and *Palmer v Associated British Ports* now [1994] ICR 97 CA. Despite the legislation the defendants have appealed to the House of Lords.

6. See *Associated British Ports v Palmer, Associated Newspapers Ltd v Wilson* [1994] ICR 97 CA (on appeal to HL; 'douceurs' given by the employer to those choosing individual contracts were unlawful attempts to deter others from maintaining union membership, on the law before the 1993 Act).

[Note: On the profound issues, including problems of representativeness and democracy, arising from the decision of the ECJ requiring United Kingdom law to designate a machinery for appointing workers' representatives for consultation under Directives 75/129 (collective dismissals) and 77/187 (transfers of undertakings), in *Commission v United Kingdom* (382 and 383/92) [1994] ICR 664, see P. Davies (1994) 23 ILJ 272; Wedderburn (1994) 11 Int. JC LL I R 339, and 1995 Giorn DLRI (forthcoming); G. Lyon-Caen, Dr. Soc. 1994, 923; and Chapter 10 below, notes 10, 317.

6

COLLECTIVE BARGAINING AT EUROPEAN LEVEL: THE INDEROGABILITY PROBLEM*

Ask labour law colleagues from the Continent what they know about British collective agreements and they will invariably tell you that these agreements are not contracts or, better, presumed not to be intended to give rise to legal obligation. They are 'gentleman's agreements' unless otherwise stated, not legally binding ('NLB'). The comparatist will add: Britain is 'rather a-typical' compared with the 'model most widely found which sees the collective agreement as an act endowed with legal effect, creating binding obligations'.[1] Important though this phenomenon is, it may be best to advise our colleagues, especially in the context of the Community, that this is not the most, and certainly not the only, important legal principle in our labour law concerning collective agreements. That is not to deny the crucial, if elementary, distinction between the 'obligatory' or (in a social sense) 'contractual' functions of the agreement, on the one hand, between the collective parties, as against the 'normative' or rule-making function, on the other, which in our system is normally brought into effect through incorporation by the individual employment contract[2] (though English courts occasionally fall into the howler of confusing the two).[3] Such 'errors', however, are all part of the game in this area where social policy and personal conviction rub shoulders uncomfortably with uncertain legal principles and fluid social relationships.[4] That is why we can expect problems in areas touched by the teleologies (usually more than one) of Community labour law.[5]

*First published in 1992 in *Industrial Law Journal*, Vol. 21.

THE COLLECTIVE AGREEMENT AS CONTRACT OR GENTLEMAN'S AGREEMENT

In Britain the legislation of 1974 confirmed the presumption that parties to a collective agreement do not normally intend to create a binding contract, whether it be a national accord or a plant agreement. This was the principle proposed in 1954, adopted in the Donovan Report 1968, applied by the High Court in 1969, overturned in 1971 but restored three years later.[6] It seems likely to stick if only because modern free market conservatives find the opposite presumption corporatist. Comparatively it is of especial interest not merely because most comparable systems of labour law take a different view, but because they did not do so (as is sometimes thought) merely by applying their private law of contract to the new collective agreements.[7] On the contrary, we find elsewhere that it is normally statute which intervenes to assert or to affirm the binding nature of the collective contract and put it on a legislative base in the modern system.[8] Labour law systems in countries which have recently broken the grip of authoritarian regimes have made such legislation a priority.[9] Two rather special cases are Italy and Denmark. In Italy, the 1948 Constitution envisaged legislation to regulate collective agreements and unions generally; but general legislation failed because, the laws envisaged by the Constitution (Article 39) not having been passed, alternative ways of introducing by law *erga omnes* effect (binding on all relevant workers) for collective bargaining were held to be unconstitutional.'[10] In this frame, Britain and Ireland[11] and Denmark are all unusual. In the last collective agreements are, however, legally binding between the parties, indeed that is the core of the system; the 'September Agreement' of 1899 reached after prolonged conflict, is still the base for centralized industrial relations without significant legislative intervention. Together with rules for conflict first agreed nationally in 1908, modern versions of the basic agreements, especially the general agreement between unions and employers (as amended 1987) and co-operation agreements (1986), rule the labour market, along with the disciplinary powers of State conciliators.[12] The Arbitration Court set up by statute of 1910 and 1919 became the Labour Court now (under the Act of 1973), the key piece of legal machinery in a system which works largely by way of national legally binding collective contracts.[13]

This not unfamiliar area of comparative study has come to be of new importance in face of the impact of laws and (with the slow implementation of the 'social dimension') proposals for laws within the competence of the European Community. Indeed, it will be suggested that in two complementary ways our thinking (not just in Britain) has not focused sufficiently sharply on the multiple classifications we should give to collective agreements in a European context. There may even be a blinkered belief shared with colleagues abroad that the status of 'legally binding' (LB) or 'not legally binding' (NLB)[14] is the only serious comparative way of looking at collective agreements. It will be suggested, on the contrary, that for all its importance the distinction tied to NLB status is less relevant than other models or tools for comparative classification – not least because through them we may more clearly keep in mind the law's dependence not, or not only, on legal characteristics but on its roots 'in different methods of collective bargaining – probably also in differences in political and social history which become legally relevant through the "intention of the parties" ', a point which 'it is impossible to over emphasise'.[15] The two issues which therefore demand investigation here are found, first, in the 'obligatory' or collective level of agreements and, secondly, in the different approaches to 'normative' machinery translating the collective terms (or some of them) to the individual level. These may be described as follows.

First, given that the British NLB principle is exceptional in presuming the parties had no intention to constitute legal relations in what others might take to be a contract, is it helpful to categorize European laws on collective agreements along this boundary, that is simply according to whether they ensure that collective agreements do normally have legally binding effect? This is a common habit. But it is suggested it is not always a helpful categorization. It is sometimes confusing because it lumps together jurisdictions which are as different from each other *inter se* as they all are from the British. More, its apparently neutral language hides the fact that it is the employer who usually relies on the binding effect of 'peace clauses' or the like to prevent action by the union. Signs of this undifferentiated categorization have appeared in the Community. The second issue is more difficult. It reveals a yawning gap between British juridical ideas and most of the Continental systems, in whatever manner they are grouped – 'civil law', 'Roman-Germanic' or 'Nordic'[16] – on the interaction between normative clauses in the collective agreement and the individual employment relationship. Indeed, English contains no word, certainly no term of art, apt to describe one of the very starting points in the legal vocabulary elsewhere. The terms of a collective agreement can in our system be excluded, adopted, varied or adapted by the facade which we are still pleased to call the individual employment 'contract', but in those other systems the classical point of departure (with varying degrees of emphasis) has been precisely the opposite. No derogation from the norms in an applicable collective agreement is permitted in the ordinary case, except it be for the benefit of the employee. It is not surprising that no English word is available for the Italian, nor for the equivalent German term.[17] The concept is (unhappily) deeply offensive to classical common law 'freedom of contract'. It is no accident that Coke CJ spoke of 'new and subtle inuentions (*sic*) in derogation of the Common Law'.[18] That dominant doctrine is still divided by a chasm from most labour law systems in Europe on just this point.[19] Their doctrine limits the individual contract because of its limitations as a bargained contract in a real sense within the foundations of labour law. Here, authoritative books on the common law – telling it as it is, as they must – still describe legislated protection of employees as importing 'inroads on the principle of freedom of contract – to redress some real or supposed imbalance of bargaining power', thereby regulating 'many service contracts'.[20] Fifty years of labour law have scarcely dented the pachydermatous cornucopia of self-esteem that is the life style of the English common law.[21]

Italian labour law refers to the doctrine as '*inderogabilità*', applicable to norms from which in the ordinary way you may not derogate. If the collective agreement sets a 'going rate', the employer may not contract with individual workers to work for less. It is not, of course, the whole modern story in Italy or anywhere else. Each of the systems has areas where the old presumption of *inderogabilità in pejus* once applied but has had to change or give way. There authorities may say of new laws: 'Here we find the introduction of the unheard-of legislative formula of *inderogabilità in melius* (unalterable upwards), reversing the traditional relationship between law and collective bargaining and transforming legislative minima into decrees on maxima, a ceiling not to be transgressed.'[22] At least in order to understand, compare and avoid confusion we need a term to describe this approach, where the law prohibits the employment contract made under the *droit commun* or *diritto commune* from derogating from the applicable collective agreement to the detriment of the protected party.[23]

We need a new word. That has never bothered our language nor should it hold up our labour law. Perhaps we could describe the doctrine as *inderogability*. (The word has the advantage of being less barbarous than 'subsidiarity'.) Not all systems apply the doctrine of inderogability in precisely the same way, but it is central to many different European traditions just as its absence is critical to ours. But there is no easy boundary 'civil law/common law' here either. Inderogability is not unknown in the labour laws of some 'common law' countries. The labour law of the United States, otherwise living largely in a world of its own, in a formative period prohibited just this variation by way of an individual contract of the terms of a collective agreement made by a union elected as the bargaining agent,[24] and a very strict form of inderogability it was, prohibiting variation whether more or less favourable to the individual employees (in Continental terms, inderogability both *in pejus* and *in melius*). A similar doctrine has very recently been enacted in New Zealand.[25] All sorts of labour law systems are tempted to solve the problems of collective bargaining and individual employment by adopting a version of inderogability.

In Italy, moreover, as in some other civil law systems, 'legal safeguards over the terms of the collective agreement at individual level break down ... into two sub-problems: the efficacy of the agreement *erga omnes* and so-called inderogability *in pejus*'.[26] This agenda is at least familiar to us, though we must understand the special problem of extending the collective agreement to all relevant workers (*erga omnes*) when unions are organized on a base of ideological pluralism as in France and Italy (such systems tend to invent advantages also for the established 'representative' unions). Further, unless we know just how different the 'inderogability' of normative terms is from our own 'incorporation' of collective terms into individual contracts (where the latter are dominant), we shall mistake the meaning of Italian writers when they call for a new balance between rigid protections and flexibility, to avoid control by a 'market which is not a source of just rules', with 'a firm base of collective bargaining machinery' *and* 'inderogable rights for workers (*diritti inderogabili dei lavoratori*)'.[27] In that legal culture the appeal is not to our 'freedom of contract' but to a freedom from fragmentation of the gains won collectively for those who are the weaker parties individually.

COLLECTIVE AGREEMENTS AND THE EUROPEAN COMMUNITY

We may try here for an agenda rather than answers, a few new lines on the map for legal cultures that have long passed each other in the night. First, we might re-examine the fate of British collective agreements within the optic of Community law, some examples (it is not possible to offer a comprehensive list) to improve our understanding of classification at collective level or, in the light of inderogability, on the normative level. Broadly one might take three areas: some brief encounters between British and Community concepts; Community instruments which contain collective bargaining machinery within their very structures; and, last, how far collective bargaining is a permitted method for implementation of Directives (that is, a 'method' permitted to Member States in Article 189 of the Treaty, especially in the light of ILO practice).

Encounters with collective agreements necessarily occur when terms of a collective agreement are offered as a material factor for pay unequal between men and women, or justification for unequal treatment,[28] or in a specifically British brush with the Court when it insisted that British collective agreements, even if not legally binding, must be made subject to judicial review in order to satisfy Community law on unequal treatment.[29] Even if governed by the NLB principle, between the parties collective agreements 'nevertheless have important de facto consequences for the employment relationships to which they refer' indicating rights and conditions which those 'relationships must satisfy or need not satisfy'.[30] It is of interest that a majority of judges came from systems where 'inderogabilità' principles applied.

Moving into the second area, Directive 77/187 requires that the transferee of an undertaking must continue to observe the terms and conditions of a collective agreement, other than on excepted matters, as they applied to the transferor (until its termination or expiry or for one year if the State adopts that option: Article 3(2)(3)). Regulation 6 of the British TUPE Regulations[31] sought to implement this by enacting, 'without prejudice to section 18 of TULRA', that a transferor's collective agreement has effect as if made by the transferee 'in its application to the employee'. Where the collective agreement is of the NLB kind, the transferee may as regards the union rescind it without liability, so it may be said that the United Kingdom had not complied with the Directive.[32] But with inderogability in mind, we can more readily see the collective norms rehoused in the individual contract (as reg. 6 seems to provide) so that neither the amendment nor even rescission of the collective agreement as such varies that individual contract, as is the case even under English case law.[33] Clearly though, and maybe unfortunately, Directive 77/187 did not effect a replacement of incorporation with inderogability.

Next come Directives or proposals which include collective

agreements in their own structure. For example, the proposal for European Works Councils (EWCs) in Community-scale undertakings or groups for informing and consulting with employees or their representatives.[34] A written agreement should be negotiated 'in good faith' by management and a 'special negotiating body' of employees' representatives, determining the composition and procedures of the EWC (Articles 5, 6, 7) or determining that no EWC shall be set up. But short of agreement to the contrary, the minimum floor of conditions in the Annex must be met; these provide for minimum numbers in a council and give it the right to be informed and consulted on a range of matters (including those likely to have serious consequences for employees) at the European level of the enterprise. It is here that we might expect Community lawyers to repeat the demand for legally enforceable collective agreements,[35] as the Legal Service of the Council has done on parallel matters.[36] But that issue may not arise here at all. The proposed Directive itself imposes the obligation to implement its rights and obligations. More, it specifically provides that the national law must 'ensure that adequate procedures exist *at the suit of the EWC* for the enforcement of obligations under this Directive' (Article 10(2)). Almost by analogy with the old actions in trespass and 'on the case', the EWC would sue not in contract on the agreement but on the statute (the Directive or the implementing national Law or regulations). Broadly similar arguments can be made about the 'collective agreement options' in the proposed 'European Company' Statute (Regulation and Directive)[37] and the draft Fifth Directive on company law harmonization.[38] The same appears to be true in other Community proposals for worker participation.[39] It would not follow inevitably, therefore, that the British domestic NLB presumption would be compelled to change generally.

But this solution is scarcely available if a Directive determines that a 'hard core' of employment rights in a Member State (such as hours of work, holiday rights, minimum wage rights, safety, equal treatment etc.) must apply to a worker 'posted' from another State as long as they are laid down by laws, regulations, administrative provisions or 'collective agreements or arbitration awards covering the whole of an occupation and industry concerned having an *erga omnes* effect and/or being made legally binding in the occupation or industry concerned'.[40] Of course, national or industry-wide agreements in Britain are open to variation at collective level (because they are NLB) and insecure at individual level (within the doctrine of incorporation). But the Directive finds a response among industrial parties who have long treated them socially as 'binding' collectively and as inderogable at individual level, a tradition not yet dead in Britain as the UCATT evidence on the proposed Posting Directive illustrates.[41]

So too, when it is urged that in the Community the 'methods' available to a State for implementing a Directive include collective bargaining, objections are likely to be lodged to agreements which are not legally binding. Indeed, we have seen that some Advocates General have argued that collective agreements are *never* available as a 'method' of implementation to reach 'the result to be achieved' under Article 189 of the Treaty.[42] But the Court has not gone that far.[43] It has rejected, however, circulars or reversible practices as not satisfying Community tests of legal certainty and clarity,[44] and (especially in the cases against Italy) criticized collective agreements not applicable *erga omnes*, but supported by legislation which gave most workers a higher degree of protection than anything in the Directive (75/219, consultation on redundancies) yet nevertheless let some workers fall through the net.[45] The Court appears not to take the view of the Experts of the Council of Europe that implementation may be proved by covering 'a great majority of workers' (perhaps 80 per cent).[46] If anything the Court has shown a recent tendency to be more strict about implementation *erga omnes*.[47]

It would be a pity if in a quest for legal formalism this tendency threw aside the long experience of the ILO, where there has gradually been developed a flexible policy towards implementation of Conventions by way of 'such measures as may be necessary to make [the ratified Convention] effective', including collective agreements.[48] That could be of great value to the Court of Justice, where Directives add to the normal formula (requiring Member States to 'bring into force the laws, regulations and administrative provisions necessary to comply with this Directive') the additional method: 'or shall ensure, at the latest two years after adoption, that the employers' and workers' representatives introduce the required provisions by way of agreement, the Member States being obliged to take the necessary steps enabling them at all times to guarantee the results imposed by this Directive' (the formula in Article 2, of the 1992 Directive 92/56, amending Directive 129/75 on approximation of laws on collective redundancies)[49] – if you like, collective bargaining with a legislative back-up guarantee.

A parallel appears in the 'Agreement on Social Policy' attached to the Maastricht *Protocol on Social Policy*, the 'Social Chapter' expanding on Article 118b of the existing Treaty, where a Member State may entrust implementation of Directives (within the specified employment fields: Article 2(1)(3)) to management and labour so long as the State guarantees the results by back-up measures if need arises by legislation (Article 2(4)). The Commission will give management and labour nine months to consider proposals in the social field (Article 3). More, the social dialogue may not only 'lead to contractual relations including agreements' but to agreements at Community level ('European level collective bargaining' in the eyes of the optimists)[50] which may be implemented in accordance with national procedures and practices between management and labour or, if they jointly request it, by a Council decision on a qualified majority (Article 4(1)(2)). The United Kingdom is not of course a party to the Protocol, Agreement and accompanying Declarations; and those instruments can do little or nothing for fundamental values (freedom of association and the right to strike, for example, are excluded: Article 2(6)). Beyond that there is much disagreement as to the legal results if the Maastricht Treaties are ratified.[51] What is significant here is the determination of eleven Member States to expand the area of Community rule-making by collective agreements without, it seems, confining this as such to agreements legally binding. Of course, the Agreement is a circle of mazes. At first it seems that 'contractual relations including agreements' (Article 4(1)) means that the agreements are binding so as to have some contractual force. Yet around the next corner we meet with agreements being 'implemented' in accordance with national collective procedures in all their diversity (in Britain agreements non-binding and with fragile, individualist incorporation; in France automatically enforced *erga omnes* and inderogable and open to further *extension*).

THE NEED FOR MORE FLEXIBLE CLASSIFICATIONS

A glance at legal developments in the Community suggests that it is inherently unlikely that just one classification or typology – between those 'legally binding' and those not legally binding (NLB) – will be sufficient. There are many other useful lines to be drawn. Some of the more prominent must suffice: the place of the agreement as regulation; the 'extension of agreements'; and bargaining for benefits-for-members-only. In terms of legal regulation, for example, one may legitimately put France, Italy, Belgium and Spain into one category – the *Code du Travail* is scarcely matched elsewhere for regulation, as though the Acts and orders on safety at work which we take for granted as an obvious area for regulation, were spread to many other employment conditions (as they nearly were before the turn of the century – on working hours, for example).[52] We can then put Germany, the Netherlands, Denmark and Sweden in a second category (where centralized bargaining dominates in a somewhat less regulated, though to British eyes still legalistic, system). Such a classification can be justified by reference to the labour movements, so often the key to understanding labour law: in the former group, ideologically pluralist and centrifugal, a movement of 'opposition'; in the latter, unitary and centralist with power based on membership, funds and property (with a minor exception in the Netherlands where we find pluralist unions).[53]

In formal terms the Member States in both groups regard collective agreements as legally binding. But when we ask after the operation of this principle on bargaining, not only do national divergencies appear (even on unexpected matters like the 'check-off')[54] the proposed legal classification begins to disintegrate, especially in regard to machineries of 'extension'. In France, Belgium and Spain (Group 1) and in Germany and the Netherlands (Group 2) a legal power exists, after a variety of complex procedures, for the public authorities (the Minister) to 'extend' a collective agreement to new employers and workers by order (or, in the German phrase, declare it 'generally binding'). This machinery is a central part in these jurisdictions for making agreements binding *erga omnes*.[55] Yet in Italy (Group 1) and Sweden and Denmark (Group 2), extension is unacceptable as contrary to contractual principles (which in a purist sense it clearly is). In Italy, moreover, it risks being unconstitutional.[56] In comparative considerations about applying agreements *erga omnes*, the variety of the real systems takes the place of a simplistic debate about 'binding' and 'not binding' agreements. Indeed, even Britain has had experience of weak forms of such machinery in decades of unilateral arbitration machineries now recently repealed.[57]

A similar classification, however, fares better when applied to the 'peace obligation'. That is said by indiscriminate British commentary to arise from Continental collective agreements just because they are legally binding.[58] That is broadly true in German, Swedish and Danish labour law; indeed, the role of the peace obligation there cannot be exaggerated.[59] But on France and Italy it is a crude misdescription which breeds misunderstanding. Collective agreements are contracts there too, but for union officers or members to be liable for causing a breach of a collective agreement in France, the act done must be deliberate and direct; and the rare cases of liability of the union itself rest more on *alter ego* principles than anything like English principles of vicarious liability.[60] Nor can the union expunge the individual right to strike of its members. Authorities remark that, whereas 'in Germany the peace obligation is strictly applied, in France and Italy one scarcely speaks of it'.[61] Nor are categories of 'tort' and 'contract' helpful; what matters is the extent of liability, not its name; and in Britain we now have unheard-of new rules for vicarious liability of trade unions (with the regulated route to 'repudiation' offered like a booby-trapped oasis in the legal minefield) with extensions of liability in tort, in restitution and for contempt of court, on the one side, and, on the other, the common law uncaged by Parliament's dismantling of the trade dispute 'immunities'. All this produces liabilities for workers and unions far beyond the wit of *responsabilité civile* – laws in breach of minimum standards of the ILO, so dour they surprise even German colleagues whose law on strikes is hardly docile.[62] Just so, French and Italian principles carry the effect of their law far beyond the formalities of any 'binding effect' doctrine, basing collective rights (not least, a right to strike) not on contractual models but on individualist rights seen as civil liberties. British legal culture has here been more akin to, though not the same as, German or Danish law; but its individualist rhetoric is idiosyncratic.[63]

Finally, before leaving the normative effect, we must note that there is no simple typology of systems even in respect of inderogability. Of course the doctrine does not mean that a collective agreement 'enforceable *erga omnes*' must be binding on every employer and employee in the land, or even a district.[64] A lively French jurisprudence illustrates the way in which in all systems courts may be called on to interpret the extent to which (in the words of the proposed Directive on 'Posting of Workers', Article 3(1)(a)) it covers 'the whole of an occupation and industry and has *erga omnes* effect'.[65] There are more difficult issues. Systems have their own hierarchy of norms;[66] but there are strong and weak versions of inderogability as between collective agreement and individual contract. The strong version causes the normative part of a relevant agreement to attach at once to the employment relations of any employer and worker within the scope of the agreement. Then, runs this version, 'these terms apply to employment contracts concluded with him, except for provisions more favourable [to the employee]'.[67] The machinery here is not, French writers insist, 'incorporation' of the English or any other kind, but a process in which the application of the collective agreement is 'automatic, immediate, and imperative'.[68] The agreement binds as *règlement*. The law in Sweden is in similar, if not even stricter, terms.[69] In Spain, normative terms attach to workers' contracts not by incorporation, but by law so that individually negotiated terms which are less favourable are not licit.[70]

But there is a weaker version, still based on inderogability but materially different, resting on agency. In these systems – notably Germany, Italy, the Netherlands and (oddly) Sweden – the union (and the employers' association, if one is a party) is taken to contract normatively only as agent for its *members*. This conjures up the nightmare of all modern collective labour law systems: how to cover the non-union employee also by an agreement negotiated by the union to which he has given no authority, i.e. one species of the *erga omnes* problem.[71] Writers stress that, whatever the law says, in practice employers in Germany, Sweden and elsewhere, do grant the same terms to non-union employees;[72] but that does not, of course, solve the legal problem. In the Italian system, similar but more complex problems arise; the doctrine of *inderogabilità in pejus* and the agency of the unions rest, the majority of writers say, on the Civil Code which subjects terms of the employment contracts of union members to relevant collective agreements, save for provisions more advantageous to the worker; an amendment to the Code of 1973 confirmed that a worker may not renounce the inderogable advantages of the agreement.[73] But in order to produce a scope wider than 'agency', more like *erga omnes*, writers and courts rely too on a range of other sources, for example Article 36 of the Constitution giving every worker the right to a wage adequate for a free and dignified life for him and his family (as well as specific provisions such as that in the Workers' Statute 1970 requiring employers receiving public benefits or contracts to maintain terms and conditions 'not less favourable' than those in relevant collective agreements, as once did our sadly rescinded Fair Wages Resolution).[74]

Moreover, the typologies so far offered encounter further difficulties if we ask after just one further item of a crowded agenda: whether the union can bargain for benefits available *only* to its members. Those who see this practice as part of a banned closed shop or other prohibited union security practices, will be likely to regard benefits-for-members-only-agreements as equally illicit, possibly as pressure on non-members. At once yet another classification opens up. Germany, France and Portugal follow that logic, making members-only-bargaining illegal (though for rather diverse reasons). So too (on the majority view) Italy. But Spain and the Netherlands do not rule out members-only-benefit-agreements *per se* (the latter theoretically allowing for union security so long as there is a choice of union) while in Belgium the apparent inconsistency between opposition to the closed shop and acceptability of members-only-bargaining is defended on grounds of convenience (such agreements are even open to extension, which in the Netherlands they are not). Curiously little attention has been paid, even by British union officials, to the new prohibition on union-members-only-bargaining in Britain since 1988.[75] If the recession grows worse, union leaders in these countries may find members demanding that the (or some) advantages in new collective agreements should be reserved for them. Otherwise, why bother to pay subscriptions? One may legitimately ask too whether such discrimination would 'distort competition', though it would offend profound principles of ideologically pluralist systems and doubly offend where (as in France) collectively bargained terms immediately bind all the relevant contracts of employment.

So, most national patterns gravitate around poles of strong or weak inderogability in its diverse forms, a force which affects the shape of a whole range of related issues. The variations are a product of legal cultures, forged by social developments, and their multi-faceted divergence is all the more reason not to lump them into a falsely simplistic category of 'foreign-systems-that-have-binding-collective-agreements'. In general, those other systems make collective agreements binding but some are much less 'binding' than others. Instead, we might elaborate a pattern of collective agreements in Europe in which the 'contractual' status is just one item alongside others: for example, inderogability (*in pejus* and *in melius*), incorporation, 'extension', the 'peace' clause and the right to strike, protection of minimum standards or members-only-bargaining in the new labour market. To these traditional items there must now be added others: for example, the relationship, or lack of it, to vocational training, provisions on redundancy and job creation. In that venture we can not only remedy a defect in comparative labour law scholarship, one by no means confined to Britain; we may also promote more fruitful dialogue with those from East of the Neisse who are eager to create their own forms of the autonomous collective bargaining which for decades has not been available to them.[76] To refine a comparative concept of inderogability would be a useful step along that path. Equally, we shall have need of it at home because the introduction of forms of inderogability will be useful to moderate the common law of incorporation, as part of the next structural reform to modernize British law on collective labour relations.

NOTES

1. B. Veneziani, *Stato e autonomia collettiva: diritto sindacale italiano e comparato* (1992 Bari) 154, and Chap 5 for a comparative review.
2. O. Kahn-Freund, *Labour and the Law* (3rd edn eds P. Davies and M. Freedland) pp 158-199; Wedderburn, *The Worker and the Law* (1986 3rd edn) 318-54.
3. See *Marley* v *Forward Trust Group* (1986) IRLR 43 EAT, set right by the CA [1986] IRLR 369.
4. An example is the prolonged argument in Italy about the applicability of 'peace clauses': e.g. G. Giugni, in B. Aaron and K. Wedderburn, *Industrial Conflict: A Comparative Legal Survey* (1972) 143, criticizing lawyers whose 'static conception of law' leads them to deny, not only the presence of any peace obligation, but also the 'existence of a collective contract binding in law'. See below n 61ff.
5. See especially the revealing essay by P.L. Davies, 'The Emergence of European Labour Law' Chap 10 in W. McCarthy (ed.) *Legal Interventions in Industrial Relations* (1992); also Wedderburn, 'European Community Law and Workers' Rights: Fact or Fake in 1992?' (1991) 13 Univ. Dublin LJ 1, 13-33, reprinted in this volume, chap. 8.
6. Trade Unions and Labour Relations Act 1974, section 18, now section 179 Trade Union and Labour Relations (Consolidation) Act 1992 [hereafter 'TULRCA']: presumed not to have been intended by the parties to be a legally enforceable contract unless the opposite is stated in writing; O. Kahn-Freund, in A. Flanders and H. Clegg (eds.) *The System of Industrial Relations in Great Britain* (1954) 43-5, (changing his view in (1943) 5 MLR 112); Donovan *Royal Commission Report* (1986, Cmnd 3623) Chap VIII; *Ford Motor Co* v *AUEF* [1969] 2 QB 303; Industrial Relations Act 1971, section 34. A proposal to reverse the presumption again and promote legal enforceability in *Industrial Relations in the 1990s* (1991 Cm 1602) appears to have been dropped in face of policies to promote an individualized labour market (*People, Jobs and Opportunity* 1992 Cm 1810), see Parl Deb HC 11 February 1992, col 809).
7. In some countries legal effect was first pronounced by the courts and only later put on a statutory basis, e.g. Sweden, 1915 NJA 233; legislation set up a Labour Court and extended binding effect to members of associations party to the agreement in 1928 (Collective Agreements Law section 2); see Folke Schmidt, *The Law of Labor Relations in Sweden* (1962) 28-9. The modern law is in the Joint Regulation of Working Life Act ['JRWLA'] 1976, sections 26 and 27, see Folke Schmidt, *Law and Industrial Relations in Sweden* (1977) 238, and Chap 9.
8. See, for example, *France:* Law of 25 March 1919 (now Code du Travail Article L 135-5); *Germany*: Weimar *Tarifsvertragsordnung* 23 December 1918, today Article 2 Law of 9 April 1949, as amended 1969 and 1974; *the Netherlands*: after amendments to the Civil Code in 1907, Article 1 Law on Collective Agreements 24 December 1927. Legislation in *Belgium* (Articles 19, 26, Law of 5 December 1968) came relatively late. In *Norway*, the 1915 legislation on disputes regulated the effect of collective agreements and set up a Labour Court, penal sanctions being added for breach of an agreement

by workers; and in *Finland* an Act on collective agreements was passed in 1924 soon after independence (though a Labour Court was not added until 1946). For greater detail of some jurisdictions, A. Jacobs in B. Hepple *The Making of Labour Law in Europe* (1986) Chap 5; and on Denmark see n 12 below.

9. *Spain*, Article 82 Workers Statute 10 March 1980; *Portugal*, Decree Law no. 164/A 28 February 1976, modified in Decree Laws no. 887 29 December 1976, and no. 519 20 December 1979; *Greece*, Law no. 3239/1955 (a not wholly liberal measure) later modified e.g. Law no. 1915 28 December 1990 (see 1991, 204 *EIRR* 20). For concern by the ILO Committee of Experts about the law in Greece see *Report of the Committee of Experts* ILO 78th Session 1991 Report III (Part 4A) pp 176-7.

10. A temporary Law no. 741/1959 making agreements binding *erga omnes* (i.e. on all relevant employers and employees) was upheld, but the Constitutional Court's judgments rendered permanent machinery of this kind unconstitutional: G. Giugni, *Diritto sindacale* (9th edn 1991) Chap 6; the 'reception' of some agreements into the law under the 1959 Law left many subsequent collective agreements to the 'common law' and the Civil Code. The problem of *'erga omnes'* effect was pronounced as pluralist trade unions, ideologically rivals, attempted to make agreements covering a whole sector or industry: *ibid*. pp 74-7. The device of 'representative unions' has moderated, but not solved this problem: *ibid*. 68-99. See further S. Sciarra, 'The Rise of the Italian Shop Stweward' (1977) 6 ILJ 35.

11. It would appear that Ireland still shares the common law approach of Britain, without any statute equivalent to section 179 TULRCA 1992: A. Kerr and G. Whyte, *Irish Trade Union Law* (1985) 153-158. But other statutory interventions make for differences in practice (e.g. the need for the union party to an agreement to be licensed, *ibid*. pp 50-69 and Industrial Relations Act 1990, sections 20, 21, and the effects of registration of collective agreements, pp 146-52).

12. The Conciliation Act, as amended 1971, gives the official conciliators power to postpone a strike or lock-out (sections 3, 4(4)); and where a stoppage would 'affect vital functions' or be of 'far-reaching social consequence' or would 'exert a vitally unfortunate influence on a peaceful settlement', they may require postponement for up to two weeks (Article 4(5)). The role of conciliators is confirmed by the Danish Report in the European Commission's, *First Report on the Application of the Community Charter of the Fundamental Social Rights of Workers, Social Europe*, 1/92, p 51; 'it is not as a general rule lawful to strike during the currency of a collective agreement' (the so-called 'peace clause'); i.e. an absolute, not a relative, peace obligation. Large fines on unions are common in the Labour Court, in contrast with Sweden: T. Sigeman, 'Damages and Bot: Remedies for Breach of Collective Agreement in Nordic Law' (1987) 8 Comp. Lab. Law Jo. 155, 163-81; and on the history, see A. Adlercreutz, *Scandinavian Studies in Law* 1958, 32-5. Danish governments have often intervened by legislation to extend collective agreements to defeat strikes, often in breach of ILO Conventions 87 and 98 (see for example, ILO Committee on Freedom of Association, Case 1443, *Computer Workers Union (PROSA) v Denmark*

1988, 259th Report, 21 November 1988; Committee of Experts, *Report on Application of Conventions* 1991, III (Part 4A) 78th Session ILO p 167).

13. The 1899 Agreement 'could have become the Magna Carta of modern Western European industrial relations'; one of the reasons it did not was perhaps the 'inaccessibility of the Danish language': A. Jacobs, in B. Hepple (ed.) *The Making of Labour Law in Europe, op.cit.* above n 8, 224. On Nordic Labour Courts, see T. Sigeman, *op.cit.* above n 12, (1987) 8 Comp. Lab. Law Jo. 155, 156-73.

14. See on the absence of binding effect in Britain and on 'TINALEA' clauses excluding legal remedies (in line now with section 179 TULReCA 1992) Wedderburn, *The Worker and the Law* (3rd edn 1986) 318-321; and on 'incorporation' 329-343; and on public policy in this area see P. Davies and M. Freedland, *Labour Law: Text and Materials* (1984 2nd edn) 127-61.

15. O. Kahn-Freund, *'Pacta Sunt Servanda* – a Principle and its Limits: Some Thoughts Prompted by Comparative Labour Law' (1974) 48 Tulane LR 894, 902-3.

16. Groupings found in the Commission's, *Comparative Study on Rules Governing Working Conditions in the Member States* (1989) SEC (89) 1137, pp 10-15, in contrast to the 'Anglo-Irish' system of labour law.

17. The writer takes heart from the difficulty Jon Clark had, despite his consummate skill in the language, in translating the German term *Unabdingbarkeit* in *Labour Law and Politics in the Weimar Republic: O. Kahn-Freund* (eds. R. Lewis and J. Clark 1981) 243: he suggested 'unalterability, irrevocability', a ban on employers contracting out of collective terms to the detriment of the employee; see Sinzheimer's justification for this, 82. The Spanish principle *'la condicion mas beneficiosa de origen contractual'* plays a similar role, but is also touched by a notion of contractual 'incorporation': T. Sala Franco (ed.) *Derecho del Trabajo* (5th edn 1990) pp 266-71; and 272-8 on the issues on inderogability of workers' rights.

18. *Shorter Oxford English Dictionary*, Vol. 1 p 526.

19. *Simpson v Kodak Ltd* [1948] 2 KB 184; *Hulland v Saunders* [1945] KB 78. The strength of the early English insistence on inderogability of the *common law* is matched even today when we find attempts by employers, albeit unsuccessful, to enforce a contractual wage in place of the higher (inderogable) rate fixed by a wages council order under *statute* in almost the only exceptional case left in British law: *Reid v Camphill Engravers* [1990] ICR 435, EAT (Scot.) on Wages Councils Act 1979, section 15, restricted in Wages Act 1986 sections 13-16 [repealed by s. 35 TURER Act 1993].

20. G. Treitel, *The Law of Contract* (8th edn 1991) 3.

21. On the common law and British labour law, see Wedderburn, 'The Social Charter in Britain – Labour Law and Labour Courts?' (1991) 54 MLR 1; and on links with free market philosophies: *Employment Rights in Britain and Europe* (1991) Chap 8.

22. L. Mariucci, *Le fonti del diritto del lavoro* (1988) 48, describing Italian 'crisis legislation' (to some degree, incomes policy) of the 1980s which began to block negotiated increases for seniority, cost of living, and wage-indexation etc. (the last was finally abolished in 1992). Compare the interaction of incomes policy legislation and the law of contract, *Allen v*

Thorne Electrical Industries [1968] 1 QB 487, CA.

23. Confusion is not all on the British side. R. Blanpain and J.C. Javillier, *Droit du Travail Communautaire* (1991) 67-8, describe *l'effet obligatoire* of British collective agreements entirely in terms of its NLB character at collective level, without taking account of incorporation into employment contracts. See too the very different approaches to collective agreements in a transnational setting in A. Lyon-Caen and G. Lyon-Caen, *Droit Social International et Européen* (7th edn 1991) pp. 16-18, and Felice Morgenstern, *International Conflicts of Labour Law* (1984) pp 100-6 (especially on 'extension').

24. *JI Case* v *NLRB* 321 US 332 (1944), said to be a consequence of the 'exclusive representation' principle: L. Merrifield, T. St. Antoine, and C. Craver, *Labor Relations Law* (8th edn 1989) 494-7. There is a limited parallel here with the concepts of *interesse collettivo or interêts collectifs*: see Lord Wedderburn and S. Sciarra, 'Collective Bargaining as Agreement and as Law', in A. Pizzorusso, *Law in the Making* (1988) 192-4 (also 1989 35 Riv. dir. civ. 45, 52-4).

25. When a 'collective employment contract' applies, the employee may negotiate with the employer 'on an individual basis' but only for terms and conditions which are '*not inconsistent* with any terms and conditions of the applicable collective contract': section 19(2) Employment Contracts Act 1991 (New Zealand).

26. G. Vardaro, *Contratti collettivi e rapporto individuale di lavoro* (1985) 21 (the term *inderogabilità* was not common before the 1940s in Italy because the problem did not arise in corporative, fascist labour law, pp 31-2 and n 12). The writer pays a sincere tribute to the work of Gaetano Vardaro, whose untimely death robbed comparative labour law of a remarkable scholar.

27. Silvana Sciarra, '*Uno "Strabismo di Venere": Le politiche sociali comunitarie verso il completamento del mercato interno*' 1991, 81 *Prospettiva sindacale* 33, 38. Parallel French sentiments appeal to the 'rights of man': see J.M. Verdier, '*En Guise de Manifeste: Le Droit du Travail, Terre d'Élection pour les Droits de l'Homme*', *Écrits en l'Honneur du Jean Savatier* (1992) 427-37.

28. For example, see *Enderby* v *Frenchay Health Authority* [1991] IRLR 44; *Handels-og-Kontorfunktionaererenes Forbiund i Danmark* v *Dansk Arbejdsgiverforening (Danfoss)* (Case 109/88) [1989] IRLR 532 (ECJ); *Nimz* v *Freie und Hansestadt Hamburg* (Case 184/89) [1991] IRLR 222 (ECJ); *Kowalska* v *Freie und Hansestadt Hamburg* (Case 33/89) [1990] IRLR 447 (ECJ); R. Nielsen and E. Szyszczak, *The Social Dimension of the European Community* (1991) 81-132.

29. Directive 76/207, Article 4(b); *Commission* v *United Kingdom* (Case 165/82) [1984] ICR 192 (ECJ); J. Shaw (1984) 47 MLR 348.

30. *Commission* v *United Kingdom, op.cit* n. 29, 215. The consequence was the unsatisfactory section 6, Sex Discrimination Act 1986, applying section 77 of the 1975 Act. The remedy is of doubtful efficacy: B. Hepple (1990) 53 MLR at p 652, n 62.

31. Transfer of Undertakings (Protection of Employment) Regulations 1981, SI 1794; P. Davies and M. Freedland, *Transfer of Employment* (1982). The

view that Article 3 means nothing in the British context because of the NLB character of agreements was a common political evaluation, see Parl Deb HL December 10th 1981, col 1500; Parl Deb HC 7 December 1981 col 679.

32. See B. Hepple and A. Byre, cited in B. Hepple (1990) 53 MLR p 652; and P. O'Higgins, in R. Lewis (ed.) *Labour Law in Britain* (1986) 588-90.

33. See on such 'pendant' employment contracts: *Robertson v British Gas* [1983] ICR 351 CA; *Gibbons v Assoc. British Ports* [1985] IRLR 376. On the range of employees protected see J. McMullen, *Business Transfers and Employment Rights* (2nd edn, 1992) 238-40. Also, the judges have stepped up their unfortunate practice of deciding whether terms are 'apt' for incorporation: *Alexander v Standard Telephones* (no 2) [1991] IRLR 286; *British Leyland v McQuilken* [1978] IRLR 245 (Scot); and procedural clauses are often regarded as inappropriate for incorporation (Wedderburn, *The Worker and the Law cit.* 339-43). Inderogability might assist on the last point: see the German category of '*collective* normative regulations' (which may include certain procedures, though they are 'a source for never ending controversies': M. Weiss, *Labour Law and Industrial Relations in the FRG* (1987) 126-7). Compare A. Adinolfi, 'Implementation of Social Policy Directives through Collective Agreements?' (1988) 25 CMLR 291, 300-15.

34. COM (91) 345 final, British objections were maintained: *EIRR* 1992, 220 p 3. Such undertakings have 1000 employees and [now 150] in each of two establishments within the Community (in two different Member States). See M. Hall (1991) 20 ILJ 147, 149-50, and on the UK and 'Vredeling', C. Docksey (1986) 49 MLR 280, 302-6 [now the amended text adopted by Eleven States under the 'Social Chapter': (1994 EIRR 250, 14].

35. Sir Gordon (now Lord) Slynn, when Advocate General, said that collective agreements were not 'laws, regulations or administrative provisions' within Article 7 of Directive 77/187: so 'a Directive cannot be implemented by collective bargaining agreements unless they are given the force of law by legislation': *Commission v Italy* (Case 235/84) [1987] 3 CMLR 115; so too, Advocate General Van Themaat, *Commission v Italy* (Case 91/81) [1982] ECR 2133, 2145. But the Court has refrained from going that far and repeated that a State might 'leave the implementation of the social policy objectives in the first instance to management and labour': *Commission v Denmark* (Case 143/83) [1985] ECR 428 (equal pay). On the ILO and implementation by collective bargaining, see below n 48, and Adinolfi *op.cit* n. 33 above.

36. Excluding NLB agreements from the permissible methods of implementing Directives: 10550/84 IUR 148 SOC 323; C. Docksey (1986) 49 MLR pp 302-6.

37. See *Revised Proposal for a European Company Statute: Consultative Document*: Dept Trade and Industry, January 1992 (the Regulation and the Directive: OJ C 176/1, 8 July 1991); also HL Select Committee on European Communities *European Company Statute* 19th Report 1989/90, 10 July 1990. The collective bargaining option of the draft Directive (in Article 6: 'other models') complements participation on a two-tier Supervisory Board or an administrative board of directors (Article 4), or in

a 'separate body' representing employees (Article 5). Recently proposed amendments (to Articles 5 and 9 of the Regulation, and Article 3(1) (1a) (1b) of the Directive) aim to prevent shareholders moving the registered office of the *Societas Europaea* to a new State where the option agreed upon for employee participation might not be permitted, with the agreement of the employees' representatives: see the new Article 3(5). On this problem: Wedderburn, *The Social Charter, European Company and Employment Rights* (1990) pp 59-70; P.L. Davies, 'The Emergence of European Labour Law' in W. McCarthy (ed.) *Legal Interventions in Industrial Relations* (1992) 336-8.

38. Proposal for a Fifth Company Law Directive, first presented 9 October 1972 (OJ C 72/49), as now amended: COM (91) 372 final-SYN 3; in *Consultative Document: Amended Proposal for a Fifth Company Law Directive*, Dept of Trade and Industry January 1990. The proposal now allows for a 'collective bargaining' option (Articles 4e and 21f) alongside options for an 'organ' representative of employees (Article 4e and 21e) or participation on a company board (Articles 4b and 4c, and 21d). Collective agreements concluded under this third option must make provision for rights of employee participation equivalent to rights in the models for institutional participation: Articles 4e(2), 21f(2). As with the EWC proposal, the 'fall back' floor in the Directive itself sets out rights for employee representatives. For enforcement if a Member State fails to implement the Directive, see *Francovich and Boniface* v *Italy* (Cases 6 and 9/90) [1992] IRLR 84 (ECJ); P. Duffy (1992) ELR 133.

39. For promotion of 'agreements' between management and employees' representatives about information and consultation on a wide range of matters in co-operative societies, see Articles 3 and 4, of proposed Directive on European Co-operative Societies: COM (91) 273 final-SYN 389 (OJ C99/37, 21 April 1992). If the registered office is moved to another Member State, any change in the participation arrangements must be negotiated (compare the European Company Statute, above n 37).

40. Proposal for Directive on 'Posting of Workers' (Provision of Services): COM (91) 230 final, 1 August 1991, Article 3(1)(a); for the 'hard core' of rights Article 3(1)(b) and the Commission's Explanatory Memorandum paras 24-26; see now *Protection of Posted Workers* HL Select Committee on European Communities, 14 July 1992, 5th Report 1992-3 (see the note by the present writer p 52, who did not share the conclusions of the Report on 'fair competition' p 22). On the relationship to the Rome Convention, see pp 7-8 and Evidence cited [see too below pp. 421ff, nn. 163, 173].

41. See HL Select Committee Report *Protection of Posted Workers, cit.* n 40, where UCATT argued that in the building industry the National Joint Council agreement had effect throughout the industry and, as implied terms in all building workers' employment contracts, must satisfy the *erga omnes* test even though the agreement is 'not legally binding in the way that some continental agreements are' (*Evidence* p 28). The Department of Employment did not fully distinguish the two dimensions (the NLB collective agreements and the separate question of incorporation) Appendix 3, p 25; compare the Ministry of Labour *Written Evidence* to

the Donovan Royal Commission (1965, paras 26-32).

42. See Advocates General Slynn (as he was then) and van Themaat above n 35; *Commission* v *Italy* (Case 235/84) [1987] 3 CMLR 115; *Commission* v *Italy* (Case 91/81) [1982] ECR 2133, 2142; the Opinion of the Legal Service of the EC Council 23 November 1984, 10550/84 JUR 148 Soc 323 (NLB collective agreements not suitable for implementation); also, B. Hepple and A. Byre (1989) 18 ILJ 129, 138-42; the British employer's ability to escape from the obligations of Directives 75/219 and 77/187, by refusing to recognize or to continue to recognize, a trade union, which has since 1980 been a voluntary choice: B. Simpson *Trade Union Recognition and the Law* (1991), Wedderburn *Employment Rights in Britain and Europe, cit.* 52-3, 212-4, 364-7. This question of 'recognition' is bound to be central to the cases launched against the UK for failure to implement these Directives [see now below p. 411, n. 10].

43. For example, a State may leave the implementation of the social policy objectives in the first instance to management and labour: see *Commission* v *Denmark* (Case 143/83) [1985] ECR 428 (equal pay).

44. *Commission* v *Belgium* (Case 102/79) [1980] ECR 1473; but not, it appears, where the State has already satisfied the Directive's standards before its adoption: *Commission* v *Germany* (Case 29/84) [1985] ECR 1459. See A. Adinolfi, *op.cit.* above n 33 (1988) 25 CMLR 291, 298-310.

45. For a critique of both Community and Italian law: G. Ghezzi and U. Romagnoli, *Il rapporto del lavoro* (2nd 2d 1987) pp 318-321. Implementation of Directives 75/129, 77/187 and the insolvency Directive 80/987, has now been effected in (respectively) Law no. 428, 29 December 1990; Law no. 223, 23 July 1991; and Law no. 80, 27 January 1992.

46. O. Kahn-Freund, 'The European Social Charter' in F. Jacobs, *European Law and the Individual* (1976) 190-2; D. Harris, *The European Charter* (1984) 279.

47. See the Court's refusal to permit exceptions, by law or through bargaining, to the ban on special rules to protect women on night work: *Re: Stoeckel* (Case 345/89 25 July 1991) OJ C220/7, 23 August 1991; *Re Protection of Women* (Case 312/86) [1989] 1 CMLR 408 (ECJ). Compare ILO Convention no. 171 (27 June 1990) on Night Work which would limit it with interim measures for groups of workers, and introduce tighter health checks. Compare the draft EC Directive on pregnant women and new mothers: (1990) *EIRR* 203, 16, (1992) 217 *ibid.* 14; 222 *ibid.* 2 (alternatives to night work) [see N. Wuiame (1994) 23 95].

48. ILO Constitution Article 19(5)(d); see N. Valticos, *Droit International du Travail* (2nd edn 1985) 595-7; A Adinolfi, *op.cit.* above n 33, 296-8, citing ILO Convention 135 on workers' representatives, to be implemented 'through national laws or regulations or collective agreements or in any other manner consistent with national practice' (Article 6); J.M. Servais, 'Flexibility and Rigidity in International Labour Standards' (1986) 193, 197; O. Kahn-Freund, *Labour and the Law, op.cit.* (3rd edn 1983 eds. P. Davies and M. Freedland) pp 52-9. Effect may often be given to a Convention by collective agreements even if they are not mentioned expressly in it.

49. Directive 92/56 adopted 24 June 1992; but many radical clauses proposed in earlier drafts have disappeared (such as those rendering dismissals in contravention of consultation procedures null and void). The employer's obligations on information and consultation are somewhat increased, consultations 'must cover ways of avoiding collective redundancies', and a company is less able to plead the default of a controlling undertaking as an excuse for ineffective consultation [now TURER Act 1993, s. 34].

50. For a pessimistic view (or realistic, according to taste) see M. Weiss, 'Social Dialogue and Collective Bargaining in the Framework of Social Europe' in G. Spyropoulos and G. Fragnière, *Work and Social Policies in the New Europe* (1991) 59-75 (arguing that, with such diverse systems, no European collective agreements can be concluded through the social dialogue; it can only be a forum for reaching joint positions relayed to 'the actors of collective bargaining' at national level, at best ending in 'co-ordinated bargaining').

51. This paper was written before the French referendum of September 1992, and before any steps had been reported to reverse the negative result of the Danish referendum. If ratification does ensue, one difficult question will be the extent to which instruments adopted under the Social Protocol and Agreement by the eleven Member States form part of the *acquis communautaire*. Although that issue cannot be discussed fully here, we may note that it might be especially difficult to convince the Court that this was the case if reliance were placed on the Declaration on Article 4(2) (envisaging standards set by collective bargaining and agreements but declaring that there is 'no obligation ... to apply the agreements directly or to work out rules for their transposition, nor any obligation to amend national legislation in force to facilitate their implementation'). Clearly the legal effect of collective agreements would remain different in different States. The fact that this Declaration dispenses with the State's duty to provide a legal effect, if need be back-up legislation, might add to the difficulty of arguing that these provisions fall within enforceable Community law: compare E. Vogel-Polsky, *Le Volet Social du Traité sur l'Union* (1992) p 11: the 'directives' under the Protocol will not be Community law. It may be significant that the Declaration was added after the Agreement of 31 October 1991 between UNICE, CEEP (employers) and ETUC on which the Agreement is founded. See too B. Bercusson, 'Maastricht: A Fundamental Change in European Labour Law' (1992) 23 Ind Rel Jo 177; and B. Fitzpatrick, 'Community Social Law after Maastricht', above p 199.

52. See Wedderburn, 'The Social Charter in Britain: Labour Law and Labour Courts?' (1991) 54 MLR 1, 2-14.

53. For references and comparisons see Wedderburn, *Employment Rights in Britain and Europe* (1991) Chaps. 3 and 10; also (1991) 54 MLR 1, 2-14.

54. In 'Group 1 States', the variations are enormous: the check-off of union subscriptions is illegal in France (Law of 27 April 1956, see Folke Schmidt, *Discrimination in Employment* (1978) Chap 6 on the origins of that law) whereas in Italy it is a fundamental right for the worker and the union (*Workers' Statute* Law no 300 1970, Article 26), it is encouraged in Spain (*Ley Organica de Libertad Sindical* Law no 11/1985 Article 8). Yet French

232

authorities describe it as 'le check off des pays anglo-saxons': G. Lyon-Caen and J. Pelissier, *Droit du Travail* (1990) 15th edn) 835, and it is sometimes equated to the closed shop. See *Industrial Relations in the 1990s* Cm 1602, Chap 6 [now ss. 68, 68A TULRCA 1992]. Greece has only recently shrugged off what were (in practice), obligatory check-off practices, part of the 'workers' hearth' funds: ILO Committee of Experts *Report 1991*, 78th Session, III (Part 4A) p 177. An analysis of national differences on the check-off appears in the writer's study for the Commission, *Freedom of Association and Community Protection*.

55. The detailed account by B. Venziani, *Stato e autonomia collettiva cit.* n 1 above, 162-90, understandably places 'extension' at the centre of the comparative debate about *erga omnes* and *inderogabilità*, and describes projects for law reform in Italy to repair the absence of *erga omnes* effect and to improve 'representativity'. The two issues go together: applicability of collective agreements and representativity of the bargaining parties. For general references to the sources, see Wedderburn, *Employment Rights in Britain and Europe, op.cit.* p 360; and on details of diverse national procedures, Wedderburn and S. Sciarra, 'Collective Agreement as Bargaining and as Law, *op.cit.* n 24 above, pp 220-4 [also below p. 389].

56. On the special problems in Italy concerning *erga omnes* applications, see above nn 10, 26, 27; and G. Ghezzi and U. Romagnoli, *Il diritto sindacale* (3rd edn 1992) pp 149-54.

57. The unilateral arbitration provisions of Sched 11, Employment Protection Act 1975 (repealed section 19 Employment Act 1980) and the Fair Wages Resolution 1946, rescinded in 1982 (see P. Wood (1978) 7 ILJ 65; M. Jones (1980) 9 ILJ 13) [see too above p. 13ff].

58. The legal enforceability of collective agreements as contracts in most Western countries 'imposes upon those parties a "peace" or "no strike, no lock out" obligation', making industrial action unlawful 'while it is in force': *Trade Union Immunities* (1981 Cmnd 8128) pp 54-5. Absolute peace obligations are not there distinguished from 'relative' obligations, i.e. related to the contents of the agreement, as in Germany: M. Weiss, *Law and Industrial Relations in the FRG, op.cit.* 124-5. On the once dominant problem of judicial creation of 'invisible clauses' in Nordic agreements: A. Suviranta 'Invisible Clauses in Collective Agreements' (1965) 9 Scandinavian Studies in Law 177-215.

59. For some comparative sources on 'peace obligations' and the associated division between 'conflicts of rights' and 'conflicts of interests', see Wedderburn, *Employment Rights in Britain and Europe op.cit.* 297-314. Neither in French nor Italian law can a peace clause render the right to strike wholly ineffective.

60. For rare French decisions on deliberate wrongdoing, see Soc 5 May 1960; and Soc 8 December *Tanneries de Sireuil* (union delegates ignoring agreed safety measures for goods in case of a strike); G. Lyon-Caen and J. Pelissier, *Droit du Travail* (1990 15th edn) pp 1021-82 [see above chap. 4]. Liability may arise where statute creates a floor of 'peace' obligations, e.g. on strike notice, which the parties may enlarge by collective agreement (as under Italian Law no 146 of 1990, Articles 2, 4, 5, on strikes in essential services: G. Ghezzi and U. Romagnoli, *Il diritto sindacale* (1992 3rd edn)

p 161; but the root of the obligation here is the legislation, even if the agreement has extended the obligations above the floor prescribed.

61. A Lyon-Caen and G. Lyon-Caen, *Droit Social International et Européen* (1991 7th edn) p 305. In Italy the majority view attaches peace or 'armistice' clauses only to a union party to the agreement at a given level: F. Carinci, R. De Luca Tamajo, P. Tosi, T. Treu, *Il diritto sindacale* (2nd edn 1987) 285-94; G. Ghezzi and U. Romagnoli, *op.cit.* above n 60, pp 157-61 (there are further procedural problems arising from, *inter alia*, unions' legal capacity: *ibid*: 70-5, 275-84).

62. Wedderburn (1991) 54 MLR 1, 17-25, and for detailed comparisons, 'Vicarious Liability and *Responsabilité Civile* in Strikes' (1991) 20 ILJ 188-200 (especially the cases involving *la Société les Papeteries de Maudit* and *la Société Générale Sucrière* pp 195, 198) [above chap. 4]. In Britain, see now on the extensions of 'vicarious liability', section 6 Employment Act 1990 (sections 20, 21 TULRCA 1992); and on comparative judicial creativity, Wedderburn, '*Le législateur et le juge*' in *Transformations du Droit du Travail: Études offertes à Gerard Lyon-Caen* (Dalloz 1989) 123-58; and '*Limitation législative et judiciaire en matière d'action syndicale et droit de grève*' (1990) 37 Rev Int de Droit Comparé 1-113.

63. See O. Kahn-Freund, '*Pacta Sunt Servanda...*', *op.cit.* n 15 above (1974) 48 Tulane Law Rev 894, 904-5; Wedderburn, 'Laws about Strikes' in W. McCarthy (ed.) *Legal Interventions in Industrial Relations* (1992) 147, 184-91. For the mixture in the Swedish law on peace obligations, see Folke Schmidt, *Law and Industrial Relations in Sweden* (1977) 160-90.

64. This heresy threatened to encumber the House of Lords EC Select Committee's Report, *Protection of Posted Workers*, HL 5th Report 1992-93, *op.cit.* nn 40, 41, see paras 49-51; and the writer's note, pp 52-3.

65. See G. Lyon-Caen and J. Pelissier, *Droit du Travail op.cit.* n 60, above pp 956-962. Special problems beset '*la pluralité d'activités dans une même établissement*'; they were well known to the CAC in Britain before the repeal of Sched 11 Employment Act 1975; see P. Wood (1978) 7 ILJ 65, 72-77.

66. For example, Belgium enjoys nine levels of sources, said to operate via incorporation: at the top mandatory law and extended collective agreements ('declared to be generally binding') down through agreements concluded in the National Labour Council, joint committees' resolutions and finally to a 'verbal individual contract' and 'custom': see R. Blanpain and C. Engels, *Encyclopaedia: Belgium*, p 247.

67. *Code du Travail* Article L 135-2. Even an express renunciation by the worker of the terms is ineffective, Cass Soc 3 March 1988, *Gagnepain c. Tiraboschi*.

68. G. Lyon-Caen and J. Pelissier, *Droit du Travail*, *op.cit.* pp 963-7.

69. 'Employers and employees who are bound by collective agreement shall not have power to enter into any contract which is not consistent with that collective agreement' section 27 JRWLA 1976; but whether the employee can contract for better terms may depend on the terms of the collective agreement: Folke Schmidt, *op.cit.* n 7 above, pp 145-6. Compare the New Zealand Employment Contracts Act 1991, above n 25 and below n. 72.

70. Workers Statute 1980, Articles 3(1)(3) and 82(3); T. Sala Franco *Derecho*

del Trabajo (1990) 201, 253-69.

71. English law does not espouse a general 'agency' relationship between union and member: see *Assoc. British Ports* v *TGWU* [1989] IRLR 291, 300-1 (aff'd on other grounds [1989] 1 WLR 939 HL); *Boxfoldia Ltd* v *NGA* [1988] IRLR 383; *Ellis* v *Brighton Co-op Soc.* [1976] IRLR 419.

72. See, e.g., M. Weiss, *Law and Industrial Relations in the FRG, op.cit.* p 127 (noting, however, that *'collective* normative regulations' apply to all employees, e.g. clauses referring to activities of the Works Council); Folke Schmidt, *Law and Industrial Relations in Sweden, op.cit.* 141-4 (agreements binding on members and future members; extended to non-members in practice). German difficulties are compounded by uncertainties about the hierarchy of norms concerning individual and collective interests: see Federal Labour Court (Big Senate) *Der Betrieb* 1987, 383, GS 1/82 [1983] 6 Int. Lab. Law Reps 220 (individually contracted fringe benefits cut down by works agreement, disadvantages or advantages to workers judged collectively: weak inderogability) nd GS 3/85, 7 November 1985, [1990] 10 Int. Lab. Law Reps 425 (works agreement modifying contractual retirement age binding on a worker only if it is more favourable individually: strong inderogability).

73. Civil Code Article 2077, and Article 2113 as amended by Article 6 Law no 533, 1973 (on procedure in labour cases): G. Ghezzi and U. Romagnoli, *op.cit.* n 56 pp 161-5.

74. See a helpful short account of this difficult area in G. Giugni, *Diritto sindacale, op.cit.* pp 147-58, including the bequests of the Law of 1959, above n 10; Wedderburn, 'The Italian Workers' Statute' (1990) 19 ILJ 154 and Chap. 9 in *Employment Rights in Britain and Europe* (1991). On judicial tendencies to exclude *inderogabilità*, especially where there are successive collective agreements, see V. Leccese, *'Transazioni collettive e disposizione dei diritti del lavoratore'* (1991) 50 Giorn. DLRI 283, 295-323; G. Ghezzi and U. Romagnoli, *Il diritto sindacale* (1992, 3rd edn) 170-3.

75. See France *Code du Travail* Article L 135-1; Germany, Federal Labour Court BAG 20, 175, 29 November 1967; Portugal, M. Pinto, *Encyclopaedia 'Portugal'* (1989) 198; Britain, section 10 Employment Act 1988 (now TULRCA 1992, section 222). On Spain, see M. Rodriguez-Pinero on Constitutional Court practice: *Transformations du droit du travail: Études offertes à Gérard Lyon-Caen* (1989) 113-25; Italy, G. Giugni, *Diritto sindacale* (1991 9th edn) 57-9 (discrimination); G. Ghezzi and U. Romagnoli, *op.cit.* n 56. 43-4, 144-70; Belgium, *Encyclopaedia op.cit.* n 66, 159-60; the Netherlands, H. Bakels, *Encyclopaedia 'Netherlands'* (1990) 65-72 (also on extension); and see too, N. Aliprantis, *La Place de la convention dans la hiérarchie des normes* (1980) 127-131. On earlier developments in members-only-bargaining, see T. Treu, *Condotta antisindacale e atti discriminatori* (1974) 155-77; Wedderburn in F. Schmidt, *Discrimination in Employment* (1978) 401-58.

76. See the reports of conferences, M. Felicioli (ed.) *Est e Ovest: il sindacato nell'economia di mercato:* (1990); and (1991) *L'iniziativa pentagonale;* in the latter, U. Carabelli, *'Occupazione e protezione nell'economia di mercato',* suggests there is not one correct formula for collective bargaining, but the internationalization of markets and technological

change have opened new opportunities for joint control 'suited to the culture and traditions of each country', albeit transnational in perspective. On new forms of bargaining objectives, see too F. Guarriello, 'Accordi di gruppo e strutture di rappresentanza europee' (1992) 53 Giorn. DLRI 21-72 (especially recording demands by Italian and German unions for notification to the unions when an undertaking assumes a 'transnational character', successful in the textile sector: 59-67).

7

MULTI-NATIONAL ENTERPRISE AND NATIONAL LABOUR LAW*

Less than four years ago a Cabinet Minister could still shock by saying that international companies would soon reduce national governments, including the British Government, to 'the status of a parish council'.[1] Since then wider recognition has grown of the power of multi-national enterprises conducting business in a setting of internationalised capital. Berle and Means had foreseen competition between State and corporation,[2] but in 1970 a TUC paper rightly stated

> the international company is rapidly replacing the nation state as the basic operating and accounting unit in the international economy.[3]

In a world in which the turnover of General Motors exceeds the national budgets of all but four of Western countries; where 'exports' frequently involve only intra-group transactions of multi-national organisations (accounting by now for perhaps a third of Britain's exports); when the advantages of flexibility of investment, transfer-pricing, tax havens and co-ordinated planning accrue above all to the multi-national enterprise – that form of business has naturally become the object of intense study by economists. Already the rapid growth of internationalised (mainly American) capital has been charted in such countries as Britain[4] and Canada;[5] and the penetration of such enterprises (not exclusively American-based) into Europe and Asia is well documented.[6] Moreover, management thereby derives at the bargaining table new power of immeasurable importance. The trade unionists frequently have little idea whether they face men with a power of decision or whether that power now lies in a far-off land. Indeed:

* First published in 1972 in *Industrial Law Journal* Vol. 1.

The whole basis of the game is changed when a national union is negotiating with a firm that can adjust both its production and its profits to suit some overall international strategy.[7]

The general response of national systems of law to the internationalisation of capital is neither uniform nor developed;[8] but in the field of labour relations, apart from the pressures for the release of more information by such corporations,[9] the demands for change have been few. The evidence by British trade unions to the Donovan Royal Commission made scarcely any reference to the new framework within which national labour law operates; and trade union leaders have on occasion agreed that the real solution is to be found in internationally imposed 'fair labour standards' to prevent the world-wide enterprise picking off at leisure the weaker labour force in any one country.[10] But voices have been heard demanding new national laws to establish:

> some form of democratic control over the action of the large international enterprise. Their arbitrary decisions are likely to become the main source of disputes in industry.[11]

While the decisions of the multi-national firm are very likely to become the source of disputes, they are often not 'arbitrary' from the point of view of the enterprise. Indeed, when in 1971 Fords decided to switch the production of engines for the Pinto car from Germany and Britain (a few months before Henry Ford was welcomed by the British Prime Minister in a royal style that befitted an economic monarch), German and US trade union leaders could declare, in support of strikers at British Fords, that Fords' international power would not be permitted by them to 'crush trade unionists in Britain or anywhere else'.[12] But nothing stopped the switch of a £30 million expansion project, which, said *The Times*, was 'an entirely sensible decision for an international company to take'[13] from the company's point of view, whatever the effects upon employment prospects in parts of Britain.

A recent survey of foreign firms in Britain suggests that unions might find recognition more difficult to obtain from them and more important,

> the multinational often has more opportunity to produce elsewhere, and even if this threat is costly to implement, the possibility of expanding elsewhere is a credible threat. This can alter the bargaining position of trade unions, as well as leading to competition between countries to attract investment.[14]

Institutions are, however, developing (as yet in embryonic form) which are likely to exert pressures on national systems of labour law to permit the emergence of a 'countervailing power' to the vast resources of the multinational enterprises. The scope for international trade union action has so far been 'limited';[15] and no-one could claim that in any economic sector has the aim been reached of international bargaining for common collective contracts 'which would prevent the employers from exploiting international wage differentials'.[16] Many factors have contributed to the slow development of international trade union action – among them the ideological division between the World Federation of Trade Unions and the International Confederation of Free Trade Unions (from which the AFL-CIO is now further alienated); in Europe itself the different character of the movements, the centralised unions of Sweden and Germany (the latter with its eyes dazzled by aims of 'co-determination' which, as recent steel mergers have shown,[17] can be absorbed without difficulty by international capital), the unified yet fragmented British movement, the ideologically divided unions of France and Italy (where, however, the three groupings are now about to make common cause), so that even co-ordinated bargaining among unions within the EEC is 'still a long way off'.[18] The embryonic institutions of an organised opposition are the international trade secretariats, notably the International Federation of Chemical and General Workers' Union (ICF), the International Metalworkers' Federation (IMF), International Union of Food and Allied Workers (IUF) and the International Transport Workers' Federation (ITF), all of which are 'limbering up for a long struggle'.[19]

Sporadic skirmishes have already been fought by some of these federations, all of which, especially the ICF and IMF have busily been preparing machinery for the computerised handling of international information for their affiliated unions. The IMF has since 1966 established international councils to match various automobile multinationals (such as Fords, Chrysler, and so on), and has more recently at its twenty-second Congress in 1971, reported the operation of permanent co-ordinating groups in the electrical industry (Philips, General Electric, AEG-Siemens, and Honeywell), the latter group attempting to co-ordinate bargaining demands thereby forbidding Honeywell 'to play off the workers of the various countries against each other'.[20] In February 1971, pressure from German unions affiliated to IMF was instrumental in the winning of a recognition strike by workers in South Carolina employed by a sister company in the Korf Industries group. The ITF has long organised common action among, for example, port workers whose interests are more likely to be obviously concurrent than those of workers in apparently competing manufacturing companies. The IUF has only just begun to take effective international action (especially in connection with Nestlé's).

The most spectacular successes have so far been won by the ICF which may be explained by the fact that its interests lie in capital-intensive industries where transnational co-ordination of small groups of workers can more easily make a serious impact. The most notable case was the co-ordinated bargaining in 1969 operated effectively by ICF unions in Italy, Germany and the USA against the subsidiaries of St. Gobain, the French-owned glass firm. There St. Gobain lost the advantage of the tool, long prized by multi-nationals, of 'the adjusted profitability of subsidiaries',[21] and acceded to co-ordinated wage demands in those three countries.[22] The local union in the USA fought on the basis of the healthy *international* profits of the St. Gobain group, and the ICF secretariat co-ordinated the fight. More recently the ICF has warned Deutsche Texaco in December 1971 that action would be taken on an international level, including possibly interruption of supplies from abroad, unless it acceded to the wage demands of German Texaco workers, but with what success is as yet uncertain. Indeed, a close study of such actions, even by ICF, leaves one commentator with the feeling that, as a response to the multinational firm, it is 'rather discouraging'.[23] Certainly the crunch – a test of solid, international, co-ordinated industrial action – has not yet come.

Even so, the legal dimension in England of the kind of phenomena just described is not hard to find. Under the law as it stood before 1972, union officials who took action to support industrial demands by colleagues overseas risked liability, despite the protections of the Trade Disputes Acts 1906 and 1965. In 1966, for example, a wage dispute between Olympic Airways, the Greek airline owned by Mr Onassis, and its pilots in Greece, led the striking Greek union to ask for support from the ITF. Thereafter, three English unions affiliated to the ITF instructed members to 'black' Olympic Airways whose operations were allegedly hampered in consequence. An *ex parte* injunction was granted by Orr J. against the three trade unions and against the ITF and International Federation of Airline Pilots. The writ alleged 'intimidation, conspiracy, and actionable interference' and the injunctions were *mandatory* in form, ordering the organisations and their officials to withdraw any 'blacking' instructions.[24] The main liability incurred appeared to be the interference with commercial contracts, which no statute protected even in a trade dispute. Five days later after argument *inter partes*, the judge refused to continue the injunctions, partly because no such order should have been made against trade unions as such in the light of section 4 of the Trade Disputes Act 1906, and partly because there was insufficient proof of deliberate interference with contracts. Proceedings were then discontinued because of a settlement of the dispute in Greece. Various legal issues were left unsettled (such as whether it was *per se* unlawful to strike in Britain in support of a strike which was a criminal offence in another country, i.e. whether the British courts would ignore for this purpose the rule that they refuse to enforce the 'penal laws' of another country, a result which would have 'put in jeopardy the sympathetic strike which crosses national boundaries').[25]

Subsequent developments in British labour law made it even more risky for officials to organise international trade union action in Britain. Indeed, one wonders whether an organisation such as ITF can continue to have a headquarters in London – most other international secretariats are in Geneva – rather than move to (say) Sweden where tort liability for sympathetic action and interference with contracts is unknown.[26] Even before 1972, liability might be encountered for a conspiracy to use 'unlawful means', or for inducing breach of contract, or (*per* Lord Denning MR) for deliberately interfering with contractual relations short of inducing breach.[27] Moreover, despite what the members of the Court of Appeal said in the *Hull Trawlers* case (1970)[28] it has remained the practice of many High Court judges in the Chancery Division to grant *ex parte* injunctions of a *mandatory* character.[29]

This area of the law of tort still remains relevant even *after* the Industrial Relations Act 1971, because if the industrial action is taken otherwise than in contemplation of an 'industrial dispute' as defined in that statute,[30] none of the 'unfair industrial practices' would come into play but, by the same token, the protections provided by section 132 of the Act against the pristine liabilities of the law of tort similarly will not apply. Such a case might arise for example if the action were held to be in furtherance of a 'political' objective.[32] In that connection, we may recall that in the disputes concerning the employment of General Aviation Services by the London Airport Authority, an interlocutory injunction was obtained in 1970 against shop stewards whose complaints included one of 'creeping denationalisation' and whose actions were alleged to that extent to have 'political' not 'industrial' objectives. The intricate relationships between the multi-national firm and Government, could easily lead to a strike having a 'political' complexion which would allow a court to exclude it from the category of 'industrial dispute' and apply to it the old law of tort in which creative judges have recently enlarged liabilities for those daring to take industrial action.[33]

The impact of the Industrial Relations Act 1971 will, however, now be felt directly when action in furtherance of an 'industrial dispute' *is* established. The Act cannot be discussed here in detail; but two important sections of immediate relevance are clearly (1) section 96, establishing the unfair industrial practice of inducing a breach of contract (except for registered trade unions and their agents); and (2) section 98, making unlawful any strike or 'irregular industrial action'[34] for the purpose of preventing performance or inducing breach by an 'extraneous party',[35] of a contract made with an employer who is engaged in an industrial dispute. Both liabilities require the existence of an 'industrial dispute'; but the statute does not appear to confine the *locus* of such a dispute to the confines of British shores. Indeed, there is good precedent to indicate that British labour legislation will take account of disputes outside the jurisdiction when that suits its purposes.[36] It seems, therefore, that sympathetic industrial action in Britain as part of an internationally co-ordinated campaign against a multi-national group would run (even within the area of 'industrial disputes') grave risks of liability for preventing performance of commercial contracts (section 98); or, if the trade union in question is an unregistered 'organisation of workers', for inducing breach of contract *simpliciter* (section 96). In regard to the former liability, it must be remembered that where there are 'associated' companies within one group (as defined in section 167 (1)) each counts as an *extraneous* party for the others.[37] The units of internationalised capital in the multi-national enterprise are highly likely to be organised as separate, if associated, companies. Just as their intra-group transactions may take on the unreal economic appearance of an 'export' from or 'import' to Britain, so their transactions will be legally shrouded in the garb of 'contracts' between independent legal persons. By this mystification of reality, the law sets up its pegs upon which more easily to hang liability.

Britain is by no means alone in Western Europe in having severe – and after 1971 very severe – restrictions upon the right to take industrial action in sympathy or in solidarity with other workers, at home or overseas.[38] But it may be regarded as strange that the limitations upon strike action, embodied for example in sections 96 and 98 of the British 1971 Act, were enacted without discussion of their effects upon the new economic world of dominant multi-national enterprises, in which international trade union action is widely regarded as one of the few methods of establishing a countervailing power to that of international management. A similar failure of analysis underlies the original Treaty of Rome setting up the EEC. Title III Chapter 2 provides for the free right of establishment within the Community, and Chapter 4 seeks to establish the removal of 'all restrictions'[39] from movements of capital between member States, a provision now largely in effect. But what was to be the 'freedom' correlative to these freedoms established by Community law for international capital? The correlative right for workpeople was pronounced to be their freedom to accept work and be employed, within certain limitations, freely in each of the member States.[40] Such a freedom of movement for 'labour' is not, however, in any way the social correlative of a freedom of movement for 'capital', partly because it relates to individual movement whereas rights for 'capital' are essentially rights for collectivised, accumulated capital. The logical correlative, of a freedom of trans-national movement for 'capital' would be a legal right of trans-national, collective industrial action for 'labour'.

In other words, the international function of the trade union movement as a countervailing power to management in the multi-national enterprise demands recognition by *national* systems of labour law of a right to take collective action in support of industrial action in other countries against companies which are, in an economic sense, part of the same unit of internationalised capital. It is as true on an international as on the national plane that the legality of industrial action goes to the heart of the bargaining power. At the very least, sympathetic action in support of such action which is lawful in the country of the primary dispute must be made lawful, whether 'contracts' are incidentally broken or not, in order that this function should be fulfilled. Until some such recognition of the international realities is undertaken by each system of national law, it will remain the social function of that law to assist in the fragmentation of the international labour and trade union movement, and by so doing to inhibit the development of industrial action across national frontiers through the emergent secretariats of trade union co-operation. In the next reform of British labour law, the very existence of dominant multi-national enterprises will demand that Parliament should legalise in some form multi-national trade union activity organised from and in Britain.

NOTES

1. Tony Benn, then Minister of Technology, *The Times*, November 28, 1968.
2. *The Modern Corporation and Private Property* (1932: revised 1968 ed.), p. 313.
3. *International Companies: Report of a Conference* (TUC, 1970), p. 3.
4. See especially J.H. Dunning, 'The Role of American Investment in the British Economy' (PEP no. 507, 1969) and Chap. 6 in Kindleberger (ed.), *The International Corporation: A Symposium* (MIT, 1970); also J.H. Dunning (ed.), *The Multinational Enterprise* (1971); and Robin Murray, 'The Internationalisation of Capital and the British Economy' in *The Spokesman*, No. 11 (1970), pp. 17-38.
5. Notably the *Watkins Task Force Report. Foreign Ownership and the Structure of Canadian Industry* (1968); A.E. Safarian, *Foreign Ownership of Canadian Industry* (1966); K. Levit, *Silent Surrender: The Multinational Corporation in Canada* (1970).
6. *Growth and Spread of Multinational Companies*, Economist Intelligence Unit (1969); J.J. Servan Schreiber, *The American Challenge* (1968); S. Hymer and R. Rowthorn, 'Multinational Corporations: The Non-American Challenge' Chap. 3 in Kindleberger (ed.), *op.cit.*; Rolfe and Damm (eds.). *The Multinational Corporation in the World Economy* (1970); Brooke and Remmers, *The Strategy of Multi-national Enterprise* (1970); S. Holland, Parts 3-5 in *Sovereignty and Multinational Companies* (Fabian Tract 409, 1971).
7. Hugh Stevenson, *The Times*, April 9, 1970, reviewing *The Multinational Corporation in the World Economy* (papers of the Atlantic Council of the United States conference 1969, Pall Mall Press, 1970). For a useful analysis, produced after this article was written, see J. Gennard, *Multinational Corporations and British Labour* (1972).
8. See D.F. Vagts, 'The Multinational Enterprise: A New Challenge for Transnational Law,' (1970) 83 Harv. LR 739.
9. *Cf.* H. Scanlon, in *Trade Union Register 1970*, p. 45. See further, K.W. Wedderburn, 'The Multinational Enterprise and Industrial Relations', in *Nationalism and Multi-National Enterprise* (papers of conference at McGill University 1971, ed. H.R. Hahlo). More recently, Herr Vetter of the West German Trade Union Confederation has demanded constant disclosure of multinational companies' future plans to trade unions, *The Times*, October 25, 1971.
10. For example, Leonard Woodcock of the United Automobile Workers of America has frequently made such demands.
11. W. Paynter, *Bulletin of the Industrial Law Society* (1969) No. 5, Supplement, Report of Conference, p. 32.
12. See L. Woodcock and O. Brenner, Transport and General Workers' *Record*, April 1971, p. 16.
13. *The Times*, 24 February 1971.

14. J. Gennard and M. Steuer, 'Industrial Relations of Foreign Owned Subsidiaries in the UK (1971) 9 BJIR, 143, 158.
15. The conclusion of the TUC's special study, *Economic Review 1970*, p. 38.
16. Ernest Mandel, 'International Capitalism and Supra Nationality', *Socialist Register 1967*, p. 39.
17. The merger of Hoesche of Germany and Hoogovens of Holland in November 1971 created an international giant with 'workers' participation' on the Supervisory Board. Similarly, the proposed EEC Regulation for a Statute for European Companies (Brussels, June 24, 1970) incorporates a variety of possibilities in Title V, Arts. 137-145, for employees' representation on supervisory boards. But in the giant multi-national, such representatives would inevitably be remote from their constituencies and would exercise relatively little countervailing power to that of the managers.
18. L. Olslager, 'Trade Unions in the EEC: A long way from a Common Front', *Financial Times*, 27 July 1971. The very different character of the 'labor unions' of the USA from the working-class movements of Europe is another factor impeding joint action. On the effect of this difference on US labour law, see D. Bok (1971) 34 Harv. LR 1394, 1401.
19. 'The Unions: the Multinational Opposition Responds', *Multinational Business* (Economist Intelligence Unit, 1971, Vol. 1, no. 1), p. 21.
20. *The Times*, 25 October 1971. On problems of North America, see J.H.G. Crispo, *The Role of International Unionism in Canada* (1967).
21. G. Merritt, *Financial Times*, 14 October 1971.
22. See L. Turner, *Politics and the Multinational Company* (Fabian Research Series 279; 1970), Part 3, for an excellent account of this and other international trade union actions. The French St. Gobain company escaped the ICF campaign largely because of the ideological estrangement of the French CGT from the ICF.
23. L. Turner, *op.cit.*, p. 18. For his proposals for new laws controlling British emanations of the multi-nationals, see pp. 30-31 [and see p. 309ff below, and above Chap. 6].
24. *Olympic Airways* v *International Transport Workers Federation*, *Financial Times*, 25 August 1966. For later proceedings, see *Financial Times*, 3 September 1966.
25. 'Justinian', commenting in *Financial Times*, 3 September 1966. See too, *Slade and Stewart Ltd* v *Haynes* (1969) 5 DLR (3d) 736 (Sup. Ct. Brit. Col.); [1970] ASCL 306 (solidarity with American farmworkers to enforce grape boycott no justification for inducing breach of contract).
26. See Folke Schmidt, *The Law of Labour Relations in Sweden* (1962), pp. 193-195, 201-203.
27. *Torquay Hotel Ltd* v *Cousins* [1969] 2 Ch. 106. For details of the law of tort in this area, see Clerk and Lindsell, *Torts* (13th ed.) Chap. 11; Winfield and Jolowicz, *Tort*, Chap. 21. See too, *Acrow (Automation) Ltd* v *Rex Chainbelt Inc.* [1971] 3 All E.R. 1175.
28. *Boston Deep Sea Fisheries Ltd* v *Transport and General Workers Union*, *The Times*, 13 March 1970, *per* Russell and Sachs LJJ; described in Wedderburn, *The Worker and the Law* (2nd ed. 1971) pp. 379-384 on the 'Labour Injunction'.

245

29. As in *Astons Transport Ltd* v *Cowdrill*, 15 October 1971, Foster J. (unreported: order to shop stewards to withdraw instructions or recommendations to black plaintiff's vehicles). But Brightman J. refused to do so in a similar case: *Hull and Humber Cargo Handling Ltd* v *TGWU, The Times*, 16 December 1971.
30. See s. 167 (1).
31. With the possible exception of action in breach of obligations arising from a binding collective agreement; ss. 36 (1) and (2) of the Industrial Relations Act 1971.
32. See *e.g. Associated Newspapers Group Ltd* v *Flynn* (1971) 10 KIR 17 (injunction to prevent the tort of inducing breach of employment contracts in threatened strike against the Industrial Relations Bill).
33. See *The Worker and the Law* (2nd ed. 1971), pp. 374-379 on the innovations connected with unlawful interference with trade and interference with contracts. [See now the wide modern liabilities: Clerk and Lindsell, *Torts* (17th ed. 1995 forthcoming) Chap. 21.]
34. Defined respectively in ss. 167 (1) and 33 (4).
35. Preventing performance by the *employer* alone seems to import no liability under s. 98 (1) (*b*), though it might fall within s. 96. The National Industrial Relations Court will be able to issue mandatory interim orders (s. 101 (3); Sched. 3, para. 22, Industrial Relations Act 1971) but not *ex parte* since the defendant must be given an opportunity to make representations (Sched. 3, para. 22 (3) *ibid.*). [The Industrial Relations Act 1971 was repealed by TULRA 1974; but compare the liability for secondary action and the new definition of 'trade dispute' today: TULRCA 1992, ss. 219-244.]
36. See e.g., s. 7 (3) of the Redundancy Payments Act 1965 (no account taken of short-time or lay-off attributable to a strike or a lock-out 'whether it is in Great Britain or elsewhere'). [On turning action lawful abroad into a wrong in England: see *Dimskal Shipping SA* v *ITF* [1992] 2 A.C. 152 HL; below p. 358.]
37. s. 98 (3) (*a*); unless ones gives 'material support' to the other in furtherance of *that* dispute: s. 98 (2) (*b*). But such support is not given if the 'extraneous' company merely increases supplies in accordance with obligations incurred under a contract made before the industrial dispute began: s. 98 (3) (*d*). When a dispute 'begins' may be a nice question. [See *Dimbleby* v *NUJ* [1984] ICR 386 HL (contracts with subsidiary company).]
38. See on Germany, T. Ramm in *Labour Relations and the Law* (ed. Kahn-Freund (1964) p. 207). See too *Industrial Conflict: a Comparative Legal Survey* (eds. Aaron and Wedderburn: 1972).
39. Art. 67 (2).
40. Arts. 48-51.

8

EUROPEAN COMMUNITY LAW AND WORKERS' RIGHTS AFTER 1992: FACT OR FAKE?*

Some thirty years ago Frances Moran, in whose honour I am privileged to offer this paper, took part in a series of broadcast talks about 'The Migration of the Common Law'.[1] She opened her scholarly contribution by reminding her audience that Ireland was 'the first adventure of the common law'. Today, she might have perceived our two systems of law, in Ireland and in Britain, engaged upon a different, this time a joint, adventure through unmapped juridical territory in the European Community. By the end of 1992, the twelve Member States are pledged to create a single market and consider further union. Gradually Directives and Regulations adopted by the Council of Ministers, on the proposal of the Commission and possibly on a widening basis of majority voting, will make parallel or common ever greater areas of our social laws. What will be the effects of these developments on the rights of ordinary men and women at work, rights against dismissal or on equal treatment or to a fair remuneration? In asking how far changes in labour laws may affect the level of rights for people at work – that is, not rights in the law books, but rights that can be actually enforced – I am aware (especially here in the presence of the Irish Centre for European Law)[2] that I leave aside the other half of the coin: the right to work, or at least the welfare rights of those not in work, whose numbers may well grow in the early stages of the internal market.

But the laws about employment and labour relations are in another sense at the heart of the social process. They concern relationships which reflect in each of these comparable countries, not merely limits on managerial prerogative or protections for employees as the weaker

*The sixth Frances Moran memorial lecture, Trinity College, Dublin, 6 December 1990; published in 1991 *Dublin University Law Journal*, Vol. 13.

parties to the work-wage bargain; they also touch the nerves of deeply-rooted social structures, above all the collective organisations of workers which in democratic industrial societies derive both their *raison d'être* and their legitimacy from the individual employee's subordinate status which is cloaked by the text of the contract of employment itself.[3] Although the law provides protections, the protection which comes from freedom to negotiate collectively is everywhere recognised as essential for workers in these jurisdictions.

LABOUR LAWS IN THE COMMUNITY

Yet the forms differ extravagantly. Despite their adherence to shared values and their significantly similar social systems, what is remarkable about these twelve countries is the sharp diversity of their labour laws. The variety of the labour laws for the most part mirrors patterns of industrialisation and, above all, the history of each of the labour movements. Collective bargaining became a common European heritage but it is expressed in very different forms, dangerous to translate: the *convention collective* is crucially different from the collective agreement; neither is the same as the *Tarifvertrag* or the *contratto collettivo*. Collective agreements which are not normally contractually binding baffle our French and German colleagues, just as the French criteria of a 'representative trade union' (qualifying a union to conclude binding agreements) baffle us; and we often forget, when we speak of 'works councils', the profound differences between the German Works Council and the French *comité d'entreprise* (or more important still, the *comité de groupe de sociétés*) or, again, the unique character of the *rappresentanza aziendale sindacale* (the workers' guaranteed 'presence' in unionised form at plant level since the Workers' Statute of 1970 in Italy).[4] Instead of the positive rights found in most Continental systems, Britain shares with Ireland the 'immunities' of collective labour law (which, I see from the latest statute, are ineradicable), not for any legal reason but by reason of our trade union movements in the fifty years before 1906.[5]

The contrasts are not all one way – common law systems against 'Continental' systems. Far from it. German labour law like French law permits a Minister power to 'extend' collective agreement to bind new employers who were not parties to it, but neither Italian nor Swedish labour law can accept such a practice.[6] German and Swedish law are at one in vesting the right to strike in the union alone, while France and Italy insist that this right inheres in the individual worker. The French limit their right to strike in ways not found elsewhere: for example, the doctrine of *'autosatisfaction'*, rendering illegal industrial action which itself achieves the strikers' demand (so that stopping work on a Saturday in furtherance of a demand for an end to Saturday work is unlawful when a strike would have been lawful on Friday).[7] Yet it is envisaged in the Community that some of the social advances will be put into effect by collective bargaining or through the 'social dialogue', involving (to use the words of the draft Directive on rights of workers to be consulted through a 'European Works Council' in enterprises of European-scale, adopted by the Commission just two days before this paper was given) 'representatives of workers elected or appointed as provided for in the legislation or practice of each Member State'. It remains to be seen whether these vastly different legal systems or usages about trade union representation of workers can provide institutions at Community level that will work. Sometimes even meaningful comparative conversation between these very different systems is possible only with difficulty. Scratch any major labour law institution and you find the contours of its particular trade union history.

What chance is there then of harmonisation or approximation (to use the phrase which has been the Commission's guiding star for many years) 'in an upward direction'? A common internal market in the Community manifestly implies free movement of individual workers. But what of collective labour? Free movement of *individual* workers may increase, but collective labour organisations, trade unions, cross frontiers only with difficulty. That is why collective bargaining at transnational level is still little less than a dream. Not so collective capital: personified by law with the privilege of limited liability it leaps across national boundaries at the press of a computer key. This is the 'employer', at least in the private sector; normally a company, often part of a corporate group, increasingly a transnational group. This reopens Labour Law questions, as it were, from the back door. If there is to be a 'level playing field' of competition in a single market, how far must the conditions for these corporate enterprises be equivalent in all twelve countries, in the way they treat employees or in the manner in which employees may participate in decision making within them.

This is one reason why from an early date the Commission had no choice but to be concerned with harmonisation of employees' rights within Company Law, in areas as it were contiguous to Labour Law. These projects first appeared in the 1960s, then developed in the era that gave rise to the 'Social Action' programmes. It so happened that in

Germany, and in different form in the Netherlands, worker representation (or codetermination) was found within the framework of company law.[8] The Commission has since then advanced proposals, on an increasingly flexible basis and in pursuit of what it called in 1975 a 'democratic imperative',[9] for employee representation within the institutions of the company – in the proposed Fifth Directive on harmonisation of the company laws and in the proposed Directive on the European Company (*Societas Europaea*).[10] On the Labour Law side, there have been proposals for rights to consultation (as in the now defunct 'Vredeling' proposals) and recently in the legislation for 'balanced participation' in the Framework Directive of 1989 on safety at work.[11] The draft 'Vredeling Directive'[12] has been overtaken under the Action Programme on the Community Social Charter where the Commission has now proposed workers' rights to information and consultation in a European Works' Council in undertakings with at least 1000 employees which have establishments of 100 [later 150] workers or more in more than one Member State.[13] All of these proposals have so far been blocked by the opposition of the United Kingdom Government in the 1980s. Naturally many employers not accustomed to workers' participation within the company also felt menaced by proposals to put a few employees into the board room. The Institute of Directors in 1981, which had bitterly resisted the proposals of the 'Bullock Committee' in 1977 in Britain for workers' representatives on the boards of large companies (as did some unions), resisted too the Commission's proposed Fifth Directive which, they declared, was no better than a 'Trojan Bullock'.[14]

Plans for employee participation are still part of the Commission's programme, but are now concentrated on the 'European Company' (*Societas Europaea*) and the proposal for the European Works Council. The question remains, therefore, how far the rights of employees to participate in decision-making or (more meaningfully) to enjoy effective rights of consultation before strategic decisions are taken or implemented, might be effectively undertaken, whether as rights within the walls of the corporate institutions, or as rights to either consultation or negotiation in bargaining on a more conflictual model. The two are sometimes counterposed more sharply than is necessary; for the reality of collective bargaining is not perpetual strife; any trade union official knows that the 'joint administration' of a collective agreement is often more important than its negotiation.[15] After all, 'industrial democracy' or 'codetermination' in Sweden has been pursued not primarily by workers' representation on company boards (though that plays a supportive role) but by way of legislative support for the expansion of collective bargaining.[16] This is why the Commission has been able to build in a 'collective bargaining' model as one option available for workers' participation, for example in the 1989 version of the *Societas Europaea*.

THE BASES OF COMMUNITY LABOUR LAW

But what is the basis of Community intervention in labour law? Professor Mancini, a distinguished labour lawyer, then an Advocate General and now a judge at the Court of Justice in Luxembourg, delivered a provocative lecture on 'Labour Law and Community Law' here in Dublin in 1985.[17] The Treaty of Rome, he said, was concerned primarily with the creation of a 'European market based on competition'; employed labour is 'inextricably involved'; for the single competitive market is inconceivable without free movement of labour. The abolition of restrictions on free movement may have 'beneficial social effects', for example, on discrimination or low pay: if so, all the better – but 'it is *nothing more* than that'. He insisted: 'Community law is only marginally labour law'; the fundamental criteria are those of competition. On the other hand, 'a market intended to enjoy genuine freedom of competition will not function if, in the regions to which it extends, employment is subject to excessively disparate rules.' In other words, extensive harmonisation of Labour Law is a condition of level competition.

There is a good reason today to reexamine this thesis. For we are now on the brink of the single internal market of 1992, and of what is termed 'the social dimension' of that market, three years on from the Single European Act and only a few days away from the Intergovernmental Conferences with the task of revising the Treaty itself. We are also in something of a crisis. Barely one year ago, the 'Community Charter of Fundamental Social Rights' for workers was adopted by eleven Member States as a solemn declaration, a code which overlaps, but is not in every respect as strong as, the half-forgotten Council of Europe's Social Charter of 1961. Then the Commission set out its 'Action Programme' to implement parts of that Charter into Community Law.[18] In Britain, the Charter received widespread attention as part of the 'social dimension' of 1992, not least because of its affirmation that workers were entitled to high standards in their employment conditions, including a decent minimum wage. In 1988, the President of the Commission, Jacques Delors, in a widely publicised speech, described this forthcoming programme as 'the establishment of a platform of guaranteed social rights', establishing 'every worker's right to be covered by a collective agreement', with rights for temporary part-time and other (mistakenly so-called) 'atypical' workers, as part of the programme to resist 'the dismantling of the labour market', plus the 'participation of workers or their representatives' in European Companies and the 'right to a life-long education in a changing society'.[19] It would not be going too far to say that this and similar speeches finally cemented Britain, or at least its labour movement, into a Community commitment.

The crisis, though, arises from two divergent tendencies in recent events. On one side, the Commission has proposed that 'qualified majority voting' be the basis of adoption of many important social Directives (e.g. the central Directive on part-time workers). It will follow this policy by proposing to the Intergovernmental Conference that this be 'extended to cover certain social provisions ... in a new Chapter of the Treaty' on the social dimension.[20] On the other hand, the Commission's first major proposal to implement its Social Charter 'Action Programme', on rights for part-time and temporary workers, fell at the first hurdle. Submitted to the Council of Ministers late in November 1990, it was rejected and referred back to the Commission, not by reason of a British veto – that would hardly be news in a Community context – but because the Ministers of at least four other Member States also rejected it, both (it seems) because of the contents of the proposal and because of the Treaty base selected by the Commission for its adoption by majority vote (article 100A). The Italian presiding Minister is reported to have remarked tartly that some States must have been unaware of the legal consequences of the Social Charter they signed in 1989. The British Minister gleefully commented that there was now a 'realisation that the social action programme is very difficult territory'.[21] The Action Programme could hardly have had a more unfortunate baptism.

The determination of the Commission to carry through the Action Programme is, of course, not in doubt. But this early rebuff suggested tht it was necessary to be vigilant, and to ask how far the social advantages guaranteed in the declarations of the Social Charter are still on the cards or on the agenda, and just which parts of the Programme are crucial to the social dimension. Economic forecasts have, after all, predicted (and this before the volcanic changes in the East) that the internal market in its first years will see a loss of more than half a million jobs in Western Europe, but that with the right policies far greater job gains could be expected in the longer term.[22] The Commission, moreover, has been firmly opposed to 'social dumping'.[23] This is a difficult term, too little analysed; it was admitted to be a 'vague' concept in the words of the Commission's own interdepartmental working party of 1988.[24] There is a danger in defining it too loosely, for example as investment by companies in regions where 'wages and conditions are the cheapest and thereby force the workers in other countries with higher standards to accept lower standards and consequently downgrade employment conditions'.[25] The trouble with a simplistic definition of this sort is that it appears to include within 'social dumping' all investment in low wage cost areas when that is regarded by a company as more efficient; that is to say, it includes the very process which many employers would think of as part of competition itself in a single market.

The working party report of 1988, however, took the further step of linking 'social dumping' to the maintenance of 'fair labour standards', especially those of the ILO – as the Commission itself has occasionally done[26] – concluding that the danger to less developed Member States arises only in certain sectors of economic activity. Even limited in this way, however, the concept of 'social dumping' obviously draws inspiration from norms outside those of pure and unrestricted competition. In fact, 'social dumping' is not a value-free term – nor should it be. Writers have recently suggested that there is 'social dumping' when Fords, as was alleged recently, invests in Portugal instead of Ireland because of the permissive rules there about women's night work, or when General Motors threatens to invest in Belgium unless German unions (and government) agreed to more extensive continuous shift work.[27] The answer of employers has often been that too rapid or rigorous an approximation of employment conditions in the internal market, with fixed exchange rates but very different levels of productivity and efficiency, can only work to the disadvantage of the less developed societies in it and constitutes 'a kind of social dumping in reverse'.[28]

Such conceptual problems serve to heighten the importance of the concrete priorities chosen by the Commission. To judge these one must have in mind two further features of Community law making. First, the 'Treaty Base' problem. Proposals by the Commission for adoption by the Council must have a base in the Treaty; and since the Single European Act 1987, many have been framed for the Council of Ministers as suitable for the qualified majority procedure. The draft Directive on worker participation in the European Company, many

Directives on safety at work, and the strongest of three 1990 drafts on employment rights for 'atypical' workers, are examples of proposals made under articles of the Treaty which allow for adoption by majority. The British government has challenged the propriety of a majority vote on such matters where they 'relate to rights and interests of employed persons', in the Single Act amendments [though it later had to accept equal rights for part-time workers on dismissal, based on the logic of the law banning discrimination against women workers].[29] Much may turn on how the Court of Justice eventually interprets that phrase.[30]

Secondly, the Commission has developed the principle of 'subsidiarity' – 'whereby the Community acts when the set objectives can be reached more effectively at its level than at that of the Member States'.[31] This goes further than limitations on the powers of the Commission in the Treaty, or even in the articles of the Charter which oblige the Commission to take account of 'national legislation and practice'.[32] In its latest formulations of 'subsidiarity' the Commission has put a new brake upon itself, self-regulation which fits the direction of its current preference for progress through the social dialogue between the 'social parties', rather than by normative Directives. Both of these, genuflection to 'subsidiarity' and the constitutional need for each proposal to have a legitimate base in the Treaty, have contributed to the Commission's decision not to initiate Community legislation on many of the matters within the Social Charter's ambit, including the principle that 'all employment shall be fairly remunerated' and all workers must have 'an equitable wage', sufficient for a 'decent standard of living'.[33]

THE 1990 PROPOSALS

On the contrary, in the Action Programme we find: 'wage-setting is a matter for the Member States and the two sides of industry alone'. The Commission may express its views, but it is not its task to fix a decent reference wage. Moreover, even in the areas in which it aims to take legislative action, the Commission is notably more cautious in 1990 than was the Programme in 1989. To implement the Programme, it has at the time of this paper proposed three Directives on part-time and temporary employment,[34] one on working time,[35] one on pregnant women and new mothers at work,[36] one on workers' rights to information and consultation through European Works Councils[37] with one more to follow shortly on the written proof of terms of the employment contract.[38]

Of the three drafts relating to part-time workers, one is based on article 100 of the Treaty (requiring unanimity) aiming to provide for them equality in such matters as vocational training and non-contributory social security benefits *pro rata* with full-time workers. Another, based on article 118A (which allows for majority voting) requires particular protection of temporary workers in regard to health and safety at work. It is the fate of the third draft Directive, however, (proposed under article 100A, which permits adoption by a majority) which is of greatest importance to the present theme. In its memorandum on the drafts on part-time and fixed term temporary workers, the Commission noted the value to employers of these flexible forms of employment but it noted too, as it had in the Action Programme, the dangers of 'distortions of competition' as between different States. This is the factor which led it in the third of these Directives to propose a compulsory equality *pro rata* between part-time and full-time workers on certain terms of employment: occupational social security schemes, holidays, dismissal and seniority allowances – but *not* pay.

The systems of law of some Member States do protect part-time workers even in respect of pay. For example, we find that the primary rule in France in the Code du Travail is that they must enjoy *pro rata* the benefits of collectively agreed conditions and remuneration 'proportional to full time employees'.[39] In Italy, the Law of 1984 equalises their position in social security, encourages collective bargaining about their conditions, numbers, jobs and overtime, in the knowledge that general principles and, indeed, the Constitution itself secures them equivalent basic rates of pay (especially Article 36 which states that the wage must be both proportionate to the work and sufficient for a decent family life).[40] Also, in Italy as in France the part-time worker has priority in the filling of full time posts if and when they are available. In Germany, it was the courts which first developed a principle that there must broadly be equal treatment for full time and part time workers, an approach confirmed by the legislature in 1985.[41]

The Commission might have been expected to move some way towards a *pro rata* protection of part-time workers even in respect of remuneration. But it did not feel able to do so because of its new analysis of the ways in which part-time work can 'distort competition' (which, it must be remembered, was the Treaty base on which it offered the draft, though British Ministers had throughout objected that this was inappropriate for majority voting since they saw the proposal as relating to the rights and interests of employees). As we have seen, for once other Ministers too raised objections to even this constricted proposal and its Treaty base. Despite its rejection, however, the draft has lessons to teach. In substance, it would require Member States to provide for temporary and part time workers defined, as in the new Irish legislation, as those working 8 hours a week or more (significantly lower than the British 16 or the old Irish 18 hour threshold), *pro rata* protection to full-time workers on such matters as occupational social security schemes, annual holidays, dismissal and seniority allowances. It would also limit short fixed term contracts to a maximum of 36 months; and, with other drafts, control employment agencies. The application of a threshold is significant; all such limits to basic employment rights have been cogently criticised (a threshold marks their secondary status, 'downgrading the wages and hours of part-time workers as employers seek to qualify themselves for what can only be regarded as artificial savings on taxation and employment protection obligations').[42] The limitation of 8 hours opens the proposals on a conservative note.

The reason why the proposals omit a central feature of the 1983 proposal on part-time voluntary work, namely the requirement that part-time workers must enjoy rates of pay within ranges proportional to those of full-timers, is justified by an analysis of pay and competition. Employers, of course, had fiercely resisted such a move in 1983; in the CBI's words, such differences reflect 'the different value of part-time and full-time work. Any move compulsorily to equalise wages between part-time and full-time employees is a form of reverse discrimination and ... probably contrary to the proper operation of the common market'.[43] In perhaps one of its most important statements to accompany a proposed Directive on the social dimension, the Commission appears to have conceded this central point in 1990 as a matter of economic analysis. Wage determination, it asserts, is a matter for management and labour at Member State level (that is, on the basis of subsidiarity). But more than that, variations in wages and working conditions 'broadly speaking ... do not hamper the operation of healthy competition in the Community'. Differences in productivity 'attenuate these differences in product unit costs to a considerable degree' in the different countries.[44] The Commission made a similar point in its 1990 *Employment in Europe* report:

> differences in wages and labour costs across the Community largely reflect differences in labour productivity. Labour costs per unit of

output do not vary much from one part of the Community to another ... A policy focused primarily on low rates of pay will therefore not necessarily secure a shift in market shares towards the weaker countries in the Community.[45]

It is noteworthy that, *per contra*, where wage rates are in issue such an analysis also makes the reality of 'social dumping' questionable.

On the other hand, the Commission argues there are cost differences which are 'not offset by factors such as productivity'; these do not help to improve social or economic cohesion; they amount to 'veritable distortions of competition'. States which produce lower labour costs by such means, not related to productivity or other allowable factors, have 'a comparative advantage which cannot be considered permanent and runs counter to common interests'.[46] This is especially apparent in frontier areas. Such indirect cost differences (stemming from legislation or collective agreements) are 'nothing to do with productivity' and are 'not justified by the workers' performance per time unit'; they are impermissible; they arise especially from social protection, annual holidays, seniority and allowances on dismissal. The proposed Directive would therefore require them to be brought into line. Thus, the Commission no longer founds upon a general proposition that undistorted competition requires part-time workers to be treated proportionally to full time workers, but on the more limited argument that this requirement attaches only to certain 'indirect costs', but not to pay. By this point, the requirements of 'subsidiarity' are found to coincide with the dictates of this economic analysis: there must be no Community control of the rates of pay of part-time workers in their local markets because these do not distort competition.

In face of this new analysis, various questions come to mind. First, whether economists generally, or only certain schools, will support it? Second, whether it will be accepted that the ratio of pay for part-time and of full-time workers is always determined in a precisely parallel manner in the different labour markets of various Member States (one might have expected, for example, that the relationship to productivity might not always be the same, as the analysis implies). And is the point one of theory or of evidence? One must add that the Commission more than once states that it will monitor the position in the future; the purpose of acquiring such new evidence would presumably be to allow an empirical challenge to the conclusions. When one contrasts the rich diet of principles in the Social Charter of 1989 with the nourishing but thinner offerings of the Action Programme and now with the bare gruel of the draft Directives on atypical workers, the refusal of the Ministers to stomach even the last may be doubly significant. We may contrast the Commission's active and successful intervention in other areas. The Community legislation on accidents at work, for example, offers a different perspective. The many existing Community instruments are now put in the shade by the Framework Directive of 1989 and a series of Directives flowing from it, including a serious attempt to reduce accident rates on mobile worksites.[47] This is an area in which – happily – the ideology of the British government of the 1980s has permitted its full collaboration. More, it is producing rights for workers at the workplace which at present they do not have, including the right to stop work in face of a serious danger.[48] The rationale of high safety standards cannot be explained solely by the principles of the competitive market; and in terms of welfare, there is no more important right for a worker than the right to survive the working day alive and unscathed.

WELFARE, COMPETITION AND THE TREATY

In more general terms, as the Action Programme puts it:

> The Commission has ... limited its proposals for directives or regulations to those areas where Community legislation seems necessary to achieve the social dimension of the internal market and more generally to contribute to the economic and social cohesion of the Community.[49]

On 'economic and social cohesion' five new articles were added to the Treaty in 1987 (though their emphasis is the rectifying of regional imbalance) but there is no specific article on 'the social dimension'. There is, if not a contradiction, at least a tension underlying the concept of the 'social dimension', a problem which attached, too, to the earlier notion in the 1970s of a 'social action programme'. We may approach it by asking a different question: Is the social dimension something which will result from the operation of the internal market with free and level competition? Or is it an extra ingredient which must be added, as it were a flavouring *ab extra*, to make the market work in a socially acceptable manner? Does social advance result from the hidden hand alone, or virtually alone? Or is it an objective to be pursued by major interventions *ab extra* in order to achieve 'a Europe which links democracy, social justice and economic success?'[50]

One does not answer those questions by ambiguous propositions such as: 'The economic, industrial and social aspects of the internal market form a whole'.[51] Nor even: 'The European Councils of Hanover, Rhodes and Madrid considered that, in the context of the establishment of the single European market, the same importance should be attached to the social aspects and to the economic aspects and that they should therefore be developed in a balanced manner'.[52] What percentage of each makes up the 'whole'? If economic times grow hard, whose bottom line is to determine the balance? In the Commission's 1992 proposals on part-time and temporary workers the division is drawn between unequal wages which are part of 'healthy competition' and other indirect costs which promote distortions. But the question remains: when the Community accepts that it must intervene, is the basis always 'competition' defined in such a narrow compass? Is it not sometimes welfare? Unless it is welfare on a significant number of occasions can the 'social dimension' be said to retain its integrity?

This is not a new problem. The Spaak Report which preceded the signing of the Rome Treaty in 1957 held that a greater 'coalescence' of social policies would eventuate but as the result of more free competitive forces; intervention would be needed to correct only 'the effect of specific distortions'.[53] 'The spontaneous tendency towards the harmonisation of the social systems and wage levels and also the pressure exercised by the trade unions in order to obtain a co-ordination of the conditions of labour will be supported by the gradual creation of the Common Market'. The Treaty took a similar view, though it also looked forward more clearly to improvements in working and living conditions, with co-operation and consultation on such matters as labour law, social security and collective bargaining.[54] On that basis, inroads into harmonising labour law were made in the 1970s. But the number of Directives in that category – what we may call the Labour Law Directives[55] – was not great: in 1975, obligations on employers to consult on proposed redundancies: 1977, protection of acquired rights of workers and rights to consultation on the transfer of the undertaking; 1980, rights in the insolvency of the employer, in addition to the health and safety measures.[56] Further steps, such as the 'Vredeling' proposals of 1982-3, were blocked, largely by the British Government.

I add immediately that I have not omitted from this list, out of some fit of sexist amnesia, the great Directives, to which many would indeed give pride of place – on equal pay for men and women, on equal treatment, on sex equality in social security and occupational pensions. On the contrary, they are omitted here precisely because they are so important. Their basis is different from, more secure than, the Labour Law Directives. We return to them later.

Throughout the Action Programme, as in earlier proposals, reliance has been placed upon two different justifications: first, the need to secure undistorted competition; and, secondly, the need to provide for the welfare of workers in the context of the internal market, frequently of the working environment. So, the Commission argued in the Action Programme that the 'anarchical' spread of atypical work relationships could lead to 'distortions of competition' and to social dumping (though when it came to make its legislative proposals on atypical workers, as we saw, it has been more cautious). Similarly, too great a diversity of working hours, the Action Programme declared, could lead to 'an adverse effect on the well-being and health of workers'; but the organisation and flexibility of working hours was crucial, too, for competitiveness. So too, dangers to health and hygiene at work could affect workers' well-being and also 'the business environment and the labour markets'.[57] This dualism, an almost Manichaean counterpoint of competition and welfare, was also the subject of Professor Mancini's analysis in his Dublin lecture in 1985. He could find little justification based upon competition for the 1980 Directive, with its rights for employees to recover sums in their employer's insolvency. By contrast, the Directive of 1975 which demanded consultation of workers' representatives when redundancies were proposed rested upon a model not of welfare but, he emphasised, of competition.[58] Unemployment of workers is undesirable, he agreed; but that was not the basis of the 1975 Directive on redundancy:

> like it or not, upstream from enlightenment and welfare there is no getting away from the conditions of competition. If a country can authorise redundancies on less stringent conditions than other countries its industry will be given *an incalculable advantage*. And it is against the advantage that war is being declared.[59]

The reason for the employers' obligation to consult workers' representatives and notify public agencies about proposed redundancies is – despite appearances – not, or not primarily, to protect the employees. It is to ensure that all employers are players on a level field of competition, where each must go through the same procedural hoops. The Court of Justice has pointed out that the Directive does not require the employer to foresee dismissals by reason of redundancy, still less to abstain from them. As two Italian writers say, the Community regulation imposes 'no limits of a substantial character on the freedom of the employer to reduce the number of employees in the workforce'.[60] The Directive, in the Court's words, 'does not affect the employer's freedom to effect or refrain from effecting collective dismissals. Its sole object is to provide for consultation with the trade unions and for notification of the competent public authorities prior to such dismissals'. Even if they see redundancies coming, workers cannot force the employer into consultation by terminating their employment contracts themselves.[61] The Court twice found Italy to be in contravention of the Directive,[62] even though its Constitutional Court held that such Community law could be directly enforced and even though domestic Italian labour law put workers and their unions in a much better position than any other in the Community to challenge the need for the collective dismissals themselves.[63] The Court held that Italy was in breach of its Community obligations, whatever its substantive law and industrial practice and even though its law about dismissals was 'heavily weighted in favour of workers', as it had not enacted all the required procedures for consultation and notification. No clearer proof could be given that this Directive – despite the description of it as having been adopted to improve living standards and promote improved working conditions under article 117[64] – is based on competition, not primarily the welfare of employees (whose primary interest is manifestly not to put redundancies through a procedure but to prevent them altogether). Indeed, it was a misunderstanding about the purpose of the same 1975 Directive which in part caused the mismatch in the British legislation of that year which sought to implement it.[65]

THE LABOUR LAW DIRECTIVES

Paradoxically this conservative explanation entails radical conclusions. If the reason for compulsory consultation had been the welfare of workers, it might have been confined to redundancies or similar situations; but if it is the procedural onus put upon the employers that matters, so that a failure to observe it breaches rules of competition, the frame widens. How many other rules of employment or industrial relations might be considered crucial to a floor of undistorted competition? In order to create a level playing field, free from 'incalculable advantages' to employers in one State or another, is it really enough to have Directives only on redundancy consultation, insolvency payments and workers' rights on the transfer of the employer's undertaking? Even if differences in pay can be put aside on grounds of productivity (whatever 'pay' means in this context), as the Commission now appears to do in its 1990 proposals on part-time workers, what about working hours? (As we shall see, proposals made in 1990 on working hours are not based primarily upon distortions of competition.) And is competition undistorted when one employer is under no legal obligation to bargain with workers' unions (as in Britain) but his counterpart falls under some such obligation (as in France, at any rate once a year) while, without any general duty to bargain, law and practice together make it virtually impossible for others to refuse to bargain (as in Italy)?[66]

Put this way, the avoidance of a competitive advantage not enjoyed by others might be thought to require a total harmonisation of the twelve systems of Labour Law. That would be, of course, totally unrealistic. What is more, it is a well known principle of comparative labour law that 'harmonisation can work rather more directly on traditional areas of individual employment law than in collective labour relations'.[67] We have seen that the skein of collective labour relations is more closely interwoven into the social fabric; the sheer technical difficulties of harmonisation are greater in collective than in individual employment law (consider the similar starting points in various countries on individual dismissals with the differences in concept and practice affecting the right to strike).[68] At all levels, too, the bargaining realities in each country make a difference: 'the substantive effects of labour law norms in practice depend on the relative strengths of employers and workers in collective bargaining at local and workplace level.'[69]

But disparities can be cured, and it is odd that some remain unremedied so long even where they constitute a failure to implement a Directive. For example, the 1975 Directive demands that an employer contemplating redundancies must begin consultations with workers' representatives within stated periods. But the British Act converts this into a duty to consult with the representatives of an 'independent trade union which is recognised by him'.[70] When that formula was enacted in 1975, a residual procedure did exist whereby an employer could be obliged to 'recognise' (i.e. to bargain with) a trade union recommended by ACAS; but that procedure was repealed by the Employment Act 1980.[71] Since 1980, therefore, the British employer has been under no legal obligation to recognise a union, however well it represents his employees. The British statute, in other words, now converts the Directive's mandatory requirement to consult into an obligation to consult only while the employer chooses to 'recognise' a union. This defect has not gone unnoticed by the Commission which aims during the review of the 1975 Directive under the Action programme[72] to challenge it.[73] A visiting comparative lawyer may only speculate whether a comparable problem will arise in Ireland under the Protection of Employment Act 1977.[74]

Similar problems can arise, of course, in respect of the employer's obligation to inform and consult employees' representatives on a transfer of the undertaking.[75] The Directive of 1977, however, illustrates the degree of formalism which, via subsidiarity, can limit the value of Community institutions in a further respect; where, for example, there is a transfer of the undertaking, the contract of employment is transferred to the new owner. This transfer is a matter of 'public policy'; but the Directive 'does not aim to set up a uniform level of protection [for employees] for the whole of the Community', so the worker cannot displace the rights of the transferee employer to alter the legal position once the transfer is complete, even by dismissal 'in so far as national law allows'.[76] Thus, the real position of the Danish worker in that case could be quite different from a French or German worker under their national laws the day after the operation of the Community rule has ensured the transfer of their contracts of employment.

SEX EQUALITY

It is at this late stage of the discussion that the significance of Community law on sex equality, including equal pay, demands attention. Whereas we have seen that the precise objective of the Labour Law Directives can be debated, as between promotion of welfare or (more often) prevention of distortions of competition, the aim of these provisions, beginning with article 119 of the Treaty, appears to be clear (at least as interpreted by the Commission and the Court). It is equality of the sexes. This was perhaps the most remarkable feature of the Treaty of 1957. The founding fathers spoke in the Spaak Report of the need to assimilate 'conditions of labour, such as the relation between the wages of men and women, the systems of working hours, overtime or vacation with pay'.[77] But (apart from an ineffective mention of paid holidays) only equal pay for men and women appeared in substantial form in the Treaty,[78] and ever since it has been treated quite differently from 'overtime' or 'conditions of labour' in general. Here we can do no more than note the rapid development of this area of law: the manner in which the 1975 Directive built on article 119, confirming the right to equal pay for work of equal value;[79] how the thrust of the 1976 Directive led to rights to equal treatment in employment, training and social security; and how courts at national and Community level developed the principles of equality and, not least, have extended the meaning of 'pay'.[81] More important, from the 'equal pay' in the Treaty the Directives leapt to demand equal pay for work of equal value, and then to equal treatment and a ban on direct or indirect discrimination. As the 1976 Directive recorded, 'Community action to achieve the principle of equal treatment ... appears to be necessary'; it is 'one of the objectives of the Community'.

All this was done with a dragging of feet by some Member States but without serious challenge to the Treaty base of the legislation. The Directives on equal pay and equal treatment never had to prove their legitimacy as corrections to distortions of competition in the manner required of the central draft Directive on part-time work in 1990. It would, after all, be possible to run a common market with pay that was, at least within limits, unequal between the sexes, just as today we run it with unequal pay between adult and younger (and elderly) workers. The reason for the foundation of sex equality as a Community value was not a series of careful calculations about the distorting market effects of unequal pay or conditions. Historically, at the outset in 1957, on one side there was the influence of an aggressive ILO inquiry on equal pay of 1952; on the other, the 'fear of the French who already had equal pay for women, that without [article 119] they would be at a competitive disadvantage, compared with Member States with no such legislation'.[82] From French fears and ILO standards were created Community standards. As Davies and Freedland put it: 'The pursuit of the principle of equal pay for men and women has always been a prominent objective of the EEC. The principle lies within an area of consensus in which the member states can convince themselves that economic liberalism can be combined with social progress'.[83] (How different things might have been on discrimination generally if the founding fathers had also identified racial discrimination as worthy of equal attention, instead of leaving it to be treated as an aspect of immigration).

The consequence material to the present purpose is that Community law often takes a bifocal view of a worker. Looked at through the lens of part-time work, the analysis now offered in 1990 by the Commission denies protection on pay through proportionality with full-time workers as that is not required to avoid distortions of competition. But we know that everywhere a very high percentage of part-time workers are women. The curious result is, therefore, that if they are looked at through the other optic of sex discrimination, these same workers may receive just that protection which they cannot acquire from the 1990 proposals. Once the concept of pay is extended, as the *Bilka Kaufhaus* judgment confirmed – for example, where the employer supplements a non-contributory occupational pension scheme applicable only to full-time workers where women constitute the mass of the part-time work force – then the part-time women workers may secure a remedy where the 'global pay given to full-time employees is higher than that for part-time employees'.[84] In such cases there is a way of securing equal *pro rata* rates so long as the women workers can secure a comparison with a 'male comparator'; for the law on equal pay is of course less helpful to 'those part-timers who are in female ghettoes of unskilled and semi-skilled jobs or doing homework or "casual" jobs'.[85]

The equal treatment principles have become almost a separate citadel in the fortress of Community law, built to protect these values of social progress. Once the part-timer can establish that a pay structure favours full-timers in an indirectly discriminatory manner, it now appears she or he can challenge it in the national court, and unless the employer can prove that the difference is objectively justified 'the members of the group which is disadvantaged must be treated in the same way and have the same system applied to them as the other workers, in proportion to their hours of work'.[86] But the sex equality laws are not totally invulnerable to the pressures of competition in the market. That is the meaning of the difficulties encountered about 'justification' in indirect discrimination, or 'genuine material factors' and market forces as an excuse for unequal pay. Economists tell us that, although women's pay is affected by social status, 'in many employments there are objective reasons for the work of women being of lower net value than that of men'.[87] It is in the measurement of these justifications for indirect discrimination or 'genuine factors' permitting unequal pay that the courts now judge the legitimacy of such reasons, whether they arise from flexible increments, degrees of training or qualification, or criteria attached to quality or quantity of work or seniority of workers.[88] If the onset of the internal market in 1992 brings a dip into recession, we may expect employers to press hard to legitimise new forms of whatever can be seen as, in Lord Keith's words, 'a difference which is connected with economic factors affecting the efficient carrying on of the employer's business or other activity'.[89] But even though judges call it 'objective', the interpretation of 'justifiability' invariably requires a value judgment, a balance of the needs of the discriminator and the effects upon the victim, a process that is highly subjective.[90]

REMEDIES AND ENFORCEMENT

But rights are worth little without effective remedies and these are in the hands of the domestic jurisdictions. Even where the applicant is able to bring an action in the national courts, perhaps relying on the Treaty on equal pay or upon a remedy in domestic procedure (say, through Equality Officers in Ireland or in Britain the industrial tribunals)[91] there may still be a question whether the sanction and remedy in the national tribunals is, as it must be according to Community principles, an 'appropriate system of sanctions' affording a 'real and effective judicial protection' or whether the compensation offered has a 'real deterrent effect on the employer' and is 'adequate in relation to the damage sustained'.[92] The English Court of Appeal has recently had difficulty in deciding whether the compensation available under the Sex Discrimination Act 1975, s.65(2), to a worker retired at an discriminatorily early age was, in the light of these tests, so inadequate that it should be put aside for a higher measure more in conformity with the Directive on equal treatment.[93] Some remedies are manifestly inadequate, such as the notorious British Regulations purporting to implement the Directive on transfers of undertakings; the sanction for the employer's failure to consult union representatives is measured by compensation with a maximum of two weeks wages to each individual employee who sues after a successful union application to the tribunal – but minus any contractual or similar sums payable to him.[94] The availability of penal sanctions in the equivalent Irish Regulations is of considerable comparative interest.[95]

But even an adequate remedy needs a suitable engine to set the legal process in motion. This puts in issue the range of parties who have locus standi to do so. How far can Community law leave the enforcement of employment obligations of the employer at national level to the individual employee? In principle, this would seem inadequate especially where it is the isolated and exposed employee whom the law is attempting to protect. Under the U.K. transfer of undertakings Regulations – which, it must be observed, have also had the admirable result of leading the Law Lords into revolutionary new canons of construction to rewrite domestic statutory texts in order to achieve the purposes of the Directive[96] – and under the provisions for redundancy consultation,[97] a trade union is allowed a rare opportunity to initiate proceedings in an industrial tribunal; but once it establishes that the employer is at fault, only individual workers can enforce an award for slender compensation. So too, sex discrimination cases may reflect a hinterland of collective industrial problems behind individual cases; yet we now find enforcement only by individual complaint in the tribunals – with no legal aid. The British Equal Opportunities Commission may assist individual applicants,[98] but after the repeal of the jurisdiction of the Central Arbitration Committee in 1986, there is no body competent to review and rectify the collective consequences of discriminatory practices.[99]

There is, therefore, an active interest (now that a reform of British Labour Law is on the political cards) to know how far this tendency towards individualistic assessment has affected procedures elsewhere, as in the Irish procedure of 'group applications'.[100] It is commonly said in England that one answer lies in the American style 'class action'.[101] A different and more attractive solution might be to seek analogies with the 'action syndicale' – the right of the union to appear in court to protect the rights of its members. In France, this now includes cases of individual sex discrimination and equal pay, the union appearing as a collective entity defending the individual worker's rights, whilst retaining the other, traditional species of the action to defend l'intérêt collectif de la profession.[102] A new proposal of the Commission may also point in that direction. In the draft Directive for rights of consultation in undertakings of 'European scale' the proposal for a 'European Works Council' is matched by a requirement that Member States must provide appropriate remedies and 'adequate procedures at the suit of the European Works Council for the enforcement of obligations under this Directive'.[103]

WORKING TIME AND WELFARE

It would be wrong, however, to conclude that, outside the area of sex equality, the drive to secure better welfare for workers has disappeared from the Community programme for 1992. For example, in the proposals on working hours the Action Programme proposed regulation both for young and for adult workers. On the first it declared: 'The working hours of young workers aged under 18 will have to be limited to protect their health and safety, to take account of their development ... [and] with a view to protecting the health and safety of young people night working must also be prohibited with the exception of very few specific jobs'.[104] The precise proposals of the Commission on young workers will appear in the second wave; but they seem bound to confront British policy in a manner more than usually direct. For as recently as 1989 the British Government swept away virtually all protections for young workers on rest periods and night shifts on the argument that there was no health risk: 'There is little evidence of adverse health effects for any age group as a result of working at night or on shifts beyond the disruption of sleep patterns and circadian rhythms'.[105] In their memorandum introducing the 1990 draft Directive on hours of work for workers generally the Commission cites many studies supporting the opposite view, isolating 'above all night work which entails adverse consequences for the health of the workers concerned'.[106]

The draft Directive of 1990 on the organisation of working hours, applicable to all workers, is proposed under Art. 118A, relating to improvement of the working environment, the safety and health of workers, accidents at work and occupational diseases, and within the context of the 'Framework Directive' 1989, for a floor on hours for all workers. This fulfils the promise of action on working hours set out in the Social Charter and the Action Programme (though a Community commitment to shorter working hours was indirectly present even at the time of the Treaty in 1957). The substantive proposals are for minimum rest periods (essential for the improvement of workers' health), limits on night work, a ban on night overtime, limits on shift and night work, especially in hazardous or heavy work, and health assessments for night workers, together with notification of inspectors by each employer who uses night work.[107] Derogations are permitted – rather extensively – to allow for flexibility in seasonal work and under collective agreements. The latter reflects a widespread Continental pattern whereby the collectively agreed norms become the mechanism for local adjustment of statutory criteria or even relaxations of limits (a method highly developed in Italy).[108] In the case of the 48 hour week an exception is allowed by way of an *individual* agreement.

But the new floor of controls over working hours is not proposed on grounds that relate to competition. It is 'to encourage improvements in the safety and health of workers', because 'the completion of the internal market must lead to an improvement in the living and working conditions of workers' and it is 'indispensable ... in the social dimension of the internal market that minimum rules should ... establish a ceiling for daily and weekly working time'.[109] It is sometimes said that State regulation of working time is typical of the 'Continental systems' whereas *laissez-faire* on hours of work for adult male workers is the mark of the 'common law' countries.[110] But this boundary to legislative regulation occurred in Britain more by reason of historical than of logical factors,[111] and the fact that Ireland has known of general regulation on hours of work since the Conditions of Employment Act 1936, shows that the division cannot be mapped out in quite that simple manner.[112] The British system will need to change in face of such an intervention. It is perhaps ironic to find that the British TUC in 1988, the very year in which it swung its weight behind the Social Charter, deleted from its objects the century-old demand for a 'legal working week of not more than 40 hours'.[113]

WELFARE, PARTICIPATION, BARGAINING AND TRADE UNIONS

The welfare of workers makes its presence felt in the social dimension by extending their rights and protections, especially where issues of the working environment or safety and health at the workplace within article 118A of the Treaty are concerned. Moreover, the meaning of the 'working environment' is itself as yet uncertain: does it, for example, include sexual harassment? The Commission, too, has pointed out that 'health', according to the World Health Organisation, means 'a state of complete psychic, mental and social wellbeing', not merely 'an absence of disease or infirmity' – though few would be so ambitious as to expect either legislation or collective bargaining to produce that condition. But terms in the Treaty can be understood widely; the safety of pregnant women workers and new mothers at work, for example, includes, in the 1990 draft Directive under article 118A of the Treaty, their protection against dismissal.[114] There is plenty of room there for creative play in the Treaty base game.

On the other hand, some features of the 1990 proposals appear to be coloured by the general ideological movement of the past decade towards flexibility imposed on labour by expanded management prerogative. Only seven years ago, in the 1983 proposals of the Commission, part-time workers were to be afforded *pro rata* rates of pay as against full-time workers, and the draft explicitly guaranteed them their trade union rights. Moreover, there would have been rights of consultation with the union on their deployment, rather on the French or Italian pattern.[115] In 1990 there is no mention of trade union rights. Nor is any consultation with a union required, merely a requirement that the employer should 'inform in good time the workers' representative bodies' of his intention to introduce temporary or part-time workers.[116]

Similar problems are to be found in areas often quoted as marking the greatest extension of workers' rights, the Company Law Directives. The latest version of the Draft Fifth Directive on harmonisation of Company Law retains a threefold option for obligatory workers' participation (by minority representation on a company board, or representation in a separate organ, or a negotiated structure through collective bargaining with parallel rights of participation). These proposals are still totally rejected by the British Government; and the amendments circulated for further consideration in 1990 are concerned only with its traditional company law aspects, prompting some to think that the Commission might be about to surrender the battle of two decades and proceed to harmonisation without obligatory employee representation.[117]

Like the Fifth Directive, the draft for the European Company (*Societas Europaea*), normally formed by a voluntary merger of two companies from different Member States, is proposed as a Directive under article 54(3)(g) of the Treaty (with its company law aspects separated as a Regulation proposed under article 100A), permitting adoption by qualified majority vote in the Council of Ministers. At first, the employee participation opportunities of the European Company appear to be substantial. An SE would be obliged to adopt one of three models: a German-style system in which worker participation constituted between one third and one half of the members of the supervisory board (or administrative board, if a one-tier board company); or a corporate organ composed of worker representatives with defined powers of consultation; or a 'collective bargaining option' with a negotiated structure but equivalent powers of consultation before decisions are taken, or in some cases 'implemented'.[118] The Preamble sets out the aims: *inter alia*, to promote the 'economic and social objectives of the Community' and to arrange for 'employees to participate in the supervision and strategic development of the SE'.

Unhappily, the draft proposed by the Commission is not a strong form of industrial democracy. The rights of consultation in the three different models are not equivalent. Most serious of all, however, the draft Directive proposes that the Member State in which the SE chooses to place its registered office shall have the right to limit the choice of models to two, or even to one. In addition, even if the host State permits a choice, when on formation of the SE the management and the representatives of workers from the founding companies cannot agree about the model to be applied to the new company, the management 'shall choose the model applicable to the SE' (art. 3(1)). This insecure base for workers' participation is remarkable enough in the context of what the Commission once identified as the 'democratic imperative' for workers' participation; but further proposals weaken the structure further. Control over geographical changes in the registered office (and therefore over the State-permitted available options) vests, through the power to amend the articles, in the shareholders' meeting (draft Regulation art. 81(h)) which also has power to disapprove a change of model (draft Directive art. 3(5)). The 'employees' participation in supervision and in strategic decision making' by this point depends so far upon the blessing of the shareholders and the management that it can be terminated or amended more or less at their pleasure. Given that the SE will be chosen as a form of enterprise in cross-frontier mergers largely for other reasons, such as taxation benefits, it seems doubtful how far this structure could afford effective worker-participation. [Amendments made later required an agreement with employee representatives when a change of the SE's national seat would affect participation.[119]]

An understanding of such deficiencies caused many to await with anticipation the proposals of the Commission not in the Company Law, but in the Labour Law field, to fulfil the promise in the Social Charter that 'information, consultation and participation for workers must be developed along appropriate lines'. The Action Programme promised an 'instrument' to provide for rights of consultation and information for workers' representatives in undertakings of 'European scale' (defined as those with more than 1,000 employees and establishments with 100 [and later 150] workers in more than one Member State). Here the Commission proposes a 'European Works Council' agreed between management and workers' representatives, with a model as a fall-back in the absence of agreement. More, the proposal included a plan for a 'Group Works Council' where undertakings are in a corporate group under the same 'control' (a delicate relationship to define in this context), rather like the French *Comité de Groupe de Sociétés*.[120] One important feature of the European Works Council (especially in corporate groups) might be the impetus it would give to collective negotiation with independent union representatives at European level, acting too as an obstacle to what some modern managements like to call 'direct employee relations', managing 'human resources' without the mediation of any inconvenient trade union presence. But the European – and even more, the Group – Works Council would still demand a solution on the workers' side of the problems arising from the transnational confluence of streams of trade unionism of kaleidoscopic variety from the twelve countries of the Community. The gap here in imaginative thinking is equally unfortunate, one which should be remedied quickly by the European trade unions.

This mention of independent trade unions touches on a final, but crucial difficulty for workers' rights in 1992 within the social dimension. Although the Conventions of the ILO are often mentioned – the Preamble to the Social Charter itself says it draws 'inspiration' from them and from the Council of Europe's 'Social Charter' of 1961 – there is little or nothing in the Action Programme to promote the rights to organise, to bargain and to strike. These are the three basic human rights of modern democratic labour law, however they are expressed, whether in immunities or in positive rights, in constitution, legislation or case law. Not only does the Action Programme consign this entire area of collective labour law to the level of Member States, 'in accordance with their national traditions and policies' in a massive dose of subsidiarity; it also asserts that the right to freedom of association (within which the ILO locates also the right to strike), together with the right to collective bargaining, 'exists in all Member States'.[121]

Yet only a few months earlier in 1989 the ILO Committee of Experts had condemned the British Government for contravening the minimum international standards in the ILO Conventions both in respect of collective bargaining (in the 1987 law banning collective bargaining for teachers) and of the right to strike inherent in freedom of association (by the legislation of the 1980s, in its limitations on industrial action and in its controls over internal union affairs – not to speak of the Government's interventions at GCHQ).[122] Britain is not the only Member State which has failed adequately to implement ILO standards. One hears questions put about the ban on strikes by German *Beamter*, about compulsory arbitration in Greece, even about the Irish laws on licensed trade unions. But the British case is the most comprehensive condemnation for many years of a Western European country for breaches of the elementary fundamental standards of the basic ILO Conventions – on freedom of association (no. 87 of 1948) and on the right to collective bargaining (no. 98 of 1949). In the face of that, it is remarkable that the Commission omitted from its programme any action for the strengthening of collective liberties in the Labour Laws of Member States (it promises no more than a 'communication' on 'the development of collective bargaining, including collective agreements at European level with special reference to the settlement of disputes'). Whatever else it means, the principle of subsidiarity does not demand that degree of abstentionism.

It would, of course, be absurd to expect the Action Programme to achieve harmonisation of the twelve collective labour laws. But there is much that could be done to ensure that all the systems have a floor in common. Indeed, the concept of diversity built on a common floor of standards applies equally to collective as to individual employment rights. It is here that the Commission forges inadequate links with the ILO, the appointed agency of the United Nations in these matters. The representation of workers, for example, whether it be in the European Company or in a European Works Council, should be composed of representatives from organisations of workers which are independent of management, in the ILO sense. Few would disagree; yet in British law even that would require specific, new provision. Similarly, without making a fruitless attempt to standardise union structures, the Community could adopt minimum standards of autonomy and freedom from State control, inspired by ILO norms.

Such a policy for minimum Community standards would make its impact first, not upon strikes or collective bargaining, but on the individual worker, because everyone knows that rights on the shop floor are more effectively protected where there is a strong and autonomous union presence. Indeed, the effects of labour law principles 'will usually depend on the relative strengths of employers and workers in collective bargaining at local and workplace level'.[123] A commitment to minimum collective standards, therefore, feeds into the application of individual workers' rights which the Action Programme promotes. The proposals on working hours are a paradigm example. Nor would promotion of trade unionism do anything but good to such Community values as sex equality, where new mechanisms of enforcement involving the union would be an attractive development. At first it is not clear why the Commission chose to say no more about these issues in an Action Programme which is otherwise so finely balanced and confined its chapter to a solitary page of generalities about the 'social dialogue'. The explanation lies perhaps in that very page. The Commission's chosen collective instrument appears to be the 'social dialogue', which it is indeed obliged to encourage after the Single Act.[124] But for all its virtues, the 'social dialogue' is not, and cannot replace, collective bargaining. What it shares with collective bargaining is the need of free trade unions. It overlaps but is not co-terminous with the methods of collective bargaining. It is consensual not conflictual; it may or may not aim at an agreement; and it cannot in the same manner aim to resolve conflict by 'joint administration' in the workplace.

It would be quite wrong to say that the Action Programme is hostile to collective bargaining; but – and this is the litmus test – it gives no priority to it. On the other hand, it is perhaps surprising that European trade unions have not insisted on such priority; at times they have blurred the distinction. If agreements and social plans can be made consensually through 'dialogue', well and good; but in real life there are conflicts of interests which require tougher negotiation. Indeed, if the employer walks away from the bargaining table, workers are left mouthing a social monologue until their union uses such legal and industrial muscle as it can muster to induce him to return. It is in the lack of commitment to the promotion of workers' rights by collective bargaining, to the fostering of independent trade union organisation and to the taking of concrete steps for a floor of rights in the Community on freedom of association that the defects appear most clearly in the Commission's plans for workers' rights in 1992 and beyond. Those who found the Social Charter in general attractive have a special duty to offer this criticism; for it is not too late to influence its application. Action may yet be taken at Community level to adopt collective bargaining (like sex equality) as a Community value. Indeed, features of the European Works Council proposal are swallows that allow one to hope for the summer to follow. Otherwise, the unhappy paradox of 1992 may turn out to be that, despite all the qualities of the Social Charter and Action Programme requiring at Community level a range of individual employment rights, the fundamental debates about workers' rights in their collective dimension will continue to be fought out on twelve separate 'subsidiary' national agendas. In that event, trade unions will not be able adequately to protect workers' rights of any kind in face of employers who are increasingly transnational.

NOTES

1. 'The Migration of the Common Law: The Republic of Ireland' (1960) 76 LQR 69.
2. See, for example, Philippa Watson in Whyte (ed.) *Sex Equality, Community Rights and Irish Social Welfare Law: The Impact of the Third Equality Directive* (Irish Centre for European Law, 1988).
3. See for a recognition of subordination even in the case of management executives: *Provident Group plc* v *Hayward* [1989] ICR 160, 169, *per* Dillon LJ.
4. On France see, Lyon-Caen and Pélissier, *Droit de Travail* (15 ed, 1990) pp 919 *et seq*; on the Italian *rappresentanza*, Wedderburn, 'The Italian Workers' Statute' (1990) 19 ILJ 154.
5. See Kerr and Whyte, *Irish Trade Union Law* (1985) Chaps 1, 2; Wedderburn, *The Worker and the Law* (3rd ed, 1986) Chap. 1.
6. See Wedderburn and Sciarra, 'Collective Bargaining as Agreement and as Law: Neo-Contractualist and Neo-Corporative Tendencies' in Pizzorusso (ed.) *Law in The Making* (1988), pp 185-237.
7. See further Wedderburn, 'The Right to Strike: Is there a European Standard?' in *Employment Rights in Britain and Europe: Selected Papers* (1991).
8. On the history of the introduction of 'co-determination' into German Company law of the 1950s, see Spiro, *The Politics of German Codetermination* (1957).
9. See *Employee Participation and Company Structure* (1975, E.C. Bull. Supp. 8/75) p 9.
10. Proposal for Directive COM(89) 2768 final-SYN 219, parallel to the proposed Regulation on the 'company' aspects, *ibid.* SYN 218: Wedderburn, *The Social Charter, European Company and Employment Rights* (Institute of Employment Rights, 1990).
11. Arts. 10 and 11 in Directive 89/391 EEC, 12 June 1989; see (1990) 173 *Health and Safety Info. Bull.* 14.
12. See Docksey, 'Information and Consultation of Employees: the United Kingdom and the Vredeling Directive' (1986) 49 MLR 281-313.
13. Adopted by the Commission on 5 December 1990; see *Financial Times* 5 and 6 December 1990 [see now Com (90) 581 final].
14. *The EEC Vth Directive: A Trojan Bullock?* (Institute of Directors, 1980).
15. On 'joint regulation' and collective bargaining, see Flanders, *Management and Unions* (1970), pp 220-226.
16. On the Joint Regulation at Work Act 1976, see Schmidt, *Law and Industrial Relations in Sweden* (1977).
17. Mancini, 'Labour Law and Community Law' (1985) 20 *Ir. Jur. (n.s.)* 1 at pp 2, 12, 15.
18. E.C. Commission *Action Programme Relating to the Implementation of the Community Charter of Basic Social Rights for Workers* COM (89) 568, 27 November 1989. See in the special Community number of the MLR: Hepple, 'The Implementation of the Community Charter' (1990) 53 MLR 643; Bercusson, 'The European Community's Charter', *ibid* p 624; and the special number of the *Comparative Labor Law Journal* (Summer

1990), especially Weiss, 'A German Perspective' (1990) 11 *Comp. Lab. Law Jo.* 411; Treu on Italy at p 441; von Prondzynski on Ireland p 498.

19. Delors, speech to the TUC, see *TUC Report* 1988 at pp 568-570.
20. Delors, speech, 'What Social Europe?', 4 October 1990, *Fourth Forum of Works Councils*; the Commission made its proposals on 21 October 1990.
21. *The Times,* 27 November 1990. Art. 100A of the Treaty as amended in 1987 allows the Council, for the establishment or functioning of the internal market, to act by qualified majority voting; but under paragraph (2), this does not apply to 'fiscal provisions, to those relating to the free movement of persons nor to those relating to the rights and interests of employed persons'.
22. See Cecchini, *The European Challenge 1992: The Benefits of a Single Market* (1988). On the omission from the final draft of the Preamble to the Charter of combating unemployment, see Bercusson, (1990) 53 MLR 624, 626; also, *Employment in Europe* (1990 COM (90) 290 final) p 15 and Chaps 10, 11. For the British government's argument that the Action Programme will cause further loss of jobs, see DE *People Jobs and Progress* (1990).
23. For example, part-time working might give rise to 'problems of social dumping or even distortions of competition': *Action Programme* Part II, p 16 [see *R* v *Sec. of State for Employment ex parte EOC* [1994] ICR 317 HL: the UK government accepted this extension of rights of part-time workers on redundancy and unfair dismissal based on the law of sex discrimination whilst still opposing Directives to extend their rights further: *The Times* 21 December 1994].
24. *The Social Dimension of the Internal Market* (Social Europe Special Edition) 1988 Part 3, pp 63-66 (interdepartmental working party).
25. Blanpain, '1992 and Beyond' (1990) 11 *Comp. Lab. Law Jo* 403, 404 n 3.
26. As in its *Report on Naval Construction: Industrial, Social and Regional Aspects* (1987) COM(87) 275, 11.6.87, p 16.
27. See Pochet, 'Dumping Social – Un Concept Opérationnel?' (1990) L'Observatoire Social Européen, 56 *Nota Bene* 4; and (1989) 187 EIRR 12.
28. Treu, 'Pubblico e privato nell' Europa sociale' (1990) Lav. Dir. 329, 336.
29. Treaty of Rome art. 100A (2); see DE *People Jobs and Progress* (1990) [and see n. 23 above].
30. The common view is that there must be a substantial relationship, but others take a narrower view of the exception: compare Hepple, (1990) 53 MLR 643, 647-648; Vogel-Polsky, (1990) 19 ILJ 65, 69-71.
31. *Action Programme* Part I para 3.
32. E.g. the *Social Charter* arts. 5 (fair wage), 8 (rest periods and holidays), 12 (collective bargaining), 17 (information), 21-22 (young workers).
33. *Action Programme*, Part II pp 14-15.
34. COM(90) 228 final-SYN 280 and SYN 281, 13 August 1990; see (1990) 200 EIRR 12 and 203 EIRR 11.
35. COM(90) 317 final-SYN 295, 20 September 1990; see (1990) 200 EIRR 29; Hepple, *Working Time: A New Legal Framework?* (IPPR, 1990).
36. OJ 90/C 281/04, 9 November 1990.
37. *Financial Times*, 5 December 1990 [see Com (90) 581 final]. See too, Gold and Hall, *Legal Regulation and the Practice of Employee Participation in*

the EC (European Foundation for the Improvement of Living and Workers Conditions, 1990).

38. Draft of 4 December 1990 [see now generally (1991) 423 IRLIB 2].

39. Lyon-Caen and Pelissier, *Droit du Travail* (1990 15th ed.) pp 497-502 (but collective agreements may reserve certain advantages for full-time workers).

40. Law 863/84, 19 December 1984, especially art. 5. On remuneration, see Gherra, *Diritto di Lavoro* (1989) pp 210-5; on art. 36 Constitution, de Crisofero in Garofalo (ed.) *Crisi, Occupazione, Legge* (1985) pp 84-88; and Maresco in D'Amato (ed.) *Occupazione flessibile e nuove tipogie del rapporto di lavoro* (1988) pp 63-67.

41. Weiss, *Law and Industrial Relations in the Federal German Republic* (1987) pp 48-49 (art. 2 of the Act of 1985); and in Blanpain and Kohler (eds.) *Legal and Contractual Limitations to Working Time in the EC Member States* (European Foundation for the Improvement of Living and Working Conditions, 1988) pp 224-225.

42. Muckenberger and Deakin, 'From Deregulation to a European Floor of Rights' (1989) ZIAS 153, 204. [Proposals for proportional rights for part-time workers were revived in 1994, but were opposed by the UK in order to 'have as flexible a labour market as we can'; *Parl Deb HL* 16 December 1994 col 1469.]

43. CBI Evidence to HL Select Committee, *Voluntary Part-time Work*, Session 1981-2, 19th Report, 27 July 1982, on Draft Directive 4053/82 COM (81) 775 final; see too OJ C62/1983; and on temporary work OJ C128/2/1982.

44. EC Commission, *Explanatory Memorandum on Proposals for Directives. Concerning Certain Employment Relationships* COM(90) 228 final-SYN 280, SYN 281, p 12; the later quotations are from the analysis in pp 12-31 (referred to below as *Memorandum* COM(90) 228).

45. *Employment in Europe*, COM(90) 290 final, p 13, and see Chap 4.

46. *Memorandum* COM(90) 228, pp 11-14, see too, pp 20-28.

47. See *Proposal for Council Directive on Temporary or Mobile Work Sites* (8th individual Dir within art. 16 Directive 89/391; COM(90) 275 final – SYN 279 23 July 1990 [adopted later as Directive 92/57, OJ L. 245/92].

48. See *Framework Directive* 391/89 12 June 1989, art. 10. On the dispute whether a stoppage in protest at unsafe conditions can be 'industrial action' within the Employment Act 1990, s.9, see: Wedderburn, (1991) 54 MLR 1, 5 n. 23 [now overtaken by ss. 22A, 57A EPCA 1978, in TURER Act 1993, Sched. 5].

49. See *Action Programme* Part I, pp 4-5.

50. Breit, President of ETUC, *TUC Report 1988*, p 258.

51. *Action Programme*, Part I para. 9.

52. EC Commission, *Explanatory Statement on Directives on Employment Relationships* COM(90) 228 final p 3; also *Proposal for Directive Concerning Aspects of the Organisation of Working Time*, COM(90) 317 final – SYN 295, p 2; and see Kahn-Freund, 'Labour Law and Social Security' Chap VI in Stein and Nicholson, *American Enterprise in the European Common Market* Vol 1 (1960) pp 299-310.

53. *Comité Intergouvernemental créé par la conference de Messine: Rapports des Chefs de Delegations* (21 April 1956) Part 1, p 65.

54. See arts. 117, 118 Treaty of Rome, and after 1987 art. 118A.
55. On the slow rate of harmonisation in labour law see Hepple, in Adams (ed.) *Essays for Clive Schmitthoff* (1983) pp 14-28.
56. See EC Directives 75/117 of 10 February 1975, 77/187 of 14 February 1977 and 80/987 of 20 October 1980.
57. *Action Programme* Part II, pp 18, 23, 48.
58. Mancini, *op.cit.* in 17, above, at pp 11-12.
59. *Ibid.* p 12.
60. Ghezzi and Romagnoli, *Il rapporto del lavoro* (2nd ed., 1987) p 318.
61. Case 284/83, *Dansk Metalarbejderforbund* v *Nielsen* [1985] ECR 553, para 10.
62. Case 91/81, *EC Commission* v *Italy* [1982] ECR 2133; Foglia, 'Obblighi comunitarii e licenziamenti collettivi, *Dir. Lav.* 1982, p 387; and Case 131/84, *EC Commission* v *Italy* [1985] ECR 3531; Adinolfi, *Rev. Dir. Internat.* 1985, 76; Pera, *Diritto del lavoro* (3rd ed. 1988) p 530.
63. See Carinci, de Luca Tamajo, Tosi and Treu, *Diritto del lavoro* (2nd ed 1987) p 322; Ghezzi and Romagnoli, *op.cit.* n 60 above at pp 316-320; Corte costit. 140/1984.
64. See the first judgment on Italy [1982] ECR 2133, para 11; also Case 215/83, *EC Commission* v *Belgium* [1985] ECR 1039.
65. See Freedland, 'Employment Protection: Redundancy Provisions and the EEC' (1976) 5 ILJ 24, 34, on Part IV of the Employment Protection Act 1975.
66. For France: Lyon-Caen and Pelissier, *Droit du Travail* (15th ed), pp 976-997; Italy: Sciarra, *Contratto collettivo e contrattazione in azienda* (1985) pp 118-148; Wedderburn and Sciarra, *op.cit.* n 6 above in Pizzorusso, *Law in the Making* (1988) pp 210-228; and for a comparative assessment, see Biagi, *Rappresentanza e democrazia in azienda* (1990) pp 268-324.
67. Treu, *op.cit.* n 28 above at p 337.
68. Wallyn, *La Politique Sociale de la Communauté et la participation des partenaires sociaux à la formation des decisions au niveau européen* (1987) Europe Sociale (no 1) 13.
69. Bercusson, 'The European Community's Charter of Fundamental Social Rights of Workers' (1990) 53 MLR 624, 642.
70. See EC Directive 75/129 of 17 February 1975, arts 2, 4; and Employment Protection Act 1975, ss 99-105.
71. Employment Act 1980, s 19. The procedure, under s 11 of the Employment Act 1975, was unsatisfactory by reason of lack of criteria for recommendation and hostile interpretation by the courts: see Simpson. 91979) 8 ILJ 69; Wedderburn, *The Worker and the Law* (3rd ed., 1986) pp 278-289.
72. *Action Programme* Part II, p 19, announcing a 'revision' of the 1975 Directive.
73. See Hepple, (1990) 53 MLR 643, 650; Wedderburn, 'The Social Charter in Britain' (1991) 54 MLR 1, 13; Hepple and Byre, 'EEC Law in the UK. A New Approach' (1989) ILJ 129.
74. See Kerr and Whyte, *Irish Trade Union Law* (1985) Chap 7.
75. EC Directive 77/187 of 14 February 1977, implemented in Ireland by

European Communities (Safeguarding of Employees Rights on Transfer of Undertakings) Regulations 1980, and in Britain by Transfer of Undertakings (Protection of Employment) Regulations 1981 (SI No 1794). See Kerr, 'Implementation of Directive 77/187 into Irish Law' in *Acquired Rights of Employees* (Irish Centre for European Law, 1989) 1-23, and on the UK position, McMullen, *ibid.* pp 24-60.

76. Case 324/86, *Foreningen af Arbejdsledere* v *Daddy's Dance Hall* [1988] ECR 739, 754. Compare Rideout, 'The Great Transfer of Employee Rights Hoax' (1982) 35 *Current Legal Problems* 233 [now *Katsikas* v *Konstantinides* [1993] IRLR 179 ECJ, and s. 33(4) TURER Act 1993].

77. *Report, op.cit.* Pt 1, Title 2, Ch 2, p 63.

78. It was by no means clear at first that this was immediately binding or that it meant equal pay for work of equal value: see Kahn-Freund, in Stein and Nicholson, *op.cit.* fn 52 above, pp 325-328.

79. EC Directive 75/117 of 10 February 1975; on the effect in Britain see Rubenstein, *Equal Pay for Work of Equal Value* (1984).

80. EC Directive 76/207 of 9 February 1976; see, on the history, Davies in McCrudden (ed.) *Women, Employment and European Equality Law* (1987).

81. See McCrudden, *op.cit.* above n 80; Townshend-Smith, *Sex Discrimination in Employment* (1989). On 'pay' see now, Case C262/88, *Barber* v *Guardian Royal Exchange Assurance Group* [1990] ICR 616.

82. Townshend-Smith, *op.cit.* p 33; Rowe in Cappelletti, Secombe and Weiler (eds.) *Integration through Law* (1986) Vol 1, p 470-472.

83. Davies and Freedland, *Labour Law: Text and Materials* (2nd ed, 1984) p 380, and generally pp 380-421.

84. Case 170/84, *Bilka Kaufhaus GmbH* v *Von Hartz* [1986] ECR 1607, para. 27; Case 96/80, *Jenkins* v *Kingsgate (Clothing Productions) Ltd* [1981] ECR 911; but see too, Case 109/88, *Handels-OG Kontorfunktionaerernes Forbund i Danmark* v *Dansk Arbejdsgiverforening (Danfoss)* [1989] IRLR 532.

85. Hepple, *Working Time: A New Legal Framework?* (IPPR, 1990) p 18.

86. Case 33/89, *Kowalska* v *Freie und Hansestadt Hamburg* [1990] IRLR 447, 449; it has been said that the ECJ thereby brought into effect parts of the proposed Directive on part-time work: Rubenstein [1990] IRLR at p 411. See too now, Case C262/88, *Barber's* case, *cit.* n. 81 above [and now *Coloroll Pension Trustees* v *Russell* (case 200/91) [1994] IRLR 586 ECJ].

87. Phelps Brown, *The Inequality of Pay* (1977) p 158.

88. See Case 109/88, *Handels-OG* (etc.) v *Dansk Arbejdsgiverforening (Danfoss)* [1989] IRLR 532 (accepting seniority).

89. *Rainey* v *Greater Glasgow Health Authority* [1987] ICR 129, 140, relying on the *Bilka* decision, above n 84.

90. Case 96/80, *Jenkins* v *Kingsgate (Clothing Productions) Ltd* [1981] ECR 911; cf *Hampson* v *Department of Education and Science* [1991] 1 AC 171. See too, *Benveniste* v *University of Southampton* [1989] IRLR 122, where the final decision excluding the 'financial constraint' as a legitimate factor was admirable, but value laden.

91. On the Labour Court and sex discrimination, see von Prondzynski and McCarthy, *Employment Law* (1984) pp 199-206; on Britain, see Smith and

Wood, *Industrial Law* (4th ed, 1989) pp 81-85, 236-265.

92. Case 14/83, *Von Colson v Land Nordrhein Westfalen* [1984] ECR 1891, paras 22-23.

93. *Marshall* v *Southampton and S.W. Hampshire AHA (No 2)* [1990] IRLR 481. [The ECJ later struck down the limits on compensation for sex discrimination: *Marshall* v *Southampton and S.W. AHA* (No 2) [1993] ICR 893 ECJ; now Sex Discrimination (etc.) Regulations 1993, S.I. 2798, and the parallel Race Relations (Remedies) Act 1994; McColgan (1994) 23 ILJ 226.]

94. Transfer of Undertakings (Protection of Employment) Regulations 1981, SI 1794, reg 11(5) (7) (11). [But see now ss. 33(7) (11) TURER Act 1993, rescinding the deductions and making the maximum period four weeks: *quaere* whether that is an adequate measure of compensation?]

95. Reg 9(1)(a) of the European Communities (Safeguarding of Employees' Rights on Transfer of Undertakings) Regulations 1980 (SI No 306 of 1980); see Kerr, *Acquired Rights of Employees* (Irish Centre for European Law, 1988) 1, 20 ('To date, no prosecutions have been instituted and, as far as can be ascertained, the powers under reg. 8 [giving the Minister the right to demand information and papers] have never been used').

96. See *Litster* v *Forth Dry Dock & Engineering Ltd* [1990] AC 546; Szyszczak (1989) 52 MLR 7093.

97. Employment Protection Act 1975, ss 99-103; see Wedderburn, *The Worker and the Law* (3rd ed, 1986) pp 296-301.

98. Sex Discrimination Act 1975, s 75; Townshend Smith, *op.cit.* above n 81, pp 189-196.

99. Sex Discrimination Act 1986, repealing s 3 of the Equal Pay Act 1970; on the relationship of CAC and High Court, see Davies, (1980) *Current Legal Problems* 196.

100. von Prondzynski and McCarthy, *op.cit.* above n 91, pp 202-204.

101. See Pannick, *Sex Discrimination Law* (1985) pp 284-301.

102. See Lyon Caen and Pélissier, *Droit du Travail* (15th ed 1990) pp 727-735: on the *action syndicale* see *Code du Travail* art L. 122-6 (sex equality) and art L. 411-11 (granting a right to appear in all courts in civil cases where workers' 'collective interest' is threatened). [See the valuable review by Fitzpatrick (1992) 8 Int. Jo CLLIR 208.]

103. Art 10(2) of the proposed 'Directive on the Establishment of European Works Councils in European-scale Undertakings' (under Art. 100 of the Treaty) 5 December 1990 [but this right of action for the Works Council appears not to have survived into the final text: see text of 22 June 1994, 7436/94.].

104. *Action Programme*, p 50; on adult working hours, *ibid* Chap 3 [now adopted as a Directive 22 June 1994; 1994 EIRR 246, 2].

105. *Restrictions on Employment of Young People and Removal of Sex Discrimination in Legislation: Consultative Document* (December 1987 D.E.) para 8.2, a document much relied upon by Government in debates on the 1989 Bill; see Deakin, (1990) 19 ILJ 1, 11-13.

106. See Memorandum COM (90) 317 final SYN 295 p.13, and pp.5-12; and on the 1957 Treaty, Kahn-Freund on the original 'Protocol relating to Certain Provisions of Concern to France', which aimed to spread the 40

hour week throughout the market: Stein and Nicholson, *op.cit.* above n 52 pp 333-335.

107. (1990) 313 IRLIB pp 5-10. [As amended, this became Directive 93/104; von Prondzynski (1994) 23 ILJ 92. In a set-back for the collective approach, it permits *individual* agreements to contract out of the 48 hour week.]

108. See Mariucci, *Le fonti del diritto del lavoro* (1989) Chaps 2-4.

109. Preamble to proposed Directive on working time COM(90) 317 final SYN 295 [now Directive 93/104].

110. Blanpain in *Legal and Contractual Limitations to Working Time in the EC Member States* (European Foundation for the Improvement of Living and Working Conditions, 1988) p 18; Hepple, *Working Time: A New Legal Framework?* (IPPR, 1990) p 25.

111. See Wedderburn, 'The Social Charter in Britain, Labour Law and Labour Courts' (1991) 54 MLR 1, 3-6. Even as late as 1893 and 1908 the control of adult male hours was effected by legislation in Britain.

112. See Redmond, 'Ireland' in *Legal and Contractual Limitations to Working Time in the EC Member States* (1988) chap 6, pp 261-294.

113. *TUC Report*, 1988 p 709-710.

114. COM (90) 406 final SYN 303; (1990) 203 EIRR 16 and 28 (text).

115. See the draft proposals OJC 62/1983.

116. Art 2(3) Draft Directive on Certain Employment Relationships, COM (90) 228 final p 37.

117. *Amended Proposal for a Fifth Directive on the Harmonisation of Company Law* (DTI, January 1990).

118. *Proposals for a Council Regulation and Directive* COM (90) 268 final-SYN 218 and 219; see Wedderburn, *The Social Charter, European Company and Employment Rights* (1990).

119. On new limits to shareholders' powers to move SE's national seat: above p. 113 n. 8; below p. 386-7.

120. Commission proposals of 5 December 1990. [Later texts do not name a Group Council separately; but the Directive requires a Council 'in every Community-scale undertaking and every Community-scale group of undertakings' (art. 1(2)), unless otherwise agreed. The Eleven States adopted it under the Social Chapter (22 September 1994). The UK is not bound, but UK undertakings operating in those States must comply there. The Directive will not apply to undertakings with agreements already in place by 1996 for 'transnational consultation of employees'.]

121. *Action Programme* Part II p 29.

122. See Ewing, *Britain and the ILO* (1989), [see too now, ILO governing body condemnation of the UK in Case 1540, 27 February 1991, *NUS* v *UK* adopting 277th Report of Freedom of Association Committee].

123. Bercusson, (1990) 53 MLR 624, 642.

124. Treaty of Rome as amended 1987, Art 118B [and now the 'Social Chapter' procedures for Eleven States]. The social dialogue may facilitate the creation of machinery for framework agreements bargained at European level; but that prospect remains uncertain.

APPENDIX TO CHAPTER 8

ON THE MAASTRICHT 'SOCIAL CHAPTER'*

Lord Wedderburn of Charlton: I ask: why is it that the Government withdrew their support from the social dimension of the market? After the Commission's White Paper in 1985 and the Cecchini Report of 1988, it was agreed by all 12 heads of state that there was a need for a social dimension. I quote the words of the conclusions of the Madrid Summit:

> in the context of the establishment of the single European market, the same importance must be attached to the social aspects as to the economic aspects.

It is quite clear that the social aspects involve intervention in the market, which some Ministers were once prepared to do but it now seems that that is offensive. Why was that? It was because one of the predictions of those reports was that in at any rate the first phase of the single internal market there might be – indeed, in one case there would be – a serious loss of jobs and that the redeployment and restructuring which were inevitable would need some protection for those upon whom otherwise the main costs and burdens would fall and are now falling.

Noble Lords who speak about these matters must remember that, a return of the reserve army of unemployed of 18 or 19 million in the Community (whoever is doing a little better or a little worse in the member states), discloses a shocking situation. It is that situation that the social dimension addressed.

The Government supported the social dimension. I shall give one example as evidence, because I see that that statement creates something of a shock across the Chamber. On 8th November 1989, the Minister for Employment, Mr. Eggar, speaking for the Government, told your Lordships' Select Committee that they were,

> committed ... to fulfilling the social dimension

He said a little later, taking account of the doctrine of subsidiarity, that there was no basic challenge to the need to fulfil a social dimension. He said that the Government were guided by the Madrid conclusions; and there are many statements of that kind. I do not remember any great wave of protest from the

---

* Speech in a debate to note the Government's policy on the Agreement attached to the Protocol on Social Policy in the Maastricht Treaty: Parl. Deb. HL 22 July 1993, cols. 829-833.

Conservative Party or the Conservative Benches against that statement. Of course, it then depends on what one puts into the social dimension. Some of the contents proposed were far-reaching. It is well known that M. Delors convinced the British labour movement that there was something in it at the TUC conference in 1988 when he said that the social dimension should include lifelong retraining, employees' participation in European companies and,

every worker's right to be covered by a collective agreement.

None of that is in the social chapter.

Yet by 1990 the Government had resiled from their support for a social dimension and will not now support even the minimal procedures for the social chapter. I insist that these are procedures. They are often publicised as though they were a set of substantive norms for employment law, but they are a set of procedures. In that historical context I believe that we can heavily discount the recent rhetoric about 'burdens on business', competitiveness and loss of jobs which came later than the change of government policy.

I say to the noble Lord, Lord Aldington, that the Government are not against European collective bargaining because it is European. They are against European collective bargaining because it is collective bargaining and may negotiate protection for workers. The noble Lord has a distinguished record on collective bargaining which I appreciate. However, the Government now believe that all the structures which he helped to build in the port industry and elsewhere should be dismantled into individualised employment. That is, of course, the key to the change.

If we look at the social chapter what do we find? I submit that we find three categories. First, we find a group of bipartisan matters; that is to say, the pursuit of policies concerning equality of the sexes and a ban on discrimination, although, alas, not a ban on race discrimination, which may be the hole in the heart for the Community in many ways. Further, we find improved measures on health and safety at work, which historically this country saw on its statute book earlier and which in some respects are now better than, and at any rate as full as, those of any other member state.

If health and safety legislation is acceptable, whether it be at European level or otherwise for the Government, by what divine ordinance is the permission retracted when we pass across the boundary into modest legislation on working hours? Why is there that line, other than by reference to history and the work of Professor von Hayek? Apart from that, I can find no justification for drawing the line in this ideological manner. All other social legislation appears to them to be bad, apart from those two now traditional policies, on sex and safety.

Secondly, it is true that Community competence in the Council of Ministers is extended by the social chapter's agreement on decisions by qualified majority, but only over a comparatively modest range – for me, far too narrow in many respects.

What do we find? It does not extend to social security, to collective interests of workers or to the employer's right to dismiss workers. Under Article 2(6) it does not extend at all to freedom of association – something which the Commission ought to face up to but will not. It does not extend to pay. It does not extend to rights to strike or rights to lock out. The Minister—

Baroness Elles: My Lords, I am most grateful to the noble Lord for allowing me to intervene. Did I understand him to say that the social policy agreement did not include social security? I draw his attention to Article 2, paragraph 3, where it says,

> the Council shall act unanimously on a proposal from the Commission
> ... in the following areas:
> —social security and social protection of workers.

I may have misunderstood the noble Lord, in which case I apologise, but I should like to draw his attention to that paragraph.

Lord Wedderburn of Charlton: My Lords, the noble Baroness is quite right in what she reads. But I was referring to the *qualified* majority provisions. It is from that narrow area in the chapter that all these provisions are excluded, by two different paragraphs of Article 2. There is no minimum wage, despite what the noble Lord the Lord Privy Seal said. He is not here, but I am sure that he will correct me if I get it wrong. He said that all sorts of trade union rights could be introduced. How you do that by not being able to pass any decision at all upon freedom of association, rights to strike, lock out and so on, defeats me. I have no idea.

Thirdly, the main areas set out in the social chapter – and this is what it comes to – are: first, consultation with employees; secondly, integration of persons excluded from the labour market; and thirdly, working conditions. Those are the three main areas of new possibilities for qualified majority decisions.

The historian will find it difficult to understand how noble Lords on the Benches opposite, who played such a distinguished role in introducing the Industrial Relations Act in 1971 and passing new, if misguided, laws on rights of association and unfair dismissal, can object to this extraordinarily minimal document of procedures. What has happened is due to the Government's unquenchable appetite to strip away, on the one hand, employment protection legislation and, on the other, collective bargaining from the market. Those aims were made quite explicit in their White Paper of last year, in which they state that they wish to replace collective arrangements with individualised employment relations. That is the Government's norm; it is the star which they follow – black holes which are not shared in Bonn, or indeed in Paris, or in Italy.

It is true that many national labour laws have changed and been adapted over the years. But the notion that you should not approach large areas of the labour market on a collective basis is one which is not shared in other member other member states. That curious and unique belief of the Government is the problem in regard to the Social Charter, not its contents.

Finally, in another part of the chapter, (I say this for completeness) Articles 3 and 4 aim to facilitate collective mechanisms at European level for consultation or negotiation. I must admit that some are more optimistic about that route than I am. It is not at all clear how the legal and industrial difficulties of Community-level negotiations could be overcome in the translation or transposition of European level agreements or arrangements to national or sectoral level in the domestic labour markets. Two examples show the extraordiarily narrow range of this part of the chapter. Declaration No. 2 attached to the agreement clearly states that there is,

> no obligation on the Member States to apply the agreements directly ... nor any obligation to amend national legislation ... to facilitate their implementation.

What is this part about? This part is about agreements. No employers need go further than they wish to go in these arrangements, even were the arrangements to work rather more easily than I would foresee. Nor is there anything in the social chapter to breathe new life into Community plans for the protection of part-time workers; nor in regard to worker participation in a European company, and so forth.

The reality of the social chapter is not the normative Frankenstein, even if all the procedures were used to the full, that exists in the nightmares of Ministers; nor is it, in my submission, the passport to more sun and cheaper wine, which those who support it appear sometimes to suggest. It is a very careful and narrow document for a beginning of a social dimension.

It is well documented that many, many ordinary people have a sense of disillusionment about the Community. The impoverishment of the social dimension has been a major cause in that. If you lose a job and you have been led to believe that something will perhaps come from Brussels to protect you, when you find that it is not there, that is a rather more serious situation than most of us experience most of our lives. It is that disillusion to which the Government have contributed. They have done that rather than support this first fragile set of procedures to protect workers and their families who will be the victims in the coming economic storms.

9
LABOUR LAW AND THE INDIVIDUAL: CONVERGENCE OR DIVERSITY?*

In the dark time of 1933, the year of his inaugural lecture in Amsterdam, Sinzheimer wrote:

> The powers in control of the current economic system have failed to ensure the realisation of the most elementary human right, the right to earn one's daily bread by work ... The problem of labour law has in fact become the problem of an entire economic order. A renovation of labour law is no longer possible without a renewal of that economic order ... The social requirements of labour law are no longer compatible with the individual character of the economic system.[1]

Yet today we hear on all sides of the triumphs of that individualism. Not so much perhaps in the labour law debates in Continental Europe – for many jurisdictions there continue to pursue flexibility not through market forces alone but with 'objectives of social purpose combined with objectives of efficiency'.[2] But elsewhere they are trumpeted increasingly. Is this then to be an age of labour law individualism? Must the economic system once more demand primarily individual legal relations between the employee and his or her employer? Should legal policy concentrate now on protection against the 'colonialisation' of the individual employee by public and private power, not least through computerised data?[3] Must we accept the paradox that the global rise of multinational employers, in

* The Sinzheimer Lecture 1993, given at the Hugo Sinzheimer Institute, University of Amsterdam, 5 November 1993, to the conference *Labour Law in the Post-Industrial Era.*

international coalitions of collective capital, will be matched by the irretrievably atomised decollectivisation of their employees? As policies of 'globalised localisation' in transnational enterprises seek the cheapest labour market – Swissair now handles its revenue accounting in Bombay[4] – are national economic systems in a 'post-industrial' condition still, or increasingly, unable to combat structural unemployment ('that terrible expression', as Sinzheimer put it)? Yet do we find, even so, the same 'individual character' that Sinzheimer described within the economic market and is that the cause of the failure by the European Community – despite the theatre of some of its measures – so far to ensure protection for elementary labour standards in the face of contraventions by its Member States to adhere to minima in the ILO Conventions, even on freedom of association?[5]

There are in Britain those who refuse to address this agenda, even though it has been constructed by 'those in control of the economic system'. It may be unwise for those at the other end of the tunnel to ignore it altogether, even if it seems a little remote to their practices based rather more upon consensus. The legal dimension of such issues invites us to address, first, the ideology and policy of the law (where some recent British developments offer a good example), secondly, the call for convergence but the divergent responses of industrial relations systems and of labour law in the Community, and thirdly, the need for new mechanisms for protection of the individual dignity and private interests of workers in an internationalised market.

INDIVIDUAL BARGAINING?

Until recently such questions would have been regarded as rhetorical. As long ago as 1897 Sidney and Beatrice Webb gave a firm answer about individualism:

> Individual bargaining between the owner of the means of subsistence and the seller of so perishable a commodity as a day's labour must be, once for all, abandoned. In its place, if there is to be any genuine 'freedom of contact', we shall see the conditions of employment adjusted between equally expert negotiators acting for corporations reasonably comparable in strength.[6]

This new 'collective bargaining' would be supplemented by laws from Parliament 'in the interests of the community as a whole'. Such negotiation was quite different from mere 'consultation' – indeed that is the ground on which different brands of 'pluralists' have later stood, placing collective bargaining at the centre of industrial and 'post-industrial' society. But in Britain today, government and others promote the virtues of 'personalised contracts of employment', freed from collective bargaining, and of individual negotiations by the vendors of labour power lucky to be chosen for work from the reserve army in the market. One brand of such policies of 'deregulation' and individualism has been favoured by the British Parliament in its Acts of the 1980s, and now 1990 and 1993 – curtailing union rights, seemingly in breach on several occasions of ILO Conventions 87 and 98,[7] now even empowering an employer lawfully to discriminate against union members when his purpose is to 'change his relationship' with employees (for example, on pay and conditions) intending explicitly thereby to discriminate against those who retain their trade union membership.[8]

There is perhaps a need respectfully to warn colleagues elsewhere in Europe who still enjoy *consensus*-based labour law, not to write off these developments as some short term Anglo-Saxon deviation from the natural course of history in 'post industrial societies'. Those who have subscribed to the new individualism believe that they have seen the future and that it works. It is a proselytising faith which is not dependent on any particular political party or leader. Many in Britain, including the Government, find these policies convincing and the latter has sought inward investment by explicitly advertising that in Britain labour costs are 'significantly below other European countries' with the 'least onerous labor (sic) regulations'.[9] Throughout the world it is reported that this individualist flower is flourishing, albeit sometimes with a little force feeding from management or government. In the United States, the density of union membership – crucial to a system which depends on membership – has fallen below 12 per cent in the non-agricultural, private sector; bargaining elections are won much less often, millions of workers suffer annually under the employment-at-will doctrine[10] (proudly defended by neo-liberals)[11] and 'runaway' multinational employers increasingly avoid collective industrial relations altogether.[12] 'Corporate executives have begun to envision the total demise of American unions.'[13] Japanese investment and 'lean production' methods frequently opt for union avoidance.[14] Recent legislation in New Zealand[15] and now in the Australian State of Victoria in 1993, have introduced new forms of individualism; the latter, promoting employment agreements 'preferably "individual" rather than "collective" ', now 'strips Victorian employees (other than those covered by federal awards) of their collective voice ... obliged to work for very low pay and with little or no employment security.'[16] This statute, which is likely to be counteracted in Federal legislation by the Commonwealth government, is said to owe much to the New Zealand Act and to the British legislation.[17]

Some British scholars, whilst accepting that the relation 'between worker and boss' has 'contractual elements', have tried to change the axis of debate by insisting that the best way to understand the relationship as a whole today is

> to recognize that between them personally no contract exists and that the power relation springs from the organisation of which they are both members.[18]

But this may reflect inadequately the conflict of interest within the employment relationship and (more important to the present purpose) run counter to the deeply rooted 'freedom of contract' philosophy which is the mainspring of the common law and central still to the rhetoric and direction of legal policy. Official British thinking of the 1980s, moreover, has developed a policy reliant upon similar premises by putting the individual contract first, claiming that patterns of collective employment relations are 'increasingly inappropriate', that more employees now should and do negotiate pay and conditions 'for themselves on an individual basis and directly with their employers', and that an 'increasing trend to move away from collective bargaining' and decline in national bargaining are 'valuable and healthy developments'.[19]

IDEOLOGY: THE RECENT BRITISH CASE

In an era of reduction in the coverage of collective agreements, curtailment of union and employment protection rights and decline of employers' associations as bargaining parties,[20] ideological considerations have played an unusually prominent rôle in shaping British labour law legislation in the 1980s, especially the neo-liberal individualist philosophy of Hayek[21] (one not unknown elsewhere).[22] British analysis is comfortable with pragmatism, but more anxious in the realm of ideology, prone to minimise its effect on real political life, at times thinking that ideologues with scant knowledge of legal detail can have little influence on governments which react to day to day events. But it is not necessary for an ideologue to sit at the right hand of the prime minister or to master legal niceties[23] so long as his ideas sufficiently permeate the minds of law makers, as Hayek's did; his theses suited Ministers who sought the path of individualism plus strong government (strong, not weak – how else was the obstacle of effective trade unionism to be removed from the operation of the market?).[24] He knew enough about the common law, approving fervently of its doctrine of restraint of trade[25] and its reliability to uphold the 'natural spontaneous order',[26] to embrace it as the executioner does the axe.

A reference to Hayek's ideology 'does not explain everything, but it illuminates much'.[27] It should be taken seriously by those in other jurisdictions who wish to come to grips with the new British individualism. Its close structural links with the common law and freedom of contract, on the one hand, and the neo-liberalism of the Thatcher statutes, on the other, compounded the difficulty which has always existed for those who wished to see British labour law aim overtly at a general 'protection' of employees in relations of subordination, in the way of, say, Italian law where 'protective intervention' is an avowed, general objective,[28] or German law where the judges developed strong, protective presumptions of equality between employees quite different from British freedom of contract.[29] As always, particular pressures and events had their effect upon the shape of the 1980s legislation; but it would flout the record to believe that there was no compass guiding the legislative programme, planned in the 1970s to be executed 'step by step' in order not to make the mistake of trying to do everything at once, as in 1971.[30] Ideology is not, of course, a book from which government reads out answers, but here the legal measures on social conflict were manifestly connected to 'the ideological forms in which men become conscious of this conflict and fight it out' – and here a woman too.[31] Each 'step' was not a pragmatic note in a score without a tune. Sometimes Ministers were frank about this: 'I have not,' said one in 1982, 'sought to use the law – *this time at any rate* – to reform the structures or internal affairs of trade unions'.[32] In 1984, with no significant events intervening, regulation of their internal affairs was introduced, then tightened in 1988 and in 1990, just as Hayek had indicated, declaring: 'The very term "freedom of organisation" … carries overtones which are not in accord but in conflict with the reign of law on which a free society rests'.[33] It was wrong to think that the 'collective action of organisations should not be restricted by rules which do not apply to individuals'.[34] Special rules could apply to such groups – a thesis

Ministers used to the full as the threads unwound after 1982, avowing that special laws were needed to deal with 'special' organisations both for the 'protection of the individual' and for promoting the 'competitiveness of the economy'.[35] This is a philosophy which makes common law and free-market individualism feel comfortable, with its direct appeal to the morality of individual 'freedom of contract', doubting the very legitimacy of action 'on the part of a collectivity'.[36] Nor was ideological commitment missing in the twists and turns of the legislation, sometimes departing from previous party manifestos, at others creating novel ways to squeeze out the influence of unions, especially after the final break with traditional thinking in 1982, but always ending within the same general axis of advance.[37]

COLLECTIVE ORGANISATION

Of course, there are common elements shared among different employment ideologies. In a democratic society, for example, few would deny that the law must protect some aspects of the individual relationship in employment, in particular the right to refuse a particular employment – and in modern society to refuse it without loss of all welfare rights. Without that, forced labour is only a gulag away. But the new proposals go much further. Collective values are no longer part of the shared premises. What is more, they are often supported by the increasingly important school of 'human resource management', holding that there may be a place for a 'mix of individual and collective regulation' so long as 'the latter is of a non-union character or a co-operative type of union arrangement.'[38] Frank exponents of the art write that 'the smart money' is being placed on 'a wholehearted commitment to an individually based human resource programme',[39] even if managers in 'non-union HRM' firms find it necessary to maintain employees' conditions in face of union organisation elsewhere.[40] On the other hand, it has been a truism of much of labour law as we have known it, that the reality of even 'individual' employee protection itself requires a lasting presence of collective autonomous organisation, expressing the demand for collective representation with freedom of association, collective bargaining and, if need arises, the struggle of industrial conflict. In 1991 the German Federal Constitutional Court reaffirmed the need for 'collective bargaining autonomy ... to balance the structural inferiority of the employee'.[41] Where central protections are expressed in the form of individual legal guarantees,[42] the reliance on formal individualism that is magnified in times of danger must be interpreted within the strategies of current social relations – in Sinzheimer's phrase: 'It is only in legal policy that the meaning of jurisprudence is fulfilled'[43] – as when voices cry: *'Faut-il brûler le Code du Travail?'*[44] or when sacrifices are demanded in the name of 'flexibility'[45] or when labour law is ambushed by competition law (as in the *Genoa Port* case, where the Court of Justice exposed labour relations to the full blast of competition regulation, as if it were resurrecting the *Danbury Hatters* philosophy for Europe long after it was officially dead in the United States).[46] British competition laws permit a formal inquiry into allegedly anti-competitive labour practices, so far without sanctions, but the unions have defeated attempts to use them by proving the allegations groundless.[47] Were the legislature to extend the teeth of 'anti-competition' laws to labour, the paucity of individual workers' rights in British law would be further exposed.

NON-INTERVENTION

Classical British labour law had its own ideology, one to which 'post-industrial pluralists' made their contribution, predicting that, as unions 'matured' concentrating on pragmatic collective bargaining and pressure group activities, they would become an acceptable and integral part of a pluralist society within systems of 'voluntary' labour relations.[48] Voluntarism became the buzz word; even in 1980 Ministers laid claim to the same rationale, saying: 'We want to get back to a voluntary system'.[49] Aspects of pluralist thinking fed into Kahn-Freund's classic analysis that British law was 'abstentionist' or 'non-interventionist', affording primacy to collective bargaining – 'if you like, collective *laissez faire*'.[50] This was a philosophy which could co-habit easily with individualism so long as social consent was forthcoming on all (or for a sufficient number of) sides – hence the 'if you like'. Protection of employees' conditions could be effected by social rather than legal means. Reports of the death of this concept are much exaggerated and debates have been bemused by misunderstandings about it in Britain, especially on individualism, which have lapped over into European debate.[51] So a brief word about relevant aspects of it is fitting.

Most industrial systems have abstentionist elements, especially once trade unions acquire the strength to bargain.[52] Some systems where originally employers and unions relied on 'self-government' have seen the unions use their political influence to obtain protective legislation.[53] But from its special history, there evolved three overlapping senses of 'abstentionism' in Britain which are not always distinguished: the idealist, the historical and the ideological. In all of them there were of course 'pluralist' elements.[54] Kahn-Freund himself made little reference to the first as a principle after his pronouncement in 1954 that there is 'something like an inverse correlation between the practical significance of legal sanctions and the degree to which industrial relations have reached a state of maturity'. British industrial relations were therefore 'fundamentally healthy'.[55] He designated the State as 'neutral' in labour conflicts (perhaps 'a momentary semantic victory of Hegel over Marx or Weber').[56] In 1959, he added the grand (but surely erroneous) pronouncement: 'What the State has not given, the State cannot take away.'[57] Secondly, the historical sense. Here 'non-intervention' was a description of the British system in order to understand it, for undeniably, as against comparable societies, its industrial relations were – and to a degree are – governed remarkably little by legal (certainly legislative) sanction. This was explicable largely by social developments at the time of early trade union development.[58] The thesis asserted not that there was 'no law' (how could it in face of massive regulation on health and safety at work?), but that a special type of labour law structure had arisen which regulated collective activities very little, especially bargaining (though it had the potential for more, especially the judges, hence from time to time the 'abstention'). The main exception, legislation on health and safety at work developed from 1833, was similarly explicable. Judicial interventionism in the 1960s threatened to upset the balance apparently forged in the preceding century.[59] This might threaten the British 'equilibrium', which by 1959 Kahn-Freund had come to think impregnable. The new legislative threat was expressed in a repressive Act of 1971 which appeared to try to cast aside the 'attitude of abstention which was the outstanding virtue of British law'.[60] More generally, this was a moment when the British middle class upon whose 'acquiescence' the balance had rested, began to return to its earlier hostility against trade unions.[61] This change, greatly encouraged by the media, had consequences also for the 1980s. Previously, it could be said that there had been 'not so much an "abstention" on the judges' part as an exclusion by them' by legislation, which was later rationalised as 'abstention' or 'non-intervention'.[62] But that balance of social forces, framed in laws to exclude judicial interventions, was secured only temporarily from time to time as the pendulum swung between courts and Parliament. As the threats of hostile legislation came to be perceived 'non-intervention' became

an enlightened strategy (though rarely the religion some critics detected)
... At times it was a language, at others a code, for the defence of
autonomous trade unionism.[63]

The ideological battle was hard fought. Some suggested there was a
contradiction in proposing legislation to ban racial discrimination (at
work as everywhere else) while resisting at the same time proposed
anti-union legislation designed to have 'more law and order' by
subjecting trade unions and their members to State control.[64] In the
'Donovan' Royal Commission some members took this line – behind
its pragmatic face there was a sharp, if unacknowledged, struggle of
ideologies. Those who held to 'non-intervention', some said, should be
opposed to all legislation affecting industrial relations, including
discrimination laws: 'Why', they asked, 'do you make *an exception* in
fact in favour of racial or ethnic discrimination?'[65] It was here that the
historical analysis was mobilised by those who saw the coming threat
of attacks upon freedom of association. This reaction is not unknown
in other systems;[66] but in a jurisdiction where no constitutional right
to associate was on the agenda, the 'immunities' were the only territory
to defend: they were, despite their form, central to non-
interventionism since without them trade unions and their activities
would be largely unlawful. As the attack took up the crude cry that
immunities were 'privileges', social forces were unleashed against these
legal protections, ultimately to be manifested in the 1980s legislation
by different techniques. The labour movement itself, calmed by
decades of soft pluralism, had no profound understanding of its danger
before 1970 and was uneasy with ideological explanation. But
strategically, at the time, there was only one answer to the question:
'Where else was there to go?'.[67] There were no prospects of 'positive
rights' no more than minimal individual employment protection, so to
cast off the anchor of 'non-intervention' altogether would have been to
emigrate from collective bargaining. Here, therefore, the ideological
and historical context of non-intervention were merged, expressly and
avowedly; events proved that there was indeed a threat of 'tight legal
regulation' of unions, made more severe in the 1980s.[68] It was a
'vocation' which no other school of thought was able to articulate – in
Sinzheimer's sense, a conviction allied to scholarship.[69] The suggestion
that collective *laissez-faire* was somehow an obstruction to laws
against racism stands as a tasteless insult to the memory of Sinzheimer
and Kahn-Freund, both in their day, victims of Nazi tyranny. The

citadel to be protected was not 'non-intervention' in the abstract, but concrete autonomous trade unionism. It was a use of historical analysis (itself not yet widely understood) in order to enlarge general understanding and consciousness[70] which became part of a social movement opposing judicial and legislative threats to dismantle the legal bases of workers' autonomous organisations. Only through such an understanding could the trade unions have taken such measures as withdrawing their 'wingperson' judges from the local industrial tribunals in 1972 (80 per cent actually resigned).[71]

INDIVIDUAL RIGHTS AND REMEDIES

But in all the modern debates, the contract of individual employment itself has remained the cornerstone of positive British jurisprudence, albeit for the vast majority of workers a fictitious bargain and in reality 'a command under the guise of an agreement'.[72] Moreover, the intervention of State law alone – which is so much more important in some systems than others – is in itself not necessarily an adequate protection. That is why the ILO has long stressed that governments should collaborate with free trade unions and employers' organisations in the *implementation* of minimum labour standards in its Conventions.[73] Autonomous collective organisations are as important for enforcing or supplementing remedies as they are in the establishment of standards. Entrusted only to the hands of individual litigants, social change is slow and precarious, and a jurisdiction like the British desperately needs to adopt a suitable version of *l'action syndicale*,[74] analogies to which are found in a surprisingly large number of Community States, in some, as part of a more advanced extension of *locu standi* for interest groups.[75] To take an example from the domain where Community law has had its deepest and most positive impact in Britain; since the implementation in 1983 of the principle of equal pay for 'equal value', only 23 cases have succeeded in the British courts, all brought by individuals, some lasting six years or more [actions brought by the EOC for part-time workers have had much greater effect]. [76] Individual law suits, like individual bargaining, rarely suffice in themselves. We may recall Kahn-Freund's maxim: 'on the labour side, power is collective power'.[77] Autonomous collective power is not *necessarily* weakened by laws on the statute book – indeed, systems with constitutional or other positive legal protection sometimes leave development to 'autonomous collective bargaining' even to the extent of derogating from binding statute.[78] Non-interventionism has in reality never been the preserve of the British system. Its colours appear in different patterns in many systems. Being 'for' or 'against' it generally is rather like being on principle for or against orange.

The question of remedies is much discussed in Britain now in 'public' law, amending the earlier practice whereby 'public' sector employees have this century been largely governed by 'private' labour law (give or take a few exceptions for Crown servants).[79] Some remedies applied to an uncertain range of 'public employment' promise wider relief than the old common law or the new legislation about unfair dismissal;[80] but recent experience on the closure of coal mines illustrates the need for caution. In 1992 the British Coal Corporation and the Government announced plans for closure of 31 coal mines but after immense public protests 21 pits were reprieved. The High Court quashed the decisions as 'unlawful' because the Corporation had failed to consult with the recognised trade unions under agreed procedures, the primary duty to consult being laid down by the nationalisation statute of 1946.[81] The remedy awarded was a 'declaration of rights' stating that the decisions were unlawful, a remedy which normally cannot give rise to sanctions for disobedience (such as contempt of court).[82] Hopes ran high to save the mines from immediate closure, until in 1993 the court declared that, in respect of ten pits, the Corporation had engaged in satisfactory consultation,[83] and official statements thereafter indicated the impending closure of the others after consultation. The legal proceedings had perhaps won a short extension of the redundancy payments scheme or a few months longer employment for some miners, but to many they illustrated 'the near impotence of the legal consultation requirements'.[84] Public law failed to satisfy claims that it maintains 'dignity, liberty and self-determination' and protects citizens 'by upholding the principles of the Rule of Law which prevent the agencies of government from overstepping their delegated powers'.[85] It must be added, though, that private law could not have offered anything better. In such a situation of social disintegration legal rights, both individual and collective, had a marginal impact on workers and their families, succeeding mainly in raising expectations dashed within the year. Protection might in earlier times have lain in industrial action; but the capacity for that was low among miners who had been defeated and dubbed 'the enemy within' in the bitter strike of 1984-85.[86]

PERCEPTIONS OF THE INDIVIDUAL AND THE COLLECTIVE

Of course, such comparison as we can make does not necessarily allow us to transfer or superimpose concepts of one system to another, still less institutions which prise open the variable meanings of the 'individual' and the 'collective'.[87] There is no internationally agreed realm of the 'collective' or the 'individual'. The 'right to strike', inherently collective in Germany and available only to the trade union, vests in the individual worker in France, albeit exercised collectively. Moreover, French courts refuse to apply doctrines of collective 'fault' to affect the exercise of the constitutional right to strike, while individual fault may do so, and confine the liability of unions by what seem to outsiders a narrow doctrine of vicarious liability.[88] In Britain such liberty to strike as exists is not in the hands of individual strikers (who are invariably perceived to break their employment contracts) but is a narrow liberty for the organisers, usually the union (to which the law granted a collective protection in 1906, removing it in 1982 with an extension, after 1990 a massive extension, of vicarious liability and in 1993 the demand for a postal ballot).[89] In this context, however, the advocacy of individual bargaining is recognisable in many different legal cultures as implying the reduction or exclusion of the collective role of the trade union. The British legislation of 1980-1993 points not merely to deregulation but also to 'union exclusion' aiming

> to deny workers access to the resources of collective power, thereby commensurately increasing employers' discretion to determine the terms of the employment relationship both within and outside collective bargaining.[90]

The 'shift from collectivism towards individualism'[91] has been marked; British employers have gone gradually along the road towards 'derecognition' of unions, partly no doubt because there is no legal obligation to bargain[92] – though equally in many jurisdictions that impose no duty to bargain in their positive law employers do engage in bargaining, even if they show hostility to its extension in face of union decline.[93] The precise progress of derecognition is uncertain partly because employers often opt for partial derecognition[94] or instigate creeping derecognition[95] or secure a more 'malleable form of unionism'[96] in seeking the 'rediscovery of management prerogative',[97] all traditional aims of management made easier in an age of information technology. In contrast, when confronted by workers collectively organised in an improved market situation, management becomes 'less able than before, as it were, to fill in the "silences" in the employment contract to its own advantage'.[98]

Yet we are in a prolonged economic crisis of a system which has vanquished its enemy but not yet proved its integrity for the future, when the spectre haunting working people in Europe is unemployment. Even where there is no direct loss of employment in prospect, employees feel the weakness in their position sensing a great fear of discipline or selection for dismissal in a sudden 'restructuring' of the enterprise through the power which recession puts into the hands of management and – however civilised it may be – forces it to use. In seven of the last ten years unemployment in the Community has exceeded 10 per cent of the labour force; it now rises above 18 million and we are told that, according to the policies adopted, it may be between 5 and 30 million in the year 2000.[99]

COMMUNITY LEVEL BARGAINING AND INDIVIDUAL RESULTS?

Comparisons with British labour law may shed some light on the degree to which labour laws of Member States and the Community differ in their essential approach to issues inherent in collective bargaining or, if you like, 'social dialogue' – though since the latter appears to allow very little space for a right to strike, one may legitimately ask whether they are the same. What is crucial here is the 'normative effect' of collective agreements, the concept Sinzheimer introduced as 'a Copernican revolution of labour law'.[100] Without some shared understanding about the role of the collective and the individual here Community labour law will remain a fragmented adjunct to the integration of markets, not part of any social dimension.[101] Indeed, the Community, it seems, has come to regard collective *and* individual bargaining as acceptable methods of implementation of standards, without necessarily giving the former precedence over the latter. That appears to be the case in the Maastricht Social Protocol and Agreement (or 'Social Chapter') and curiously also in the Working Time Directive of 1993.[102] On the first, under the Social Chapter Agreement the use of collective bargaining could allow for a crippling number of individual exceptions because the second Declaration attached to the Agreement article 4(2), declares that in using the method of collective bargaining to *create* standards within the social dialogue at European level, a State is under no obligation.

to apply the agreements directly or to work out rules for their transposition, nor any obligation to amend national legislation in force to facilitate their implementation.[103]

At the request of the parties, in matters covered by Article 2 the Commission may propose to the Council that an agreement be made law by way of a Decision (binding all referred to in it, thereby moving the norms from autonomous bargained rules to the realm of regulation). Presumably even without a Decision, the standards of implementation should apply *erga omnes*, and be equivalent in all States, yet few State laws require this. When at the request of management and labour, Directives are *implemented* by collective agreements, in case that implementation does not cover all relevant workers, each Member State must have to hand laws enabling it to 'guarantee the results' of the Directive (art. 2(2), a provision which would require new legislation in Britain). The general principle has so far been that where collective agreements leave gaps in implementing Directives, the State must by legislative or administrative means ensure in those 'residual cases' that '*all* workers ... are afforded the full protection provided for in the directive'.[104] So, unless it be said they are not Community law at all, how can instruments *setting* standards, adopted under article 4(2), escape a similar principle? The Social Chapter Agreement purports to offer new methods for social measures;[105] but the viability of that method remains doubtful while there is no Community instrument incorporating the very sensible principle of the Council of Europe that labour provisions of its Social Charter may be implemented by agreements that are 'applied by law to the *great majority* of workers concerned'.[106] But even if such a principle were adopted in the British (and probably Irish) situation new law would still be required to prevent employers giving notice to renegotiate individual contracts of employment and to remove the collective standards altogether – which in those jurisdictions they could currently do, Euro-agreement or not. What emerges, of course, is that the transposition of Community-level collective agreements to national level cannot be satisfactory in Britain, Ireland and probably some other States, either for creation of standards or for implemention of Directives without changes in the law about the normative effect of such agreements, in some cases, as we shall see below, fundamental changes.

On its part, the draft Working Time Directive permits derogations not only generally by collective agreement, but also significantly exceptions (technically not 'derogations') from maximum working hours with no more than an individual worker's 'agreement', subject to the 'general principles' on safety, notification to the public authorities and a review within seven years.[107] Here protection through 'agreement' of individuals against the employer may, unless they have the backing of a strong union, be little more than a pipe dream. This is not to deny that the imagination that inspires experiment dares to imagine a different outcome in Community labour law; the subject of 'European collective agreements' has been allotted its fair share.[108] But the practical difficulties have long defied solution. They arise in part from vastly diverse national laws and institutions; these alone have led some to deny the very possibility of 'European collective bargaining'.[109] At the least, they would require special mechanisms to translate and transmit the equivalent supra-national agreed standards to each jurisdiction – with some consideration of the representativity of those who bargain at European level[110] (the concepts of 'representativity' are totally diverse in different States, and in some are in crisis). These problems, though, are not quite as novel as is sometimes believed. In 1959 Paul Durand and others proposed plans for 'European collective agreements' in coal and steel concluded according to each of the six national laws and practices but based upon 'recommendations' made by committees of delegates from unions and employers meeting at European level. 'Not uniform working conditions imposed by European collective agreements,' he proposed, 'but closely similar working conditions imposed by national collective agreements'.[111] Others have promoted wider plans on a similar basis and one agreement, for agricultural workers, was concluded in 1968;[112] but such experience speaks to the difficulties of the venture.

COMMON GROUND OR DIVERGENCE?

There is ground for thinking that the divergence in industrial relations institutions, law and practice may even have widened in Europe since then, not because – or not only because – of the idiosyncratic polices in labour legislation of the British government since 1980 (there have been seven major Acts, the most recent in 1993, with maybe more to come).[113] At a deeper level, comparative examination suggests that the very foundations of the common law system, rooted in doctrines of 'freedom of contract' but also of master's authority,[114] cannot support principles which are for some Continental systems (though in different measure) an intrinsic and necessary party of labour law architecture.

Take regulation and the effect of collective agreements. If we try to display in our scholastic laboratory a spectrum of basic principles, with European systems put, as it were, through a refracting prism for individualist and collective characteristics, British law would in most such experiments emerge in the ultra violet band – often adjacent to Ireland and sometimes Denmark – in the colours of 'voluntarism' amid a blaze of 'freedom of contract', whereas most others would come to rest in the colours of rather greater State regulation. Perhaps we might take for our first essay in refraction two principles recently described as 'basic principles of labour law':[115] first, the principle of 'inequality compensation', and secondly the principle that 'collective rights precede individual rights'. The first affords priority to the weaker party by way of employment protection rights, making that protection a central party of labour law itself, part of its very essence. Whether this is expressed in individual rights is a further question; it may include guarantees for and legal 'promotion' of their trade unions,[116] but this model of labour law aims expressly to remedy the inequality of the parties in a relation that is essentially one of subordination.[117] Other systems (common law, for example) do not; they have to add on protection as an extra. From the second principle, priority for collective rights over individual rights, derives the rule that 'deviation [from the collective standard] however greatly desired by the employer or the individual employee, is not permitted legally', where there is an attempt to vary the standard *in pejus* to the worker's disadvantage. It is here that a recent tendency towards individualism, 'the wish for decentralisation and conditions tailored to individuals', has put new pressure on the legitimacy of collective regulation.[118] Here – in the machinery of normative effect of collective agreements which was, Kahn-Freund said, 'Sinzheimer's most individual contribution to the practical realisation of the principle of autonomy in labour law'[119] – is the orange to infra-red zone shared in greater or lesser degree by most Continental systems but into which British labour law rarely enters and then only with trepidation, because it is still dominated by the individual employment contract. So too is Irish law – though the Irish legislation on rights of part-time workers demonstrates that systems with this common law base are not disabled from adding on more civilised standards for atypical workers.[120]

ERGA OMNES SINGILLATIM?

The strong version of a protective species of labour law is nowhere illustrated better than in provisions on the normative effect. In fact, British and French law form a contrast at each end of the spectrum. The Code du Travail says:

> When an employer is bound by the clauses of a collective agreement … these clauses apply to contracts of employment concluded with him, except for provisions more favourable [to the employee][121]

Even express renunciation of these benefits by an employee does not oust the principle, which applies equally to all employment contracts whether made before or after the agreement; but the worker takes the benefit of any special clause more favourable to him.[122] Once the employment in the enterprise is recognised as one covered by the relevant agreement, application of the terms is 'automatic, immediate and imperative', binding those concerned (signatories and their members being obliged to do nothing which would endanger its faithful performance).[123] French authorities state that these principles conform to the 'character of labour law' which operates a 'one way street of advantage for the individual worker'; the collective agreement becomes a source of minimum conditions on which the individual contract can only improve; the individual contract is to the collective agreement what the collective agreement is to the law.[124] These principles are different from the common law concept of 'incorporation'; indeed, if the employee ceases to be bound by the collective agreement, he can no longer claim its advantages; for its provisions are not 'incorporated' into his individual contract.[125] It is not a matter of contract but of regulation. The fundamental rules in Britain on the collective agreement and the personal employment contract stand all these principles on their heads. Here, it is individual contract all the way. The individual contract is paramount, and the common law judge regards it as obvious that

> the so-called normative effect … has to be one of incorporation into the individual contracts of employment and the extraction of a recognisable contractual intent as between *the individual employee and his employer.*[126]

The personal contract of employment determines the outcome, not the collective agreement, and one must seek incorporation in *its* express or (often) implied terms and interpret them on normal contractual principles[127] to see what is incorporated, whether from a collective agreement or any other document.[128] The union is not the agent of the workers such that its actions *ipso facto* change the terms of their employment relationships, certainly not for non-members and not even of members unless there is very clear evidence indeed.[129] Nor does the result depend upon the fact that the collective agreement is not (as it usually is not) intended to be, and therefore not, legally enforceable between the collective parties, i.e. the employer and trade union,[130] and the fact that the presumption to that effect is central to an understanding of the British position is well known in comparative labour law (perhaps too well known because the individualist ideology can produce the same doctrine of incorporation even if the collective agreement is contractually binding).[131] What is missing from British law may be called broadly 'inderogability', a term coined not to match, but merely catch the flavour of, the sophisticated Italian term *inderogabilitá* indicating the character of norms which cannot be varied by individual consent.[132] In its modern legislation no system applies a doctrine of strict 'inderogability' without exception; legislation everywhere places some limits to the normative effects of collective bargaining as inalienable minimum conditions.[133]

The individualist approach to collective agreements may of course work in favour of a particular worker. For example, if the employment contract has incorporated terms of a collective agreement, the employer cannot displace them by unilateral action, but only by evidence that meets the ordinary contractual principles of a common intention to vary or rescind the contract.[134] Even a subsequent collective agreement which appears to vary it will not do so successfully if there is inadequate evidence of its effect on individual contracts – though equally it is lawful for the employer to stipulate for a reservation in the individual contract of a right for him to change terms unilaterally.[135] That is why English courts are much concerned with the *evidence* of the individual worker's contractual conditions, usually found in the 'statement of written particulars' which since 1963 the law has obliged the employer to give to each employee.[136] A parallel obligation is now required by the EC Directive 91/533 which aims to make conditions more 'transparent' for employees working 8 hours or more (though its provisions on 'reference' to collective agreements available at the workplace seem to be less satisfactory than the earlier British provisions – which might perhaps have been retained as arguably 'more favourable to employees').[137] In a further move, British courts have developed an even more extreme individualism: even if the employment contract appears to incorporate clauses of a collective agreement, judges hold from time to time that these form no part of the employee's contract because, in the court's view, they are not 'apt for incorporation'. This may be understandable when clauses are concerned with collective issues, such as dispute procedures between union and employer,[138] but in other cases the court has regarded clauses as not 'apt to be a term in a contract' even when they relate to what seems to be workers' rights (judges have even applied this to clauses on agreed selection procedures in the event of redundancy).[139] The ambit of this judicial intervention is still unclear.

FOR WORKERS OR MEMBERS?

Of course, this account of the law does not paint a canvas of industrial reality. In such jurisdictions one finds the claim made, as in Germany, that whilst the normative effect of bargained minimum standards bites in law only for employees who are members of the contracting union and whose employer is a member of the employers' association, in practice strict agency notions give way and 'non-union members normally receive the same conditions as union members'.[140] In Italy many ingenious ways have been found to expand the legal effects beyond members of the contracting organisations;[141] and even in Britain agreements for 'members-only benefits' were found rarely even in the 1960s (today pressure for such arrangements would be unlawful).[142] This area, however, seems oddly to be of little interest to the commentators. Yet in a competitive market and in an era of individualism, would it not be of great importance in practice to know how far the law forbids unions and their hard working officials to obtain preferences for their members. A trade union's capacity to bargain for members-only is a curious footnote in most systems even when it is not offensive to basic principle, usually because it has not been the practice of trade unions to seek such bargains. The practice does entail a risk of illegality in some countries (Germany, France,[143] and Britain, Portugal, Ireland[144] and now Denmark[145]) despite its apparent legality in others (which seems to be the case in the Netherlands[146] or Belgium).[147] This could become a factor of great tactical importance to union members faced with loss of their employment.[148] Some labour movements have accepted remarkably easily the State demand that they must be more altruistic than other organisations in not seeking advantages for their needy members. A similar example of policy and culture suffused with legal technique rather than logic arises in respect of 'extension' of collective

agreements – again an invention of Sinzheimer.[149] Here the
jurisdictions line up in different teams and the split is not common-law
versus civil-law. With the exception of Britain,[150] Denmark, Italy and
(save for a weak mechanism of registration) Ireland,[151] all other
European Community jurisdictions permit, sometimes encourage, the
administrative authorites, usually after long procedures of consultation
but otherwise in very different terms, to 'extend' collective agreements
to bind new employers and workers not party to them – in Germany if
half the relevant workforce is covered, in France under two procedures
on the initiative of the Minister, in the Netherlands if the Minister
finds that a 'significant majority' of the industry's workers and
employers are already covered. But there is no 'fit' or convergence
with other classifying factors. Germany proffers a set of unitary unions
which are the beneficiaries of an organic right to strike, but a similar
right is vested in the Netherlands' mildly pluralist unions, while in
France ideologically pluralist unions with (necessarily) an individual
right to strike enjoy the benefits of extension[152] so long as they are
'representative'.[153]

All of these, with pluralist unions, have knowledge of the fruit of
'extension'. Yet in 1960 the pluralist trade unions in Italy found that
legislation to make their collective agreements binding *erga omnes*
there was declared unconstitutional.[154] The unitary unions of
Denmark and Sweden pursue the extension of negotiated terms by
increased organisation, while the competitive (*soi-disants* unified)
unions in Britain saw the fragile law that gave them a skeleton
extension machinery for minimum terms in agreements snuffed out in
1980.[155]

DIVERSE CAUSES OF DIVERGENCE

To speak of classifying factors which these divergences in labour law
systems do not 'fit' may refer to various levels or different
significancies of causation. First, the cause may lie in just that
formative period of labour law systems when the very language and
grammar of each was created by its social, rather more than its legal,
history, in European systems above all the history of its labour
movement. 'Without a smattering of that vocabulary, comparataive
conversation is impossible.'[156] The pragmatism of British unions and
with it the system of 'immunities' and 'voluntarism' in place of positive
rights, derived mainly, not from any decision of principle to play the
cards that way, but from the fact that they achieved industrial strength

(at times an apparent strength) and won collective bargaining early in a developed industrial society devoted to 'freedom of contract', before the onset of universal male franchise and long before any political party appeared as the flagbearer of the new proletariat. In every other European country trade unions were accompanied or even preceded by such political parties, a product, it has been said, of later industrialisation in the Latin countries, while in Northern Europe unions and parties 'kept approximate pace with one another'.[157] In most of these constitutional development and even the political franchise was in place and in several the tradition of State regulation (France and Germany, for example) significantly affected the formulation of regulated rights.[158] At another level, later social or legal developments may cause a system to respond with a different logic from that which influenced its formative years: take the Irish Constitution 1937, causing a partial break with the old common law.[159] Yet again, even supervenient events may stick in a system, causing even greater diversity. Take the example of the arrangement where employer, employee and union freely agree that the employer will deduct a sum from wages and pay it over to the union as the member's contributions – the 'check off', a practice some but not all trade unions encourage. Far from being an 'Anglo Saxon' practice linked to union security practices, as is sometimes alleged, it has positive legal support in many countries which have never accepted the closed shop or anything like it, such as Italy and Spain,[160] both with ideologically pluralist unionism, and it is lawful in other systems.[161] In Britain, where some 7 million union members pay subscriptions by check off, the vast majority not now affected by any form of 'closed shop', it is lawful but administrative obstacles have lately been put in its way,[162] while in Greece an authoritarian arrangement for contributions to the 'Workers' Hearth' fund – virtually a compulsory check off – has been replaced with the advent of democracy.[163] But in France, the check off is illegal, not because of any draconian logic imposed by freedom in ideologically pluralist unions (Italy and Spain show the contrary) but as the result of traumatic industrial and legal battles, especially attempts by the CGT to maintain a union monopoly in the Paris newspaper industry which gave rise to the Law of 27 April 1956[164] rendering the check off illegal along with other union security practices, while union rights to collect subscriptions within the enterprise were later improved.[165]

Such divergencies – some profound, some adventitious – are the legal dimension of tendencies in industrial relations which rebut the once fashionable predictions of 'convergence towards a pluralist system', in place of which industrial sociologists have found 'divergence in modes of institutional regulation in advanced Western societies'.[166] The industrial pluralists of the 1960s, notably Dunlop and Clark Kerr, in describing the 'post-industrial society', were confident that industrial systems would converge as new technology with its 'standardising tendencies' was developed and exchanged, and as the industrial actors negotiated within a 'web of rules ... more explicit and formally constituted in the course of industrialisation'.[167] This would rest largely on an élite in management and unions, the former recognisably similar to the technocracy envisaged by Berle and Means, who assumed wrongly that 'managerial firms will acquiesce readily to social pressures or needs'.[168] In this vision of a 'mature system' of industrial pluralism, institutionalised mutual recognition of the differing goals of management and unions carried 'implied recognition in principle of management's right to manage',[169] and has made modern pluralists more than average doubtful of schemes for cooperation or worker participation.[170] Other theoreticians even foresaw the 'end of ideology'.[171]

FREEDOM OF ASSOCIATION: COMMUNITY PROTECTION?

Social issues not yet confronted by the policies, albeit often by the rhetoric, of the Community include the continuing, perhaps widening, disparities in the various jurisdictions of Member States' labour relations laws and practices, to which *renvoi* often has to be made because Community law refers to national law or practice – and this despite the advent of multinational employers. At best it would here be 'unwise to predict any strong convergence',[172] even if divergencies in the law are said to disturb the market for investors, e.g. in dismissal law.[173] Indeed, given the varieties of industrial relations, and especially trade union, structures, diversities are likely to persist,[174] some of them even sanctified by the holy water of 'subsidiarity' – and not merely the kaleidoscope of labour relations law and practice, but also the legal offspring of varied State interventions on employment and welfare, structures dependent as much on international market links or the make-up and segmentation of the labour force as on narrower industrial relations factors.[175] More generally, a profound change in Community policy would be required in order to release the 'social dimension' from the grip which its policies (other than sex equality)[176] suffer from the hegemony of market integration. It has not escaped attention that Community legislation which appears to be aimed at the welfare of workers, turns out on inspection to be as much, if not more, concerned with market integration.[177]

The Commission has been particularly coy in its failure to examine the concrete situation in Member States concerning freedom of association, despite its formal adherence to ILO principles.[178] Concepts of subsidiarity cannot excuse the blind eye cast by the Commission over contraventions of workers' fundamental rights.[179] Indeed, the Commission's energy in regard to the ILO has been directed more to its claim that the Community has exclusive competence in many areas to represent Member States at the ILO, which has set off a long tripartite wrangle, energy which might have been better expended in furthering the enforcement of ILO standards rather than Byzantine questions of international status.[180] It is not as if the Community does not recognise ILO standards of 'trade union freedom'. The 'inspiration' of the ILO was recorded in the Social Charter of 1989, and more specifically, the same fundamental liberty was the basis of decisions of the Court holding that trade unions of which Community employees were members enjoy trade union rights, including the capacity to sue or be sued, citing 'general principles of labour law' and 'the freedom of trade union activity' which had also been recognised by Community staff regulations.[181] In reliance on that analysis, the Court held that no penalty could be imposed on trade union representatives who wished to take time off for their duties.[182] Such ground rules should set equivalent standards on collective liberties framed in ILO minima throughout the Community. The problem is not confined to Britain and countries which have a proud record of not deviating from these standards (notably France and Italy) may think it is time that all other Member States should be required to meet them. In fact, a satisfactory framework of transnational industrial relations cannot flourish if any national standard on freedom of association is seriously defective.[183] Trade union freedoms are not an optional extra in plans for workers' rights on consultation and information or in power sharing schemes for workers' representatives within a 'social dialogue'.[184] Community guarantees of fundamental freedoms would give no offence to subsidiarity nor to those States that already enforce them. The Commission, however, erred in 1989 by stating that the right to freedom of association (with its concomitant right to strike) is already fully enjoyed in all Member States.[185] National laws now face ever more severe difficulties in a world of transnational industrial relations.[186] and the proposed 'European level' works councils are, in that setting, weaklings compared with the councils created by Sinzheimer's article 165 in the Weimar Constitution – 'the show piece of the Republic'.[187] Indeed, the new Commission budget item offering finance for meetings and activities of workers' representatives in transnational enterprises may turn out to be more important – and more popular (except no doubt for those who are refused a grant). But to build a pattern of consultation between 'social partners' without adequate and transparent inquiry into – and express criteria on – the autonomy and representativity of highly diverse national organisations on the invitation list, is a procedure defensible neither intellectually nor pragmatically. The trade unions involved should also reflect that, quite apart from issues of principle, the power to send invitations to the dialogue table is in the hands of the Commission, with its associated power to dispense moneys for approved meetings.[188]

TRANSNATIONAL REALITIES

Post industrial pluralism demanded freedom of association, but its predictive theses – the 'inner logic of industrialisation' and with it the 'withering away of the strike' – suffered severe blows, not least from empirical work doubting the automatic 'embourgeoisement of the working class'.[189] The question remained and remains, of course, as to the future 'identity incentives' of workers' movements.[190] As Crouch writes: '[Trade] unions may have a long-term future, but do union movements?'[191] Here the advance of the multinational and 'transnational' enterprise has outflanked the analysis completely, leading to an international division of labour and global markets. Few foresaw in the 1960s that three decades later these networks would dominate the world economy with a 'globalisation of production' and their own brand of capital concentration.[192] That growth, facilitated by information technology, has enfeebled both positive law and autonomous trade unionism at national level and has led workers' representatives to the ILO to propose that access to world trade through GATT should be conditional upon adherence to 'social clauses' on freedom of association and other minimum ILO labour standards.[193] One may ask what the response of the Community is to that challenge.

So far the main international instruments aiming to provide countervailing power to transnational employers are in two Codes, the International Labour Organisation's (ILO) *Tripartite Declaration of*

Principles on Multinationals and Social Policy (first adopted in 1977 and applied primarily through a special Committee) and the *Guideline on Employment and Industrial Relations* (1976, now 1992) of the Organisation for Economic Co-operation and Development (OECD) which also deals with labour relations, though the primary concern of the OECD is investment.[194] Both call upon multinational enterprises to observe basic employment standards, including consultation, and to some extent negotiation, with autonomous representatives of employees. More, the Declaration seeks the observance of fundamental rights of labour and of a wide range of ILO Conventions. But, not surprisingly, in neither do we find a claim to effective limitation of the power of the multinational enterprise to transfer capital or resources and thereby evade inconvenient local labour standards or costs (employees are rarely, if ever, given a right in law to have the enterprise kept *in situ* or in being as it is).[195] Frequently the Codes can do little more – again, understandably – than ask for terms 'not less favourable than those offered by comparable employers in the host country concerned.'[196] Indeed the need to build from the bottom is well illustrated by the OECD's elementary requirement that 'negotiations should take place in a language understood by both sides'.[197] There may be difficulty, too, in ascertaining which legal rules apply to employees, for example mobile transfrontier employees or the directorial managers at headquarters who operate under a common code, who may enjoy not a contract but almost an autonomous status.[198] The multinational employer may operate intra-firm welfare which obtains benefits from normal social insurance, may play one law or one labour market or one group of employees off against another, may according to its production and marketing patterns construct transnational consultation processes so as to need no significant change in management practice and, if vigilant, may ensure that its employees, individually and collectively, will themselves oppose the entry into the enterprise of an autonomous union (IBM is a famous example).[199] At a lower level, the problems of contractors 'posting' workers across frontiers has led to special Community legislation – itself difficult to enforce in jurisdictions which do not normally give collective agreements or arbitration awards an *erga omnes* effect.[200] Beyond that the Community has shown little will or capability to enforce ILO minimum employment standards.[201] Multinationals have not led to the 'homogenisation of everything' in a post-industrial world, but rather to 'global webs' in which individual employees can more easily be controlled and organised by powerful mobile employers. From the common genetic code, the single helix of international capital, a 'plurality' of establishments, with diverse products, markets and services, though often recognisably national styles of management, utilises powerful methods of communication with employees,[202] a power yet to be effectively addressed by Community or trade union policies.

That is the setting which highlights the modern call for priority of individual rights and interests – even to speculation by some whether 'particularistic' demands may upset regulatory mechanisms as stable as German co-determination.[203] In this we need to identify separately what the employer gains by introduction of new types of *individual* rights or interests, on a more sophisticated footing than the conventional calculation of the 'union mark up'.[204] He may be very willing to exchange a law which compensates in money the individual worker for arbitrary treatment for a union which has rights to fight for the individual at work. Apart from workers' 'particularistic' demands at work (including now security of pensions after working life)[205] we find that systems are adapting to the new individualism in a variety of ways. For some, like the British, New Zealand or American and in part Australian, it is, as we have seen, an opportunity to disestablish collectivism, roll back the frontiers of workers' collective organisation, fragment employment protection laws and dismantle machineries of corporatist consensus in the name of 'competitiveness', even to the point of restricting the scope of consensual, tripartite machinery, such as ACAS in Britain.[206]

NEW TRIM FOR THE COLLECTIVE?

Conversely, some systems which enjoy entrenched individual rights, whether or not in a Constitution, have placed reliance upon them in attempts to reformulate conditions for the exercise of collective rights, precisely because this is seen as a way to move to a new social balance. A recent example is the Italian law of 1990 on strikes in essential services, passed in face of the waves of strikes by unions and even more by the COBAS.[207] The Law sets up a range of remedial steps in an attempt to prevent or cut short such strikes (not least in schools and transport), requiring notice of the strike action, initially ten days. (This is a point where we may notice how different philosophies produce similar results: the British Acts of 1984-93 require seven-day notices from a union about the obligatory ballot and the strike action).[208] The Italian Law contains a great variety of enforcement procedures, including executive orders by the Prefect requiring maintenance of a minimum service (which are still much used) and disciplinary sanctions and administrative fines against employees and employers. Trade unions, however, are encouraged to make collective agreements on essential services; these have proved in some sectors to be central to the implementation of the Law; procedures and details of definition for 'essential minimum services' have been specially negotiated in many sectors, as well as in self-regulating Codes (long common in Italy). But unions which contravene the new rules may be suspended from the bargaining table and lose their right to check off for two months (again it is noteworthy that the British Act of 1993 regulates the check off). An adventurous step was the establishment of a 'Committee of Guarantee' (nine Professors) which has a quiver full of powers, from conciliation to proposals for awards, operating a 'complex mechanism' of geared sanctions so as to measure the deterrent effect and retain a base 'above all in the self-regulation of the parties to industrial conflict'.[209] The new Law has been described as 'an extreme case of pluralistic regulation'.[210] It strikes the eye, however, as massive intervention to observers who have previously recognised the non-interventionist character of Italian law in collective labour relations. Domestic authorities, though, see it as justified in the 'so-called post-industrial society' by the 'tertiarization of conflict', even referring to Kahn-Freund's ultimate image of the strike as 'an internecine civil war' among workers[211] (an analogy perhaps valid only if the Italian context is that of the Barcelona 'civil war' between the Trotskyite POUM and the Republican Communists which helped the Fascists to seize Spain).[212] Already some success is claimed for the Law; the new regulations arose, it is said, from pressure 'inside the labour movement itself', and have reduced the number of strikes among members and non-members of unions.[213] These limitations on the exercise of the constitutional right to strike (vested in the individual, but exercisable collectively) – it would be 'naive or misleading' to underestimate the way the Law aims 'to restrict the scope of the right to strike'[214] – apply to areas described by reference to constitutional rights of the *individual*. Essential services are therefore defined by reference to safeguarding the enjoyment of personal rights protected by the Constitution, broadly life, health, liberty, safety, freedom of movement, social security, education and communication. Thirty five specific areas are then added (from public health to urban refuse collection and guardians of cultural possessions, to transport, schools and post and telecommunications; the list is not exclusive – some banking services are within, others outside the definition in the view of the Commission).[215] The object is said to be creation of reflexive rules interacting with the persons involved.[216] The Law itself speaks of the right of the Prefect or Minister, after reference to the Commission and talks with the unions and employers 'where possible', to make an Ordinance, ordering that minimum services be maintained, under which daily fines can eventually be imposed on workers, when grave damage is imminent to *personal rights* of others protected by the Constitution.[217] It is clear that others might use this technique to render the lawful exercise of the right to strike more difficult, if not impossible.[218] From a different perspective, it is noteworthy that the need for this new 'balance' between collective and individual interests arose when it did – part of an attempt at re-ordering in which the subsequent, tripartite 'Protocol on Incomes Policy and Employment, Bargaining Order, Labour Policies and Support for the Productive System' was also a part.[219]

THE PRIVACY OF THE INDIVIDUAL WORKER

But in this same period, some systems of labour law have relaunched the quest for protection of the individual worker in a different direction, one which once might have been called 'privacy' – 'an instance of the right of the individual to be let alone'[220] – but now is usually given a more complex range in an information society.[221] Few systems other than those that tolerate conditions of slavery envisage that in the work-wage bargain the employee offers to the employer with his labour power control over his entire private life, thereby giving up his civil liberties to the master. It has long been thought that today there is a

> general principle concerning the non-relevance of private affairs to the establishment, performance and termination of the employment relationship.[222]

In some instances, as with the Italian Workers' Statute 1970 and French constitutional principles now supplemented by legislation of 1922 plus protection found in the Civil Code for 'private life', principles of non-discrimination and privacy are applied to hiring.[223] An influential report by Gérard Lyon-Caen recently declared that at work the worker has become subject to subordination only for the execution of the work, and even in that execution he still cannot 'consent to the surrender of his liberty'; his personal liberties are 'inalienable'.[224] This tendency is in line with ILO Conventions which aim to outlaw discrimination in employment based on race, colour, sex, religion, political opinion, national extraction or social origin.[225] But there is diversity in the implementation of such standards even among European systems. In some they relate to enforceable standards in a Constitution which proclaims 'human dignity' and looks to the removal of obstacles to equality, liberty and the 'full development of the human person'.[226] 'Hiring no longer absorbs the entire personality of the worker'.[227] Elsewhere, one finds these standards supplemented by the European Convention on Human Rights, such as freedom of expression, in support of remedies against dismissal.[228] There is, too, a plethora of international instruments designed to uphold fundamental human rights in employment most of which have had less influence on positive labour law: for example, the UN Universal Declaration of Human Rights 1948, the two UN Covenants of 1966, and the Council of Europe Social Charter 1961. While the Conventions of the ILO have had stronger effects, their structures have not kept pace with new forms of invasion of private life; nor have all European States developed such laws to maturity; and Community law itself knows little of the problem.[229] British labour law confines protection of the employee to a relatively narrow ambit, permitting, for example, a refusal to hire by reason of personal details or opinions discovered by special inquiry,[230] and even legalising dismissals by reasons of discovery of a history of medical illness which had not marred performance of the job, or of possession of cannabis in a park after work, or of mere personal sexual orientation.[231] The burden on the employer is merely to demonstrate that management acted, not fairly, but within the 'range of reasonable responses'.[232] Protection in France, building on the civil law protection of private life, granted the employer the right to discipline where the employee's private characteristics cause disturbance at work, but not otherwise.[233] To this, we shall see, a Law of 1992 now adds a restriction on his enquiries to those having 'a direct and necessary link' with the work or the worker's qualifications.[234] The distance between the Members States' systems is illustrated, too, by the provisions in the Italian Workers' Statute which as early as 1970 not only protected workers' private opinions at work but made it unlawful for the employer to carry out inquiries, before the hiring or during the employment, 'about the worker's political, religious or trade union opinions or about any facts not relevant to the assessment of the worker's aptitude for his employment',[235] a provision at times applied strictly by the courts.[236] All European workers have a private life but some are much more private than others.

DATA-PROTECTION FOR WORKERS?

It is perhaps surprising in an age of information technology, when new protections are necessary against the compilation and use of computerised personal information, that Italy remains one of the few Western European jurisdictions which does not have a special law directed at data protection. One of the reasons is undoubtedly found in the existence of the Workers' Statute of 1970, which contained provisions making unlawful the use of 'audio-visual and similar equipment for supervising and controlling workers at a distance' (where these are necessary for safety or for the work itself they can be installed only by agreement with the plant union body or if the Inspector agrees). These provisions have been variously applied by the courts as complainants have tried to bring within them new methods of worker-control by management.[237] Elsewhere, legislation specific to data protection has been passed, in some cases added to controls over methods of surveillance of workers (as in Germany), in others allowing for a flexible if stern régime.[238] Simitis has laid out the requirements for the regulation of practices which can amount to closer monitoring and control than ever before, employers' methods which have become 'astonishingly similar' everywhere, namely (a) recognition of the unique nature of personal data, (b) specification of the purposes for which data will be used, (c) regular updating of the protection regulations, and (d) an independent authority.[239] Lyon-Caen trenchantly formulates the primary requirement as follows:

> An individual has the right to know *who* collects the data on him, for what *purpose*, in what *context* and for *how long*.[240]

An independent authority to regulate data processing is now a feature of many laws, for example the *Commission Nationale de l'Informatique et des Libertés* in France, the Data Protection Registrar in Britain.[241] The activities of the data protection authorities, together with authoritative studies, public appeals and resolutions of legislatures, have 'greatly influenced the retrieval of employee data' and restricted its use, but:

More than ever [employers] consider that systematically collected, continuously updated information on employees is an elementary condition for rational planning and successful monitoring of personnel.[242]

New developments – novel magnetic devices attached to workers or camera videos which control working behaviour and process the information or mechanisms much more difficult to detect – are likely to escape from the static grip of legal restraint unless there is effective on-the-spot inspection;[243] and the advent of telework or other 'distance-work' now increases the possibility of distance-control.[244] Some legislation, however, has overlooked rather elementary precautions. The British Act of 1984, for example, incorporates basic principles which require personal data to be acquired 'fairly and lawfully', for specified purposes, not excessive to the purpose, accurate and up to date and open to access and correction by the individual concerned.[245] So far, so good. Unhappily, it appears to have made no provision on 'enforced subject access', the practice whereby an employer or prospective employer of a worker whose record is stored on computer records, including criminal police records, requires him to exercise his right of access to them in order to obtain the information so that the employer can then see it.[246] Although this coercion of the worker to use his or her rights to the benefit only of the employer has been repeatedly criticised, the Data Protection Registrar was compelled to report yet again in 1993 that this 'misuse of rights given to individuals' under the Act had continued; but he failed to convince the Government on the need to stop it.[247] His Report also shows that there is a growing number of enforced subject access requests to both the police and other authorities. Moreover, for the year 1992-93 the number of prospective employers (other than those specially concerned with the welfare of children, taxis or national security) who obtained from the police information from (mainly) computerised criminal records about applicants for employment – which the applicants could, it seems, neither see nor answer – was estimated at 150,000.[248] A British consultation document recognises that there is a problem about enforced subject access but suggests that applicants for jobs might be 'required by a prospective employer to obtain from the police a note of any criminal record relating to them'. If they preferred not to tell the employer, it went on, then they might 'effectively rule themselves out of contention for particular forms of employment' – scarcely a generous interpretation of the civil liberties of employees.[249]

In an era of multinational firms and theoretically free movement of workers, 'data processing is also internationalised'.[250] This makes the enforcement of control doubly difficult. Administrative practice is, as usual, important apart from specific laws on data protection. Some States, for example, operate a system of 'good conduct' or 'no convictions' certificates, usually obtained from the police or other authorities.[251] Are these, one wonders, a modern version of the *livret* or *Arbeitsbüch*?[252] One might think that free movement of workers is inhibited by such national practices. In face of these transnational problems, the Council of Europe adopted a Convention in 1981 and a Recommendation in 1989, recommending national legislation for the protection of data subjects in the employment relationship.[253] It is not yet clear whether the proposed Directive of the European Community on data protection will effectively ban such practices as 'enforced subject access'. Its scope is wide – it would cover manually recorded data as well as computerised information – and it provides for subject access, though it also allows wide exceptions to that right based upon national security, defence, public safety, criminal proceedings, any 'paramount' State economic interest, public authority monitoring activities, and equivalent rights of other persons.[254] It is based, as the Preamble repeatedly makes clear, upon the twin planks of, first, the 'fundamental rights and freedoms of individuals, notably the right of privacy',[255] and secondly, economic needs for a 'cross-border flow of personal data necessary for the expansion of international trade.' But these two foundations are directed primarily at the employer and only then (for what he can make of it) at the individual worker. The draft omits the crucial provision in the Council of Europe's Recommendation to the effect not only that the individual employee must have adequate access to data and opportunity for rectification, but procedures should be agreed between an employer and *the employeees' representatives* concerning the introduction and operation of information retrieval systems, rights of access and correction, the purposes of the data collection, any risks to the employee's privacy and personal dignity and any third parties to whom information is regularly communicated.

COLLECTIVE PROTECTION OF THE INDIVIDUAL

It is only if the collective mechanisms for implementing worker' rights are kept on the agenda that the individual, as these examples show, can be adequately protected. That is not to say that collective agreements, desirable as they may be, could operate effectively on such matters without an adequate base of legislation. But collective bargaining has never anywhere operated free from some legislative framework – in its most 'abstentionist' mode British law, for example, never operated with 'no law on industrial relations', as less than well informed commentators often put it. Take the mass of factory and other legislation in the shadow of which voluntary labour relations flowered. Where European systems have differed *inter se* is in the location and culture of legislation and the 'mix' of statutory and negotiated norms. The differences have new relevance, but less justification, now in regard to defence of workers' human rights. The central requirement is to spell out the logic of article 87(1)(6) of the German Works Constitution Act 1972, which gives powers of co-determination to the works council over the introduction and use of devices for monitoring employees' performance or behaviour. Community plans for 'Euro-level' works councils have long included consultative functions for such a body on matters likely to have 'serious consequences for the interests of the employees', but it is not entirely clear how far this would go in limiting management's powers to introduce a new technology of control or plans to acquire and use information.[256] Legislation on data protection which omits the trade union dimension in practice torpedoes the individual rights of the ordinary worker; for the employer can then unilaterally computerise the business and (rather like Mr Boulwar in take-it-or-leave-it 'collective bargaining')[257] present his 'objective' decisions (say, for lay offs) as in reality the only possible plan. As Simitis puts it: 'The computer generated list is the end of all dialogue'.[258] Lacking any such rights as those of the German works council, British workers have already tried to use their limited rights of industrial action to struggle against the employer's ability to use the new information technology to their disadvantage, for example where the employer replaced the customary LIFO principle ('last in first out') on redundancy dismissals by a new points system, drawn from – in a sense 'individualised' from – data about each employee (their attendance, disciplinary record, performance assessment, personal reliability and on on).[259] It is these developments which have led to the view that what the individual needs most of all is protection from 'colonisation' of his behaviour by law and even collective agreements, from both State *and* trade unions.[260] Neither the 'general needs of society', it is said, nor the 'general interest' of workers will 'tolerate alternatives'; therefore the individual must be preserved for the enjoyment of new possibilities for his or her self-realisation as an individual person.[261] Even if in the protection of such individual interests, both law and unions have their place, the 'renewal' of man requires the 'radical renunciation of all attempts by the state or corporatists to instrumentalise and colonise the individual workers'.[262]

This view may be thought a rather idealised conception of the individual worker who must, it seems, find the strength to resist 'colonisation' without State law or collective unions. Yet the essence of the employment problem is subordination, the very weakness of the individual worker. There is a different perspective of the most recent French statute on the subject, the remarkable Law of 1992, based on the report by Gérard Lyon-Caen which, like the German law, suggests that the worker needs both law and union. More, at the very 'heart of the subject' there is proposed a reconsideration of the individual employment relationship itself:

> The field is open for an evolution in the link of subordination. But it is also open to a better evaluation of what exactly is exchanged in the contract of employment, what is stipulated for by the employer and what is promised by the employee.[263]

The data protection problem is here put into proper context for employment law: just what part of his private life does the worker sell with his labour power? The Law of 1992 includes provision for protection of a worker at the time of recruitment and during the employment contract, with further strengthening of protections for personal liberty within the enterprise.[264] First, in recruitment obligatory procedures are required and the information demanded of an applicant may seek only to reveal his capacity for the job and his occupational qualifications, not his morality or private life as such. The information must have

> a direct and necessary link with the relevant work or with evaluation of occupational qualifications.

In return, the candidate for employment must answer permissible questions 'in good faith', but to invalid questions he may refuse to answer or (it seems) even give a false answer. The applicant must be told about techniques used to evaluate him for recruitment; these must be pertinent and the results kept confidential; nor may personal data be collected in advance by methods not brought to his notice.[265] Parallel protections are extended to the employee already hired. Moreover the works council must be notified of such methods before they are utilised. Secondly, before they are introduced into the workplace, the employer must inform the works council of a decision to instal automated management systems and techniques 'and consult it on techniques permitting control of workers' activities' (which covers computerised surveillance). The Law goes further. No restrictions may be imposed on personal rights or personal or collective liberties that are not justified by the nature of the job or not proportional to the purpose. Further, any invasion of these rights and liberties may give rise to an immediate claim by, not only the employee, but also the elected *délégué du personnel* whom the employer must meet without delay. If the employer denies the contravention, the employee or (if the employee does not object in writing) the *délégué* may commence interlocutory proceedings. The court may order the cessation of the contravention with the final sanction of a fine which is here payable to the public Treasury.[266] It is this element of a collective character, the elected *délégué* joined in the defence of individual interests, which marks the 1992 Law as one which attempts to preserve a very real protection for the individual even in the workplace.

> The employee is not merely a 'creature of work'. Respect must be paid to his or her intimate identity.[267]

The protection of an individual private identity and of dignity at work requires recognition that the individual is a member of the work group. The victories won for the unlawfulness of sexual harassment at work have been laudable and remarkable extensions of protection and equality; but there are many other dimensions of dignity as yet unprotected in Member State jurisdictions. These new moves to defend workers' dignity come at a time when convention demands that they be ever more flexible and submissive, challenging programmes for the future of labour law – at Community as well as at domestic level. National systems confronting this demand through traditional legal remedies backed by collective bargaining in different styles and proportions must allow too the exercise of imagination for new mechanisms;[268] and the task of Community law is to ensure that the space for that is adequate and equivalent, through protection both individual (in an improved Data Protection Directive, for example) and collective (not least by guaranteeing freedom of association and other trade union freedoms at ILO standard). It is because the worker needs individual protection that the collective apparatus provided by autonomous trade unions is crucial, not only in negotiation and consultation with the employer but, since law is not self-executing, in the general support and enforcement which unions provide of legal standards. Union members have a right to no less; even the British courts have accepted that membership of a trade union gives the member not merely possession of a union card, but the right to assistance from a union official:

> the activities of a trade union officer in negotiating and elucidating terms of employment are, to use a prayer book expression, the outward and visible manifestation of trade union membership.[269]

The Webbs' belief that the employer would inevitably be compelled to abandon individual bargaining was misplaced partly because at that time, we can now see, the employer was relatively weak. Now that the employer has in his hands an unprecedented armour of weapons for control – information technology backed by unemployment – and employers in many markets have begun to seek individuated employment relations once more, the individual worker has need of the collective shield as never before. If we are to recover the perspective of seeking steps towards 'emancipating the flexible employment contract from its economic subordination',[270] we shall have need of legal and social initiatives at both collective and individual level. To Sinzheimer the connection was crucial. Collective bargaining and autonomous trade unions stood at the heart of democratic labour law; even his favoured works councils were not to trespass on trade unions' functions.[271] But the final purpose was always equally clear. Workers are persons, not things; that was the 'fundamental idea' running through his proposals. And that, he insisted,

> means treating the worker no longer as part of a machine, regarded merely as eyes and hands; now at last workers are to take on full human dignity and expand the range of their human relationships.[272]

NOTES

1. *Die Krisis des Arbeitsrechts* (1933: a paper to celebrate the founding of the journal *Arbeitsrecht*; taken here from *La crisi del diritto del lavoro*, in G. Arrigo and G. Vardaro (eds.), *Laboratorio Weimar* (1982) 85-6). On how far Sinzheimer was here a Marxist, see F. Mestitz 1989, no. 4 Lav. Dir.

661-76 and R. Erd 1989, 44 Giorn. DLRI, 643-55. Most British students come to Sinzheimer through O. Kahn-Freund's lecture, 'Hugo Sinzheimer 1875-1945' (1976), now in R. Lewis and J. Clark (eds.), *Labour Law and Politics in the Weimar Republic* (1981); also Wedderburn, R. Lewis and J. Clark (eds.) *Labour Law and Industrial Relations* (1983) 90-102, on Sinzheimer's effect on Kahn-Freund.

2. G. Giugni, '*Il dirrito del lavoro negli anni 80*' 1982, 15 Giorn. DLRI 373, 408 (now *Lavoro leggi contratti*, 1989, 334). On legal styles suiting corporatist consensus, see Wedderburn (1991) 54 MLR 1, 10-17.

3. See S. Simitis in his review of the *Loi Chapelier* (1990) 48 Giorn. DLRI 743, 764-7, citing J. Habermas, *Nachmetaphysisches Denken* (1988) 179, 223ff. The translation is sometimes rendered as 'colonisation', n. 261, below.

4. United Nations Centre for Trade and Development (UNCTD), *World Investment Report 1993; Transnational Corporations and Integrated International Production* (1993); and see J. Dunning, *Multinational Enterprises and the Global Economy* (1993) 128-33; see below n. 192ff.

5. On Britain, see ILO Committee of Experts Reports for 1989, and 1990-1992, see too below notes 179-186; K. Ewing, *Britain and the ILO* (Institute of Employment Rights, 2nd ed. 1994); generally, W.B. Creighton, 'An ILO Perspective', R. Trask (ed.) *Trade Unions in a Single Market* (1992).

6. S. and B. Webb, *Industrial Democracy* (1897, 1914 ed.) 842.

7. And the Council of Europe *Social Charter* 1961, art. 5; see W.B. Creighton and K.Ewing, *op.cit.*, n. 5 above; D. Brown and A. McColgan, 'UK Employment Law and the ILO' (1992) 21 ILJ 265; J. Hendy, *A Law Unto Themselves: Conservative Employment Laws* (1993, 3rd ed. Institute of Employment Rights) Chap. 7.

8. See s. 13 Trade Union Reform and Employment Rights Act 1993, (TURER) amending s. 148, Trade Union and Labour Relations (Consolidation) Act 1992 (TULRCA); see too on s. 14, B. Simpson (1993) 22 ILJ 181; also S. Auerbach, *Derecognition and Personal Contracts: Fighting Tactics and the Law* (1993, Institute of Employment Rights). The section was introduced to nullify Court of Appeal decisions holding that 'persuading employees to give up trade union representation' by enhanced pay and conditions, given as 'douceurs' to the non-unionists, was unlawful under ss. 146-148, first introduced in 1975: *Wilson v Associated Newspapers; Palmer v Associated British Ports* [1993] IRLR 336, CA [on appeal to HL].

9. *Britain the Preferred Location: An Introduction for Investors* (1993 Dept. of Trade and Industry) 6; compare S. Deakin and F. Wilkinson, *The Economics of Employment Rights* (1991 Institute of Employment Rights). The Government programme for 1993-94 includes legislation to sweep away many hundreds of 'unnecessary' regulations.

10. On State reforms of employment-at-will: T. St Antoine, 'A Seed Germinates', Nebraska LR 67 (1988); on the uncertain exceptions: H. Winterbauer, 'Wrongful Discharge in Violation of Public Policy', Ind. Relns Law Jo. (1993) 386; L. Blades, 'Employment at Will v Individual Freedom' 67 Col. L.Rev. 1404 (1967). The doctrine guarantees unilateral management

discretion: P. Selznick, *Law, Society and Industrial Justice* (1969) 135.

11. For example, R. Epstein, 'In Defense of the Contract at Will' 61 Univ. Chi. L.Rev. 947-82 (1984).

12. See generally C. Craver, *Can Unions Survive?* (1993) 34-51, 91-123, to which I am much indebted.

13. C. Craver, *op.cit.*, 73; see too, P. Weiler, 'Promises to Keep; Securing Workers' Rights to Organisation', 96 Harv. L.Rev. 1778-81 (1983); and on the use by management of schemes for 'cooperation': W. McLeod, 'Labor-Management Cooperation: Competing Visions and Labor's Challenge' 12 IRLJ. 233 (1990); on union avoidance, D. Meyer and W. Cooke (1993) 31 BJIR 531-552.

14. See N. Oliver and B. Wilkinson, *The Japanization of British Industry* (1992, 2nd ed. 'Human Resource Management in Action') Chaps. 10, 11.

15. New Zealand Employment Contracts Act 1991; the individual contract may not escape the impact of a 'collective contract': s. 19; this is not in itself an individuating characteristic (see below note 121 on the *Code du Travail*). But collective contracts may be made directly with 'all of the employees' or not at all, as the employer chooses: s. 20(1)(2), and the thrust of the Act is towards individualist employment relations. See too P. Brook, *Freedom at Work: Reforming Labour Law in New Zealand* (1990), on the transfer from compulsory arbitration.

16. R. Mitchell, *Note on the Employee Relations Act 1992 (Victoria)* (Working Paper 70, Dept. Management and Industrial Relations, Univ. Melbourne, 1993) 25.

17. W.B. Creighton, 'Employee Agreements and Conditions of Employment Under Employee Relations Act 1992 (Vic.)' (1993) 6 AJLL 140, 158, commenting that many workers will seek to 'escape' into the Federal system of labour law (I am much indebted to him on the Australian position). Liberty to strike is even more severely restricted than is usual under State law, apparently with criminal sanctions: M. Pittard (1993) 6 Aus. JLL 159. For Australian State and Federal systems, see W.B. Creighton and A. Stewart, *Labour Law: An Introduction* (1990) Chap. 3; on changing policies in industrial relations, K. Hancock and D. Rawson (1993) 31 BJIR 489-514 [on the Industrial Relations Reform Act 1993, see (1994) 7 Aus. JLL, no. 2].

18. H. Collins, 'Organization and the Limits of Contract', Chap. 5 in J. McCahery, S. Picciotto and C. Scott, *Corporate Control and Accountability* (1993) 99, understandably criticising the 'implicit contract' analysed by Professor K. Stone, *ibid.*, Chap. 4 'Labour Markets, Employment Contracts and Corporate Change' – the workers 'can police their implicit contracts by unionizing', p. 84, quoting O. Williamson, *The Economic Institutions of Capitalism* (1985). One can appreciate Collins' 'agnosticism' about the utility of this model.

19. *People Jobs and Opportunity* (UK White Paper Cm. 1810 Feb 1992) paras. 1.15, 4.2-4.6.

20. See W. Brown, 'The Contraction of Collective Bargaining in Britain' (1993) 31 BJIR 189; N. Millward, M. Stevens, D. Smart, W. Hawes, *Workplace Industrial Relations in Transition* (1992).

21. In particular, *Law Legislation and Liberty* (Vols. I, II, and III 1979) and

The Constitution of Liberty (1960); see on Hayek and the 1980s legislation: Wedderburn, 'Freedom of Association and Philosophies of Labour Law' (1989) 18 ILJ 1 (now also in *Employment Rights in Britain and Europe* (1991) Chap. 8). See too, U. Mückenberger and S. Deakin, 'From deregulation to a European floor of rights' (1989) 3 ZIAS (Zeitschrift für ausländisches und internationales Arbeits-und Sozialrecht) 153, esp. 171-5 on Hayek.

22. For example, J. Garello and B. Lemennicier, *Cinq Questions sur les Syndicats* (1990), on which see J. Dupeyroux, '*Les néo-liberaux et les syndicats*' D. Soc. 1991, 1; compare, Kronberg Kreis, *Mehr Markt schafft Wohlstand* (1987); B. Rüthers, *Die offene Arbeitsgesellschaft* (1986); U. Mückenberger and S. Deakin *op.cit.*, 21 above, 162-183.

23. Compare K. Ewing, in C. Graham and T. Prosser, *Waiving the Rules: The Constitution under Thatcherism* (1988) 142-6. See too the useful reviews by K. Miller and M. Steele, 'Employment Legislation – Thatcher and After' (1993) 24 *IRJ* 211; and P. Fosh, H. Morris, R. Martin, P. Smith, R. Undy, 'Politics, Pragmatism and Ideology; the Wellsprings of Conservative Union Legislation' (1993) 22 ILJ 14.

24. See Wedderburn *op.cit.*, n. 21, at 15; and Wedderburn, R. Lewis and J. Clark (eds.), *Labour Law and Industrial Relations* (1983) 221, on Margaret Thatcher's evaluation of Hayek's major works: 'superb'.

25. The common law doctrine from which British trade unions still need a special 'immunity' to avoid being unlawful: s. 11 TULRCA 1992. On the use of 'restraint of trade', see O. Kahn-Freund's classic account in (1944) 7 MLR 192.

26. One function of the 'general principles of the common law' (the 'rules of the law of property, contract and tort' as Hayek says) is, if unrestrained, to render a range of trade union activity unlawful, a factor of primary importance to the 'ideological pedigree' or 'blueprint' of the new legislation. The interesting analysis in S. Auerbach, *Legislating for Conflict* (1990) 230-9, seems to underestimate this factor and overlooks that Hayek explicitly advocated supplementary legal rules specifically to enfeeble unions (just as the legislation came to do): see *Law Legislation and Liberty* Vol. III, 80-93, 114-128, 143-152; and for his 'detailed programme' on employments where concerted stoppages of work must be made specifically 'illegal': *The Constitution of Liberty* (1960) Chap. 18, especially 267-9. Compare s. 22 TURER Act 1993 (avoiding the corporatist approach of strikes in 'essential services': compare Italy, below n. 210ff.).

27. Wedderburn *op.cit.*, n. 21 above, (1989) 18 ILJ at 25, and for the future programme 34-5; see too, W. McCarthy, 'The Rise and Fall of Collective Laissez-Faire' in *Legal Interventions in Industrial Relations* (1992) 55.

28. See on employees' inalienable rights of protection in Italian law, G. Ghezzi and U. Romagnoli, *Il rapporto del lavoro* (1987 2nd ed.) 330-50.

29. See for example, the judicial presumption against fixed term contracts: M. Weiss, *Labour Law and Labour Relations in the Federal German Republic* (1987) 46-9.

30. The specific influence of the 'New Right' is plain here, not least because it had articulated the general programme years earlier: for example, among the politicians K. Joseph, 'Solving the Union Problem is the Key to

Britain's Recovery' (1974), and the planning behind N. Ridley, 'Appotatox or Civil War?' *The Economist*, 27 May 1978. Doubtless there were many sources of inspiration for the government besides Hayek (e.g. Milton Friedman and his school in economics) and Hayek's views were manifestly not 'the sole determinants of Government policy' (Wedderburn *op.cit.* (1989) 18 ILJ, above n. 21, p. 8); nor does a 'Hayek thesis' ascribe a 'detailed programme' in each Act to him (as may be suggested in Auerbach's *Legislating for Conflict* (1990) 235) though he did formulate a list of very specific proposals in 1959; *The Constitution of Liberty* (1960) Chap. 18 (trade unions' activity should be restricted to that of 'friendly societies', 275-7).

31. K. Marx, 'Preface' *Critique of Political Economy* (1859, 1904 ed. N. Stone) 11.

32. N. Tebbit, Secretary of State for Employment, Parl. Deb. HC 8 Feb. 1982, col. 744 (emphasis supplied): 'though there may come a time when there is great public pressure to do that'! Regulation of internal affairs followed in the Acts of 1984, 1988, 1990 and 1993, with a special Commissioner, whose sole purpose is to assist workers to sue their trade union, and a ban on union discipline of members who refused to follow union decisions to strike, even if taken lawfully and democratically.

33. *Law Legislation and Liberty, op.cit*, n. 21 above, Vol. III, 89-90: the term was 'hallowed by its use as a battle cry not only by labour' but by others; and such organisations' activities would 'probably require limitations ... far more narrow than those it has been found necessary to impose by law on the actions of individuals'. Compare Auerbach, *op.cit.*, n. 26 above.

34. *Ibid.*: trade union activity should be restricted to that of 'friendly societies', *The Constitution of Liberty* (1960) 275-7.

35. Such phrases were paralleled in most Government responses – see for example, Secretaries of State N. Tebbit, Parl. Deb. HC 8.2. 1982 col. 737ff. and G. Shepherd, 7.11.1992 col. 168ff. – and were used frequently to repulse complaints that trade unions were being unfairly treated compared with other associations or companies: see Wedderburn (1989) 18 ILJ 1, 25-6. These later debates were of greater significance than those on the prefatory 1980 Bill, when Secretary of State Prior tried to maintain a traditionally pragmatic stance but must have known his Bill could not be the final 'step' because overall government strategy was to enact in *tranches* so as to avoid the mistake, as they saw it, of doing everything at a stroke, as in the Industrial Relations Act 1971; compare the evaluation by P. Davies and M. Freedland, *Labour Legislation and Public Policy* (1993) 441-525.

36. C. McCarthy, *Elements in a Theory of Industrial Relations* (1984, Dublin) 130.

37. The tactical changes were influenced by events, but invariably were one way ideologically – for example: imposing strike ballots in 1984 (with tighter rules in 1988, 1990 and 1993) after the 1983 Green Paper listed the objections (*Democracy in Trade Unions* Cmnd. 8778, Chap. 3); dropping the corporatist proposal to make collective agreements into contracts (*Industrial Relations in the 1990s* 1991, Cm. 1602, Chap. 8); preventing the lawful operation of union security arrangements in 1988, after permitting

reliance on a 'closed shop' if supported by a ballot; inaction on the commitment to ban strikes in 'public' or 'essential services' in the 1983 manifesto and the 1991 Green Paper (Cm. 1602, Chap. 4, on 'public services') followed by the individual's right to stop industrial action in 1993; replacing the union option to have workplace or postal ballots by a demand for postal ballots (even in ballots on industrial action) in 1993.

38. I. McLoughlin, in J. Clark (ed.), *Human Resource Management and Technical Change* (1993) 181; see too, P. Edwards (1992) 30 BJIR 361, 387.

39. Karen Legge, *Human Resource Management and Technical Change*, *op.cit.* 35; F. Foulkes, *Personnel Policies in Large Non-Union Companies* (1980), unions will become 'irrelevant', 342; and see, K. Sisson, 'In Search of HRM' (1993) 31 BJIR 201.

40. Lloyd Ulman, 'Why Should Human Resource Managers Pay Higher Wages?' (1992) 30 BJIR 177, 207-8, and F. Foulkes, *Personnel Policies in Large Non-Union Companies* (1980) 61.

41. *Der Betrieb* 1991, 1678, 16 June 1991, so as to 'ensure an almost fair level of negotiations on wages and conditions'; U. Zachert, 'Trade Unions in Europe; Dusk or New Dawn?' (1993) 9 Int. J. Comp. LLIR 15, 21.

42. Central protections are expressed in collective terms in some systems, for example Sweden or Germany.

43. *Über soziologische und dogmatische Methode in der Arbeitsrechtswissenschaft* (1922) quoted by O. Kahn-Freund, in R. Lewis and J. Clark (eds.), *Labour Law and Politics in the Weimar Republic* (1981) 100.

44. See B. Teyssié *et.al*, '*Faut-il brûler le droit du travail?*' 1986, Dr. Soc. 559; B. Boubli, '*A propos de la flexibilité de l'emploi: vers le fin du droit du travail?*' 1985, D. Soc. 240. 45. See for example, G. Lyon-Caen, *La bataille truquée de la flexibilité* Dr. Soc. 1985, 809; on flexibility in this period: A. Jeammaud, *Flexibilité du droit du travil: Objectif ou réalité?* (1986 ed. leg admin); A. Roudil, '*Flexibilité de l'emploi et droit du travail: 'la beauté du diable'* 1985, Dr. Soc. 84.

46. See, *Merci Convenzionali Porto di Genova* v *Soc. Siderurgica Gabrielli*, Case C.179/90, 10 December 1991, ECJ; G. Lyon-Caen, '*L'Infiltration du Droit du Travail par le Droit de la Concurrence*' 1992, Dr. Ouvr. 313. *Loewe* v *Lawlor* 208 US 274 (1908) ('*Danbury Hatters*') applied anti-trust law to labour relations – a decision 'devastating for organised labor': W. Gould, *A Primer on American Labor Law* (1982) 15.

47. See the Monopolies and Mergers Commission, *Report under section 79 Fair Trading Act 1973* (Cm. 66 1989); J. Campling (1990) 19 ILJ 46.

48. See the description by J. Goldthorpe, *Order and Conflict in Contemporary Capitalism* (1984) 322, discussing H. Clegg, *A New Approach to Industrial Democracy* (1960); Clark Kerr, J. Dunlop, F. Harbison, C. Myers, *Industrialism and Industrial Man* (1960); A. Ross and P. Hartman, *Changing Patterns of Industrial Conflict* (1960); they failed to foresee the emergence of 'maximising militancy' in collective bargaining, and the growing concern of unions with macroeconomic issues. Compare the analysis in R. Hyman and I. Brough, *Social Values and Industrial Relations* (1975) 62-100, 157-83. For the influences on O. Kahn-Freund, see his, 'Intergroup Conflicts and their Settlement' (1954) 5 Brit. Jo. Sociology 193.

49. Earl Gowrie (Employment Minister) Parl. Deb. HL 20 May 1980 col. 902. See A. Flanders, 'The Tradition of Voluntarism' (1974) 7 BJIR 352.

50. O. Kahn-Freund, in M. Ginsberg (ed.), *Law and Opinion in England in the 20th Century* (1959) 215, 224 (but see note 70 below). On pluralism in England, compare H. Clegg, 'Pluralism in Industrial Relations' (1975) 13 BJIR 309-16, A. Flanders, 'The Tradition of Voluntarism' (1974) 12 BJIR 354-70, with the radical critique of A. Fox, 'Collective Bargaining, Flanders and the Webbs' (1975) 13 BJIR 151-74.

51. For example, see the severe criticisms by W. Streeck in 'Revisiting Status and Contract: Pluralism, Corporatism and Flexibility', now Chap. 2, *Social Institutions and Economic Performance* (1992), especially of Fox and Kahn-Freund; see below n. 169.

52. Italian law 'abstains' from control over union organisation and imposes no duty to bargain: T. Treu, *'Diritto del lavoro'* (1987) 36 Giorn. DLRI 685, 706-8, pointing out that such a duty may be regarded as among the most regulatory incidents of juridification: see S. Simitis in G. Teubner (ed.), *Juridification of Social Spheres* (1987) 123-6 (legislation on collective bargaining causes the collective agreement to be 'integrated into a regulatory system governed by state intervention', citing parallel examples in France, Germany and the United States). In all these, of course, constitutional issues arise.

53. In Sweden (F. Schmidt, *Law and Industrial Relations in Sweden* (1977) 13-14); so too in Britain the 'Social Contract' legislation, P. Davies and M. Freedland, *op.cit.*, n. 35 above Chap. 8.

54. See *Labour Law and Politics in the Weimar Republic op.cit.*, n. 1 above, 85. For helpful, if rather different, analyses: R. Lewis, 'Kahn-Freund and Labour Law: an Outline Critique' (1979) 8 ILJ 204-22; A. Wilson, 'Contract and Prerogative' (1984) 13 ILJ 1-29; and W. McCarthy, 'The Rise and Fall of Collective *Laissez-Faire*' Chap. 1, *Legal Interventions in Industrial Relations* (1992): all he meant by collective *laissez-faire*, was a 'preference for collective bargaining', 6.

55. In A. Flanders and H. Clegg (eds.), *The System of Industrial Relations in Great Britain* (1954) Chap. 11 'Legal Framework', 43-4. Sometimes this took a weaker form: 'excessive legalism' must be avoided in industrial relations: 'Industrial Democracy' (1977) 6 ILJ 65, 83.

56. K.W. Wedderburn (1971) 11 Bulletin of Industrial Law Society 2, 3. Kahn-Freund had himself criticised Sinzheimer's treatment of the State as a *'corpus mysticum'*: *Law and Politics in the Weimar Republic op.cit.*, n. 1 above, 80.

57. In Ginsberg (ed.), *Law and Opinion in England in the 20th Century op.cit.*, n. 50, 244-5; see J. Clark and Wedderburn in R. Lewis, J. Clark and Wedderburn (eds.), *Labour Law and Industrial Relations: Building on Kahn-Freund* (1983).

58. See Kahn-Freund in Ginsberg (ed.), *Law and Opinion in England in the 20th Century op.cit.*, n. 50 above, 244; H. Phelps Brown, *The Growth of British Industrial Relations* (1959) Chaps. 4 and 7 and *The Origins of Trade Union Power* (1983) Chaps. II-V; also W. McCarthy, 'The Rise and Fall of Collective *Laissez-Faire*', Chap. 1 in *Legal Interventions in Industrial Relations* (1992); Wedderburn, *The Worker and the Law* (1986

3rd ed.) Chap. 1, and *Employment Rights in Britain and Europe op.cit.*, n. 21 above, 41-51, and sources cited in (1991) 54 MLR 1, at 2-25.

59. Kahn-Freund feared that 'the repressive tendencies of the courts, which in the 19th and 20th centuries had to be repeatedly counteracted by Parliament, are on the point of being revived' (1964) 14 Federation News (GFTU) 30, 41. On his faith in British 'social equilibrium' see R. Lewis, *op.cit.*, n. 54, 218-221; and Wedderburn, Clark and Lewis *op.cit.*, n. 57, at 38-41.

60. *Labour and the Law* (1972) 270; now (1983 3rd ed., eds. P. Davies and M. Freedland).

61. K.W. Wedderburn, 'Labour Law and Labour Relations in Britain' (1972) 10 BJIR 270, 281.

62. K.W. Wedderburn, *The Worker and the Law* (1965) 20, (2nd ed. 1971), 25.

63. Wedderburn, *The Worker and the Law* (1986 3rd ed.) 846.

64. Compare P. Davies and M. Freedland, *Labour Legislation and Public Policy* (1993) 225-6 (who cite the odd analysis of the state of industrial relations in 1966 by H. Street, G. Howe and G. Bindman, later published in *Report on Anti-Discrimination Legislation* (1967), 73). Already an adumbration could be sensed by those who attached importance to 'non-intervention' in this sense, of the forthcoming State control over the internal autonomy of the unions, which reached a new level in the Trade Union Act 1984 and now s. 14 TURER Act 1993.

65. Lord Tangley's question to the writer in evidence to the Donovan Commission: *Royal Commission on Trade Unions and Employers Association: Minutes of Evidence*, 22 March 1966, Qn. 4888 (emphasis added). Notably he resisted new rights for employees summarily dismissed (Qns. 4734-9) and was opposed to the legality of trade union activity which could put the employer out of business (see Qns. 4926-38: 'much worse' than driving the employer 'off the premises with a whip'). Lord Tangley was one of the bare majority to advocate sharp curtailment of basic union protections in the Act of 1906 (*Report of Royal Commission* 1968 Cmnd. 3623, para. 800) parallel to those effected in the legislation of 1980, 1982 and 1988. The notion, currently held in some quarters, that curtailment of immunities was an original idea in 1980 is shown not to be the case by a perusal of the evidence given to, and the Report of, the Royal Commission. [On racism and collective laissez-faire, see also p. 53.]

66. When the Swedish trade union federation LO feared impending attacks recently that might destroy the legislative base of collective organisation, its President said: 'It is the individual rights at work which we are defending, not the legislation as such. The best thing would be for the labour legislation's protection to be written into collective agreements' (Stig Malm, *LO News*, October 1993, 2).

67. See H. Collins, 'Against Abstentionism' in *Oxford Essays in Jurisprudence* (3rd Series 1987) 79-99: the question was not 'rhetorical', as he suggests, but practical, as are many of his other very pertinent questions, *ibid.* 80-90. It is notable that the only book of the period to advocate some positive rights, C. Jenkins and J. Mortimer, *The Kind of Laws the Unions Ought to Want* (1968), had little influence until the 1980s. Even among academic commentators, demands for 'positive rights' generally did not

take off before the early 1980s: see Wedderburn, *Employment Rights in Britain and Europe* (1991) Chap. 4. Nor were the laws of the 'Social Contract' period 1974-1976 a success; they contained no consistent policy for 'maintaining and extending independent trade union strength', Clark and Wedderburn, *Labour Law and Industrial Relations*, op.cit., n. 1 above, 190-4.

68. See, for example, Wedderburn: *On the Industrial Relations Bill*, TUC, Royal Albert Hall Rally, 12 January 1971 above p. 158.

69. 'No scholarship is possible without conviction, without a view of the totality.' *Philip Lotmar* (obituary) *Arbeitsrecht* 9 (1922) 587-600. It is difficult for any school in labour law to avoid a 'vocation': see the teasing treatment by H. Collins, 'Labour Law as a Vocation' (1989) 105 LQR 468, 482.

70. Kahn-Freund promoted the historical analysis at first (see for example, his notes to *Renner: The Institutions of Private Law and their Social Functions* (1949) 172, and *Labour Law: Old Traditions and New Developments* (1968) 7-10) but sometimes he became rather uncertain about it without clear explanation, except that political developments were perhaps as important: *Labour and the Law*, op.cit. (1983 3rd ed.) 53-4.

71. TUC *Report, 1971*, 368-70, and *Report, 1972*, 96.

72. O. Kahn-Freund, 'Introduction', Renner, *The Institutions of Private Law and their Social Functions* (1949) 28. Such analysis is not unknown to the conservative tradition: '... the workman, by himself, is at a disadvantage compared with the employer who has greater knowledge and resources at his disposal', Inns of Court Conservative Society, *A Giant's Strength* (1958) 9.

73. See for example *Report* of the Committee of Experts 1990, 77th Session Report III (Part 4A) para. 63, a formula used by the Experts in most of their reports; see too, N. Valticos, *International Labour Law* (1983) paras. 608-34.

74. G. Lyon-Caen and J. Pélissier, *Droit du Travail* (1992 16 ed.) 566-72. Proposals for 'class actions', for example on equal pay, are desirable but a trade union right to launch proceedings would have a more secure base. In France the union can appear in defence of a collective interest but to protect individual interests it must be a representative union and not encounter the objection of the worker (as in cases of sex equality at work: *Code du Travail* Art. L-123-6).

75. See B. Fitzpatrick, 'Towards Strategic Litigation?' (1992) 8 Int. J. Comp. LLIR 208, 218-22; on the Netherlands, 222-3.

76. *The Independent*, 11 October 1993; Equal Pay (Amendment) Regulations 1983, SI 1794, amending the Equal Pay Act 1970. [For part-time workers' rights in redundancy and unfair dismissal won by the EOC, see *R v Sec. of State for Employment, ex parte EOC* [1994] ICR 317 HL; the law on equality, in Directives 75/117 and 76/207, and equal pay, art. 119 Treaty of Rome, was used to strike down requirements for longer qualifying periods of service by such workers, the great majority of whom are women, a decision the UK government accepted.]

77. *Labour and the Law* (3rd ed. 1983; eds. P. Davies and M. Freedland) 17.

78. See G. Ghezzi and U. Romagnoli, *Il rapporto del lavoro* (1987 2nd ed.) 60.

79. See generally S. Fredman and G. Morris, *The State as Employer: Labour Law in the Public Services* (1989).
80. Notably by judicial review, but the narrow scope of the remedies is illustrated in: *R v Hertfordshire CC ex parte NUPE* [1985] IRLR 258 CA (failure to abide by national agreements not fatal to public body's decisions); on remedies for unions, see *Council of Civil Service Unions* v *Minister for the Civil Service* [1984] 1 WLR 1174, HL.
81. The employer had also contravened duties to consult the unions under EC Directive 75/129 and in the national legislation implementing it, (probabaly unsatisfactorily) now TULRCA 1992, s. 188; *R v British Coal Corpn. and Secretary of State for Trade and Industry ex parte Vardy* [1993] IRLR 104, 114-121. The procedures could not be enforced in private law as they were collective agreements not intended to be contracts under the presumption in: s. 179 TULRCA 1992, below n. 130.
82. But see *Webster v Southwark LBC* [1983] QB 698 where sequestration was available to support the declaration of rights. It must be questionable too whether, if there had been a contravention of the Directive of 1975 the principle that there must be effective sanctions to enforce a Community norm was here itself satisfied: *Von Colson v Land Nordrhein-Westfalen* (14/83) [1984] ECR 1891. The remedy for breach of s. 188 TULRCA 1992 is a 'protective award' of compensation paid, to the individual employees after the union has established failure to consult about 'collective redundancies'; s. 34 TURER Act 1993 improves the amount recoverable but arguably still fails to implement the directive with an effective remedy. The employers had argued they were exempt by reason of art. 1(2)(b) of the Directive, but the mines were not establishments 'governed by public law'.
83. After refusing to vary the declaration: *R v British Coal Corpn. ex parte Price, The Times* March 5 1993; and *ibid* (No. 3) *The Times* May 28, 1993. By September 1993, most of the pits were destined for closure and British Coal Corpn. was 'pessimistic' as to 12 further pits: *The Times* 13 September 1993.
84. G. Pitt (1993), 22 ILJ 211, 213. See too H. Collins, *Justice in Dismissal* (1992) 128-32; H. Carty, 'Dismissed Employees: Search for a More Effective Range of Remedies' (1989) 52 MLR 449 ('injunctions and judicial review – remain exceptional remedies').
85. H. Collins, *Justice in Dismissal* (1992) 191, citing Lord Woolf (1986) *Public Law* 221.
86. On the strike, see M. Adeney and J. Lloyd, *The Miners' Strike* (1986), and on litigation arising: Wedderburn, *The Worker and the Law* (1986 3rd ed.) 680-752.
87. See T. Treu, *'Pubblico e privato nell' Europa sociale'* 1990 LD, no. 3, 329, 337.
88. See Soc. 4 November 1992, no. 3799, *Jilaki c. France Glaces Findus* (for which I am much indebted to Professor A. Lyon-Caen); Wedderburn, 'Vicarious Liability and *Responsabilité Civile* in Strikes: Comparative Notes' (1991) 20 ILJ 188.
89. See ss. 17-20, TURER Act 1993; generally Wedderburn, 'The Right to Strike – Is There a European Standard?' Chap. 10, *Employment Rights in*

Britain and Europe (1991) and for the five threads of British labour legislation of the 1980s, 'Freedom of Association and Philosophies of Labour Law' Chap. 8, 211-26. For a comparative review, see '*Limitation Législative et Judiciaire en Matière d'Action Syndicale et de Droit de Grève*' 1990 Rev. Int. de Droit Comparé, n. 1, 37-114.

90. P. Smith and G. Morton, 'Union Exclusion and Deregulation of Industrial Relations in Contemporary Britain' (1993) 31 BJIR 97, 100. On 'union exclusion' see J. Goldthorpe (ed.) Chap. 13 'The End of Convergence', *Order and Conflict in Contemporary Capitalism* (1984); but contrast G. Baglione, in G. Baglione and C. Crouch (eds.), *European Industrial Relations* (1990) 12-13.

91. R. Hyman, in M. Regini (ed.), *The Future of Labour Movements* (1992) 151 *et.seq.*

92. On the question whether Britain should adopt a legal duty to bargain: B. Simpson, *Trade Union Recognition and the Law* (1991, Institute of Employment Rights).

93. See J. Visser in A. Ferner and R. Hyman (eds.), *Industrial Relations in the New Europe* (1992) 350-1, on Dutch employers' refusal to concede greater bargaining roles to local union representatives or works councils; J. Visser, 'In Search of Inclusive Unionism' (1990) 18 Bull. Cop. Lab. Relns. 12.

94. See T. Claydon, 'Union Derecognition in Britain in the 80s' (1989) 27 BJIR 214; G. Gall and S. McKay, *Trade Union Derecognition in Britain 1988-93* (1993); Smith and Morton, *op.cit.*, n. 90 above; Wedderburn, (1989) ILJ 1, at 19; and *Labour Research* November 1992, p. 6 (over 200 employers ceased to recognise unions in 1988-92); P. Beaumont and R. Harris, 'Trade Union Recognition and Employment Contraction' (1991) 29 BJIR 49; ACAS *Annual Report* 1992, 18-20.

95. See the gradual but accelerating derecognition by Shell, BP and other oil companies: *Financial Times* 27 *May 1993* [N. Millward *The New Industrial Relations?* (1994).]

96. J. Visser, in M. Regini (ed.), *The Future of Labour Movements* (1992) 42; for a cautious prognosis, H. Gospel and G. Palmer, *British Industrial Relations* (1993) Chap. 11.

97. See J. Purcell (1991) 7 Ox. Rev. Econ. Policy 33-43.

98. J. Goldthorpe, in T. Clark and L. Clements (eds.), *Trade Unions Under Capitalism* (1978) 193. On the legal authority of the employer and its master and servant background in Britain: Wedderburn, 'Companies and Employees' (1993) 109 LQR 220, now above Chap. 2.

99. EC Commission, *Datastream*, Economist Survey, 3 July 1993, 9. On the year 2000 see J. Delors, *The Times* 15 October 1993 (30 million) but if flexibility, job-sharing, wage flexibility and more part-time work, were adopted, he thought unemployment could fall to 7 per cent (*Financial Times* 11 October 1993) or even 5 per cent (*Financial Times* 27 October 1993). Not all the figures are comparable: the British of 2.9 million would on the ILO basis be nearly 4 million: *Financial Times* 29 October 1993.

100. O. Kahn-Freund in R. Lewis and J. Clark (eds.), *Labour Law and Politics in the Weimar Republic op.cit.*, n. 1 above, 82.

101. See on this aspect of certain labour law Directive, P.L. Davies, 'The Emergence of Community Labour Law' Chap. 10 in W. McCarthy (ed.),

Legal Interventions in Industrial Relations (1992).
102. See EC Draft Directive on Working Time [now Directive 93/104]; see (1993) 233 *EIRR* 2 and 238 *ibid* 3; adopted 23 November 1993) and the analysis by B. Bercusson, *Working Time in Britain: Part I The Directive* and *Part II: Collective Agreements* (Institute of Employment Rights, 1994, to which I am greatly indebted): derogations may be made generally by collective agreement (art. 17) but the limit on maximum weekly working hours (48) may also be displaced with the *individual* worker's 'agreement', subject to the 'general principles' on safety, conditions concerning notification to the authorities and to workers not suffering any detriment if they refuse (all to be reviewed in seven years time): art. 18 (1)(b).
103. Declaration to Article 4(2) Agreement on Social Policy 1993 (Cm.1934, p. 117), the 'Social Chapter'.
104. *Commission* v *Denmark* (143/83) [1985] ECR 427 ECJ; and see *Commission* v *Italy* (91/81) [1982] 3 CMLR 468 ECJ, and *Commission* v *Italy* (235/84) [1987] 3 CMLR 115 ECJ. It is sometimes argued that, whereas implementation under art. 2(4) must be complete *erga omnes*, this is not required under art. 4(2); yet the paragraph says the agreements 'shall be implemented', which can hardly mean partially.
105. The Commission has an opportunity in the forthcoming Green Paper on European Social Policy 1993, to outline implementation mechanisms in relation to the divergent enforcement of normative clauses in Member states, a problem not hitherto addressed.
106. Council of Europe, *Social Charter* 1961 art. 33. See the helpful discussion by A. Adolfini, 'The Implementation of Social Policy Directives through Collective Agreements' (1988) 25 CMLR 291; the figure sometimes used is 80 per cent; Wedderburn 'Inderogability, Collective Agreements and Community Law' (1992) 21 ILJ 245, below n. 132.
107. Arts. 17(3) and 18. See Bercusson *op.cit.*, n. 102, 33-41, questioning the meaning of a worker's *individual* agreement; e.g. can it be given *via* a collective agreement?
108. See for optimistic reports: F. Guarriello, *Ordinamento comunitario e autonomia collettiva* (1992), and B. Bercusson, 'Maastricht: a fundamental change in European labour law' (1992) 23 Ind. Rel. Jo. 177, and 'The EC Charter of Fundamental Social Rights for Workers' (1990) 53 MLR 624; compare B. Hepple *ibid*. 643; B. Fitzpatrick (1992) 21 ILJ 199 and Wedderburn (1991) 54 MLR 1, 25ff. For trade unions optimism: D. Lea, 'Time for Turning Weakness Into Strength' 1993 *International Union Rights*, 8-10.
109. Rather than 'coordinated collective bargaining': M. Weiss in G. Spyropoulos and G. Fragnière, *Work and Social Policies in the New Europe* (1991), 59, 68-75. For recent discussion: P. Langlois, *La négotiation collective d'entreprise; la politique communutaire* Dr. Soc. 1990, 673; and in relation to the Social Dialogue: M. Roccella and T. Treu, *Diritto del lavoro della Comunità* (1992), 336-60.
110. See B. Hepple, *European Social Dialogue Alibi or Opportunity* (1993 Institute of Employment Rights).
111. See P. Durand in G. Spyropoulos (ed.) *Le Droit des Conventions*

collectives de Travail dans les Pays de la Communauté Charbon et de l'Acier (1959) xi–xv.

112. See G. Schnorr, *Les possibilités d'une convention collective sur le plan Européen* (1959) 26; and H. Günter (ed.), *Transnational Industrial Relations* (1972): see the views at that time of O. Kahn-Freund 352, M. Despax 318, R. Blanpain 300, J. van Dierondonck 274 (on the Commission's view).

113. Trade Union Reform and Employment Rights Act 1993; (under the Major administration, enabling the employers to discriminate against trade unionists when making personal contracts); see on the Act: B. Simpson (1993) 22 ILJ 181; G. Morris *ibid.* 194 (new liabilities for industrial action).

114. See Wedderburn *op.cit.* (1993) 109 LQR 220, above n. 98.

115. P.F. van der Heijden, *Nederlanse Juristenblad*, 1993, n. 9, March 4 (English translation kindly supplied by the author).

116. On the dichotomy integrated in the Italian, *Statuto dei lavoratori*, Law no.300, 1970, see T. Treu, '*Lo Statuto dei lavoratori: Vent' anni dopo'* 1989 *Quaderni di diritto del lavoro e delle relazioni industriali*, 7-44; on the *rappresentanza sindacale aziendale* (plant level union presence) see M. Terry (1993) 24 Ind. Rels. Jo. 138, and Wedderburn (1990) 19 ILJ 154.

117. J.-M. Verdier, *Droit du travail* (1990 9th ed.) 9, noting the 'new possibilities for provisions derogating *in pejus* in collective agreements'; see *Code du Travail* arts L.212-2, al. 3, L.132-26 (unless the majority unions exercise the rights of opposition, collective agreements may derogate in regard to pay and working hours).

118. P.F. van der Heijden, *Nederlanse Juristenblad* 1993, *op.cit.*, n. 115.

119. 'Hugo Sinzheimer 1875-1945' (1976) in R. Lewis and J. Clark, *Labour Law and Politics in the Weimar Republic* (1981) 82.

120. See the Worker Protection (Regular Part-time Employees) Act 1991; B. Wilkinson (1992) 14 Comp. Lab. Law Jo. 33-41, and (1991) 20 ILJ 224-6.

121. *Code du Travail* Art. L.135 2. See the similar Italian approach as to the *inderogabilitá* of the collective terms, based by the courts especially on the Civil Code arts. 2077 and 2113 (as revised in 1973): Cass. 21 November 1977; G. Giugni, *Diritto sindacale* (1991 9th ed.) 143-52.

122. Soc. 3 March 1988 Jur. UIMM, n. 501.88 (renunciation); Soc. 15 1981 (personal contract entitlement to severance payment which the collective agreement excluded).

123. See G. Lyon-Caen and J. Pélissier, *Droit du travail* (1992 16th ed.) pp. 749-5 (and see p. 748 on the difficult doctrine concerning *avantages aquis*) and *Code du Travail* Arts. L-135-1, L-135-3. The obligation concerning performance is stricter than the good faith obligation imposed on a contracting party by the Code Civil art.1134: see generally D. Harris and D. Tallon, *Contract Law Today* (1989) 234; B. Rudden, *A Source-Book on French Law* (1991) 399. In the short period when English law attempted to place contractual obligations on the parties to a collective agreement, it also imposed a duty in regard to performance which was more strict than the normal contractual duty: see s. 36(2)(3) Industrial Relations Act 1971; R. Simpson and J. Wood, *Industrial Relations and the 1971 Act* (1973), 136.

124. See G. Lyon-Caen and J. Pélissier, *Droit du travail op.cit.*, n. 123, 750.
125. *Ibid.* 751; a collective agreement is considered to be of a nature réglementaire and incorporation has been explicitly rejected by the courts as a correct understanding of the normative effect: Soc. 21 June 1967, Bull. IV no. 415, Dr. Soc. 1968 177. Legislation has made numerous exceptions to the principle of non-incorporation, e.g. Law of 13 November 1982 (denunciation of agreement by all signatories).
126. Hobhouse J., *Alexander v Standard Telephones and Cables Ltd* (No. 2) [1991] IRLR 286, 292 (emphasis supplied); *McLaren v Home Office* [1990] ICR 824, 834, 839 CA.
127. Which apply throughout: *Hooper v British Railways Board* [1988] IRLR CA, especially Ralph Gibson LJ, 527-7.
128. For example, from an employer's Works Rules. A number of difficult decisions concern incorporation from documents other than collective agreements, see e.g. *Cadoux v Central Regional Council* [1986] IRLR 131 Ct. Sess.; the courts are sometimes willing to interpret the 'intention' of the parties by reference to the nature of such a document: see Connell J. *Lee v GEC Plessey Telecommunications* [1993] IRLR 383, 390; and see Wedderburn, *The Worker and the Law* (1986 3rd ed.) 326-43.
129. *Boxfoldia v NGA* [1988] ICR 752; *Ellis v Brighton Co-op. Soc.* [1976] IRLR 419; the reasoning of Denning LJ in *Chappell v Times Newspapers Ltd* [1975] ICR 145 must be doubted on this point. British courts here reach Sinzheimer's conclusion, though for different reasons: see O. Kahn-Freund *Labour Law and Politics in the Weimar Republic* (1981, eds. R. Lewis and J. Clark) 83.
130. Unless the parties signify otherwise in writing: s. 179 TULRCA 1992.
131. As in the period 1971-1974 when s. 34 of the Act of 1971 reversed the presumption, deeming that the parties did intend to make collective agreements enforceable: see Simpson and Wood *op.cit.*, n. 123 above, 138-40.
132. Wedderburn, 'Inderogability, Collective Agreements and Community Law' (1992) 21 ILJ 245; Chap. 6 above. On the niceties of *inderogabilità* see the account in L. Mariucci *Le fonti del diritto del lavoro* (1988), 24-64, and on its historical development in this century, G. Vardaro, *Contratti collettivi e rapporto individuale di lavoro* (1985).
133. 'On many matters legislation has made possible derogation *in pejus* from legal control by the collective contract, even a plant agreement': G. Giugni, *Diritto sindacale op.cit.*, n. 121 above, 158.
134. *Robertson v British Gas Corpn.* [1983] IRLR 302 CA.
135. *Lee v GEC Plessey Telecommunications* [1993] IRLR 383, 390.
136. 'There is a heavy burden upon a party who asserts that the actual contract is different from the statement of terms and conditions', Connell, J. in *Lee v GEC Plessey Telecommunications cit.* 390-1.
137. As permitted by art. 7 of the Directive. The British law before 1993 allowed conditions to be incorporated and varied generally by reference to a copy of a relevant collective agreement provided it was reasonably accessible to the worker at the workplace (especially ss. 2(3) and 4(3) Employment Protection (Consolidation) Act 1978). This was designed to avoid an ocean of paper every time a worker's terms were changed; but

the Directive appears to allow reference to operate now only over a more narrow range: see art. 3 as implemented in new ss. 2(2)(3), 4(3)(4), Schedule 4 TURER Act 1992; compare K. Ewing (1993) 22 ILJ 165, 168-9. It is difficult, on this practical point, to share the enthusiasm shown by some commentators for the Directive: (see J. Clark and M. Hall, 'The Cinderella Directive?' (1992) 21 ILJ 106, 112-16).

138. *National Coal Board* v *National Union of Mineworkers* [1986] IRLR 439.
139. *Alexander* v *Standard Telephones and Cables Ltd* (No. 2) [1991] IRLR 286; *British Leyland UK Ltd* v *McQuilken* [1978] IRLR 245 (Scot.); *Lee* v *GEC Plessey Telecommunications* [1993] IRLR 383; Wedderburn, *The Worker and the Law* op.cit., Chap. 4; S. Auerbach, *Derecognition and Personal Contracts: Fighting Tactics and the Law*, n. 8 above, 15-26.
140. M. Weiss, *Labour Law and Industrial Relations in the Federal Republic of Germany* (1987) 126. The Labour Court has prohibited union efforts to reserve bargained rates to members: W. Däubler, 'The Individual and the Collective' (1989) 10 J. Comp. Lab. Law 505, 511. The reasoning is of course bound up with the constitutional right not to be a member: F. von Prondzynski, *Freedom of Association and Industrial Relations* (1987) 90-2, 190-4.
141. See M. Magnani, '*Contrattazzione collettiva e governo del conflitto*' 1990, 48 Giorn. DLRI 687; and n. 121 above and 154 below. The question is posed differently where, as here, there are many ways in which the law directly or indirectly ascribes benefits of collective bargaining to employees, not least art. 2077 Civil Code: see G. Ghezzi and U. Romagnoli, *Il diritto sindacale* (1992), 154-70.
142. Even in open shops: S. Dunn and J. Gennard, *The Closed Shop in British Industry* (1984) 99; for examples, (1977) 163 IRRR 12. See today, s. 222 TULRCA. The amendment by TURER Act 1993, s. 13, of s. 148 TULRCA 1992, permitting the employer to discriminate against union members (see n. 8 above) appears to remove most of such legal risks for him as were revealed in *National Coal Board* v *Ridgway* [1987] ICR 641 CA. Some British agreements are expressed to be made by the union 'on behalf of the members' but this has not had significant legal effect; nor could the union lawfully bargain for members' benefits without the risk of illegality under s. 222 TULRCA.
143. See *Code du Travail*, Art. L-412-2, expressing constitutional values.
144. *Meskell* v *Córas Iompair Eireann* [1973] IR 121 explained in M. Redmond, *Dismissal Law in the Republic of Ireland* (1982) 34-7; T. Kerr and G. Whyte, *Irish Trade Union Law* (1985) 11-15. The practice is illegal in Greece and Portugal (*International Encyclopaedia of Labour Law and Industrial Relations* (ed. R. Blanpain 1990) 'Greece' 176, 'Portugal' 198) and of uncertain status in Spain: M. Rodriguez Piñero in *Transformations du droit du travail: Études offertes à Gérard Lyon-Caen* (1989) 113.
145. See 1992 European Industrial Review n. 218, 4, on the Blicher Hansen decision (reinstatement of non-unionists under new legislation of 1990).
146. See H. Bakels, 'Netherlands' in R. Blanpain (ed.), *International Encyclopaedia of Labour Law and Industrial Relations* 65.6, 69-70.
147. Despite the protection of a right not to join a union, special benefits for

members and exclusion of non-members appear, for reasons which are not wholly clear, to be accepted: see R. Blanpain and C. Engels, 'Belgium' in *International Encylopaedia of Labour Law* (above n. 146), 159-61.

148. See the discussions in N. Aliprantis, *La Place de la Convention dans les Hiérachies des Normes* (1980) 127 *et seq.*; T. Treu, *Condotta antisindacale e atti discriminatori* (1974) 142-70; Wedderburn Chap. 6 in Folke Schmidt (ed.), *Discrimination in Employment* (1978).

149. See O. Kahn-Freund in *Labour Law and Politics in the Weimar Republic op.cit.*, n. 1 above.

150. Unilateral arbitration machinery designed in 1940 during the war was continued (with a gap in 1958) and became Schedule 11, Employment Protection Act 1975, under which a union could obtain conditions for workers whose terms were less favourable than those established by collective agreements representing a substantial proportion of workers and employers in the trade or industry nationally or in a district. It was repealed in 1980.

151. Under the Industrial Relations Act 1946, an Irish collective agreement may, if the union holds a 'negotiating licence' and if it has the necessary content (e.g. no-strike clauses), be registered by the Labour Court and then becomes binding in the industry on employers and workers not party to it; but relatively few agreements are registered, even after the amendments made in ss. 44-50 Industrial Relations Act 1990.

152. *Code du Travail* Art. L-133-11 and -12; G. Lyon-Caen and J. Pelissier, *Droit du Travail op.cit.*, note 123 above, 1002-14 (*extension* and *élargissement*); M. Weiss, *Labour Law and Industrial Relations in the Federal Republic of Germany op.cit.*, 297-300 (*Allgemeinverbindlicherklärung*); Netherland, Laws of 25 May 1937 and 24 December 1977, H. Bakkels 'Netherlands' (1981) *op.cit.*, para. 243. See too for administrative action to extend collective agreements: Spain, Workers' Statute 1980 art. 92; Portugal, Decree-law no. 519-C1, 1979; Greece, Law of 1955, n. 3239, amended 1957, n. 3755; Belgium, Law of 5 December 1968: B. Veneziani, *Stato e autonomia collettiva* (1992) 162-190.

153. The complex French concept of 'representative' unions – '*proportionnelle et non majoritaire*' – usually rests on affiliation to one of the accepted national organisations: G. Lyon-Caen and J. Pelissier *op.cit.*, n. 123 above, 566-71. The parallel but different Italian concept is similarly based: G. Giugni, *op.cit.* above n. 121, 86-98 (*sindacato maggiormente rappresentativo*). But in Spain it rests on a set proportion of votes in workers' ballots: M. Casas Baamonde, '*Sulla rappresentatività sindacale ...*' 1990 Lav. Dir. 493-61. In Greece a judicial decision is needed: T. Koniaris, 'Greece' in *Encyclopaedia of Labour Law op.cit.*, above n. 144, at 174. The huge variations in such legal concepts may be accommodated by the Community principle of 'subsidiarity'; but if that is the base of Community labour law, Community laws on such matters will in real life have vastly divergent implementations in different States, thereby frustrating the aim of building a floor or equivalence of employment conditions, let alone a concrete harmonisation of laws.

154. See G. Giugni, *Diritto sindacale op.cit.*, n. 121, 136-42 on the Laws of 1959

no. 741, and 1960 decree, no. 1019, and 150-160. Italian courts are able to promote the standards of collective agreements in various other ways, including the worker's constitutional right to a wage sufficient to provide him and his family 'with a dignified existence': Constitution of 1948, art. 36.

155. By the Employment Act 1980; see also Wedderburn and S. Sciarra, 'Collective Bargaining as Agreement and as Law' in A. Pizzorusso, *Law in the Making* (1988) Chap. 6, 221-4. The divergencies are such that it is difficult realistically to envisage a 'dialogue' at European level in the medium term producing concrete norms; but for another view compare S. Sciarra, '*La contrattazione collettiva (ordinamento communitario e nazionale del lavoro*' (1992) 56 Giorn. DLRI 715, 746-52.

156. Wedderburn, 'The Social Charter in Britain, Labour Law and Labour Courts?' (1991) 54 MLR 1, 7. On the proposals to introduce 'positive collective rights' see Wedderburn, '*The New Politics of Labour Law*' (1983) in *Employment Rights in Britain and Europe* (1991) Chap. 4; K. Ewing, 'Rights and Immunities in British Labour Law' (1988) 10 Comp. Lab. L. Jo. 1-35.

157. See C. Maier in J. Goldthorpe (ed.) *Order And Conflict in Contemporary Capitalism* (1985); Wedderburn, *Employment Rights in Britain and Europe* (1991) 41-51, and other sources cited in (1991) 54 MLR 2-25; H. Phelps Brown, *The Origins of Trade Union Power* (1983) Chaps. II-V; compare on Kahn-Freund n. 70 above.

158. See A. Lyon-Caen, 'Labour Law Looking Ahead: A French Viewpoint' (1990) 6 Int. J. Comp. LLIR3: on the 'State pre-eminence on French labour culture'.

159. Especially Art. 40. 6.1; see T. Kerr and G. Whyte, *Irish Trade Union Law op.cit.*, 4-37. See too, on the ambiguous legacy of Weimar and modern 'suspicion' in Germany of the 'options of Sinzheimer and his school', see W. Daübler *Lavoro nel diritto della Repubblica Federale Tedesa* (1993) *Digesto* (IV ed.) vol. VII (Commerciale) 13.

160. Art. 26 Workers' Statute 1970, Law no. 300 (a right to collect dues at the workplace and to a checkoff so long as secrecy about the union chosen is maintained); U. Romagnoli and G. Ghezzi, *Diritto sindacale* (1987 2nd ed.) 282-91; *Ley Organica de Libertad Sindical* 1985, No. 11 (in Spain it is 'relatively common', A. Martin Verde, *European Employment and Industrial Relations Glossary: Spain* (1991) 66; M. Rodriguez Piñero and J. Cruz Villalon (1987) 33 Giorn. DLRI. 77, 102-5). In the former, an employer's failure to execute the agreement gives a right of action to the employee and to the signatory union.

161. It is permitted in Portugal (Law 57/1977), Belgium (R. Blanpain and C. Engels, *International Encyclopaedia of Labour Law and Industrial Relations* (1980) 159), Denmark (Per Jacobsen, Chap. III, A. Jaspers and L. Betten (eds.), *25 Years of the European Social Charter* (1988)), Ireland, (T. Kerr and G. Whyte, *Irish Trade Union Law* (1985) 96-8), and probably in Germany (W. Daübler and H. Hege, *Koalitionsfreiheit* (1976)).

162. TULRCA 1992 ss. 68, 68A, inserted by s. 15, TURERA 1993 (the employee's consent must be signified every three years). Part of the

subscription may, if the member has not 'contracted out', be paid as a political subvention to the Labour Party. On whether such members are subject to 'coercion', see M. Regini, *The Future of Labour Movements* (1992) 22 and sources cited.

163. See R. Fakiolas in G. Spyropoulos (ed.), *Trade Unions Today and Tomorrow* (1985) 124-36; A. Papaionnou, 'The Greek Labour Movement in the 1980s' (1990) 11 Comp. Lab. Law Jo. 295, 301-16; and (1991) 204 EIRR 20.

164. Article L-412-7, al.2 *Code du Travail*. J-M. Verdier, *Syndicats et Droits Syndical* Vol. I, *Liberté, structure, action* (1987) 228-41 and on collection of subscriptions, Vol. II, *Le Droit Syndical dans l'Entreprise* (1984 2nd. ed) 173. The right to collect union subscriptions *within* the enterprise was extended in 1982: now Art. 412-7 *Code du Travail*.

165. See on the details of the *Roger* cases, which extended into the 1960s, Wedderburn in F. Schmidt, *Discrimination in Employment* (1978) 397-8, 438-45, and the removal in 1975 of *Parisien Liberé* to centres outside Paris which has, with hindsight, remarkable affinities to the conflict over the relocation to Wapping of *The Times*; see K. Ewing and B. Napier [1986] Camb. LJ 285.

166. D. Gallie in J. Clark, C. Modgil, S. Modgil (eds.), *John Goldthorpe: Consensus and Controversy* (1990) 32, summarising J. Goldthorpe, 'The End of Convergence' in *Order and Conflict in Contemporary Capitalism* (1984) 12-13; see too *ibid.* 41-4 on the absence also of the predicted convergence between capitalism and State socialist societies.

167. C. Kerr, J. Dunlop, F. Harbison, C. Myers, *Industrialism and Industrial Man* (1960) 198-9 and *passim*; and J. Dunlop, *Industrial Relations Systems* (1958); and see parallels in J.K. Galbraith, *The New Industrial State* (1967) Chap. 6. It must be added that Kerr later retracted the more general convergence thesis: *The Future of Industrial Societies: Convergence or Continuing Diversity* (1983).

168. E. Herman, *Corporate Control, Corporate Power* (1982), 264, and Chap. 7 on A. Berle and G. Means, *The Modern Corporation and Private Property* (1932); for a convincingly sceptical view of managerialism, see J. Scott, Chap. 15, 'Ownership and Employer Control' in D. Gallie (ed.), *Employment in Britain* (1988).

169. W. Streeck, *Social Institutions and Economic Performance* (1992) 57. See too, A. Fox in A. Child (ed.), *Man and Organisation: The Search for Explanation and Relevance* (1973) and A. Fox, *Beyond Contract: Work, Power and Trust Relations* (1974).

170. See W. McLeod, 'Labor Management Cooperation' 12 IRLJ 233 (1990). Predictably, critical legal scholars are more prepared than traditional pluralists to advocate workers' participation beyond collective bargaining: see K. Stone, 'Labour and the Corporate Structure' 55 Univ. Chi. LR (1988) 79, and 'The Post-War Paradigm in American Labor Law' 90 Yale LJ 1509 (1981); K. Klare, 'The Labor-Management Cooperation Debate' 23 Harv. CR-Civ.Lib. L.Rev. 39 (1988).

171. D. Bell, *The End of Ideology* (1960) and his *The Coming of Post-Industrial Society* (1973).

172. C. Crouch in M. Regini (ed.), *The Future of Labour Movements* (1992)

185; compare J. Goldthorpe in *J.H. Goldthorpe: Consensus and Controversy op.cit.*, n. 166, 431-4 on co-existence of corporatism and dualism. But see W. Streeck, *Social Institutions and Economic Performance op.cit.*, n. 169, 66-72, who detects a possible convergence of 'dualist' societies. On the puzzling difficulty of measuring convergence or divergence of trade unionism in Canada and the United States: L. Troy (1992) 30 BJIR 1, and (1993) 31 BJIR 305; J. Rose and G. Chaison (1993) 31 BJIR 293; M. Thompson (1993) 31 BJIR 299.

173. R. Blanpain and J.-C. Javillier, *Droit du Travail Communautaire* (1991) 64-5.

174. See M. Weiss Chap. III in G. Spyropoulos and G. Fragnière (eds.), *Work and Social Policies in the New Europe* (1991) 59-75. See too, P. Lange, G. Ross, M. Vanicelli, *Unions, Change and Crisis: French and Italian Unions and the Political Economy 1945-80* (1982); P. Gourevitch, A. Martin, G. Ross, S. Bernstein, A. Marcovits, C. Allen, *Unions and Economic Crisis (Britain, Germany and Sweden)* (1984); G. Spyropoulos, *L'Adaptation des syndicats aux mutations en cours: à la recherche d'un Modèle d'analyse comparative: Études Offertes à Marcel David* (1989) especially 430-441.

175. See J. Due, J.S. Madsen, and C.S. Jensen, 'The Social Dimension: Convergence or Diversification of I.R. in the Single European Market?' (1991) 22 Ind. Rels. Jo. 85. On the delayed proposals on atypical workers, see the Commission *Second Report on the Application of the Community Charter* (COM (92) 562 Final, 23 December 1992); this flexibility of labour is needed to satisfy the 'needs of businesses' and the 'aspirations of workers', para. 14. On British species of atypical workers, P. Leighton (1986) 8 Comp. Lab. Law J. 34.

176. Equality of men and women now has its own independent place in Community values, not least because of art. 119 of the Treaty: see C. Docksey (1991) 20 ILJ 258; so too in a different manner has safety at work, on which neo-liberals accept regulation: F. Hayek, *Law, Legislation and Liberty* (1979) Vol. III, 115 (though he naively believed protection could be ensured by 'general rules'). Freedom of movement for workers is directed to the operation of markets; so to some extent are measures proposed for re-insertion of those suffering 'social exclusion'.

177. See on the dominance of market integration and the uncertain purpose of existing Community labour law Directives: P.L. Davies, 'The Emergence of Community Labour Law' Chap. 10 in W. McCarthy, *Legal Interventions in Industrial Relations* (1992), and 'Acquired Rights, Creditors' Rights, Freedom of Contract and Industrial Democracy' (1990) 9 *Yearbook of European Law* (1990) 21. Also, on the supremacy of competition not welfare in Community labour law: G.F. Mancini, 'Labour Law and Community Law' (1985) 20 Ir. Jur. (NS) 1; B. Hepple, *European Social Dialogue - Alibi or Opportunity* (1993 Institute of Employment Rights): will the social dialogue be 'an alibi for inaction'?; Wedderburn, 'European Community Law and Workers' Rights: Fact or Fake?' (1991) 13 Dublin UL 1, and 'The Social Charter in Britain: Labour Law and Labour Courts?' (1991) 54 MLR 1,10-17 (the 'logic of Community labour law').

178. See for example the Commission's *Second Report on the Application by the EC of the Community Charter of Fundamental Social Rights for Workers*

(COM(92) 562 fin. 23 December 1992) paras 10 to 49, where freedom of association escapes the detailed attention of the Commission despite the fact that all Member States (except the United Kingdom) report upon it: see *ibid*. Annex.

179. See W.B. Creighton, 'An ILO Perspective', *Trade Unions in a Single Market* (1992, ICTUR) who records breaches of Conventions 87 and 98 in laws on collective bargaining or strikes between 1981 and 1990 by Belgium (1), Denmark (5), Germany (1), Greece (9), the Netherlands (1), Portugal (7), Spain (6), United Kingdom (3), in addition to further criticisms of the Committee of Experts (such as the GCHQ case in Britain): note 185 below.

180. See the Commission's *Communication to the Council: ILO Report V(1)* '*Safety and Health in Mines' (81st Session June 1994)*, 3 September 1993, SEC (93) 1291 final, relying on Opinion 2/91 ECJ (concerning similar issues on ILO Convention 170); see F. Maupin, *Particularismes institutionnels et vocation universelle: les défis croisés des relations CEE-OIT* (1990) Rev. Générale de Droit Interl. Public, no. 1, 49-90. The ILO is, of course, a tripartite UN agency, where government representatives have regular communication with their national employer and union sides. The ILO was unlikely to accept demands for a change in representation which appeared to need a change in its practices and constitution.

181. *Union Syndicale-Amalg. Euro. Public Service Union, Massa and Kortner v EC Council* (Case 175/73) [1974] ECR 917 (First Chamber); *Syndicat Général du Personnel des Organismes Européens v EC Commission* (Case 18/74) [1974] ECR 933.

182. *Maurissen and European Public Service Union v Court of Auditors* (Cases C-193/87 and 194/87) [1990] ECR 95 ECJ (First Instance): quite apart from the agreement made with the unions, the Court accepted here that trade union freedoms covered such representatives generally, as evidenced in the regulations.

183. W.B. Creighton, *op.cit.*, n. 179 above; Wedderburn, *Freedom of Association: Protection in the Community* (1992, Report for the Commission); there should at least be a Community Recommendation on freedom of association which, although not binding, could be taken into account in Community law: *Grimaldi v Fonds des Maladies Professionelles* [1989] ECR 4407. Compare the searching inquiry by A.Lo Faro 'EC Social Policy and 1993: the Dark side of European Integration?' (1992) 14 Comp. Lab. Law J. 1.

184. On Community support for workers' councils in transnational enterprises within the social dialogue pending the adoption of a Directive, see: I. Roberts, 'Where are European Works Councils?' (1993) 24 Ind. Rels. J. 178, see too n. 188 below; compare M. Gold and M. Hall, *European-level Information and Consultation in Multinational Companies* (1992); and see (1993) 228 EIRR 13, and 239 EIRR 14, 20 (on the possible emergence of a procedure for obtaining information rights). Ford Motor Co. has agreed to establish a works council covering employees in five European countries: *Financial Times* 1 October 1993 (representativity problems have been solved – at least temporarily – by

officials and conveners attending from Britain and members of existing works councils from Germany; it is not clear what would happen if workers in one jurisdiction wished to be represented in a way used by law or national practice in another).

185. Commission, *Action Programme on the Implementation of the Community Charter of Basic Social Rights for Workers* (COM (89) 568, 27 November 1989) Part II, Chap. 6, p. 29. The most persistent European culprit in recent times is the United Kingdom: see the *Reports* of the ILO Experts (see especially 1989, 76th Session, 234-41, 302-3; 1991 78th Session, 217-23, 289-91; 1992, 79th Session, 242-9, 264-5) to which the UK Government has responded with legislation enlarging the offences against Convention 87 and 98; see ss. 13-21 TURER Act 1993.

186. See P. Marginson, 'European Integration and Transnational Management-Union Relations in the Enterprise' (1992) 30 BJIR 529 (and on employer opposition 536-42). The Commission's forthcoming studies on European Social Policy will need to consider how far individual Member States can solve such problems without Community standards.

187. E. Fracnkcl, *'Die politische Bedeutung des Arbeitsrecht'* (1932) cited in R. Lewis and J. Clark (eds.), *Labour Law and Politics in the Weimar Republic op.cit.*, n. 1 above, 36.

188. On the Commission's budget for transnational meetings of workers' representatives from multinational enterprises ('B3 4004'), see (1993) 238 EIRR 15 (applications from some workers' groups were rejected by the Commission: 19). And see the problems caused by requests to the Commission from the autonomous CEC and CESI unions, not affiliated to the ETUC, for recognition at Community level on grounds of freedom of choice and 'union pluralism', (1993) 230 EIRR3 and 236 *ibid.* 3-4. A number of other similar employees' organisations exist in Europe, especially in the public sector. Maverick employers' organisations outside UNICE or CEEP might cause even greater difficulty if they wished to join the dialogue.

189. Especially J. Goldthorpe, D. Lockwood, F. Bechhofer, J. Platt, *The Affluent Worker in the Class Structure* (1969), J. Goldthorpe, 'The End of Convergence' and W. Streeck, 'Neo-Corporatist Industrial Relations' in J. Goldthorpe (ed.), *Order and Conflict in Contemporary Capitalism* (1984) and G. Marshall, H. Newby, D. Rose, C. Vogler, *Social Class in Modern Britain* (1988). See too on industrial pluralism, R. Hyman and I. Brough, *Social Values and Industrial Relations* (1975); D. Gallie (ed.), *Employment in Britain*, Chap. 16; and see above n. 48. On co-existence of different models within the industrial relations of one country, see the helpful discussion by G. Cella and T. Treu, *Relazioni industriali (voce per una enciclopedia)* 1986 31 Giorn. DLRI 475, 518.

190. For a summary, see M. Regini, 'Introduction: Past and Future of Social Studies of Labour Movements', *The Future of Labour Movements* (1992) citing the prognosis of P. Schmitter and W. Streeck in 'Euro-pluralism and pressure politics', 12-13.

191. *European Industrial Relations op.cit.*, n. 90 above, 359.

192. Among 37,000 TNC's 1 per cent owns one half of all foreign assets; see J. Dunning, *Multinational Enterprises and the Global Economy* (1993):

'international production has become a structural characteristic of the world economy' 128; UNCTAD *World Investment Report 1993; Transnational Corporations and Integrated International Production* (1993); and S. Gill and D. Law, *The Global Political Economy* (1988).

193. Some commodity trade agreements already include such commitments: *Financial Times*, 15 November 1993.

194. I am most indebted here to Peter Muchlinski for sight of his *Multinational Enterprises and the Law: a Study of Evolution and Change in International Business Regulation* (1995) which offers a full discussion. See too, P. Davies 'Labour Law and Multinational Groups of Companies' in K. Hopt (ed.), *Groups of Companies in European Laws* (1982) 208-28, and pp. 238ff. above.

195. See for the United States: *First National Maintenance Corp.* v *NLRB* 452 US 666 (1981); *Dubuque Packing Co.* 303 NLRB (66) 137 LRRM 1185 (1991); Britain: *Newns* v *British Airways plc.* [1992] IRLR 575, 577, CA; Italy: G. Ghezzi and U. Romagnoli *Il diritto sindicale* (3rd ed. 1992) 156-7 (no duty to bargain though the duty not to engage in 'anti union conduct' still applies); but see in France the wide duty to consult the *comité d'entreprise*: (applying since 1982 to cases of transfer of control by share acquisition, which are of course not covered in Britain by the TUPE Regulations 1981 SI 1794): *Code du Travail* Art. L-432-1; G. Lyon-Caen and J. Pélissier, *Droit du Travail* (1992 16th ed.) 680-6.

196. ILO *Declaration cit.* above p. 309-10, para, 33; but in special circumstances the employer can drop below national standards: Muchlinski *op.cit.* n. 194, who points out that in some cases multinationals have, however, shown determination to improve on minimum local entitlements (as in the Levi-Strauss case: *Financial Times* 8 May 1993).

197. P. Muchlinski *op.cit.*, Chap. 13, n. 194 above, citing the decision on *Citibank* (Denmark) and R. Blanpain, *The OECD Guidelines for Multinational Enterprises and Labour Relations: Experience and Review* (1985) Vol. III, 97-100.

198. See the discussion in G. Lyon-Caen and A. Lyon-Caen, *Droit Social International et Européen* (8th ed. 1993) 69, and the helpful Chap. III in F. Mogenstern, *International Conflicts of Labour Law* (1984 ILO).

199. Employees of IBM in a ballot in 1977 rejected ASTMS as a recognised union: J. Stopford and L. Turner, *Britain and the Multinationals* (1985) 146. Many American employers use strong methods to resist union incursions: C. Craver, *op.cit.*, n. 12 above, 47-51. United States experience suggests that control by law over the employer's manipulation of employees' views is not easy to achieve. On industrial relations in different types of MNE, see P. Marginson (1992) 3 BJIR 529; on intra-firm welfare (especially the Airbus exemption in the EC): G. Esping-Anderson, 'Labour Movements and Welfare States' in M. Regini (ed.), *The Future of Labour Movements* (1992) 133, 145.

200. See the Directive proposed on protection of 'posted workers': OJ C187/93, 9 July 1993; the worker should receive the same minimum conditions on core employment matters as apply to work of the same character where it is temporarily carried out; but those conditions must be laid down by law, administrative provision, collective agreements or

arbitration awards binding the whole occupation or industry or otherwise with an 'erga omnes' effect: Art. 3. See on the erga omnes problem, above n. 121ff. On the background to the Posted Workers Directive, see Rush Portugesa Lda. v Office National d'Immigration (Case 113/89, 27.3.1990) [1991] 2 CMLR 818 ECJ.

201. One test of the Commission's forthcoming Green Paper on European Social Policy 1993 will be whether it offers mechanisms to enforce ILO standards.

202. See Thriving on Diversity: informing and consulting employees in multinational enterprises (1993, Multinational Business Forum). See too, C. Bartlett and S. Ghoshal, Managing Across Borders – The Transnational Solution (1989).

203. See W. Streeck in (1981) 19 BJIR 149, 164-8, and Chap. 3 in G. Teubner (ed.), Regulating Corporate Groups in Europe (1990).

204. See on that issue D. Metcalf (1989) 27 BJIR 1 and (1990) 28 BJIR 249; P. Nolan and P. Marginson (1990) 28 BJIR 227-47; W. Brown and P. Nolan (1988) 26 BJIR 339; T. Kochan, H. Katz, R. McKersie, The Transformation of American Industrial Relations (1986).

205. See on Spain and Britain, R. Nobles, Controlling Occupational Pensions Schemes (1992, Institute of Employment Rights).

206. The public conciliation agency, ACAS, a tripartite body, was deprived of its function of improving collective bargaining by s. 43, TURER Act 1993, which Act also gave the Minister power to require it to levy charges on parties assisted by conciliation work (s. 44). Neo-liberals had long demanded such changes: see e.g. C. Hanson and G. Mather, Striking Out Strikes (1988) 90-1. ACAS made clear its continuing availability to advise on various matters, including collective bargaining: Financial Times 21 October 1993.

207. Comitati di base or unofficial rank and file groups outside and within trade unions; the law is Law of 12 June 1990, n. 146; T. Treu, M. Roccella, A. Grilli, P. Pascucci, Sciopero e servizi essenziali (1991); M. Rusciano and G. Santo Pasarelli, Lo sciopero nei servizi essenziali (1991). In France unofficial coordinations have played a similar rôle.

208. TULRCA 1992 ss. 226-35, amended by ss. 17-21 TURER Act 1993 (the strike ballot must now be a postal ballot).

209. S. Sciarra, '...Tutela giurisdizionale v giustizia privata' 1992, Lav. Dir. 493, 500. See too, on the position in practice, E. Gragnoli, 'L'individuazione delle 'prestazioni indispensabili' nel comparto della scuola e gli interventi della Commissione di garanzia' 1992, Lav. Dir. no. 2, 340-60.

210. T. Treu, Chap. XXII, 'Strikes in Essential Services' in R. Blanpain and M. Weiss (eds.), Changing Face of Labour Law and Industrial Relations (1993) 333, on the Commission and collective bargaining, see 348-49; this 'regulation of conflict in essential services derives from a combination of a possible maximum of ten different sources', 333. The 'complexity of the regulatory sources has sometimes caused deadlocks' and agreements are often inadequate 'in their procedural rules'; the defects are not failures in regulatory drafting; they stem from inadequate social legitimacy of the parties, unions and employers: 351-3.

211. G. Giugni, 'Recent Trends in Italian Strike Law', Chap. XXIII, *Changing Face of Labour Law and Industrial Relations op.cit.*, n. 210 above, 355-8; the reference is to O. Kahn-Freund, *Heritage and Adjustment* (1979) 78; so too, in his 'Postscript' to *Labour Law and Politics in the Weimar Republic op.cit.*, n. 1 above, he wrote: 'I am coming increasingly to the conclusion ... that what the state represents is the consumer: in intention, not in actuality'. Such a leap challenges both the nature of the employment relationship and the 'interests' of consumers, both individual and corporate; for as to the latter, he insisted that a company's interests must always be those of the shareholders alone: *Industrial Democracy* (1977) 6 ILJ 65, 76-7; *contra* P. Davies and Wedderburn (1977) 6 ILJ 197, 200-1.

212. See G. Orwell, *Homage to Catalonia* (1938).

213. G. Giugni *op.cit.*. The causes of fluctuations in strikes are notoriously uncertain: M. Shalev, Chap. 3, M. Regini (ed.), *The Future of Labour Movements* (1992); W. Brown and S. Wadhwani 1990, 131 Nat. Instit. Econ. Rev. 2, and Paper 376 Centre for Labour Economics LSE.

214. Treu *op.cit.*, n. 210 above, at 338.

215. The test for marginal activities may be whether the sub-sector is required for 'fundamental consumer interests' (e.g. a catering service in an airline): Treu *op.cit.*, 344.

216. G. Giugni, *op.cit.*, n. 211 above, refers to G. Teubner (ed.), *Dilemmas of Law in the Welfare State* (1986), and also to H. Sinzheimer, *Über den Grundgedanken und die Möglichkeit eines einheitlichen Arbeitsrecht für Deutschland* (1914). But it may be open to question whether the new Law is concretely 'reflexive'.

217. Arts. 8, 9; the parties may challenge an Ordinance within 7 days: art. 10: see A. Zoppoli in M. Rusciano and G. Santo Passarelli, *Lo sciopero nei servizi essenziali* (1991) 104-132.

218. See L. Mariucci on the 'most delicate relationship between the individual ownership of the right [to strike] and the relative impossibility of exercising it in face of a programme of guarantees for minimum services,' *Notiziario Giuridico* 1991, no. 2/3, 30; and further in (1990) Lav. Dir. 533. Few other Italian authors appear to have probed this aspect. On laws about strikes in essential services, see Wedderburn, *Employment Rights in Britain and Europe* (1991) 316-15. On Britain, S. Fredman and G. Morris, *The State as Employer* (1989).

219. Signed after long negotiations on 3 July 1993, a four year national contract on labour relations, limiting plant bargaining benefits to those 'strictly related' to the results of joint programmes for increases in productivity; see too *Financial Times* 5 July 1993. Further labour law legislation is proposed, probably including a Bill on representativity of unions, likely to introduce new 'rules of the game' that may favour established unions.

220. E. Warren and L. Brandeis, 'The Right to Privacy' 4 Harv. L. Rev. 193, 205 (1890). In what follows I am greatly indebted to participants at the 'Pontignano' comparative labour law seminar held at Sitges, Barcelona, 12-18 September 1993, in particular to M. Magnani, R. Romei, Salvador del Rey Guanter, S. Deakin, A. Lyon-Caen and W. Daübler.

221. See the seminal article by S. Simitis, 'Reviewing Privacy in an Information Society', 135 Univ. Penn. L.Rev. 707-46 (1987). On other aspects, see B. Napier, 'Computerisation and Employment Rights' (1992) 21 ILJ 1.

222. G. Giugni, 'Political, Religious and Private Life Discrimination' Chap. 4 in F. Schmidt (ed.), *Discrimination in Employment* (1978), 191. See the Italian Workers' Statute 1970, Law 300, in particular arts. 1, 4, 8, 15, 16.

223. See J-M. Verdier, *Droit du Travail* (9th ed. 1990) 158; Law of 31 December 1992, discussed below; also the Civil Code art. 9.

224. G. Lyon-Caen, *Les libertès publiques et l'emploi* (1992) 154-5, discussing J. Savatier on subordination, *La liberté dans le travail* Dr. Soc. 1990, 49.

225. Convention nos. 111, 1958, on discrimination; and on dismissal Convention no. 158, 1982; Napier, 'Dismissals – the New ILO Standards' (1983) 12 ILJ 17, and (1984) 13 ILJ 130: the UK Government refused to ratify the 1982 Convention or accept the associated Recommendation no. 166, by reason of the burdens this would throw on British employers; ironically, here it preferred the method of collective bargaining.

226. Italian Constitution 1948, art. 3.

227. T. Ramm, '*Diritti fondamentali e diritto del lavoro*' (1991) 50 Giorn. DLRI 359, 364, on the German Constitution arts. 1, 2. On the practice of commentators and courts of looking for tests in 'human dignity', 'fundamental values' and the like, rather than to 'the specific societal, political and economic factors' behind the privacy debates, see S. Simitis *op.cit.*, n. 221 above, 135 Univ. Penn. L.Rev. 708.

228. As in *Dunlop c. Clavaud* Soc. 28 April 1988, (employee reinstated when dismissed by reason of his exercising the right to freedom of expression outside the enterprise); see J-M. Verdier, '*Liberté et travail: problématiques des droits de l'homme et rôle du juge*' 1988 D. Chron, 63-70. On the '*droit d'expression*' within the enterprise, see G. Lyon-Caen and J. Pelissier, *Droit du Travail op.cit.*, n. 123 above, 366-73.

229. On the draft Community Directive on data protection, see below n. 254.

230. Legislation in 1990 banned discrimination in hiring on grounds of trade union membership or non-membership, but not trade union activity; also banned is discrimination on grounds of sex (1975) or race (1976). On hiring, employers may rely on information secretly gathered about militancy in union activities. On the availability of criminal records, below notes 246-251 below.

231. *O'Brien* v *Prudential Assurance* [1979] IRLR 149 (work 'completely satisfactory'); *Saunders* v *National Camps Assoc.* [1980] IRLR 174 (camp handyman found to be homosexual); *Matthewson* v *RB Wilson Dental Laboratories* [1988] IRLR 512.

232. *Boychuk* v *Symons Holdings Ltd* [1977] IRLR 395 (wearing of lesbian badges). See H. Collins, *Justice in Dismissal op.cit.* n. 18 above, 37-40, 73-80, 118-22, for a revealing analysis of this crippling test, invented by the courts on top of the inadequate provision by the legislature; also Wedderburn, *The Worker and the Law* (1986, 3rd ed.) 453 (courts provide no 'fairness for the unconventional').

233. Soc. 17 April 1991, Dr. soc. 1991, 489 (private morality of the employee

cannot justify dismissal unless it disturbs the workplace); Soc. 22 January 1992, Dr. soc. 1992, 334 (activity as a consumer does not affect his position as employee). See G. Lyon-Caen, *Les libertés publiques et l'emploi* (1992).

234. Law no. 92-1446, 31 December 1992; below, n. 264.

235. Arts. 1 and 8, *Lo Statuto dei lavoratori* Law 300, 1970; with criminal sanctions; see on art. 8, S. Sciarra in G. Giugni (ed.), *Commentario al Statuto dei lavoratori* (1979) 100.

236. See Cass. 11 March 1987, no. 1535 (unlawful discipline of Alitalia hostess for refusing to answer question from US consulate about membership of Communist Party, so that she could be employed on flights to America); see also on art. 4, G. Ghezzi and F. Liso (1986) 8 Giorn. DLRI 353.

237. See art. 4; see Pret. Milan 12 July 1988 (electronic systems for determining the presence and activities of workers); compare on the subjective element, Pret. Pen. Milan 4 October 1988 (all such machines are covered strictly, including '*Kienzle* machines' which can record the details of the worker's presence and activity, even if the employer had no subjective intent to offend); Pret. Milan 5 December 1984 (computerised system automatically recording details of work can be a prohibited system if intended to control workers).

238. See on the new technology and control over behaviour and work of the worker: G. Lyon-Caen, *Les libertés publiques et l'emploi* (1992) 142-51, and in particular the delicate lines of illegality surrounding the use of video camers, '*telemetrie*' and the manner in which 'the system of control is incorporated into the process of production' *ibid*. 150.

239. S. Simitis *op.cit*, n. 221 above, 135 Univ. Penn. L.Rev 707 (1987) 737-8 (who was himself the Hesse Land Commissioner); and see the remarkable devices of control described at 729-35, including the total surveillance possible through a modem by 'Videotex': 720-34.

240. G. Lyon-Caen, *Les libertés publiques et emploi* (1992) 132; compare his list of necessary rights to achieve transparency – a right to prior notice of the purposes, to access, to rectification, to exinguishment of spent information, to object to processing of certain information and to a remedy: 79.

241. In France under Law no. 78-17 of 6 January 1978 (the Commission is independent of all other authorities: art. 13); and in Britain the Data Protection Act 1984, on which see D. Bainbridge, *Computers and the Law* (1990).

242. S. Simitis, 'Developments in the Protection of Workers' Personal Data', *Conditions of Work Digest*, Vol. 10 (1991) 7, 8, and 14-21, especially for Reports of the Commissioners in Canada. The thirst for information gathering is said to have begun with Ford shortly after 1900 sending inspectors to investigate employees' life styles: A. Nevins, *Ford: the Man and the Company* (1954) 54.

243. J. Fayssinet, '*Nouvelles technologies et protection des libertés dans l'entreprise*' Dr. Soc. 1992, 596-602.

244. See Simitis, 'Juridification of Labor Relations' in G. Teubner (ed.), *Juridification of the Social Spheres* (1987) especially on 'relocation of work' 149-52; compare the extensive review by B. Veneziani, '*Nuove*

technologie e contratto di lavoro: profili di diritto comparato' (1987) 33
Giorn DLRI 1-60, in English in Wedderburn, B. Veneziani, S. Ghimpu,
Diritto del lavoro in Europa (1987) 61-131. So far, however, the more
extreme predictions of 'cottage' industries where most work is done at
distant, suitably equipped locations, do not seem justified.

245. Section 2 and Schedule 1, and s. 21 Data Protection Act 1984. Special
protection can be given by Order as to information on racial origin,
political or religious or other beliefs, physical or mental health, sexual life
and criminal convictions: s. 2(3).

246. The Rehabilitation of Offenders Act 1974 was designed to render many
convictions 'spent' after varying periods of time; but the Minister has
exercised his powers liberally to create many exception by Order to the
operation of that Act: see the extraordinary *Disclosure of Criminal
Records for Employment Vetting Purposes – A Consultative Document*
(1993 Cm. 2319) 21, Annex E, for the 43 wide areas of employment
exempted under the 1974 Act and 17 more under other powers in related
Acts.

247. *Ninth Report of the Data Protection Registrar* 1993, Section 3 (i), (ii),
(vii).

248. *Disclosure of Criminal Records for Employment Vetting Purposes* (1993
Cm. 2319) 7; many of these convictions were not 'spent' under the
Rehabilitation of Offenders Act 1974, see at 18. The Report advocates
that records should be managed by a *privatised* agency, making charges
for disclosure.

249. *Ibid.* 18: spent convictions might be ignored 'if the technical systems
permitted'. It is admitted that this would 'blur the borderline' between
individual application and enforced subject access. But compare the
practices on 'certificates', p. 317 above, and n. 251 below.

250. S. Simitis, *Conditions of Work Digest op.cit.*, n. 242, especially at 18.

251. See *Disclosure of Criminal Records for Employment Vetting Purposes
op.cit.* 7, 9, 12 and 17 and Annex F: citing notably, Belgium, Denmark,
Germany, Greece, Italy, Luxembourg, and in lesser measure Spain and
Portugal.

252. See on these controls over workers in earlier eras, B. Veneziani in B.
Hepple (ed.), *The Making of Modern Labour Law* (1986) 40-4 on France,
and T. Ramm, 293-4 on Prussia.

253. Council of Europe, *Convention for the Protection of Individuals with
regard to Automatic Processing of Personal Data*, in effect 1 October
1985; *Protection of Personal Data Used for Employment Purposes:
Recommendation R(89)2*, 13.1.89. Previously the OECD had issued a
helpfully succinct code: *Guidelines on the Protection of Privacy and
Transborder Flow of Personal Data*, 1978.

254. Articles 13, 14 of the revised proposal for a *Council Directive on the
Protection of Individuals with regard to the Processing of Personal Data
and on the Free Movement of Such Data* COM(92) 422 fin.-SYN 287,
OJ. 311/30, 27.11.92; A. Mole, *'Au delà de la loi informatique et libertés'*
Dr. Soc. 1992, 603.

255. As protected by the Council of Europe Convention of Human Rights
1950, article 8.

256. On the Commission's strategy on works councils: M. Hall (1992) 30 BJIR 549. This project has been adopted for a Directive under the Social Chapter by 'the Eleven': *Financial Times* 24 November 1993.
257. See W. Gould, *A Primer of American Labor Law* (1982) 119-22, on the Vice President of General Electric who took to announcing his final position at the outset of bargaining.
258. S. Simitis, *Conditions of Work Digest* n. 242 above, at 12; see too, A. Mole, '*Au delà de la loi informatique et libertés*' Dr. Soc, 1992, 603, 604-5.
259. See the dispute at British Telecommunications, *Financial Times* 8 October 1993. Of course, neither system makes a dismissal for redundancy necessarily 'fairer' in any given situation; but the new system put unilateral control more firmly into the hands of management.
260. The thesis holds that each step towards detailed regulation is an interference with the worker's 'life world and colonises his behaviour by forcing it into a pre-fixed scheme that excluded alternatives'. S. Simitis, 'Juridification of Labor Relations' in G. Teubner (ed.), *Juridification of the Social Spheres* (1987) 132, and above n. 244.
261. S. Simitis, '*Il diritto del lavoro e la riscoperta dell'individuo*' (1990), 45 Giorn. 59, 89-91. On 'colonisation' (there expressed as 'colonialisation') see S. Simitis, 'Juridification of Labour Relations' in G. Teubner (ed.), *Juridification of the Social Spheres* (1987) 132-4, where the weight of *legislation* is claimed frequently to depersonalise the worker and leave him with no choice; see too, the helpful note by W. Murphy, 'The Habermas Effect' 1989, *Current Legal Problems* 135, 140-8. But it may be suggested that a similar loss of choice eventuates for the individual if market forces become the 'guiding star' of policy, leading to deregulation and decollectivisation, as in Britain in the 1990's, especially where choice is further limited by extensive unemployment. Contrast also, Simitis' own requirement of consultation with the employees' representatives: *Conditions of Work Digest op.cit.* n. 242 above (employees can be categorised and controlled through the processing of data; the experience of even the protective German judicial decisions shows that only a right of 'informational self-determination' will suffice to protect them: 20-21).
262. Simitis *op.cit.* n. 261 above, (1990) 45 Giorn. DLRI at 113, citing Sinzheimer's call for a 'renewal of man within the productive processes': *Philipp Lotmar und die deutsche Arbeitsrechtswissenschaft, Arbeitsrecht* 1922, 587.
263. G. Lyon-Caen, *Les Libertés publiques et l'emploi* (1992) 12.
264. Law no. 92-1446, 31 December 1992; the details of this law repay study but cannot be discussed here; for an analysis see: J. Grisnir, '*Les dispositions nouvelles relatives "au recrutement individuel et aux libertés individuelles"* ', Dr. Ouvr. 1993, 237.
265. French employers appear to have taken to using 'exotic and doubtful' methods of selection in hiring including occult sciences, graphology and 'psycho-morphology': J. Grisnir *op.cit.*, n. 264 above, 239.
266. This is an exception to the normal payment in a civil action of an *astreinte* when (with a few exceptions) the money is paid to the *plaintiff* by a defendant who is in breach of a court order; this may perhaps be seen as a

small move towards the common law practice of fines for civil contempt of court: see Wedderburn, 'The Injunction and the Sovereignty of Parliament' in *Employment Rights in Britain and Europe* (1991), Chap. 7, 174-84.

267. G. Lyon-Caen, *Les libertès publiques et l'emploi* (1922), 158.

268. See *ibid*. 166-9, for a pungent discussion of remedies; see too the proposal to introduce a new 'elected representative for individual liberties' alongside the other elected representatives in French enterprises; the legislature would not go that far and assigned the job to the existing elected *délégué du personnel*.

269. *Discount Tobacco & Confectionery* v *Armitage* [1990] IRLR 15, 16, *per* Knox, J.

270. A phrase used by Bruno Veneziani in his valuable, '*La flessibilità del lavoro e i suoi antidoti*' (1993) 58 Giorn. DLRI 235, 310.

271. See O. Kahn-Freund in *Law and Politics in the Weimar Republic* n. 1 above, 89-90 (borrowing a phrase from Flatow, he says Sinzheimer saw the works councils as the 'extended arm' of the trade unions – a dramatic contrast with the works councils currently proposed for transnational companies in the Community in 1993).

272. Hugo Sinzheimer's speech to the Constituent Assembly, 21 June 1919: O. Kahn-Freund and T. Ramm (eds.), *Arbeitsrecht und Rechtssoziologie: Gesammelte Aufsätze und Reden* (1976) Vol. 1, 356-72, and G. Arrigo and G. Vardaro, n. 1 above, 45-47.

10

FREEDOM AND FRONTIERS OF LABOUR LAW

The problems of establishing an alternative labour law for 2000 lie not so much in selecting the reforms to be addressed. Many are well known and waiting for action; others will arise from the diversity of the new tasks that may be assigned to labour legislation and the pressures put by other legal policies at its frontiers. But the core function of an alternative labour law will remain a quest to extend the freedoms of those who in our society are ordinarily strangers to power, even when they are fortunate enough to be granted employment – that avenue for the sale of labour power which is for most people their only asset. It is a truism of labour relations law everywhere that, whilst individual rights are important in this ambition, workers' interests cannot be protected, let alone advanced, without legitimising and promoting collective action by them in autonomous organisations, within laws that provide 'adequate protection against acts of anti-union discrimination in respect of their employment'.[1] The key issues in these areas of British labour law are fairly well known, though some have been overlaid by myth in the decade just ended. It is worth examining them briefly before turning to other influences on labour law policy.

SOME KEY ISSUES

The issues include: improved protection for workers individually, by objective standards of conduct at work, testing the substance and procedure of management behaviour on hiring, discipline and dismissal against standards, not of 'the reasonable employer', but of civil liberties;[2] an effective remedy of reinstatement to the job, as well as compensation, for those unfairly sacked;[3] and a general recognition of workers' rights as citizens in the workplace,[4] including rights to family leave, equal treatment and a realistic drive against racist and other forms of discrimination. Just as crucial are measures ensuring

350

rights to trade union activity at work and protecting the autonomy of unions in their internal affairs; rights to organise and to take industrial action, to end the scandal whereby British workers are still held to break their contracts of employment in taking even lawful strike action; and new obligations requiring employers to fund training courses and offer training and retraining to their workers in schemes negotiated with trade unions – the most conducive method for efficient change[5] – given that 'most firms will most of the time have a tendency to invest less in training than they should in their own interest'.[6] At tribunal level, the reforms required are legion, including a release from some bizarre features, such as the rule whereby a worker may be required to pay a monetary deposit before he or she can pursue a complaint about the unlawful loss of a job.[7] More generally, British law must make good its shameful contraventions of ILO standards, in particular the Conventions on freedom of association and collective bargaining, contraventions brought about by the incestuous mingling of the common law and the new legislation since 1980.[8] At European level, the government will be obliged to introduce protections for young workers (whose safeguards were scandalously deregulated in 1989)[9]: and it is already bound to provide for workers' representatives a structure for consultation on workers' rights in collective dismissals and transfer of the employer's undertaking (other than one by sale of shares, by means of which capital is still able to change the nature of the enterprise without such consultation).[10] And a real drive for educational opportunity must be mounted, on which new ventures of industrial democracy can be built. That is an area where action at domestic and European level has been most dismal. Jacques Delors converted the labour movement, when it hungered after something better than Thatcherism, by setting out his 'social manifesto',[11] emphasising such promises as workers' rights to 'access to training throughout their working lives', adding that 'the right to continuing training is enshrined in the first framework agreement between management and labour at European level'.[12]

It would be quite wrong to suggest that the twin ambitions of contributing to the battle against structural unemployment and of constructing a code of labour law on adequate standards of employment rights can be attained without excising swathes of Thatcher and post-Thatcher labour legislation from the statute book, as well as making profound changes in the common law. Both will be required. No doubt there can be no 'return to 1974', but nor should alternative labour law tolerate a prolongation of the barbarisms in the

1980s statutes. For example, the principle of ballots inside trade unions can no doubt continue to be one (though not the only) measure of internal democracy; but colleagues in Europe just cannot believe that British legislation has so far distorted this principle, and departed from elementary industrial liberties, as to require, as it now does, trade unions to notify to employers the identities of their individual members involved in industrial action both at the time of the ballot and at the time of the strike.[13] 'Retaining a law on ballots' is a slogan that tells us little; we need to see the small print. There must, above all, be an end to interventions by the common law which hark back to the era of master and servant and which still dominate doctrines and procedures in the High Court (not least procedure for injunctions), with perhaps – if it is done skilfully – a carefully constructed labour court.[14] Fortunately, it is now clear that there need be no argument of principle about whether the legislation should utilise 'immunities' or 'positive rights. Both are needed in the peculiar British circumstances. Our lack of a constitution with fundamental collective rights for workers is matched by the persistent presence of the common law, so that even in 1994 the same courts which centuries ago invented doctrines of illegality to put upon workers' unions, now refuse to alter them, holding that, by the very process of collective bargaining as such, trade unions are still threatening to act illegally under the common law, because they 'negotiate with employers under threat of committing against them ... acts which that same law regards as wrongful' (that is, threatening to induce members to break their contracts by taking industrial action).[15] There is no more fundamental demand upon alternative labour law than that it must introduce a suspension of the employment contract in lawful industrial action. The authoritarian laws of 1980 to 1993 have, additionally, imposed in Britain, alone of European systems, conditions which aim to end effective trade union influence in the labour market and ultimately make them into friendly societies.[16] These legislative measures were not the result of an ideological conspiracy; they were just the working out, in a somewhat zigzag fashion, of a socio-legal ideology applied to changing events.[17] They now include measures directly controlling admission to unions, which threaten not only the TUC Bridlington procedures but even 'the ability of mainstream unions to function as a movement co-ordinating their activities, rather than as separate competing units.'[18] A new policy for labour law would not merely aim to produce law that was 'fair'; that is necessary, but not sufficient. Reform must go further to match and affect the realities of social power. A labour law which tries to disengage from the conflict of interest between those who buy and those who sell labour power, and therefore from workers' collective organisations, is the labour law of the eunuch.

Furthermore, an alternative labour law will always have in mind the overriding importance in the real world of the pursuit of full employment and the growing difficulties of achieving it in a world of global capital, where the employer – or the effective force behind what the law still sees as the 'employer', especially in corporate 'employers' – is a multinational network of capital capable of using new technologies to switch its focus rapidly from one jurisdiction to another.[19] Such a policy will have many tasks to perform, not least to prevent the transformation of any endowment of rights and obligations to support new and flexible, negotiated relationships at work into a harness for new forms of exploitation. The struggle against unemployment[20] and the relevance of the multinationals (and their quick fingered cousins on the global money markets) will at times dominate the life of any alternative government. As for the 'reserve army' of unemployed, the need for which many said had disappeared,[21] it is stubbornly present, and when its numbers fall in Europe, they do not fall to the previous level of a similar point in the economic cycle. This is a context where, managerial powers being so acutely enlarged by the facts of economic life, each and every protection enacted for employees and those seeking employment must be studied closely for its impact on the labour market, not merely its excellence in principle.

ARGUMENTS OF LABOUR LAW

In all this, alternative labour law will find that many seek to narrow the frontiers within which its writ is said legitimately to run. The scope of 'competition' law, for example, is gradually on the increase, especially in the growing competence of European competition law. There is a long frontier between competition law and labour law, which must be adequately mapped for serious study of social and legal policy, including the 'Social Chapter'. In face of practices which may not satisfy the bottom line of competition laws, the scope for a court to take account of protection for jobs or employment standards for the workers is under question in many sectors of the law of the European Union. To this frontier between labour law and competition, the battle between lowest cost and minimum welfare, we return later in this

Chapter (including the important area of 'public procurement' law, so far little studied by lawyers concerned about employment law). That inquiry will lead us to look again at a different 'frontier' between national law and European Law concerning fundamental rights affecting employment, where lines have already been drawn which neither doctrines of 'subsidiarity' nor the terms of the 'Social Chapter' agreed by Eleven States at Maastricht readily explain.

This chapter looks primarily at such contextual issues in Britain and Europe, and at European labour law, on which it may be time to ask whether – despite remarkable advances on such matters as the law of equal treatment between women and men at work – there may sometimes have been a lack of realism in the labour movement. As we shall see, the limits even of the 'Social Chapter' machinery are narrower than many believe. In such assessments it is essential to look closely at the meanings of the words offered by those in charge of the debate. No one doubts, for example, the shifting meaning of 'flexibility' or 'subsidiarity'.[22] In such inquiries it is also to be noted that the agenda for argument is often set by those who have power which they are unwilling to share. Control of the agenda often implies control over the language of debate and the meanings given to events. This is of great importance in British labour law where the terms employed are often unusually technical. The easiest examples are the 'immunities' which the emergent labour movement won for the bare legality of its activities at the turn of the century, for example in 'trade disputes', there being no demand for, or possibility of, 'positive rights' to organise, to bargain and to strike.[23] Because the collective legal framework has been built largely on 'immunities', it has been easy to misrepresent these as 'privileges' for trade unions (when without such protections they would be hourly threatened by illegality) and to call for the total withdrawal of this 'licence to use coercion conceded to unions'[24] (that is, making them unlawful) as the way to solve the nation's troubles.

Of course, the very language in which we speak of such social objectives is itself a weapon of change or of resistance, not only about trade unions, but also, for example, about the difference between 'training' (for other people's children?) and 'education' (for our children?). Labour law is a well known crucible for the fusing of the ideology and semantics inherent in arguments that claim to rest on 'facts' or 'principle'. Many have written, for example, about the ambiguities of 'freedom' in labour relations – freedom to associate, freedom to dissociate, freedom of the worker by protection by confining the freedom of the employer,[25] freedom from unemployment, or 'freedom for private economic enterprise';[26] and that key British concept 'freedom of contract', as applied to the employment contract (which in social reality remains for virtually all workers 'a command under the guise of an agreement').[27] There is no neutral usage, and writers should not conceal their preferences under that pretence. Nor do the meanings remain constant over the generations. Just as concepts of 'class' or 'revolution' or 'competition' develop new meanings with social change,[28] or with new social and political forces,[29] so an understanding of the legal context matches new appreciations of freedom. Such changes do at times affect even the courts (though British judges are unlikely to copy the Italian High Court of Appeal which in 1980 seized the semantic bull by the horns and declared that henceforth it would avoid any direct definition of a 'strike', the legal meaning of which would in future be governed, under the constitutional right to strike, by 'what the word, and the concept supported by it, carry in ordinary language in the current social context').[30]

There is a direct relationship between the legal and social limits to the pressures which workers can bring to bear on a situation by autonomous organisation and the prospects for improvement of their condition. This is one measure of the freedom which they claim in a democratic society. We have seen that this equation is greatly influenced by the extent to which the State itself recognises a sufficient legitimacy of trade union organisation essential to their condition,[31] and the extent to which employers accept, or are obliged to accept, collective bargaining by way of 'recognition of trade unions' – although some have doubted the 'retreat from collective bargaining',[32] the latest surveys tell us that *derecognition* by British employers to erode or end collective bargaining has proceeded more quickly than had previously been thought.[33] There can be no doubt that the legal changes of the 1980s are one reason for this development, though only one. There is no more difficult item on the agenda of an alternative labour law than devising legal interventions to turn round the drift from collective bargaining (and, perhaps more important, to avoid legal measures which do damage to the evolution of collective bargaining).[34] Workers' fragile 'freedoms' in the labour market will continue to reflect the contradictions of Bobbio's remark: 'Better a freedom always in danger than a freedom that is unable to develop ... Freedom which is incapable of renewing itself sooner or later becomes a new form of servitude'.[35] That dynamic renewal is the relentless task of leadership, both in the law and in social action.

British unions may be said to have often responded slowly to events in the courts. Recently they have learned that a quiet response does little to avert unprecedented onslaughts from press and Parliament. A legal judgment is perhaps the more difficult because it will normally be couched in terms claiming that the law was always so, whereas in many cases the judges will have 'developed' the legal doctrines – especially common law doctrines – which are at their disposal, so that action which was accepted as lawful before the judgment turns out to be unlawful. On such judicial decisions, union members may need rapid interpretation to shed light on the interests lurking behind the obfuscations of legal jargon. In 1964, for example, a flurry of explanation was needed to unravel the Law Lords' decision that an official who was protected (by an 'immunity') in a trade dispute for inducing members to break their employment contracts in a trade dispute, was nevertheless liable in tort, despite the statutory immunity, for 'conspiring' with members who threatened to break their contracts because, the Law Lords said, overturning the unanimous view of the Court of Appeal, of a little known wrong called 'intimidation' (which happened not to be mentioned in the statute of 1906 which gave the immunity and which was based upon a bizarre precedent concerning competing sea captains firing cannon to frighten off customers from their rival off the African coast in 1793).[36] More recently there has been little discussion of similar judgments. A Court of Appeal decision, for example, on the dock strike of 1989 which introduced new judge-made liabilities for trade unions, excited little attention, partly because the House of Lords decided for the union but on a much more limited point, leaving the Court of Appeal judgment intact as a precedent in future legal actions (especially for interlocutory injunctions).[37] Also, few union members seem to have heard of the doctrine of 'economic duress', a time bomb liability ticking away under labour law after decisions of the Law Lords in the 1980s. In the latest case, international union action had organised a boycott of a flag of convenience ship in a Swedish port, because of the extreme exploitation evident in the crew's wages and conditions. This industrial action by a boycott keeping the ship in port was lawful in Sweden. In a settlement to release the ship, the owners paid various sums to the unions and crew; the ship sailed to England, whereupon the owners sued to recover the money because in an English court the boycott would be illegal as 'economic duress'. The House of Lords held in their favour. Until the mid-1970s, 'duress' was confined to duress to the person; but the judges (not Parliament) had then decided to extend its scope to economic pressure, and they have now introduced it into labour law where, in the absence of any statutory 'immunity' its consequences could be extensive.[38] Workers can readily see the class content of such innovation so long as the confusing rhetoric is pared away – we ought not to be afraid to call it what it is merely because the phrase is unfashionable, for 'conscience' need not make cowards of us all. Moreover this is a continuing problem, whether or not we choose to enact 'positive rights'.[39] Alternative labour law should also pay heed to the more directly political effect of the language employed in the system. What greater victory in public relations has there been than the Thatcher government's description as 'trade union power' of a winter when discontent came from the rank and file, or its label of 'trade union reform' pasted on to legislation which from 1980 to 1993 progressively contravened the international minimum standards of labour law?[40] As a law to promote effective trade unionism the law 'reform' of the 1980s was as meaningless as Chomsky's famous sentence, 'Colourless green ideas sleep furiously'[41] and it was as mystifying as the announcement 'the market rose today', by which operations of finance capitalists are presented nightly in the media as if they were movements of natural forces. Labour legislation should be couched in a form available to workers, a style reviving the English radical tradition which insists that economic ills are not the product of divine 'competitive forces' but are the product of visible hands and therefore remediable by human effort.[42] Many workers have been confused, too, even about down to earth questions such as 'unfair dismissal' rights, which are often presented as including a right to a job, cloaking the inadequacy of our legal remedies (of all the applicants to tribunals concerning unfair dismissal, those successfully reinstated in their jobs were 0.33 per cent in 1989 falling to 0.17 in 1993: and the median compensation award in 1993 was £2773 – contrary to legend, there are few riches in tribunal awards).[43] Alternative labour law must concentrate as much on remedies as on rights, for rights are of little value if there is no adequate remedy. At a less exalted level, labour relations tends to be a field where even the naming of institutions becomes a battle ground. The special industrial court set up in 1971 never recovered from being labelled 'the NIRC',[44] and the public official established with the sole function of financing workers' legal actions against their own unions – business has been less than brisk – was less than happily launched with an acronym quite properly rendered as 'CROTUM'.[45]

There is one other area where the language of labour relations law has been particularly important, here as in other jurisdictions, to which it is helpful to turn before inspecting the role of competition law. This is 'incomes policy', or as it is sometimes put: 'prices and incomes policy'. This special nomenclature tends, on the one hand, to conceal the fact that any rational government programme, including the labour law programme, must have a close relationship to government economic and social policies as a whole. On the other hand, it focuses attention upon the problem of inflation, with an ideological implication in its semantics that central solutions are to be found by way of restraint on incomes, especially using weapons available to government to try to stop what it sees as 'wage-push' inflation. In one sense, every government has an 'incomes policy', since its economic policies affect incomes, deliberately or sometimes with unintended effects. A government with an alternative labour law programme will understandably call for assistance in the fight against unemployment and inflation, and that might revive an incomes policy under whatever title. The history of the British 'incomes policy' saga helps to keep the problems thereby created in perspective, just as it helps to make plain the need for trade unions to deal with the most friendly government in terms that do not allow for misunderstanding. In a sense. even Thatcherite governments inevitably pursue an 'incomes policy' whilst rejecting them in principle; it is inescapable in the public sector, if only through 'pay review' exercises. But monetarist administrations are disinclined to intervene, or to be seen to intervene, other than indirectly on collective bargaining, not least because they encourage its replacement by 'individually negotiated reward packages'.[46] The Thatcher administration's policies of deregulation and measures to relieve burdens on business', on the other hand, had a natural relationship to their economic policies; the truncation of labour rights and displacement of collectivism was part of the overall drive for 'competitive' market policies.[47] It was uncertain how far the Major government's covert intervention in the signal staff strike of 1994 heralded a more general intervention: one Minister warned 'public and private sector organisations' against paying 'inflationary pay increases'.[48] In recent years, less has been heard of the relationship between labour law and 'incomes policy'; but past experience suggests that, if inflation rose, politics based on consensus would encounter pressures to turn to formal incomes policy.

It is useful, therefore, to re-examine this area, asking especially after the role of the labour movement in the post-war years when the policy emerged; and in the light of the useful intervention of Davies and

Freedland who suggested that in the 1960s successive governments of all colours 'were never able to view the Donovan prescription as a sufficient response to the problems as they viewed them'. This 'Donovan prescription' was, as we have seen, a modernised version of collective *laissez-faire*, For government, they added, 'the inflation problem was the more significant one and that is why Donovan was of limited impact from their point of view'.[49] In one sense this insight must be correct, for government after government wrestled with inflation as a central issue. But if the suggestion is that policy on inflation and 'incomes policy' dominated all government policies on labour relations, ousting the 'Donovan culture' and its predecessors, a second opinion may be needed. Certainly some Ministers did not think so at the time: there was effectively no discussion of incomes policy in Labour's *In Place of Strife.* nor in the Conservatives' *Fair Deal at Work*.[50] Even in the 140 pages of the Ministry of Labour's *Evidence* to the Donovan Royal Commission, prices and incomes policy was given only a few lines, and then only because the National Board for Prices and Incomes might seem to have 'certain resemblances' to arbitration bodies.[51] For its part, the newly created Department of Economic Affairs wanted collective bargaining to be drawn into a much closer relationship with incomes policy, 'voluntarily' if possible, but by regulation if it became 'necessary to make the policy effective' – the first incomes policy legislation was enacted a year later – though it was compelled to say that 'as a Department' it was 'not technically competent to discuss industrial relations issues which are really matters for the Ministry of Labour'.[52] This was the clear division of functions and territory within government at the time of Donovan's deliberations in 1966.

INCOMES POLICY AND LABOUR RELATIONS LAW

This issue is not easily settled, and lessons for the future need further inquiry on this important period. As we shall see, it was a Labour Chancellor of the Exchequer who proved that the Treasury had an eye on labour relations law. Nor is the term 'incomes policy' itself easily pinned down; it is usually applied to attempts by law, sometimes soft-law or even government persuasion (often a mixture of the three) to intervene directly on wage bargaining 'in the public interest', and not merely by policies working through fiscal or market or rigged market mechanisms.[53] Nor are the attitudes towards such a policy always congruent with conventional 'left' or 'right'; whilst the consensual right has approved, the philosophy of the extreme right finds no place for such a disturbance of the 'spontaneous order of the market' which, like other moves seeking 'social justice', are, they hold, bound to fail.[54]

There are policies in many States within the European Union that pursue aims of this character, often through tripartite structures. Italy has recently built on its consensus policies a 'Protocol on Incomes and Employment Policy' of 3 July 1993,[55] a semi-voluntary system built on the corpse of wage-indexation (and accepted, so it says, even by the new, free-market Berlusconi government). Member States are now under an obligation to develop their economic policy in accordance with the 'convergence criteria' (under articles 103 and 104c of the Maastricht Treaty and the December 1993 summit decisions); and the analysis in the Commission's 1993 White Paper on economic policy, later broadly accepted by the Council of Ministers,[56] suggests that 'some part of the high wages and social costs being paid are not fully justified by the levels of productivity'.[57] Also, the Commission 'thinks that wage increases should be kept below the rate of growth in productivity'.[58] The Finance Ministers' Recommendation of 13 December 1993 (ECOFIN), prompted by the Commission, urged that 'pay developments [be] consistent with improvement in the profitability of investment and in the competitiveness of European enterprises'. In the short term 'the need to create new jobs will not permit real pay growth in most countries and may result in real pay reductions in certain sectors of the economy'.[59] For their part, European industrialists have not been slow to state their view vigorously about wages, stressing the extortionate price of labour power today:

> Labour costs are the single major cause of falling competitiveness and rising unemployment. Work is there but not at these prices'.[60]

Wages, therefore, seem to face a prospect of containment or possibly even reduction at national, perhaps one day even at Community, level, while capital maintains or increases its return and is free to extend its international mobility, the factor that above all else increases uncertainty for labour. These are conditions which echo occasions which have heralded the entry of 'incomes policy', at least as an item on the agenda.

British post-war policy is always traced from Stafford Cripps' Labour White Paper in 1948 (associated with the 1944 White Paper on full employment), followed by many others, most requiring in the words of a Conservative Paper of 1956: 'self-restraint in making wage claims and fixing profit margins and prices'.[61] But it was only in the mid-1960s that governments began to introduce the unthinkable – legislation to impose limits on incomes (mainly on wages) by law.[62] First came Labour's Prices and Incomes Acts 1966, 1967 and 1968, putting the National Board for Prices and Incomes on a statutory footing and for short periods empowering the government to halt certain wage or price increases. A Conservative government passed two not dissimilar Acts in 1972 and 1973. In both these periods the attempt to impose wage restraint by law was tentative and limited in time; and eventually it failed. In the 'Social Contract' period 1974-79 legal sanctions were abandoned. Throughout the period, such agreements as there were between unions and government were often unclear, and the commitment of government to any radical plans from the unions was in Britain (as in the comparable developments in Germany) rather limited.[63] The return to a less conditional 'voluntarism' in 1974 was significant when a general or 'secular' trend towards greater use of 'regulation' (of many different kinds) was apparent in labour law as a whole.[64] The interpretation of these complex periods, however, may have given rise to misunderstandings of importance to future policy. Commentators have noted, as we have seen, that governments in those periods had been greatly occupied with anti-wage inflation strategies and felt that the inflation problem was more significant than the Donovan proposals for reform of industrial relations and labour law.[65]

Of course, other economic events, such as the oil crisis, claimed the attention of governments. But the Treasury's lively interest in conventional theories of wage-push was dramatically emphasised in 1969 when the Chancellor of the Exchequer, Roy Jenkins, in what the TUC called the government's 'overnight decision', announced in his budget speech that an interim Bill was imminent on 'incomes policy and industrial relations', a move widely interpreted as an attempt to influence not only the Bank of England at home, but also international bankers and the IMF abroad by illustrating just how 'responsible' a Labour government could be.[66] In a formal sense the statutory interventions of 1966-8 and 1972-3 were indeed, as Kahn-Freund noted, a totally 'new departure' which limited the 'freedom of collective bargaining'.[67] In the last resort, theoretically, it made criminal both the payment of wages (collectively bargained or not) above permitted levels and also trade union pressure inducing an employer by industrial action to make such payment,[68] though naturally, employers were protected if in accordance with the policy they refused to pay.[69]

But this 'novel departure' of statutory incomes control has been identified further as 'a major departure ... from the doctrine of collective *laissez-faire* ... If collective *laissez-faire* could be abandoned in one area, was it vulnerable elsewhere?'[70] This analysis may be limited by the equivalence it makes between 'collective *laissez-faire*' and 'abstention',[71] for, as we saw in Chapter 1, here 'collective *laissez-faire*' symbolises the very tradition of encouraging autonomous trade unionism as against the more simplistic model of 'abstentionism'. At a different level it does not merit a theoretical answer, for the question was factual – 'was it vulnerable elsewhere?'. To describe the 1972-1973 Counter Inflation Acts as a 'retreat from voluntarism' is more helpful;[72] pay legislation under an incomes policy confines 'voluntarism' in a variety of ways.[73] But at a practical level, in terms of what actually happened, the policy was not effective; and by 1970, it had in truth failed. It certainly had not occupied the territory of autonomous trade unionism; nor had the immunities and other paraphernalia of labour law been blotched out by the ink of wage restraint. In fact, soon after the 1973 Act, contemporary observers thought that the statutory policy was all bluff. On the pay side the law was never invoked.[74]

First, incomes policy could not be made to work by trying to make trade union officials 'act as policemen'.[75] This was not just a matter of drafting. But it is useful not to overlook the manner in which pay policy *legislation* and its accompanying soft-law instruments (Codes etc.) were buffeted both by the law of contract and by their own need of reference points in collective bargaining. The incomes policy legislation bent in the face of both. So, one finds a Secretary of State, near the end of the game in 1973, falling at what had been one of the earliest, contractual hurdles: the employers' promise-to-pay-after-the-freeze, so building up a dam of promises to pay wage increases in the future after the policy had been changed, which could wreck the policy itself. 'What is completely legal is to reach an agreement now to pay [the wage increase] at the end of the standstill'.[76] And as to the need for reference points in collective bargaining, his Consultative Document said of new jobs: 'The rate for new work should not be more than the current rate paid in the locality for the same or most nearly similar work by the same or other employers'. In the majority of cases that meant fixing it by, or by reference to, collectively bargained standards.[77] Moreover, rises obtained in the arbitration procedures of labour law, bringing low pay 'into line' with minimum conditions in representative collective agreements, were generally exempt from the controls of incomes policy law.[78] If the main question is: did the new 'incomes policy law' cause collective *laissez-faire* to be 'abandoned', or threaten such an outcome, the evidence suggests that this would be too extreme a view.[79] That reflection does not rest, it must be said at once, on an assumption 'excluding, as a matter of definition, legislation enforced by criminal sanctions from the ambit of labour law'.[80] That would be a very odd idea indeed. Of course, criminal sanctions did, and still do, sometimes touch labour relations; but, apart from the general criminal law which applies everywhere (on, say, theft or bigamy) the crimes are mainly ancient in origin (1875, 1909, 1919) and in the modern era have been progressively contrary to the spirit of the system in peace time, ever since the repeal of the Master and Servant Acts in 1875.[81] To resurrect any criminal sanctions in incomes legislation was dramatic. It was asked: if seeking a pay rise made workers into – or look like – criminals, what liberties were safe?[82] That was why the Attorney-General was given control over prosecutions. If we inquire after the reasons why statutory incomes policy was resisted by traditional industrial relations policy, both through the trade union movement and partly in the State bureaucracy (the Ministry of Labour) as well as by sections of employers, we must not insert *a priori* assumptions but consider the wider canvas that showed how statutory incomes policy was '*not* allowed to invade and conquer' the traditional land of industrial relations. That it could have attempted this – that is, attempted to use legal sanctions to drive collective organisation out of its territory of pay bargaining – is manifest if we look further at home and abroad. Two pertinent examples suggest themselves.

THE MEADE PLAN

Many British economists have wished to give incomes policy control over the structure of labour relations law, above all of collective bargaining. Some even wished to introduce a general 'economic judiciary' or, in more modest vein, to institute automatic loss of employment benefits or even social security rights if incomes norms were transgressed.[83] Professor Meade refined such a plan which can still be found in the drawers of Whitehall.[84] In his plan, if industrial action were taken by 'recusant workers and trade unionists' in contravention of pay norms, they would lose social security, redundancy and employment protection rights (some benefits would become loans). The workers would be taken to have terminated their employment contracts and lose unfair dismissal rights. Moreover, significantly, the immunities applicable in trade disputes would be withdrawn from any action taken for any purpose offending a pay norm, trade dispute or no trade dispute. That norm would be set by arbitration in a permanent body, in what he called 'not quite compulsory arbitration'. It is especially important to note how quickly such schemes are driven to the remedy of obligatory arbitration. Trade union immunities from tort liability would also be lost, and expulsion from unions of members who wanted to abide by an arbitral award would be unlawful (a remarkable forecast of the Thatcherite law of 1988 banning 'unjustified' union discipline).[85] Damages could be recovered against workers who infringed this regime by deduction from wages at source. 'The rule of reason,' he said, 'would replace the rule of muscle power'. Now that is no design for a namby pamby incomes policy law. That is a plan for grown men in uniform, ready to take over labour law and social policy and feed them into the economic model.

THE NETHERLANDS

Secondly, if we look abroad, we find that some systems of European labour law experienced very strict controls after the war, at a time immediately after liberation when trade unions were too weak to object or, in some cases, preferred for a time a comfortable accommodation inside State machinery. In the Netherlands, for example, a Decree of 1945 took control of wages and working conditions, through boards of conciliators and a Foundation of Labour through which government worked.[86] It is a significant contrast with the British story, one illustrating the fate of a union movement which no longer, perhaps never had, an ideological faith in the conflict underlying collective *laissez-faire*, that the unions were said by the 1970s to have become 'belated supporters of a centralised policy which no longer worked'.[87] After revisions in 1963 and in 1970 when the law acknowledged 'the principle of free wage bargaining' but in practice granted the Minister power to freeze wages for six months, and after complaints by Dutch unions to the ILO, government powers to regulate wages were restricted in 1986 to 'acute economic emergencies'.[88] Remnants remained of government powers to intervene in collective bargaining for 'reasons of national economic interest', and controls over collective bargaining continued in breach of the ILO Convention on freedom of association even into the 1990s.[89] One can correlate the Dutch saga of the gradual but slow disintegration of this system of total control with the development of Dutch law on freedom of association and the right to strike. In 1960 the courts reaffirmed that a strike in the Netherlands was a breach of employment contracts; but later that doctrine was modified for official union stoppages (many strikes arose from wage freeze interventions) and in 1988 the Supreme Court adopted a right to strike, basing it upon the Council of Europe Social Charter 1961 (art. 6(4)).[90] Here there was a take-over of labour law by incomes policy law, albeit working through corporatist structures, but over a period of fifty years a gradual fight back took place to loosen its hold.

THE BRITISH LEGISLATION

The first impact of incomes policy regulation by law in Britain fell not in wartime, nor even immediately post-war, but in 1966 after a long tradition, and freedom from government control, of collective bargaining. That tradition was the outward and visible manifestation of collective *laissez-faire*.[91] Incomes policy never took over that structure not because of some inherent virtue, but out of the interaction of social forces. After all, why was it that neither the Labour nor the Conservative version of a wage-freeze tried to take the form of a Meade-type plan or to match the controls of a Netherlands model? The answer seems to lie – and is indicated in the structure of the legislation itself – in that tradition of effective union autonomy, its presence in the 'industrial relations' culture of the time, exemplified in 'Donovan' and in the presence of a strong, autonomous trade union movement. This strength of the facets of collective *laissez-faire* appeared at various levels. The central opposition to various forms of pay norm[92] was curiously symbolised, for example, by the struggle against the 1966 Bill waged by Frank Cousins.[93] So too, the Acts went much further in the direction of an accommodation with traditional labour relations than is often remembered. The 1966 Act explicitly provided that a dispute between employers and workers or workmen and workmen connected with the statutory restrictions was a 'trade dispute' for the purposes of immunities under the Trade Disputes Act 1906 and specifically included also 'differences of opinion as to the manner in which account is to be taken' of the Act.[94] Even more important, the 1966 Act set the precedent in highly significant provisions that the sections creating the statutory offences 'shall not give rise to any criminal or tortious liability for conspiracy or any liability in tort' (s.16(5)).[95] When the Conservative government took its turn, its legislation was based on precisely the same dichotomy between incomes policy and (its version of) labour law: nothing in the Acts gave rise to 'any tortious or criminal liability for conspiracy, or to any other liability in tort or to any liability under the Industrial Relations Act 1971 in respect of an unfair industrial practice'.[96]

There was of course no inherent reason for the legislation to take that form. But it was certainly not the language of a draconian Meade-plan, striking at the heart of labour law. He could have no truck with retention of the immunities in his scheme for 'not-quite-compulsory' arbitral awards. His plan would have enacted – and the legislation of 1966 to 1973 *could* have enacted if there had been no adequate social force protecting labour law to stop it – a wholesale destruction of the trade dispute immunities so that the sanctions of criminal and tort law would come down on the heads of those obstructing the purposes of the pay planners. Instead, wide areas of the traditional labour law were preserved, even expressly protected. The provision redefining trade disputes was even slightly wider than traditional trade dispute law (the 1906 definition did not so explicitly include differences of opinion about the meaning of the law: and the Conservative Opposition thought this went too far and actually tabled an amendment so as to exclude disputes about whether an employer should observe pay restrictions).[97] The provisions excluding conspiracy and general tort liability extended to forms of civil liability which at the time were unclear. Of course the criminal offences sanctioning the pay norms were enacted, though it seems to be agreed they were little more than symbolic.[98] A union taking action in a dispute about members' pay to secure payment above the statutory norm might, if unlucky, offend the complex prohibitions about inducing the employer to pay and (if the Attorney-General decided it was worth it)[99] risk a minor fine; but it would not thereby be in peril of an interlocutory injunction at the hands of employers because of these Acts. Contraventions were not unlawful means in the law of tort.[100] Other provisions concurred. Whereas a manager consenting to an offence by a company was liable along with it, an official of a trade union who failed to comply with a pay order or notice had a defence in the 1973 Act if he showed that he acted within his authority on behalf of the union.[101] More generally, as we have seen, incomes policy laws did not catch labour law machinery which aimed to help the low paid, including the unilateral arbitration provisions in the Terms and Conditions of Employment Act 1959, awards under the Fair Wages Resolution, and progress towards equal pay. Legislation of this kind was a 'prop' to collective bargaining, and defence of these minima based on collective bargaining standards protected the process itself from incomes policy norms.[102] The Central Arbitration Committee knew very well that its awards under such procedures were sometimes used as a way round incomes policy : 'at one stage it appeared as if ratification of a proposed low pay remedy through the Fair Wages (or Schedule 11) procedure had become a recognised but unacknowledged feature of pay policy'.[103] An incomes policy plan going for the jugular of labour law would have plugged those loopholes.

THE SURVIVAL OF LABOUR RELATIONS LAW

It is therefore more than tenable, once misunderstandings are cleared away, to hold that the incomes policy legislation in the 1960s and 1970s did not, other than in a purely theoretical sense, effect 'the reconstruction of labour law'. It certainly did not secure complete 'abandonment of collective *laissez-faire*'. The most important reason for this failure – perhaps more accurately, this coerced disinclination to use the methods needed for success – may be ascribed externally to the strength of trade unions and internally to an enforced respect for, or acquiescence in, the values of collective bargaining. This does not, of course, exclude the possibility that the issue 'might come back on the agenda'.[104] Incomes policy laws today might be less shy about smashing collective *laissez-faire*. That is one reason why the debate has relevance, not least for trade unions and for their relationship to a new Labour government. Two other points may be added to avoid misunderstandings. First, the temporary nature of the legislation of the 1960s and 1970s did not represent an overall choice by government, Whitehall and their economists to inaugurate only a limited period of pay restriction, though each regulation was for a limited period. Many would have tried out a Meade-plan if they could. Secondly, this interpretation of the story does not try to fix trade union responses in stone. Every crisis is different. Trade union responses, like those of politicians or even economists, will vary amidst economic change. Some trade union leaders in the 1970s, for example, eventually sought voluntary agreement on forms of pay restraint because they judged the crisis to be so deep that without it, 'unemployment will become Britain's incomes policy for a long time to come'.[105] But the last thing they would have accepted was a take over of labour law. In fact in three decades after 1948, the philosophy and practice of collective *laissez-faire* were preserved despite laws directly regulating pay. Support for it was forthcoming not only in the trade unions. Ministers in the Department of Employment supported the Department's inheritance of 'the true doctrine of the Ministry of Labour', by which they meant: 'the first thing to be done is to pursue consultations' with the parties in a dispute, and the 'next thing is to turn to the [tripartite] National Joint Advisory Committee'.[106] By 1973 the same Department was also in charge of the pay policy. 'If there is any schizophrenia it is within my Department, because we are not only a Department for consultation, we are charged with carrying out the pay side of the policy.'[107]

As has been pointed out, the policy, perhaps better, the philosophy, of the Ministry of Labour, even during wartime, was one of 'free collective bargaining', and the debate continued into the 1960s, as Freedland puts it, 'between those who like James Meade, believed in a moderate wage policy and those who, like the Ministry of Labour, put their faith in free collective bargaining'.[108] It is highly arguable, too, that in the 1960s and 1970s the legislation, though temporary in its terms, may have represented a policy 'which government wished to establish on a permanent basis'.[109] Yet one administration after another disappointed its economists by expressing the legislation in tentative, temporary , scarcely enforceable and eventually indefensible terms. Why did they refrain from grasping labour law to tear it up by the roots? Why did the new law, which on its face was such a theoretical threat to 'free collective bargaining', within a decade fall away like the autumn leaves? In part it was because its sponsors knew it was unenforceable in the criminal courts. But there were deeper reasons pointing back to the strength of collective *laissez-faire* in industrial relations and in public policy. These administrations could do no other. Like it or not, that was the root cause of the Donovan Report treating 'incomes policy' as a separate issue from the structure of labour law.[110] As was said pungently by a member of the Commission who wanted to go further in a legal reconstruction of labour law, but did not include incomes policy legislation:

> What the fashionable exponents of 'incomes policy' seemed constantly to ignore was that they were asking wage-earners to accept that the existing division of wealth and the income derived from it was basically fair.[111]

That, not some slide rule calculations, is what incomes policy is about. Collective organisation by labour is the countervailing power to the social initiatives employing legislation to confine it – another reason why the concept of 'trade dispute' must, in a system of 'immunities', always be considered free from philosophically *a priori* limiting factors.[112] Finally, it is accepted that 'there *was* a continuity in government's mind between prices and incomes legislation and other types of labour law, even if it existed only at the level of impressing foreign creditors by 'doing something about the trade union problem'; and with this went a 'need to maintain the confidence of foreign creditors, on the one hand, and an increasingly ineffective incomes policy, on the other ...'[113] But it cannot be doubted that, had union rank and file opposition been less effective, one government administration or other would have moved to impress the IMF and foreign bankers even more deeply by a Meade-type plan to take over the central citadels of labour law and 'deal with the trade union problem'. Armies of economists, and not just the monetarists, would have been false to their creeds had they not preferred to see the overthrow – at least for a period – of autonomous collective bargaining and with it the muzzling of the unions.It was the orthodox belief that, with less unemployment and increased demand, pressure on pay 'can be contained only through some form of incomes policy.'[114] It is ironic that the effective attack on autonomous labour law came from administrations in the 1980s which disavowed formal incomes policies to control pay directly (other than 'pay review' and cash limits mechanisms in the public sector). But today social change comes fast. Italy, home of social consensus, saw no threat to constitutional trade union freedom in the comprehensive 'prices and incomes' deal struck on 3 July 1993, after exhausting sessions with the Minister of Labour, reminiscent of Labour governments' beer and sandwiches at 10 Downing Street; but suddenly in 1994 the appearance of neo-fascist Ministers in an Italian government raised new questions about this consensus. Conversely, constitutions which purport to guarantee 'freedom of association' are held, as in Canada, to provide no defence against a statutory ban on collective bargaining or pay freeze (another danger signal for those who would rely on 'positive' legal methods alone).[115] We cannot know whether any administration in Britain will ever wish, or in the face of pressures from international capital will feel compelled, to revive a version of open or covert, legal 'incomes policy'. If the trade union movement – and employers – were prepared to negotiate anew on such matters with government, one lesson of the past legislation for the former may be that a discussion on incomes policy and overall economic programmes needs from the outset to spell out explicitly how far it is proposed that employment rights, old or new, individual or collective, should be suspended or foregone in the package under negotiation. The citadel of collective autonomy within labour law, which was neither abandoned nor taken in the post-war period, should not be lightly ceded.

COMPETITION LAW AND LABOUR LAW

There are other areas of law which probably carry a greater threat to labour law in the long run. These appear most clearly in various aspects of the law on 'competition', the source of which has come to be found increasingly over the last decade in European Community law. To explain how the movements at the frontier constitute a threat which is more than a theoretical possibility, it is necessary to glance at the relation between the many statutes on competition and workers. We have noted already that the Conservative lawyers' tract in 1958, *A Giant's Strength*, proposed that restrictive practices by workers or unions should be put before the Restrictive Practices Court, if necessary by the Attorney General.[116] The authors regarded it as of 'paramount importance' to take action here. It should be 'an offence to continue, or to organise the continuance of, a restrictive practice that had been declared contrary to the public interest'. Individual workers should be subject to fines with 'deterrent effect' and for unions, 'only the risk of putting in peril substantial quantities of the union funds would be a sufficient deterrent'.[117] This represented a rediscovery of that tradition which in the nineteenth century made unions subject to the common law doctrine of 'restraint of trade' which, until the statutory immunity of 1871, made their rules unenforceable and left them as associations with no protection in the courts.[118] It was a time when much play was made about 'restrictive practices' in general, and some Conservative opinion turned to the idea of control by courts composed of judges and lay wingpersons (it was the decade too in which the industrial tribunals were in gestation).[119] New legal controls over trade unions' practices had earlier been discussed as a riposte to the Attlee Government's repeal of the anti-trade union Act of 1927. But in 1956 the government carefully omitted from the legislation on restrictive practices or agreements 'any restriction which affects or otherwise relates to the workmen to be employed by any person or as to the remuneration, conditions of employment, hours of work or working conditions of such workmen'.[120] This, as Lord Hailsham put it, on a patrician note, excluded from registration as restrictive agreements 'restrictions from the other side of industry'.[121] Many post war capitalist societies reflected that policy; this type of statutory exclusion matched the 'laws of other industrialised states'.[122] The same formula excluded such restrictions in competition legislation of 1973 and 1976.[123] The courts have interpreted such sections strictly, holding that they did not exclude an agreement not to publish newspapers made to combat an unofficial strike, even though it clearly 'affected' the workmen involved.[124] The judges were reluctant to let slip from their jurisdiction an arrangement which appeared to them to be 'contrary to the public interest' in general terms, 'simply because it related to certain aspects of employment'.[125]

The justification, though not always the reason at the time, for this exclusion of labour relations from laws concerned with monopolies and arrangements restricting competition is the qualitative difference between a 'contract of employment', or even a contract for services, and a commercial contract. It was illustrated by some early developments in the labour law of the United States. In the *Danbury Hatters* decision of 1908 the Supreme Court decided that the prohibition of the Sherman Act 1890 applied to labour unions.[126] That statute made unlawful every 'combination ... or conspiracy, in restraint of trade or commerce among the several states ', and the conclusion of any such agreement or any attempt to 'monopolise any part of the trade or commerce among the several states' was deemed to be a misdemeanour. English lawyers will recognise the threat not only from 'restraint of trade' but also from broad notions of 'combination'. In traditional common law thinking one combination was much like another; books on the subject always traced the common law line of thinking from laws on monopolies in the seventeenth century through restraint of trade to the various 'trade combinations and conspiracy' known in the nineteenth century, which included trade unions.[127] The *Danbury Hatters* decision was 'devastating for organised labor'; the Act provided for treble damages in addition to criminal sanctions, and these were recoverable from individual members.[128] A measure of protection was secured six years later in the Clayton Anti-Trust Act 1914, which declared that the Sherman Act prohibitions did not 'forbid the existence and operation' of the unions, though this was in turn interpreted adversely by the courts in a manner which for many years to come left them open to repression, not least through the use of 'labour injunctions'. Despite a section in the Act which appeared to ban such injunctions, they were granted in forms even easier for employers to obtain than in the English procedures, and by the development, significantly, of liabilities for 'secondary boycotts' in which workers attempted to recruit the solidarity of colleagues outside the walls of the enterprise.[129] The unions had to wait for the Roosevelt administration of the 1930s for some protection against what the Supreme Court still saw as an 'actual combination or conspiracy in restraint of trade'.[130] But for us the real significance of the Clayton Act lay in the blunt statement it made in section 6, namely:

> the labor of a human being is not a commodity or article of commerce.

The sale of human labour power is not, therefore, to be treated as parallel to the substratum of the commercial combinations or transactions to which competition law is directed. This is why 'it is a common feature of anti-cartel legislation to regard collective agreements between employers and employees as being outside its scope',[131] though legal writing on competition law rarely acknowledges it. The same rationale emerges by rather different routes in many Continental legal systems. In France, for example, the trade union is normally prohibited from becoming party to any 'commercial' activity (even if its rules permit it); it is there to defend workers' 'occupational' interests (*les intérêts professionnels*) and must not enter into a 'commercial' agreement (*entente*) which means that it is not therefore normally subject to the law on anti-competitive agreements.[132]

The frontier, therefore, between labour law and 'competition law' is one along which a fundamental aspect of the worker's freedom is defended, not merely to have the right to organise in combination for the sale of labour power but also not to be treated, combination or not, as a commodity to be traded. But it is on that very frontier that a guerrilla campaign has been carried on in many of these jurisdictions, including Britain. For example, in legislation on resale price maintenance in 1956, the then general protection of a trade union against liability in tort was cast aside, whether or not there was a trade dispute, making possible liability for inducing breach of contract or conspiracy.[133] In a little quoted section, the Donovan Report put up a spirited resistance against the proposal of the Engineering Employers' Federation[134] to have union 'restrictive practices' assessed by a tribunal with penalties and contempt of court fines available against unions and their officials (Andrew Shonfield proposed an alternative tribunal which would aim to persuade people to change practices, as had happened with the 'smoke-controlled zone' laws).[135] In many of the disagreements about working practices cited to it, the Commission saw 'essentially a bargaining situation', a basic 'disagreement about what would constitute a reasonable bargain'. Recent research on the struggle for the 35 hour week in engineering suggest that this is the realistic way of looking at the problem.[136] To be effective a tribunal would in effect be imposing arbitration decisions, a resort to legal sanctions which would not produce 'increased co-operation'. One member remarked: 'Almost everything a trade union does is restrictive in one way or another.'[137]

That the Thatcher government still had this matter very much in mind was demonstrated in 1988 when it announced that the Monopolies and Mergers Commission would investigate labour agreements and customary practices in film and television companies and the BBC (the Prime Minister having called the BBC the 'last bastion of restrictive practices'). The statutory power to refer to the MMC 'restrictions or requirements' relating to workers had never been used before. It gives government the right to ask for a report on whether practices not necessary for the 'efficient conduct' of the enterprise (other than those exclusively relating to rates of pay) are against the public interest. But it stops at that point; the legislation offers no legal machinery to enforce any recommendations.[138] The Report[139] found that the unions were not party to restrictive practices with management, other than those representing actors and musicians in which cases the agreements were not operating against the public interest. But before and during the period of the investigation, the agreements in ITV and the BBC were greatly refurbished. More, the ITV companies went ahead in this period with dismissals for redundancy of up to 15 per cent of the employees, some of them unusually cruel. The MMC commented that it was 'shooting at a moving target' and wondered whether restrictive practices abolished before its Report would return later. In most circles it was felt that this Government's 'first and probably last attempt to use the MMC as a tool for exposing restrictive working practices ... [and] to launch a witchhunt on restrictive working practices ... gave organised labour and the television companies a major propaganda victory'.[140] To that two caveats may be added. The period of the MMC investigation itself saw a number of profound changes in practices, in a labour market where workers were in an increasingly weaker position. Government might believe that the investigation failed because it gave the unions too much time to guard their flanks. And, secondly, it cannot be guaranteed that a government will not in the future give to the MMC or to itself power to refer 'restrictive practices' to a tribunal for legally binding adjudication with suitable penalties attached. After all, even the Labour Government in 1970 was committed to combining the Monopolies Commission with the National Board for Prices and Incomes, while the (then not so monetarist) Conservative Party wanted to replace the latter with a 'Productivity Board'; if therefore present policies give way to a more consensual or corporatist approach to labour market policies, some such body may well be proposed with powers to control 'restrictive practices'. Such legislation might – logically but dangerously – be combined with laws to diminish managerial prerogatives over employees, claiming to remove workplace practices to the level of 'the public interest'. These are phrases which come easily off the civil service tongue. In introducing their plans for closing the gaps against the pre-entry closed shop and secondary action, the present government remarked of the first, with little empirical evidence: 'This is a restrictive practice' which 'can push up labour costs very significantly'. The desire to drive industrial action further into the ground is not yet dead in (mainly) Conservative circles. We should not exclude a campaign whipped up at a time of higher inflation, seeking an incomes policy or outlawing 'restrictive practices' and perhaps adding new penalties for those who dare to challenge industrial discipline.

Australia is a case to consider. For a century after 1871, there had been 'a tacit assumption in Britain and Australia that the same regulatory criteria should not be applied to the anti-competitive activities of capital and of labour'.[141] Australian legislation too had excluded employment relations from the Federal competition laws. But following the report of the Swanson Committee in 1976 which declared that 'no section of the community should be entitled to be the judge in its own cause on matters directly aimed at interfering with the competitive process between firms', section 45D was added to the Trade Practices Act, in 1977, with 'extraordinarily convoluted drafting', ostensibly to stop anti-competitive 'secondary boycotts' by unions. A further section 45E was added in 1980 to penalise employers who settled with unions if the agreement interfered with commercial relationships between third parties.[142] In fact, these additions gave a new 'range of legal weaponry' to employers against unions for 'various forms of industrial action extending far beyond 'secondary boycotts' in the conventional sense of the term'[143] and made illegal much industrial action by unions in furtherance of policies applicable to workers outside the enterprise primarily in dispute.[144] The reform of industrial relations law in Australia in 1993 contained a positive 'right to strike' expressly based upon the ILO and other international instruments; but a revised, if somewhat less extensive liability for secondary boycotts remains under the Industrial Relations Reform Act 1993, and a version of section 45D also remains in the Trade Practices Act to ban some concerted action 'causing a substantial lessening of competition in any market'.[145] Limitations on industrial action in respect of interference regarded as anti-competitive 'trade practices' are, it seems, not easily removed once introduced, even in this enlightened legislation expressly enacted to 'give effect in particular situations to Australia's international obligation to provide for a right to strike' arising under the United Nations International Covenant on Economic, Social and Cultural Rights, art. 8, the ILO Conventions No. 87 and No. 98 and the ILO Constitution and 'customary international law relating to freedom of association and the right to strike'. That task is, British observers should note, performed by both 'positive' sections and 'negative' immunities.[146] Protection of workers is also provided across the face of discrimination, equal treatment, notice and unfair dismissal, minimum wages and consultation rights for any union that has members among employees threatened with collective dismissal. Australia is both an encouraging and a dangerous precedent. The danger lies in the way the easy formulae of 'anti-competition' boycotts can be used to introduce horrendous attacks on the right to strike. The encouragement arises from the bold attempt, especially just now in the Asian markets of which Australia is increasingly a part, to secure a new footing for organised workers, including a positive right to strike, alongside adaptations of the framework, traditional in that jurisdiction since 1904, of compulsory arbitration. Government policy contains a refreshing base of modernised, legally structured collective *laissez-faire*: 'With the enactment of this bill the onus will be on the industrial relations players – it is their opportunity'.[147]

LABOUR LAW AND PERSPECTIVES ON EUROPEAN COMPETITION LAW

Because 'competitiveness' is a key factor in the policies of the European Community, its dimension is bound to increase in importance. Unless the labour law implications are discussed expressly, it is likely that 'competition' law – including in the term here the law buttressing a free market between Member States – will, as has already happened, slowly extend its language into the dominant dialogue of labour relations. It is a very complex area and can be discussed only in outline, but its importance is clear in the Recommendations with which the Council approved the Commission's *White Paper* of 1993.[148] The relevance of concerns about inflation, unemployment and competitiveness is, we have already seen, both general and immediate: 'the need to create new jobs' will restrict pay increases in most countries and 'may result in real pay reductions in certain sectors'.[149] The earlier report on the *European Economy* had struck a similar note: it is the capacity of 'individual companies to perceive new openings which have been created by the internal market and their ability to capitalise on them which will drive forward the process of market integration and unleash the wider economic benefits described in the Cecchini report'. But employment creation requires a removal of 'rigidities' making 'wage-setting procedures more adaptable to macroeconomic conditions'.[150] The Council, Commission and now the employers and even European unions (in the Joint Opinion of 1993) have emphasised the importance of the new articles in the Treaty of European Union (arts. 103 and 104c) whereby Council economic guidelines, implemented by majority decision, have greater effect on national policies, and a lack of 'convergence' by way of an 'excessive deficit' may cause a Member State to be penalised. The aspirations of the Commission's *Green Paper* on the 'social dimension' do not reassure gloomy forecasts that the economic pressures have priority; policies 'will require new links between macroeconomic, structural and social policies'.[151] The precise mechanism by which we are to prevent competition introducing what are called 'unacceptably low social standards' is less than clear. The *White Paper* on competitiveness took on a different tone in its demands for a drive towards 'flexibilisation' and a 'more efficient' labour market: social protections have

> in the main, tended to protect people at work, making their situation more secure and consolidating certain advantages. They have in effect proved to be an obstacle to the recruitment of job-seekers …[152]

Whatever else these crucial documents of 1993 may be, they are not the clarion call which many had hoped for, proclaiming a belief that high social labour standards 'must precede improved economic performance' because they offer opportunities 'to improve productivity and profitability through innovation and flexibility'.[153] Still less is there any enthusiastic commitment affirming that: 'In an advanced industrial society, an efficient labour market system has as its first pre-condition the establishment of a high level of social protection by the state'.[154] Such progressive approaches are swept aside in the quest for 'flexibility' (of labour power). We are reminded of Jacques Delors' view that 'the social dimension is the Achilles heel of a Community that is misunderstood, that lacks grassroots support'.[155] In part this is because it has not built labour standards into its grass roots' rights.

We must be clear about the mid-term context in which Community labour law is developing. It is one in which (for all the admirable trade union rights in the *national* constitutions and laws of many Member States) there is little or no countervailing transnational power, no tradition of collective *laissez faire* at European level, nor any other procedures to match the power of global capital (although the Commission has, in a policy of some originality, recently begun to offer funds to promote transnational meetings of workers' representatives from multinational enterprises).[156] It is scarcely surprising (with hindsight, few predicted it) that at this point there has appeared on the horizon of labour law the cloud of 'competition law' in the European, just as in the domestic, dimension. (We use 'competition law' here in its widest sense to include the law which aims to integrate the cross-frontier internal market in the Union.) The Byzantine structure of the Commission, in whose diverse corridors different 'Directorates General' run social, commercial and, in the narrower sense, competition policy, may inhibit legislative rationalisation but it leaves the functionaries concerned with 'social' issues (in D.G. 5) isolated; meanwhile the Court of Justice develops the case law. It is this which has attracted attention to a number of articles of the Treaty. Distinguished commentators have said 'labour law is subject also, and perhaps above all, to the weight of Community competition law'.[157] For example, the provisions in the Treaty prohibiting quantitative restrictions on imports (art. 30) and exports (art. 34) and measures of 'equivalent effect'[158] can determine the legality of steps which directly affect employment conditions, such as working hours. Limits on working conditions which affect inter-State trade are not prohibited under these articles, so long as the restrictions are not applied differently to domestic and other goods, are necessary in pursuit of a justified objective and do not exceed effects intrinsic to rules of that kind, tests extending the range of judicial control. So, limits on working hours on Sundays were held to be lawful as a 'legitimate part of economic and social policy'.[159] The Treaty also contains provisions allowing measures to be justified under specific headings which set their own policy problems – public morality, public policy or security, protection of health or life, etc. (art. 36). Thus, national regulations on hours of work in bakeries have been judged to be part of economic and social policy and justified.[160] The importance for labour law lies in the prospect that further decisions may extend the scope of control by the Court in assessing the 'objectives' of, or justification for, social measures; the Commission has agreed that it is 'too early to say what the practical implications' of the Court's decisions in this field will be.[161] But the validity of regulations in breach of article 30 has been tested by whether the laws applied reflect social choices 'relating to particular national or regional socio-cultural characteristics' or are excessive under 'the principle of proportionality', and here the Court has taken to assessing all the issues itself.[162] A similar point has been raised on freedom of movement for services (Treaty, art. 59). The person (normally a company) providing a service may pursue his activity in the State where the service is provided, under the same conditions as are imposed by that state on its own nationals (art. 60); but there are limits to the rule that the employees of that person fall under the host country's employment laws. Of course, there must not be any regulation specially restricting freedom to provide services except 'to the extent strictly necessary', and a company can come with its own workers to render the services.[163] Conditions must not be imposed that duplicate conditions already met in the country of origin (as where social security contributions are demanded for workers still affiliated to a scheme in that State)[164] and any other conditions must be 'proportionate' in the eye of the court.[165] This has been said to risk not harmonisation upwards, as envisaged in art. 117 of the Treaty: harmonising improved standards for workers 'while the improvement [in standards of living and in working conditions] is being maintained', but 'harmonisation downwards' (*vers le bas*).[166]

The highly complex Community competition rules, especially those concerned with restrictive practices and abuse of a dominant position, naturally affect public undertakings which are subject to the régime set out in articles 85–94. When they provide services of 'general economic interest' or are a 'revenue-producing monopoly' they are subject to the rules of competition so far as they do not obstruct, in fact or in law, performance of tasks assigned to them (art.90). No development of such trade must infringe the 'interests of the Community'. The Court has considerable powers of interpretation here too. It has held that the German Employment Office (a public monopoly 'undertaking') was subject to the competition articles; it had abused its 'dominant position' under article 86 by keeping out private companies, a contravention made worse by its inability to satisfy demand for the services it rendered.[167] In the *Port of Genoa* judgment of 1990 the Court caused further concern. Companies were required to employ Italian dock workers who were granted exclusive rights for loading and unloading in Genoa's port in a dock labour scheme.[168] That requirement of nationality was by itself unlawful (under art. 48 on free movement of workers). But the Court held that there was also an abuse of a dominant position (the ship owners would have been able to unload with their own personnel 'at lesser cost' and with more 'modern technology'). Articles 90 and 86 were infringed (the undertaking was not a 'service of general economic interest') and article 30 was also contravened.[169] The ship owners had rights which 'the national courts must protect'. This appears to extend the range and flexibility of articles 30 and 90, and alarm has been expressed about whether it requires a national enterprise to pay the lowest possible wage and to cut costs, including labour costs, to satisfy the court.[170] The Commission has paid special attention to the decision.[171] It is not difficult to envisage Community law subjecting further areas of labour relations to the demands of the economic 'laws' of competition that suffuse the judgments of the Court. Recently, it has ruled that the hiring by German ship owners of Philippine seafarers on rates of pay some 20 per cent of the normal German rates, and without any social security charges being incurred for them (as opposed to German seafarers) under German law, did not constitute 'State aid' contrary to article 92 of the Treaty.[172] Such a decision does little for the alleged Community objection to 'social dumping'. In fact, in these judicial trends on the law of market competition, labour power is not adequately distinguished by the Court's judges from commodities. Competition law creeps forward, therefore, to occupy territory which labour law or 'social law' is supposed to safeguard.

PUBLIC PROCUREMENT LAW AND CONTRACT COMPLIANCE

Similarly, the Community rules on 'public procurement', operating in conjunction with articles 30, 52 (freedom of establishment) and 59 (freedom of services)[173] may be used to limit national measures taken to counter unemployment, protect collective bargaining or to improve employment conditions, not least by the methods of 'contract compliance' where public bodies impose labour standards as a condition of contracting. Procurement rules on public bodies and tendering are set out in Directives 93/37 on public works contracts, 93/36 on public supply contracts,[174] and 92/50 on public services contracts, all of them implemented in Britain by recent Regulations.[175] This is a complex area[176] which the Commission scrutinises with increasing interest,[177] one of the most important areas in which neo-liberal economics has been successfully put into action from Brussels.[178] We can illustrate it by the rules governing public works contracts. Broadly speaking, all relevant contracts[179] must be awarded to the tender which 'offers the lowest price or is the most economically advantageous', and criteria for the exclusion of tenders are restricted, e.g. to other permissible 'objective' criteria, particularly standards of economic or financial standing or technical capacity,[180] though national authorities are permitted to interpret these grounds by reference to local requirements.[181] Even the rejection of 'abnormally low tenders' is regulated; it must not be effected by procedures outside the range of those laid down.[182] Local legislation which allows awards of contracts only to national companies will be set aside, unless there is exceptional urgency, in the interests of EC companies and competition.[183] Nor are public authorities permitted to allocate contracts only to companies owned by the government.[184]

The issue arises immediately for labour law: can tenderers be excluded from public contracts because they impose exploitative terms and conditions on their workers, for example below the minima found in collective agreements? Or because they refuse to recognise trade unions for bargaining? Apart from the Thatcherite law of 1988 on local authorities, to which we come below, it is important for any British government to know whether the Community-based regulations on public bodies' contracts generally prevent or inhibit such mechanisms as a new 'Fair Wages Resolution' or more general 'contract compliance' requirements.[185] For a decade it has been a commonplace of Labour Party pronouncements that minimum labour conditions should be enforced by contract compliance in the public sector and, more widely, on all employers awarded public contracts, both on substantive minima and procedurally. Policies of 'contract compliance' are, it is rightly said, appropriate to promote union recognition.[186] Unhappily little attention has been paid to the uncertain effects of 'European procurement law' – another example of 'European' law being applauded in general and in prinicple, but inadequately examined or researched in particular. For it appears that Community rules in this field may have registered yet more unannounced victories for competition law as against protection to employees, offering not even the ambivalent protections found in the Directive on transfers of undertakings.[187] The central problem, still unsolved, is whether the Directive 'regulates exhaustively the factors which may be taken into account in selecting a contractor', restricting 'suitability' largely to technical and financial factors and strictly enforcing the 'lowest price or most economically advantageous' principle. Or does the Directive permit conditions to be added by the public authority across a discretionary range of social factors?[188] Contracts of employment are excluded from the Directive and Regulations on 'public services contracts',[189] but that does not mean public bodies necessarily have a general power to impose employment conditions on tenderers by contract compliance relating to their general employment practices or to their pay rates as employers – quite apart from the obvious risk that some such conditions might be more difficult for non-national employers to meet, given their experience in a very different industrial relations system. The Court of Justice has considered several criteria added by public authorities touching employment. Italian regulations, for instance, which retained 30 per cent of public bodies' purchases from the South to assist with regional unemployment, were held to infringe both articles 30 and 36 of the Treaty and the procurement rules.[190] But offers by public bodies in the Netherlands offering contracts (as required by national regulations) to employers willing to hire quotas of unemployed workers were upheld, given that the condition had been advertised and might facilitate the most economically advantageous tender, being a precondition and not a criterion discriminating between tenderers.[191] But in Britain, the High Court recently had difficulty in salvaging legitimacy (under the Directives and the implementing Regulations) for conditions and inquiries about tenderers' records even on such a crucial issue as health and safety at work. By a teleological interpretation it was able (but only just) to uphold these inquiries and conditions as relevant to the (permitted) head of 'information on technical capacity' and to questions to tenderers permitted under the Directive about their 'satisfactory completion' of previous work.[192] It is not at all clear that the same reasoning could save conditions about minimum terms of employment or about recognition of trade unions.[193] Moreover, a narrow interpretation of the procurement Directive was suggested in 1994 when the Court held that a company cannot be excluded from participation merely because it aims to execute the work through subsidiaries or 'agents' (i.e. sub-contractors), so long as it meets, through them, the criteria of 'suitability' concerning 'economic and financial standing and technical knowledge and ability' (the same approach led the Court to overlook inter-corporate arrangements which left a company about to be transferred without employees, but with labour supply arrangements with other companies in the group, thereby evading the Transfer of Undertakings Directive 77/187 outlawing termination of employment by reason of a transfer).[194] The public authority could not require company groups 'to assume a specific legal form'. By parallel reasoning the Court might hold that no such compliance-control could be exercised over the legal arrangements about the tenderer's sub-contracts, or atypical workforce, or employment conditions or labour costs, if he entered the lowest bid and met the economic and technical 'suitability' requirements.[195] If the logic of the procurement rules were not to be smashed, that might well rule out further compliance conditions other than those mandatory by law.

These provisions can be attractive to governments devoted to market mechanisms. In 1994, the British government let it be known it would apply a Community procurement provision on public supply contracts to terminate the longstanding practice giving disabled workers in 'sheltered workshops' some priority by way of a second bid if they failed the first time round (although a formula for small contracts was later found to assist the disabled).[196] The surprise this event caused revealed the widespread ignorance about the effects that Community competition laws may have upon labour law and practice. The policy had been signalled earlier in the same year when, in resisting calls for contract compliance requiring local labour, Ministers in the House of Lords said this 'would contravene provisions of the Treaty of Rome', and 'where EC public procurement directives apply', infringe them too; they also expressed concern that support for the hiring of disabled workers might be in breach of Community obligations.[197] Other factors are relevant to contract compliance. First, the public works contract Directive in its modern form permits the contracting authority to draw the *attention* of the tenderer to the 'authorities' from whom he may 'obtain information' about relevant national or regional legal obligations relating to 'employment protection provisions and working conditions which are in force', and applicable to the work to be carried out. Moreover, the State may require the contracting authority to do so. It may also request tenderers to indicate that 'they have *taken into account* such conditions when drawing up their tender.[198] This provision could perhaps legitimise cautiously worded requirements for 'attention' to be given to minimum employment conditions;[199] but the very fact that the provision is needed suggests that a public authority may not be permitted always to impose compliance further with its own chosen labour standards via the procurement conditions – it is notable too, that in the 'supplies' Directive exclusion of tenderers is permitted only for default in social security or tax, not employment law, obligations. Moreover, attention can be drawn to 'local labour and employment protection *laws*'.[200] It must be doubtful whether such an article can justify demands for compliance by tenderers with terms fixed by voluntary collective bargaining, or for union recognition for bargaining – at any rate in systems where the law imposes no legal obligation to bargain. Not surprisingly the British Government long ago took a narrow view of such provisions, advising local authorities that they should not make requirements about tenderers using local labour as that could imply an illegal preference for local firms.[201] A requirement that a contractor should negotiate with a British trade union, or with one of a number of unions claiming 'representative' status (in any meaning of the word) might risk a similar charge of discrimination against non-national tenderers; and where there were 'posted' workers from, say, Portugal, the requirement would at least need to leave room for their Portuguese union. It is true that, like the 'works' Directive, the Luxembourg court has affirmed (in *Rush Portugesa*) the general right of a Member State to enforce its own employment laws, if it wishes, on a workforce from another State,[202] and the draft 'posted workers' Directive would reinforce that policy with additional protection. But the procurement Directives cannot confidently be said to express the right of each public body, even if national discrimination is avoided, to require by contract that its own code or a union's code on employment practice be adopted by tenderers whether or not that offends the principles of competition on which the procurement régime manifestly rests. (Policing such obligations can be swift: the Commission expects to receive the reasons for rejecting tenderers.) Lastly, support for contract compliance might perhaps be fortified if Britain re-ratified ILO Convention 94 of 1949 (requiring labour clauses as to minimum conditions in public contracts), 'denounced' by the Thatcher administration in 1983. The Directive does not apply to contracts awarded in pursuance of international agreements or pursuant to procedures of an international organisation.[203] It must, however, be regarded as uncertain whether the ILO Convention falls into that category.

If, then, in the light of this inquiry alternative labour law found that the procurement Directives seriously obstructed policies of contract compliance (for example on union recognition), a British government would need to press hard for changes in European law, so as to accommodate new domestic policies and, even more important, ultimately to promote 'social clauses' to uphold employment standards in transnational and international trade and other agreements. In its 1994 plans, the Commission, indeed, favoured social clauses to help 'developing countries' to adopt labour standards, especially a ban on child and forced labour along with 'the right to association and of collective bargaining'[204] – rights which, we shall see below, it has chosen not to build into the structure of European law. These issues can no longer be ignored by leaders of the labour movement who aim to strengthen minimum conditions of employment by way of contract compliance in Britain. It is but one example of the need for vigilance where European competition laws by their natural evolution threaten to erode social protection.

But British labour law of the 1980s has added further regulation of local authorities to Community developments on the frontier between labour law and market-competition law. In 1988 local authorities were forbidden to continue the practice of requiring reasonable or negotiated terms and conditions for the employees of their contractors.[205] These new regulations, which appear to ban even requirements about sex equality or safety at work in the employment terms as conditions to be observed by the contractor, were dubbed 'non-commercial' considerations which, under the 1988 Act, local authorities must ignore. They have been strictly interpreted by the courts, even in regard to discrimination or safety matters forming part of the employment conditions.[206] Nor are public bodies permitted to refer to many other matters, such as the record of the employers in industrial disputes or their interests in 'irrelevant fields of Government policy'; and the same applies to a contractor's subcontractors or the suppliers or customers of either of them. There is no clearer example than this of free market policies on 'competitiveness' inhibiting employment protection, excluding the normal rights of the local authority under contract law to use enforcement by contract compliance of basic labour standards even when they are themselves laid down by law (as in the case of requirements on safety or sex discrimination). Moreover, it is noteworthy that the 1988 Act, in banning contract compliance through employment conditions by public authorities, gives to the private contractor a specific advantage. It is time to sweep away this obnoxious piece of legislation.

WORKERS' FREEDOMS AND THE 'SOCIAL DIMENSION'

An alternative labour law policy would clear the ground in this area where there are so many pressure points to enforce minimum standards, including union recognition. Competition or no competition, there is a more than respectable argument for refusing public contracts or assistance to employers who grant their workers breadline conditions, below negotiated or arbitrated minima. Why should such exploitation receive the benefit of public moneys under a contract from which it profits at the expense of its employees? There is no general objection in European law for a State to impose minimum employment standards (consider the many jurisdictions which use the 'extension' of collective agreements for this purpose).[207] Nor do most Member States see any problem about requiring collective negotiation with unions as the basis of market relationships – Italian labour law, though it does not impose a general duty to bargain, is replete with such notions: article 36 of the Workers' Statute 1970 makes it a basic principle of the law on public contracts.[208] No doubt the Community ban on improper discrimination among those who tender will remain and require delicate drafting for contract compliance conditions. But the alliance of competition law and the law on free movement of goods, capital and services at Community level should not be allowed to displace the subsidiary competence of each State to maintain non-discriminatory conditions set by public bodies for their contractors in support of social standards. Nor is the existing law a good foundation for a 'balanced social dialogue'. An alternative labour law will find that the adoption of policies of contract compliance will require some agile steering round the corners of Community law on free movement of goods and services and on public procurement. This is a European issue to which urgent, practical attention should be paid by the labour movement. It is a frontier of labour law and competition law along which battle will be increasingly joined about how far labour law is free to protect exploited workers.

The national labour laws on the Continent have in the last decade been more firmly based on social consensus and respect for trade union liberties than in British law, most seeking a system which 'participates in the values of our industrial relations culture and is able to marry together objectives of social purpose and objectives of efficiency'.[209] Of course, that does not mean that each of these laws is preferable in every way to the British: British civil servants would not stomach for long the lack of civil rights suffered, for all their job security, by the German *Beamte* (State officials); and the French law on strikes, for all that it is a constitutional right, has limitations such as the doctrine of *autosatisfaction* that look bizarre to us.[210] Many Community Directives from Brussels which also claim to promote a similar policy deserve a close look; sometimes the small print discloses a more mixed effect. We saw one example above in the drafting of the 1991 Directive on a worker's right to written particulars, a Directive beneficial to part-time workers but otherwise decidedly not superior to the earlier British law.[211] Another area yet to be tested out concerns declarations about rights we have been told to expect in the future, for example, the prediction that was influential in 1988 in turning the British labour movement away from its agnosticism about free-market Community economics, to the effect that among forthcoming 'social rights' would be a guarantee of 'every worker's right to be covered by a collective agreement'.[212] A legal innovation of that kind would go to the root of British problems, especially in days when 'derecognition' appears to be extensive.[213] Progress (if any) on this has been slow. And on similar benefits promised through changes in company law for workers to participate in decision-making within the enterprise – the draft 'Fifth Directive' on harmonisation of company law and the draft 'Statute' (a Regulation and a Directive) for a 'European Company', progress has been insignificant. The proposals for workers' participation in company structures have now, it is true, been cross-fertilised by concepts based on collective bargaining – largely through contributions by the British TUC – as noted in Chapter 8;[214] negotiated procedures would be one of four basic models available on present plans: minority representation on a company board of directors or a supervisory board, or by way of a special body similar to a works council or other channels collectively negotiated (though the Member State in which the company's head office is sited can restrict the options available in its jurisdiction). A minimum 'standard model' is provided to seek equivalence in effect among these options. But these proposals have been around for two decades or more. Some technical improvements have been made – for example the latest drafts of the 'European Company' Regulation and Directive would (at long last!) at least prevent the management and shareholders from wrecking an agreed model of participation by simply moving the head office to a different Member State which has excluded that model.[215] But all these proposals 'are still blocked in the Council' (through the UK veto but not only the UK veto) along with two other Directives which propose workers' participation in cross border mergers. In any event the European Company would be no more than an 'option for business wishing to take it up'.[216] Business could equally put it down at its convenience. The prospect of company law changes transforming the place of workers in the midst of the crisis is virtually nugatory. Yet this was prominent in the offers made to them in the 1980s about the social dimension. Why has it failed to deliver? The answer, it will be suggested, is integrally related to the failure to make freedom of association and collective bargaining central European values.

COMPETITION UPSTREAM FROM WELFARE

In view of the overall economic objectives of the Treaty (of Rome, now of Maastricht) it is not surprising that competition values play a role in its labour law. Although some lip service has been paid to the 'equal' place of the 'social dimension' with economic ambitions, it is impossible to recognise this in the real world of the Community. Social policy was 'subsidiary to the market economies' in 1957, when it was believed that social progress would emerge from the common market and the Treaty procedures (art. 117) including promotion by the Commission of 'co-operation between Member States in the social field' including labour law and (significantly) 'the right of association and collective bargaining' (art. 118). The agreement in article 117 to maintain improvement of workers' standards and conditions was merely programmatic, was not a separate purpose but merely an 'aid for interpretation' of the rest of the Treaty.[217] The addition of article 118A in 1986 extended the scope of Council decisions by majority to health and safety issues, but the new article 100A made clear that unanimous decisions under it are needed on matters affecting 'the rights and interests of employed persons' (art.100A(2) – a highly uncertain phrase). Amidst this confusion of competences, the Treaty made specific provision for only two 'social' items, while a third has risen subsequently to prominence.[218] First, the pressures of an ILO Report and of France resulted in inclusion in the 1957 Treaty of a requirement of equal pay (art. 119) later to be transformed into equal treatment between men and women. That equality has now become a fundamental right in the Community.[219] No similar Community provision was included for race or ethnic equality which is, as a consequence, a poor relation in face of the need for a 'firm Community policy on racial discrimination which includes equal rights for non-EC citizens settled in the Community'.[220] But in Britain the insistence on adequate remedies for sex discrimination has rubbed off on to the domestic law on race relations and the law on sex equality has afforded rights to part-time workers generally.[221] Secondly, free movement of (individual) workers without discrimination is a condition of the internal market (art. 48ff). Thirdly, measures on the working environment and safety at work (under article 118A by majority) including the Framework Directive (89/391), caused less difficulty to the British whose long history of safety legislation made even Thatcherites accept regulation here (which 'should not be subordinated to purely economic considerations').[222] The ideological objection was also absent.[223]

Some instruments adopted in the field of labour law clearly have as one object the welfare and protection of workers, such as protection of wages in an employer's insolvency (80/987) or transparency of the terms and conditions of the employment relationship (91/533). The same may be said of the recent Directive on Working Hours (93/104) passed as a 'safety and health' instrument (the UK government aims to appeal to the Court of Justice against that base for it),[224] though it is noteworthy that this Directive departs from the practice, common in many Continental jurisdictions, of making all important derogations the subject of *collective* negotiation. Here a State may permit the weekly limit of 48 working hours to be exceeded (within the limits of safety) under an *individual* agreement made between worker and employer (the possibilities for pressure by employers on workers in a severe labour market are obvious). Other Directives, even if they make reference to article 117 of the Treaty, are more ambiguous. These include the central Directive 75/129 requiring employers to consult with representatives of workers (that is representatives provided for by law or practice in that State: art.1(b)) and inform public authorities within certain time limits, when contemplating collective dismissals (as amended by 92/56).[225] They also include the 'TUPE' Directive 77/187 (also being reviewed by the Commission) which maintains the employment contract (for a period) and many other rights of an employee on the 'transfer of an undertaking' and requires similar consultation with the employees' representatives (similarly defined, but excluding members of company boards).[226] These Directives, the Court has ruled, are intended *both* to ensure comparable protection for workers' rights in the different member States *and* to harmonise the costs which such protective rules entail for Community undertakings' (emphasis supplied).[227]

Competition rules making costs equivalent are central even to the most important protections for workers. Even experienced authorities sometimes make the mistake of speaking as though the law requires some kind of consent from the workers, for example to the conditions of the transfer.[228] It does not. The right of the employer to make the decisions on redundancy or transfer is not fettered by the duty to consult; and even if he fails to consult, none of the British remedies compels him to do so. Nor does Community law declare void a transfer or redundancy effected in defiance of the consultation rules, as might on occasion be required if workers' interests were at the heart of the Directives. Interim impediments can sometimes result, as when, in the absence of proper consultation, the High Court declared unlawful the British Government's decision in 1992 to close most of the coal mines without proper consultation; but little more than a year later, having made the necessary formal, procedural moves, it closed vast sectors of the coal industry, leaving less than 10,000 miners (ripe for privatisation) where a decade before there had been twenty times that number. Rights of consultation rarely stop closures.

Nor is this central place of competition rules new. It was in respect of the employers' duty to consult on redundancy under the 1975 Directive that one authority, soon to become a judge of the Court, wrote a decade ago:

> A market intended to enjoy genuine freedom of competition will not function if ... employment is subject to excessively disparate rules ... Like it or not, upstream from enlightenment or welfare there is no getting away from the conditions of competition. If a country can authorise redundancies on less stringent conditions than other countries its industry will be given an incalculable advantage.[229]

The rationale of the rules here is not 'welfare' but competition. Similarly, it has been persuasively argued that a central object (though not the only object) of the 'TUPE' Directive, 77/187, is market integration.[230] Certainly, employees who object to being transferred like commodities along with an undertaking for the convenience of capital's restructuring have a 'fundamental right' to object to their transfer but no specific rights thereafter safeguarded by Community law. If they object to being 'transferred' to a new employer, they are left to the mercies of national law which, in the British case, wipes out all their rights, even in respect of dismissal, flinging them into the ocean of unemployment like flotsam as the price of their objection.[231] The recusant employee is not necessarily better off in practice than under the old British right not to be transferred to a new master as an object or a 'serf',[232] though it must be noted that long before the Treaty of Rome some systems took the opposite view to the common law and transferred the employee automatically to the new employer.[233] Yet the Luxembourg Court claims that the 'subject matter of this Directive' is the 'safeguarding of employees' rights' (relying especially on its title).[234] Harmonisation and interpretation of such labour laws is in many respects 'a function of competition principles' and labour standards may become less a protection of workers than rules 'contingent upon the operation of the market'.[235] Even the Community's Economic and Social Committee reported in 1989 that 'basic social rights' in the Community should be protections in the Member States themselves plus 'those social measures which are a *sine qua non* for the internal market to operate smoothly'.[236] That notion – doing what is enough to keep the workers going for the market – is a different concept from a dimension of social laws enacted primarily to benefit workers as in, say, an ILO perspective.[237] The Commission has recently justified its proposals for new workers' rights of consultation (which do not, of course, afford any rights of bargaining) as a way of making 'socially acceptable' the implementation of the restructuring needed by the ever greater concentrations of capital in Europe.[238]

The question is how far 'workers' rights' are to be shaped by the needs of the free market rather than the needs or human rights of the workers themselves. The Commission, for its part, usefully and consistently summarises the three 'cardinal principles' which govern the way in which it aims to implement social policy in the Community 'Social Charter'. These are 'subsidiarity'; 'diversity of national systems, cultures and practices, where this is a positive element'; and the 'preservation of the competitiveness of the enterprises, reconciling the economic and social dimensions'.[239] This has been its consistent set of priorities in the 1990s, in which a 'social dimension' has had to struggle with the 'economic dimension' in a context where all the other priorities, especially 'competitiveness', favour the latter. In the general field of competition the economic is a stronger player than the social.

The social can, of course, contribute to competitiveness, but where it conflicts with the economic, whatever the rhetoric it has few friends. That analysis is not confined to the Commission and labour law. Writers have seen the Court's aim, too, in cases involving fundamental human rights as primarily 'economic integration', not 'social rights' or 'human rights', even though judgments may use the 'high rhetoric of human rights protection ... as a vehicle'.[240] Both Commission and Court have failed to propose or establish an effective code of fundamental rights for real people in the Community.

INTERNATIONAL LABOUR STANDARDS AND THE EUROPEAN 'SOCIAL CHAPTER'

The consequential limitations of 'European labour law' as a part, not exactly of a robust 'social dimension' for welfare, but in a great measure as an adjunct of competition to assist market integration, mean that some of the early dreams have become irrelevant. The belief, not unknown in the labour movement, that a European magic wand would somehow be waved to solve problems – to stop the drift to derecognition or the downward slide of union membership or the relentless advance of unemployment – has somewhat melted. No longer is it thought that 'signposts point unmistakably to a European labour law in which the control of jobs is increasingly removed from the power of management to the power of organised labour' – if indeed they ever did.[241] Instead commentators have begun to find no 'coherent body of principles' that can constitute an 'overall external reference point for socially active labour law'.[242] The labour jurist tends to quail once competition is found at the heart of European policies, where it had been hoped some civilised concern for people had been lodged (even if by stealth or doublespeak). Indeed it is the relative failure of Community law – despite the honourable efforts of some central players – to absorb and express, as was once planned, the standards set by the Council of Europe Social Charter and by (above all) the ILO, especially the Conventions on Freedom of Association and Collective Bargaining (Nos. 87 of 1948 and 98 of 1949), that has produced 'a hole in the heart of the "social dimension",'[243] one detected increasingly behind the rhetoric by ordinary working folk as the economic crisis is not miraculously reversed. Plans for employment rights to become 'fundamental social rights in the same way that the free movement of persons and equal treatment provisions have been recognised as such' began, as we moved into the 1990s, to have a jaded look against the background of economic recession.[244] It is remarkable that only a few years separate us from imaginative, but what now must seem almost millennialist, plans for a comprehensive labour law of Europe, even for a European Labour Court.[245] This in its turn prompted great interest in plans for a more effective 'social dialogue' between employers and unions at Community level, which the Commission is obliged to develop (Treaty art. 118B, added in 1986 in language somewhat distant from the spirit of collective *laissez-faire*)[246] and which may now evolve particularly under the 'Social Chapter' to which Eleven States adhered under the Protocol and Agreement on Social Policy in the Maastricht Treaty, under which the Commission is required to promote the consultation of management and labour on social policy (Agreement, art. 3(1)). Unhappily, debate on that instrument has often presented to the public a charter of substantive rights for workers, whereas in fact the 'Social Chapter' contains a series of procedures the results of which may or may not be desirable.

Of the myriad problems arising, two are of primary interest here: the problems of 'representativeness' and of trade union freedom itself. Both require a brief look at aspects of the 'Social Chapter' of the Eleven States (hereafter 'SC11') which provides the framework for the discussion. It is not, contrary to accounts in the media, a list of substantive rights but a set of procedures on particular matters. First, SC11 'Directives' may be adopted by qualified majority under art. 2(1) concerning: health and safety, working conditions, consultation of workers, sex equality and integration of those excluded from the labour market. Other subjects need unanimity, such as social security, dismissal law, representation of workers and co-determination, employment of third-party nationals or funds for job-creation (art. 2(3)). Such Directives may be implemented in a Member State, if management and labour request, by collective agreements (art.2(4)) but the State must guarantee by enforcement mechanisms the results required. Secondly, article 4(2) provides that collective agreements concluded 'at Community level shall be implemented' either by way of 'procedures and practices specific to management and labour and the Member States' or, if the matter falls within art. 2(1), at their joint request by the Council in a 'decision taken by qualified majority'. If the agreement contains items on matters within art. 2(3) – matters that require unanimity – the Council must act unanimously.[247] But the second 'Declaration' to the Agreement affirms that article 4(2) permits application at national level by 'collective bargaining'; but here this 'implies no obligation on the Member States to apply agreements directly ... nor any obligation to amend national legislation in force to facilitate their implementation'. In an important clarification of its views in 1993, the Commission indicated that the Declaration does mean that a Euro-level agreement would have no greater force in a Member State than under its existing 'practices and procedures specific to them in their respective Member States', a meaning which effectively rules out this route of advance in Britain unless we have new rules on 'inderogability'.[248] It also stated that 'the Community nature of the measures taken under the Agreement is beyond doubt' and accepted that such a 'decision' would not be able to change the terms of the agreement, a confirmation according priority to the agreement of 'management and labour', a rare moment of Euro-collective *laissez-faire*. Even more important, the Commission expressed the 'need to ensure that the social dimension progresses at the same pace as other Community policies', though no new source of fuel to speed its progress was indicated, other than the Commission itself; it is strategically in command since it will decide on a 'case by case' basis about moving issues into the procedures of the SC11 Agreement.[249]

Of course, the international implementation of standards by collective bargaining is not new. The ILO and the Council of Europe have had long experience of it.[250] But their relaxed methods of implementation – neither the ILO nor the Council of Europe have demanded strict standards of universal extension ('*erga omnes*', that is, covering everyone) – are light years away from the legalistic approach necessarily applied in the Community,[251] a factor which the Commission sometimes overlooks.[252] The Community rule requiring that national measures to implement Directives without undue delay cover all relevant workers is strictly applied by the Court of Justice: a State 'may not plead provisions, practices or circumstances existing in their internal legal system in order to justify a failure to comply'.[253] We have seen above that enforcement of 'Euro-level' collective agreements at Member State level, by respecting national diversity, accords with 'subsidiarity' and the demands of sheer practicability (there is no army of European inspectors ready to supervise enforcement). But this also renders implementation of a 'European-level' agreement more difficult by reason of the vastly varied national laws and practices on the so-called *erga omnes* issue, that is, on whether and how such collective agreements could enter into the employment relationship and become binding, at least as a floor, in the employment terms of relevant workers by way of their 'normative' effect (that is, their effect upon the conditions of individual workers). Indeed, the difficulties of implementing a 'Euro-level' agreement by transposition to the relations between employers and workers in each State may have been understated in our earlier discussion.[254] One key issue is how to bind the employer in dealings with each employee to a floor of terms bargained by Euro-level union negotiators. Contrast the lack of 'inderogability' in the British doctrines of freedom of contract (the worker's individual contract can in law be given terms *inferior* to those in the collective agreement) with systems where the exact opposite applies. In France a relevant collective agreement is applied 'imperatively' *by law*, so that even the worker's consent to take inferior terms is ineffective to vary his or her rights – a legal principle which recognises the subordination behind the contract. Other systems seek to implement the agreement without an absolute rule; they run into problems such as lack of authority in unions to contract for non-members in the workforce (as in Italy and Germany where unions contract for members and complex practical and legal manoeuvres are needed to cover other employees). All these laws cross-connect with rules about bargaining for benefits to members only (illegal in France, Portugal and Britain; lawful in Spain, Belgium) and with diverse mechanisms available for 'extending' collective agreements to employers who are not parties to them (as in the Netherlands, Germany, France, and Spain, but not Italy nor, after 1980, in Britain) – in many systems permissible only so long as they are made by 'representative unions', a phrase of many meanings originating from the ILO, to which each brand of law and practice has given its own gloss. The ILO's flexible use of 'representative' status might have been of assistance,[255] but the Commission seems unwilling to accept ILO usage here. Indeed, here and elsewhere, relations between the two entities have for years been soured by the Commission's demand to represent Member States within the ILO (a United Nations agency in which it is an observer) in a manner barely consistent with its tripartite constitution,[256] and by its insistence on denunciation of the ILO Convention on night work for women despite careful ILO studies leading to a new and less 'discriminatory' Convention on night hours generally being prepared.[257] It took the Court of Justice to stop the Commission from taking greater competence for itself;[258] but in 1994 the Commission began infringement proceedings against five Member States for failure to repeal immediately all their laws protective of women working at night.[259] One must ask oneself whether these policies in Brussels concentrated adequately on safety at work – and on travelling to and from work, where protective legislation has played an important rôle for women.

The enormous national variations in understandings of 'representativeness' reflect the differences within and outside union movements: in Belgium representative unions must have 50,000 members and membership of national bodies at the instance of government, similarly in the Netherlands a 'not inconsiderable number of members'; in France 'representative' status, necessary for concluding collective agreements, may be acquired either by affiliation to one of the big national federations or by sufficient presence (tested not merely by membership) at enterprise level;[260] in Italy, where many organisational advantages go with the 'most representative' status under the 1970 Workers Statute,[261] affiliation to a big national union or proof of local bargaining status is required; in Spain similar advantages, including negotiation of agreements binding for all workers (*erga omnes*) go to unions gaining a certain proportion of votes in works council elections, usually 10 per cent; in Greece what matters is the number of members voting for the national union committee; and – curiously in what is thought of as one of the less conflictual jurisdictions – in Germany proof of sufficient 'social power' to bargain is the key test.[262]

When we add to this the variety of methods through which workers' representatives at enterprise level are selected – in France, for instance, one finds four types elected by employees: general personnel representatives, members of the works council, the safety committees and judges in the labour tribunals – with 'representative' trade unions having an exclusive monopoly of nomination in the first round[263] – in addition to the appointed trade union delegates. Any harmonisation which aims to work through the 'laws and practices of each Member state' to identify workers' representatives, needs great comparative acuity to achieve equivalent results. It is unthinkable to break down the deep seated social structures represented in the phenomena of these labour movements in the immediate future, though one may modify them. So, for example, under the proposed 'European Works Councils in Community-scale Undertakings and Community-scale Groups for Information and Consultation of Employees' (adopted by the Eleven States party to the 'Social Chapter' in the Maastricht Protocol and Agreement)[264] workers' representatives are to constitute a 'special negotiating body' (SNB) whose job it is to negotiate the consultation agreement or procedures with management. Workers' representatives are naturally defined as those provided by 'national laws and/or practice'. In the various drafts before 1994, though, the members of the SNB were apparently to be drawn from existing representatives, in the British case shop stewards or local officials; but as so often, important changes were made in the last minute compromises to the 1994 versions. Now the Member State must determine 'the method to be used for election or appointment' to the SNB – a formula which in the hands of some governments could result in new forms of legal regulation displacing established union channels of representation.[265] One thinks of the British TURER Act of 1993 suddenly imposing control over the rights of unions to admit or exclude their members.[266] It is well known that, with undertakings of 'European scale' defined as those having, broadly, 1000 employees and (now) 150 in at least two Member States (or an equivalent group of companies), even an SC11 Directive not applicable in Britain would catch many British multinational companies operating in the Eleven States. That has led to predictions that, even though their British plants were territorially exempt because of the British 'opt out', some might 'voluntarily' afford to their British employees representation in the European-level obligatory consultative body.[267] But it is unlikely that management can maintain control over the forms of consultative bodies by use of compliant staff associations, which the Court appears to have excluded as a way of implementing the duty to consult about redundancies.[268]

Despite the bewildering variety of national laws and practices, some writers are confident that they can be overcome to establish not merely co-ordinated national bargaining,[269] but bargaining at Community-level producing agreements which can then be legally transposed to national and regional level. They see the SC11 as capable of supporting a new form of European-level negotiation – just as some saw earlier Community developments as 'the stimulus to negotiation ... furnished by the threat of legislative Community intervention',[270] or as 'bargaining in the shadow of the law'.[271] That is, bargaining under threat or prospect of an SC11 'Directive' promoted by the Commission, if 'management and labour' cannot reach a satisfactory conclusion. There is no doubt that the trade union side had a vision, perhaps too readily,[272] of an opportunity to put pressure on employers to bargain at a transnational level. A central thrust of the analysis envisages that such collective agreements, probably at first over a sectoral area of employers and employees, would develop flexible standards of a new European labour law,[273] and that the SC11 in referring to 'agreements at Community level' does not require that all Member States be represented in the bargaining.[274] We cannot judge here if it is right to doubt whether European unions will have the strength to maintain bargaining at supranational level in the emergent Community market;[275] it is enough to note that employers could still cause problems by withdrawal from the bargaining table. For on top of the legal problems of diverse normative effects in different jurisdictions (in part reflecting the state of trade unionism, as with the weak French unions) and of new problems such as the effect of the mysterious Declaration to article 4(2), the 'employers' involved here are mainly multinational companies. Although in some cases willing to set up their own versions of transnational consultative councils for their employees,[276] they are virtually unanimous in rejecting the idea of increasing, or in some cases introducing, machineries of consultation which can lead to bargaining with outside trade unions.[277] And it is the admirable intention to proceed, as the Commission says, 'from consultation to negotiation' which marks out what could, if it is for real, be a positive feature of the post-Maastricht arrangements.[278] Prospects of Euro-level negotiation, however, by aiming at a Europe-wide bargained 'floor' of conditions, bring back into prominence the rationale of European labour law analysed by Mancini in 1985, that Community labour law requires not a wholesale harmonisation of labour laws or even standards (a complete harmonisation would of course not be possible) but a sufficient equivalence of rules in respect of employment, not in order to raise 'the level of welfare and the quality of life', but in order to avoid differences in the market which are 'liable to distort competition between undertakings'.[279] In 1994 the Court saw the purposes of the 1975 Directive on redundancy-consultation as to ensure 'comparable protection for workers' rights' in the various Member States and to 'harmonise the costs which such protective rules entail for Community undertakings'.[280] If employers in State X can dismiss at pleasure, while those in Y can do so only after laborious procedures, that is a constraint on competition. Again, other proposals of the Commission for workers' rights are justified to a major degree as a way of obtaining 'social acceptance' for changes which capital requires. Proposals for a Directive on workers' rights to consultation at Community level in undertakings of 'Community scale', discussed below,[281] were premised by the Commission on the need to accommodate and promote restructurings 'in socially acceptable conditions', to gain workers' assent in a context of inevitable 'major corporate reorganisations in the Community' and 'concentrations' of capital that are causing 'more and more employees' to fall under corporate decisions taken outside the country where they work. There may well, of course, be a hard headed case for this approach if capital will otherwise draw stumps and go elsewhere, making Community workers unemployed. But that is rather different from workers' rights in a 'social dimension'. The main aim of the proponents of 'European-level' collective agreements is no doubt the admirable objective of promoting improved living and working standards under the influence of workers' collective organisation; but the relationship of enterprise 'competitiveness' and market integration to such labour relations aims is not of course simple. Not every breakdown of industrial peace automatically damages competitiveness. Strikes by British unions in 1989, for example, led to many employers accepting their demands for shorter hours in reorganisations which 'involved no sacrifice of competitiveness'.[282]

The concept of a 'European' labour law, with transnational bargaining rising above the national markets in an attempt realistically to confront multinational capital amidst guarantees given by Community machinery, is therefore an attractive vision, especially for trade unions weakened by the recession. The case for it in terms of real workers' struggles, however, has often owed rather more to idealism than to realistic analysis. Some would construct it on a social constitution of fundamental rights, or a gradual formulation of essential rights which would extend to labour law.[283] Unhappily this is built on questions as yet unanswered, some not yet asked. Beyond that, what has been established since 1957 may carry the seeds, if not of its own destruction, at least of its own malaise. Its rhetoric is endangered by its contradictions. As examples we take two points fundamental to the bargaining system itself and the law surrounding it. First the identification of the parties, the bodies claiming legitimacy or accorded the status to bargain on behalf of workers – and indeed of employers – at European-level. The Commission understandably stresses that a 'European system' cannot be created 'in the short term', and that the parties must enter it voluntarily; but when it adds that these organisations must be 'representative' without further clarification, it injects, as we have seen, a comparative muddle.[284] Naturally, employee representation must be based upon national law and practice (not because of 'subsidiarity', but out of common sense). But there must be reasonable links with basic standards of union freedom. One must feel concern if, in order to be 'representative', as in one jurisdiction, unions must satisfy shadowy, 'unwritten' criteria, probably in contravention of international standards.[285] Here the

Commission has not always been well served in its legal research.[286] Second: what kind of 'bargaining' takes place in the 'social dialogue' and how does it relate to the rights and freedoms of the parties? The Commission quite rightly stresses the 'autonomy' or 'bargaining independence' of the parties; but that is a first step only. Until the 'Social Chapter' took effect, it was not clear whether the 'social dialogue' necessarily imported collective bargaining at all.[287] Now the Social Chapter and the Commission have confirmed that it may do so, if management and labour 'desire'. The fundamental question arises – and a body as worldly wise as the Commission must have seen it coming: What rights to combination or to action connected with the bargaining are guaranteed to workers and their unions? What happens in the event of a breakdown of negotiations or in face of employers' unwillingness to bargain? The term 'European level negotiation' imports an analogy with national or sector level collective negotiation: but is that analogy valid?

The social dialogue has been continued since its reactivation at Val Duchesse in 1985, between the same participants – the main European trade union confederation (ETUC), one body representing private sector employers (UNICE) and one public sector 'centre' (CEEP).[288] It must immediately be said, though, that the authority of these bodies, if any, to bargain on behalf of national unions or of members of affiliated organisations, is highly uncertain. It is assumed by some that a Euro-level agreement could bind at national level automatically. They often think that British collective agreements are the obstacle to progress because they are not binding at collective level, but this is quite wrong, as we have seen.[289] We saw too that the real problem lies in the diversity of the national doctrines of 'normative' effect. Beyond that lies the generic variation among national union federations. Whereas German or French central union confederations bargain with employers, the British TUC does not. German unions act legally as agents of their members but English courts have been careful to demand unusually clear evidence of any 'authority', beyond the ordinary rule book, if a trade union claims to act as its members' agent in law.[290] Moreover, fewer agreements are made with national employers' associations in Britain than in Continental systems. Again, in Britain, parties to the European 'dialogue' may not be bargaining bodies (the CBI, for example, a member of UNICE). On the other hand, an agreement signed at Community level might be 'transposed' to national level with equivalent effect by diverse national agreements, though with obvious risks of national variations, not least on 'normative' effects. Nor are these the only points to consider. Other organisations have sought entry to the dialogue, such as 'Eurocommerce', claiming to represent over a million commercial and retail employers in all Member States and the Commission appears to have retained the power in practice to decide which organisations shall represent 'management' or 'labour', just as it retains the legal competence whether to move for a Directive in the SC11 Agreement. The Commission needed more precise guidelines, though, than vacillating tests of 'representativity' in the national systems (the meaning of 'representative union' is quite different in Spain, Italy and France). Among the criteria there needed to be something going to the effectiveness of organisations on the one hand, and, on the other, to their ability to represent their members – in the broad sense their democratic structure. No 'Euro-level' agreement would be worth much that had no democratic legitimacy at ground level. We have seen that most Continental systems of labour law contain relatively little regulation of trade unions' internal affairs, certainly when compared with the British laws of 1980 to 1993.[291] The Commission had an opportunity, then, ingeniously to promote bargaining that was effective *and* representative *and* democratic, bargaining which supported fundamental labour standards. In this difficult task, abundant advice might have been found in the ILO, where the idea of 'representative unions' was born in 1919, and from the established 'Internationals' of the trade union movement. No such link was forged. The criteria set out by the Commission are in consequence disappointing. As 'a matter of general principle' to enter the social dialogue, the Commission requires an organisation to meet three requirements –

(i) be cross industry or relate to 'specific sectors' and organise at a European level; (ii) consist of organisations that are an 'integral and recognised part of Member State partner structures and with the capacity to negotiate agreements, and which are representative of all Member States, as far as possible'; and (iii) have 'adequate structures to ensure effective participation in the consultation process'.[292]

This static, bureaucratic vision of the trade union purpose, leaves largely vacant the relationship of union to ILO standards and thereby to union members. The criteria rest on Statist bureaucratic approval more than on members' approval. They include bodies for which collective bargaining is a remote purpose or activity – no less than 25 employers' organisations may qualify. The 'substantial body of experience behind the social dialogue' has sustained so far the priority of the ETUC, UNICE and CEEP in this 'multiplicity of potential actors'; but there are many other 'potential candidates'. The Commission would concentrate on 'the development of new linking structures between all the social partners', possibly creating an 'umbrella liaison committee' for the procedure under article 3 of SC11, under which the Commission is to promote consultation of management and labour by 'ensuring balanced support for the parties' and to consult them on social proposals. Beyond that, the Commission intends to consult with 'all European or where appropriate, national organisations which might be affected by the Community's social policy'.[293]

What is more, the obligation of the Commission to give *balanced support* to the parties cannot be discharged except by a recognition of the degree of imbalance in existence at the outset. The strength of the multinationals outweighs that of the trade unions at Community-level even more than employers outweigh the unions in national markets. The Commission is therefore not fulfilling its obligation to give 'balanced' support unless it tries to provide incomparably greater support to unions which speak on behalf of workers, so as to create a countervailing potential between the parties, devising its criteria to this end, promoting a dynamic mixture of administrative effectiveness and direct democracy. The experience of the ILO is helpful here too. It has not been starry eyed and is acutely aware of the need to include 'all those actors whose support is necessary for political success', in order to be effective.[294] The sustained work of its Credentials Committee in striving to meet the need for organisations that are, in the words of its Constitution, 'most representative of employers and workpeople', has been remarkably effective since the first dispute on workers' representatives' credentials which went to the International Court of Justice in 1922.[295] While interpretations have been realistic and practical, one element at the centre of ILO considerations has inevitably been the requirement of 'freedom of association'.[296] This element is noticeably lacking in the Commission's express discussion. Freedom of association, and all that goes with it, plays little part in its long survey – and missing with it is the ILO interpretation of that freedom, including a right to strike, 'one of the essential means available to workers and their organisations for the promotion and protection of their economic social interests'.[297]

Now it may be said that all these freedoms are implied or assumed in the intention of the Commission. It is true that the Community Charter of Fundamental Rights of Workers of 1989 (the 'Social Charter' accepted by eleven States) set out a right to freedom of association, with a right to join and not to join a union, and a 'right to strike'. It also claimed to draw 'inspiration' from ILO Conventions and the Council of Europe Social Charter 1961. But its concept of a right to strike was comparatively narrow, covering disputes of interest only, limited by the terms of collective agreements and not necessarily extending to the 'civil service' (arts. 11, 13, 14) – noticeably narrower than the rights declared by the ILO Conventions of 1948 (No. 87) and 1949 (No. 98).[298] It was also considerably narrower than in many of the national systems.[299] Moreover, when the Commission came to proposals in its *Action Programme* it stated:

> The right to freedom of association and collective bargaining exists in all the Member States. The ... Charter reiterates a number of fundamental principles (for example the right to strike) responsibility for the implementation of which rests with the Member States in accordance with their national traditions and policies.[300]

It would therefore 'develop the social dialogue', and merely 'prepare a communication on collective bargaining'. The dialogue has been strongly promoted; the collective bargaining paper has suffered unexplained delay; it was still 'not yet scheduled' four years later.[301] More important, the statement by the Commission in 1989 was erroneous. Proper standards of freedom of association did not exist in all the Member States, at least if judged by normal ILO standards, and yet these were said in the Preamble of the Social Charter to be an 'inspiration'. Between 1981 and 1990, 33 successful complaints were made against Member States other than France, Italy, Ireland and Luxembourg to the ILO Committee on Freedom of Association; and in the year 1989–90 alone the Committee of Experts reported breaches of the Convention on Freedom of Association in the same Member States other than Spain.[302] Defects appeared, of course, inside and out of the Community; invasions of the right to strike were reported in Norway (1988) and Greece (1989), of public employees' rights in the Netherlands (1990), of government control of union status as bargaining parties in Belgium (1991, 1993). Some of the problems have long roots, as with German State officials (*Beamte*, 1991). The worst recent case has undoubtedly been the United Kingdom. It has been criticised for contravening basic standards in the two Conventions in regard to its legislation in the 1980s, especially the ban on union discipline of members who insist on breaking a lawful strike, new liabilities on union officials, reduced 'immunities' of unions in trade disputes, the ban on collective bargaining for school teachers and on union membership for a group of government employees (GCHQ), and to the retention of the common law principle that a strike breaks the employment contract of the employee.[303] The reaction of the U.K. government was twofold. It pursued further legislation that made the position worse, for example the Employment Act 1990 granting employers a new power to dismiss at their whim employees who take unofficial strike action (now TULRCA 1992, s. 237). It also replied to criticisms of the Committee of Experts with blank denials of any breach of the Conventions and little reasoned argument on the particular charges.[304] These were all developments which rendered the proposition that 'the right to freedom of association and collective bargaining exists in all the Member States' at best inappropriate and, in the eyes of many, curiously inaccurate.

For a time it was possible to think that, faced with the undoubted difficulties of the matter, the Commission was biding its time, and colleagues elsewhere who enjoyed constitutional rights satisfying the ILO standards preferred to think that the 'British problem' would given time go away (a view less common in Italy after the elections of 1994 when neo-fascists joined the Berlusconi government). The problem, however, was more deeply seated than this analysis allowed, as the 'Social Chapter' in the Maastricht Treaty demonstrated. The 'social dialogue' was based upon consultation but, it was said, would extend gradually to bargaining. It is becoming clear that few concentrations of capital intend to have it go that far. At first, the 'social partners' were unlikely to object to imperfections in this plan, certainly not the unions who were grateful for a new field of action in days of recession and macho management. British unions sighed with relief at this rare opportunity to outflank derecognition by employers and the stream of authoritarian legislation by government and offered little resistance to new rights for non-unionists that punctured union-security.[305] Moreover, other States did not want to see their progressive practices, laws and constitutions on freedom of association, bargaining and strikes affected by alien concepts from Britain. It seemed better to all to leave even the flimsiest version of freedom of association out of the Community rights. At Maastricht, therefore, there was inserted into article 2 of the Social Chapter Agreement – now a main engine of social advance by way of SC11

Directives – a paragraph which read: '(6) The provisions of this Article shall not apply to pay, the right of association, the right to strike or the right to impose lock-outs'.

At a stroke, article 2(6) dims the prospect of Community trade union rights, or even Community-level machinery for collective bargaining. Directives under the SC11 could not deal with this matter. But what kind of 'social dialogue' negotiation is there then under the Agreement? At national level, if negotiation fails, industrial action of some kind must be a lawful option. At European level, when the dialogue turns into bargaining the union side not only has little industrial muscle, it is not to be protected by rights to transnational action. That position is one which the Commission defends. When members of the European Parliament in November 1993 protested against derecognition of MSF by Zurich Insurance based in Switzerland, Commissioner Flynn expressed sympathy but stressed that it was for the Member States alone to lay down rules on collective bargaining.[306] This leaves national trade unions in the exposed position made apparent two decades or more ago.[307] Their own national histories are sufficiently common – to the point where their struggle shook off the penal laws making their activities criminal – [308] for them to know that there is a correlation between real bargaining and liberty to strike. It was not for nothing that so many labour movements struggled for these rights or, in the British case, for immunities which gave them elementary protection before the 1980s on which to build bargaining. And it was not quirkish for the ILO to station the right to strike at the very centre of freedom of association itself, as an 'essential means' of protection. One is driven to ask why the Commission has pointedly given no support to this basic right at European level.

LABOUR RIGHTS AND EUROPEAN LAW

There is, in truth, a contradiction at the core of Community labour law. It encourages 'dialogue', which is sometimes collective bargaining, sometimes not. But it averts its eyes from, or is blind to, freedom of association and the right to strike which are essential to that process for workers' interests. Its attitude to these rights is at best ambiguous. It favours a 'dialogue', even bargaining, yet it will do little to empower trade unions. It calls on the Commission to give 'balanced support' to parties whose different strengths make a mockery of 'balance' at the outset. It fails to make the connection with international labour standards, to the necessary advantage of capital. Such defects make for danger to other rights too; experience demonstrates, for example, that rights to equal treatment or to safety at work thrive best in an active trade union environment. These defects colour Community labour law with an ideology which leans in favour of the *status quo* of power. Nor is this contradiction caused by the inability of Community law in its nature to cope with concepts of fundamental trade rights: the judges of the Court of Justice have been prepared to apply fundamental trade union rights in connection with Community employees;[309] and the individual worker's right of freedom of movement carries with it a fundamental right to be a member of a trade union in the host State, including a right to take part in its internal affairs.[310] Why then should workers who exercise the right of free movement, say from France to England, find that their right to take action in such unions is minuscule compared with the substantial fundamental rights enjoyed in the State from which they came? Most proponents of Community-level bargaining – let it be repeated, in itself an admirable objective – have preferred not to discuss this central theme. The writer expressed doubts some years ago about the reality of workers' collective rights in these arrangements if they did not include clear rights to freedom of association and to collective bargaining.[311] Parallel conclusions were reached by Bercusson in 1994,[312] seeking the reason for the 'auto-exclusion' of the Community from rights to associate and to strike: 'The Maastricht Agreement does not address even the possibility of industrial conflict at European level. Indeed, Article 2(6) explicitly withholds regulatory competences which would be most relevant.' The lesson drawn from this goes nearer to the heart of it: 'The logic of the auto-exclusion is, perhaps, that the current state of Community level social dialogue is qualitatively different in that the normal means of pressure – strikes – are not (yet) operational at Community level'. The dialogue 'implies rather a tripartite process', with the Commission as a 'dynamic factor';[313] and this scenario is also said to be part of 'bargaining in the shadow of the law'. But the shadow surely falls mainly on the workers' side. The qualitative difference in Community dialogue, at any rate from most systems in Western Europe, is that here it fails (rather like the British system) to support the rights that go to make up freedom of association. At Euro-level therefore it is even easier for employers to walk away from the table, unless perhaps the Commission puts pressure on them. It is ironic how many of those who understandably seized on Kahn-Freund's mistaken designation of a 'neutral State' brooding over collective bargaining, have been induced to accept a supra-national 'dialogue' in the benign presence of a Commission obliged to give 'balanced' support to the parties. Fundamentally, this is not because of some defect of drafting in the Treaty or some procedural inadequacy in majority voting. It is because the workers' side has little power to take transnational industrial action of meaningful proportions and because the Member State is allowed to infringe fundamentally minimum labour standards without a Commission eyebrow being raised, at least in public. This is not to ask the Community, absurdly, to propose some explosive Community right for strikes, the exercise of which the sinews of labour could anyway presently not easily bear. The Commission, though, has a responsibility, even in its 'balanced support to the parties', to recognise the needs of workers' organisations which it has itself encouraged to come to the table.

A Community 'floor' to freedom of association is imperative, however unpleasing it may be to the multinationals. It would require in flexible forms broadly equivalent standards nationally within the Community to those which appear in the ILO's Conventions 87 and 98; this would threaten none of the national laws or constitutions which already meet them but would assist immeasurably trade union movements in and between the States that do not. Such a move could create a base from which new elements of equivalence in freedom could emerge over time. If Community labour law does not carry even the commitment to fundamental labour standards, including rights to take action, its promoters are obliged to devise some alternative at Community level which can render the social dialogue effective as negotiation, though it is hard to see what that can be. Without some such guarantee, the dialogue will ultimately appear to workers to be a false prospectus, the script of a monologue echoing to serve the needs of multinational capital. Such an analysis does not at all devalue the benefits of workers' rights to consultation, even though management takes the decisions in the end. Nor does it ask the Commission to solve the peculiar British problem of derecognition.

Although in 1994 the Court held that the British government must oblige employers to consult workers' representatives under specific Directives (such as 75/129 on consultation about redundancies),[314] Community law does not impose any general 'duty to bargain' on European employers; it would make little sense to try to impose a common pattern at that level in present conditions, especially when overall duties to bargain are not found in half the States in the Union. What is needed is collective bargaining in fact backed by legal rights to associate as a minimum floor for Member States. There are many other legal mechanisms that can contribute. Bringing employers to the bargaining table in Britain whilst insisting upon regulation of an adequate set of fundamental rights for workers, will require a mixture of industrial and collateral legal pressures – such as making recognition a condition of public contracts, devised within Community procurement rules[315] – perhaps with a central right to representation by any independent union sufficiently present at the workplace to provide consultative and bargaining opportunities.[316] There have been and are four main legal problems about recognition: Which union(s)? Which unit of employment? What duty on the employer? and What sanction for enforcement? The last is notoriously the most difficult to answer. Similar problems beset the UK in face of the Community obligation, now clarified by the Court, to provide a structure for workers' representatives with whom the employer must consult on redundancies and transfers of the enterprise.[317] Also in 1994, after three years of discussion about an agreement on measures to afford rights of information and consultation for workers' representatives in multinational, 'Community-scale' undertakings (and, crucially, of corporate groups), the negotiations ended with a flurry that seemed to wreck the dialogue. The motive force was the British CBI which suddenly resisted any obligatory requirements in the scheme; UNICE found itself in difficulties and the ETUC regarded the dialogue as at an end.[318] The ETUC thought minimum requirements had already been agreed in principle; but the CBI now asserted UNICE had gone beyond its mandate. In 1994 the impact of the residual 'minimum (later called: subsidiary) requirements' was altered; the right of consultation on 'all management proposals likely to have serious consequences for employees' interests' became a right to consult (when there was no other agreement) on the progress and prospects of the Community-scale undertaking, including working methods, mergers, cut-backs or closures, redundancies and (significantly) investments; and 'where there are *exceptional circumstances* affecting the employees' interests to a considerable extent', a right to consult with any level of management on relocations, closures etc; and on 'measures significantly affecting employees' interests' (Annex paras. 2 and 3). The residual, fall-back provisions in the Annex do not now apply at all if the parties reach agreement on different machinery, no matter how weak the workers' position may be.[319] The Commission proposed a new draft Directive to be adopted through the SC11 procedure; and a 'common position' was reached on a text, amended, in June 1994. The employers had carried on with 'social dialogue' up to the strategic moment. The multinationals had noted that the agenda was about consultation, not rights to collective bargaining – and that the Directive will not apply wherever any agreement for consultation already exists by the end of 1996 (art. 13). The outcome, a Directive under the SC11 procedures on European works councils, is an important new venture on consultation at Community level. What effect it will have below that level is uncertain.[320]

ALTERNATIVE LABOUR LAW AND SOCIAL POWER

Some of these threads may now be drawn together. The European law issues connect with the discussion on 'incomes policy' and competition law and our earlier inquiry into freedoms ideologically inherent in developed forms of collective *laissez-faire*. As we have seen, belief in a 'European' solution of central labour law problems is presently an unrealistic assessment of Community law – despite its achievements in some areas such as safety at work or equal treatment of men and women where its positive character and contribution have been undoubted. Otherwise, 'Euro-euphoria must be kept under control',[321] preferably by accurate analysis. Forms of regulation by way of positive rights must be welded to trade union organisation consistently with its autonomous nature. Assertions that the trade union has 'had its day' will come to be seen like the phoney war which broke out in 1939, as 'a matter of historical curiosity'.[322] Many in Europe look forward to trade union collective organisation becoming a channel of 'common experience, not only in workplace activity but also in our daily lives'.[323] More fashionable, and more misleading, are formalistic explanations of what are legal isues related to social power. Sometimes the suggestion is made, for example, that the weakness which allowed the Thatcher legislation to triumph was the very form of the British legal 'immunities', born out of the social struggles of the labour movement,[324] and carried over from 1906 in the laws of 1974 to 1978. In fact, even if the form of 'immunity' could be dispensed with altogether in face of the common law (which it plainly cannot, though it can be melded with positive regulation) this explanation would remain unsatisfactory. It undervalues the determination and unified resolve of the authors of the 1980s legislation, and of the class forces sustaining them, to attack the already weak legal protections of workers' organisations in Britain. They were not one single bit daunted by legal form.[325] Moreover, explanations of history by reference to the formalities of the law are in themselves implausible. They also run the risk of accepting the charge that 'immunity' meant 'privilege', rather than being, as they were, a modest way of removing the worst excesses of the property-related 'ordinary law of the land'.[326] What matters is the content of the law and the enforceability of the rights afforded, not the form, save in so far as that may inhibit or encourage autonomous organisation.

Indeed, the concentrated concern for the forms of positive rights – whether individual or collective – is sometimes accompanied by the suggestion that they can be made immutable whereas, like the immunities, in the British context, with one exception, none of the rights is immune to repeal by a subsequent Parliament. The one exception lies, of course, in the areas of competence now filled by European Community law. These fundamental rights and duties the Westminster Parliament alone cannot now change short of a political revolution. That is the reason why the gap in European law on freedom of association and collective bargaining (a gap which art. 2(6) of the Social Chapter Agreement confirms) is of such importance to British workers. That is why an alternative labour law cannot be satisfied by reform which merely offers to 'opt in' to the Social Chapter. It must go further and propose, consistently with its programme at home and with its partisan advocacy of ILO standards, a strengthening of the freedoms upheld by European labour law. That means collective rights at ILO standards , as a mandatory floor in labour law, a right to organise and a right to strike along with liberties promoting collective bargaining.[327] If European law says the State must provide a scheme for independent workers' representatives, as it does for consultation purposes (and even British courts may require real representation by independent unions)[328] how can it draw back from guaranteeing the negotiating autonomy and freedom of association upon which any such representation must rest? And beyond Europe, realistic solutions in which workers can trust must now grapple with the global social relations enveloping us, in a determination to press for countervailing power and democracy at work, and for full employment. Or shall we settle for government by global banks and multinational corporations?

Here, then, in the heart of labour law the European Union, the Commission whose job it is to look after these things, has missed an historic opportunity in failing to promote measures for freedom of association. It has failed to issue even a 'Recommendation' about the very basis of democratic societies at work – freedom of association and collective bargaining.[329] Formulae on 'subsidiarity' are no substitute for the protections of basic labour standards; and paradoxically it has been the United States which has now set out a minimum programme in the 'Reich formula', to insert into trade agreements a modest minimum, on the one hand rejection of child or forced labour and on the other protection of freedom of association at ILO level.[330] Such values only gain in relevance when they are denied by those who purport to fly their flags of 'competition' to defend the poor in developing countries from 'hidden protectionism'. Of course, a balance of regulation and bargaining is needed at national and at Community level; but any such 'balance' must avoid the errors of some 'voluntarists' of the past in not taking account of the real imbalance of social power, nationally and transnationally. We should instead adhere to the radical spirit inherent in the tradition of collective *laissez-faire*, a vision of democracy upheld by laws, but forged in change by autonomous movements of ordinary people, those who are despised in their suffering and trivialised in their understanding by the knowing clients of those who wield global power. The world is not as friendly a place as it was only a few years ago for those who take seriously the bonds of community and class and who refuse to submit to the hollow individualism mockingly offered by propertied exploiters to the powerless for whom labour law was created. Yet there is good reason for trade unionists in every continent to hold their heads high. There is even greater need for their message to reach the honest, inquiring eyes of our daughters and sons who are not yet warped by an increasingly competitive society. In that tradition, the authors of a labour law reform pledged to expand freedom for working people, touching new frontiers of human rights, will pass to their heirs a finer testament in action, endorsed with Winstanley's preface to the Diggers:

When these clay bodies are in grave, and children stand in place,
This shows we stood for truth and peace and freedom in our days.[331]

NOTES

1. Art. 1(1) International Labour Organisation (ILO) Convention No. 98 (1949), on The Right to Organise and Collective Bargaining.
2. See H. Collins, *Justice in Dismissal* (1992).
3. There were signs early in 1994 that the Government might paradoxically propose more extensive remedies of reinstatement on terms suited to the employer, because that might be less costly than compensation, especially

where European law has displaced the domestic maximum, as in sex discrimination: *Marshall* v *Southampton and SW Hampshire AHA* (No.2) (271/91) [1993] ICR. 893 ECJ; and now Race Relations (Remedies) Act 1994. The decision on an order for reinstatement or re-engagement must already give due weight to the employer's 'commercial judgment' about its practicability: *PLA* v *Payne* [1994] ICR 555 CA.

4. The 'concept of the citizen worker' will be crucial in Britain: R. Taylor, *The Future of the Unions (1994)* 232. French literature is more developed and rich on this concept, especially on the 'Auroux' reforms of 1982; see too, the Italian Workers' Statute 1970 (Wedderburn (1990) 19 ILJ 154, with text).

5. J. and R. Winterton, *Collective Bargaining and Consultation over Continuing Vocational Training* (Dept. of Employment 1994).

6. W. Streeck, 'Skills and the Limits of Neo-Liberalism' (1989) 3 Work, Employment and Society, 94.

7. Schedule 1, para. 7, Industrial Tribunals (Constitution and Rules of Procedure) Regulations 1993, S.I. 2687.

8. See W.B. Creighton, 'The ILO and Protection of Freedom of Association in the UK' in K. Ewing, C. Gearty, B. Hepple (eds) *Human Rights and Labour Law* (1994).

9. See the Employment Act 1989; the European Directive on Young People at Work was adopted finally on 22 June 1994, with some derogations for the UK: 1994 EIRR 247, 31.

10. See *Commission* v *United Kingdom* (382 and 383/92) [1994] IRLR 392, 412 ECJ; see P. Davies (1994) 23 ILJ 272; Wedderburn (1995) 11 Int.J.C.LL IR 339; G. Lyon-Caen, Dr. Soc. 1994, 923.

11. S. Sciarra, 'Regulating European Unions: An Issue For 1992' (1990) 11 Comparative Labor Law Journal 141, 160.

12. J. Delors, President of the Commission *Address to the European Parliament* 10 February 1993, Bull. EC Supp. 1/93, 9.

13. TURER Act 1992, s. 21 (inserting s. 234A TULRCA 1992); see *Blackpool and the Fylde College* v *NATFHE* [1994] IRLR 227 CA ('a ballot of all our members in your institution' was not, the court held, adequate).

14. See on the master and servant elements in modern employment relations under British law, Chapter 2 above. On the common law, injunctions, imunities and labour courts see, Wedderburn *Employment Rights in Britain and Europe* (1991) Chapters 6, 7 and 11.

15. Nicholls VC *Boddington* v *Lawton* [1994] ICR 478, 487.

16. On this see Wedderburn 'Freedom of Association and Philosophies of Labour Law: the Thatcher Ideology' Chap. 8, *Employment Rights in Britain and Europe* (1991), also in (1989) 18 ILJ 1.

17. See S. Fredman, 'The New Rights: Labour Law and Ideology in the Thatcher Years' (1992) 12 Ox.Jo.L.S. 24, 25-6. For a different analysis emphasising the events to the exclusion of the ideology, S. Auerbach, *Legislating for Conflict* (1990).

18. B. Simpson on section 14 of the Trade Union Reform and Employment Rights Act 1993 (1993) 22 ILJ 181, 199.

19. On multinationals, see the valuable study by P. Muchlinski, *Multinational Enterprises and the Law* (1995); see too Chapter 7 above.

20. For a realistic immediate programme, see TUC *Budget for Jobs: Towards Full Employment* (1994).
21. 'We have learned that, contrary to a Marxist assumption, the "industrial reserve army" is not a pre-established fact of any economic system, capitalist or socialist, nor more is equilibrium', O. Kahn-Freund, *Labour Law: Old Traditions and New Developments* (1968)11.
22. 'Flexibility' about which '… many (false) quarrels are uselessly sustained by mere words of which the content seems to have become obscure as the passions have increased', J.-C. Javillier, *'Dynamique des Relations Professionnelles et Evolution du Droit du Travail'* in N. Aliprantis and F. Kessler (eds.) *Le Droit collectif du Travail* (1994) 219, 232.
23. See Wedderburn, 'The New Politics of Labour Law: Immunities or Positive Rights' (1983), now Chap 4 in *Employment Rights in Britain and Europe* (1991).
24. F. Hayek, *1980s Unemployment and the Unions* (1980) 62.
25. O. Kahn-Freund, *Labour and the Law* (eds. P. Davies and M. Freedland 3rd. ed. 1983) 24 and 236. See too the revealing treatment by S. Fredman, 'The New Rights: Labour Law and Ideology in the Thatcher Years' (1992) 12 Ox.Jo.L.S. 24-44, especially 38-40; C. Hill on the word 'revolution' and Chapter 7, 'Gerrard Winstanley and Freedom' in *A Nation of Change and Novelty* (new ed. 1993).
26. The last is proclaimed in art. 41 Italian Constitution 1947 though it is confined immediately by the notion of 'social usefulness'and a ban on 'damage to safety, liberty and human dignity'.
27. O. Kahn-Freund, *Introduction to Renner, The Institutions of Private Law and their Social Functions* (1949) 28.
28. See A. Briggs, 'The Language of Class in Early Nineteenth Century England' in A. Briggs and J. Saville (eds.) *Essays in Labour History* (1960); and on origins of 'class consciousness', E. Thompson, *The Making of the English Working Class* (1963) Chapter 16.
29. E. Thompson, *op. cit.* especially on the populist radicals, 660-711 and Postcript 932ff. ; see too, the discussion in G. Stedman-Jones, *Language of Class* (1983) Chapter 3 'Rethinking Chartism'.
30. Cass. 30 January 1980, No. 711, where the court also engaged in a comparative review of legality of action less than a strike, especially those equivalent to Italian 'hiccup' strikes and 'checkerboard' strikes; G. Giugni 'Sciopero' Vol. XXVIII *Enciclopedia Giuridica* (1991) 1, 6; M. Magnani and P. Tosi 'Lo sciopero articolato' in *Diritto sindacale: casi e materiali* (1994) 225ff.
31. See Chapter 1 above; as P. Davies and M. Freedland conclude, thereby 'capturing those strengths of collective *laissez-faire*': *Labour Legislation and Public Policy* (1993) 666.
32. See W. Brown and S. Wadhwani, 'The Impact of Recent Industrial Relations Laws on the Economy' Nat. Inst. Econ. Rev., 1990, no. 131.
33. See N. Millward, *The New Industrial Relations* (1994) and his *Change Within the Workplace* (1994, PSI, data from the WIRS panel) and 1994 IRRR No. 571, 2. Between 1984 and 1990 workplaces recognising unions fell from 48 to 40 per cent In engineering, 23 per cent of establishments surveyed had derecognised. Union membership in workplaces derecognis-

ing a union fell from 53 to 14 per cent. There was a marked increase in 'partial' derecognition, i.e. employers gradually reducing the matters on which they were willing to bargain.

34. For a careful examination, B. Simpson, *Trade Union Recognition and the Law* (1991 Institute of Employment Rights).

35. N. Bobbio, *L'età dei diritti* (1990) 250.

36. *Rookes* v *Barnard* [1964] A.C. 1129 HL; *Tarleton* v *M'Gawley* (1793) Peake NP 270: see the Appendix to Chapter 1 above.

37. *Associated British Ports* v *TGWU* [1989] 1 WLR 939 CA, (rv'sd on other grounds HL); B.Simpson (1989) 18 ILJ 234.

38. See *Dimskal Shipping Co. SA* v *ITWF* (No.2) [1992] IRLR 78 HL; Wedderburn, *The Worker and the Law* (1986 3rd ed.) 650-4.

39. On the difficult subject of judges and 'labour courts', see R. Ragowski, in R. Ragowski and T. Wilthagen (eds.) *Reflexive Labour Law* (1994) 76-93; Wedderburn, *Employment Rights in Britain and Europe* (1991) Chapter 11, originally (1991) 54 MLR 1.

40. See W.B. Creighton, *op.cit* above n. 8; K. Ewing, *Britain and the ILO* (2nd ed. 1994, Institute of Employment Rights).

41. Illustrating the grammatical sentence which may lack meaning: N. Chomsky, *Language and Responsibility* (1979) 138; and see S. Pinker, *The Language Instinct* (1994) Chap. 1.

42. See Henry Hetherington, *Poor Man's Guardian*, 4 April 1835, on the teachings of Robert Owen: 'solely the work of man and by man *therefore* remediable'. Given the date, Hetherington may perhaps be forgiven the sexist formulation.

43. *Employment Gazette* (1994) 283 and (1979) 866; also Parl. Deb. H.C. 8 July 1994, col. 332.

44. The 'National Industrial Relations Court', pronounced 'Nerk'; for its appellation, see the Appendix to Chapter 3 above, 158.

45. Commissioner for the Rights of Trade Union Members; s. 19 Employment Act 1988 (now s. 266 TULRCA 1992). The draftsman did somewhat better with the Commissioner for 'Protection Against Unlawful Industrial Action', s. 235B TULRCA 1992, inserted by s.22 TURER Act 1993. In 1993/94, 6 cases of assistance were ongoing, 502 enquiries were received, 7 new cases were given assistance, and just one case gave rise to a court order: CROTUM, *Annual Report 1993/94*. The total membership of trade unions was just under 9 million: *Annual Report of the Certification Officer*, 1993, Appendix 4. Having in mind (*Companies 1993* DTI, p. 41 and note) the regular disqualification of company directors, one might conclude that trade unions are relatively well administered.

46. *People, Jobs and Opportunity* (White Paper 1992, Cm. 1810) para.1.16, where opposition to all collectively negotiated remuneration became more pronounced.

47. See S. Deakin, 'Labour Law and the Developing Employment Relationship in the UK' (1986) Camb. Jo. Econ. 225; K. Ewing, 'Economics and Labor Law in Britain: Thatcher's Radical Experiment' (1990) 28 Alberta L.R. 632; S. Deakin and F. Wilkinson, *Labour Law, Social Security and Economic Inequality* (1989 Institute of Employment Rights).

48. J. McGregor, Secretary of State for Transport, *Financial Times* 16 June 1994.
49. P. Davies and M. Freedland, 'Introduction' to O. Kahn-Freund, *Labour and the Law* (3rd ed. 1983) 5; see their *Labour Legislation and Public Policy* (1993) for a less tentative version of the thesis.
50. *In Place of Strife: A Policy for Industrial Relations* (1969 Cmnd. 3888); *Fair Deal at Work* (Conservative Political Centre, 1968).
51. *Written Evidence of the Ministry of Labour* (1965 HMSO) in the Fourth Memorandum on *Arbitration and Inquiry*, para 36. The NBPI was then a Royal Commission but was about to be put on a statutory basis.
52. Dept. of Economic Affairs, Day 18, 25 January 1966, *Evidence to Royal Commission*, para. 2639; see too below n. 11.
53. S. Kessler rightly adds the need of 'some means or procedures whereby the policy can be implemented': 'Incomes Policy' (1994) 32 BJIR 181, 182.
54. See F. Hayek, *Law, Legislation and Liberty* (1979) 94-95.
55. The *Protocol on Incomes and Employment Policy, on Collective Bargaining, Policies on Work (including training) and Support for Productive Industries*, 3 July 1993, made between the union confederation (other than the neo-fascist CISNAL) and employers in industry, commerce and co-operatives. See below note 115.
56. Commission, *Growth, Competitiveness, Employment: The Challenges and Ways Forward into the 21st. Century* (White Paper: Bull. EC Supp. 6/93), largely accepted by the Council of Ministers: December 1993 OJ L.9, 11 January 1994.
57. Treasury (H. Evans), Evidence to House of Lords Select EC Committee *Growth, Competitiveness and Employment in the EC*, 7th Report: Paper 43, 19 April 1994, 9.
58. House of Lords Select EC Committee *Growth, Competitiveness and Employment in the EC*, 7th Report: Paper 43, 19 April 1994, 92.
59. As recommended by the Commission to the Community Finance Ministers (ECOFIN): reported in 1994 EIRR, 240, 2, 3.
60. *European Round Table of Industrialists*, 'Beating the Crisis: A Charter for Europe's Industrial Future' in Appendix 3, *Evidence* to House of Lords Select EC Committee, *Growth, Competitiveness and Employment in the EC*, 7th Report: Paper 43, 19 April 1994, 49.
61. *The Economic Implications of Full Employment* (1956, Cmnd. 1417) 17. For a useful table of varying policies on pay 1960-90, see H.Gospel and G. Palmer, *British Industrial Relations* (2nd ed.1993) 230; also W. McCarthy (1993) 15 Emp. Relns. 3.
62. For a very useful list of soft-law Papers and Reports on incomes policy 1944-1980, see S. Kessler (1994) 32 BJIR 181, 199.
63. See J. Clark, H. Hartmann, C. Lau, D. Winchester, (eds.) *Trade Unions, National Politics and Economic Management* (1980, Anglo-German Foundation): a helpful comparative study of the TUC and DGB.
64. J. Clark and Wedderburn, in Wedderburn, R. Lewis, J. Clark, *Labour Law and Industrial Relations* (1983), 184-6.
65. P. Davies and M. Freedland, 'Introduction' to O. Kahn-Freund, *Labour and the Law* (3rd ed.1983) 5, above note 49.
66. See Wedderburn, *The Worker and the Law* (2nd ed.)34; R. Jenkins Parl.

Deb. H.C. 15 April 1969 col. 1003-6; details were given by Barbara Castle, Secretary of State for Employment next day: HC 16 April 1969 col 1181. Authorities suggest that confidence of the IMF and banks abroad was a dominant factor: D. Barnes and E. Reid, *Governments and Trade Unions* (1980) 100-6; on the Labour Governments and international capital and the IMF: see C. Crouch, *The Politics of International Relations* (1979) 153-6.

67. *Labour Law: Old Traditions and New Developments* (1968) 20-1; on the details of the 1966 Act, see *ibid.* 16-20.
68. Prices and Incomes Act 1966 s. 16(1)(4); Counter Inflation Act 1973, s. 17(2)(3).
69. The Act of 1966, for example, in s.30; and see ss.14,15 and 16 on what the employer's duties were. Compare the compulsory modification of employment terms in s. 3 Counter-Inflation (Temporary Provisions) Act 1972.
70. P. Davies and M. Freedland, *Labour Legislation and Public Policy* (1993) 181 and 178.
71. See Chapter 1 above. This implicit conflation of the two ideas goes to the heart of the analysis of parts of the Davies and Freedland volume, *op. cit.* note 70.
72. P. Davies and M. Freedland, *op. cit.* note 70 above, 329-31, where the analysis takes less account of the developments relating to tort liability described below.
73. See Chapter 1 p. 17ff.
74. B. Sewill, *British Economic Policy 1970-74* (1975) 55.
75. H. Clegg, *How to Run an Incomes Policy and Why We Made Such a Mess of the Last One* (1971) 88. See too, the study by R. Davies, 'Incomes and Anti-Inflation Policy' in G. Bain, *Industrial Relations in Britain* (1983) 419-55; Wedderburn, *The Worker and the Law* (3rd ed. 1986) 354-62.
76. M. Macmillan, Secretary of State for Employment, on the Counter Inflation Bill 1973, Parl. Deb. H.C. 27 February 1973 col. 1421.
77. *The Price and Pay Code: A Consultative Document* (1973 Cmnd. 5427) para 106 .The formula contained parallels with the Fair Wages Resolution and Sched. 11 Employment Protection Act 1975.
78. *Ibid.* Appendix p. 28, explaining para. 107; see below notes 85-93.
79. See Wedderburn, 'Labour Law Now – A Hold and a Nudge' (1984) 13 ILJ 73-78.
80. P. Davies and M. Freedland, *Labour Legislation and Public Policy* (1993) 178, ascribe that idea to the writer in the article of 1984 *op. cit.* previous note. The argument in that article was rather different – not that 'incomes policy *should* be kept in a large degree in a separate category from labour law' but that it *was* still separate in the period 1966-1974 when it *might* have been subjugated or colonised. Despite the survival of some criminal sanctions, such sanctions were in fact increasingly 'anathema' to modern labour law after 1875, after the repeal of Master and Servant laws; even the legislation of the 1980s did not return to them.
81. For instance, criminal liability for breach of employment contracts in certain public utilites (1875, 1919, repealed in 1971); for breach causing injury to persons or property (Conspiracy and Protection of Property Act

1875 s. 5 – never applied); for intimidation and watching etc. within s. 7, *ibid.* (still important in picketing but confined by modern judgments: *Thomas* v *NUM (South Wales)* [1986] Ch. 20); *DPP* v *Fidler* [1992] 1 W:LR 901, and sanctions for non-payment of wages in Wages Councils industries (from 1909). Other liabilities, e.g. under the Public Order Act 1986 and (except for prison officers, ss. 126-128) the Criminal Justice and Public Order Act 1994, are part of the general law. The Act of 1927, imposing criminal penalties, now looks quite exceptional and was repealed in 1946. On master and servant laws, see Chapter 2 above. The sanctions of the criminal law in factory law and safety at work generally, are of course important but irrelevant to the present point.

82. See the classic commentary by H. Clegg, *How to Run an Incomes Policy and Why We Made Such a Mess of the Last One* (1971) 58.

83. A. Shonfield, *Modern Capitalism* (1965) 154, see too 211-20; see R. Taylor, *Workers and the New Depression* (1982) 52-9; and see complementary proposals for automatic sanctions for breach of procedure agreements rejected in the *Report of the Donovan Commission* (Cmnd. 3623 1968) paras. 489-519.

84. J. Meade, *Wage Fixing: Stagflation Volume 1* (1984) 114-18 and Chapter VIII generally. For a time these plans attracted favourable comment from the then Social Democrats. But Meade accepted that a centralised wage-fixing system could not be 'a permanently acceptable and workable system in a free society' (106).

85. Now s. 64 TULRCA 1992. The primary object is to protect strike breakers.

86. See M. Levenbach, 'Collective Bargaining and Government Wage Regulation in the Netherlands' (1953) 16 MLR 453; *ibid.*, 'The Law Relating to Collective Agreements in the Netherlands' Chapter 8 in O. Kahn-Freund (ed.) *Labour Relations and the Law* (1965); J. Pen, 'The Strange Adventures of Dutch Wage Policy' (1963) 1 BJIR 318-30; J. Windmuller, *Labour Relations in the Netherlands* (1969). For a general view see J. Visser in A. Ferner and R. Hyman, *Industrial Relations in the New Europe* (1992) 323-56. Contemporary French discussion is largely concerned with the national minimum wage: that apart, 'today the very idea of intermeddling by the State is rejected': G. Lyon-Caen and J. Pélissier, *Droit du Travail* (1992 16th. ed.) 450.

87. J. Pen in A. Sturmthal and J. Scoville, *The International Labour Movement in Transition* (1973) 261.

88. H. Bakkels, Vol. 7, *International Encyclopaedia for Labour Law and Industrial Relations* (eds. R. Blanpain and C. Engels) paras 248-256.

89. See especially ILO Governing Body, *Report May-June 1990 Session*, paras. 161-209; Committee of Experts *Report 1990*, 195-6; and *Report 1993*, 214.

90. H. Bakkels, *Ibid.* note 88 above, paras 260-79; Wedderburn in W.McCarthy (ed.) *Legal Interventions in Collective Bargaining* (1992) 163-4.

91. See the discussion above in Chapter 1.

92. The five Acts between 1966 and 1973 included a variety of pay norms details of which cannot be discussed here: see H. Clegg, and other references above nn. 61, 62.

93. Seconded from his post as General Secretary of the TGWU he became an MP and a Minister, but resigned and fought against the Bill before returning to his union post; he complained that under the policies of the Bill the trade union movement could eventually become 'the adjunct of government' (Standing Committee B, H.C. 4 August 1966, col. 673). He always made it clear in discussing its clauses (with the writer) just how far he foresaw each one going in that regard and carefully distinguished in his speeches between the bad and the worse.

94. Prices and Incomes Act 1966, s. 17, bringing such disputes within s.5 Trade Disputes Act 1906; extended to Part IV by s.28(6). It appeared that the pay policy contributed to an increase in the number of strikes: J. Durcan, W. McCarthy, G. Redman, *Strikes in Post-War Britain* (1981) 395 and generally Chapter 11.

95. In Scotland, infringements of the section were made 'irrelevant for the purposes of civil proceedings': s. 16(6).

96. The Act of 1972, s. 5(8); see the equivalent provision in the Act of 1973, s. 17(8). On the equivalent provision in Scotland, ss. 6(4) and s. 19(b), respectively.

97. See Standing Committee 'B' Order Paper, 4 August 1966, at 2632; lack of time prevented it from being called in the notorious all-night sitting: Standing Committee H.C. 4 August 1966, col. 710 (sitting suspended at 6.30a.m. until 8.0 a.m.).

98. See P. Davies and M. Freedland, *op. cit.* note 70 above, 180, where they also note that the legislation was 'only a temporary part' of labour law.

99. Whose consent was required for a prosecution: s. 22, 1966 Act; s. 5(9), 1972 Act; s.17(9) 1973 Act.

100. It is true that at the time an alternative base for an injunction might possibly have been found by reason of criminal acts and in 'defence of property': see Malins VC *Springhead Spinning Co.* v *Riley* (1868) LR 6 Eq. 551. But even the Court of Appeal in *Associated British Ports* v *TGWU* [1989] 1 WLR 939, did not favour the survival of that arcane liability.

101. S.17(4) of the 1973 Act.

102. See Wedderburn, 'Labour Law Now – A Hold and a Nudge' (1984) 13 ILJ 73, 74 and sources cited note 5. On the later Social Contract provisions, see M.Foot, Secretary of State for Employment, Parl.Deb. H.C. 24 July 1975, col.864 (Remuneration, Charges and Grants Bill 1975).

103. Central Arbitration Committee *Report 1982* 17; some cases appeared to be 'collusive' by the parties to evade pay policy, there being insufficient 'machinery' for dealing with anomalies which may 'lead to covert breach of the policy': *ibid* 17 and 222-3.

104. Wedderburn, *The Worker and the Law* (3rd. ed. 1986) 362.

105. TUC, *Annual Report 1975*, 460 (Jack Jones).

106. H. Watkinson, Parliamentary Secretary to the Ministry of Labour, Parl. Deb. H.C. 23 June 1955, cols. 1628-9.

107. M. Macmillan, Secretary of State for Employment, *Parl. Deb.* H.C. 27 February 1973, cols. 1419-20.

108. M. Freedland, in W. McCarthy (ed.) *Legal Interventions in Collective*

Bargaining (1992) 275, quoting A. Cairncross, *Years of Recovery: British Economic Policy* (1985) 39. He goes on to suggest that the modern Department of Employment has been weakened both in its status and in its adherence to collective bargaining:280-294. Cairncross' description of Meade's programme as 'moderate' relates to the earlier period of Meade's thinking in the 1940s.

109. Davies and Freedland, *op.cit.* note 70 above, 180.

110. *Report* (Cmnd 3623 1968)paras. 207-211; but for an obligation on arbitrators to take account of incomes policy, see 276-287. It thought the Prices and Incomes legislation was 'a unique situation without parallel in industrial relations' (para. 487). It seems wider discussion took place among the Commissioners: W. McCarthy (1993) 15 Emp. Relns. 3.

111. Andrew Shonfield, *Modern Capitalism* (1965) 217.

112. See Wedderburn, in W. McCarthy (ed) *Legal Interventions in Industrial Relations* (1992) 153-4: the division between the 'political' and the 'economic' is 'conventional not ontological'. Compare Italian labour law which renders licit strikes in protest against social conditions but not strikes which 'subvert the constitution' or prevent the expression of the 'people's sovereign will': *ibid.* 154 and sources cited.

113. Davies and Freedland, *op.cit.* note 70 above, 181.

114. S. Kessler, 'Incomes Policy' (1994) 32 BJIR 181, 198: not 'rigid controls'. For the helpfully put 'stark choices', see 187-9.

115. In Italy, under the *Contractual Aspects of the Protocol on Policies on Incomes and Employment*, 3 July 1993, the results of collective bargaining at plant level were to be'strictly related' to agreements between employer and unions, which must respect the 'competitiveness of the enterprise': clause 2(3). For the latest of a line of cases in Canada rejecting the constitutional freedom of association as a defence against such legislation, see: *NSTU* v *Att.-Gen. Nova Scotia* (1993) 102 DLR (4th) 267 (NSSC).

116. Above Chapter 1, p. 13.

117. *Ibid.* 34-5: removal of the fear of unemployment was 'largely an educational problem' plus an increase in the obligatory notice (normally not less than one month) before a worker was sacked.

118. See *Boddington* v *Lawton* [1994] ICR 478, for the law on restraint of trade: *per* Sir Donald Nicholls VC: the contract in the rules was unenforceable and void, but that did not stop the administration of the property by the trustees in accordance with them. The Prison Officers Association was not a 'trade union' since its members were not 'workers', because they had by statute powers of a constable. See now the amendments protecting the POA status, but removing rights to take industrial action, in ss. 126-128 Criminal Justice and Public Order Act 1994.

119. See the Conservative Political Centre, *Monopolies and the Public Interest* (1963); at the time many people 'exhibited a conversion to a belief in the judicial solution of economic problems': R. Stevens and B. Yamey, *The Restrictive Practices Court* (1965) 8.

120. Restrictive Trade Practices Act 1956 s.7(4). Workmen was, as usual, a wider term here than employees, and included persons providing services.

121. Viscount Hailsham and R. McEwan, *The Law Relating to Monopolies, Restrictive Trade Practices and Resale Price Maintenance* (1956) 29.
122. N. Green, *Commercial Agreements and Competition Law: the UK and EEC* (1986) 26.
123. Fair Trading Act 1973, s. 114(6); Restrictive Trade Practices Act 1976, ss. 9(6), 18(6).
124. *Re Sheffield Daily Newspapers Society* (No. 1) (1970) LR 7 RP 379 (RP Ct).
125. See Lincoln J. in *Re Assoc. of British Travel Agents Ltd.* Agreement [1984] ICR 12, 51: the arrangements affected workers, but they were a 'mixed bag ... a member of a family' or 'cluster' of restrictions about trading, which went wider than employment matters.
126. *Loewe v Lawlor* 208 U.S. 274 (1908).
127. See for examples R. Wilberforce, A. Campbell, N. Ellis, *Restrictive Trade Practices and Monopolies* (1957) Chapter 2; also A. Haslam, *The Law Relating to Trade Combinations* (1930).
128. W. Gould, *A Primer on American Labor Law* (1982) 15.
129. Especially *Coronado Coal Company v United Mine Workers* 268 US 295 (1925). See the story told in C. Gregory, *Labor and the Law* (2nd. ed. 1961) Chapter VIII, and the classic work: F. Frankfurter and N. Greene, *The Labor Injunction* (1930).
130. *Duplex Printing Press Co. v Deering* 254 US 443, 469 (1921).
131. J. Cunningham, *The Fair Trading Act 1973* (1974) 248.
132. J-M. Verdier, *Syndicats et Droit Syndical* (2nd ed. 1987) Vol 1, para 162; and Cour d'Appel Paris, 1 Ch. sec. concurrence, 14 Mars 1991, D. 1991 I.R. 100 (atypical agreement made by television unions on transmission fees held, exceptionally, to be an agreement within the Ordinances on Competition, 1 December 1968). See the exposé by A. Lyon-Caen, *'Droit social et droit de la concurrence'* in *Orientations sociales du droit contemporain: écrits en l'honneur de J. Savatier* (1992 PUF) 331-43.
133. See s. 24(8) Restrictive Trade Practices Act 1956; R. Wilberforce, A. Campbell, N. Ellis, *Restrictive Trade Practices and Monopolies* (1957) para. 924.
134. The EEF made the bizarre suggestion that the matter might go to an industrial tribunal (*Evidence* para. 77, in *Selected Written Evidence Submitted to the Royal Commission* (HMSO 1968) 396).
135. Donovan *Royal Commission Report* (1968 Cmnd. 3623) paras. 312-329; A. Shonfield, *Note of Reservation* paras. 23-32. See too, the development of thinking on the Commission described by its Director of Research, W. McCarthy, *Legal Interventions in Collective Bargaining* (1992) 15-18.
136. See D. Metcalf and S. Milner (eds.) *New Perspectives on Industrial Disputes* (1993) 11, and Chapters 9 (D. Metcalf, J. Wadsworth, P. Ingram) and 10 (R. Richardson, M. Rubin).
137. Professor H. Clegg at Qn. 3093 of the Engineering Employers' Federation *Evidence* to the Royal Commission, Day 48, 20 September 1966.
138. Fair Trading Act 1973, s. 79. See too on MMC powers to investigate Competition Act 1980, s.11 (into nationalised industries), Fair Trading Act 1973, s. 78 (general uncompetitive practices). Competition lawyers

tend therefore to think it 'has little, or no, use': N. Green, *Commercial Agreements and Competition Law: the UK and EEC* (1986) 571.

139. Monopolies and Mergers Commission *Report under Section 79 Fair Trading Act 1973* (1989 Cm. 666).

140. J. Campling, 'Labour Practices in TV and Film Making' (1990) 19 ILJ 46, 47. There was 'no evidence' that old practices would return.

141. W.B. Creighton, W. Ford. R. Mitchell, *Labour Law: Text and Materials* (1993 2nd. ed.) 1268, 1271.

142. On penalties and remedies, see Trade Practices Act ss. 76, 77. In Britain, of course, action by way of secondary boycott does not today attract any protection from civil liability even in a trade dispute: s. 224, TULRCA 1992, and see ss. 222, 225, 244.

143. See W.B. Creighton, A. Stewart, *Labour Law: An Introduction* (1990) 240-9 for a very helpful explanation. See too: W.B. Creighton, (1991) 4 Aus. Jo. Lab. L. 197-225.

144. See the *Mudginberri* case where a dispute about payment methods led to 'orders, damages awards, fines, legal costs and sequestration orders': V. Pittard (1988) 1 Aus. Jo. Lab. L. 23, 57.

145. See Industrial Relations Reform Act 1993, ss. 36-38 Part 6, Division 1 (new Division 7A-F, ss 156-164 in the 1988 Act; remedies are now subject to a conciliation pause of up to 72 hours, ss. 163D-H, and are not available for peaceful picketing: s.162A) and ss. 42-48 Part 6, Division 2 (amendments to the Trade Practices Act retaining the 'anti-competition' measures); see too J. Palmos 'Sections 45D and 45E Reviewed' (1994) 7 Aus. Jo. Lab. L. 102-4; G. McCarry on sanctions and industrial action, *ibid*. 198, 217-23.

146. See Industrial Relations Reform Act 1993, s.31, inserting ss.170PA-170PP in the 1988 Act. See especially s. 179PA on the international obligations; and for the exclusion of State laws banning peaceful industrial action (including, it seems, common law liability), s.170PM(3).

147. The Minister for Industrial Relations introducing the Bill, 28 October 1993, quoted in B. Moore, 'The Industrial Relations Act 1993: A New Era for Industrial Relations in Australia' (1994) 7 Aus. Jo. Lab. L. 69,76.

148. *'White Paper'* : *Growth, Competitiveness, Employment: The Challenges and Ways Forward into the 21st Century* Bull. E.C. Supp. 6/93 especially Chapters 2 and 6.

149. See Council (ECOFIN) Recommendation 13 December 1993; 1993 EIRR 240, 3; see above note 59.

150. *European Economy:Broad Economic Policy Guidelines and Convergence Report* (Commission, Directorate General for Economic and Financial Affairs) No. 55, 1993, 16 and for the *Joint Opinion* of the 'social partners' on broad economic guidelines, see pp. 19-21.

151. European Commission (*'Green Paper'*) *European Social Policy: Options for the Union* 1993, COM(93) 551, 18. A White Paper followed: *European Social Policy*, COM (94) 333, which was similar in nature.

152. *'White Paper' op. cit.* note 148 above, Bull. E.C. Supp. 6/93, 124; also 130-1: 'Existing collective bargaining and related taxation and labour cost arrangements have the effect of causing gains from economic growth to be absorbed mainly by those already in employment, rather than creating

new jobs.'
153. W. Sengenberger, 'The Role of Labour Standards in Industrial Restructuring: Participation, Protection and Promotion' (IILS, 1990) 1.
154. S. Deakin and F. Wilkinson, *The Economics of Employment Rights* (1991, Institute of Employment Rights) 9.
155. J. Delors, President of the Commission, *Address to the European Parliament* 10 February 1993, Bull. EC Supp. 1/93, 9.
156. See 1993 EIRR 238, 15; and I. Roberts, 'Where are the European Works Councils? An Update' (1993) 24 Ind. Rel. Jo. 178.
157. See Antoine Lyon-Caen, '*Droit social et droit de la concurrence: Observations sur une rencontre*' in *Orientations sociales du droit contemporain: écrits en l'honneur de J. Savatier* (1992 PUF)331, 338, a chapter to which I am most indebted. See too, the assessment of 'fundamental' rights: M. Roccella (1993) Giorn. DLRI 1-9, who sees a less pronounced threat from competition law developments.
158. See generally N. Green, T. Hartley, J. Usher, 'Quantitative Restrictions and Measures Having Equivalent Effect: Equally Applicable Measures' Chapter 6 in *The Legal Foundations of the Single European Market* (1991) 60-71; also Chapter 7 on 'The Express Exceptions'. The articles include anything which makes importation more difficult or costly than the disposal of the domestic production: Directive 70/50 art.2(1).
159. *Torfaen B.C.* v *B & Q. plc* (145/88) [1990] 2 QB19, ECJ; on the availability of injunctions: *Kirklees MBC* v *Wickes Building Supplies* [1993] A.C. 227 HL; compare *André Marchandise* (332/89) [1989] ECR 3851 (ECJ). Laws banning Sunday trading have now been held not to infringe art. 30: *Stoke-on-Trent City Council* v *B & Q. plc* [1993] AC 900 ECJ and HL. No intention to discriminate is required if the national rule has unjustified effects: '*Cassis de Dijon*', *Rewe-Zentral* v *Bundesmonopolverwaltung* (120/78) [1979] ECR 649; but see now *Keck and Mithouard* (267-8/91) 24 November 1993; C. Barnard (1994) 57 MLR 449.
160. *Re Oebel* (155/80) [1981] ECR 1993, ECJ.
161. A. Lyon-Caen, note 157 above, 339-40; Commission *Eleventh Annual Report on Monitoring the Application of Community Law* (1993) p.16, discussing *Keck and Mithouard* (267-8/91) 24 November 1993 ECJ; and *Hünermund* (292/92) 15 December 1993 ECJ.
162. *Stoke-on-Trent City Council* v *B & Q plc* (169/91) [1993] AC 900 H.L. and ECJ.: Sunday trading laws affecting both imports and domestic goods not a breach of art.30; but the court added also that the legislation 'pursued an aim which was justified under Community law' 946; and it also preserved its jurisdiction to say when restrictions were 'excessive', since 'such an assessment cannot be allowed to vary according to the findings of fact made by individual courts in particular cases.' 947, following *Conforama* (3212/89) [1991] ECR I-997, and *Marchandise* (332/89) [1991] ECR I-1027 ECJ. (retail employment prohibited on Sunday; restrictions not excessive).
163 *Rush Portuguesa Lda* v *Office National d'Immigration* (113/89) [1990] ECR I-1147, ECJ. A Directive is proposed for the protection of 'posted' employees: see COM(93) 225 final; see on the objective of preventing

'social dumping': M. Rocella and T. Treu, *Diritto del lavoro della Comunità europea* (1992) 115-118; above p. 230, n. 41, below note 173.

164. *Seco* (62 and 63/81) [1982] ECR 223 ECJ; and *Van Wesemael* v *Follachio* (110/78) [1978] ECR 35 ECJ.

165. *Commission* v *France* (154/89) [1991] ECR I-659 ECJ.

166. A. Lyon-Caen, *op. cit.* note 133, above, 341.

167. *Höfner* v *Macrouton* (41/90) 23 April 1991 ECJ; R.Slot (1991) 28 CMLR 964, 972-88. But a national office running a comprehensive national insurance service is not such an undertaking: *CANAM* v *CANCAVA* (159 and 160/91) 17 February 1993 ECJ.

168. Aspects of which are familiar to us (decasualisation; guaranteed wage; obligation to attend for work; register of dock workers) in the light of the British dock labour scheme privatised in 1989 after the dock strike had been the subject of litigation: *Associated British Ports* v *TGWU* [1989] 1 WLR 939 CA, (rv'sd on other grounds HL).

169. *Merci Convenzionali Spa* v *Siderurgica Gabriella Spa.* (179/90) [1991] ECR I-5889.

170. D. Wyatt and A. Dashwood, *European Community Law* (3rd ed. 1993) 556; A. Lyon-Caen and G. Lyon-Caen, *Droit social international et européen* (8th ed. 1993) 265. Professor G. Lyon-Caen recently wrote of the 'infiltration' of labour law by competition law: 1992 *Droit Ouvrier* 313-9.

171. See Commission *Eleventh Annual Report on Monitoring the Application of Community Law* (1993) p.52: Italy must 'genuinely and definitively abolish the monopoly' in the docks.

172. *Firma Sloman Neptun Schiffahrts AG* v *Seebetriebsrat Bodo Ziesmer* (72 and 73/91) ECJ, *Financial Times* 23 March 1994; see E. Szyszczak (1994) 1 Jo. Soc. Welfare and Fam. L. 121-6.

173. On freedom to supply services in another State with one's own workforce: see *Rush Portugesa Lda* v *Office National d'Immigration* (113/89)[1990] ECR I-1417 ECJ. A State *must* allow the freedom to supply services and *may* enforce its own employment laws; but if it chooses not to do the latter, the host labour market will see local standards undermined: J. Shaw, *European Community Law* (1993) 324-6. Collective bargaining will thereby be weakened.

174. OJ L.199, 9.8.1993, at p.1 and p. 54. These consolidated respectively, Directives 71/305 and 77/62, as later amended (notably by 89/440 and 88/265). See generally, C. Bright, *Public Procurement Handbook* (1994); F. Weiss, *Public Procurements in the European Community* (1993); A. Geddes, *Public Procurement: A Practical Guide* (1992); J. Schrab (1991) 10 Ox. J. L.S. 522. The procurement rules tend to catch all types of public bodies: *Gebr. Beentjes BV* v *Netherlands* (31/87) [1990] 1 CMLR 287, ECJ; compare *Commission* v *Italy* (296/92) 12 January 1994 ECJ. In total, public procurement accounts for about 15 per cent of Community GDP: J. Shaw, *European Community Law* (1993) 316.

175. See the Regulations implementing the relevant Directives on public works contracts: SI 1991 No.2680 and SI 1992 No.3279; on public supply contracts, SI 1993 No. 2679; on public services contracts, SI. 1993 No. 3228. For special rules on utilities, see Directives 90/531 and 93/38 and

Regulations SI 1993 No. 3227. The main enforcement remedy in Britain is a civil action for those improperly excluded from tendering, see e.g. reg. 31, SI 1991 No. 2680: M.Bowsher (1994) PPLR 30. For the earlier contextual British law, see: C. Turpin, *Government Procurement and Contracts* (1989).

176. See the series by the Birmingham University Research Unit on *Public Procurement in the European Community*: A. Cox, Vol.1 *The Single Market Rules* (1993); S. Arrowsmith, Vol.II *A Guide to the Procurement Cases of the ECJ* (1993); A. Cox, F. Lamont, Vol.III *The Texts of the Community Directives (etc.)* (1993); S. Arrowsmith, Vol. IV *Remedies for Enforcing the Public Procurement Rules* (1993), especially S. Weatherill, Chapter 8 on the UK; S. Arrowsmith, *Remedies for Enforcing the Utilities Rules* (1994).

177. See the Commission's, *Eleventh Annual Report on Monitoring the Application of Community Law* (1993) pp. 34-36.

178. See the account in Chaps.1 and 2 of A. Cox, *The Single Market Rules, op. cit.* note 176.

179. For public works contracts, 5mn. ECU or more in value: Reg. 7(1) SI 1991 No. 2680 (C. Bock (1994) PPLR CS137). There are three types: the open, restricted and negotiated procedures: *ibid.* Regs. 10-13; see A. Cox, *op.cit.* note 176, 80-88.

180. See e.g. Public Works Contracts Regulations 1991, SI No. 2680, regs. 14 to 20; see below n. 192.

181. *Constructions et Enterprises Industrielles SA (CEI) v Société Coopérative Association. Intercommunale pour les Autoroutes des Ardennes* (27-29/1986) [1987] ECR 3347 ECJ (*'Bellini'*: enquiries about financial standing beyond those set out in the Directive permitted). But technical criteria that confine tenders to one local company ('grandfather clauses') are not acceptable as they discriminate contrary to art. 30, Treaty: *Commission v Ireland* (45/87) [1989] 1 CMLR 225, ECJ; contrast *Apple and Pear etc Council v Lewis* Ltd (222/82) [1983] ECR 4083 ECJ (descriptive campaign did not discriminate against imported goods).

182. *Fratelli Costanzo SpA v Comune di Milano* (103/88) [1989] ECR 1839 ECJ (art. 29(5) of 71/305, now art. 30(4) of 93/37: low bid for World Cup stadium); see in Britain the Regulations SI 1991 no. 2680, reg.20(60). See too, *Transporoute v Minister of Public Works* (76/81) [1982] ECR 417 ECJ (the Directive limits the information which can be demanded); and *Impresa Donà Alfonso & Figli v Consorzio per lo sviluppo industriale del Comune di Monfalcone* (295/89) 18 June 1991; S. Arrowsmith, *Guide to the Procurement Cases, op. cit.* above note 176, 227.

183. *Re an Italian Incinerator Contract: Commission v Italy* (194/88) [1990] CMLR 813 ECJ (environmental urgency disallowed; six year delay by authorities misallocating national contracts); also, *Commission v Spain* (24/91) March 18, 1992 ECJ (private contracts offending procurement rules).

184. *Re Data Processing Companies; Commission v Italy* (3/88) [1991] 2 CMLR 115 ECJ.

185. On the Fair Wages Resolutions 1891 to 1946, see B. Bercusson, *Fair Wages Resolutions* (1978); Wedderburn, *The Worker and the Law* (1986

3rd.ed.) 347-54.

186. See TUC, *Trade Union Recognition: A Consultative Document* (1991) and *Representation at Work* (1994); W. McCarthy, *Freedom at Work* (1985) (where the 'stages' for a union to advance from 'representation' rights to consultation and then to negotiation, might make it even easier for management to hold it on a lower rung); K. Ewing, 'Trade Union Recognition – A Framework' (1990) 19 ILJ 209 (where proposals for swingeing sanctions, including imposing new managers to negotiate, might cause the enterprise to founder, and bring no benefit to the workers). This is part of the old problem of how to compel capital to invest and carry on enterprises on terms suited to the workers' interests); and B. Simpson, *Trade Union Recognition and the Law* (1991 Institute of Employment Rights) 19-21; see below note 316.

187. On the protections in Directive 77/187 and its rationale as a measure for market integration, see P. Davies, 'Acquired Rights, Creditors' Rights, Freedom of Contract and Industrial Democracy' (1989) 9 Yearbook of European Law 21; and see his 'The Emergence of European Labour Law' Chapter 10 in W.McCarthy (ed.) *Legal Interventions in Collective Bargaining* (1992). See now *Commission v United Kingdom* (382 and 383/92) [1994] IRLR 392 and 412 ECJ on the obligation of employers to consult with workers' representatives even where they do not recognise a union. On the project for a Directive to protect the core employment conditions of workers 'posted' to another Member State into which the employer is exercising his freedom to render services: see COM (93) 230; above p. 219, n. 41; compare *Rush Portugesa Lda v Office National d'Immigration* (113/89) [1990] ECR I-1147, ECJ: above note 163.

188. See S. Arrowsmith, *Guide to the Procurement Cases, op. cit.* note 152, 77-79, on the *Beentjes* case, note 191 below, who supports the wider view. See too, J. Winter, note 190 below; and on support for social policies in Northern Ireland, C. Turpin, *op. cit.*, note 175 above, 78-9; but see now Fair Employment (Northern Ireland) Act 1989, ss. 38, 41, 42 (public authorities not to contract with employers in breach of legal duties on fair employment practices, there including religious equality).

189. Public Services Contracts Regulations 1993 SI No. 3228, reg.2(10), implementing 92/50.

190. *Du Pont de Nemours Italiana* (21/88) [1990] ECR I-889 (infringement of art. 30 Treaty); *Commission v Italy* (351/88) July 11, 1991 (similar restriction infringing also arts. 30 and 92 Treaty); *Commission v Italy* (360/89) June 3, 1992 ECJ (where part of a tender reserved work for local sub-contractors the tender was unlawful as national firms could indirectly benefit, infringing art. 59 of the Treaty on freedom of establishment and Directive 71/305 on procurement: now arts. 26 and 27 of 93/37) ; and on the position in 1990, J. Winter, 'Public Procurement in the EEC' (1991) 28 CMLR 741,766-82.

191. *Gebr. Beentjes BV v Netherlands* (31/87) [1990] 1 CMLR 287 ECJ; Winter, *op. cit.* note 190 above ,773-80.

192. *Greenwich Building and Maintenance plc v Greenwich BC* [1993] IRLR 535: the 'ability competently to carry out the operations of their trade in these days includes ability to carry them out with proper regard for the

health and safety of those whom they employ and members of the public whom they affect', Sir Godfray le Quesne QC. The judgment unhappily overlooked the existence of the 'Framework Directive' (89/391) on safety at work which might have strengthened its reasoning.

193. But see Winter, *op. cit.* note 190, who suggests States 'are free to use public contracts in order to further social, industrial, political and other goals of their own societies', 775; *sed quaere* now, as this seems inconsistent, despite *Beentjes* (note 191 above), with the approach of the ECJ in several recent cases, for example *Commission* v *Italy* (360/89) June 3, 1992, ECJ.

194. *Ballast Nedam Groep NV* v *Belgium* (389/92) *The Times* 18 May 1992 ECJ; decided on Directives 71/304 and 305; J.F.Martin (1994) P.P.L.R.. CS200. On the Directive 77/187, *BIFU* v *Barclays Bank* [1987] ICR 495. This is one of many ways of evading the Directive ably analysed by C. Whelan, 'Employment Protection and Business Transfers: Limits in European Law' (Paper of 1992, Conference at Exeter University).

195. The *Beentjes* decision, note 191 above, allowing prior conditions on general social policy grounds, might be distinguished by the ECJ from a case where the public authority sought to control the contractor's (and sub-contractors') employment conditions, labour relations or labour costs, even though those tenderers had complied with domestic *legal* requirements.

196. The Secretary of State for Employment, Mr Portillo, in implementing the new Directive 93/36 on public supply contracts, ended the sheltered workshops' advantage for disabled workers to bid again after the lowest bid is known: 1994, 57 Eq.O. R. 7. But the employers (Remploy) acknowledged the scheme was 'illegal under EU Directives': *Financial Times* 24 August 1994. Various preferential arrangements ended in 1992 (C.Serveney (1994) PPLR 163). The Commission ironically indicated that, had it asked, Britain might have obtained an exemption for the scheme: *The Times* 22 August 1994. A new arrangement allows disabled workers (anywhere in the Community) to have priority for small supply contracts below the Directive's threshold (normally £96,403): Written answer H.C. 30 November 1994, col. 637.

197. Lord Henley (Employment Under-Secretary of State) Parl. Deb. 20 July 1994 HL cols. 330-331, 345-346. He also threw in for good measure the principles of 'free movement of workers, the freedom to provide services, or discrimination on the ground of nationality' col. 330. Opposition spokespersons, appeared to discount the relevance of procurement Directives, saying of domestic legislation permitting contract compliance clauses for the disabled:'Surely nothing the EC says can override [it]' : Bnss. Hollis col.347; and also Lord Peston col. 331. The Government thought contract compliance clauses on employment of women might also be unlawful under the Sex Discrimination Act 1975 ss. 6 and 77 (as amended in 1986, 1989, in part implementing EC Directive 76/207): Lord Henley *ibid* col. 337. [A Bill is forthcoming on disabled persons, replacing the Act of 1944: Parl. Deb. HC 24 November 1994, col. 740.]

198. Art. 23(1)(2) Directive 93/37, implemented in the UK by SI. 1991 no. 2680, reg. 27; introduced by amending Directive 89/440, art. 18. See the

same provision in reg. 26, Public Services Contracts Regulations SI 1993 no. 3228, implementing Directive 92/50 (see now art. 29 of Directive 93/38).

199. British labour law could benefit here if the Court adopted the stance of many Continental systems in seeing collective agreements as quasi-law, setting out an indispensable minimum: see Wedderburn and S. Sciarra 'Collective Bargaining as Agreement and as Law' in A. Pizzorusso, *Law in the Making* (1988), and on 'inderogability' see Chapter 6 above.

200. A. Cox, *The Single Market Rules, op. cit.* note 152, 84: 'at the same time ensuring that these laws cannot be used to discriminate unfairly against non-national contractors'. Once more, it is important to reflect on the informational nature of art. 23, prompting observance of the law rather than permitting contractual conditions requiring observance of negotiated local labour standards.

201. Circular from Dept. of Environment, 14 September 1989: see A. Geddes, *Public Procurement op. cit.* note 174 above, 28. The inference of the unsatisfactory judgment in *Greenwich Building and Maintenance plc* v *Greenwich BC* [1993] IRLR 535, above note 192, is that the narrow view of the Directive is correct in regard to social conditions additional to what is explicitly set out in the Directive.

202. See the *Rush Portugesa* decision, above note 173.

203. Directive 93/37, art. 5(a)(b) and implementing Reg. 6(c)(iii) of S.I.1991 no.2680, an 'international organisation of which only States are members'; *quaere* whether the ILO falls within this provision, and whether its Convention sets out a relevant 'procedure'?

204. See the White paper on *European Social policy* (COM (94) 333, 61).

205. Local Government Act 1988, ss. 17-19 (provisions against race discrimination are exceptionally allowed: s. 19). Also now, Local Government Act 1992, ss. 8-11, extending compulsory competitive tendering to services, white collar and blue: see S. Arrowsmith (1994) PPLR CS157-173.

206. See *R* v *Islington LBC, ex parte Building Employers' Confederation* [1989] IRLR 382.

207. See Chapter 6 above. Alternative policy would also require repeal of what are now ss.186, 187 and 225 TULRCA 1992, which ban parallel measures by a union to extend recognition.

208. See Wedderburn, *Employment Rights in Britain and Europe* (1991) 273: 'a specific clause shall be inserted' in the contract stating that the contractor's employees shall be paid not less favourably than under relevant collective agreements, in effect a form of 'extension'. On the enforcement of procurement rules in Italy, see F. Mastrogostine, Chapter 4 in S. Arrowsmith, *Remedies for Enforcing Public Procurement Rules*, above note 176.

209. G. Giugni, *Lavoro, legge, contratti* (1989) 334.

210. *Autosatisfaction* (gaining the objective sought by the industrial action itself) is illegal: Wedderburn, *Employment Rights in Britain and Europe* (1991) 288.

211. Directive 91/533, above Chapter 1, p. 4ff. Although it was open to the UK to implement the Directive with measures more favourable to the workers (Art.7) Sched. 4 of TURER Act 1993 appears not to have done so.

212. J. Delors, speech 8 September 1988, *TUC Report 1988*, 570.
213. See the work of N. Millward, above n. 33 above
214. Chapter 8 above, p. 248ff. Amendments have recently been made to the draft Fifth Directive on company law points which are only indirectly relevant, for example limiting shareholders' voting rights in proportion to their capital and the powers of majorities in general meeting: COM(90) 629 final-SYN 3, and COM(91) 372 final-SYN 3.
215. See the new art. 5a of the draft Regulation COM(91) 174 final-SYN 218, OJ 8,7,91, C 176/1, and art. 3, of the Draft Directive, COM(91) 174 final-SYN 219 (in DTI Consultative Docment January 1992). See Wedderburn, *The Social Charter, European Company and Employment Rights: An Outline Agenda* (1990) 59-61; and on the 1991 amendments A.Wehlau (1992) 29 CMLR 473.
216. Commission, *Communication: Making the Most of the Internal Market* COM(93) 632 final, 22.12.1993, 33; and *Reinforcing the Effectiveness of the Internal Market* COM(93) 256 final, 9.6.1993, 35. Worker participation on similar lines was proposed for European Co-operative Societies: Treasury, *Consultative Document* June 1992, on the proposal COM(91) 273 final-SYN 389, OJ C.99/37, 21.4 1992. Workers' representatives have a right to be heard by the Commission on anti-competitive mergers with a Community dimension (art. 18(4), Regulation 4064/89, OJ L 257/14) which the Commission sees as complementary to competition in public procurement: A. Brown (1994) PPLR 16. But the First Instance Court appears to restrict this right to cases where damage attributable to competition measures can be proved: *Grandes Sources Works Council et al* v *Commission* (T-96/92R) 15.12.1992,: *Vittel Works Council et al* v *Commission* (12/93R) 2.4. 1993; S. Anderman (1994) 23 ILJ 318 (arising from Nestlé's bid for Perrier).
217. See the discussion in R. Neilsen and E. Szyszczak, *The Social Dimension of the European Community* (1991) 16-23.
218. See also Chapter 8 above.
219. See C. Docksey, 'The Principle of Equality between Women and Men as a Fundamental Right under Community Law' (1991) 20 ILJ 258-80.
220. M. Spencer, *1992 and All That: Civil Liberties in the Balance* (1990) 122. See E. Szyszczak, on 'Race Discrimination' Chapter 8 in B. Hepple and E. Szyszczak (eds.) *Discrimination: The Limits of Law* (1992).
221. See *Marshall* v *Southampton and SW Hampshire AHA* (No. 2) [1993] IRLR 445, ECJ; Race Relations (Remedies) Act 1994 [and now *R* v *Sec. of State for Employment, ex parte EOC* [1994] ICR 317 HL, which the UK government accepted on 20.12.1994; see above p. 329, n. 76].
222. Preamble to Framework Directive, 17th indent: OJ L 183, 29 June 1989.
223. F. Hayek agreed that the tasks of the State included regulations of safety and health: *Law Legislation and Liberty* (1979) 115 ('what used to be called safety legislation').
224. See the comprehensive treatment in B. Bercusson, *Working Time in Britain: Towards a European Model* Part I, *The Directive*, and Part II *Collective Bargaining in Europe and the UK* (1994 Institute of Employment Rights).
225. See ss. 188-198 TULRCA 1992, as amended by s.34 TURER Act 1993,

bringing many items into proper accord with the Directives, not least the basic definition *here* of 'redundancy' to include any dismissal for a reason not related to an individual.

226. See in Britain, Transfer of Undertakings (Protection of Employment) ['TUPE'] Regulations 1981 No.1794, amended by TURER Act 1993 s. 33; on the transferee's right to vary the employment terms after the transfer, see the useful review by B. Napier, *CCT, Market Testing and Employment Rights* (1993 Institute of Employment Rights) 26ff. On the issue of 'representatives' of the workers involved and union recognition, see below note 260ff.

227. *Commission* v *United Kingdom* (382 and 383/ 92) [1994] IRLR392, 409, 420 ECJ, the judgment declaring that the U.K. was in default in having no scheme for workers' representatives to be consulted by an employer who chose not to recognise a union.

228. See Advocate General van Gerven: who spoke of making it 'subject to conditions acceptable to the workers', in *Commission* v *United Knigdom* (382/92 and 383/92) Opinion 2 March 1994, [1994] I.R.L.R. p. 403 (a view not shared in the judgments of the Court on 8 June 1994, above note 227). On the British position of dissentient workers, see *Newnes* v *British Airways plc* [1992] IRLR 575 CA; and on remedies (though transient) compelling consultation before the closure of pits, *R* v *British Coal Corpn. and Secretary of State for Trade ex parte Vardy* [1993] IRLR 104; *Financial Times* 5 February 1994.

229. G.F. Mancini, 'Labour Law and Community Law' (1985) 20 The Irish Jurist 1, 2, 12. See too above, Chapter 8, 'European Community Law and Workers' Rights after 1992: Fact or Fake?' originally in (1991) 13 Univ Dublin L.J. 1.

230. See P. Davies, 'Acquired Rights, Creditors' Rights, Freedom of Contract and Industrial Democracy' (1989) 9 Yearbook of European Law 21; and see his 'The Emergence of European Labour Law' Chapter 10 in W. McCarthy (ed.) *Legal Interventions in Collective Bargaining* (1992).

231. The employment contracts of the dissenting employees are automatically terminated with no right to complain because British law now determines that it is not a 'dismissal': s. 33(4) TURER Act 1993, enacted after the Court had held the status of such employes is a matter for national law: *Katsikas* v *Konstantinidis* (132/91)[1993] IRLR 179 ECJ.

232. See *Nokes* v *Doncaster Amalgamated Collieries* [1940] AC 1014: the classical common law attitude assumes there is enough employment to go round: 'the right to choose for himself whom he would serve ... the main difference between a servant and a serf' (Lord Atkin).

233. See for example, the French law of 19 July 1928 (now in Code du Travail art.L. 122-12), and the Italian Civil Code art. 2112 was to the same effect, now amended in the light of the Directive: Law 428/1990, art. 47.

234. *Christel Schmidt* v *Leikhasse der früheren Ämter Bordesholm* (392/92) [1994] IRLR 302 ECJ.

235. Wedderburn, 'Labour Standards, Global Markets and Labour Laws in Europe' in D. Campbell and W. Sengenberger (eds.) *International Labour Standards in the Globalised Economy* (1994 IILS 245, 259-64).

236. *Opinion of the Economic and Social Committee on Basic Community Social Rights* OJ C126, 32, 4, 23 May 1989.
237. On 'why the world needs the ILO' to maintain human rights at work, see B. Brett, *International Labour Law in the 21st. Century* (1994) Chapter 2.
238. Commission *Explanatory Memorandum* to the *Directive on Works Councils* (etc.) on consultation and information rights for workers in undertakings of Community scale, text of 13 April 1994, paras. 6 and 8; the text was amended beofre the common position at the Council 22 June 1994, see M. Gold and M. Hall (1994) 25 Ind. Rels. J. 177, below note 265ff.
239. *Third Report from the Commission On the Application of the Community Charter* COM(93) 668 final (21.12.1993), 3. So too in *Intergovernmental Conferences: Contributions by the Commission* 1991, Bull. E.C. Supp. 2/91, p.130 on 'principles and method' in the 'new Community social framework'.
240. J. Coppel and A. O'Neill, 'The European Court of Justice: Taking Rights Seriously?' (1992) Legal Studies 227, 245.
241. B. Hepple, 'Community Measures for Protection of Workers against Dismissal' (1977) CMLR 489, 500; and see his seminal 'Crisis in EEC Labour Law' (1987) 16 ILJ 77 calling for Community labour law to be based on the fundamental rights in the Council of Europe Social Charter ('CESC').
242. P. Davies and M. Freedland, *Labour Legislation and Public Policy* (1993) 662-3.
243. Wedderburn, 'Labour Standards, Global Markets and Labour Laws in Europe', above note 235, p. 266.
244. E. Szyszczak, 'L'Espace Sociale Européenne: Reality, Dreams or Nightmares?' (1990) 33 German Yearbook of International Law 284, 306; compare on fundamental social rights, W. Däubler, *Market and Social Justice in the EC* (1991) 37-160.
245. See A. Cassese, A. Clapham, J.Weiler, *1992: What Are Our Rights?* (1990 EUI) 31; B. Bercusson, 'Fundamental Social and Economic Rights' in Cassese, Clapham and Weiler (eds.) 'Human Rights and the European Community: Methods of Protection' especially Part VI; Bercusson 'The European Community's Charter of Fundamental Social Rights for Workers' (1990) 53 MLR 624.
246. The Statist style of the drafting is illustrated by the phrasing: 'Should management and labour so desire, the dialogue between them at Community level may lead to contractual relations, including agreements'. In more liberal régimes no such permission is juridically needed for agreements to become contractual provided they do not offend under the general law.
247. Some suggest, partly because of the German and Dutch text, that this does not mean a 'Decision' within article 189 Treaty (e.g. P.Davies 'The Emergence of European Labour Law' note 230 above, 352; compare B. Hepple, *European Dialogue-Alibi or Opportunity?* (1993 Institute of Employment Rights) 30-1; such a Decision binds those to whom it is

addressed. Perhaps a Decision could define the employers to whom it was addressed and make the terms binding on employment within that sphere of industry, in the manner of the *Code du Travail* art. L. 135-2: see chapter 6 above. However the machinery is arranged, there would have to be some definition of the employment covered, e.g. in a sectoral agreement at Community level, where a statement from the Council (whatever it was called) would need to define the area of employment bound; compare B. Bercusson, 'The Dynamic of European Labour Law After Maastricht' (1994) 23 ILJ 28-9. On similar problems of definition under the now repealed Sched. 11, Employment Protection Act 1975, see P. Wood (1978) 7 ILJ 65, 72; above Chapter 6, text to note 64ff.

248. *Communication Concerning the Application of the Agreement on Social Policy* COM(93) 600 final, 14.12.93, at para 37, an important instrument which needs to be more widely known.

249. *Ibid.*, COM(93) 600 final, 14.12.93, at paras. 38-42 and para. 8 respectively, the second being a declaration of an astonishing character. The Commission speaks of a 'Council decision' in a way that does not wholly solve the problem in note 247 above.

250. See A. Adinolfi, 'The Implementation of Social Policy Directives Through Collective Agreements' (1988) CMLR 291 (also on EC developments). On the acceptance by the Community of this method: above Chapter 6, p. 218f.

251. See Wedderburn, 'Labour Standards, Global Markets and Labour Laws in Europe' in D. Campbell and W. Sengenberger (eds.) *International Labour Standards in the Globalised Economy* (1994) 245.

252. See paras. 43-44 in the *Communication Concerning the Application of the Agreement on Social Policy* COM(93) 600 final, 14 December 1993.

253. *Commission v Belgium* (215/83) [1985] 3 CMLR 624; and *Commission v Italy* (235/84) [1982] ECR 2291; *Commission v Denmark* (143/83) [1985] 1 CMLR 44, ECJ (implementation 'in the first instance to representatives of management and labour' but the State guarantee must cover all cases not receiving 'the full protection' of a Directive, e.g. non-unionists).

254. See Chapter 6 above, pp. 216-23; compare B. Hepple, *European Dialogue-Alibi or Opportunity?*, above note 247; on Germany, W. Däubler (1989) 10 CL. J 505.

255. See on the ILO, F. Morgenstern, 'Participation in International Organisations: Representation and Representativity' Chapter II in *Legal Problems of International Organisations* (1986) especially 78 – 90.

256. The problems are more than formal; the ILO is concerned with labour standards and 'competition' in their setting; the Community's priorities are the reverse: see F. Maupin, *'Particularisme institutionnelles et vocation universelle: les défis croisés CEE-OIT'* 1990 *Rev Gén. de Droit International Public*, no.1, 49-90; see too now, Wedderburn, 'Labour Standards, Global Markets and Labour Laws in Europe' in D. Campbell and W. Sengenberger (eds.) *op.cit.*n. 251 above. The matter has not been settled by the Commission's trenchant *Proposal for a Council Decision on the Community's External Competence at ILO Conferences*, COM(1994) 2 final, 12. 1. 1994, under which, after the Court's Opinion (2/91), 'joint competence' in the ILO would lead to Member States losing their

separate competence to vote.
257. ILO Convention no. 89 of 1948, now overtaken by Convention no. 171 of 1990. See *Stoeckel* (345/89) [1991] ECR I-4047 ECJ; but see, *Ministère Public du Direction du Travail* v *Levy* (158/91) [1994] IRLR 138 ECJ (international obligations incurred before the Treaty are dominant, even against the principle of equal treatment: art. 234). See the ILO report 'Women Workers: Protection or Equality?' Conditions of Work Digest, vol.6, 1987, and see 1992 EIRR 219, 16 and 1989 EIRR 200, 25.
258. *Advisory Opinion on Ratification of ILO Convention No. 170, 1990* (2/91) 19 March 1993, ECJ: the Community must conclude an ILO Convention 'through the medium of the Member States' (para. 37). The Commission's later proposals were not reassuring: *Proposal for a Council Decision, op. cit.* COM(94) 2 final, 12. 1. 1994.
259. See 1994 EIRR 244, 3. Member States can now be fined for default.
260. The five elements include membership, independence, level of subscriptions, age of organisation and attitude during the occupation: art. L. 133-2 Code du Travail. One finds small local unions trying to prove their representativeness: Trib. G.I. Valence, 13 October 1992 (union with subscriptions from 51 members bringing in 165 francs in two years, failed): *Droit Ouvrier* 1993, 25.
261. The *rappresentanza* (local union presence which must be formed within the ambit of a representative union: art. 19) is being supplanted by a new 'unified union presence' (*rappresentanza sindacale unita*) elected by the workforce (Agreement of 3 July 1993) though so far only by an agreement as changes in the law were overtaken by the new government elected in 1994.
262. For a summary of types of 'representative unions', see Wedderburn, *Employment Rights in Britain and Europe* (1991) 301; on Italy see Chapter 9. An analysis has been belatedly attempted by the Commission in the rather patchy Annexes I and II to the *Communication Concerning the Application of the Agreement on Social Policy* [i.e. SC11] COM(93) 600 final, 14 December 1993 ('the Social Partners study'). The national reports in Annex III are somewhat more helpful.
263. See G. Lyon-Caen and J. Pélissier, *Droit du Travail* (1992 16th. ed.) 596-708; unions which are not 'representative' may not nominate even jointly with those that are: Soc. 16 November 1993, *Syndicat CGT Dassault Falcon Service c. Sté Dassault Falcon Service*, Droit Ouvrier 1994, 169 (the representative union may however nominate workers who are members of other unions). A union has standing to correct the employer's omission of workers from the electoral list: Soc. 3 March 1993, *SM Enterprise H.Reinier c Union Syndicale CGT Soc*, Droit Ouvrier 1994, 191.
264. Reference is to the text on which a 'common position' was reached at the Council of Ministers, 22 June 1994: 7436/94.
265. See the European Works Council Directive, arts. 2(d) and 5(2)(a). Previous drafts had spoken of members of the special negotiating body (SNB) as being 'drawn from the representatives of the employees', which seemed to mean selected from existing union representation. Of course, members of the consultative council or body might well be different

persons. For earlier proposals, see *Commission Proposal for a Council Directive* COM(90) 581 final, 25.1.1991, and COM (91/345) 16.9.1991, the *Menrad Report*, Committee on Social Affairs, Employment and Working Environment (European Parliament) C3-0065/91, 25.6.1991; see too, DTI *Proposal for a Directive on a European Works Council* (Consultative Document) February 1991, and below note 267.

266. TURER Act 1993, s. 14 (amending s. 174 TULRCA 1992); and see B. Simpson, 'Individualism versus Collectivism: an Evaluation of section 14 TURER Act 1993' (1993) 22 ILJ 181; also J. Elgar and B. Simpson, 'A Final Appraisal of 'Bridlington'?' (1994) 32 BJIR 47, on the TUC procedures rendered in part unlawful by s.14; and see now the new TUC *Disputes Principles and Procedures* (1993). See Chapter 5 and Appendix, pp. 180, 208.

267. See P. Marginson, M. Hall, K. Sisson, *European-Level Employee Information and Consultation Structures in Multinational Enterprises* (1993 Institute of Personnel Management/ IRRU Warwick Univ Issues in People Management 7); K. Sisson, J. Waddington, C. Whiston, *The Structure of Capital in the European Community* (IRRU, Warwick Univ Paper no. 38). Compare policy at Vauxhall: 1994 EIRR 250, 15.

268. *Commission v United Kingdom* (383/92) [1994] IRLR 412, 8 June 1994, ECJ, above n.10 rejecting the UK contention that where the local 'law and practice' imposed no obligation on the employer, nor did Directive 75/129; and see parallel the reasoning on Directive 77/187 (382/92) [1994] IRLR 392. But under the Social Chapter Directive, if the employer fails to agree a structure for a Works Council, the minimum requirements apply giving elected workers' representatives rights to consult: art. 7 and Annex, 'Subsidiary Requirments'.

269. For a sustained argument that the most we can expect is co-ordinated, not supranational, bargaining, see M. Weiss in G. Spyropoulos, G. Fragnière, *Work and Social Policies in the New Europe* (1991) 59-75.

270. F. Guarriello, '*Autonomia collettiva e dimensione Europea: profili organizzativi e funzionali*', in *Quaderni di dir. del lav e delle relaz. ind.* 1991 No. 10, 91 (on the proposed Directive on European works councils and rights to consultation in transnational groups).

271. B. Bercusson, 'Maastricht: a Fundamental Change in European Labour Law' (1992) 23 Ind. Rels.Jo. 177, 188.

272. For a determinedly optimistic trade union view, see D. Lea, 'Time for Turning Weakness into Strength' (1993) 1 International Union Rights 8.

273. B. Bercusson, 'Maastricht: a Fundamental Change in European Labour Law' (1992) 23 Ind. Rels.Jo. 177; and see his 'European Labour Law and Sectoral Bargaining' (1993) 24 Ind. Rels. Jo. 257.

274. Four types of agreements are suggested: interconfederal/intersectoral; industry/ sector/branch; transnational with a multinational enterprise; national in one State: B. Bercusson, 'The Dynamic of European Labour Law after Maastricht' (1994) 23 ILJ 1, 22-23.

275. See W. Streeck, *Social Institutions and Economic Performance* (1992), Chapter 7 (with P. Schmitter), and *La dimensione sociale del mercato unico europeo: verso un' economia non regolata?* (1990) 29 *Stato e mercato* 43ff.

276. Mainly French based enterprises: see the series in 1993 EIRR 228, 13 and 20; 229, 14; 1994 *ibid.* 242, 13 and 250 *ibid.* 14. On the financial assistance from the Community for workers' representatives (budget B3-4004) see 1993 EIRR 238, 15 (some £200,000 was reported to be available for the British TUC unions in 1993).

277. See M. Gold and M. Hall, *Report on European-Level Information and Consultation in Multinational Companies* (1992 Dublin); M. Hall, 'Behind the European Works Council Directives' (1992) 30 BJIR 547; and now, M. Gold and M. Hall 'Statutory Works Councils: the Final Count-Down?' (1994) 25 Ind. Rels. Jo. 177 (postscript, 186).

278. Commission, *Communication Concerning the Application of the Agreement on Social Policy* COM(93) 600 final, paras. 29-36.

279. G.F. Mancini, 'Labour Law and Community Law' (1985) note 229 above, 2; see too, Wedderburn (1990) now 'European Community Law and Workers' Rights after 1992' Chapter 8 above; and P. Davies, 'The Emergence of European Labour Law' Chapter 10 in W. McCarthy (ed.) *Legal Interventions in Collective Bargaining* (1992).

280. *Commission v United Kingdom* (383/92) *cit.* above n. 10, para. 16.

281. Commission, *Explanatory Memorandum* in *Proposal for a Council Directive* (etc). *on consultation and information rights for workers in undertakings of Community-scale*, 13. 4. 1994, paras. 5, 6 ['socially acceptable conditions'] and 8.

282. R. Richardson and M. Rubin, 'The Shorter Working Week in Engineering: Surrender without Sacrifice?' Chapter 10 in D. Metcalf and S. Miller (eds.) *New Perspectives on Industrial Disputes* (1993) 223.

283. Compare W. Däubler, *Market and Social Justice in the EC: the Other Side of the Internal Market* (1991); S. Sciarra, '*Uno 'strabismo di Venere':* le politiche sociali comunitarie verso il completamento del mercato interno' 1991 Prospettive Sindacali 33.

284. See Commission, *Communication Concerning the Application of the Agreement on Social Policy* COM(93) 600 final, paras. 22-37 for these matters. On representativeness, see above note 260ff. above.

285. ILO Committee of Experts, *Report* 1993, 80th. Session (III Part 4A) 174, on the position in Belgium.

286. See, for example, *Regulation of Working Conditions in the Member States of the European Community* EC Bull. Supp 4/92, 'Comparative Labour Law of the Member States' (as at 1990, eds. H. Zeijen, R. Blanpain, and 'ERL') where it is erroneously stated that United Kingdom 'safety representatives must be elected by workers' (114: this is the case only with offshore oil workers). For a review, see D. Walters, A. Dalton and D. Gee, *Worker Representation on Health and Safety in Europe* (1993).

287. See above Chapter 8, especially pp. 270-4.

288. None of these is comprehensively 'representative'; even the ETUC leaves out some unions, e.g. the CGT in France; no British public sector enterprise is affiliated to CEEP. Six other employers' side bodies (such as Eurocommerce) and two other union federations (CESI and CEC, for *cadres* and white collar staff) are claiming *locus standi* to be consulted: see Appendix II *Communication Concerning the Application of the Agreement on Social Policy* COM(93) 600 final. On CEC and 'the new

social partners' accepted by the Commission, see (1994) EIRR, 245, 31.

289. See above Chapter 6.

290. See *Boxfoldia Ltd v NGA* [1988] IRLR 383, Saville J.; on the union not normally acting as 'agent' of members, see Wedderburn, *The Worker and the Law* (3rd ed. 1986) 326-9.

291. See Chapter 5 'Trade Union Democracy and State Regulation' above.

292. *Communication Concerning the Application of the Agreement on Social Policy* COM(93) 600 final, para. 24. On the bodies that 'broadly comply with these criteria', see Annex 2 to the main *Communication*; and also paras. 25-27.

293. See the admission of CEC, a European body comprising unions organising management and professional staff: 1994 EIRR 245, 31.

294. E. Suy (former legal counsel) 'Status of Observers in International Organisations' 1978, 160 RCA DL-II, 75. For the need to strengthen the ILO approach, see B. Brett, *International Labour in the 21st Century* (1994).

295. *Re Designation of Workers' Delegation for the Netherlands* PCIJ Series B no.1 (1922); 1 Ann. Dig. 316.

296. See F. Morgenstern, *op. cit. Legal Problems of International Organisations* (1986) 74-86, to which I am much indebted; see too, A. Alcock, *A History of the International Labour Organisation* (1971).

297. This is the long established ILO formula on the right to strike inherent in freedom of association: *Freedom of Association and Collective Bargaining: General Survey by the Committee of Experts* (1983) para. 200; see too the analysis by R. Ben-Israel, *International Labour Standards: The Case of Freedom to Strike* (1987) especially Part II.

298. See Wedderburn, 'Laws about Strikes' Chapter 4 in W. McCarthy, *Legal Interventions in Collective Bargaining* (1992).

299. See Wedderburn, *The Social Charter, European Company and Employment Rights: An Outline Agenda* (1990) 29-36.

300. *Communication from the Commission ('Action Programme')* COM (89) 568, 27. 11. 1989, Part II, 29; and on the Communication on collective bargaining, p. 30.

301. Commission, *Green Paper: European Social Policy: Options for the Union* COM(93) 551, 17 November 1993, 96. Later in 1994, a White Paper on Social Policy followed COM(94) 333, but was no more radical than the final version of the Green paper.

302. W.B. Creighton, 'An ILO Perspective', R. Trask (ed.) *Trade Union Rights in the Single Market* (1992) 54-66. See the *Reports* of the ILO Committee of Experts for 1988-1992, especially on the UK in regard to Conventions 87 and 98. W.B. Creighton, 'The ILO and Protection of Freedom of Association in the UK' (1994), *op.cit.*, n. 8 above. Ireland had earlier carried on a long battle about its system of 'licensing' unions for bargaining under the Council of Europe's Social Charter 1961, which was also a source of 'inspiration': P. Conlan Chapter II in A. Jaspers and L. Betten, *25 Years: European Social Charter* (1988) 568-72.

303. See K. Ewing, *Britain and the ILO* (1994, 2nd. edition, Institute of Employment Rights). The employees worked at the government 'spy centre' (GCHQ). The criticisms of the Committee of Experts are

contained in their *Reports* for 1988 to 1992 (sections on the United Kingdom and Conventions 87 and 98).

304. *Reports of the United Kingdom Government on Measures to Give Effect to (the ILO Conventions)* for 1 July 1991-30 June 1992, on Convention no.87, and 1 July 1991 to June 1993, on Convention no.98. Previous responses were made available only to the TUC and CBI.

305. See the important speech by T. Blair, then Labour Party spokesperson, 17. 12.1989, accepting the legal 'right not to join a trade union'; the TUC then spoke of seeking 'how unions can most effectively pursue 100 per cent membership consistent with the Social Charter' *Employment Law: a New Approach*, 27. 6. 1990; see too, Wedderburn, *The Social Charter, European Company and Employment Rights: An Outline Agenda* (1990) 29-42. It is arguable that the conversions to the rights of non-unionists went further than the Social Charter required.

306. See 1994 EIRR 240, 3. Limited recognition was subsequently obtained.

307. See above Chapter 7.

308. The second level of development in the classic analysis of P. Calamandrei, *'Significato costituzionale del diritto di sciopero'* (1952) 1 Riv Giur. Lav 221; see Wedderburn, *Employment Rights in Britain and Europe* (1991) 276-83.

309. See *Maurissen and European Public Service Union v Court of Auditors* (193 and 194/87) [1990] ECR 95; *Union Syndical-Amalgamated European Public Service Union, Massa and Kortner v Council* (175/73) [1974] ECR 917 (First Chamber). Fundamental trade union rights were relied upon also by Advocate General Trabucchi in *Syndicat Général du Personnel des Organismes Européens v Commission* (18/74) [1974] ECR 933, 947-9.

310. Regulation 1612/68, article 8, including also a right to sit as workers' representative on a board in a national system of co-determination.

311. See Wedderburn, 'European Community Law and Workers' Rights after 1992: Fact or Fake?' Chapter 8 above, republished from (1991) 13 Univ Dublin L.J. 1.

312. B. Bercusson, 'The Dynamic of European Labour Law after Maastricht' (1994) 23 ILJ 1. He seems to identify the problem as coming from the 'timing of the initiative of the process of social dialogue during the Commission's consultations', under art. 3(4): p. 20-1; but the causes would seem to be more profound. See too, for an optimistic assessment of European-level bargaining: F. Guarriello, *op, cit.* note 242 above.

313. Bercusson, *ibid.*, 20, and 23 for next citation. See too the Community policy of obtaining workers' consent to change in order to create the 'socially acceptable conditions' for the restructuring of capital: Commission, *Explanatory Memorandum* in *Proposal for a Council Directive* (etc.) 13. 4. 1994, paras. 5, 6 and 8; above note 253.

314. See the judgments of the ECJ in in *Commission v United Kingdom* (382 and 383/92) 8 June 1994 [1994] IRLR 392 and 412 ECJ, rejecting the UK's assertion that it had properly implemented Directives 75/129 and 77/187 (duty to consult on redundancies and transfer of the undertaking) even though employers have since 1980 had a free choice about whether to recognise a trade union and therefore, under UK law, whether to

consult. The Court required the Member State to ensure that workers' representatives are designated for the purpose of consultation on proposed redundancies and on transfers of undertakings; above n. 10.

315. See above, pp. 380-7. The procurement rules have ambushed labour law making it the harder to escape from the net because of the European source of the regulation.

316. See, however, the careful and cautious assessment of proposals for legal sanction by B. Simpson, *Trade Union Recognition and the Law* (1991 Institute of Employment Rights); and see note 186 above.

317. See *Commission v United Kingdom* (382 and 383/92) [1994] IRLR 392 and 412 ECJ. Representatives elected *ad hoc* after redundancies are announced would seem to be inadequate; but must there be permanent representatives, awaiting redundancies? Most Member States do have 'permanent' workers' representatives to whom the task can be allotted.

318. See *Financial Times* 28 and 30 March 1994.

319. Compare Commission *Explanatory Memorandum to Proposal for a Council Directive* on the earlier draft, 13 April 1994, para. 31. The Council and Commission made a joint statement (Annex II) stating that the 'collective redundancies' requiring consultation means here a 'significant number of employees' in relation to the size of the Community-scale undertaking or group, or the establishment. Art. 12 of the European Works Council Directive now declares that it is adopted 'without prejudice' to Directives 75/129 and 77/187.

320. See OJ C 199/94; common position by the Eleven 22 June 1994: see 1994 EIRR, 246, 2.

321. S. Sciarra, 'Regulating European Unions: an Issue for 1992' (1990) 11 Comp. Lab.L.J. 141, 163.

322. A.J.P. Taylor, *The Origins of the Second World War* (1963) 336, because the 'real world war' began in 1941. Without democratic legitimacy, social resistance could turn into a 'real' struggle of a more violent character on lines unhappily winessed already in many countries.

323. Bruno Trentin (until 1994 general secretary of the Italian union federation CGIL) *Lavoro e libertà* (1994) 62.

324. See Wedderburn, 'Industrial Relations and the Courts' (1980) 9 ILJ 65 and Chapter 3 in *Employment Rights in Britain and Europe* (1991).

325. Consider the example of picketing: s. 15 TULRA 1974 (as amended now s. 220 TULRCA 1992). On positive rights, see Wedderburn, 'The New Politics of Labour Law' (1983) now Chapter 4, *Employment Rights in Britain and Europe* (1991).

326. See Wedderburn, *The Worker and the Law, op. cit.* Chapter 1, and *Employment Rights in Britain and Europe* (1991) Chapters 8 and 11.

327. This level was not in every respect attained by the 'Community Social Charter 1989', to which all Member States except Britain adhered: see Wedderburn, *The Social Charter, European Company and Employment Rights: An Outline Agenda* (1990 Institute of Employment Rights).

328. Under Directives 75/129 and 77/187: *Commission v United Kingdom* (382 and 383/92) [1994] IRLR 392 and 412 ECJ; Wedderburn (1994) 11 Int. J CLLIR 339; P. Davies (1994) 23 ILJ 272. On workers' representatives under Directive 75/219, see *Griffin v South West Water*,

High Court, 25 August 1994, Blackburn J.; J. Eady (1994) 23 ILJ 350.

329. In a report to the Commission, *Freedom of Association and Community Protection* (1992), the writer proposed a Recommendation on freedom of association as a floor from which Community bargaining and freedom of association could develop; although non-binding in law, this could be taken into consideration by the Court: *Grimaldi* v *Fonds des Maladies Professionnelles* (322/88) [1990] IRLR 400 ECJ.

330. See the position of Robert Reich, US Secretary of Labor, on 'labour clauses' in trade agreements, taking account of the need not to produce a new protectionism contrary to the perceived interests of developing countries: *Financial Times* 10 June 1994; compare M.Hansenne, *Defending Values, Promoting Change* (ILO, Report of the Director General 1994 Part 1) above Chapter 1 note 22. Support for these values was repeated in the Essen 'summit' Council (*Resolution*, 6 December 1994, para. 9), but no action was proposed.

331. In C. Hill, *A Nation of Change and Novelty* (1993, revised ed.) Chapter 7 'Gerrard Winstanley and Freedom' 152.

INDEX

(SUBJECT MATTER AND COUNTRIES)

INDEX OF NAMES

(MAIN REFERENCES)

INDEX OF LEGAL SOURCES